W9-CBG-825

THIS REGISTRATION CODE GIVES YOU ACCESS TO

🅔 Ebook | 📖 *The Little Seagull Handbook* Ebook

📲 InQuizitive for Writers | 📑 Tutorials | 📖 Plagiarism Tutorial

FOR *They Say / I Say with Readings*, Fifth Edition

ACTIVATE YOUR REGISTRATION CODE!

1) Scratch the foil to view your code

TJW-ALH-YPM

2) Go to digital.wwnorton.com/theysayreadings5
3) Follow the instructions to register your code

A code can be registered to only one user. Used codes are nontransferable and nonrefundable.

For more help, see the back of this card.

What if my code is scratched off?

You can purchase access at
digital.wwnorton.com/theysayreadings5

What if I need more help?

For additional support, visit **support.wwnorton.com**

ISBN 978-0-393-53871-7

9 780393 538717

9 0 0 0 0

WHAT THEY'RE SAYING ABOUT "*THEY SAY / I SAY*"

"Like a Swiss army knife for academic writing, 'They Say / I Say' has long served as a multipurpose tool for students learning how to make the 'moves' that are second nature to more experienced writers. The fifth edition adds several useful implements to the knife, including new chapters with practical, how-to advice on revision and inquiry-driven research."

—Steven Bailey, *Central Michigan University*

"It is so invigorating to have a concise, smart chapter on research writing that thinks past the 'standard' process we are all so used to reading and teaching."

—Ana Cooke, *Penn State University*

"The new theme, 'Why Care about the Planet?,' is very appealing and one I will certainly teach with the new edition. You've made it easy for students to do original local research as part of the unit. 'They Say / I Say' rocks!"

—Courtney Danforth, *College of Southern Nevada*

"I am thrilled to see your new Planet readings. They are diverse and inviting—even to a student who might be disinterested or unaware." —Greta Skogseth, *Montcalm Community College*

"These new readings invite students to think about the more challenging questions facing our world."

—Christian Smith, *Coastal Carolina University*

"The best book that's happened to teaching composition— ever!" —Karen Gaffney, *Raritan Valley Community College*

"This book demystifies rhetorical moves, tricks of the trade that many students are unsure about. It's reasonable, helpful, nicely written . . . and hey, it's true. I would have found it immensely helpful myself in high school and college."

—Mike Rose, *University of California, Los Angeles*

"A beautifully lucid way to approach argument—different from any rhetoric I've ever seen."

—Anne-Marie Thomas, *Austin Community College, Riverside*

"Students need to walk a fine line between their work and that of others, and this book helps them walk that line, providing specific methods and techniques for introducing, explaining, and integrating other voices with their own ideas."

—Libby Miles, *University of Vermont*

"*'They Say' with Readings* is different from other rhetorics and readers in that it really engages students in the act of writing throughout the book. It's less a 'here's how' book and more of a 'do this with me' kind of book."

—Kelly Ritter, *University of Illinois, Urbana-Champaign*

"It offers students the formulas we, as academic writers, all carry in our heads." —Karen Gardiner, *University of Alabama*

"Many students say that it is the first book they've found that actually helps them with writing in all disciplines."

—Laura Sonderman, *Marshall University*

"The best tribute to '*They Say / I Say*' I've heard is this, from a student: 'This is one book I'm not selling back to the bookstore.' Nods all around the room. The students love this book."

—Christine Ross, *Quinnipiac University*

"My students love this book. They tell me that the idea of 'entering a conversation' really makes sense to them in a way that academic writing hasn't before."

—Karen Henderson, *Helena College University of Montana*

"It's the anti-composition text: Fun, creative, humorous, brilliant, effective."

—Perry Cumbie, *Durham Technical Community College*

"A brilliant book. . . . It's like a membership card in the academic club." —Eileen Seifert, *DePaul University*

FIFTH EDITION

"THEY SAY/I SAY"

WITH READINGS

FIFTH EDITION

"THEY SAY / I SAY"

The Moves That Matter in Academic Writing

WITH READINGS

GERALD GRAFF
CATHY BIRKENSTEIN

both of the University of Illinois at Chicago

RUSSEL DURST

University of Cincinnati

With **LAURA J. PANNING DAVIES**

SUNY Cortland

W. W. NORTON & COMPANY
Independent Publishers Since 1923

W. W. Norton & Company has been independent since its founding in 1923, when William Warder Norton and Mary D. Herter Norton first published lectures delivered at the People's Institute, the adult education division of New York City's Cooper Union. The firm soon expanded its program beyond the Institute, publishing books by celebrated academics from America and abroad. By midcentury, the two major pillars of Norton's publishing program—trade books and college texts—were firmly established. In the 1950s, the Norton family transferred control of the company to its employees, and today—with a staff of five hundred and hundreds of trade, college, and professional titles published each year—W. W. Norton & Company stands as the largest and oldest publishing house owned wholly by its employees.

Composition: Cenveo
Manufacturing: King Printing Co., Inc.

Permission to use copyrighted material is included in the credits section of this book, which begins on page 739.

Library of Congress Cataloging-in-Publication Data

Names: Graff, Gerald, author. | Birkenstein, Cathy, author. | Durst, Russel K., 1954- author.
Title: "They say / I say" : the moves that matter in academic writing with readings / Gerald Graff, Cathy Birkenstein, both of the University of Illinois at Chicago, Russel Durst, University of Cincinnati.
Other titles: They say/I say with readings
Description: Fifth Edition. | New York : W.W. Norton & Company, [2021] | Fourth edition: 2018. | Includes bibliographical references and index.
Identifiers: LCCN 2020045140 | ISBN 9780393427509 (Paperback) | ISBN 9780393538335 (ePub)
Subjects: LCSH: Writing. | Authorship. | English language—Rhetoric—Handbooks, manuals, etc. | Persuasion (Rhetoric)—Handbooks, manuals, etc. | Report writing—Handbooks, manuals, etc.
Classification: LCC PE1431 .G73 2021b | DDC 808.06/6378—dc23
LC record available at https://lccn.loc.gov/2020045140

W. W. Norton & Company, Inc., 500 Fifth Avenue, New York, NY 10110
wwnorton.com

W. W. Norton & Company Ltd., 15 Carlisle Street, London W1D 3BS

7 8 9 0

To the great rhetorician Wayne Booth,
who cared deeply
about the democratic art
of listening closely to what others say.

CONTENTS

CONTENTS

New to this edition

Contents

New to this edition

CONTENTS

*New to this edition

PREFACE
TO THE FIFTH EDITION

———◻———

WHEN WE FIRST SET OUT TO WRITE THIS BOOK, our goal was simple: to offer a version of *"They Say / I Say": The Moves That Matter in Academic Writing* with an anthology of readings that would demonstrate the rhetorical moves "that matter." And because *"They Say"* teaches students that academic writing is a means of entering a conversation, we looked for readings on topics that would engage students and inspire them to respond—and to enter the conversations.

Our purpose in writing *"They Say"* has always been to offer students a user-friendly model of writing that will help them put into practice the important principle that writing is a social activity. Proceeding from the premise that effective writers enter conversations of other writers and speakers, this book encourages students to engage with those around them—including those who disagree with them—instead of just expressing their ideas "logically." We believe it's a model more necessary than ever in today's increasingly diverse—and some might say divided—society.

Our own experience teaching first-year writing students has led us to believe that to be persuasive, arguments need not only supporting evidence but also motivation and exigency and that the surest way to achieve this motivation and exigency is to generate one's own arguments as a response to those of others—to something "they say." To help students write their way into the often daunting conversations of academia and the wider public sphere, the book provides templates to help them make sophisticated rhetorical moves that they might otherwise not think of attempting. And of course learning to make these rhetorical moves in writing also helps students become better readers of argument.

The two versions of *"They Say / I Say"* are now being taught at more than 1,500 schools, which suggests that there is a widespread desire for explicit instruction that is understandable but not oversimplified, to help writers negotiate the basic moves necessary to "enter the conversation." Instructors have told us how much this book helps their students learn how to write academic discourse, and some students have written to us saying that it's helped them to "crack the code," as one student put it.

This fifth edition of *"They Say / I Say" with Readings* includes forty-one readings—over half of them new—on five compelling and controversial issues. The selections provide a glimpse into some important conversations taking place today—and will, we hope, provoke students to respond and thus to join in those conversations.

WHAT'S NEW IN THIS EDITION

"But as Several Sources Suggest": Research as Conversation. This new chapter, written with the help of librarian and social scientist Erin Ackerman, focuses on the research essay, as it is traditionally called, and on research writing more broadly. It suggests that the research paper is not just about amassing information, as is often assumed, but also about entering into conversation with other researchers. With a variety of templates and examples from academic writing, the chapter offers advice on such issues as how to craft a good research question (spoiler alert: it's one that can be debated), how to find relevant sources, how to synthesize sources into a common conversation, and how to locate online sources that are reliable and credible. The chapter concludes with an annotated student essay that shows how the advice we offer might look in a final piece of writing.

"What I Really Want to Say Is . . .": Revising Substantially. This new chapter takes on one of the more formidable challenges faced by college students: how to move beyond superficial revision and improve a composition in a genuinely substantial way. It presents revision not as a matter of simply correcting spelling or moving a sentence or two but as a process students can use to discover what it is they really want to say. More specifically, the chapter encourages students to reread their writing with an eye to whether, for instance, they have accurately represented their sources, inadvertently contradicted themselves or lost their train of thought, or included "uh-oh" moments, as we refer to them, that are out of step with their larger intentions and aims.

New Exercises. Each core chapter (Chapters 1–15) now includes three exercises, which give students an opportunity to apply the chapter's advice. Instructors can either use these exercises for in-class work or assign them as homework. Many exercises include a short passage for reading and writing practice and also prompt students to join conversations on **theysayiblog.com.**

More than half the readings are new, including an entirely new chapter, Why Care about the Planet?, which brings together diverse perspectives on pressing environmental questions—from

Naomi Klein's thoughts on how to tackle climate change to a Texas congressman's views on why conservatives should own the issue. Scholars, scientists, students, and popular writers present a multitude of perspectives on everything from plastic bags to the preservation of a sacred mountain in Hawaii.

Every chapter features new readings in conversation, such as a sociologist's response to J. D. Vance's *Hillbilly Elegy* alongside a selection from the best-selling memoir; linguist John McWhorter's provocative analysis, "Could Black English Mean a Prison Sentence?," next to a selection from Michelle Alexander's *The New Jim Crow* and college student Kelly Coryell's textual analysis of what's wrong with saying "all lives matter."

Three new chapters on writing in the disciplines are complemented by new writing from students who used *"They Say / I Say"* and whose essays were nominated for the Norton Writer's Prize. These essays, documented in MLA and APA styles, not only model the rhetorical moves across disciplines and in researched writing but also offer lively examples of writing that engages with other people's views.

WHAT'S ONLINE

"They Say / I Say" comes with more online options than ever—all of which are packaged automatically with all new copies of the book and are also available separately for a low cost. Visit **digital.wwnorton.com/theysayreadings5** for access, or contact your Norton representative for more information or help with any of the resources below.

Ebooks, available for both "They Say / I Say" and "They Say / I Say" with Readings, provide an enhanced reading experience. Convenient and affordable, the Norton ebooks can be used on any device and let students highlight ideas, bookmark passages, take notes, and even listen to the text.

Online tutorials give students hands-on practice using the rhetorical moves that this book emphasizes. Each tutorial helps students analyze an essay with an eye to these "moves that matter" and then use the book's templates to craft a response.

InQuizitive for Writers delivers adaptive, game-like exercises to help students practice editing and working with sources, including fact-checking. InQuizitive for Writers includes *The Little Seagull Handbook*, so students get two books for the price of one with all new copies of *"They Say / I Say."*

Instructor's Guide includes expanded in-class activities, sample syllabi, summaries of each chapter and reading, and a chapter on using the online resources, including the tutorials and the book's blog.

"They Say / I Blog" provides current readings that use the rhetorical moves covered in the book, along with questions that prompt students to join conversations online. Updated twice a month by Laura J. Panning Davies of the SUNY Cortland, the blog provides a rich archive of additional readings on important issues. Check it out at **theysayiblog.com**.

Resources for your learning management system (LMS) provide high-quality Norton content for your online, hybrid, or in-person course. Customizable resources include assignable writing prompts from **theysayiblog.com**, quizzes on editing and documentation, style guides, student essays, and more.

HALLMARK FEATURES

Forty-one readings that will prompt students to think—and write. Taken from a wide variety of sources, including the *Chronicle of Higher Education*, the *Washington Post*, the *New York Times*, the *Wall Street Journal*, *Medium*, best-selling books, policy reports, student-run journals, celebrated speeches, and more, the readings represent a range of perspectives on five important issues, which we've organized into the following chapters:

- Why Care about the Planet?
- How Can We Bridge the Differences That Divide Us?
- What's College For?
- How Is Technology Changing Us?
- What's Gender Got to Do with It?

The readings can function as sources for students' own writing, and the study questions that follow each reading focus students' attention on how each author uses the key rhetorical moves taught in the book. Additionally, one question invites students to write and often to respond with their own views.

Two books in one, with a rhetoric up front and readings in the back. The two parts are linked by cross-references in the margins, leading from the rhetoric to specific examples in the readings and from the readings to the corresponding writing instruction. Teachers can therefore begin with either the rhetoric or the readings, and the links will facilitate movement between one section and the other.

A chapter on reading (Chapter 14) encourages students to think of reading as an act of entering conversations. Instead of teaching students merely to identify the author's argument, this chapter shows them how to read with an eye for what arguments the author is responding to—in other words, to think carefully about why the writer is making the argument in the first place and thus to recognize (and ultimately become a part of) the larger conversation that gives meaning to reading the text.

We hope that this new edition of *"They Say / I Say" with Readings* will spark students' interest in some of the most pressing conversations of our day and provide them with some of the tools they need to engage in those conversations with dexterity and confidence.

Gerald Graff
Cathy Birkenstein
Russel Durst

PREFACE

Demystifying Academic Conversation

—◻︎—

EXPERIENCED WRITING INSTRUCTORS have long recognized that writing well means entering into conversation with others. Academic writing in particular calls on writers not simply to express their own ideas but to do so as a response to what others have said. The first-year writing program at our own university, according to its mission statement, asks "students to participate in ongoing conversations about vitally important academic and public issues." A similar statement by another program holds that "intellectual writing is almost always composed in response to others' texts." These statements echo the ideas of rhetorical theorists like Kenneth Burke, Mikhail Bakhtin, and Wayne Booth as well as recent composition scholars like David Bartholomae, John Bean, Patricia Bizzell, Irene Clark, Greg Colomb, Lisa Ede, Peter Elbow, Joseph Harris, Andrea Lunsford, Elaine Maimon, Gary Olson, Mike Rose, John Swales and Christine Feak, Tilly Warnock, and others who argue that writing well means engaging the voices of others and letting them in turn engage us.

Yet despite this growing consensus that writing is a social, conversational act, helping student writers actually participate in these conversations remains a formidable challenge. This book aims to meet that challenge. Its goal is to demystify academic writing by isolating its basic moves, explaining them clearly, and representing them in the form of templates. In this way, we hope to help students become active participants in the important conversations of the academic world and the wider public sphere.

HIGHLIGHTS

- *Shows that writing well means entering a conversation*, summarizing others ("they say") to set up one's own argument ("I say")
- *Demystifies academic writing*, showing students "the moves that matter" in language they can readily apply
- *Provides user-friendly templates* to help writers make those moves in their own writing
- *Includes a chapter on reading*, showing students how the authors they read are part of a conversation that they themselves can enter—and thus to see reading as a matter not of passively absorbing information but of understanding and actively entering dialogues and debates

HOW THIS BOOK CAME TO BE

The original idea for this book grew out of our shared interest in democratizing academic culture. First, it grew out of arguments that Gerald Graff has been making throughout his career that schools and colleges need to invite students into the conversations and debates that surround them. More specifically, it is a practical, hands-on companion to his book *Clueless in Academe: How Schooling Obscures the Life of the Mind*, in which he looks at academic conversations from the perspective of those who find them mysterious and proposes ways in which such mystification can be overcome. Second, this book grew out of writing templates that Cathy Birkenstein developed in the 1990s, for use in writing and literature courses she was teaching. Many students, she found, could readily grasp what it meant to support a thesis with evidence, to entertain a counterargument, to identify a textual contradiction, and ultimately to summarize and respond to challenging arguments, but they often had trouble putting these concepts into practice in their own writing. When Cathy sketched out templates on the board, however, giving her students some of the language and patterns that these sophisticated moves require, their writing—and even their quality of thought—significantly improved.

This book began, then, when we put our ideas together and realized that these templates might have the potential to open up and clarify academic conversation. We proceeded from the premise that all writers rely on certain stock formulas that they themselves didn't invent—and that many of these formulas are so commonly used that they can be represented in model templates that students can use to structure and even generate what they want to say.

As we developed a working draft of this book, we began using it in first-year writing courses that we teach at UIC. In classroom exercises and writing assignments, we found that students who otherwise struggled to organize their thoughts, or even to think of something to say, did much better when we provided them with templates like the following:

▸ In discussions of _____, a controversial issue is whether _____. While some argue that _____, others contend that _____.

▸ This is not to say that _____.

One virtue of such templates, we found, is that they focus writers' attention not just on what is being said but also on the *forms* that structure what is being said. In other words, they make students more conscious of the rhetorical patterns that are key to academic success but often pass under the classroom radar.

THE CENTRALITY OF "THEY SAY / I SAY"

The central rhetorical move that we focus on in this book is the "they say / I say" template that gives our book its title. In our view, this template represents the deep, underlying structure, the internal DNA as it were, of all effective arguments. Effective persuasive writers do more than make well-supported claims ("I say"); they also map those claims relative to the claims of others ("they say").

Here, for example, the "they say / I say" pattern structures a passage from an essay by the media and technology critic Steven Johnson:

> For decades, we've worked under the assumption that mass culture follows a path declining steadily toward lowest-common-denominator standards, presumably because the "masses" want dumb, simple pleasures and big media companies try to give the masses what they want. But . . . the exact opposite is happening: the culture is getting more cognitively demanding, not less.
>
> STEVEN JOHNSON, "Watching TV Makes You Smarter"

In generating his own argument from something "they say," Johnson suggests *why* he needs to say what he is saying: to correct a popular misconception.

Even when writers do not explicitly identify the views they are responding to, as Johnson does, an implicit "they say" can often be discerned, as in the following passage by Zora Neale Hurston:

> I remember the day I became colored.
>   ZORA NEALE HURSTON, "How It Feels to Be Colored Me"

In order to grasp Hurston's point here, we need to be able to reconstruct the implicit view she is responding to and questioning: that racial identity is an innate quality we are simply born with. On the contrary, Hurston suggests, our race is imposed on us by society—something we "become" by virtue of how we are treated.

As these examples suggest, the "they say / I say" model can improve not just student writing but student reading comprehension as well. Since reading and writing are deeply reciprocal activities, students who learn to make the rhetorical moves represented by the templates in this book figure to become more adept at identifying these same moves in the texts they read. And if we are right that effective arguments are always in dialogue with other arguments, then it follows that in order to understand the types of challenging texts assigned in college, students need to identify the views to which those texts are responding.

Working with the "they say / I say" model can also help with invention, finding something to say. In our experience, students best discover what they want to say not by thinking about a subject in an isolation booth but by reading texts, listening closely to what other writers say, and looking for an opening through which they can enter the conversation. In other words, listening closely to others and summarizing what they have to say can help writers generate their own ideas.

THE USEFULNESS OF TEMPLATES

Our templates also have a generative quality, prompting students to make moves in their writing that they might not otherwise make or even know they should make. The templates in this book can be particularly helpful for students who are unsure about what to say or who have trouble finding enough to say, often because they consider their own beliefs so self-evident that they need not be argued for. Students like this are often helped, we've found, when we give them a simple template like the following one for entertaining a counterargument (or planting a naysayer, as we call it in Chapter 6):

> ▸ **Of course some might object that** _____. **Although I concede that** _____, **I still maintain that** _____.

What this particular template helps students do is make the seemingly counterintuitive move of questioning their own beliefs, of looking at them from the perspective of those who disagree. In so doing, templates can bring out aspects of students' thoughts that, as they themselves sometimes remark, they didn't even realize were there.

Other templates in this book help students make a host of sophisticated moves that they might not otherwise make: summarizing what someone else says, framing a quotation in one's own words, indicating the view that the writer is responding to, marking the shift from a source's view to the writer's own view, offering evidence for that view, entertaining and answering counterarguments, and explaining what is at stake in the first place. In showing students how to make such moves, templates do more than organize students' ideas; they help bring those ideas into existence.

"OK—BUT TEMPLATES?"

We are aware, of course, that some instructors may have reservations about templates. Some, for instance, may object that such formulaic devices represent a return to prescriptive forms of instruction that encourage passive learning or lead students to put their writing on automatic pilot.

This is an understandable reaction, we think, to kinds of rote instruction that have indeed encouraged passivity and drained writing of its creativity and dynamic relation to the social world. The trouble is that many students will never learn on their own to make the key intellectual moves that our templates represent. While seasoned writers pick up these moves unconsciously through their reading, many students do not. Consequently, we believe, students need to see these moves represented in the explicit ways that the templates provide.

The aim of the templates, then, is not to stifle critical thinking but to be direct with students about the key rhetorical moves that it comprises. Since we encourage students to modify and adapt the templates to the particularities of the arguments they are making, using such prefabricated formulas as learning tools need not result in writing and thinking that are themselves formulaic. Admittedly, no teaching tool can guarantee that students will engage in hard, rigorous thought. Our templates do, however, provide concrete prompts that can stimulate and shape such thought: What do "they say" about my topic? How would a naysayer respond to my argument? What is my evidence? Do I need to qualify my point? Who cares?

In fact, templates have a long and rich history. Public orators from ancient Greece and Rome through the European Renaissance studied rhetorical *topoi* or "commonplaces," model passages and formulas that represented the different strategies available to public speakers. In many respects, our templates echo this classical rhetorical tradition of imitating established models.

The journal *Nature* requires aspiring contributors to follow a guideline that is like a template on the opening page of their manuscript: "Two or three sentences explaining what the main result [of their study] reveals in direct comparison with what was thought to be the case previously, or how the main result adds to previous knowledge." In the field of education, a form designed by the education theorist Howard Gardner asks postdoctoral fellowship applicants to complete the following template: "Most scholars in the field believe _____ . As a result of my study, _____ ." That these two examples are geared toward post-doctoral fellows and veteran researchers shows that it is not only struggling undergraduates who can use help making these key rhetorical moves but experienced academics as well.

Templates have even been used in the teaching of personal narrative. The literary and educational theorist Jane Tompkins devised the following template to help student writers make the often difficult move from telling a story to explaining what it means: "X tells a story about _____ to make the point that _____ . My own experience with _____ yields a point that is similar / different / both similar and different. What I take away from my own experience with _____ is _____ . As a result, I conclude _____ ." We especially like this template because it suggests that "they say / I say" argument need not be mechanical, impersonal, or dry and that telling a story and making an argument are more compatible activities than many think.

WHY IT'S OK TO USE "I"

But wait—doesn't the "I" part of "they say / I say" flagrantly encourage the use of the first-person pronoun? Aren't we aware that some teachers prohibit students from using "I" or "we" on the grounds that these pronouns encourage ill-considered, subjective opinions rather than objective and reasoned arguments? Yes, we are aware of this first-person prohibition, but we think it has serious flaws. First, expressing ill-considered, subjective opinions is not necessarily the worst sin beginning writers can commit; it might be a starting point from which they can move on to more reasoned, less self-indulgent perspectives. Second, prohibiting students from using "I" is simply not an effective way of curbing students' subjectivity, since one can offer poorly argued, ill-supported opinions just as easily without it. Third and most important, prohibiting the first person tends to hamper students' ability not only to take strong positions but also to differentiate their own positions from those of others, as we point out in Chapter 5. To be sure, writers can resort to various circumlocutions—"it will here be argued," "the evidence suggests," "the truth is"—and these may be useful for avoiding a monotonous series of "I believe" sentences. But except for avoiding such monotony, we see no good reason why "I" should be set aside in persuasive writing. Rather than prohibit "I," then, we think a better tactic is to give students practice at using it well and learning its use, both by supporting their claims with evidence and by attending closely to alternative perspectives—to what "they" are saying.

HOW THIS BOOK IS ORGANIZED

Because of its centrality, we have allowed the "they say / I say" format to dictate the structure of this book. So while Part 1 addresses the art of listening to others, Part 2 addresses how to offer one's own response. Part 1 opens with the chapter

"Starting with What Others Are Saying," which explains why it is generally advisable to begin a text by citing others rather than plunging directly into one's own views. Subsequent chapters take up the arts of summarizing and quoting what these others have to say. Part 2 begins with a chapter on different ways of responding, followed by chapters on marking the shift between what "they say" and what "I say," on introducing and answering objections, and on answering the all-important questions "so what?" and "who cares?" Part 3, "Tying It All Together," includes a chapter on connection and coherence; one on academic language, which encourages students to draw on their everyday voice as a tool for writing; and others on the art of metacommentary and using the templates to revise a text. Part 4 offers guidance for entering conversations in specific academic contexts, with chapters on entering class discussions, writing online, and reading and writing in the social sciences. Finally, we provide forty-one readings and an index of templates.

WHAT THIS BOOK DOESN'T DO

There are some things that this book does not try to do. We do not, for instance, cover logical principles of argument, such as syllogisms, warrants, logical fallacies, or the differences between inductive and deductive reasoning. Although such concepts can be useful, we believe most of us learn the ins and outs of argumentative writing not by studying logical principles in the abstract but by plunging into actual discussions and debates, trying out different patterns of response, and in this way getting a sense of what works to persuade different audiences and what doesn't. In our view, people learn more about arguing from hearing someone say, "You miss my point. What I'm saying is not _____ but _____," or "I agree with you that _____ and would even add that _____," than they do from studying the differences between inductive and deductive reasoning. Such formulas give students an immediate sense of what it feels like to enter a public conversation in a way that studying abstract warrants and logical fallacies does not.

ENGAGING WITH THE IDEAS OF OTHERS

One central goal of this book is to demystify academic writing by returning it to its social and conversational roots. Although writing may require some degree of quiet and solitude, the "they say / I say" model shows students that they can best develop their arguments not just by looking inward but by doing what they often do in a good conversation with friends and family—listening carefully to what others are saying and engaging with other views.

This approach to writing therefore has an ethical dimension, since it asks writers not simply to keep proving and reasserting what they already believe but also to stretch what they believe by putting it up against beliefs that differ, sometimes radically, from their own. In an increasingly diverse, global society, this ability to engage with the ideas of others is especially crucial to democratic citizenship.

Gerald Graff
Cathy Birkenstein

INTRODUCTION

Entering the Conversation

—◻—

THINK ABOUT AN ACTIVITY that you do particularly well: cooking, playing the piano, shooting a basketball, even something as basic as driving a car. If you reflect on this activity, you'll realize that once you mastered it you no longer had to give much conscious thought to the various moves that go into doing it. Performing this activity, in other words, depends on your having learned a series of complicated moves—moves that may seem mysterious or difficult to those who haven't yet learned them.

The same applies to writing. Often without consciously realizing it, accomplished writers routinely rely on a stock of established moves that are crucial for communicating sophisticated ideas. What makes writers masters of their trade is not only their ability to express interesting thoughts but their mastery of an inventory of basic moves that they probably picked up by reading a wide range of other accomplished writers. Less experienced writers, by contrast, are often unfamiliar with these basic moves and unsure how to make them in their own writing. Hence this book, which is intended as a short, user-friendly guide to the basic moves of academic writing.

One of our key premises is that these basic moves are so common that they can be represented in *templates* that you can use right away to structure and even generate your own writing. Perhaps the most distinctive feature of this book is its presentation of many such templates, designed to help you successfully enter not only the world of academic thinking and writing but also the wider worlds of civic discourse and work.

Instead of focusing solely on abstract principles of writing, then, this book offers model templates that help you put those principles directly into practice. Working with these templates will give you an immediate sense of how to engage in the kinds of critical thinking you are required to do at the college level and in the vocational and public spheres beyond.

Some of these templates represent simple but crucial moves, like those used to summarize some widely held belief:

▸ Many Americans assume that _____.

Others are more complicated:

▸ On the one hand, _____. On the other hand, _____.

▸ Author X contradicts herself. At the same time that she argues _____, she also implies _____.

▸ I agree that _____. However, _____.

▸ This is not to say that _____.

It is true, of course, that critical thinking and writing go deeper than any set of linguistic formulas, requiring that you question assumptions, develop strong claims, offer supporting reasons and evidence, consider opposing arguments, and so on. But these deeper habits of thought cannot be put into practice unless you have a language for expressing them in clear, organized ways.

2

STATE YOUR OWN IDEAS AS A
RESPONSE TO OTHERS

The single most important template that we focus on in this book is the "they say _____; I say _____" formula that gives our book its title. If there is any one point that we hope you will take away from this book, it is the importance not only of expressing your ideas ("I say") but of presenting those ideas as a *response to some other person or group* ("they say"). For us, the underlying structure of effective academic writing—and of responsible public discourse—resides not just in stating our own ideas but in listening closely to others around us, summarizing their views in a way that they will recognize, and responding with our own ideas in kind. Broadly speaking, academic writing is argumentative writing, and we believe that to argue well you need to do more than assert your own position. You need to enter a conversation, using what others say (or might say) as a launching pad or sounding board for your own views. For this reason, one of the main pieces of advice in this book is to write the voices of others into your text.

In our view, then, the best academic writing has one underlying feature: it is deeply engaged in some way with other people's views. Too often, however, academic writing is taught as a process of saying "true" or "smart" things in a vacuum, as if it were possible to argue effectively without being in conversation *with* someone else. If you have been taught to write a traditional five-paragraph essay, for example, you have learned how to develop a thesis and support it with evidence. This is good advice as far as it goes, but it leaves out the important fact that in the real world we don't make arguments without being provoked. Instead, we make arguments because someone has said or done something (or perhaps *not* said or done something) and we need to respond: "I can't see why you like the Lakers so much"; "I agree: it was a great film"; "That argument is contradictory." If it weren't for other people and our need to challenge, agree with, or otherwise respond to them, there would be no reason to argue at all.

"WHY ARE YOU TELLING ME THIS?"

To make an impact as a writer, then, you need to do more than make statements that are logical, well supported, and consistent. You must also find a way of entering into conversation with the views of others, with something "they say." The easiest and most common way writers do this is by *summarizing* what others say and then using it to set up what they want to say.

"But why," as a student of ours once asked, "do I always need to summarize the views of others to set up my own view? Why can't I just state my own view and be done with it?" Why indeed? After all, "they," whoever they may be, will have already had their say, so why do you have to *repeat* it? Furthermore, if they had their say in print, can't readers just go and read what was said themselves?

The answer is that if you don't identify the "they say" you're responding to, your own argument probably won't have a point. Readers will wonder what prompted you to say what you're saying and therefore motivated you to write. As the figure on the following page suggests, without a "they say," *what* you are saying may be clear to your audience, but *why* you are saying it won't be.

Even if we don't know what film he's referring to, it's easy to grasp what the speaker means here when he says that its characters are very complex. But it's hard to see why the speaker feels the need to say what he is saying. "Why," as one member

of his imagined audience wonders, "is he telling us this?" So the characters are complex—so what?

Now look at what happens to the same proposition when it is presented as a response to something "they say":

We hope you agree that the same claim—"the characters in the film are very complex"—becomes much stronger when presented as a response to a contrary view: that the film's characters "are sexist stereotypes." Unlike the speaker in the first cartoon, the speaker in the second has a clear goal or mission: to correct what he sees as a mistaken characterization.

THE AS-OPPOSED-TO-WHAT FACTOR

To put our point another way, framing your "I say" as a response to something "they say" gives your writing an element of contrast without which it won't make sense. It may be helpful to think of this crucial element as an "as-opposed-to-what factor" and, as you write, to continually ask yourself, "Who says otherwise?" and "Does anyone dispute it?" Behind the audience's "Yeah, so?" and "Why is he telling us this?" in the first cartoon above lie precisely these types of "As opposed to what?" questions. The speaker in the second cartoon, we think, is more satisfying because he answers these questions, helping us see his point that the film presents complex characters *rather than* simple sexist stereotypes.

HOW IT'S DONE

Many accomplished writers make explicit "they say" moves to set up and motivate their own arguments. One famous example is Martin Luther King Jr.'s "Letter from Birmingham Jail," which consists almost entirely of King's eloquent responses to a public statement by eight clergymen deploring the civil rights protests he was leading. The letter—which was written in 1963, while King was in prison for leading a demonstration against racial injustice in Birmingham—is structured almost entirely around a framework of summary and response, in which King summarizes and then answers their criticisms. In one typical passage, King writes as follows:

> You deplore the demonstrations taking place in Birmingham. But your statement, I am sorry to say, fails to express a similar concern for the conditions that brought about the demonstrations.
>
> MARTIN LUTHER KING JR., "Letter from Birmingham Jail"

King goes on to agree with his critics that "it is unfortunate that demonstrations are taking place in Birmingham," yet he hastens to add that "it is even more unfortunate that the city's white power structure left the Negro community with no alternative." King's letter is so thoroughly conversational, in fact, that it could be rewritten in the form of a dialogue or play.

King's critics:
King's response:
Critics:
Response:

Clearly, King would not have written his famous letter were it not for his critics, whose views he treats not as objections to his already-formed arguments but as the motivating source of those arguments, their central reason for being. He quotes not only what his critics have said ("Some have asked: 'Why didn't you give the new city administration time to act?'"), but also things they *might* have said ("One may well ask: 'How can you advocate breaking some laws and obeying others?'")—all to set the stage for what he himself wants to say.

A similar "they say / I say" exchange opens an essay about American patriotism by the social critic Katha Pollitt, who uses her own daughter's comment to represent the patriotic national fervor after the terrorist attacks of September 11, 2001.

> My daughter, who goes to Stuyvesant High School only blocks from the former World Trade Center, thinks we should fly the American flag out our window. Definitely not, I say: the flag stands for jingoism and vengeance and war. She tells me I'm wrong—the flag means standing together and honoring the dead and saying no to terrorism. In a way we're both right. . . .
>
> KATHA POLLITT, "Put Out No Flags"

As Pollitt's example shows, the "they" you respond to in crafting an argument need not be a famous author or someone known to your audience. It can be a family member, like Pollitt's daughter, or a friend or classmate who has made a provocative claim. It can even be something an individual or a group might say—or a side of yourself, something you once believed but no longer do, or something you partly believe but also doubt. The important thing is that the "they" (or "you" or "she") represent some wider group with which readers might identify—in Pollitt's case, those who patriotically believe in flying the flag. Pollitt's example also shows that responding to the views of others need not always involve unquali-fied opposition. By agreeing and disagreeing with her daughter, Pollitt enacts what we call the "yes and no" response, reconciling apparently incompatible views.

See Chapter 4 for more on agreeing, but with a difference.

While King and Pollitt both identify the views they are responding to, some authors do not explicitly state their views but instead allow the reader to infer them. See, for instance, if you can identify the implied or unnamed "they say" that the following claim is responding to:

> I like to think I have a certain advantage as a teacher of literature because when I was growing up I disliked and feared books.
> GERALD GRAFF, "Disliking Books at an Early Age"

In case you haven't figured it out already, the phantom "they say" here is the common belief that in order to be a good teacher of literature, one must have grown up liking and enjoying books.

COURT CONTROVERSY, BUT...

As you can see from these examples, many writers use the "they say / I say" format to challenge standard ways of thinking and thus to stir up controversy. This point may come as a shock to you if you have always had the impression that in order to succeed academically you need to play it safe and avoid controversy in your writing, making statements that nobody can possibly disagree with. Though this view of writing may appear logical, it is actually a recipe for flat, lifeless writing and for writing that fails to answer what we call the "so what?" and "who cares?" questions. "William Shakespeare wrote many famous plays and sonnets" may be a perfectly true statement, but precisely because nobody is likely to disagree with it, it goes without saying and thus would seem pointless if said.

But just because controversy is important doesn't mean you have to become an attack dog who automatically disagrees with everything others say. We think this is an important point to underscore because some who are not familiar with this book have gotten the impression from the title that our goal is to train writers simply to disparage whatever "they say."

LISTEN BEFORE YOU LEAP

There certainly are occasions when strong critique is needed. It's hard to live in a deeply polarized society like our current one and not feel the need at times to criticize what others think. But even the most justified critiques fall flat, we submit, unless we really listen to and understand the views we are criticizing:

▸ While I understand the impulse to _____, my own view is _____.

Even the most sympathetic audiences, after all, tend to feel manipulated by arguments that scapegoat and caricature the other side.

Furthermore, genuinely listening to views we disagree with can have the salutary effect of helping us see that beliefs we'd initially disdained may not be as thoroughly reprehensible as we'd imagined. Thus the type of "they say / I say" argument that we promote in this book can take the form of agreeing up to a point or, as the Pollitt example above illustrates, of both agreeing and disagreeing simultaneously, as in:

▸ While I agree with X that _____, I cannot accept her over-all conclusion that _____.

▸ While X argues _____, and I argue _____, in a way we're both right.

Agreement cannot be ruled out, however:

▸ I agree with _____ that _____.

THE TEMPLATE OF TEMPLATES

There are many ways, then, to enter a conversation and respond to what "they say." But our discussion of ways to do so would be incomplete were we not to mention the most comprehensive way that writers enter conversations, which incorporates all the major moves discussed in this book:

▸ In recent discussions of _____, a controversial issue has been whether _____. On the one hand, some argue that _____. From this perspective, _____. On the other hand, however, others argue that _____. In the words of X, one of this view's main proponents, "_____." According to this view, _____. In sum, then, the issue is whether _____ or _____.

My own view is that _____. Though I concede that _____, I still maintain that _____. For example, _____. Although some might object that _____, I would reply that _____. The issue is important because _____.

This "template of templates," as we like to call it, represents the internal DNA of countless articles and even entire books. Writers commonly use a version of it not only to stake out their "they say" and "I say" at the start of their manuscript, but—just as important—to form the overarching blueprint that structures what they write over the entire length of their text.

Taking it line by line, this master template first helps you open your text by identifying an issue in some ongoing conversation or debate ("In recent discussions of _____, a controversial issue has been _____") and then map some of the voices in this controversy (by using the "on the one hand / on the other hand" structure). The template then helps you introduce a quotation ("In the words of X") and explain the quotation in your own words ("According to this view"). Then, in a new paragraph, it helps you state your own argument ("My own view is that"), qualify your argument ("Though I concede that"), and support your argument with evidence ("For example"). In addition, the template helps you make one of the most crucial moves in argumentative writing, what we call "planting a naysayer in your text," in which you summarize and then answer a likely objection to your own central claim ("Although it might be objected that _____, I reply _____"). Finally, this template helps you shift between general, overarching claims ("In sum, then") and smaller-scale, supporting claims ("For example").

Again, none of us is born knowing these moves, especially when it comes to academic writing—hence the need for this book.

BUT ISN'T THIS PLAGIARISM?

"But isn't this plagiarism?" at least one student each year will usually ask. "Well, is it?" we respond, turning the question around into one the entire class can profit from. "We are, after all, asking you to use language in your writing that isn't your own—language that you 'borrow' or, to put it less delicately, steal from other writers."

Often, a lively discussion ensues that raises important questions about authorial ownership and helps everyone better understand the frequently confusing line between plagiarism and the legitimate use of what others say and how they say it. Students are quick to see that no one person owns a conventional formula like "on the one hand / on the other hand." Phrases like "a controversial issue" are so commonly used and recycled that they are generic— community property that can be freely used without fear of committing plagiarism. It *is* plagiarism, however, if the words used to fill in the blanks of such formulas are borrowed from others without proper acknowledgment. In sum, then, while it is not plagiarism to recycle conventionally used formulas, it is a serious academic offense to take the substantive content from others' texts without citing the authors and giving them proper credit.

"OK—BUT TEMPLATES?"

Nevertheless, if you are like some of our students, your initial response to templates may be skepticism. At first, many of our students complain that using templates will take away their originality and creativity and make them all sound the same. "They'll turn us into writing robots," one of our students insisted. "I'm in college now," another student asserted. "This is third-grade-level stuff."

In our view, however, the templates in this book, far from being "third-grade-level stuff," represent the stock-in-trade of sophisticated thinking and writing, and they often require a great deal of practice and instruction to use successfully. As for the belief that preestablished forms undermine creativity, we think it rests on a very limited vision of what creativity is all about. In our view, the templates in this book will actually help your writing become *more* original and creative, not less. After all, even the most creative forms of expression depend on established patterns and structures. Most songwriters, for instance, rely on a time-honored verse-chorus-verse pattern, and few people would call Shakespeare uncreative because he didn't invent the sonnet or the dramatic forms that he used to such dazzling effect. Even the most avant-garde, cutting-edge artists like improvisational jazz musicians need to master the basic forms that their work improvises on, departs from, and goes beyond, or else their work will come across as uneducated child's play. Ultimately, then, creativity and originality lie not in the avoidance of established forms but in the imaginative use of them.

Furthermore, these templates do not dictate the *content* of what you say, which can be as original as you can make it, but only suggest a way of formatting *how* you say it. In addition, once you begin to feel comfortable with the templates in this book, you will be able to improvise creatively on them to fit new situations and purposes and find others in your reading. In other words, the templates offered here are learning tools to get you started, not structures set in stone. Once you get used to using them, you can even dispense with them altogether, for the rhetorical moves they model will be at your fingertips in an unconscious, instinctive way.

But if you still need proof that writing templates need not make you sound stiff and artificial, consider the following opening to an essay on the fast-food industry that we've included in Chapter 14:

> If ever there were a newspaper headline custom-made for Jay Leno's monologue, this was it. Kids taking on McDonald's this week, suing the company for making them fat. Isn't that like middle-aged men suing Porsche for making them get speeding tickets? Whatever happened to personal responsibility?
>
> I tend to sympathize with these portly fast-food patrons, though. Maybe that's because I used to be one of them.
>
> DAVID ZINCZENKO, "Don't Blame the Eater"

Although Zinczenko relies on a version of the "they say / I say" formula, his writing is anything but dry, robotic, or uncreative. While Zinczenko does not explicitly use the words "they say" and "I say," the template still gives the passage its underlying structure: "*They say* that kids suing fast-food companies for making them fat is a joke; but *I say* such lawsuits are justified."

PUTTING IN YOUR OAR

Though the immediate goal of this book is to help you become a better writer, at a deeper level it invites you to become a certain type of person: a critical, intellectual thinker who, instead of sitting passively on the sidelines, can participate in the debates and conversations of your world in an active and empowered way. Ultimately, this book invites you to become a critical thinker who can enter the types of conversations described eloquently by the philosopher Kenneth Burke in the following widely cited passage. Likening the world of intellectual exchange to a never-ending conversation at a party, Burke writes:

> You come late. When you arrive, others have long preceded you, and they are engaged in a heated discussion, a discussion too heated for them to pause and tell you exactly what it is about. . . . You listen for a while, until you decide that you have caught the tenor of the argument; then you put in your oar. Someone answers; you answer him; another comes to your defense; another aligns himself against you. . . . The hour grows late, you must depart. And you do depart, with the discussion still vigorously in progress.
>
> KENNETH BURKE, *The Philosophy of Literary Form*

What we like about this passage is its suggestion that stating an argument (putting in your oar) can only be done in conversation with others; that entering the dynamic world of ideas must be done not as isolated individuals but as social beings deeply connected to others.

This ability to enter complex, many-sided conversations has taken on a special urgency in today's polarized red state / blue state America, where the future for all of us may depend on our ability to put ourselves in the shoes of those who think very differently from us. The central piece of advice in this book—that we listen carefully to others, including those who disagree with us, and then engage with them thoughtfully and respectfully—can help us see beyond our own pet beliefs, which may not be shared by everyone. The mere act of crafting a sentence that begins "Of course, someone might object that _____" may not seem like a way to change the world; but it does have the potential to jog us out of our comfort zones, to get us thinking critically about our own beliefs, and even to change minds, our own included.

Exercises

1. Write two paragraphs in which you first summarize our rationale for the templates in this book and then articulate your own position in response. If you want, you can use the template below to organize your paragraphs, expanding and modifying it as necessary to fit what you want to say:

   In the Introduction to *"They Say / I Say": The Moves That Matter in Academic Writing,* Gerald Graff and Cathy Birkenstein provide templates designed to _____. Specifically, Graff and Birkenstein argue that the types of writing templates they offer _____. As the authors themselves put it, "_____." Although some people believe _____, Graff and Birkenstein insist that _____. In sum, then, their view is that _____.

   I [agree / disagree / have mixed feelings]. In my view, the types of templates that the authors recommend _____. For instance, _____. In addition, _____. Some might object, of course, on the grounds that _____. Yet I would argue that _____. Overall, then, I believe _____ —an important point to make given _____.

2. Read the following paragraph from an essay by Emily Poe, written when she was a student at Furman University. Disregarding for the moment what Poe says, focus your attention on the phrases she uses to structure what she says (italicized here). Then write a new paragraph using Poe's as a model but replacing her topic, vegetarianism, with one of your own.

   The term "vegetarian" tends to be synonymous with "tree-hugger" in many people's minds. *They see* vegetarianism as a cult that brainwashes its followers into eliminating an essential part of their daily diets for an abstract goal of "animal welfare." *However*, few vegetarians choose their lifestyle just to follow the crowd. *On the contrary*, many of these supposedly brainwashed people are actually independent thinkers, concerned citizens, and compassionate human beings. *For the truth is* that there are many very good reasons for giving up meat. Perhaps the best reasons are to improve the environment, to encourage humane treatment of livestock, or to enhance one's own health. *In this essay, then*, closely examining a vegetarian diet as compared to a meat-eater's diet will show that vegetarianism is clearly the better option for sustaining the Earth and all its inhabitants.

ONE

"THEY SAY"
Starting with What Others Are Saying

—▢—

NOT LONG AGO we attended a talk at an academic conference where the speaker's central claim seemed to be that a certain sociologist—call him Dr. X—had done very good work in a number of areas of the discipline. The speaker proceeded to illustrate his thesis by referring extensively and in great detail to various books and articles by Dr. X and by quoting long passages from them. The speaker was obviously both learned and impassioned, but as we listened to his talk, we found ourselves somewhat puzzled: the argument—that Dr. X's work was very important—was clear enough, but why did the speaker need to make it in the first place? Did anyone dispute it? Were there commentators in the field who had argued against X's work or challenged its value? Was the speaker's interpretation of what X had done somehow novel or revolutionary? Since the speaker gave no hint of an answer to any of these questions, we could only wonder why he was going on and on about X. It was only after the speaker finished and took questions from the audience that we got a clue: in response to one questioner, he referred to several critics who had

The hypothetical audience in the figure on p. 5 reacts similarly.

vigorously questioned Dr. X's ideas and convinced many sociologists that Dr. X's work was unsound.

This story illustrates an important lesson: that to give writing the most important thing of all—namely, a point—writers need to indicate clearly not only what their thesis is but also what larger conversation that thesis is responding to. Because our speaker failed to mention what others had said about Dr. X's work, he left his audience unsure about why he felt the need to say what he was saying. Perhaps the point was clear to other sociologists in the audience who were more familiar with the debates over Dr. X's work than we were. But even they, we bet, would have understood the speaker's point better if he'd sketched in some of the larger conversation his own claims were a part of and reminded the audience about what "they say."

This story also illustrates an important lesson about the *order* in which things are said: to keep an audience engaged, writers need to explain what they are responding to—either before offering that response or, at least, very early in the discussion. Delaying this explanation for more than one or two paragraphs in a very short essay or blog entry, three or four pages in a longer work, or more than ten or so pages in a book reverses the natural order in which readers process material—and in which writers think and develop ideas. After all, it seems very unlikely that our conference speaker first developed his defense of Dr. X and only later came across Dr. X's critics. As someone knowledgeable in his field, the speaker surely encountered the criticisms first and only then was compelled to respond and, as he saw it, set the record straight.

Therefore, when it comes to constructing an argument (whether orally or in writing), we offer you the following advice: remember that you are entering a conversation and therefore need to start with "what others are saying," as the title of this chapter recommends, and then introduce your own ideas as a response. Specifically, we suggest that you summarize what "they say" as soon as you can in your text and remind readers of it at strategic points as your text unfolds. Though it's true that not all texts follow this practice, we think it's important for all writers to master it before they depart from it.

This is not to say that you must start with a detailed list of everyone who has written on your subject before you offer your own ideas. Had our conference speaker gone to the opposite extreme and spent most of his talk summarizing Dr. X's critics with no hint of what he himself had to say, the audience probably would have had the same frustrated "why is he going on like this?" reaction. What we suggest, then, is that as soon as possible you state your own position and the one it's responding to *together*, and that you think of the two as a unit. It is generally best to summarize the ideas you're responding to briefly, at the start of your text, and to delay detailed elaboration until later. The point is to give your readers a quick preview of what is motivating your argument, not to drown them in details right away.

Starting with a summary of others' views may seem to contradict the common advice that writers should lead with their own thesis or claim. Although we agree that you shouldn't keep readers in suspense too long about your central argument, we also believe that you need to present that argument as part of some larger conversation, indicating something about the arguments of others that you are supporting, opposing, amending, complicating, or qualifying. One added benefit of summarizing others' views as soon as you can: you let those others do some of the work of framing and clarifying the issue you're writing about.

Consider, for example, how George Orwell starts his famous essay "Politics and the English Language" with what others are saying:

Most people who bother with the matter at all would admit that the English language is in a bad way, but it is generally assumed that we cannot by conscious action do anything about it. Our civilization is decadent and our language—so the argument runs—must inevitably share in the general collapse. . . .

[But] the process is reversible. Modern English . . . is full of bad habits . . . which can be avoided if one is willing to take the necessary trouble.

GEORGE ORWELL, "Politics and the English Language"

Orwell is basically saying, "Most people assume that we cannot do anything about the bad state of the English language. But I say we can."

Of course, there are many other powerful ways to begin. Instead of opening with someone else's views, you could start with an illustrative quotation, a revealing fact or statistic, or—as we do in this chapter—a relevant anecdote. If you choose one of these formats, however, be sure that it in some way illustrates the view you're addressing or leads you to that view directly, with a minimum of steps.

In opening this chapter, for example, we devote the first paragraph to an anecdote about the conference speaker and then move quickly at the start of the second paragraph to the misconception about writing exemplified by the speaker. In the following opening, from an opinion piece in the *New York Times Book Review*, Christina Nehring also moves quickly from an anecdote illustrating something she dislikes to her own claim—that book lovers think too highly of themselves:

"I'm a reader!" announced the yellow button. "How about you?" I looked at its bearer, a strapping young guy stalking my town's Festival of Books. "I'll bet you're a reader," he volunteered, as though we were two geniuses well met. "No," I replied. "Absolutely not," I wanted to yell, and fling my Barnes & Noble bag at his feet. Instead, I mumbled something apologetic and melted into the crowd.

There's a new piety in the air: the self-congratulation of book lovers.

CHRISTINA NEHRING, "Books Make You a Boring Person"

Nehring's anecdote is really a kind of "they say": book lovers keep telling themselves how great they are.

TEMPLATES FOR INTRODUCING WHAT "THEY SAY"

There are lots of conventional ways to introduce what others are saying. Here are some standard templates that we would have recommended to our conference speaker:

▸ **A number of sociologists have recently suggested <u>that X's work has several fundamental problems</u>.**

▸ **It has become common today to dismiss _____.**

▸ **In their recent work, Y and Z have offered harsh critiques of _____ for _____.**

TEMPLATES FOR INTRODUCING "STANDARD VIEWS"

The following templates can help you make what we call the "standard view" move, in which you introduce a view that has become so widely accepted that by now it is essentially the conventional way of thinking about a topic:

- Americans have always believed that <u>individual effort can triumph over circumstances</u>.

- Conventional wisdom has it that _____.

- Common sense seems to dictate that _____.

- The standard way of thinking about topic X has it that _____.

- It is often said that _____.

- My whole life I have heard it said that _____.

- You would think that _____.

- Many people assume that _____.

These templates are popular because they provide a quick and efficient way to perform one of the most common moves that writers make: challenging widely accepted beliefs, placing them on the examining table, and analyzing their strengths and weaknesses.

TEMPLATES FOR MAKING WHAT "THEY SAY" SOMETHING *YOU* SAY

Another way to introduce the views you're responding to is to present them as your own. That is, the "they say" that you respond to need not be a view held by others; it can be one that you yourself once held or one that you are ambivalent about:

- I've always believed that <u>museums are boring</u>.

- When I was a child, I used to think that _____.

▶ Although I should know better by now, I cannot help thinking that _____ .

▶ At the same time that I believe _____ , I also believe _____ .

TEMPLATES FOR INTRODUCING
SOMETHING IMPLIED OR ASSUMED

Another sophisticated move a writer can make is to summarize a point that is not directly stated in what "they say" but is implied or assumed:

▶ Although none of them have ever said so directly, my teachers have often given me the impression that <u>education will open doors</u>.

▶ One implication of X's treatment of _____ is that _____ .

▶ Although X does not say so directly, she apparently assumes that _____ .

▶ While they rarely admit as much, _____ often take for granted that _____ .

These are templates that can help you think analytically—to look beyond what others say explicitly and to consider their unstated assumptions, as well as the implications of their views.

TEMPLATES FOR INTRODUCING
AN ONGOING DEBATE

Sometimes you'll want to open by summarizing a debate that presents two or more views. This kind of opening demonstrates your awareness that there are conflicting ways to look at your subject, the clear mark of someone who knows the subject and therefore is likely to be a reliable, trustworthy guide. Furthermore, opening with a summary of a debate can help you explore the issue you are writing about before declaring your own view. In this way, you can use the writing process itself to help you discover where you stand instead of having to commit to a position before you are ready to do so.

Here is a basic template for opening with a debate:

> ► In discussions of X, one controversial issue has been _____.
> On the one hand, _____ argues _____. On the other
> hand, _____ contends _____. Others even maintain
> _____. My own view is _____.

The cognitive scientist Mark Aronoff uses this kind of template in an essay on the workings of the human brain:

> Theories of how the mind/brain works have been dominated
> for centuries by two opposing views. One, rationalism, sees the
> human mind as coming into this world more or less fully formed—
> preprogrammed, in modern terms. The other, empiricism, sees the
> mind of the newborn as largely unstructured, a blank slate.
>
> MARK ARONOFF, "Washington Slept Here"

A student writer, Michaela Cullington, uses a version of this template near the beginning of an essay to frame a debate over online writing abbreviations like "LOL" ("laughing out loud") and to indicate her own position in this debate:

> Some people believe that using these abbreviations is hindering
> the writing abilities of students, and others argue that texting is

actually having a positive effect on writing. In fact, it seems likely that texting has no significant effect on student writing.

MICHAELA CULLINGTON, "Does Texting Affect Writing?"

Another way to open with a debate involves starting with a proposition many people agree with in order to highlight the point(s) on which they ultimately disagree:

▸ **When it comes to the topic of _____, most of us will readily agree that _____. Where this agreement usually ends, however, is on the question of _____. Whereas some are convinced that _____, others maintain that _____.**

The political writer Thomas Frank uses a variation on this move:

That we are a nation divided is an almost universal lament of this bitter election year. However, the exact property that divides us—elemental though it is said to be—remains a matter of some controversy.

THOMAS FRANK, "American Psyche"

KEEP WHAT "THEY SAY" IN VIEW

We can't urge you too strongly to keep in mind what "they say" as you move through the rest of your text. After summarizing the ideas you are responding to at the outset, it's very important to continue to keep those ideas in view. Readers won't be able to follow your unfolding response, much less any complications you may offer, unless you keep reminding them what claims you are responding to.

In other words, even when presenting your own claims, you should keep returning to the motivating "they say." The longer and more complicated your text, the greater the chance that readers will forget what ideas originally motivated it—no matter how clearly you lay them out at the beginning. At strategic moments throughout your text, we recommend that you include what we call "return sentences." Here is an example:

> ▶ In conclusion, then, as I suggested earlier, defenders of _____ can't have it both ways. Their assertion that _____ is contradicted by their claim that _____.

We ourselves use such return sentences at every opportunity in this book to remind you of the view of writing that our book questions—that good writing means making true or smart or logical statements about a given subject with little or no reference to what others say about it.

By reminding readers of the ideas you're responding to, return sentences ensure that your text maintains a sense of mission and urgency from start to finish. In short, they frame your argument as a genuine response to others' views rather than just a set of observations about a given subject. The difference is huge. To be responsive to others and the conversation you're entering, you need to start with what others are saying and continue keeping it in the readers' view.

Exercises

1. Following is a list of topics people have debated. Working by yourself or with a partner, compose a "they say" argument

for each of these topics, using any of the templates from this chapter.

Example:

Self-driving vehicles. "Many people think that self-driving cars will make roads safer by reducing accidents caused by unavoidable human errors."

a. Free college tuition at public universities
b. Social media use among teenagers
c. The value of studying the humanities in college
d. Public-funded clean needle exchanges
e. Assigning homework in elementary school

When you finish, read aloud and compare your "they say" arguments with a partner or a small group. Which template moves were more challenging than others to use? Why do you think so?

2. Read the following passage from Kenneth Goldsmith's 2016 *Los Angeles Times* op-ed, "Go Ahead: Waste Time on the Internet."

The notion that the Internet is bad for you seems premised on the idea that the Internet is one thing—a monolith. In reality it's a befuddling mix of the stupid and the sublime, a shattered, contradictory, and fragmented medium. Internet detractors seem to miss this simple fact, which is why so many of their criticisms disintegrate under observation.

The way Internet pundits tell it, you'd think we stare for three hours at clickbait—those articles with hypersensational headlines—the way we once sat down and watched three hours of cartoons on Saturday morning TV. But most of us don't do any one thing on the Internet. Instead, we do many things, some of it frivolous, some of it heavy. Our time spent in front of the computer is a mixed time, a time that reflects our desires—as opposed to the time spent sitting in front of the television where we were fed shows we didn't necessarily enjoy. TV gave us few choices. Many of us truly did feel like we wasted our time—as our parents so often chided us—"rotting away" in front of the TV.

I keep reading—on screens—that in the age of screens we've lost our ability to concentrate, that we've become distracted. But when I look around me and see people riveted to their devices, I notice a great wealth of concentration, focus, and engagement.

a. Where in this passage do you see Goldsmith introducing what others are saying about the internet and the amount of time we spend on screens? What do you notice about the different ways Goldsmith introduces "they say" arguments?

b. Summarize Goldsmith's argument by using the following template for introducing an ongoing debate (p. 26):

In discussions of **how the internet affects people**, one controversial issue has been _____. On one hand, _____ argues _____. On the other hand, _____ contends _____. Others even maintain _____. My own view is _____.

3. Read over something you've written for one of your classes—a paragraph, a short response, or an essay—and then respond to the following questions. You can do this exercise with a partner or by yourself.

a. Where do you introduce what others are saying? Underline or highlight where you include a "they say." If you can't find a "they say" in your writing, add one using one of the templates from this chapter.

b. How soon in your argument do you introduce these other views? Make sure that you include a "they say" early in your writing (in the first paragraph or two for a short response or essay). If the views you're responding to are buried later in your piece, revise your writing so that they appear earlier.

TWO

"HER POINT IS"

The Art of Summarizing

IF IT IS TRUE, as we claim in this book, that to argue persuasively you need to be in dialogue with others, then summarizing others' arguments is central to your arsenal of basic moves. Because writers who make strong claims need to map their claims relative to those of other people, it is important to know how to summarize effectively what those other people say. (We're using the word "summarizing" here to refer to any information from others that you present in your own words, including that which you paraphrase.)

Many writers shy away from summarizing—perhaps because they don't want to take the trouble to go back to the text in question and wrestle with what it says, or because they fear that devoting too much time to other people's ideas will take away from their own. When assigned to write a response to an article, such writers might offer their own views on the article's *topic* while hardly mentioning what the article itself argues or says. At the opposite extreme are those who do nothing *but* summarize. Lacking confidence, perhaps, in their own ideas, these writers so overload their texts with summaries of others' ideas that their own voice gets lost. And since these summaries are not animated by the writers' own interests, they often read like mere lists of things that X thinks or Y says—with no clear focus.

As a general rule, a good summary requires balancing what the original author is saying with the writer's own focus. Generally speaking, a summary must at once be true to what the original author says while also emphasizing those aspects of what the author says that interest you, the writer. Striking this delicate balance can be tricky, since it means facing two ways at once: both outward (toward the author being summarized) and inward (toward yourself). Ultimately, it means being respectful of others but simultaneously structuring how you summarize them in light of your own text's central argument.

ON THE ONE HAND, PUT YOURSELF IN *THEIR* SHOES

To write a really good summary, you must be able to suspend your own beliefs for a time and put yourself in the shoes of someone else. This means playing what the writing theorist Peter Elbow calls the "believing game," in which you try to inhabit the worldview of those whose conversation you are joining—and whom you are perhaps even disagreeing with—and try to see their argument from their perspective. This ability to temporarily suspend one's own convictions is a hallmark of good actors, who must convincingly "become" characters whom in real life they may detest. As a writer, when you play the believing game well, readers should not be able to tell whether you agree or disagree with the ideas you are summarizing.

If, as a writer, you cannot or will not suspend your own beliefs in this way, you are likely to produce summaries that are so obviously biased that they undermine your credibility with readers. Consider the following summary:

> David Zinczenko's article "Don't Blame the Eater" is nothing more than an angry rant in which he accuses the fast-food companies of an evil conspiracy to make people fat. I disagree because these companies have to make money. . . .

If you review what Zinczenko actually says (pp. 199–202), you should immediately see that this summary amounts to an unfair distortion. While Zinczenko does argue that the practices of the fast-food industry have the *effect* of making people fat, his tone is never "angry," and he never goes so far as to suggest that the fast-food industry conspires to make people fat with deliberately evil intent.

Another telltale sign of this writer's failure to give Zinczenko a fair hearing is the hasty way he abandons the summary after only one sentence and rushes on to his own response. So eager is this writer to disagree that he not only caricatures what Zinczenko says but also gives the article a hasty, superficial reading. Granted, there are many writing situations in which, because of matters of proportion, a one- or two-sentence summary is precisely what you want. Indeed, as writing professor Karen Lunsford (whose own research focuses on argument theory) points out, it is standard in the natural and social sciences to summarize the work of others quickly, in one pithy sentence or phrase, as in the following example:

> Several studies (Crackle, 2012; Pop, 2007; Snap, 2006) suggest that these policies are harmless; moreover, other studies (Dick, 2011; Harry, 2007; Tom, 2005) argue that they even have benefits.

But if your assignment is to respond in writing to a single author, like Zinczenko, you will need to tell your readers enough about the argument so they can assess its merits on their own, independent of you.

When summarizing something you've read, be sure to provide a rigorous and thoughtful summary of the author's words, or you may fall prey to what we call "the closest cliché syndrome," in which what gets summarized is not the view the author in question has actually expressed but a familiar cliché that the writer mistakes for the author's view (sometimes because the writer believes it and mistakenly assumes the author must too). So, for example, Martin Luther King Jr.'s passionate defense of civil disobedience in "Letter from Birmingham Jail" might be summarized not as the defense of political protest that it actually is but as a plea for everyone to "just get along." Similarly, Zinczenko's critique of the fast-food industry might be summarized as a call for overweight people to take responsibility for their weight.

Whenever you enter into a conversation with others in your writing, then, it is extremely important that you go back to what those others have said, that you study it very closely, and that you not confuse it with something you already believe. Writers who fail to do this end up essentially conversing with imaginary others who are really only the products of their own biases and preconceptions.

ON THE OTHER HAND, KNOW WHERE *YOU* ARE GOING

Even as writing an effective summary requires you to temporarily adopt the worldview of another person, it does not mean ignoring your own view altogether. Paradoxically, at the same time that summarizing another text requires you to represent fairly what it says, it also requires that your own response exert a quiet influence. A good summary, in other words, has a focus or spin that allows the summary to fit with your own agenda while still being true to the text you are summarizing.

Thus if you are writing in response to the essay by Zinczenko, you should be able to see that an essay on the fast-food industry in general will call for a very different summary than will an essay on parenting, corporate regulation, or warning labels. If you want your essay to encompass all three topics, you'll need to subordinate these three issues to one of Zinczenko's general claims and then make sure this general claim directly sets up your own argument.

For example, suppose you want to argue that it is parents, not fast-food companies, who are to blame for children's obesity. To set up this argument, you will probably want to compose a summary that highlights what Zinczenko says about the fast-food industry *and parents*. Consider this sample:

In his article "Don't Blame the Eater," David Zinczenko blames the fast-food industry for fueling today's so-called obesity epidemic, not only by failing to provide adequate warning labels on its high-calorie foods but also by filling the nutritional void in children's lives left by their overtaxed working parents. With many parents working long hours and unable to supervise what their children eat, Zinczenko claims, children today are easily victimized by the low-cost, calorie-laden foods that the fast-food chains are all too eager to supply. When he was a young boy, for instance, and his single mother was away at work, he ate at Taco Bell, McDonald's, and other chains on a regular basis, and ended up overweight. Zinczenko's hope is that with the new spate of lawsuits against the food industry, other children with working parents will have healthier choices available to them, and that they will not, like him, become obese.

In my view, however, it is the parents, and not the food chains, who are responsible for their children's obesity. While it is true that many of today's parents work long hours, there are still several things that parents can do to guarantee that their children eat healthy foods. . . .

The summary in the first paragraph succeeds because it points in two directions at once—both toward Zinczenko's own text *and* toward the second paragraph, where the writer begins to establish her own argument. The opening sentence gives a sense of Zinczenko's general argument (that the fast-food chains are to blame for obesity), including his two main supporting claims (about warning labels and parents), but it ends with an emphasis on the writer's main concern: parental responsibility. In this way, the summary does justice to Zinczenko's arguments while also setting up the ensuing critique.

This advice—to summarize authors in light of your own agenda—may seem painfully obvious. But writers often summarize a given author on one issue even though their text actually focuses on another. To avoid this problem, you need to make sure that your "they say" and "I say" are well matched. In fact, aligning what they say with what you say is a good thing to work on when revising what you've written.

Often writers who summarize without regard to their own agenda fall prey to what might be called "list summaries," summaries that simply inventory the original author's various points but fail to focus those points around any larger overall claim. If you've ever heard a talk in which the points were connected only by words like "and then," "also," and "in addition," you

AND THEN HE SAYS ... THEN ALSO HE POINTS OUT... ...AND THEN ANOTHER THING HE SAYS IS ... AND THEN ...

ZZZ ZZZ

GG

THE EFFECT OF A TYPICAL LIST SUMMARY

know how such lists can put listeners to sleep—as shown in the figure above. A typical list summary sounds like this:

> The author says many different things about his subject. *First* he says . . . *Then* he makes the point that . . . *In addition* he says . . . *And then* he writes . . . *Also* he shows that . . . *And then* he says . . .

It may be boring list summaries like this that give summaries in general a bad name and even prompt some instructors to discourage their students from summarizing at all.

Not all lists are bad, however. A list can be an excellent way to organize material—but only if, instead of being a miscellaneous grab bag, it is organized around a larger argument that informs each item listed. Many well-written summaries, for instance, list various points made by an author, sometimes itemizing those points ("First, she argues . . . ," "Second, she argues . . . ," "Third . . ."), and sometimes even itemizing those points in bullet form.

Many well-written arguments are organized in a list format as well. In "The New Liberal Arts," Sanford J. Ungar lists what he sees as seven common misperceptions that discourage college students from majoring in the liberal arts, the first of which begin:

> Misperception No. 1: A liberal-arts degree is a luxury that most families can no longer afford. . . .
> Misperception No. 2: College graduates are finding it harder to get good jobs with liberal-arts degrees. . . .
> Misperception No. 3: The liberal arts are particularly irrelevant for low-income and first-generation college students. They, more than their more-affluent peers, must focus on something more practical and marketable.
>
> SANFORD J. UNGAR, "The New Liberal Arts"

What makes Ungar's list so effective, and makes it stand out in contrast to the type of disorganized lists our cartoon parodies, is that it has a clear, overarching goal: to defend the liberal arts. Had Ungar's article lacked such a unifying agenda and instead been a miscellaneous grab bag, it almost assuredly would have lost its readers, who wouldn't have known what to focus on or what the final "message" or "takeaway" should be.

In conclusion, writing a good summary means not just representing an author's view accurately but doing so in a way that fits what you want to say, the larger point you want to make. On the one hand, it means playing Peter Elbow's believing game and doing justice to the source; if the summary ignores or misrepresents the source, its bias and unfairness will show. On the other hand, even as it does justice to the source, a summary has to have a slant or spin that prepares the way for your own claims. Once a summary enters your text, you should think of it as joint property—reflecting not just the source you are summarizing but your own perspective or take on it as well.

SUMMARIZING SATIRICALLY

Thus far in this chapter we have argued that, as a general rule, good summaries require a balance between what someone else has said and your own interests as a writer. Now, however, we want to address one exception to this rule: the satiric summary, in which writers deliberately give their own spin to someone else's argument in order to reveal a glaring shortcoming in it. Despite our previous comments that well-crafted summaries generally strike a balance between heeding what someone else has said and your own independent interests, the satiric mode can at times be a very effective form of critique because it lets the summarized argument condemn itself without overt editorializing by you, the writer.

One such satiric summary can be found in Sanford J. Ungar's essay "The New Liberal Arts," which we just mentioned. In his discussion of the "misperception," as he sees it, that a liberal arts education is "particularly irrelevant for low-income and first-generation college students," who "must focus on something more practical and marketable," Ungar restates this view as "another way of saying, really, that the rich folks will do the important thinking, and the lower classes will simply carry out their ideas." Few who would dissuade disadvantaged students from the liberal arts would actually state their position in this insulting way. But in taking their position to its logical conclusion, Ungar's satire suggests that this is precisely what their position amounts to.

USE SIGNAL VERBS THAT FIT THE ACTION

In introducing summaries, try to avoid bland formulas like "she says" or "they believe." Though language like this is sometimes serviceable enough, it often fails to reflect accurately what's been said. Using these weaker verbs may lead you to summarize the topic instead of the argument. In some cases, "he says" may even drain the passion out of the ideas you're summarizing.

We suspect that the habit of ignoring the action when summarizing stems from the mistaken belief we mentioned earlier, that writing is about playing it safe and not making waves, a matter of piling up truths and bits of knowledge rather than a dynamic process of doing things to and with other people. People who wouldn't hesitate to *say* "X totally misrepresented," "attacked," or "loved" something when chatting with friends will in their writing often opt for far tamer and even less accurate phrases like "X said."

But the authors you summarize at the college level seldom simply "say" or "discuss" things; they "urge," "emphasize," and "complain about" them. David Zinczenko, for example, doesn't just *say* that fast-food companies contribute to obesity; he *complains* or *protests* that they do; he *challenges*, *chastises*, and *indicts* those companies. The Declaration of Independence doesn't just *talk about* the treatment of the colonies by the British; it *protests against* it. To do justice to the authors you cite, we recommend that when summarizing—

or when introducing a quotation—you use vivid and precise signal verbs as often as possible. Though "he says" or "she believes" will sometimes be the most appropriate language for the occasion, your text will often be more accurate and lively if you tailor your verbs to suit the precise actions you're describing.

TEMPLATES FOR WRITING SUMMARIES

To introduce a summary, use one of the signal verbs above in a template like these:

▸ In her essay X, she advocates <u>a radical revision of the juvenile justice system</u>.

▸ They celebrate the fact that _____.

▸ _____, he admits.

When you tackle the summary itself, think about what else is important beyond the central claim of the argument. For example, what are the conversations the author is responding to? What kinds of evidence does the author's argument rely on? What are the implications of what the author says, both for your own argument and for the larger conversation?

Here is a template that you can use to develop your summary:

▸ X and Y, in their article _____, argue that _____. Their research, which demonstrates that _____, challenges the idea that _____. They use _____ to show _____. X and Y's argument speaks to _____ about the larger issue of _____.

VERBS FOR INTRODUCING
SUMMARIES AND QUOTATIONS

VERBS FOR MAKING A CLAIM

argue	insist
assert	observe
believe	remind us
claim	report
emphasize	suggest

VERBS FOR EXPRESSING AGREEMENT

acknowledge	do not deny
admire	endorse
admit	extol
agree	praise
celebrate	reaffirm
concede	support
corroborate	verify

VERBS FOR QUESTIONING OR DISAGREEING

complain	qualify
complicate	question
contend	refute
contradict	reject
deny	renounce
deplore the tendency to	repudiate

VERBS FOR MAKING RECOMMENDATIONS

advocate	implore
call for	plead
demand	recommend
encourage	urge
exhort	warn

Exercises

1. To get a feel for Peter Elbow's believing game, think about a debate you've heard recently—perhaps in class, at your workplace, or at home. Write a summary of one of the arguments you heard. Then write a summary of another position in the same debate. Give both your summaries to a classmate or two. See if they can tell which position you endorse. If you've succeeded, they won't be able to tell.

2. Read the following passage from "Our Manifesto to Fix America's Gun Laws," an argument written by the editorial board of the *Eagle Eye*, the student newspaper at Marjory Stoneman Douglas High School in Parkland, Florida, in response to the mass shooting that occurred there on February 14, 2018.

We have a unique platform not only as student journalists but also as survivors of a mass shooting. We are firsthand witnesses to the kind of devastation that gross incompetence and political inaction can produce. We cannot stand idly by as the country continues to be infected by a plague of gun violence that seeps into community after community and does irreparable damage to the hearts and minds of the American people....

The changes we propose:

Ban semi-automatic weapons that fire high-velocity rounds
Civilians shouldn't have access to the same weapons that soldiers do. That's a gross misuse of the second amendment ...

Ban accessories that simulate automatic weapons
High-capacity magazines played a huge role in the shooting at our school. In only 10 minutes, 17 people were killed, and 17 others were injured. This is unacceptable ...

Establish a database of gun sales and universal background checks
We believe that there should be a database recording which guns are sold in the United States, to whom, and of what caliber and capacity they are ...

Raise the firearm purchase age to 21
In a few months from now, many of us will be turning 18. We will not be able to drink; we will not be able to rent a car. Most of us will still be living with our parents. We will not be able to purchase a handgun. And yet we will be able to purchase an AR-15 ...

a. Do you think the list format is appropriate for this argument? Why or why not?
b. Write a one-sentence summary of this argument, using one of the verbs from the list on pages 43–44.
c. Compare your summary with a classmate's. What are the similarities and differences between them?

3. A student was asked to summarize an essay by writer Ben Adler, "Banning Plastic Bags Is Good for the World, Right?

Not So Fast" (pp. 320–25). Here is the draft: "Ben Adler says that climate change is too big of a problem for any one person to solve."

a. How does this summary fall prey to the "closest cliché syndrome" (p. 35)?
b. What's a better verb to use than "say"? Why do you think so?

THREE

"AS HE HIMSELF PUTS IT"
The Art of Quoting

A KEY PREMISE OF THIS BOOK is that to launch an effective argument you need to write the arguments of others into your text. One of the best ways to do so is not only by summarizing what "they say," as suggested in Chapter 2, but also by quoting their exact words. Quoting someone else's words gives a tremendous amount of credibility to your summary and helps ensure that it is fair and accurate. In a sense, then, quotations function as a kind of proof of evidence, saying to readers: "Look, I'm not just making this up. She makes this claim, and here it is in her exact words."

Yet many writers make a host of mistakes when it comes to quoting, not the least of which is the failure to quote enough in the first place, if at all. Some writers quote too little— perhaps because they don't want to bother going back to the original text and looking up the author's exact words or because they think they can reconstruct the author's ideas from memory. At the opposite extreme are writers who so overquote that they end up with texts that are short on commentary of their own— maybe because they lack confidence in their ability to comment on the quotations, or because they don't fully understand what they've quoted and therefore have trouble explaining what the quotations mean.

But the main problem with quoting arises when writers assume that quotations speak for themselves. Because the meaning of a quotation is obvious to *them*, many writers assume that this meaning will also be obvious to their readers, when often it is not. Writers who make this mistake think that their job is done when they've chosen a quotation and inserted it into their text. They draft an essay, slap in a few quotations, and whammo, they're done.

See how one author connects what "they say" to what she wants to say, pp. 541–42, ¶ 6–8.

Such writers fail to see that quoting means more than simply enclosing what "they say" in quotation marks. In a way, quotations are orphans: words that have been taken from their original contexts and that need to be integrated into their new textual surroundings. This chapter offers two key ways to produce this sort of integration: (1) by choosing quotations wisely, with an eye to how well they support a particular part of your text, and (2) by surrounding every major quotation with a frame explaining whose words they are, what the quotation means, and how the quotation relates to your own text. The point we want to emphasize is that quoting what "they say" must always be connected with what *you* say.

QUOTE RELEVANT PASSAGES

Before you can select appropriate quotations, you need to have a sense of what you want to do with them—that is, how they will support your text at the particular point where you insert them. Be careful not to select quotations just for the sake of demonstrating that you've read the author's work; you need to make sure they support your own argument.

However, finding relevant quotations is not always easy. In fact, sometimes quotations that were initially relevant to your argument, or to a key point in it, become less so as your text changes during the process of writing and revising. Given the evolving and messy nature of writing, you may sometimes think that you've found the perfect quotation to support your argument, only to discover later on, as your text develops, that your focus has changed and the quotation no longer works. It can be somewhat misleading, then, to speak of finding your thesis and finding relevant quotations as two separate steps, one coming after the other. When you're deeply engaged in the writing and revising process, there is usually a great deal of back-and-forth between your argument and any quotations you select.

FRAME EVERY QUOTATION

Finding relevant quotations is only part of your job; you also need to present them in a way that makes their relevance and meaning clear to your readers. Since quotations do not speak for themselves, you need to build a frame around them in which you do that speaking for them.

Quotations that are inserted into a text without such a frame are sometimes called "dangling" quotations for the way they're left dangling without any explanation. One teacher we've worked with, Steve Benton, calls these "hit-and-run" quotations, likening them to car accidents in which the driver speeds away and avoids taking responsibility for the dent in your fender or the smashed taillights, as in the figure that follows.

DON'T BE A HIT-AND-RUN QUOTER.

What follows is a typical hit-and-run quotation by a student responding to an essay by Deborah Tannen, a linguistics professor and prominent author, who complains that academics value opposition over agreement:

> Deborah Tannen writes about academia. Academics believe "that intellectual inquiry is a metaphorical battle. Following from that is a second assumption that the best way to demonstrate intellectual prowess is to criticize, find fault, and attack."
>
> I agree with Tannen. Another point Tannen makes is that . . .

Since this student fails to introduce the quotation adequately or explain why he finds it worth quoting, readers will have a hard time reconstructing what Tannen argued. First, the student simply gives us the quotation from Tannen without telling us who Tannen is or even indicating that the quoted words are hers. In addition, the student does not explain what he takes Tannen to be saying or how her claims connect with his own. Instead, he simply abandons the quotation in his haste to zoom on to another point.

To adequately frame a quotation, you need to insert it into what we like to call a "quotation sandwich," with the statement introducing it serving as the top slice of bread and the explanation following it serving as the bottom slice. The introductory or lead-in claims should explain who is speaking and set up what the quotation says; the follow-up statements should explain why you consider the quotation to be important and what you take it to say.

TEMPLATES FOR INTRODUCING QUOTATIONS

▸ X states, "<u>Not all steroids should be banned from sports</u>."

▸ As the prominent philosopher X puts it, "_____."

▸ According to X, "_____."

▸ X himself writes, "_____."

▸ In her book, _____, X maintains that "_____."

▸ Writing in the journal _____, X complains that "_____."

▸ In X's view, "_____."

▸ X agrees when she writes, "_____."

▸ X disagrees when he writes, "_____."

▸ X complicates matters further when she writes, "_____."

TEMPLATES FOR EXPLAINING QUOTATIONS

The one piece of advice about quoting that our students say they find most helpful is to get in the habit of following every major quotation by explaining what it means, using a template like one of the ones below.

▸ **Basically, X is warning <u>that the proposed solution will only make the problem worse</u>.**

▸ **In other words, X believes _____.**

▸ **In making this comment, X urges us to _____.**

▸ **X is corroborating the age-old adage that _____.**

▸ **X's point is that _____.**

▸ **The essence of X's argument is that _____.**

When offering such explanations, it is important to use language that accurately reflects the spirit of the quoted passage. It is often serviceable enough in introducing a quotation to write "X states" or "X asserts," but in most cases you can add precision to your writing by introducing the quotation in more vivid

See pp. 43–44 for a list of action verbs for summarizing what other say.

terms. Since, in the example above, Tannen is clearly alarmed by the culture of "attack" that she describes, it would be more accurate to use language that reflects that alarm: "Tannen is alarmed that," "Tannen is disturbed by," "Tannen deplores," or (in our own formulation here) "Tannen complains."

Consider, for example, how the earlier passage on Tannen might be revised using some of these moves:

Deborah Tannen, a prominent linguistics professor, complains that academia is too combative. Rather than really listening to others, Tannen insists, academics habitually try to prove one another wrong. As Tannen herself puts it, "We are all driven by our ideological assumption that intellectual inquiry is a metaphorical battle," that "the best way to demonstrate intellectual prowess is to criticize, find fault, and attack." In short, Tannen objects that academic communication tends to be a competition for supremacy in which loftier values like truth and consensus get lost.

Tannen's observations ring true to me because I have often felt that the academic pieces I read for class are negative and focus on proving another theorist wrong rather than stating a truth. . . .

This revision works, we think, because it frames or nests Tannen's words, integrating them and offering guidance about how they should be read. Instead of launching directly into the quoted words, as the previous draft had done, this revised version identifies Tannen ("a prominent linguistics professor") and clearly indicates that the quoted words are hers ("as Tannen herself puts it"). And instead of being presented without explanation as it was before, the quotation is now presented as an illustration of Tannen's point that, as the student helpfully puts it, "academics habitually try to prove one another wrong" and compete "for supremacy." In this way, the student explains the quotation while restating it in his own words, thereby making it clear that the quotation is being used purposefully instead of having been stuck in simply to pad the essay or the works-cited list.

BLEND THE AUTHOR'S WORDS
WITH YOUR OWN

This new framing material also works well because it accurately represents Tannen's words while giving those words the student's own spin. Instead of simply repeating Tannen word for word, the follow-up sentences echo just enough of her language while still moving the discussion in the student's own direction. Tannen's "battle," "criticize," "find fault," and "attack," for instance, get translated by the student into claims about how "combative" Tannen thinks academics are and how she thinks they "habitually try to prove one another wrong." In this way, the framing creates a kind of hybrid mix of Tannen's words and those of the writer.

CAN YOU OVERANALYZE A QUOTATION?

But is it possible to overexplain a quotation? And how do you know when you've explained a quotation thoroughly enough? After all, not all quotations require the same amount of explanatory framing, and there are no hard-and-fast rules for knowing how much explanation any quotation needs. As a general rule, the most explanatory framing is needed for quotations that may be hard for readers to process: quotations that are long and complex, that are filled with details or jargon, or that contain hidden complexities.

And yet, though the particular situation usually dictates when and how much to explain a quotation, we will still offer one piece of advice: when in doubt, go for it. It is better to risk being overly explicit about what you take a quotation to mean than to leave the quotation dangling and your readers in doubt. Indeed, we encourage you to provide such explanatory framing even when writing to an audience that you know to be familiar with the author being quoted and able to interpret your quotations on their own. Even in such cases, readers need to see how *you* interpret the quotation, since words—especially those of controversial figures—can be interpreted in various ways and used to support different, sometimes opposing, agendas. Your readers need to see what you make of the material you've quoted, if only to be sure that your reading of the material and theirs are on the same page.

HOW *NOT* TO INTRODUCE QUOTATIONS

We want to conclude this chapter by surveying some ways *not* to introduce quotations. Although some writers do so, you should not introduce quotations by saying something like "Orwell asserts an idea that" or "A quote by Shakespeare says." Introductory phrases like these are both redundant and misleading. In the first example, you could write either "Orwell asserts that" or "Orwell's assertion is that" rather than redundantly combining the two. The second example misleads readers, since it is the writer who is doing the quoting, not Shakespeare (as "a quote by Shakespeare" implies).

The templates in this book will help you avoid such mistakes. Once you have mastered templates like "as X puts it" or "in X's own words," you probably won't even have to think about them—and will be free to focus on the challenging ideas that templates help you frame.

Exercises

1. Find an essay that is posted on **theysayiblog.com**. Read the essay, and look closely to see how the writer has integrated quotations in the argument. How has the writer introduced the quotations in the argument? What, if anything, has the writer said to explain the quotations? How has the writer tied the quotations to the essay? Based on what you read in this chapter about how to sandwich quotations, what revisions would you suggest?

2. Below is a passage from Christine Michel Carter's 2019 *Harper's Bazaar* essay, "How Feminism Is Stifling Our Sons." In this essay, Carter points out how gender stereotypes are harmful to both girls and boys, and she argues that popular media needs to present more positive models of masculinity. Read this passage and choose a phrase or sentence to quote as a "they say" for an argument of your own. Use the templates from this chapter to sandwich this quote: introduce the quote, explain what it means, and connect it to your own ideas. Your entire response (the introduction, quote, explanation, and connection to your ideas) should be three or four sentences long.

We've committed so strongly to teaching girls they're equal to boys that we've forgotten to extend the message to the boys themselves in a healthy, inclusive way. Along with our focus on feminism, we need to embrace a new men's movement too—one that pays attention to the young boys who are discovering their manhood against a backdrop of hashtags and equality campaigns that tend to either overlook or vilify where masculinity fits in.

3. Read over something you've written for one of your classes. Have you quoted any sources? If so, highlight or underline all the quotations. How have you integrated each quotation into your own text? How have you introduced it? explained what it means? indicated how it relates to *your* text? If you haven't done all these things, revise your text to do so using the list of verbs for introducing summaries and quotations (pp. 43–44) and the templates for introducing quotations (p. 51) and explaining quotations (p. 51). If you haven't written anything with quotations, revise an academic text you've written so that it uses quotations.

FOUR

"YES / NO / OK, BUT"

Three Ways to Respond

———⌐⌐———

THE FIRST THREE CHAPTERS of this book discuss the "they say" stage of writing, in which you devote your attention to the views of some other person or group. In this chapter, we move to the "I say" stage, in which you offer your own argument as a response to what "they" have said.

Moving to the "I say" stage can be daunting in academia, where it often may seem that you need to be an expert in a field to have an argument at all. Many students have told us that they have trouble entering some of the high-powered conversations that take place in college or graduate school because they do not know enough about the topic at hand or because, they say, they simply are not "smart enough." Yet often these same students, when given a chance to study in depth the contribution that some scholar has made in a given field, will turn around and say things like "I can see where she is coming from, how she makes her case by building on what other scholars have said. Perhaps if I had studied the situation longer, *I* could have come up with a similar argument." What these students come to realize is that good arguments are based not on knowledge that only a special class of experts has access to but on everyday habits of mind that can be isolated, identified, and used by almost anyone. Though there's certainly no substitute for expertise and for knowing as much as possible about one's topic, the arguments that finally win the day are built, as the title of this chapter suggests, on some very basic rhetorical patterns that most of us use on a daily basis.

There are a great many ways to respond to others' ideas, but this chapter concentrates on the three most common and recognizable ways: agreeing, disagreeing, or some combination of both. Although each way of responding is open to endless variation, we focus on these three because readers come to any text needing to learn fairly quickly where the writer stands, and they do this by placing the writer on a mental map consisting of a few familiar options: the writer agrees with those being responded to, disagrees with them, or presents some combination of both agreeing and disagreeing.

When writers take too long to declare their position relative to views they've summarized or quoted, readers get frustrated, wondering, "Is this guy agreeing or disagreeing? Is he *for* what this other person has said, *against* it, or what?" For this reason, this chapter's advice applies to reading as well as to writing. Especially with difficult texts, you need not only to find the position the writer is responding to—the "they say"—but also to determine whether the writer is agreeing with it, challenging it, or some mixture of the two.

ONLY *THREE* WAYS TO RESPOND?

Perhaps you'll worry that fitting your own response into one of these three categories will force you to oversimplify your argument or lessen its complexity, subtlety, or originality. This is certainly a serious concern for academics who are rightly skeptical of writing that is simplistic and reductive. We would argue, however, that the more complex and subtle your argument is, and the more it departs from the conventional ways people think, the more your readers will need to be able to place it on their mental map in order to process the complex details you present. That is, the complexity, subtlety, and originality of your response are more likely to stand out and be noticed if readers have a baseline sense of where you stand relative to any ideas you've cited. As you move through this chapter, we hope you'll agree that the forms of agreeing, disagreeing, and both agreeing and disagreeing that we discuss, far from being simplistic or one-dimensional, are able to accommodate a high degree of creative, complex thought.

It is always a good tactic to begin your response not by launching directly into a mass of details but by stating clearly whether you agree, disagree, or both, using a direct, no-nonsense formula such as: "I agree," "I disagree," or "I am of two minds. I agree that _____, but I cannot agree that _____." Once you have offered one of these straightforward statements (or one of the many variations discussed below), readers will have a strong grasp of your position and then be able to appreciate the complications you go on to offer as your response unfolds.

See p. 21 for suggestions on previewing where you stand.

Still, you may object that these three basic ways of responding don't cover all the options—that they ignore interpretive or analytical responses, for example. In other words, you might think that when you interpret a literary work, you don't necessarily agree or disagree with anything but simply explain the work's meaning, style, or structure. Many essays about literature and the arts, it might be said, take this form—they interpret a work's meaning, thus rendering matters of agreeing or disagreeing irrelevant.

We would argue, however, that the most interesting interpretations tend to be those that agree, disagree, or both—that
instead of being offered solo, the best interpretations take strong
stands relative to other interpretations. In fact, there would be
no reason to offer an interpretation of a work of literature or
art unless you were responding to the interpretations or possible
interpretations of others. Even when you point out features or
qualities of an artistic work that others have not noticed, you
are implicitly disagreeing with what those interpreters have said
by pointing out that they missed or overlooked something that,
in your view, is important. In any effective interpretation, then,
you need not only to state what you yourself take the work of
art to mean but also to do so relative to the interpretations of
other readers—be they professional scholars, teachers, classmates, or even hypothetical readers (as in, "Although some
readers might think that this poem is about _____, it
is in fact about _____ ").

DISAGREE—AND EXPLAIN WHY

Disagreeing may seem like one of the simpler moves a writer can
make, and it is often the first thing people associate with critical
thinking. Disagreeing can also be the easiest way to generate an
essay: find something you can disagree with in what has been
said or might be said about your topic, summarize it, and argue
with it. But disagreement in fact poses hidden challenges. You
need to do more than simply assert that you disagree with a particular view; you also have to offer persuasive reasons *why* you
disagree. After all, disagreeing means more than adding "not" to
what someone else has said, more than just saying, "Although
they say women's rights are improving, I say women's rights are

not improving." Such a response merely contradicts the view it responds to and fails to add anything interesting or new. To turn it into an argument, you need to give reasons to support what you say: because another's argument fails to take relevant factors into account; because it is based on faulty or incomplete evidence; because it rests on questionable assumptions; or because it uses flawed logic, is contradictory, or overlooks what you take to be the real issue. To move the conversation forward (and, indeed, to justify your very act of writing), you need to demonstrate that you have something to contribute.

You can even disagree by making what we call the "duh" move, in which you disagree not with the position itself but with the assumption that it is a new or stunning revelation. Here is an example of such a move, used to open an essay on the state of American schools:

> According to a recent report by some researchers at Stanford University, high school students with college aspirations "often lack crucial information on applying to college and on succeeding academically once they get there."
>
> Well, duh. . . . It shouldn't take a Stanford research team to tell us that when it comes to "succeeding academically," many students don't have a clue.
>
> GERALD GRAFF, "Trickle-Down Obfuscation"

Like all the other moves discussed in this book, the "duh" move can be tailored to meet the needs of almost any writing situation. If you find the expression "duh" too brash to use with your intended audience, you can always dispense with the term itself and write something like "It is true that _____; but we already knew that."

TEMPLATES FOR DISAGREEING, WITH REASONS

▸ **X is mistaken because she overlooks <u>recent fossil discoveries in the South</u>.**

▸ **X's claim that _____ rests on the questionable assumption that _____ .**

▸ **I disagree with X's view that _____ because, as recent research has shown, _____ .**

▸ **X contradicts herself/can't have it both ways. On the one hand, she argues _____ . On the other hand, she also says _____ .**

▸ **By focusing on _____ , X overlooks the deeper problem of _____ .**

You can also disagree by making what we call the "twist it" move, in which you agree with the evidence that someone else has presented but show through a twist of logic that this evidence actually supports your own, contrary position. For example:

> X argues for stricter gun control legislation, saying that the crime rate is on the rise and that we need to restrict the circulation of guns. I agree that the crime rate is on the rise, but that's precisely why I oppose stricter gun control legislation. We need to own guns to protect ourselves against criminals.

In this example of the "twist it" move, the writer agrees with X's claim that the crime rate is on the rise but then argues that this increasing crime rate is in fact a valid reason for *opposing* gun control legislation.

At times you might be reluctant to express disagreement, for any number of reasons—not wanting to be unpleasant, to hurt someone's feelings, or to make yourself vulnerable to being disagreed with in return. One of these reasons may in fact explain why the conference speaker we described at the start of Chapter 1 avoided mentioning the disagreement he had with other scholars until he was provoked to do so in the discussion that followed his talk.

As much as we understand such fears of conflict and have experienced them ourselves, we nevertheless believe it is better to state our disagreements in frank yet considerate ways than to deny them. After all, suppressing disagreements doesn't make them go away; it only pushes them underground, where they can fester in private unchecked. Nevertheless, disagreements do not need to take the form of personal put-downs. Furthermore, there is usually no reason to take issue with *every* aspect of someone else's views. You can single out for criticism only those aspects of what someone else has said that are troubling and then agree with the rest—although such an approach, as we will see later in this chapter, leads to the somewhat more complicated terrain of both agreeing and disagreeing at the same time.

AGREE—BUT WITH A DIFFERENCE

Like disagreeing, agreeing is less simple than it may appear. Just as you need to avoid simply contradicting views you disagree with, you also need to do more than simply echo views you agree with. Even as you're agreeing, it's important to bring something new and fresh to the table, adding something that makes you a valuable participant in the conversation.

There are many moves that enable you to contribute something of your own to a conversation even as you agree with what someone else has said. You may point out some unnoticed evidence or line of reasoning that supports X's claims that X herself hadn't mentioned. You may cite some corroborating personal experience or a situation not mentioned by X that her views help readers understand. If X's views are particularly challenging or esoteric, what you bring to the table could be an accessible translation—an explanation for readers not already in the know. In other words, your text can usefully contribute to the conversation simply by pointing out unnoticed implications or explaining something that needs to be better understood.

Whatever mode of agreement you choose, the important thing is to open up some difference or contrast between your position and the one you're agreeing with rather than simply parroting what it says.

TEMPLATES FOR AGREEING

▸ I agree that <u>diversity in the student body is educationally valuable</u> because my experience <u>at Central University</u> confirms it.

▸ X is surely right about _____ because, as she may not be aware, recent studies have shown that _____.

▸ X's theory of _____ is extremely useful because it sheds light on the difficult problem of _____.

▸ Those unfamiliar with this school of thought may be interested to know that it basically boils down to _____.

Some writers avoid the practice of agreeing almost as much as others avoid disagreeing. In a culture like America's, which prizes originality, independence, and competitive individual-ism, writers sometimes don't like to admit that anyone else has made the same point, seemingly beating them to the punch. In our view, however, as long as you can support a position taken by someone else without merely restating what was said, there is no reason to worry about being "unoriginal." Indeed, there is good reason to rejoice when you agree with others since those others can lend credibility to your argument. While you don't want to present yourself as a mere copycat of someone else's views, you also need to avoid sounding like a lone voice in the wilderness.

But do be aware that whenever you agree with one person's view, you are likely disagreeing with someone else's. It is hard to align yourself with one position without at least implicitly positioning yourself against others. The psychologist Carol Gilligan does just that in an essay in which she agrees with scientists who argue that the human brain is "hard-wired" for cooperation but in so doing aligns herself against any-one who believes that the brain is wired for selfishness and competition:

These findings join a growing convergence of evidence across the human sciences leading to a revolutionary shift in consciousness. . . . If cooperation, typically associated with altruism and self-sacrifice, sets off the same signals of delight as pleasures commonly associated with hedonism and self-indulgence; if the opposition between selfish and selfless, self vs. relationship biologically makes no sense, then a new paradigm is necessary to reframe the very terms of the conversation.

CAROL GILLIGAN, "Sisterhood Is Pleasurable: A Quiet Revolution in Psychology"

In agreeing with some scientists that "the opposition between selfish and selfless . . . makes no sense," Gilligan implicitly disagrees with anyone who thinks the opposition *does* make sense. Basically, what Gilligan says could be boiled down to a template:

- ▶ I agree that _____, a point that needs emphasizing since so many people still believe _____.

- ▶ If group X is right that _____, as I think they are, then we need to reassess the popular assumption that _____.

What such templates allow you to do, then, is to agree with one view while challenging another—a move that leads into the domain of agreeing and disagreeing simultaneously.

AGREE AND DISAGREE SIMULTANEOUSLY

This last option is often our favorite way of responding. One thing we particularly like about agreeing and disagreeing simultaneously is that it helps us get beyond the kind of "is too" / "is not" exchanges that often characterize the disputes of young children and the more polarized shouting matches of talk radio and TV.

Sanford J. Ungar makes precisely this move in his essay "The New Liberal Arts" when, in critiquing seven common "misperceptions" of liberal arts education, he concedes that several contain a grain of truth. For example, after summarizing "Misperception No. 2," that "college graduates are finding it harder to get good jobs with liberal-arts degrees," that few employers want to hire those with an "irrelevant major like philosophy or French," Ungar writes: "Yes, recent graduates have had difficulty in the job market. . . ." But then, after making this concession, Ungar insists that this difficulty affects graduates in all fields, not just those from the liberal arts. In this way, we think, Ungar paradoxically strengthens his case. By admitting that the opposing argument has a point, Ungar bolsters his credibility, presenting himself as a writer willing to acknowledge facts as they present themselves rather than one determined to cheerlead only for his own side.

TEMPLATES FOR AGREEING
AND DISAGREEING SIMULTANEOUSLY

"Yes and no." "Yes, but . . ." "Although I agree up to a point, I still insist . . ." These are just some of the ways you can make your argument complicated and nuanced while maintaining a clear, reader-friendly framework. The parallel structure—"yes and no"; "on the one hand I agree, on the other I disagree"—enables readers to place your argument on that map of positions we spoke of earlier in this chapter while still keeping your argument sufficiently complex.

Charles Murray's essay "Are Too Many People Going to College?" contains a good example of the "yes and no" move when, at the outset of his essay, Murray responds to what he sees as the prevailing wisdom about the liberal arts and college:

> We should not restrict the availability of a liberal education to a rarefied intellectual elite. More people should be going to college, not fewer.
>
> Yes and no. More people should be getting the basics of a liberal education. But for most students, the places to provide those basics are elementary and middle school.
>
> CHARLES MURRAY, "Are Too Many People Going to College?"

In other words, Murray is saying yes to more liberal arts but not to more college.

Another aspect we like about this "yes and no," "agree and disagree" option is that it can be tipped subtly toward agreement or disagreement, depending on where you lay your stress. If you want to emphasize the disagreement end of the spectrum, you would use a template like the one below:

▶ **Although I agree with X up to a point, I cannot accept his overriding assumption that <u>religion is no longer a major force today</u>.**

Conversely, if you want to stress your agreement more than your disagreement, you would use a template like this one:

▶ **Although I disagree with much that X says, I fully endorse his final conclusion that _____.**

The first template above might be called a "yes, but . . ." move, the second a "no, but . . ." move. Other versions include the following:

▶ **Though I concede that _____, I still insist that _____.**

▶ **X is right that _____, but she seems on more dubious ground when she claims that _____.**

▶ **While X is probably wrong when she claims that _____, she is right that _____.**

▶ **Whereas X provides ample evidence that _____, Y and Z's research on _____ and _____ convinces me that _____ instead.**

Another classic way to agree and disagree at the same time is to make what we call an "I'm of two minds" or a "mixed feelings" move:

▸ I'm of two minds about X's claim that _____. On the one hand, I agree that _____. On the other hand, I'm not sure if _____.

▸ My feelings on the issue are mixed. I do support X's position that _____, but I find Y's argument about _____ and Z's research on _____ to be equally persuasive.

This move can be especially useful if you are responding to new or particularly challenging work and are as yet unsure where you stand. It also lends itself well to the kind of speculative investigation in which you weigh a position's pros and cons rather than come out decisively either for or against. But again, as we suggested earlier, whether you are agreeing, disagreeing, or both agreeing and disagreeing, you need to be as clear as possible, and making a frank statement that you are ambivalent is one way to be clear.

IS BEING UNDECIDED OK?

Nevertheless, writers often have as many concerns about expressing ambivalence as they do about expressing disagreement or agreement. Some worry that by expressing ambivalence they will come across as evasive, wishy-washy, or unsure of themselves. Others worry that their ambivalence will end up confusing readers who require decisive, clear-cut conclusions.

The truth is that in some cases these worries are legitimate. At times ambivalence can frustrate readers, leaving them with the feeling that you failed in your obligation to offer the guidance they expect from writers. At other times, however, acknowledging that a clear-cut resolution of an issue is impossible can demonstrate your sophistication as a writer. In an academic culture that values complex thought, forthrightly declaring that you have mixed feelings can be impressive, especially after having ruled out the one-dimensional positions on your issue taken by others in the conversation. Ultimately, then, how ambivalent you end up being comes down to a judgment call based on different readers' responses to your drafts, on your knowledge of your audience, and on the challenges of your particular argument and situation.

Exercises

1. Below is a passage from Chris Nowinski's 2019 *Vox* essay, "Youth Tackle Football Will Be Considered Unthinkable 50 Years from Now." In this essay, Nowinski (director of the Concussion Legacy Foundation and former college football player) argues that tackle football should be banned for kids under fourteen years old.

   a. Read the passage. Then respond to Nowinski's argument using one of the templates from this chapter: one that responds by agreeing and one that responds by disagreeing.
   b. Work with a partner to compare your responses. Which response do you think is the strongest, and why?

   The science is clearer than ever: Exposure data shows children as young as 9 are getting hit in the head more than 500 times in one season of youth tackle football. That should not feel normal to us. Think of the last time, outside of sports, you allowed your child to get hit hard in the head 25 times in a day. Better yet, when was the last time you were hit hard in the head?

Scientists are now beginning to understand the long-term consequences of all those hits. Chronic traumatic encephalopathy, or CTE, is a degenerative brain disease that was once thought to be confined only to "punch-drunk" boxers. Yet in the past decade, Boston University and Veterans Affairs researchers have diagnosed CTE in American football, soccer, ice hockey, and rugby players, along with other collision sport athletes....

Our society is committed to protecting children—that's why we ban smoking, remove children from homes with lead paint, and force parents to put their children in car seats. We should also protect children from unnecessary brain damage in youth sports.

2. Working together with a partner, write a response where you agree and disagree simultaneously—the "OK, but" move. You can write your response using the Nowinski passage above as your "they say," or you can respond to a reading posted on **theysayiblog.com**. Use the templates from this chapter to compose your response. Decide if you want to emphasize disagreement or agreement, and revise your response accordingly.

3. Read an essay that is posted on **theysayiblog.com**.

   a. Is the writer agreeing, disagreeing, or both? Where do you see the writer doing this? Point to a particular sentence or passage.
   b. How connected is the writer's argument ("I say") to the larger conversation ("they say")?
   c. If the writer is disagreeing, how considerate is the writer to the views being rebutted? Why do you think being considerate while disagreeing is important in academic writing?

FIVE

"AND YET"

Distinguishing What You Say from What They Say

———□———

IF GOOD ACADEMIC WRITING involves putting yourself into dialogue with others, it is extremely important that readers be able to tell at every point when you are expressing your own view and when you are stating someone else's. This chapter takes up the problem of moving from what *they* say to what *you* say without confusing readers about who is saying what.

DETERMINE WHO IS SAYING WHAT
IN THE TEXTS YOU READ

Before examining how to signal who is saying what in your own writing, let's look at how to recognize such signals when they appear in the texts you read—an especially important skill when it comes to the challenging works assigned in school. Frequently, when students have trouble understanding difficult texts, it is not just because the texts contain unfamiliar ideas or words but also because the texts rely on subtle clues to let readers know when a particular view should be attributed to the writer or to someone else. Especially with texts that present a true dialogue of perspectives, readers need to be alert to the often subtle markers that indicate whose voice the writer is speaking in.

Consider how the social critic and educator Gregory Mantsios uses these "voice markers," as they might be called, to distinguish the different perspectives in his essay on America's class inequalities:

> "We are all middle-class," or so it would seem. Our national consciousness, as shaped in large part by the media and our political leadership, provides us with a picture of ourselves as a nation of prosperity and opportunity with an ever expanding middle-class life-style. As a result, our class differences are muted and our collective character is homogenized.
>
> Yet class divisions are real and arguably the most significant factor in determining both our very being in the world and the nature of the society we live in.
>
> GREGORY MANTSIOS, "Rewards and Opportunities:
> The Politics and Economics of Class in the U.S."

Although Mantsios makes it look easy, he is actually making several sophisticated rhetorical moves here that help him distinguish the common view he opposes from his own position.

In the opening sentence, for instance, the phrase "or so it would seem" shows that Mantsios does not necessarily agree with the view he is describing, since writers normally don't present views they themselves hold as ones that only "seem" to be true. Mantsios also places this opening view in quotation marks to signal that it is not his own. He then further distances himself from the belief being summarized in the opening paragraph by attributing it to "our national consciousness, as shaped in large part by the media and our political leadership," and then further attributing to this "consciousness" a negative, undesirable "result": one in which "our class differences" get "muted" and "our collective character" gets "homogenized," stripped of its diversity and distinctness. Hence, even before Mantsios has declared his own position in the second paragraph, readers can get a pretty solid sense of where he probably stands.

Furthermore, the second paragraph opens with the word "Yet," indicating that Mantsios is now shifting to his own view (as opposed to the common view he has thus far been describing). Even the parallelism he sets up between the first and second paragraphs—between the first paragraph's claim that class differences do not exist and the second paragraph's claim that they do—helps throw into sharp relief the differences between the two voices. Finally, Mantsios's use of a direct, authoritative, declarative tone in the second paragraph also suggests a switch in voice. Although he does not use the words "I say" or "I argue," he clearly identifies the view he holds by presenting it not as one that merely *seems* to be true or that *others tell us* is true but as a view that *is* true or, as Mantsios puts it, "real."

Paying attention to these voice markers is an important aspect of reading comprehension. Readers who fail to notice these markers often take an author's summaries of what someone else believes to be an expression of what the author himself or herself believes. Thus, when we teach Mantsios's essay, some students invariably come away thinking that the statement "we are all middle-class" is Mantsios's own position rather than the perspective he is opposing, failing to see that in writing these words Mantsios acts as a kind of ventriloquist, mimicking what others say rather than directly expressing what he himself is thinking.

To see how important such voice markers are, consider what the Mantsios passage looks like if we remove them:

> We are all middle-class. . . . We are a nation of prosperity and opportunity with an ever expanding middle-class life-style. . . .
>
> Class divisions are real and arguably the most significant factor in determining both our very being in the world and the nature of the society we live in.

In contrast to the careful delineation between voices in Mantsios's original text, this unmarked version leaves it hard to tell where his voice begins and the voices of others end. With the markers removed, readers cannot tell that "We are all middle-class" represents a view the author opposes and that "Class divisions are real" represents what the author himself believes. Indeed, without the markers, especially the "yet," readers might well miss the fact that the second paragraph's claim that "Class divisions are real" contradicts the first paragraph's claim that "We are all middle-class."

TEMPLATES FOR SIGNALING WHO IS SAYING WHAT IN YOUR OWN WRITING

To avoid confusion in your own writing, make sure that at every point your readers can clearly tell who is saying what. To do so, you can use as voice-identifying devices many of the templates presented in previous chapters.

▸ Although X makes the best possible case for <u>universal, government-funded health care</u>, I <u>am not persuaded</u>.

▸ My view, however, contrary to what X has argued, is that _____.

▸ Adding to X's argument, I would point out that _____.

▸ According to both X and Y, _____.

▸ Politicians, X argues, should _____.

▸ Most athletes will tell you that _____.

BUT I'VE BEEN TOLD NOT TO USE "I"

Notice that the first three templates above use the first-person, as do many of the templates in this book, thereby contradicting the common advice about avoiding the first person in academic writing. Although you may have been told that the "I" word encourages subjective, self-indulgent opinions rather than well-grounded arguments, we believe that texts using "I" can be just as well supported—or just as self-indulgent—as those that don't. For us, well-supported arguments are grounded in persuasive reasons and evidence, not in the use or nonuse of any particular pronouns.

Furthermore, if you consistently avoid the first person in your writing, you will probably have trouble making the key move addressed in this chapter: differentiating your views from those of others or even offering your own views in the first place. But don't just take our word for it. See for yourself how freely the first person is used by the writers quoted in this book and by the writers assigned in your courses.

Nevertheless, certain occasions may warrant avoiding the first person and writing, for example, that "she is correct" instead of "I think that she is correct." Since it can be monotonous to read an unvarying series of "I" statements ("I believe . . . I think . . . I argue . . ."), it is a good idea to mix first-person assertions with ones like the following:

▶ **X is right that <u>certain common patterns can be found in the communities</u>.**

▶ **The evidence shows that _____.**

▶ **X's assertion that _____ does not fit the facts.**

▶ **Anyone familiar with _____ should agree that _____.**

One might even follow Mantsios's lead, as in the following template:

▶ **Yet _____ are real, and are arguably the most significant factor in _____.**

On the whole, however, academic writing today, even in the sciences and social sciences, makes use of the first person fairly liberally.

ANOTHER TRICK FOR IDENTIFYING WHO IS SPEAKING

To alert readers about whose perspective you are describing at any given moment, you don't always have to use overt voice markers like "X argues" followed by a summary of the argument. Instead, you can alert readers about whose voice you're speaking in by *embedding* a reference to X's argument in your own sentences. Hence, instead of writing

> Liberals believe that cultural differences need to be respected. I have a problem with this view, however.

you might write

> I have a problem with *what liberals call cultural differences.*

> There is a major problem with the liberal doctrine of *so-called cultural differences.*

You can also embed references to something you yourself have previously said. So instead of writing two cumbersome sentences like

> Earlier in this chapter we coined the term "voice markers." We would argue that such markers are extremely important for reading comprehension.

you might write

> We would argue that "voice markers," as we identified them earlier, are extremely important for reading comprehension.

Embedded references like these allow you to economize your train of thought and refer to other perspectives without any major interruption.

TEMPLATES FOR EMBEDDING VOICE MARKERS

▸ **X overlooks what I consider an important point about <u>cultural differences</u>.**

▸ **My own view is that what X insists is a _____ is in fact a _____ .**

▸ **I wholeheartedly endorse what X calls _____ .**

▸ **These conclusions, which X discusses in _____ , add weight to the argument that _____ .**

When writers fail to use voice-marking devices like the ones discussed in this chapter, their summaries of others' views tend to become confused with their own ideas—and vice versa. When readers cannot tell if you are summarizing your own views or endorsing a certain phrase or label, they have to stop and think: "Wait. I thought the author disagreed with this claim. Has she actually been asserting this view all along?" or "Hmmm, I thought she would have objected to this kind of phrase. Is she actually endorsing it?" Getting in the habit of using voice markers will keep you from confusing your readers and help alert you to similar markers in the challenging texts you read.

Exercises

1. Look at the short passages below. Right now, it's unclear who is saying what. Use the templates from this chapter to revise these passages so they include voice markers that allow a reader to distinguish between the two voices.

Example:

Students who major in preprofessional programs like accounting or medical technology are trained for in-demand careers. Students who study the humanities learn valuable skills that prepare them for many jobs, including some that may not even exist today.

Revision:

<u>Well-meaning advisers</u> argue that students who major in preprofessional programs like accounting or medical technologies are trained for in-demand careers. <u>However, they overlook what I consider an important point</u>, that studying the humanities gives students valuable skills that prepare them for many jobs, including some that may not even exist today.

a. Fracking, or drilling deeply into the ground to reach natural gas, can contaminate drinking water in communities near the drilling operations. Natural gas is a cleaner form of energy than coal, and fracking is a cost-effective way to access the reserves of natural gas in the United States.

b. Charter schools give families in struggling school districts options to choose which schools their kids will attend. Charter schools, controlled by private individuals or corporations, divert essential funds away from the public education systems that serve all children.

2. To see how one writer signals when she is asserting her own views and when she is summarizing those of someone else, read the following passage from Anne-Marie Slaughter's essay "Why Women Still Can't Have It All." As you do so, identify those spots where Slaughter refers to the views of others and the signal phrases she uses to distinguish her views from theirs.

Seeking out a more balanced life is not a women's issue; balance would be better for us all. Bronnie Ware, an Australian blogger who worked for years in palliative care and is the author of the 2011 book *The Top Five Regrets of the Dying*, writes that the regret she heard most often was "I wish I'd had the courage to live a life true to myself, not the life others expected of me." The second-most common regret was "I wish I didn't work so hard." She writes: "This came from every male patient that I nursed. They missed their children's youth and their partner's companionship."

Juliette Kayyem, who several years ago left the Department of Homeland Security soon after her husband, David Barron, left a high position in the Justice Department, says their joint decision to leave Washington and return to Boston sprang from their desire to work on the "happiness project," meaning quality time with their three children. (She borrowed the term from her friend Gretchen Rubin, who wrote a best-selling book and now runs a blog with that name.)

It's time to embrace a national happiness project. As a daughter of Charlottesville, Virginia, the home of Thomas Jefferson and the university he founded, I grew up with the Declaration of Independence in my blood. Last I checked, he did not declare American independence in the name of life, liberty, and professional success. Let us rediscover the pursuit of happiness, and let us start at home.

3. Read over a draft of your own writing—a paragraph or an essay—and then respond to the following questions. How do you distinguish your own voice from the argument(s) you are summarizing, quoting, and responding to? How could you use a template from this chapter to clarify the distinction between *your* argument and *their* argument(s)? Where could you use first-person voice markers or embedded references in your writing?

SIX

"SKEPTICS MAY OBJECT"

Planting a Naysayer in Your Text

THE WRITER Jane Tompkins describes a pattern that repeats itself whenever she writes a book or an article. For the first couple of weeks when she sits down to write, things go relatively well. But then in the middle of the night, several weeks into the writing process, she'll wake up in a cold sweat, suddenly realizing that she has overlooked some major criticism that readers will surely make against her ideas. Her first thought, invariably, is that she will have to give up on the project or that she will have to throw out what she's written thus far and start over. Then she realizes that "this moment of doubt and panic is where my text really begins." She then revises what she's written in a way that incorporates the criticisms she's anticipated, and her text becomes stronger and more interesting as a result.

This little story contains an important lesson for all writers, experienced and inexperienced alike. It suggests that even though most of us are upset at the idea of someone criticizing our work, such criticisms can actually work to our advantage. Although it's naturally tempting to ignore criticism of our ideas, doing so may in fact be a big mistake, since our writing improves when we not only listen to these objections but also give them an explicit hearing in our writing. Indeed, no single device more quickly improves a piece of writing than planting a naysayer in the text—saying, for example, that "although some readers may object" to something in your argument, you "would reply that _____."

ANTICIPATE OBJECTIONS

But wait, you say. Isn't the advice to incorporate critical views a recipe for destroying your credibility and undermining your argument? Here you are, trying to say something that will hold up, and we want you to tell readers all the negative things someone might say against you?

Exactly. We *are* urging you to tell readers what others might say against you, but our point is that doing so will actually *enhance* your credibility, not undermine it. As we argue throughout this book, writing well does not mean piling up uncontroversial truths in a vacuum; it means engaging others in a dialogue or debate—not only by opening your text with a summary of what others *have* said, as we suggest in Chapter 1, but also by imagining what others *might* say against your argument as it unfolds. Once you see writing as an act of entering a conversation, you should also see how opposing arguments can work for you rather than against you.

Paradoxically, the more you give voice to your critics' objections, the more you tend to disarm those critics, especially if you go on to answer their objections in convincing ways. When you entertain a counterargument, you make a kind of preemptive strike, identifying problems with your argument before others can point them out for you. Furthermore, by entertaining counterarguments, you show respect for your readers, treating them not as gullible dupes who will believe anything you say but as independent, critical thinkers who are aware that your view is not the only one in town. In addition, by imagining what others might say against your claims, you come across as a generous, broad-minded person who is confident enough to be open to debate—like the writer in the figure on the following page.

Conversely, if you don't entertain counterarguments, you may very likely come across as closed-minded, as if you think your beliefs are beyond dispute. You might also leave important questions hanging and concerns about your arguments unaddressed. Finally, if you fail to plant a naysayer in your text, you may find that you have very little to say. Our own students often say that entertaining counterarguments makes it easier to generate enough text to meet their assignment's page-length requirements.

Planting a naysayer in your text is a relatively simple move, as you can see by looking at the following passage from a book by the writer Kim Chernin. Having spent some thirty pages complaining about the pressure on American women to be thin, Chernin inserts a whole chapter titled "The Skeptic," opening it as follows:

At this point I would like to raise certain objections that have been inspired by the skeptic in me. She feels that I have been ignoring some of the most common assumptions we all make about our bodies and these she wishes to see addressed. For example: "You know perfectly well," she says to me, "that you feel better when you lose weight. You buy new clothes. You look at yourself more eagerly in the mirror. When someone invites you to a party you don't stop and ask yourself whether you want to go. You feel sexier. Admit it. You like yourself better."

KIM CHERNIN, *The Obsession: Reflections on the Tyranny of Slenderness*

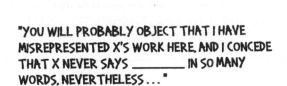

The remainder of Chernin's chapter consists of her answers to this inner skeptic. In the face of the skeptic's challenge to her book's central premise (that the pressure to diet seriously harms women's lives), Chernin responds neither by repressing the skeptic's critical voice nor by giving in to it and relinquishing her own position. Instead, she embraces that voice and writes it into her text. Note, too, that instead of dispatching this naysaying voice quickly, as many of us would be tempted to do, Chernin stays with it and devotes a full paragraph to it. By borrowing some of Chernin's language, we can come up with templates for entertaining virtually any objection.

TEMPLATES FOR ENTERTAINING OBJECTIONS

▸ **At this point I would like to raise some objections that have been inspired by the skeptic in me. She feels that I have been ignoring <u>the complexities of the situation</u>.**

▸ **Yet some readers may challenge my view by insisting that _____ .**

▸ **Of course, many will probably disagree on the grounds that _____ .**

Note that the objections in the above templates are attributed not to any specific person or group but to "skeptics," "readers," or "many." This kind of nameless, faceless naysayer is perfectly appropriate in many cases. But the ideas that motivate arguments and objections often can—and, where possible, should—be ascribed to a specific ideology or school of thought (for example, liberals, Christian fundamentalists, neopragmatists) rather than to anonymous anybodies. In other words, naysayers can be labeled, and you can add precision and impact to your writing by identifying what those labels are.

TEMPLATES FOR NAMING YOUR NAYSAYERS

▸ Here many *feminists* would probably object that <u>gender does influence language</u>.

▸ But *social Darwinists* would certainly take issue with the argument that _____.

▸ *Biologists*, of course, may want to question whether _____.

▸ Nevertheless, both *followers and critics of Malcolm X* will probably suggest otherwise and argue that _____.

To be sure, some people dislike such labels and may even resent having labels applied to themselves. Some feel that labels put individuals in boxes, stereotyping them and glossing over what makes each of us unique. And it's true that labels can be used inappropriately, in ways that ignore individuality and promote stereotypes. But since the life of ideas, including many of our most private thoughts, is conducted through groups and types rather than solitary individuals, intellectual exchange requires labels to give definition and serve as a convenient shorthand. If you categorically reject all labels, you give up an important resource and even mislead readers by presenting yourself and others as having no connection to anyone else. You also miss an opportunity to generalize the importance and relevance of your work to some larger conversation. When you attribute a position you are summarizing to liberalism, say, or historical materialism, your argument is no longer just about your own solitary views but also about the intersection of broad ideas and habits of mind that many readers may already have a stake in.

The way to minimize the problem of stereotyping, then, is not to categorically reject labels but to refine and qualify their use, as the following templates demonstrate:

▶ Although not all *Christians* think alike, some of them will probably dispute my claim that _____ .

▶ *Non-native English speakers* are so diverse in their views that it's hard to generalize about them, but some are likely to object on the grounds that _____ .

Another way to avoid needless stereotyping is to qualify labels carefully, substituting "pro bono lawyers" for "lawyers" in general, for example, or "quantitative sociologists" for all "social scientists," and so on.

TEMPLATES FOR INTRODUCING OBJECTIONS INFORMALLY

Objections can also be introduced in more informal ways. For instance, you can frame objections in the form of questions:

▶ But is my proposal realistic? What are the chances of its actually being adopted?

▶ Yet is it necessarily true that _____ ? Is it always the case, as I have been suggesting, that _____ ?

▶ However, does the evidence I've cited prove conclusively that _____ ?

You can also let your naysayer speak directly:

▶ **"Impossible," some will say. "You must be reading the research selectively."**

Moves like this allow you to cut directly to the skeptical voice itself, as the singer-songwriter Joe Jackson does in the following excerpt from a *New York Times* article complaining about the restrictions on public smoking in New York City bars and restaurants:

> I like a couple of cigarettes or a cigar with a drink, and like many other people, I only smoke in bars or nightclubs. Now I can't go to any of my old haunts. Bartenders who were friends have turned into cops, forcing me outside to shiver in the cold and curse under my breath. . . . It's no fun. Smokers are being demonized and victimized all out of proportion.
>
> "Get over it," say the anti-smokers. "You're the minority." I thought a great city was a place where all kinds of minorities could thrive. . . . "Smoking kills," they say. As an occasional smoker with otherwise healthy habits, I'll take my chances. Health consciousness is important, but so are pleasure and freedom of choice.
>
> JOE JACKSON, "Want to Smoke? Go to Hamburg"

Jackson could have begun his second paragraph, in which he shifts from his own voice to that of his imagined naysayer, more formally, as follows: "Of course anti-smokers will object that since we smokers are in the minority, we should simply stop complaining and quietly make the sacrifices we are being called on to make for the larger social good." Or "Anti-smokers might insist, however, that the smoking minority should submit to the nonsmoking majority." We think, though, that Jackson gets the job done in a far more lively way with the more colloquial form he chooses. Borrowing a standard move of playwrights and novelists, Jackson cuts directly to the objectors' view and then to his own retort, then back to the objectors' view and then to his own retort again, thereby creating a kind of dialogue or miniature play within his own text. This move works well for Jackson but only because he uses quotation marks and other voice markers to make clear at every point whose voice he is in.

See Chapter 5 for more advice on using voice markers.

REPRESENT OBJECTIONS FAIRLY

Once you've decided to introduce a differing or opposing view into your writing, your work has only just begun, since you still need to represent and explain that view with fairness and generosity. Although it is tempting to give opposing views short shrift, to hurry past them, or even to mock them, doing so is usually counterproductive. When writers make the best case they can for their critics (playing Peter Elbow's "believing game"), they actually bolster their credibility with readers rather than undermine it. They make readers think, "This is a writer I can trust."

See pp. 33–34 for more on the believing game.

We recommend, then, that whenever you entertain objections in your writing, you stay with them for several sentences or even paragraphs and take them as seriously as possible. We also recommend that you read your summary of opposing views with an outsider's eye: put yourself in the shoes of someone who disagrees with you and ask if such a reader would recognize himself in your summary. Would that reader think you have taken his views seriously, as beliefs that reasonable people might hold? Or would he detect a mocking tone or an oversimplification of his views?

There will always be certain objections, to be sure, that you believe do not deserve to be represented, just as there will be objections that seem so unworthy of respect that they inspire ridicule. Remember, however, that if you do choose to mock a view that you oppose, you are likely to alienate those readers who don't already agree with you—likely the very readers you want to reach. Also be aware that in mocking another's view you may contribute to a hostile argument culture in which someone may ridicule you in return.

ANSWER OBJECTIONS

Do be aware that when you represent objections successfully, you still need to be able to answer those objections persuasively. After all, when you write objections into a text, you take the risk that readers will find those objections more convincing than the argument you yourself are advancing. In the editorial quoted above, for example, Joe Jackson takes the risk that readers will identify more with the anti-smoking view he summarizes than with the pro-smoking position he endorses.

This is precisely what Benjamin Franklin describes happening to himself in *The Autobiography of Benjamin Franklin* (1793), when he recalls being converted to Deism (a religion that exalts reason over spirituality) by reading *anti*-Deist books. When he encountered the views of Deists being negatively summarized by authors who opposed them, Franklin explains, he ended up finding the Deist position more persuasive. To avoid having this kind of unintentional reverse effect on readers, you need to do your best to make sure that any counter-arguments you address are not more convincing than your own claims. It is good to address objections in your writing but only if you are able to overcome them.

One surefire way to *fail* to overcome an objection is to dismiss it out of hand—saying, for example, "That's just wrong." The difference between such a response (which offers no supporting reasons whatsoever) and the types of nuanced responses we're promoting in this book is the difference between bullying your readers and genuinely persuading them.

Often the best way to overcome an objection is not to try to refute it completely but to agree with part of it while challenging only the part you dispute. In other words, in answering counterarguments, it is often best to say "yes, but" or "yes and no," treating the counterview as an opportunity to revise and refine your own position. Rather than build your argument into an impenetrable fortress, it is often best to make concessions while still standing your ground, as Kim Chernin does in the following response to the counterargument quoted above. While in the voice of the "skeptic," Chernin writes: "Admit it. You like yourself better when you've lost weight." In response, Chernin replies as follows:

See pp. 63–66 for more on agreeing, with a difference.

Can I deny these things? No woman who has managed to lose weight would wish to argue with this. Most people feel better about themselves when they become slender. And yet, upon reflection, it seems to me that there is something precarious about this well-being. After all, 98 percent of people who lose weight gain it back. Indeed, 90 percent of those who have dieted "successfully" gain back more than they ever lost. Then, of course, we can no longer bear to look at ourselves in the mirror.

In this way, Chernin shows how you can use a counterview to improve and refine your overall argument by making a concession. Even as she concedes that losing weight feels good in the short run, she argues that in the long run the weight always returns, making the dieter far more miserable.

TEMPLATES FOR MAKING CONCESSIONS WHILE STILL STANDING YOUR GROUND

▸ Although I grant that <u>the book is poorly organized</u>, I still maintain that <u>it raises an important issue</u>.

▸ Proponents of X are right to argue that _____. But they exaggerate when they claim that _____.

▸ While it is true that _____, it does not necessarily follow that _____.

▸ On the one hand, I agree with X that _____. But on the other hand, I still insist that _____.

Templates like these show that answering naysayers' objections does not have to be an all-or-nothing affair in which either you definitively refute your critics or they definitively refute you. Often the most productive engagements among differing views end with a combined vision that incorporates elements of each one.

But what if you've tried out all the possible answers you can think of to an objection you've anticipated and you *still* have a nagging feeling that the objection is more convincing than your argument itself? In that case, the best remedy is to go back and make some fundamental revisions to your argument, even reversing your position completely if need be. Although finding out late in the game that you aren't fully convinced by your own argument can be painful, it can actually make your final text more intellectually honest, challenging, and serious. After all, the goal of writing is not to keep proving that whatever you initially said is right, but to stretch the limits of your thinking. So if planting a strong naysayer in your text forces you to change your mind, that's not a bad thing. Some would argue that that is what the academic world is all about.

Exercises

1. Read the following passage from "A People's Democratic Platform" by the cultural critic Eric Schlosser. As you'll see, he hasn't planted any naysayers in this text. Do it for him. Insert a brief paragraph stating an objection to his argument and then responding to the objection as he might.

   The United States must declare an end to the war on drugs. This war has filled the nation's prisons with poor drug addicts and small-time drug dealers. It has created a multibillion-dollar black market, enriched organized crime groups and promoted the corruption of government officials throughout the world. And it has not stemmed the widespread use of illegal drugs. By any rational measure, this war has been a total failure.

   We must develop public policies on substance abuse that are guided not by moral righteousness or political expediency but by common sense. The United States should immediately decriminalize the cultivation and possession of small amounts of marijuana for personal use. Marijuana should no longer be classified as a Schedule I narcotic, and those who seek to use marijuana as medicine should no longer face criminal sanctions. We must shift our entire approach to drug abuse from the criminal justice system to the public health system. Congress should appoint an independent commission to study the harm-reduction policies that have been adopted in Switzerland, Spain, Portugal, and the Netherlands. The commission should recommend policies for the United States based on one important criterion: what works.

In a nation where pharmaceutical companies advertise powerful antidepressants on billboards and where alcohol companies run amusing beer ads during the Super Bowl, the idea of a "drug-free society" is absurd. Like the rest of American society, our drug policy would greatly benefit from less punishment and more compassion.

2. Think of a debate you recently had with a friend or classmate. Compose a one-sentence summary of your argument. Then, by yourself or with a partner, brainstorm a list of possible objections or alternative perspectives on the issue. Pick one, and use it to write a naysayer objection that responds to your argument. Use the templates in this chapter to introduce and respond to this naysayer fairly.

3. Read over something you've written that makes an argument. Work with a partner to review your draft to see if you've anticipated and responded to any objections. Use these questions to guide your review: Have you anticipated all the likely objections to your argument? Whom, if anyone, have you attributed the objections to? Have you represented the objections fairly? Have you answered them well enough, or do you think you now need to qualify your own argument? Does the introduction of the naysayer strengthen your argument? Why or why not?

SEVEN

"SO WHAT? WHO CARES?"

Saying Why It Matters

BASEBALL IS THE NATIONAL PASTIME. Bernini was the best sculptor of the baroque period. All writing is conversational. So what? Who cares? Why does any of this matter?

How many times have you had reason to ask these questions? Regardless of how interesting a topic may be to you as a writer, readers always need to know what is at stake in a text and why they should care. All too often, however, these questions are left unanswered—mainly because writers and speakers assume that audiences will know the answers already or will figure them out on their own. As a result, students come away from lectures feeling like outsiders to what they've heard, just as many of us feel left hanging after talks we've attended. The problem is not necessarily that the speakers lack a clear, well-focused thesis or that the thesis is inadequately supported with evidence. Instead, the problem is that the speakers don't address the crucial question of why their arguments matter.

That this question is so often left unaddressed is unfortunate since the speakers generally *could* offer interesting, engaging answers. When pressed, for instance, most academics will tell you that their lectures and articles matter because they address some belief that needs to be corrected or updated—and because their arguments have important, real-world consequences. Yet many academics fail to identify these reasons and consequences explicitly in what they say and write. Rather than assume that audiences will know why their claims matter, all writers need to answer the "so what?" and "who cares?" questions up front. Not everyone can claim to have a cure for cancer or a solution to end poverty. But writers who fail to show that others *should* care or already *do* care about their claims will ultimately lose their audiences' interest.

This chapter focuses on various moves that you can make to answer the "who cares?" and "so what?" questions in your own writing. In one sense, the two questions get at the same thing: the relevance or importance of what you are saying. Yet they get at this significance in different ways. Whereas "who cares?" literally asks you to identify a person or group who cares about your claims, "so what?" asks about the real-world applications and consequences of those claims—what difference it would make if they were accepted. We'll look first at ways of making clear who cares.

"WHO CARES?"

To see how one writer answers the "who cares?" question, consider the following passage from the science writer Denise Grady. Writing in the *New York Times*, she explains some of the latest research into fat cells:

> Scientists used to think body fat and the cells it was made of were pretty much inert, just an oily storage compartment. But within the past decade research has shown that fat cells act like chemical factories and that body fat is potent stuff: a highly active

tissue that secretes hormones and other substances with profound and sometimes harmful effects. . . .

In recent years, biologists have begun calling fat an "endocrine organ," comparing it to glands like the thyroid and pituitary, which also release hormones straight into the bloodstream.

DENISE GRADY, "The Secret Life of a Potent Cell"

Notice how Grady's writing reflects the central advice we give in this book, offering a clear claim and also framing that claim as a response to what someone else has said. In so doing, Grady immediately identifies at least one group with a stake in the new research that sees fat as "active," "potent stuff": namely, the scientific community, which formerly believed that body fat is inert. By referring to these scientists, Grady implicitly acknowledges that her text is part of a larger conversation and shows who besides herself has an interest in what she says.

Consider, however, how the passage would read had Grady left out what "scientists used to think" and simply explained the new findings in isolation:

Within the past few decades research has shown that fat cells act like chemical factories and that body fat is potent stuff: a highly active tissue that secretes hormones and other substances. In recent years, biologists have begun calling fat an "endocrine organ," comparing it to glands like the thyroid and pituitary, which also release hormones straight into the bloodstream.

Though this statement is clear and easy to follow, it lacks any indication that anyone needs to hear it. OK, one thinks while reading this passage, fat is an active, potent thing. Sounds plausible enough; no reason to think it's not true. But does anyone really care? Who, if anyone, is interested?

TEMPLATES FOR INDICATING WHO CARES

To address "who cares?" questions in your own writing, we suggest using templates like the following, which echo Grady in refuting earlier thinking:

▸ <u>Parents</u> used to think <u>yelling at their kids was necessary</u>. But recently <u>experts</u> suggest that <u>it can be counterproductive</u>.

▸ This interpretation challenges the work of those critics who have long assumed that _____.

▸ These findings challenge the work of earlier researchers, who tended to assume that _____.

▸ Recent studies like these shed new light on _____, which previous studies had not addressed.

Grady might have been more explicit by writing the "who cares?" question directly into her text, as in the following template:

▸ But who really cares? Who besides me and a handful of recent researchers has a stake in these claims? At the very least, the researchers who formerly believed _____ should care.

To gain greater authority as a writer, it can help to name specific people or groups who have a stake in your claims and to go into some detail about their views:

▸ Researchers have long assumed that _____. For instance, one eminent scholar of cell biology, _____, assumed in _____, her seminal work on cell structures and functions, that fat cells _____. As _____ herself put it, "_____" (2012). Another leading scientist, _____, argued that fat cells "_____" (2011). Ultimately, when it came to the nature of fat, the basic assumption was that _____.

But a new body of research shows that fat cells are far more complex and that _____.

In other cases, you might refer to certain people or groups who *should* care about your claims:

▸ If sports enthusiasts stopped to think about it, many of them might simply assume that the most successful athletes _____. However, new research shows _____.

▸ These findings challenge neoliberals' common assumption that _____.

▸ At first glance, teenagers might say _____. But on closer inspection _____.

As these templates suggest, answering the "who cares?" question involves establishing the type of contrast between what others say and what you say that is central to this book. Ultimately, such templates help you create a dramatic tension or clash of views in your writing that readers will feel invested in and want to see resolved.

"SO WHAT?"

Although answering the "who cares?" question is crucial, in many cases it is not enough, especially if you are writing for general readers who don't necessarily have a strong investment in the particular clash of views you are setting up. In the case of Grady's argument about fat cells, such readers may still wonder why it matters that some researchers think fat cells are active, while others think they're inert. Or, to move to a different field of study, American literature, *so what* if some scholars disagree about Huck Finn's relationship with the runaway slave Jim in Mark Twain's *Adventures of Huckleberry Finn*? Why should anyone besides a few specialists in the field care about such disputes? What, if anything, hinges on them?

The best way to answer such questions about the larger consequences of your claims is to appeal to something that your audience already figures to care about. Whereas the "who cares?" question asks you to identify an interested person or group, the "so what?" question asks you to link your argument to some larger matter that readers already deem important. Thus, in analyzing *Huckleberry Finn*, a writer could argue that seemingly narrow disputes about the hero's relationship with Jim actually shed light on whether Twain's canonical, widely read novel is a critique of racism in America or is itself marred by it.

Let's see how Grady invokes such broad, general concerns in her article on fat cells. Her first move is to link researchers' interest in fat cells to a general concern with obesity and health:

> Researchers trying to decipher the biology of fat cells hope to find new ways to help people get rid of excess fat or, at least, prevent obesity from destroying their health. In an increasingly obese world, their efforts have taken on added importance.

Further showing why readers should care, Grady's next move is to demonstrate the even broader relevance and urgency of her subject matter:

> Internationally, more than a billion people are overweight. Obesity and two illnesses linked to it, heart disease and high blood pressure, are on the World Health Organization's list of the top 10 global health risks. In the United States, 65 percent of adults weigh too much,

compared with about 56 percent a decade ago, and government researchers blame obesity for at least 300,000 deaths a year.

What Grady implicitly says here is "Look, dear reader, you may think that these questions about the nature of fat cells I've been pursuing have little to do with everyday life. In fact, however, these questions are extremely important—particularly in our 'increasingly obese world' in which we need to prevent obesity from destroying our health."

Notice that Grady's phrase "in an increasingly _____ world" can be adapted as a strategic move to address the "so what?" question in other fields as well. For example, a sociologist analyzing back-to-nature movements of the past thirty years might make the following statement:

> In a world increasingly dominated by cell phones and sophisticated computer technologies, these attempts to return to nature appear futile.

This type of move can be readily applied to other disciplines because no matter how much disciplines may differ from one another, the need to justify the importance of one's concerns is common to them all.

TEMPLATES FOR ESTABLISHING
WHY YOUR CLAIMS MATTER

▶ *Huckleberry Finn* matters / is important because <u>it is one of the most widely taught novels in the American school system.</u>

▶ Although X may seem trivial, it is in fact crucial in terms of today's concern over _____.

▸ Ultimately, what is at stake here is _____ .

▸ These findings have important implications for the broader domain of _____ .

▸ If we are right about _____, then major consequences follow for _____ .

▸ These conclusions/This discovery will have significant applications in _____ as well as in _____ .

Finally, you can also treat the "so what?" question as a related aspect of the "who cares?" question:

▸ Although X may seem of concern to only a small group of _____, it should in fact concern anyone who cares about _____ .

All these templates help you hook your readers. By suggesting the real-world applications of your claims, the templates not only demonstrate that others care about your claims but also tell your readers why *they* should care. Again, it bears repeating that simply stating and proving your thesis isn't enough. You also need to frame it in a way that helps readers care about it.

WHAT ABOUT READERS WHO ALREADY KNOW WHY IT MATTERS?

At this point, you might wonder if you need to answer the "who cares?" and "so what?" questions in *everything* you write. Is it really necessary to address these questions if you're proposing something so obviously consequential as, say, a treatment for autism or a program to eliminate illiteracy? Isn't it obvious that everyone cares about such problems? Does it really need to be spelled out? And what about when you're writing for audiences who you know are already interested in your claims and who understand perfectly well why they're important? In other words, do you always need to address the "so what?" and "who cares?" questions?

As a rule, yes—although it's true that you can't keep answering them forever and at a certain point must say enough is enough. Although a determined skeptic can infinitely ask why something matters—"Why should I care about earning a salary? And why should I care about supporting a family?"—you have to stop answering at some point in your text. Nevertheless, we urge you to go as far as possible in answering such questions. If you take it for granted that readers will somehow intuit the answers to "so what?" and "who cares?" on their own, you may make your work seem less interesting than it actually is, and you run the risk that readers will dismiss your text as irrelevant and unimportant. By contrast, when you are careful to explain who cares and why, it's a little like bringing a cheerleading squad into your text. And though some expert readers might already know why your claims matter, even they need to be reminded. Thus the safest move is to be as explicit as possible in answering the "so what?" question, even for those already in the know. When you step back from the text and explain why it matters, you are urging your audience to keep reading, pay attention, and care.

Exercises

1. Below are two claims. Who might have a stake in these arguments? Use the templates in this chapter to answer in

one or two sentences the "who cares?" question for both arguments.

   a. The benefits of online shopping don't justify the environmental consequences of shipping items purchased online.
   b. The federal government should fund universal health care.

2. Here are two more claims. What are the possible real-world consequences of these arguments? Use the templates in this chapter to answer, in one or two sentences, the "so what?" question for both arguments.

   a. Violent video games do not cause mass shootings.
   b. Because all combat roles are now open to women, both men and women should be required to register for the Selective Service.

3. Read the following passage from Elizabeth Silkes's 2020 essay, "Cultural Heritage Reminds Us of Our Shared Humanity. That's Why Threats against Them Are So Dangerous," found on **theysayiblog.com**. Where do you see Silkes answering the "so what?" and "who cares?" questions? Who does she say should care about preserving cultural sites, and why should they?

The destruction of cultural sites—from libraries to places of worship to museums—is ultimately about erasing a people's entire history. During the Bosnian war in the early 1990s, Serb and Croat forces destroyed or damaged hundreds of mosques in their efforts to rid the region of Muslims. In Zvornik, which had been a historic Muslim trading post on the Drina River, so many traces of the town's past had been eliminated that Brano Grujic, the Serb-installed mayor there, could falsely boast in 1993 that "there were never any mosques in Zvornik." As Helen Walasek, the author of *Bosnia and the Destruction of Cultural Heritage*, writes, sites such as archives and museums were targeted in part because they reflected Bosnia's pluralistic past. Such attacks were aimed at "eradicating any trace of Bosnia-Herzegovina's historic diversity and traditions of coexistence."...

The current conversation around preservation of cultural heritage in the Middle East comes at a critical time for the region, when conflict and atrocity have put a number of marginalized cultures at risk....

While cultural heritage is not the only way we form bonds with others, it is one of the most powerful and effective means of doing so across barriers. It is heartening to see the public outcry at this latest threat, but the risk to cultural sites during conflict remains extraordinarily high. This is especially so given the limited funding for multilateral organizations dedicated to their protection such as UNESCO, from which the United States formally withdrew a year ago. If our children and our children's children cannot access the most fundamental aspects of our own histories and those of others, they will never be able to identify the common threads that bind us all. And it is only through this binding that we can tap into—and act on—our shared humanity.

4. Read over the draft of an essay you are working on. Work with a partner to identify the answers to the "so what?" and "who cares?" questions for your argument. Then revise your draft to say why your argument matters by using the following template:

My point here, that _____, should interest those who _____. Beyond this limited audience, however, my point should speak to anyone who cares about the larger issue of _____.

EIGHT

"AS A RESULT"

Connecting the Parts

WE ONCE HAD A STUDENT named Billy, whose characteristic sentence pattern went something like this:

> Spot is a good dog. He has fleas.

"Connect your sentences," we urged in the margins of Billy's papers. "What does Spot's being good have to do with his fleas? These two statements seem unrelated. Can you connect them in some logical way?" When comments like these yielded no results, we tried inking in suggested connections for him:

> Spot is a good dog, *but* he has fleas.
> Spot is a good dog, *even though* he has fleas.

But our message failed to get across, and Billy's disconnected sentence pattern persisted to the end of the semester.

And yet Billy did focus well on his subjects. When he mentioned Spot the dog (or Plato or any other topic) in one sentence, we could count on Spot (or Plato) being the topic of the following sentence as well. This was not the case with some of Billy's classmates, who sometimes changed topic from sentence to sentence or even from clause to clause within a single sentence. But because Billy neglected to mark his connections, his writing was as frustrating to read as theirs. In all these cases, we had to struggle to figure out on our own how the sentences and paragraphs connected or failed to connect with one another.

What makes such writers so hard to read, in other words, is that they never gesture back to what they have just said or forward to what they plan to say. "Never look back" might be their motto, almost as if they see writing as a process of thinking of something to say about a topic and writing it down, then thinking of something else to say about the topic and writing that down, too, and on and on until they've filled the assigned number of pages and can hand the paper in. Each sentence basically starts a new thought rather than growing out of or extending the thought of the previous sentence.

When Billy talked about his writing habits, he acknowledged that he never went back and read what he had written. Indeed, he told us that, other than using his computer software to check for spelling errors and make sure that his tenses were all aligned, he never actually reread what he wrote before turning it in. As Billy seemed to picture it, writing was something one did while sitting at a computer, whereas reading was a separate activity generally reserved for an easy chair, book in hand. It had never occurred to Billy that to write a good sentence he had to think about how it connected to those that came before and after; that he had to think hard about how that sentence fit into the sentences that surrounded it. Each sentence for Billy existed in a sort of tunnel isolated from every other sentence on the page. He never bothered to fit all the parts of his essay together because he apparently thought of writing as a matter of piling up information or observations rather than building a sustained argument. What we suggest in this chapter, then, is that you converse not only with others in your writing but with yourself: that you establish clear relations between one statement and the next by connecting those statements.

This chapter addresses the issue of how to connect all the parts of your writing. The best compositions establish a sense of momentum and direction by making explicit connections among their different parts, so that what is said in one sentence (or paragraph) both sets up what is to come and is clearly informed by what has already been said. When you write a sentence, you create an expectation in the reader's mind that the next sentence will in some way echo and extend it, even if—*especially if*—that next sentence takes your argument in a new direction.

It may help to think of each sentence you write as having arms that reach backward and forward, as the figure below suggests. When your sentences reach outward like this, they establish connections that help your writing flow smoothly in a way readers appreciate. Conversely, when writing lacks such connections and moves in fits and starts, readers repeatedly have to go back over the sentences and guess at the connections on their own. To prevent such disconnection and make your writing flow, we advise

following a "do-it-yourself" principle, which means that it is your job as a writer to do the hard work of making the connections rather than, as Billy did, leaving this work to your readers.

This chapter offers several strategies you can use to put this principle into action: (1) using transition terms (like "therefore" and "as a result"); (2) adding pointing words (like "this" or "such"); (3) developing a set of key terms and phrases for each text you write; and (4) repeating yourself, but with a difference—a move that involves repeating what you've said, but with enough variation to avoid being redundant. All these moves require that you always look back and, in crafting any one sentence, think hard about those that precede it.

Notice how we ourselves have used such connecting devices thus far in this chapter. The second paragraph of this chapter, for example, opens with the transitional "And yet," signaling a change in direction, while the opening sentence of the third includes the phrase "in other words," telling you to expect a restatement of a point we've just made. If you look through this book, you should be able to find many sentences that contain some word or phrase that explicitly hooks them back to something said earlier, to something about to be said, or both. And many sentences in *this* chapter repeat key terms related to the idea of connection: "connect," "disconnect," "link," "relate," "forward," and "backward."

USE TRANSITIONS

For readers to follow your train of thought, you need not only to connect your sentences and paragraphs to each other but also to mark the kind of connection you are making. One of the easiest ways to make this move is to use *transitions* (from the Latin root *trans*, "across"), which help you cross from one point to another in your text. Transitions are usually placed at or near the start of sentences so they can signal to readers where your text is going: in the same direction it has been moving or in a new direction. More specifically, transitions tell readers whether your text is echoing a previous sentence or paragraph ("in other words"), adding something to it ("in addition"), offering an example of it ("for example"), generalizing from it ("as a result"), or modifying it ("and yet").

The following is a list of commonly used transitions, categorized according to their different functions:

ADDITION

also	in fact
and	indeed
besides	moreover
furthermore	so too
in addition	

ELABORATION

actually	to put it another way
by extension	to put it bluntly
in other words	to put it succinctly
in short	ultimately
that is	

EXAMPLE

after all	for instance
as an illustration	specifically
consider	to take a case in point
for example	

CAUSE AND EFFECT

accordingly	so
as a result	then
consequently	therefore
hence	thus
since	

COMPARISON

along the same lines	likewise
in the same way	similarly

CONTRAST

although	nevertheless
but	nonetheless
by contrast	on the contrary
conversely	on the other hand
despite	regardless
even though	whereas
however	while
in contrast	yet

CONCESSION

admittedly	naturally
although it is true	of course
granted	to be sure

CONCLUSION

as a result	in sum
consequently	therefore
hence	thus
in conclusion	to sum up
in short	to summarize

Ideally, transitions should operate so unobtrusively in a piece of writing that they recede into the background and readers do not even notice that they are there. It's a bit like what happens when drivers use their turn signals before turning right or left: just as other drivers recognize such signals almost unconsciously, readers should process transition terms with a minimum of thought. But even though such terms should function unobtrusively in your writing, they can be among the most powerful tools in your vocabulary. Think how your heart sinks when someone, immediately after praising you, begins a sentence with "but" or "however." No matter what follows, you know it won't be good.

Notice that some transitions can help you not only move from one sentence to another but also combine two or more sentences into one. Combining sentences in this way helps prevent the choppy, staccato effect that arises when too many short sentences are strung together, one after the other. For instance, to combine Billy's two choppy sentences ("Spot is a good dog. He has fleas.") into one, better-flowing sentence, we suggested that he rewrite them as "Spot is a good dog, *even though* he has fleas."

Transitions like these not only guide readers through the twists and turns of your argument but also help ensure that you *have* an argument in the first place. In fact, we think of words like "but," "yet," "nevertheless," "besides," and others as argument words, since it's hard to use them without making some kind of argument. The word "therefore," for instance, commits you to making sure that the claims preceding it lead logically to the conclusion that it introduces. "For example" also assumes an argument, since it requires the material you are introducing to stand as an instance or proof of some preceding generalization. As a result, the more you use transitions, the more you'll be able not only to connect the parts of your text but also to construct a strong argument in the first place. And if you draw on them frequently enough, using them should eventually become second nature.

To be sure, it is possible to overuse transitions, so take time to read over your drafts carefully and eliminate any transitions that are unnecessary. But following the maxim that you need to learn the basic moves of argument before you can deliberately depart from them, we advise you not to forgo explicit transition terms until you've first mastered their use. In all our years of teaching, we've read countless essays that suffered from having few or no transitions, but we cannot recall one in which the transitions were overused. Seasoned writers sometimes omit explicit transitions but only because they rely heavily on the other types of connecting devices that we turn to in the rest of this chapter.

Before doing so, however, let us warn you about inserting transitions without really thinking through their meanings—using "therefore," say, when your text's logic actually requires "nevertheless" or "however." So beware. Choosing transition terms should involve a bit of mental sweat, since the whole point of using them is to make your writing *more* reader-friendly, not less. The only thing more frustrating than reading Billy-style passages like "Spot is a good dog. He has fleas" is reading mis-connected sentences like "Spot is a good dog. For example, he has fleas."

USE POINTING WORDS

Another way to connect the parts of your argument is by using pointing words—which, as their name implies, point or refer backward to some concept in the previous sentence. The most common of these pointing words include "this," "these," "that," "those," "their," and "such" (as in "these pointing words" near the start of this sentence) and simple pronouns like "his," "he," "her," "she," "it," and "their." Such terms help you create the flow we spoke of earlier that enables readers to move effortlessly through your text. In a sense, these terms are like an invisible hand reaching out of your sentence, grabbing what's needed in the previous sentences and pulling it along.

Like transitions, however, pointing words need to be used carefully. It's dangerously easy to insert pointing words into your text that don't refer to a clearly defined object, assuming that because the object you have in mind is clear to you it will also be clear to your readers. For example, consider the use of "this" in the following passage:

> Alexis de Tocqueville was highly critical of democratic socie-
> ties, which he saw as tending toward mob rule. At the same time,
> he accorded democratic societies grudging respect. *This* is seen in
> Tocqueville's statement that . . .

When "this" is used in such a way it becomes an ambiguous or free-floating pointer, since readers can't tell if it refers to Tocqueville's critical attitude toward democratic societies, his grudging respect for them, or some combination of both. "This what?" readers mutter as they go back over such passages and try to figure them out. It's also tempting to try to cheat with pointing words, hoping that they will conceal or make up for conceptual confusions that may lurk in your argument. By referring to a fuzzy idea as "this" or "that," you might hope the fuzziness will somehow come across as clearer than it is.

You can fix problems caused by a free-floating pointer by making sure there is one and only one possible object in the vicinity that the pointer could be referring to. It also often helps to name the object the pointer is referring to at the same time that you point to it, replacing the bald "this" in the example above with a more precise phrase like "this ambivalence toward democratic societies" or "this grudging respect."

REPEAT KEY TERMS AND PHRASES

A third strategy for connecting the parts of your argument is to develop a constellation of key terms and phrases, including their synonyms and antonyms, that you repeat throughout your text. When used effectively, your key terms should be items that readers could extract from your text in order to get a solid sense of your topic. Playing with key terms also can be a good way to come up with a title and appropriate section headings for your text.

Notice how often Martin Luther King Jr. uses the keywords "criticism," "statement," "answer," and "correspondence" in the opening paragraph of his famous "Letter from Birmingham Jail":

Dear Fellow Clergymen:

While confined here in the Birmingham city jail, I came across your recent *statement* calling my present activities "unwise and untimely." Seldom do I pause to *answer criticism* of my work and ideas. If I sought to *answer* all the *criticisms* that cross my desk, my secretaries would have little time for anything other than *such correspondence* in the course of the day, and I would have no time for constructive work. But since I feel that you are men of genuine good will and that your *criticisms* are sincerely set forth, I want to try to *answer* your *statement* in what I hope will be patient and reasonable terms.

MARTIN LUTHER KING JR., "Letter from Birmingham Jail"

Even though King uses the terms "criticism" and "answer" three times each and "statement" twice, the effect is not overly repetitive. In fact, these key terms help build a sense of momentum in the paragraph and bind it together.

For another example of the effective use of key terms, consider the following passage, in which the historian Susan Douglas develops a constellation of sharply contrasting key terms around the concept of "cultural schizophrenics": women like herself who, Douglas claims, have mixed feelings about the images of ideal femininity with which they are constantly bombarded by the media:

> In a variety of ways, the mass media helped make us the cultural schizophrenics we are today, women who rebel against yet submit to prevailing images about what a desirable, worthwhile woman should be. . . . [T]he mass media has engendered in many women a kind of cultural identity crisis. We are ambivalent toward femininity on the one hand and feminism on the other. Pulled in opposite directions—told we were equal, yet told we were subordinate; told we could change history but told we were trapped by history—we got the bends at an early age, and we've never gotten rid of them.
>
> When I open *Vogue*, for example, I am simultaneously infuriated and seduced. . . . I adore the materialism; I despise the materialism. . . . I want to look beautiful; I think wanting to look beautiful is about the most dumb-ass goal you could have. The magazine stokes my desire; the magazine triggers my bile. And this doesn't only happen when I'm reading *Vogue*; it happens all the time. . . . On the one hand, on the other hand—that's not just me—that's what it means to be a woman in America.
>
> To explain this schizophrenia . . .

Susan Douglas, Where the Girls Are:
Growing Up Female with the Mass Media

In this passage, Douglas establishes "schizophrenia" as a key concept and then echoes it through synonyms like "identity crisis," "ambivalent," "the bends"—and even demonstrates it through a series of contrasting words and phrases:

rebel against / submit
told we were equal / told we were subordinate
told we could change history / told we were trapped by history
infuriated / seduced
I adore / I despise
I want / I think wanting . . . is about the most dumb-ass goal
stokes my desire / triggers my bile
on the one hand / on the other hand

These contrasting phrases help flesh out Douglas's claim that women are being pulled in two directions at once. In so doing, they bind the passage together into a unified whole that, despite its complexity and sophistication, stays focused over its entire length.

REPEAT YOURSELF—BUT WITH A DIFFERENCE

The last technique we offer for connecting the parts of your text involves repeating yourself, but with a difference—which basically means saying the same thing you've just said but in a slightly different way that avoids sounding monotonous. To effectively connect the parts of your argument and keep it moving forward, be careful not to leap from one idea to a different idea or introduce new ideas cold. Instead, try to build bridges between your ideas by echoing what you've just said while simultaneously moving your text into new territory.

Several of the connecting devices discussed in this chapter are ways of repeating yourself in this special way. Key terms, pointing terms, and even many transitions can be used in a way that not only brings something forward from the previous sentence but in some way alters it, too. When Douglas, for instance, uses the key term "ambivalent" to echo her earlier reference to schizophrenics, she is repeating herself with a difference—repeating the same concept but with a different word that adds new associations.

In addition, when you use transition phrases like "in other words" and "to put it another way," you repeat yourself with a difference, since these phrases help you restate earlier claims but in a different register. When you open a sentence with "in other words," you are basically telling your readers that in case they didn't fully understand what you meant in the last sentence, you are now coming at it again from a slightly different angle, or that since you're presenting a very important idea, you're not going to skip over it quickly but will explore it further to make sure your readers grasp all its aspects.

We would even go so far as to suggest that after your first sentence, almost every sentence you write should refer back to previous statements in some way. Whether you are writing a "furthermore" comment that adds to what you have just said or a "for example" statement that illustrates it, each sentence should echo at least one element of the previous sentence in some discernible way. Even when your text changes direction and requires transitions like "in contrast," "however," or "but," you still need to mark that shift by linking the sentence to the one just before it, as in the following example:

Cheyenne loved basketball. Nevertheless, she feared her height would put her at a disadvantage.

These sentences work because even though the second sentence changes course and qualifies the first, it still echoes key concepts from the first. Not only does "she" echo "Cheyenne," since both refer to the same person, but "feared" echoes "loved" by establishing the contrast mandated by the term "nevertheless." "Nevertheless," then, is not an excuse for changing subjects radically. It too requires repetition to help readers shift gears with you and follow your train of thought.

Repetition, in short, is the central means by which you can move from point A to point B in a text. To introduce one last analogy, think of the way experienced rock climbers move up a steep slope. Instead of jumping or lurching from one handhold to the next, good climbers get a secure handhold on the position they have established before reaching for the next ledge. The same thing applies to writing. To move smoothly from point to point in your argument, you need to firmly ground what you say in what you've already said. In this way, your writing remains focused while simultaneously moving forward.

"But hold on," you may be thinking. "Isn't repetition precisely what sophisticated writers should avoid, on the grounds that it will make their writing sound simplistic—as if they are belaboring the obvious?" Yes and no. On the one hand, writers certainly can run into trouble if they merely repeat themselves and nothing more. On the other hand, repetition is key to creating continuity in writing. It is impossible to stay on track in a piece of writing if you don't repeat your points throughout the length of the text. Furthermore, writers would never make an impact on readers if they didn't repeat their main points often enough to reinforce those points and make them stand out above subordinate points. The trick therefore is not to avoid repeating yourself but to repeat yourself in varied and interesting enough ways that you advance your argument without sounding tedious.

Exercises

1. The statements below aren't yet connected to each other. Use any of the transitions listed on pages 111 and 112 to connect them. You can combine the statements into one sentence, or you can keep them as two separate sentences, adding or deleting words. Once you're done, compare your responses with a partner's. How does your choice of transition words affect the meaning of the statements?

   a. Herd immunity is established when 93 percent of a population is vaccinated. Vaccinations can wear off in early adolescence.

   b. Writing can look like an individual pursuit. It requires other people. Other people help writers imagine how their audience will understand and respond to their claims.

   c. Some ski resorts have begun to diversify their operations to increase year-round profitability. Some have added zip lines that draw in people in the summer months.

2. Read the following passage from the MIT professor Sherry Turkle's essay "Stop Googling. Let's Talk." (pp. 614–23). Annotate the connecting devices you see. Underline the transitions, circle the key terms, and put boxes around the pointing terms.

   Across generations, technology is implicated in this assault on empathy. We've gotten used to being connected all the time, but we have found ways around conversation—at least from conversation that is open-ended and spontaneous, in which we play with ideas and allow ourselves to be fully present and vulnerable. But it is in this type of conversation—where we learn to make eye contact, to become aware of another person's posture and tone, to comfort one another and respectfully challenge one another—that empathy and intimacy flourish. In these conversations, we learn who we are.

Of course, we can find empathic conversations today, but the trend line is clear. It's not only that we turn away from talking face to face to chat online. It's that we don't allow these conversations to happen in the first place because we keep our phones in the landscape.

In our hearts, we know this, and now research is catching up with our intuitions. We face a significant choice. It is not about giving up our phones but about using them with greater intention. Conversation is there for us to reclaim. For the failing connections of our digital world, it is the talking cure.

3. Read over something you've written with an eye for the devices you've used to connect the parts. Working either by yourself or with a partner, do the following:

   a. Underline all the transitions, pointing terms, key terms, and repetitions.
   b. Describe the patterns you see. Do you rely on certain devices more than others?
   c. Locate a passage that could use better connections. Revise it using the devices introduced in this chapter. Is it easier to read now?

NINE

"YOU MEAN I CAN JUST SAY IT THAT WAY?"

Academic Writing Doesn't Mean Setting Aside Your Own Voice

WE WISH WE HAD A DOLLAR for each time a student has asked us a version of the above question. It usually comes when the student is visiting us during our office hours, seeking advice about how to improve a draft of an essay. When we ask the student to tell us in simple words the point being made in the essay, the student will almost invariably produce a statement that is far clearer and more incisive than anything in the draft.

"Write that down," we will urge. "What you just said is sooo much better than anything you wrote in your draft. We suggest going home and revising your paper in a way that makes that claim the focal point of your essay."

"Really?" our student will ask, looking surprised. "You mean I can just say it that way?"

"Sure. Why not?"

"Well, saying it that way seems just so elementary—so obvious. I mean, I don't want to sound stupid."

The goal of this chapter is to counteract this common misconception: that relying in college on the straightforward, down-to-earth language you use every day will make you sound stupid; that to impress your teachers you need to set aside your everyday voice and write in a way that is hard to understand.

It's easy to see how this misconception took hold, since academic writing is notoriously obscure. Students can't be blamed for such obscurity when much of the writing they're assigned to read is so hard to understand—as we can see in the following sentence from a science paper that linguist Steven Pinker quotes in his essay "Why Academics Stink at Writing":

> Participants read assertions whose veracity was either affirmed or denied by the subsequent presentation of an assessment word.

After struggling to determine what the writer of this sentence was trying to say, Pinker finally decided it was probably something as simple as this:

> Participants read sentences, each followed by the word *true* or *false*.

Had the author revised the original statement by tapping into more relaxed, everyday language, as Pinker did in revising it, much of this struggle could have been avoided. In our view, then, mastering academic writing does not mean completely abandoning your normal voice for one that's stiff, convoluted, or pompous, as students often assume. Instead, it means creating a new voice that draws on the voice you already have.

This is not to suggest that any language you use among friends has a place in academic writing. Nor is it to suggest that you may fall back on your everyday voice as an excuse to remain in your comfort zone and avoid learning the rigorous forms and habits that characterize academic culture. After all, learning new words and rhetorical moves is a major part of getting an education. We do, however, wish to suggest that everyday language can often enliven such moves and even enhance your precision in using academic terminology. In our view, then, it is a mistake to assume that the academic and everyday are completely separate languages that can never be used together. Ultimately, we suggest, academic writing is often at its best when it combines what we call "everydayspeak" and "academicspeak."

BLEND ACADEMIC AND COLLOQUIAL STYLES

In fact, we would point out that many academics are highly successful writers who themselves blend everyday and academic styles. Note, for example, how Judith Fetterley, a prominent scholar in the field of literary studies, blends academic and everyday ways of talking in the following passage on the novelist Willa Cather:

> As Merrill Skaggs has put it, "[Cather] is neurotically controlling and self-conscious about her work, but she knows at all points what she is doing. Above all else, she is self-conscious."
>
> Without question, Cather was a control freak.
>
> JUDITH FETTERLEY, "Willa Cather and the Question of Sympathy: An Unofficial Story"

In this passage, Fetterley makes use of what is probably the most common technique for blending academic and everyday language: she puts them side by side, juxtaposing "neurotically controlling" and "self-conscious" from a quoted source with her own colloquial term,

See p. 548 for an essay that mixes colloquial and academic styles.

"control freak." In this way, Fetterley lightens a potentially dry subject and makes it more accessible and even entertaining.

A TRANSLATION RECIPE

But Fetterley does more than simply put academicspeak and everydayspeak side by side. She takes a step further by translating the one into the other. By translating Skaggs's polysyllabic description of Cather as "neurotically controlling and self-conscious" into the succinct, if blunt, "control freak," Fetterley shows how rarefied, academic ways of talking and more familiar language can not only coexist but can also actually enhance one another—her informal "control freak" serving to explain the formal language that precedes it.

To be sure, slangy, colloquial expressions like "control freak" may be far more common in the humanities than in the sciences, and even in the humanities such casual usages are a recent development. Fifty years ago academic writing in all disciplines was the linguistic equivalent of a black-tie affair. But as times have changed, so has the range of options open to academic writers—so much so that it is not surprising to find writers in all fields using colloquial expressions and referring to movies, music, and other forms of popular culture.

Indeed, Fetterley's passage offers a simple recipe for mixing styles that we encourage you to try out in your own writing: first state the point in academic language, and then translate the point into everyday language. Everyone knows that academic terms like "neurotically controlling" and "self-conscious"—and others you might encounter like "subject position" or "bifurcate"—can be hard to understand. But this translation recipe, we think, eases such difficulties by making the academic familiar. Here is one way you might translate academicspeak into everydayspeak:

▸ **Scholar X argues, "_____." In other words, _____.**

Instead of "In other words," you might try variations like the following:

▸ **Essentially, X argues _____.**

▸ **X's point, succinctly put, is that _____.**

▸ **Plainly put, _____.**

Following Fetterley's lead and making moves like these can help you not only demystify challenging academic material but also reinterpret it, showing you understand it (and helping readers understand it) by putting it into your own terms.

SELF-TRANSLATION

But this translation recipe need not be limited to clarifying the ideas of others. It can also be used to clarify your own complex ideas, as the following passage by the philosopher Rebecca Goldstein illustrates:

> We can hardly get through our lives—in fact, it's hard to get through a week—without considering what makes specific actions right and others wrong and debating with ourselves whether that is a difference that must compel the actions we choose. (Okay, it's wrong! I get it! But why should I care?)
>
> REBECCA GOLDSTEIN, *Plato at the Googleplex:*
> *Why Philosophy Won't Go Away*

Though Goldstein's first sentence may require several rereadings, it is one that most of us, with varying degrees of effort, can come to understand: that we all wrestle regularly with the challenging philosophical questions of what the ethics of a given situation are and whether those ethics should alter our behavior. But instead of leaving us entirely on our own to figure out what she is saying, Goldstein helps us out in her closing parenthetical remarks, which translate the abstractions of her first sentence into the kind of concrete everydayspeak that runs through our heads.

Yet another example of self-translation—one that actually uses the word "translation"—can be found on the opening page of a book by scholar Helen Sword:

> There is a massive gap between what most readers consider to be good writing and what academics typically produce and publish. I'm not talking about the kinds of formal strictures necessarily imposed

by journal editors—article length, citation style, and the like—but about a deeper, duller kind of disciplinary monotony, a compulsive proclivity for discursive obscurantism and circumambulatory diction (translation: an addiction to big words and soggy syntax).

HELEN SWORD, *Stylish Academic Writing*

In this passage, Sword gives her own unique twist to the translation technique we've been discussing. After a stream of difficult polysyllabic words—"a compulsive proclivity for discursive obscurantism and circumambulatory diction"—she then concludes by translating these words into everydayspeak: "an addiction to big words and soggy syntax." The effect is to dramatize her larger point: the "massive gap between what most readers consider to be good writing and what academics typically produce and publish."

FAMOUS EXAMPLES

Even notoriously difficult thinkers could be said to use the translation practice we have been advocating in this chapter, as the following famous and widely quoted claims illustrate:

I think, therefore I am.
—RENÉ DESCARTES

The master's tools will never dismantle the master's house.
—AUDRE LORDE

The medium is the message.
—MARSHALL MCLUHAN

Form follows function.
—LOUIS SULLIVAN

These sentences can be read almost as sound bites—short, catchy statements that express a more complex idea. Though the term "sound bite" is usually used to refer to mindless media simplifications, the succinct statements above show what valu-able work they can do. These distillations are admittedly reduc-tive in that they do not capture all the nuances of the more complex ideas they represent. But consider their power to stick in the minds of readers. Without these memorable translations, we wonder if these authors' ideas would have achieved such widespread circulation.

Consider Descartes' "I think, therefore I am," for example, which comes embedded in the following passage, in which Descartes is struggling to find a philosophical foundation for absolute truth in the face of skeptical doctrines that doubt that anything can be known for certain. After putting himself in the shoes of a radical skeptic and imagining what it would be like to believe all apparent truths to be false, Descartes "immediately ... observed," he writes:

> whilst I thus wished to think that all was false, it was absolutely necessary that I, who thus thought, should be somewhat; and as I observed that this truth, I think, therefore I am (*cogito ergo sum*), was so certain and of such evidence that no ground of doubt, how-ever extravagant, could be alleged by the sceptics capable of shak-ing it, I concluded that I might, without scruple, accept it as the first principle of the philosophy of which I was in search.
>
> RENÉ DESCARTES, "Discourse on the Method, Part IV"

Had Descartes been less probing and scrupulous, we speculate, he would have stopped writing and ended the passage after the statement "it was absolutely necessary that I, who thus thought, should be somewhat." After all, the passage up to this point contains all the basic ingredients that the rest of it goes on to explain, the simpler, more accessible formulation

"I think, therefore I am" being merely a reformulation of this earlier material. But just imagine if Descartes had decided that his job as a writer was finished after his initial claim and had failed to add the more accessible phrase "I think, therefore I am." We suspect this idea of his would not have become one of the most famous touchstones of Western philosophy.

EVERYDAY LANGUAGE AS A THINKING TOOL

As the examples in this chapter suggest, then, translating academic language into everydayspeak can be an indispensable tool for clarifying and underscoring ideas for readers. But at an even more basic level, such translation can be an indispensable means for you as a writer to clarify your ideas to yourself. In other words, translating academicspeak into everydayspeak can function as a thinking tool that enables you to discover what you are trying to say to begin with.

For as writing theorists often note, writing is generally not a process in which we start with a fully formed idea in our heads that we then simply transcribe in an unchanged state onto the page. On the contrary, writing is more often a means of discovery in which we use the writing process to figure out what our idea is. This is why writers are often surprised to find that what they end up with on the page is quite different from what they thought it would be when they started. What we are trying to say here is that everydayspeak is often crucial for this discovery process, that translating your ideas into more common, simpler terms can help you figure out what your ideas really are, as opposed to what you initially imagined they were. Even Descartes, for example, may not have had the formulation "I think, therefore I am" in mind before he wrote the passage above; instead, he may have arrived at it as he worked through the writing process.

We ourselves have been reminded of this point when engaged in our own writing. One major benefit of writing collaboratively, as the two of us do, is that it repeatedly forces us to explain in simpler terms our less-than-clear ideas when one of us doesn't already know what the other means. In the process of writing and revising this book, for instance, we were always turning to each other after reading something the other had written and asking a version of the "Can you explain that more simply?" question that we described asking our students in our office in this chapter's opening anecdote: "What do you mean?" "I don't get it—can you explain?" "Huh!?" Sometimes, when the idea is finally stated in plain, everyday terms, we realize that it doesn't make sense or that it amounts to nothing more than a cliché—or that we have something worth pursuing. It's as if using everyday language to talk through a draft—as any writer can do by asking others to critique a draft—shines a bright light on our writing to expose its strengths and weaknesses.

STILL NOT CONVINCED?

To be sure, not everyone will be as enthusiastic as we are about the benefits of everydayspeak. Many will insist that, while some fields in the humanities may be open to everyday language, colloquial expressions, and slang, most fields in the sciences are not. And some people in both the humanities and the sciences will argue that some ideas simply can't be done justice to in everyday language. "Theory X," they will say, "is just too complex to be explained in simple terms," or "You have to be in the field to understand it." Perhaps so. But at least one distinguished scientist, the celebrated atomic physicist Enrico Fermi, thought otherwise. Fermi, it is said, believed that all faculty in his field should teach basic physics to undergraduates, because having to explain the science in relatively plain English helped clarify their thinking. This last point can be stated as a rule of thumb: if you can't explain it to your aunt Franny, chances are you don't understand it yourself.

Furthermore, when writers tell themselves that their ideas are just too complex to be explained to nonspecialists, they risk fooling themselves into thinking that they are making more sense than they actually are. Translating academicspeak into everydayspeak functions as a kind of baloney detector, a way of keeping us honest when we're in danger of getting carried away by our own verbosity.

CODE-MESHING

"But come on," some may say. "Get real! Academic writing must, in many cases, mean setting aside our own voices." Sure, it may be fine to translate challenging academic ideas into plain everyday language, as Goldstein, Sword, and Descartes do above, when it's a language that your audience will understand and find acceptable. But what if your everyday language—the one you use when you're most relaxed, with family and friends—is filled with slang and questionable grammar? And what if your everyday language is an ethnic or regional dialect—or a different language altogether? Is there really a place for such language in academic, professional, or public writing?

Yes and no. On the one hand, there are many situations—like when you're applying for a job or submitting a proposal to be read by an official screening body—in which it's probably safest to write in "standard" English. On the other hand, the line between language that might confuse audiences and language that engages or challenges them is not always obvious. Nor is the line between foreign words that readers don't already know and those that readers might happily learn. After all, standard written English is more open and inclusive than it may at first appear. And readers often appreciate writers who take risks and mix things up.

Many prominent writers mix standard written English with other dialects or languages, employing a practice that cultural and linguistic theorists Vershawn Ashanti Young and Suresh Canagarajah call "code-meshing." For instance, in the titles of two of her books, *Talkin and Testifyin: The Language of Black America* and *Black Talk: Words and Phrases From the Hood to the Amen Corner*, the language scholar Geneva Smitherman mixes African American vernacular phrases with more scholarly language in order to suggest, as she explicitly argues in these books, that black vernacular English is as legitimate a variety of language as standard English. Here are three typical passages:

> In Black America, the oral tradition has served as a fundamental vehicle for gittin ovah. That tradition preserves the Afro-American heritage and reflects the collective spirit of the race.

> Blacks are quick to ridicule "educated fools," people who done gone to school and read all dem books and still don't know nothin!

> It is a socially approved verbal strategy for black rappers to talk about how bad they is.

> GENEVA SMITHERMAN, *Talkin and Testifyin:*
> *The Language of Black America*

In these examples, Smitherman blends the types of terms we expect in scholarly writing like "oral tradition" and "fundamental vehicle" with Black vernacular phrases like "gittin ovah." She even blends the standard English spelling of words with African American English variants like "dem" and "ovah" in a way that evokes how some speakers of African American English sound. Some might object to these unconventional practices, but this is precisely Smitherman's point: that our habitual language practices need to be opened up, and that the number of participants in the academic conversation needs to be expanded.

Along similar lines, the writer and activist Gloria Anzaldúa mixes standard English with what she calls Chicano Spanish to make a political point about the suppression of the Spanish language in the United States. In one typical passage, she writes:

> From this racial, ideological, cultural, and biological cross-pollinization, an "alien" consciousness is presently in the making—a new *mestiza* consciousness, *una conciencia de mujer*.
>
> GLORIA ANZALDÚA,
> *Borderlands / La Frontera: The New Mestiza*

Anzaldúa gets her point across not only through *what* she says but also through the *way* she says it, showing that the new hybrid, or "*mestiza* consciousness," that she celebrates is, as she puts it, "presently in the making." Ultimately, such code-meshing suggests that languages, like the people who speak them, are not distinct, separate islands.

Because there are so many options in writing, then, there is no need to ever feel limited in your choice of words. You can always experiment with your language and improve it. Depending on your audience and purpose, and how much risk you're willing to take, you can dress up your language, dress it down, or some combination of both. You could even recast the title of this book, *"They Say / I Say,"* as a teenager might say it: "She Goes / I'm Like."

We hope you agree with us, then, that to succeed as a college writer, you need not always set aside your everyday voice, even when that voice may initially seem unwelcome in the academic world. It is by blending everyday language with standard written English that what counts as "standard" changes and the range of possibilities open to academic writers continues to grow.

Exercises

1. Take a paragraph from this book and dress it down, rewriting it in informal colloquial language. Then rewrite the same paragraph again by dressing it up, making it much more formal. Then rewrite the paragraph in a way that blends the two styles. Share your paragraphs with a classmate and discuss which versions are most effective and why.

2. Find something you've written for a course, and study it to see whether you've used any of your own everyday expressions, any words or structures that are not "academic." If by chance you don't find any, see if there's a place or two where shifting into more casual or unexpected language would help you make a point, get your reader's attention, or just add liveliness to your text. Be sure to keep your audience and purpose in mind, and use language that will be appropriate to both.

3. Below is a short passage from Stephanie Owen and Isabel Sawhill's report, "Should Everyone Go to College?" (pp. 488–505). Use one of the translation templates on page 127 to translate the academic language in the underlined sentence into everyday language. Compare your response with a classmate.

We all know that, on average, college graduates make significantly more money over their lifetimes than those with only a high school education. What gets less attention is the fact that not all college degrees or college graduates are equal. <u>There is enormous variation in the so-called return to education depending on factors such as institution attended, field of study, whether a student graduates, and post-graduation occupation.</u> (488–89)

4. Find a reading on **theysayiblog.com** that blends academic and everyday styles, such as James Hatch's 2019 essay, "My Semester with the Snowflakes." Identify a sentence or passage where you see the author mixing everyday and academic language. Explain how this blending affects the overall argument. How did you react as a reader?

TEN

"BUT DON'T GET ME WRONG"

The Art of Metacommentary

———⌑———

WHEN WE TELL PEOPLE that we are writing a chapter on the art of metacommentary, they often give us a puzzled look and tell us that they have no idea what "metacommentary" is. "We know what commentary is," they'll sometimes say, "but what does it mean when it's *meta?*" Our answer is that whether or not they know the term, they practice the art of metacommentary on a daily basis whenever they make a point of explaining something they've said or written: "What I meant to say was _____," "My point was not _____, but _____," or "You're probably not going to like what I'm about to say, but _____." In such cases, they are not offering new points but telling an audience how to interpret what they have already said or are about to say. In short, then, metacommentary is a way of commenting on your claims and telling others how—and how not—to think about them.

It may help to think of metacommentary as being like the chorus in a Greek play that stands to the side of the drama unfolding on the stage and explains its meaning to the audience—or like a voice-over narrator who comments on and explains the action in a television show or movie. Think of metacommentary as a sort of second text that stands alongside your main text and explains what it means. In the main text you say something; in the metatext you guide your readers in interpreting and processing what you've said.

What we are suggesting, then, is that you think of your text as two texts joined at the hip: a main text in which you make your argument and another in which you "work" your ideas, distinguishing your views from others they may be confused with, anticipating and answering objections, connecting one point to another, explaining why your claim might be controversial, and so forth. The figure below demonstrates what we mean.

THE MAIN TEXT SAYS SOMETHING. THE METATEXT TELLS READERS HOW — AND HOW NOT — TO THINK ABOUT IT.

USE METACOMMENTARY TO CLARIFY
AND ELABORATE

But why do you need metacommentary to tell readers what you mean and guide them through your text? Can't you just clearly say what you mean up front? The answer is that no matter how clear and precise your writing is, readers can still fail to understand it in any number of ways. Even the best writers can provoke reactions in readers that they didn't intend, and even good readers can get lost in a complicated argument or fail to see how one point connects with another. Readers may also fail to see what follows from your argument, or they may follow your reasoning and examples yet fail to see the larger conclusion you draw from them. They may fail to see your argument's overall significance or mistake what you are saying for a related argument that they have heard before but that you want to distance yourself from. As a result, no matter how straightforward a writer you are, readers still need you to help them grasp what you really mean. Because the written word is prone to so much mischief and can be interpreted in so many different ways, we need metacommentary to keep misinterpretations and other communication misfires at bay.

Another reason to master the art of metacommentary is that it will help you develop your ideas and generate more text. If you have ever had trouble producing the required number of pages for a writing project, metacommentary can help you add both length and depth to your writing. We've seen many students who try to produce a five-page paper sputter to a halt at two or three pages, complaining they've said everything they can think of about their topic. "I've stated my thesis and presented my reasons and evidence," students have told us. "What else is there to do?" It's almost as if such writers have generated a thesis and don't know what to do with it. When these students learn to use metacommentary, however, they get more out of their ideas and write longer, more substantial texts. In sum, metacommentary can help you extract the full potential from your ideas, drawing out important implications, explaining ideas from different perspectives, and so forth.

So even when you may think you've said everything possible in an argument, try inserting the following types of metacommentary:

▸ **In other words, <u>she doesn't realize how right she is</u>.**

▸ **What _____ really means is _____.**

▸ **My point is not _____ but _____.**

▸ **Ultimately, then, my goal is to demonstrate that _____.**

Ideally, such metacommentary should help you recognize some implications of your ideas that you didn't initially realize were there.

Let's look at how the cultural critic Neil Postman uses metacommentary in the following passage describing the shift in American culture when it began to move from print and reading to television and movies:

> *It is my intention in this book to show* that a great . . . shift has taken place in America, with the result that the content of much of our public discourse has become dangerous nonsense. *With this in view, my task in the chapters ahead is* straightforward. *I must, first, demonstrate* how, under the governance of the printing

press, discourse in America was different from what it is now—generally coherent, serious and rational; *and then* how, under the governance of television, it has become shriveled and absurd. *But to avoid the possibility that my analysis will be interpreted as* standard-brand academic whimpering, a kind of elitist complaint against "junk" on television, *I must first explain that . . .* I appreciate junk as much as the next fellow, *and I know full well that* the printing press has generated enough of it to fill the Grand Canyon to overflowing. Television is not old enough to have matched printing's output of junk.

NEIL POSTMAN, *Amusing Ourselves to Death:*
Public Discourse in the Age of Show Business

To see what we mean by metacommentary, look at the phrases above that we have italicized. With these moves, Postman essentially stands apart from his main ideas to help readers follow and understand what he is arguing.

He previews what he will argue: *It is my intention in this book to show . . .*

He spells out how he will make his argument: *With this in view, my task in the chapters ahead is . . . I must, first, demonstrate . . . and then . . .*

He distinguishes his argument from other arguments it may easily be confused with: *But to avoid the possibility that my analysis will be interpreted as . . . I must first explain that . . .*

TITLES AS METACOMMENTARY

Even the title of Postman's book, *Amusing Ourselves to Death: Public Discourse in the Age of Show Business*, functions as a form of metacommentary since, like all titles, it stands apart from the text itself and tells readers the book's main point: that the very pleasure provided by contemporary show business is destructive.

Titles, in fact, are one of the most important forms of metacommentary, functioning rather like carnival barkers telling passersby what they can expect if they go inside. Subtitles, too, function as metacommentary, further explaining or elaborating on the main title. The subtitle of this book, for example, not only explains that it is about "the moves that matter in academic writing" but also indicates that "they say / I say" is one of these moves. Thinking of a title as metacommentary can actually help you develop sharper titles, ones that, like Postman's, give readers a hint of what your argument will be. Contrast such titles with unhelpfully open-ended ones, like "Shakespeare" or "Steroids" or "English Essay" or essays with no titles at all. Essays with vague titles (or no titles) send the message that the writer has simply not bothered to reflect on what is being said and is uninterested in guiding or orienting readers.

USE OTHER MOVES AS METACOMMENTARY

Many of the other moves covered in this book function as metacommentary: entertaining objections, adding transitions, framing quotations, answering "so what?" and "who cares?" When you entertain objections, you stand outside of your text and imagine what a critic might say; when you add transitions, you essentially explain the relationship between various claims. And when you answer the "so what?" and "who cares?" questions, you look beyond your central argument and explain who should be interested in it and why.

TEMPLATES FOR INTRODUCING
METACOMMENTARY

TO WARD OFF POTENTIAL MISUNDERSTANDINGS

The following moves help you differentiate certain views from ones they might be mistaken for:

▸ Essentially, I am arguing not that <u>we should give up the policy</u> but that we should monitor effects far more closely.

▸ This is not to say _____, but rather _____.

▸ X is concerned less with _____ than with _____.

TO ELABORATE ON A PREVIOUS IDEA

The following moves elaborate on a previous point, saying to readers: "In case you didn't get it the first time, I'll try saying the same thing in a different way."

▸ In other words, _____.

▸ To put it another way, _____.

▸ What X is saying here is that _____.

TO PROVIDE A ROAD MAP TO YOUR TEXT

This move orients readers, clarifying where you have been and where you are going—and making it easier for them to process and follow your text:

▸ Chapter 2 explores _____, while Chapter 3 examines _____.

▸ Having just argued that _____, I want now to complicate the point by _____.

TO MOVE FROM A GENERAL CLAIM TO A SPECIFIC EXAMPLE

These moves help you explain a general point by providing a concrete example that illustrates what you're saying:

▸ For example, _____.

▸ _____, for instance, demonstrates _____.

▸ Consider _____, for example.

▸ To take a case in point, _____.

TO INDICATE THAT A CLAIM IS MORE, LESS, OR EQUALLY IMPORTANT

The following templates help you give relative emphasis to the claim that you are introducing, showing whether that claim is of more or less weight than the previous one or equal to it:

▸ Even more important, _____.

▸ But above all, _____.

▸ Incidentally, we will briefly note, _____.

▸ Just as important, _____.

▸ Equally, _____.

▸ Finally, _____.

TO EXPLAIN A CLAIM WHEN YOU ANTICIPATE OBJECTIONS

Here's a template to help you anticipate and respond to possible objections:

Chapter 6 has more templates for anticipating objections.

▸ Although some readers may object that _____, I would answer that _____.

TO GUIDE READERS TO YOUR MOST GENERAL POINT

These moves show that you are wrapping things up and tying up various subpoints previously made:

▸ In sum, then, _____.

▸ My conclusion, then, is that _____.

▸ In short, _____.

In this chapter we have tried to show that the most persuasive writing often doubles back and comments on its own claims in ways that help readers negotiate and process them. Instead of simply piling claim upon claim, effective writers are constantly "stage-managing" how their claims will be received. It's true, of course, that to be persuasive a text has to have strong claims to argue in the first place. But even the strongest arguments will flounder unless writers use metacommentary to prevent potential misreadings and make their arguments shine.

Exercises

1. Complete each of the following metacommentary templates in any way that makes sense:

   a. In making a case for raising the minimum wage, I am not saying that _____.

   b. But my argument will do more than prove that one particular industrial chemical has certain toxic properties. In this essay, I will also _____.

   c. My point about the national obsession with sports reinforces the belief held by many _____ that _____.

d. I believe, therefore, that the war is completely unjusti-
fied. But let me back up and explain how I arrived at this
conclusion: _____. In this way, I came to believe
that this war is a big mistake.

2. Read the following passage from Pau Gasol's 2018 essay,
"An Open Letter about Female Coaches." You can find the
link to the full essay on **theysayiblog.com**. Underline where
Gasol uses the moves of metacommentary to guide his readers through the main text of his argument. Does the author
use any of the chapter's templates (see p. 144)? How do
you think the author's use of metacommentary enhances
(or harms) his writing?

The reason I wanted to start by telling you about my parents, is
that their story makes me think about today's NBA. Specifically
about how, in the 72-year history of the league, there has never
been a female head coach. Even more specifically, it makes me
think of Becky Hammon: a coach who has been the topic of much
conversation lately, and who I've had the opportunity to play for
in San Antonio.

But if you think I'm writing this to argue why Becky is qualified
to be an NBA head coach . . . well, you're mistaken. That part is
obvious: One, she was an accomplished player—with an elite point
guard's mind for the game. And two, she has been a successful
assistant for arguably the greatest coach in the game. What more
do you need? But like I said—I'm not here to make that argument. Arguing on Coach Hammon's behalf would feel patronizing.
To me, it would be strange if NBA teams were not interested in
her as a head coach.

3. Read over the draft of an essay, and try the following:

   a. Locate a passage that needs more clarification or elaboration. Revise it using the metacommentary templates included in this chapter.
   b. Add in "road map" metacommentary to help your reader follow your text, using the template on page 144.
   c. Compose a title and subtitle that function as metacommentary on your whole argument.

ELEVEN

"WHAT I REALLY WANT TO SAY IS"
Revising Substantially

ONE OF THE MOST common frustrations teachers have—we've had it, too—is that students do not revise in any substantial way. As one of our colleagues put it, "I ask my classes to do a substantial revision of an essay they've turned in, emphasis on the word 'substantial,' but invariably little is changed in what I get back. Students hand in the original essay with a word changed here and there, a few spelling errors corrected, and a comma or two added. . . . I feel like all my advice is for nothing." We suspect, however, that in most cases when students do merely superficial revisions, it's not because they are indifferent or lazy, as some teachers may assume, but because they aren't sure what a good revision looks like. Like even many seasoned writers, these students would *like* to revise more thoroughly, but when they reread what they've written, they have trouble seeing where it can be improved—and how. What they lack is not just a reliable picture in their head of what their draft *could* be but also reliable strategies for getting there. In this chapter, we supply ten such revision strategies and a revision checklist (see pp. 165–70) that are designed to work in virtually any academic setting, regardless of assignment, instructor, discipline, or course.

1. THINK GLOBALLY

Perhaps the best strategy for revising your writing in a substantial way is to think globally, as we might put it, about your draft. This involves stepping back from your writing and looking at the big picture, asking yourself what, finally, you are trying to say. You might ask: Do I have a central argument, or do I just ramble and talk *about* my subject? And if I do have a central argument, does that argument make sense? Is it coherent and unified, or do I go off on tangents or even contradict myself? Do I logically link the parts, tying them together with clear connections between them all, developing a continuous line of argument over my essay's entire length? Does my evidence match my central argument and, as we put it in our revision checklist, is it clear what is motivating my argument—why it needs to be made in the first place? That is, do I present my argument as an entry into some larger conversation or debate, as a response to something "they say"? Have I included the strongest possible objections that can be made against my argument or answered any counterarguments in a superficial way? In the end, might any such counterarguments I address be more convincing to readers—or even to me—than my own argument?

It was big questions like these that inspired a student several years ago to radically revise an essay she'd written on the Iraq War, transforming it from a series of disconnected observations about the war into a sharply focused critique of the view that the war promoted democracy. Her first draft had been a mere collection of scattered claims, all presented as if they were of equal importance: Iraq had no weapons of mass destruction. The United States has the strongest military. Saddam Hussein was evil. Many Americans and Iraqis were killed. The war increased terrorism. And so forth. But her final draft nicely subordinated all its points to a larger "they say/I say" thesis: though Saddam Hussein is an evil dictator, it makes no sense to wage war on Iraq's innocent people. The final version was virtually a different essay.

We open with this suggestion to think globally not just because it is perhaps the central way to substantially revise an essay but also because it is so frequently neglected. Because writing is often associated with local, sentence-level mechanics and grammar, some writers picture revision as a small-scale matter of dotting an occasional "i" and crossing an occasional "t." What often gets overlooked, as writing expert Nancy Sommers points out, are "strategies for handling the whole essay," ones that would help writers "reorder lines of reasoning or ask questions about their purposes and readers." It would be as if a jewelry appraiser were to assess a gem only by studying its smallest, microscopic details and never holding it back to form an overall impression.

Revising globally, then, may mean changing the way we think. It asks us to move beyond microlevel edits, beyond

The messiness of the revision process.

merely tweaking or refining an existing argument. At its best, revision is a messy process that often helps us discover what our argument is in the first place. In fact, a good way to test how substantial your revisions are is to ask how much you learned about your argument through the revision process.

2. BUT STILL SWEAT THE SMALL STUFF

But just because the global level is very important in revising, it doesn't mean that local, surface-level issues—word choice, sentence structure, grammar, style, and so forth—aren't very important too. After all, everything you write is composed of countless small-scale decisions, and if you improve enough of them your next draft has a chance of constituting a significant revision. Also, it is always possible that changing just a single word will help you radically resee your central argument and lead to major, global changes. So while we suggest you think of global revisions as more important than microlevel ones, in practice the two levels are deeply interdependent. Although writers are often told to start out by focusing on their big idea—getting that big idea down on paper and only at a later stage worrying about small-scale mechanics—seasoned writers often move back and forth between the two levels throughout the revision process.

To see how we sweat the small stuff, consider the photo on the facing page of revisions we made on our last paragraph, none of which significantly alter the paragraph's central point. The central point—about the importance of small edits and their connection to big edits—is recognizable from the one draft to the other. And yet we like to think that, taken together, these edits make the passage much more readable. The mere decision alone to move this section up in the chapter and make it the

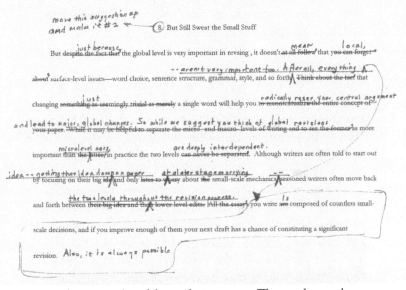

move this suggestion up and make it #2 →

8. But Still Sweat the Small Stuff

But despite *just because* the fact that the global level is very important in revising, it doesn't at all follow *mean* that you can forget *local,* —*aren't very important too. After all, everything* about surface-level issues—word choice, sentence structure, grammar, style, and so forth. Think about the fact that changing something *just* as seemingly trivial as merely a single word will help you to recontextualize the entire concept of *radically reser your central argument and lead to major, global changes. So while we suggest you think of global revisions* your paper. While it may be helpful to separate the micro- and macro- levels of writing and to see the former *microlevel ones, are deeply interdependent.* as more important than the latter, in practice the two levels can never be separated. Although writers are often told to start out by focusing on their big idea *idea--getting that idea down on paper* and only later to worry about the small-scale mechanics, *at a later stage worrying* seasoned writers often move back and forth between their big idea and their lower-level edits. *the two levels throughout the revision process.* All the essays you write are *Is* composed of countless small-scale decisions, and if you improve enough of them your next draft has a chance of constituting a significant revision. *Also, it is always possible*

second strategy listed has a big impact. The reader no longer needs to struggle to recall what we'd said several items back about thinking globally. We now have just said it.

3. READ YOUR OWN WRITING

But it is difficult to make any revisions, global or local, unless you do something even more fundamental, which is simply to read what you've written and then ideally reread and reread it again. It is very hard to set the revision process in motion if you don't do at least one initial read-through of your draft, and then do as many additional read-throughs as needed to get a solid grasp of the material with which you're dealing. As Donald Murray explains in *A Writer Teaches Writing*, "The writer reads and rereads and rereads, standing far back and reading quickly from a distance, moving in close and reading slowly line-by-line, reading again and again. . . ."

But why, you might wonder, should you read your own writing? You, after all, are the one who wrote it, so if anyone must know what your text says, shouldn't it be you? The answer is that, precisely because you're the author, you're too close to your text to know what it says. As writers, we tend to be so invested in what we've written that we need to find ways of stepping back from our text to gain some critical distance.

Perhaps the central way of gaining such distance is by reading the draft from an outsider's perspective—as if, instead of being the author, you were some other person who is on the lookout for logical glitches and inconsistencies, for better ways of stating a point, for parts that are hard to follow, for claims and subclaims that need more explanation, or for how your argument might be vulnerable to critique. You might also try reading your text aloud to yourself—or even try using text-to-speech technology on your computer or phone. And it never hurts, if you have time, to set your draft aside for a few days so that when you return to it you can reread it with fresh eyes.

4. AND HAVE OTHERS READ YOUR WRITING, TOO

Of course there are other ways to get critical distance on your work and see it from an outsider's perspective. One of the best ways is to show your work to someone who is willing to read it—a fellow student, family member, friend, or tutor—and ask for feedback. Teachers, in fact, may ask you to pair up with another student to comment on each other's work. It's a great way to get a sense of audience: how your text will be processed and received when it goes out into the world. In seeking out such readers, we often naturally gravitate toward those who share our opinions and predilections. But don't underestimate the value of readers who may know little about your subject or disagree with your position. Often, the more readers differ from you, the more likely they will be able to see things that you yourself could not have thought of.

5. GO BACK TO THE TEXT

While developing a deep familiarity with your own writing is essential in any revision process, developing a deep familiarity with your sources is also very important. It's surprising how often errors are introduced when we haven't read the text we're responding to carefully enough and start writing about it before we really understand it. It's also surprising how often errors are introduced when we fail to check and double-check our quotations against the originals and thus mistranscribe them in our texts. If we are right that the most persuasive writing responds to something that others have said, then writing that misquotes or misrepresents what those others say, as we suggested in Chapter 2 (see particularly our comments on the "closest cliché syndrome"), will be built on a false foundation.

If you're anything like us, however, you might not like going back to your source. At times we don't want to go back to a source because we don't want to take the time to unpack its difficult, challenging language. At other times, we don't want to return to a source because we fear, deep down, that it doesn't quite say what we want it to say. When this happens, there is always a danger of creating a straw man: distorting what an author says in order to pursue our own agenda, transforming the author into a mere projection of ourselves. In this respect, accurately representing what "they say" is not just an intellectual obligation but a moral one as well.

As an example, let's turn to Rosa, a student who wanted to write an essay defending the practice of meditation. In her first draft, Rosa made a strong case that meditation promotes democratic politics, but she misconstrued her essay's central source, a scholarly article by Dean Mathiowetz that reads:

Meditation Is Good for Nothing

> Does meditation bring political benefits in the sense of strengthening citizenship or democracy? Taking the Zen phrase "meditation doesn't work—it's good for nothing" as my point of departure . . . I argue that meditation can foster significant dimensions of democratic citizenship. . . .

Mathiowetz's argument here is that meditation can in fact "foster significant dimensions of democratic citizenship"—or, as he goes on to claim, that, paradoxically, because "meditation . . . is good for nothing," it can help citizens and politicians detach from their self-interested passions and biases and find common ground. Yet Rosa presented Mathiowetz as saying that meditation is literally "good for nothing" and has no political or civic benefits.

When Rosa realized her mistake, she was inspired to do a revision. And the following week, she produced a much improved draft that opens as follows:

Many people think that meditation is a waste of time. According to these skeptics, meditation is a useless activity that is only for self-absorbed flakes who have no concern for the give-and-take of politics. But I disagree. As Dean Mathiowetz argues, the very uselessness of meditation makes it a valuable political tool. It can make us less polarized—better able to listen to one another and move beyond our rigid political views, and more committed to the common good.

In this way, Rosa was able to continue using Mathiowetz as a central source in her essay but without distorting his position. Instead of casting him as a naysayer in her essay who opposes meditation, she now presents Mathiowetz as the pro-meditation ally he really is.

6. DOES YOUR EXAMPLE SAY WHAT YOU SAY IT SAYS?

Offering an example to support your argument is such a natural, familiar part of writing that it may seem easy. And yet providing examples is often a challenge, largely because of the kind of disconnection issues we discussed in Chapter 8. When giving an example—which might take the form of a statistic, a quotation, evidence, or a story or anecdote—writers often discover that the example gets away from them. That is, the example they provide turns out not to support the point they want it to support and may even contradict it. So in revising your drafts, pay special attention to whether your example actually supports your argument, whether your example and what it is supposed to exemplify are united.

A student named Jacob needed help with this issue in an essay he'd written about how, as his title put it, "We All Need to Become More Green." In an attempt to provide a model example of someone who, in Jacob's words, has admirably "stopped using toxic, traditional household cleaners" that harm the environment, Jacob cites the case of his mother:

> My mother is a perfect example. She cares a lot about the environment and has always opposed chemicals. She frequently uses cleaning products in our house that are environmentally friendly but claims they never work. She once spent almost a hundred dollars on eco-friendly cleaners for our house but ended up throwing most of them out and returning to the toxic products she's always used. Nothing ever changes. She keeps using the old-fashioned cleaners but complaining about them.

Although each sentence here is admirably clear, Jacob ran into the classic problem of his thesis being out of sync with his example. Instead of showing that we should all stop using toxic cleaners, the story of his mother actually shows just how hard giving up such cleaners can be.

With Jacob's permission, his instructor circulated his essay to his class and asked how it might be revised. One student proposed that Jacob modify his thesis so that it asserts not just that we should all be more green, but that, to echo Kermit the Frog, "it's not easy being green," which, the student added, might be a fun new title for Jacob's essay. In his next draft, however, Jacob did decide to modify his argument, but in a different way by claiming that nobody, not even his deeply committed mother, will ever be able to become fully green if they don't lower their expectations about cleanliness.

7. KEEP ASKING "AS OPPOSED TO WHAT?"

Throughout this book we suggest that writers start "with what others are saying," as the subtitle of Chapter 1 puts it, and that they use this "they say" to motivate their "I say." But writers often neglect this important rhetorical move. They get so caught up in making their claims that they forget even the truest, most accurate, and well-supported claim will seem pointless if they fail to answer the all-important "as opposed to what?" or "who says otherwise?" question.

We sometimes forget to ask these questions ourselves. For example, it was only after years of writing and rewriting this very book that we realized there was an important "they say" or "as opposed to what?" contrast buried in our manuscript that we needed to draw out. At the end of a passage describing our templates as "one of the novel features of this book," we'd written:

> This book offers model templates to help you put key principles of writing directly into practice.

When we reread this sentence, we felt that it was missing something, that it sounded flat and uninspired. But why? After experimenting with different versions of the sentence, none of which seemed to help, we realized we weren't following our own advice. "There's no 'they say' here," Cathy announced. "Nothing we push off against, no 'as opposed to what.'" With this in mind, we embarked on another round of revisions and eventually came up with the following contrast, which now appears on page 2 of this edition:

<u>Instead of focusing solely on abstract principles of writing, then,</u> this book offers model templates to help you put those principles directly into practice.

Why did we prefer this version? Because its new material, which we've underlined, not only establishes that we offer templates but also indicates why: to depart from and, we hope, improve upon writing instruction that focuses only on "abstract principles."

Had this sentence been all we changed, however, it would not have amounted to the type of "substantial" revision we've been saying is so important. But as often happens in the revision process, this one revision led to several others, setting in motion a series of revisions that significantly transformed our core argument. As we went back and reread the parts of the book we'd already written, we found several ways to extend the contrast we draw above between our templates and more abstract approaches. In the preface and introduction, we added two sections—"OK, but Templates?," and "What This Book Doesn't Do"—which help us further explain our template-based approach by contrasting it with what it isn't.

8. MOVE IT UP!

In her memoir *The Vanity Fair Diaries*, the magazine's former editor, Tina Brown, describes "the rewarding moment" in editing a manuscript

> when you see that the whole thing should start on page nine and flip the penultimate paragraph to the top of the piece, and all you want to do is call the writer immediately and tell him or her why. (73)

Brown's premise here is simple: *where* you say something matters, and the more important the point, the more it needs to be moved to "the top of the piece," where it will better get your reader's attention and infuse all you say that follows.

Imagine, after all, how frustrating it is for readers to have to slog through a lengthy text that doesn't state what its big point is until the very end, which is precisely what happens in Charles R. Morris's 333-page book, *A Rabble of Dead Money: The Great Crash and the Global Depression: 1929–1939*. Although Morris demonstrates impressive knowledge of the Great Depression and its historical era, he doesn't declare his central argument— that, contrary to what most people assume, "the 1929 stock market crash . . . did not cause the Depression"—until page 313. Had Morris foregrounded this point early in the book and used it to structure all that followed, readers wouldn't have been left wondering where he was going for the first three hundred pages: "Why is Morris telling us this?" "What's his big point?" "And this matters because . . . ?"

Delays of this kind are so common among writers that journalists long ago coined a term for it: "burying the lead" (or "lede," as it is sometimes spelled). Because writing is not a smoothly linear process of adding one perfectly polished paragraph on top of another until the last word is written, writers often don't know what their most important, or "lead," point will be until late in the writing process. As our cartoon on page 151 suggests, it is common for writers to start out thinking that their big idea will be one thing, only to realize later, just as they think their work is finished, that a different point needs to take center stage. When this happens, the best remedy, as Brown suggests, is to "flip" that point up "to the top of the piece," near the opening, and edit the rest so that your belatedly discovered argument informs your entire text from start to finish.

9. TAKE YOUR "UH-OH" MOMENTS SERIOUSLY

In our view, the best writers are always on the lookout for places in their writing that take their argument in the wrong direction. Especially when reading their work with a skeptical eye, as we suggested earlier, these self-critical writers keep looking for unanticipated implications in their writing that, for one reason or another, they are not comfortable with. As you reread your drafts, then, we suggest that you listen for any little voices in your head that say, "Uh-oh, what have I done? As I was arguing _____, I accidentally suggested _____." "Uh-oh" moments, as they might be called, can often be upsetting. But if you're willing to put in the time and to experiment with different solutions, you can head off such problems in your draft and possibly even turn them to your advantage.

Gerald had several such "uh-oh" moments as he was writing "Hidden Intellectualism" (see p. 548), in which he makes the counterintuitive claim that schools should be organized like sports. One, for instance, came when he was arguing that the worlds of academic intellectual culture and of popular sports are more similar than one might assume. He had written:

> [T]he real intellectual world, the one that existed in the big world beyond school, is organized very much like the world of team sports, with rival texts, rival interpretations and evaluations of texts, . . . and elaborate team competitions in which "fans" of writers, intellectual systems, methodologies, and -isms contend against one another. (552)

"Oh, no," Gerald thought to himself as he reread this passage. "Couldn't someone misunderstand me? Couldn't someone think that in saying schools should be organized like sports,

I'm promoting the ugly side of sports, the side that's filled with petty one-upmanship and, at times, even violence? How can I argue that schools should imitate the contentious domain of sports when schools already have too much small-minded and destructive competition?"

For a while, Gerald was disturbed enough by thoughts like these that he was tempted to simply eliminate the comparison he makes between sports and school. But after wrestling with the problem, he realized that he was defending sports not at their worst but at their best. As a result, the next chance he got, Gerald sat down with his manuscript and added the following new material, which explains that sports not only promote rivalry but

> also satisfy the thirst for community. When you entered sports debates, you became part of a community that was not limited to your family and friends, but was national and public. (552)

In this way, Gerald was able to use his "uh-oh" moment to enhance his argument. What began as a serious problem ended up helping him discover an aspect of his own argument that he hadn't seen before: that schooling should emulate not the uglier side of sports but the side that encourages camaraderie and broad, public excitement.

10. DON'T LET THE MESS SHOW

At several points in this chapter we have suggested that revising your writing in a global, substantial way is often a messy undertaking. In this final section, however, we want to suggest that to create a coherent, unified, and reader-friendly text, you need to *hide* this very mess. In other words, when you find any problems in your text, you need to do what is often a lot of hard work to correct them and make it look as if they never existed. If, for instance, you find a problem with your thesis, you need to not only reframe your thesis but also make sure that all your supporting claims, evidence, and examples, as we suggested above, match that thesis, erasing any confusing disconnects between your thesis and the rest of your text. Along similar lines, if you find that a section of your text doesn't make sense, you need to revise it until it does or eliminate that section altogether, making sure that the material that had preceded and followed the deleted material is well stitched together. And for a final example, if you realize that your best argument is buried too far back in your essay, you need not only to "move it up," as we suggested above, but also revise your entire draft so that it looks as if that best argument is what you had originally planned to say.

Joseph M. Williams and Lawrence McEnerney, writing experts, make a version of this point:

> If you find that the sentence from your conclusion is more insightful than the one from your introduction, then you have to revise your introduction to make it seem that you had this sentence in mind all along (even though when you started drafting the paper you may have had no idea how you were going to end it).

This advice holds true, we think, not just for introductions and conclusions but for virtually every part of a text. Even if you discover that your best claim appears mid-essay, you need to engage in a little smoke and mirrors, revising in a way that makes "it seem that you had" this claim in mind from the very outset, even though you hadn't.

A REVISION CHECKLIST

The checklist that follows is keyed both to this chapter on revision and to the writing advice throughout this book. It is composed of a series of questions designed to help you when rereading and revising your drafts.

Is Your Revision Really Substantial?

Look over the revisions you've made to your draft before turning it in and ask yourself if you have made enough changes to seriously improve it. If you've merely changed a few words or phrases, then you probably haven't addressed these larger issues: How coherent is your argument? Does your argument enter in dialogue with a motivating "they say"? Does your argument address a naysayer's counterargument? Is your argument consistent or contradictory?

Did you reread your draft several times and perhaps show it to other readers for feedback? If so, do you adequately respond to any concerns these readers raised, including ones possibly expressed to you by your instructor or a classmate?

Are the parts of your composition in the most effective order, or do some need to be moved? If you rearranged any of your text, have you revised the remaining material to avoid letting the "mess" show? (See pp. 163–64)

How Well Do You Represent What Others Say?

Do you start with what "they say"? If not, try revising to do so. See pages 23–28 for templates that can help.

Is it clear what is motivating your argument—why it needs to be made in the first place? If not, see pages 23–26 for templates that can help.

Do you summarize what others have said? If so, have you represented their views accurately—and adequately? Can you improve your summaries, perhaps by going back to the text and rereading the source you're summarizing?

Do you quote others? Have you carefully checked your quotations against the original sources? Do you frame each quotation in a way that integrates it into your text, explaining the quotation in your own words, and have you carefully considered whether the quotation actually supports your argument? (See pp. 49–51 for tips on creating a "quotation sandwich.")

Look at the verbs you use to introduce summaries and quotations, and consider how well they fit the action you're describing. If you've used all-purpose signal verbs such as X "said" or "believes," are there other such phrases that might be more precise, such as X "complains" or "predicts"? (See pp. 43–44 for a list of such signal verbs.)

Have you documented all of the sources you mention, both in parenthetical notations in the body of your text and at the end in a works-cited or references list?

Do you remind readers of the "they say" you're responding to throughout your text, or do you get off track and inadvertently start responding to a different "they say"? Can you revise so as to respond more continuously throughout the entire length of your text? (See pp. 27–28 for advice on using return sentences to keep your argument focused.)

How Effective Is What You Say?

Is it clear how you are responding to your "they say"? Is it clear what your position is—*agree, disagree, or a combination of both*—or might readers be unsure and need clarification? Do you use signal verbs that fit your position and clear language ("I question whether . . ." or "I'm of two minds about . . .")? (See Chapter 4 for three ways to respond and Chapter 5 for help in distinguishing the "I say" from "they say.")

If you disagree with the "they say" you're responding to, do you give reasons why in a way that moves the conversation forward, or do you merely contradict the "they say"? If you agree with the "they say," do you "agree with a difference," adding something of your own to the conversation? (For help with this move, see pp. 63–64.) And finally, if you both agree and disagree with your "they say," do you do so without contradicting yourself or seeming evasive? (See Chapter 4 for help in responding in these three different ways.)

Are your "I say" and "they say" clearly connected? Do your argument and the argument you are responding to address the same issue, or does a switch occur that takes you on a tangent? Do you use the same key terms for explaining both? (See pp. 116 for our discussion of key terms.)

What reasons—evidence, data, or examples—do you offer to support your "I say"? Do your reasons actually support your position, or is there a mismatch between them? Could a naysayer use your reasons against you to support a contrary position, and if so, could you defend your reasoning by summarizing and answering this objection? (See Chapter 6 for tips on doing so).

Will readers be able to distinguish what you say from what others say? Do you use voice markers ("My own view, however, is . . ." or "Skeptics, however, would disagree . . .") to mark the shift from the views of others to your own view and back? (See Chapter 5 for advice about using voice markers to make that distinction clear.)

Have You Introduced Any Naysayers?

Have you acknowledged likely objections to your argument? If so, have you represented these objections fairly—and responded to them persuasively? *If not,* think about what other perspectives exist on your topic, and incorporate them into your draft. (See Chapter 6 for tips on planting and responding to naysayers in your text.)

Have You Used Metacommentary?

How well, if at all, do you stand back from your writing and clarify what you do and don't mean? Might your argument be improved if you did a better job of explaining what you mean— or *don't* mean—with phrases like "in other words," "don't get me wrong," or "what I'm really trying to say here is . . ." (See Chapter 10 for examples of how to reinforce your argument with metacommentary.)

Do you have a helpful title? Does your title merely identify your topic, or does it successfully point to the position you take on that topic? Is your title lively and engaging, and might a subtitle help indicate your position?

Have You Tied It All Together?

Can readers follow your argument from one sentence, paragraph, and section to the next? Can readers see how each successive point is joined together in service of your overall argument? Are there any tangents that need to be brought in line with your larger train of thought or perhaps eliminated altogether?

Do you use transition phrases like "however," "in addition," and "in other words," which clarify how your ideas relate to one another? Are these phrases the right ones for your purposes—or do you use "however," say, when you really mean "also" or "in addition"? (See pp. 111–12 for a list of transitions.)

Do you use pointing words like "this" and "that," which help you gesture backward in your text and lead readers from one point to the next? If so, is it always clear what "this" and "that" refer to, or do you need to add nouns (e.g., "this book" or "this tendency to exaggerate") to avoid ambiguity? (See pp. 114–16 for tips on using pointing words to connect parts of your argument.)

Have you used what we call "repetition with a difference" to help connect parts of your argument? That is, do you succeed in *saying the same thing but in a slightly different way each time, which helps you move your argument forward and avoid being monotonous?* (See pp. 118–20 for help with this move).

Have You Shown Why Your Argument Matters?

Do you make clear why your argument is important—and why your readers should care? Might your draft be improved by using templates like "My critique here is important because_____" or "The stakes in how we answer this question are high, given that _____"? (See Chapter 7 for advice on addressing the "so what? and "who cares?" questions.)

Exercises

1. Read over a draft of your writing, and think about it globally. Explain to yourself the "big picture" of your argument using the following template: "Aha! Now I see! What I'm really trying to say is not, as I initially thought, _____ but _____." Use your response to write yourself a revision plan. Name two important things you need to do so that your argument matches what you're "really trying to say."

2. Read over a draft of your writing, paying particular attention to how you use sources.

   a. Go back to your sources to check how accurately you are using them. Confirm that your summaries and paraphrases are fair representations of the sources' arguments. Have you transcribed your quotations correctly? Have you properly cited all your sources?

   b. Look critically at the examples—quotations, evidence, anecdotes, and so forth—that you use to support your claims. Ask yourself, "Does this example support my argument?" Revise your writing to unify your argument and examples.

3. Read a draft of your writing out loud or listen to it using text-to-speech technology.

   a. As you read or listen, mark the places in the text that are hard to follow. Then go back to these places and revise them. Could you use better transitions? Might metacommentary help? Could you use more voice markers, such as "In Smith's opinion . . ." or "She argues . . ."?

   b. As you read or listen, also mark the places in the text where you find yourself saying "uh-oh" because your words or their implications don't reflect your underlying intentions. Then go back to these "uh-oh" moments to clarify your intentions. Consider using a template like "This is not to suggest . . . It is, however, to suggest . . ."

TWELVE

"I TAKE YOUR POINT"

Entering Class Discussions

HAVE YOU EVER been in a class discussion that feels less like a genuine meeting of the minds than like a series of discrete, disconnected monologues? You make a comment, say, that seems provocative to you, but the classmate who speaks after you makes no reference to what you said, instead going off in an entirely different direction. Then the classmate who speaks next makes no reference either to you or to anyone else, making it seem as if everyone in the conversation is more interested in their own ideas than in actually conversing with anyone else.

We like to think that the principles this book advances can help improve class discussions, which increasingly include various forms of online communication. Particularly important for class discussion is the point that our own ideas become more cogent and powerful the more responsive we are to others and the more we frame our claims not in isolation but as responses to what others before us have said. Ultimately, then, a good face-to-face classroom discussion (or online communication) doesn't just happen spontaneously. It requires the same sorts of disciplined moves and practices used in many writing situations, particularly that of identifying to what and to whom you are responding.

FRAME YOUR COMMENTS AS A RESPONSE
TO SOMETHING THAT HAS ALREADY BEEN SAID

The single most important thing you need to do when joining a class discussion is to link what you are about to say to something that has already been said.

▸ I really liked Aaron's point about <u>the two sides being closer than they seem</u>. I'd add that <u>both seem rather moderate</u>.

▸ I take your point, Nadia, that _____. Still . . .

▸ Though Kayla and Ryan seem to be at odds about _____, they may actually not be all that far apart.

In framing your comments this way, it is usually best to name both the person and the idea you're responding to. If you name the person alone ("I agree with Aaron because _____"), it may not be clear to listeners what part of what Aaron said you are referring to. Conversely, if you only summarize what Aaron said without naming him, you'll probably leave your classmates wondering whose comments you're referring to.

But won't you sound stilted and deeply redundant in class if you try to restate the point your classmate just made? After all, in the case of the first template above, the entire class will have just heard Aaron's point about the two sides being closer than they seem. Why, then, would you need to restate it?

We agree that in oral situations it does often sound artificial to restate what others just said precisely because they just said it. It would be awkward if on being asked to pass the salt at lunch, one were to reply: "If I understand you correctly, you have asked me to pass the salt. Yes, I can, and here it is." But in oral discussions about complicated issues that are open to multiple interpretations, we usually do need to resummarize what others have said to make sure that everyone is on the same page. Since Aaron may have made several points when he spoke and may have been followed by other commentators, the class will probably need you to summarize which point of his you are referring to. And even if Aaron made only one point, restating that point is helpful not only to remind the group what his point was (since some may have missed or forgotten it) but also to make sure that he, you, and others have interpreted his point in the same way.

TO CHANGE THE SUBJECT,
INDICATE EXPLICITLY THAT YOU ARE DOING SO

It is fine to try to change the conversation's direction. There's just one catch: you need to make clear to listeners that this is what you are doing. For example:

▸ So far we have been talking about <u>the characters in the film</u>. But isn't the real issue here <u>the cinematography</u>?

▸ I'd like to change the subject to one that hasn't yet been addressed.

You can try to change the subject without indicating that you are doing so. But you risk that your comment will come across as irrelevant rather than as a thoughtful contribution that moves the conversation forward.

BE EVEN MORE EXPLICIT
THAN YOU WOULD BE IN WRITING

Because listeners in an oral discussion can't go back and reread what you just said, they are more easily overloaded than are readers of a print text. For this reason, in a class discussion you will do well to take some extra steps to help listeners follow your train of thought. (1) When you make a comment, limit yourself to one point only, though you can elaborate on this point, fleshing it out with examples and evidence. If you feel you must make two points, either unite them under one larger umbrella point, or make one point first and save the other for later. Trying to bundle two or more claims into one comment can result in neither getting the attention it deserves. (2) Use metacommentary to highlight your key point so that listeners can readily grasp it.

▸ In other words, what I'm trying to get at here is _____.

▸ My point is this: _____.

▸ My point, though, is not _____ but _____.

▸ This distinction is important because _____.

Exercises

1. Choose a text you've read in class, and discuss the text's argument in a small group. Use these questions to start your conversation:

   a. Whom (or what) is the writer responding to?

b. What perspectives does the writer include, and what perspectives are missing?

c. Why does this argument matter?

2. Listen carefully to a class discussion, either in this class or another one of your courses. Notice what moves from this chapter your classmates and your instructor make:

a. How do they frame their comments to link their ideas to something that has already been said?

b. How do they change the direction of the conversation?

c. How do they use metacommentary to clarify their points?

Reflect on the conversation as a whole. Were the people in the conversation responsive to one another's ideas, or did the conversation feel more like a series of unconnected points? Explain one strategy from this chapter that would improve class discussions.

3. In your next class discussion, try using use these strategies to help your classmates follow your ideas:

a. Write down your thoughts before you say them.

b. Limit yourself to just one point per comment.

c. Use metacommentary to highlight your key idea.

How did these strategies help clarify your ideas? How did they help you listen more attentively to others? How did they invite others to respond? What was challenging about this exercise?

THIRTEEN

DON'T MAKE THEM SCROLL UP

Entering Online Conversations

THE INTERNET HAS TRANSFORMED COMMUNICATION in more ways than we can count. With just a few taps on a keyboard, we can be connected with what others have said not only throughout history, but right now, in the most remote places. Almost instantaneously, communities can be created that are powerful enough to change the world. In addition, virtually the moment we voice an opinion online, we can get responses from supporters and critics alike, while any links we provide to sources can connect readers to voices they might otherwise never have known about and to conversations they might never have been able to join.

Because of this connectivity, the internet lends itself perfectly to the type of conversational writing at the core of this book. Just the other day, we were on a discussion board in which one of the participants wrote to another, let's call him X, in a form that could have provided a template for this textbook: "Fascinating point about _____, X. I'd never thought of it that way before. I'd always thought that _____, but if you're right, then that would explain why _____."

IDENTIFY WHAT YOU'RE RESPONDING TO

Unfortunately, not all online writers make clear who or what prompted them to write. As a result, too many online exchanges end up being not true conversations but a series of statements without clear relationships to one another. All too often, it's hard to tell if the writer is building on what someone else has said, challenging it, or trying to change the discussion topic altogether. So although the digital world may connect us far more rapidly and with far more people than ever, it doesn't always encourage a genuine meeting of minds.

We've seen this type of confusion in the writing our own students submit to online discussions. Even students who use the "they say / I say" framework routinely and effectively in the essays they write often neglect to make those same moves online. While our students engage enthusiastically in online discussions, their posts are often all "I say" with little or no "they say." As a result, they end up talking past rather than to one another.

What is happening here, we suspect, is that the easy accessibility made possible by the internet makes slowing down and summarizing or even identifying what others say seem unnecessary. Why repeat the views you are responding to, writers seem to assume, when readers can easily find them by simply scrolling up or clicking on a link?

The problem with this way of thinking is that readers won't always take the time to track down the comments you're responding to, assuming they can figure out what those comments are to begin with. And even when readers do make the effort to find the comments you're responding to, they may not be sure what aspect or part of those comments you're referring to

or how you interpret them. Ultimately, when you fail to identify your "they say," you leave readers guessing, like someone listening to one side of a phone conversation trying to piece together what's being said at the other end.

It's true, of course, that there are some situations online where summarizing what you're responding to would indeed be redundant. When, for instance, you're replying to a friend's text asking, "Meet in front of the theater at 7?" a mere "OK" suffices, whereas a more elaborate response—"With regard to your suggestion that we meet in front of the theater at 7, my answer is yes"—would be not only redundant but also downright bizarre. But in more complex academic conversations where the ideas are challenging, many people are involved, and there is therefore a greater chance of misunderstanding, you do need to clarify whom and what you're responding to.

To see how hard it can be to make sense of a post that fails to identify the "they say" it is responding to, consider the following example from an online class discussion devoted to Nicholas Carr's article "Is Google Making Us Stupid?":

Blogs and social media allow us to reach many people all at once. The internet makes us more efficient.

When we first read this post, we could see that this writer was making a claim about the efficiency of the internet, but we weren't sure what the claim had to do with Carr or with any of the other comments in the discussion. After all, the writer never names Carr or anyone else in the conversation. Nor does she use templates such as "Like Carr, I believe _____ " or "What X overlooks is _____ " to indicate whether she's agreeing or disagreeing with Carr or with one of her classmates. Indeed, we couldn't tell if the writer had even read Carr or any of the other posts, or if she was just expressing her own views on the topic.

We suspect, however, that in arguing that the internet is making us more efficient, this writer was probably trying to refute Carr's argument that the internet is, as Carr puts it in his title, "making us stupid." Then again, she could also have been criticizing someone who agreed with Carr—or, conversely, siding with someone else who disagreed with Carr.

It would have been better if she had used the "they say / I say" framework taught in this book, opening not with her own "I say," as she did but with the "they say" that's motivated her to respond, perhaps using one of the following templates:

▶ X argues that _____.

▶ Like X, Y would have us believe that _____.

▶ In challenging X's argument that _____, Y asserts that _____.

It would also have helped if, in her "I say," she had identified the "they say" she is addressing, using a template like one of these:

- ▸ **But what X overlooks is that _____ .**

- ▸ **What both X and Y fail to see is that _____ .**

- ▸ **Z's point is well taken. Like him, I contend that _____ is not, as X insists, _____ but _____ .**

Here's one way this writer might have responded:

> Carr argues that Google is undermining our ability to think and read deeply. But far from making people "stupid," as Carr puts it in his title, the internet, in my view, is making people more efficient. What Carr ignores is how blogs and social media allow us to reach many people at once.

This version makes clear that the writer is not just making a claim out of the blue but that she also had a reason for making her claim: to take a position in a conversation or debate.

TECHNOLOGY WON'T DO ALL THE WORK

But still, you might wonder, doesn't the internet enable writers to connect so directly with others that summarizing their claims is unnecessary? Granted, the internet does provide several unique ways of referring to what others are saying, like linking and embedding, that help us connect to what others are saying. But as the following examples show, these techniques don't mean that technology will do all the work for you.

LINKING TO WHAT "THEY SAY"

One way the internet makes it especially easy to connect directly with others is by allowing us to insert a link to what others have said into our own text. Anything with a URL can be linked to—blog posts, magazine articles, *Facebook* posts, and so forth. Readers can then click on the words to which you've attached the link and be taken directly to that page, as we can see in the following comment in another online class discussion about how the internet affects our brains:

> In his essay "Is Google Making Us Stupid?" Nicholas Carr argues that the kind of skimming we do when we read online destroys deep reading and thinking. But I would argue the opposite: that all the complex information we're exposed to online actually makes us read and think more deeply.

By including a link to Carr's essay, this writer gives her readers direct access to Carr's arguments, allowing them to assess how well she has summarized and responded to what he wrote. But the reason the writer's post succeeds is that she introduces the link to Carr's essay, summarizes what she takes Carr to be saying, and gives her response to it.

Here are a few templates for framing a link:

▸ As X mentions in this article, " _____."

▸ In making this comment, X warns that _____.

▸ Economists often assume _____; however, new research by X suggests _____.

JUXTAPOSING YOUR "THEY SAY"
WITH YOUR "I SAY"

Another way that online forums enhance our ability to connect with others is by allowing readers to respond—not only to the original article or post but also to one another through what we might call "juxtaposition." On many online forums, when you reply to someone else's comment, your response appears below the original comment and indented slightly, so that it is visually clear whom you're responding to. This means that, in many cases, your "they say" and "I say" are presented almost as a single conversational unit, as the following example from the online discussion of Carr's article illustrates:

Lee, 4/12/20, 3:02 PM

Carr argues that the internet has harmed us by making it hard for us to read without breaks to look at other things. That might be true, but overall I think it has improved our lives by giving us access to so many different viewpoints.

Cody, 4/12/20, 5:15 PM

Like Lee, I think the internet has improved our lives more than it's hurt them. I would add that it's enabled us to form and participate in political communities online that make people way more politically engaged.

Twitter also allows for this type of close proximity, by enabling you to embed someone else's tweet inside your own. For instance, consider the following tweet:

Jade T. Moore @JadeTMoore

@willwst I agree—access to books is a social justice issue.

William West @willwst

Every child has the right to access to a school library.

Cody's response in the discussion board and Jade's on *Twitter* are effective not only because the platforms connect Cody and Jade to their "they say" but also because they take the time to make those connections clear. Cody connects his comment to his "they say" by including the words "Like Lee" and restating Lee's view, while Jade does so by including West's *Twitter* handle, @willwst, and the words "I agree." Sure, the technology does some of the work, by making the responses to comments directly available for readers to see—no scrolling or searching involved. But it can't do it all. Imagine if Cody, for instance, had merely written, "We're able to form and participate in political communities online that make people way more politically engaged." Or if Jade hadn't included an "I agree" with her comment. As readers, we'd have been left scratching our heads, unable to tell what Cody's claim had to do with Lee's claim, or what Jade's claim had to do with William's, despite how close together these claims are on the screen.

Digital communication, then, does shrink the world, as is often said, allowing us to connect with others in ways we couldn't before. But technology doesn't relieve writers of the need to use the "they say / I say" framework. A central premise of this book is that this framework is a rhetorical move that transcends the differences between all types of writing. Whether you're writing online or off, if you want others to listen to what you say, you'd better pay attention to what they think, and start with what they say. However limited your space, whatever your format, and whatever the technology, you can always find a way to identify and summarize your "they say."

Exercises

1. Look back at some of your old posts on a social media site, a class discussion board, or some other website. How well did you let other readers know whom and what you were responding to and what your own position was? What kinds of moves did you make? Does that site have any conventions or special features that you used? Revise one of your posts using the strategies described in this chapter so that your post more clearly follows the "they say / I say" format.

2. Choose an online forum (e.g., *Facebook*, *Twitter*, **theysayiblog.com**), and analyze how the site encourages users to enter conversations in response to others:

   a. Is it easy to tell whom and what people are responding to? Why or why not?

   b. What features, structures, or norms specific to that forum (e.g., embedding, hashtags, linking, etc.) influence how users formulate their "they say"?

c. Find a post that you think follows the "they say / I say" format. Describe how the writer uses the forum's specific features as well as templates from this book to clarify whom and what are being responded to.

3. Go to the blog that accompanies this book, **theysayiblog.com**. Examine some of the exchanges that appear there and evaluate the quality of the responses. For example, how well do the participants in these exchanges summarize one another's claims before making their own responses? How would you characterize the discussion? How well do people listen to one another? How do these online discussions compare with the face-to-face discussions you have in class? What advantages do each offer? Go to other blogs or forums on topics that interest you, and ask these same questions.

FOURTEEN

WHAT'S MOTIVATING THIS WRITER?

Reading for the Conversation

—⌐回⌐—

"WHAT IS THE AUTHOR'S ARGUMENT? What is the author trying to say?" For many years, these were the first questions we would ask our classes in a discussion of an assigned reading. The discussion that resulted was often halting, as our students struggled to get a handle on the argument, but eventually, after some awkward silences, the class would come up with something we could all agree was an accurate summary of the author's main thesis. Even after we'd gotten over that hurdle, however, the discussion would often still seem forced and would limp along as we all struggled with the question that naturally arose next: now that we had determined what the author was saying, what did we ourselves have to say?

For a long time we didn't worry much about these halting discussions, justifying them to ourselves as the predictable result of assigning difficult, challenging readings. Several years ago, however, as we started writing this book and began thinking about writing as the art of entering conversations, we latched on to the idea of leading with some different questions: "What other argument(s) is the writer responding to?" "Is the writer disagreeing or agreeing with something, and if so, what?" "What is motivating the writer's argument?" "Are there other ideas that you have encountered in this class or elsewhere that might be pertinent?" The results were often striking. The discussions that followed tended to be far livelier and to draw in a greater number of students. We were still asking students to look for the main argument, but we were now asking them to see that argument as a response to some other argument that provoked it, gave it a reason for being, and helped all of us see why we should care about it.

What had happened, we realized, was that by changing the opening question, we changed the way our students approached reading and perhaps the way they thought about academic work in general. Instead of thinking of the argument of a text as an isolated entity, they now thought of that argument as one that responded to and provoked other arguments. Since they were now dealing not with *one* argument but at least *two* (the author's argument and the one[s] being responded to), they now had alternative ways of seeing the topic at hand. This meant that instead of just trying to understand the view presented by the author, they were more able to question that view intelligently and engage in the type of discussion and debate that is the hallmark of a college education. In our discussions, animated debates often arose between students who found the author's argument convincing and others who were more convinced by the view it was challenging. In the best of these debates, the binary positions would be questioned by other students, who suggested each was too simple, that both might be right or that a third alternative was possible. Still other students might object that the discussion thus far had missed the author's real point and suggest that we all go back to the text and pay closer attention to what it actually said.

We eventually realized that the move from reading for the author's argument in isolation to reading for how the author's argument is in conversation with the arguments of others helps readers become active, critical readers rather than passive recipients of knowledge. On some level, reading for the conversation is more rigorous and demanding than reading for what one author says. It asks that you determine not only what the author thinks but also how what the author thinks fits with what others think and ultimately with what you yourself think. Yet on another level, reading this way is a lot simpler and more familiar than reading for the thesis alone, since it returns writing to the familiar, everyday act of communicating with other people about real issues.

DECIPHERING THE CONVERSATION

We suggest, then, that when assigned a reading, you imagine the author not as sitting alone in an empty room hunched over a desk or staring at a screen but as sitting in a crowded coffee shop talking to and engaging with others who are making claims. In other words, imagine an ongoing, multisided conversation in which all participants (including the author) are trying to persuade others to agree or at least to take their positions seriously.

The trick in reading for the conversation is to figure out *what views the author is responding to* and *what the author's own argument is*—or, to put it in the terms used in this book, to determine the "they say" and how the author responds to it. One of the challenges in reading for the "they say" and "I say" can be figuring out which is which, since it may not be obvious when writers are summarizing others and when they are speaking for themselves. Readers need to be alert for any changes in voice that a writer might make, since instead of using explicit road-mapping phrases like "although many believe," authors may simply summarize the view that they want to engage with and indicate only subtly that it is not their own.

Consider again the opening to the selection by David Zinczenko on page 199:

> If ever there were a newspaper headline custom-made for Jay Leno's monologue, this was it. Kids taking on McDonald's this week, suing the company for making them fat. Isn't that like middle-aged men suing Porsche for making them get speeding tickets? Whatever happened to personal responsibility?
>
> I tend to sympathize with these portly fast-food patrons, though. Maybe that's because I used to be one of them.
>
> DAVID ZINCZENKO, "Don't Blame the Eater"

Whenever we teach this passage, some students inevitably assume that Zinczenko must be espousing the view expressed in his first paragraph: that suing McDonald's is ridiculous. When their reading is challenged by their classmates, these students point to the page and reply, "Look. It's right here on the page. This is what Zinczenko wrote. These are his exact words." The assumption these students are making is that if something appears on the page, the author must endorse it. In fact, however, we ventriloquize views that we don't believe in, and may in fact passionately disagree with, all the time. The central clues that Zinczenko disagrees with the view expressed in his opening paragraph come in the second paragraph, when he finally offers a first-person declaration and

See Chapter 6 for more discussion of naysayers.

uses a contrastive transition, "though," thereby resolving any questions about where he stands.

WHEN THE "THEY SAY" IS UNSTATED

Another challenge can be identifying the "they say" when it is not explicitly identified. Whereas Zinczenko offers an up-front summary of the view he is responding to, other writers assume that their readers are so familiar with these views that they need not name or summarize them. In such cases, you the reader have to reconstruct the unstated "they say" that is motivating the text through a process of inference.

See, for instance, if you can reconstruct the position that Tamara Draut is challenging in the opening paragraph of her essay "The Growing College Gap":

> "The first in her family to graduate from college." How many times have we heard that phrase, or one like it, used to describe a success-ful American with a modest background? In today's United States, a four-year degree has become the all-but-official ticket to middle-class security. But if your parents don't have much money or higher edu-cation in their own right, the road to college—and beyond—looks increasingly treacherous. Despite a sharp increase in the proportion of high school graduates going on to some form of postsecondary educa-tion, socio-economic status continues to exert a powerful influence on college admission and completion; in fact, gaps in enrollment by class and race, after declining in the 1960s and 1970s, are once again as wide as they were thirty years ago, and getting wider, even as college has become far more crucial to lifetime fortunes.
>
> TAMARA DRAUT, "The Growing College Gap"

You might think that the "they say" here is embedded in the third sentence: they say (or we all think) that a four-year degree is "the all-but-official ticket to middle-class security," and you might assume that Draut will go on to disagree.

If you read the passage this way, however, you would be mistaken. Draut is not questioning whether a college degree has become the "ticket to middle-class security" but whether most Americans can obtain that ticket, whether college is within the financial reach of most American families. You may have been thrown off by the "but" following the statement that college has become a prerequisite for middle-class security. However, unlike the "though" in Zinczenko's opening, this "but" does not signal that Draut will be disagreeing with the view she has just summarized, a view that in fact she takes as a given. What Draut disagrees with is that this ticket to middle-class security is still readily available to the middle and working classes.

Were one to imagine Draut in a room talking with others with strong views on this topic, one would need to picture her challenging not those who think college is a ticket to financial security (something she agrees with and takes for granted) but those who think the doors of college are open to anyone willing to put forth the effort to walk through them. The view that Draut is challenging, then, is not summarized in her opening. Instead, she assumes that readers are already so familiar with this view that it need not be stated.

Draut's example suggests that in texts where the central "they say" is not immediately identified, you have to construct it your-self based on the clues the text provides. You have to start by locating the writer's thesis and then imagine some of the argu-ments that might be made against it. What would it look like to disagree with this view? In Draut's case, it is relatively easy to construct a counterargument: it is the familiar faith in the

American Dream of equal opportunity when it comes to access to college. Figuring out the counterargument not only reveals what motivated Draut as a writer but also helps you respond to her essay as an active, critical reader. Constructing this counter-argument can also help you recognize how Draut challenges your own views, questioning opinions that you previously took for granted.

WHEN THE "THEY SAY" IS ABOUT SOMETHING "NOBODY HAS TALKED ABOUT"

Another challenge in reading for the conversation is that writers sometimes build their arguments by responding to a *lack* of discussion. These writers build their case not by playing off views that can be identified (like faith in the American Dream or the idea that we are responsible for our body weight) but by pointing to something others have overlooked. As the writing theorists John M. Swales and Christine B. Feak point out, one effective way to "create a research space" and "establish a niche" in the academic world is "by indicating a gap in . . . previous research." Much research in the sciences and humanities takes this "Nobody has noticed X" form.

In such cases, the writer may be responding to scientists, for example, who have overlooked an obscure plant that offers insights into global warming or to literary critics who have been so busy focusing on the lead character in a play that they have overlooked something important about the minor characters.

READING PARTICULARLY CHALLENGING TEXTS

Sometimes it is difficult to figure out the views that writers are responding to, not because these writers do not identify those views but because their language and the concepts they are dealing with are particularly challenging. Consider, for instance, the first two sentences of *Gender Trouble: Feminism and the Subversion of Identity*, a book by the feminist philosopher and literary theorist Judith Butler, thought by many to be a particularly difficult academic writer:

> Contemporary feminist debates over the meaning of gender lead time and again to a certain sense of trouble, as if the indeterminacy of gender might eventually culminate in the failure of feminism. Perhaps trouble need not carry such a negative valence.
>
> JUDITH BUTLER, *Gender Trouble:*
> *Feminism and the Subversion of Identity*

There are many reasons readers may stumble over this relatively short passage, not the least of which is that Butler does not explicitly indicate where her own view begins and the view she is responding to ends. Unlike Zinczenko, Butler does not use the first-person "I" or a phrase such as "in my own view" to show that the position in the second sentence is her own. Nor does Butler offer a clear transition such as "but" or "however" at the start of the second sentence to indicate, as Zinczenko does with "though," that in the second sentence she is questioning the argument she has summarized in the first. And finally, like many academic writers, Butler uses abstract, challenging words that many readers may need to look up, like "indeterminacy" (the quality of being impossible to define or pin down), "culminate" (finally result in), and "negative valence" (a term borrowed from chemistry, roughly denoting "negative significance" or "meaning"). For all these reasons, we can imagine many readers feeling intimidated before they reach the third sentence of Butler's book.

But readers who break down this passage into its essential parts will find that it is actually a lucid piece of writing that conforms to the classic "they say / I say" pattern. Though it can be difficult to spot the clashing arguments in the two sentences, close analysis reveals that the first sentence offers a way of looking at a certain type of "trouble" in the realm of feminist politics that is being challenged in the second.

To understand difficult passages of this kind, you need to translate them into your own words—to build a bridge, in effect, between the passage's unfamiliar terms and ones more familiar to you. Building such a bridge should help you connect what you already know to what the author is saying—and will then help you move from reading to writing, providing you with some of the language you will need to summarize the text. One major challenge in translating the author's words into your own, however, is to stay true to what the author is actually saying, avoiding what we call "the closest cliché syndrome," in which one mistakes a commonplace idea for an author's more complex one (mistaking Butler's critique of the concept of "woman," for instance, for the common idea that women must have equal rights). The work of complex writers like Butler, who frequently challenge conventional thinking, cannot always be collapsed into the types of ideas most of us are already familiar with. Therefore, when you translate, do not try to fit the ideas of such writers into your preexisting beliefs, but instead allow your own views to be challenged. In building a bridge to the writers you read, it is often necessary to meet those writers more than halfway.

For more on translating, see Chapter 9.

For more on the closest cliché syndrome, see Chapter 2.

So what, then, does Butler's opening say? Translating Butler's words into terms that are easier to understand, we can see that the first sentence says that for many feminists today, "the indeterminacy of gender"—the inability to define the essence of sexual identity—spells the end of feminism; that for many feminists the inability to define "gender," presumably the building block of the feminist movement, means serious "trouble" for feminist politics. In contrast, the second sentence suggests that this same "trouble" need not be thought of in such "negative" terms, that the inability to define femininity, or "gender trouble" as Butler calls it in her book's title, may not be such a bad thing—and, as she goes on to argue in the pages that follow, may even be something that feminist activists can profit from. In other words, Butler suggests, highlighting uncertainties about masculinity and femininity can be a powerful feminist tool.

Pulling all these inferences together, then, the opening sentences can be translated as follows: "While many contemporary feminists believe that uncertainty about what it means to be a woman will undermine feminist politics, I, Judith Butler, believe that this uncertainty can actually help strengthen feminist politics." Translating Butler's point into our own book's basic move: "They say that if we cannot define 'woman,' feminism is in big trouble. But I say that this type of trouble is precisely what feminism needs." Despite its difficulty, then, we hope you agree that this initially intimidating passage does make sense if you stay with it.

We hope it is clear that critical reading is a two-way street. It is just as much about being open to the way that writers can challenge you, maybe even transform you, as it is about questioning those writers. And if you translate a writer's argument into your own words as you read, you should allow the text to take you outside the ideas that you already hold and to introduce you to new terms and concepts. Even if you end up disagreeing with an author, you first have to show that you have really listened to what is being said, have fully grasped the arguments, and can accurately summarize those arguments. Without such deep, attentive listening, any critique you make will be superficial and decidedly *uncritical*. It will be a critique that says more about you than about the writer or idea you're supposedly responding to.

In this chapter we have tried to show that reading for the conversation means looking not just for the thesis of a text in isolation but for the view or views that motivate that thesis— the "they say." We have also tried to show that reading for the conversation means being alert for the different strategies writers use to engage the view(s) that are motivating them, since not all writers engage other perspectives in the same way. Some writers explicitly identify and summarize a view they are responding to at the outset of their text and then return to it frequently as their text unfolds. Some refer only obliquely to a view that is motivating them, assuming that readers will be able to reconstruct that view on their own. Other writers may not explicitly distinguish their own view from the views they are questioning in ways that all of us find clear, leaving some readers to wonder whether a given view is the writer's own or one that is being challenged. And some writers push off against the "they say" that is motivating them in a challenging academic language that requires readers to translate what they are saying into more accessible, everyday terms. In sum, then, though most persuasive writers do follow a conversational "they say / I say" pattern, they do so in a great variety of ways. What this means for readers is that they need to be armed with various strategies for detecting the conversations in what they read, even when those conversations are not self-evident.

Exercises

1. Read Michelle Alexander's "The New Jim Crow" (pp. 408–27). Use the strategies described in this chapter to examine the conversation at the heart of her essay. Write a paragraph explaining what is motivating Alexander. What views of the US criminal justice system—and American culture— does Alexander think need correcting?

2. Annotate the concluding section of Michelle Alexander's essay, found on pages 408–27. Write "TS" in the margins where you see Alexander summarizing a "they say." Write "IS" in the margins where you see her asserting her own "I say" position. Circle the voice markers you see in the text.

3. Read over a draft of your own writing, and choose an important text you rely on in it. Reread that text, and then do the following:

   a. Ask yourself, "What view is motivating the author of this text?" Highlight where you see the writer naming or hinting at this motivating viewpoint.

   b. Examine how you use the text to motivate your own argument. Have you presented its argument thoroughly and accurately? Have you aligned the text clearly with your own "I say" position, showing whether it supports your position, challenges it, or some combination of both? If not, revise how you frame, summarize, or interpret this source accordingly.

Don't Blame the Eater

DAVID ZINCZENKO

—▣—

IF EVER THERE WERE a newspaper headline custom-made for Jay Leno's* monologue, this was it. Kids taking on McDonald's this week, suing the company for making them fat. Isn't that like middle-aged men suing Porsche for making them get speeding tickets? Whatever happened to personal responsibility?

I tend to sympathize with these portly fast-food patrons, though. Maybe that's because I used to be one of them.

I grew up as a typical mid-1980s latchkey kid. My parents were split up, my dad off trying to rebuild his life, my mom working long hours to make the monthly bills. Lunch and dinner, for me, was a daily choice between

———

DAVID ZINCZENKO, who was for many years the editor-in-chief of the fitness magazine *Men's Health*, is founder and CEO of Galvanized Brands, a global health and wellness media company. This piece was first published on the Op-Ed page of the *New York Times* on November 23, 2002.

***Jay Leno** Comedian and former host of NBC's *The Tonight Show*.

McDonald's, Taco Bell, Kentucky Fried Chicken, or Pizza Hut. Then as now, these were the only available options for an American kid to get an affordable meal. By age 15, I had packed 212 pounds of torpid teenage tallow on my once lanky 5-foot-10 frame.

Then I got lucky. I went to college, joined the Navy Reserves and got involved with a health magazine. I learned how to manage my diet. But most of the teenagers who live, as I once did, on a fast-food diet won't turn their lives around: they've crossed under the golden arches to a likely fate of lifetime obesity. And the problem isn't just theirs—it's all of ours.

Before 1994, diabetes in children was generally caused by a genetic disorder—only about 5 percent of childhood cases were obesity-related, or Type 2, diabetes. Today, according to the National Institutes of Health, Type 2 diabetes accounts for at least 30 percent of all new childhood cases of diabetes in this country.   5

For tips on saying why it matters, see Chapter 7.

Not surprisingly, money spent to treat diabetes has skyrocketed, too. The Centers for Disease Control and Prevention estimate that diabetes accounted for $2.6 billion in health care costs in 1969. Today's number is an unbelievable $100 billion a year.

Shouldn't we know better than to eat two meals a day in fast-food restaurants? That's one argument. But where, exactly, are consumers—particularly teenagers—supposed to find alternatives? Drive down any thoroughfare in America, and I guarantee you'll see one of our country's more than 13,000 McDonald's restaurants. Now, drive back up the block and try to find someplace to buy a grapefruit.

Complicating the lack of alternatives is the lack of information about what, exactly, we're consuming. There are no calorie information charts on fast-food packaging, the way there are on grocery items. Advertisements don't carry warning labels the way tobacco ads do. Prepared foods aren't covered under Food and Drug Administration labeling laws. Some fast-food purveyors will provide calorie information on request, but even that can be hard to understand.

For example, one company's Web site lists its chicken salad as containing 150 calories; the almonds and noodles that come with it (an additional 190 calories) are listed separately. Add a serving of the 280-calorie dressing, and you've got a healthy lunch alternative that comes in at 620 calories. But that's not all. Read the small print on the back of the dressing packet and you'll realize it actually contains 2.5 servings. If you pour what you've been served, you're suddenly up around 1,040 calories, which is half of the government's recommended daily calorie intake. And that doesn't take into account that 450-calorie super-size Coke.

Make fun if you will of these kids launching lawsuits against   10
the fast-food industry, but don't be surprised if you're the next plaintiff. As with the tobacco industry, it may be only a matter of time before state governments begin to see a direct line between the $1 billion that McDonald's and Burger King spend each year on advertising and their own swelling health care costs.

And I'd say the industry is vulnerable. Fast-food companies are marketing to children a product with proven health hazards and no warning labels. They would do well to protect themselves, and their customers, by providing the nutrition information people need to make informed choices about their products. Without such warnings, we'll see more sick, obese children and more angry, litigious parents. I say, let the deep-fried chips fall where they may.

FIFTEEN

"BUT AS SEVERAL SOURCES SUGGEST"

Research as Conversation

So, you've been asked to write a research essay. What exactly does that mean? What is your instructor asking you to do?

The best answer to these questions, of course, will always come from your instructors and from any assignment prompt or prompts that they may provide. Although most instructors will want a traditional paper or essay, some will want a web-page, podcast, or a poster that includes a visual component and may even be produced collaboratively with your classmates. Yet other instructors will urge you to produce what is often referred to as a "literature review," in which you summarize a variety of sources on a topic ("literature," in this case, referring not to poems and novels but to published commentary, such as the literature on the French Revolution). Chances are, however, if you've been assigned this book, your instructor will want whatever final project you produce to follow our "they say / I say" model. In our opinion, even the best literature reviews are not just disconnected summaries of various sources but coher-ent, unified documents that highlight the connections among these sources, framing—and very often entering—the conver-sation among them. As a result, though we speak throughout this chapter about "the research essay," we hope you'll be able to translate what we say about the conversational pattern at the heart of such essays to any alternative versions of the genre you may be producing. Regardless of what form it takes, the research essay, as we conceive it, is always about entering into conversation with others.

This might mean rethinking some common assumptions. In high school, you may have been asked to write research essays that involve reading various sources on a topic, learning as much as you could about it, and then reporting on what you learned in an essay or oral report. As a result, you may have formed the impression that the research essay is a kind of "data dump," as it is often called, in which you gather a lot of data or information and then dump it into some prescribed number of pages. College-level research, however, as compositionist Joseph Bizup points out, generally means *doing something* with the information you gather, which for us above all means using it to take a stance in response to other researchers. "Sources," in this model, are not merely storehouses of information that you cite, usually to support a thesis, but conversationalists like you who hold views that need to be challenged, agreed with, or some combination of both (for more on these three ways of responding, see Chapter 4). For this reason, we believe that the best research essays rely on the same "they say / I say" format that we've been describing for academic writing in general.

That being said, it does not follow that the college research essay and your standard college writing assignment are one and the same. As we illustrate below, the research paper poses special challenges, one of which has to do with its greater length; in most courses, including first-year writing, it is usually the longest paper you'll be asked to write. How do you fill all those pages? How do you develop an argument or thesis that you can focus on over your essay's entire length? And what about all the sources (articles, book chapters, and so forth) you need to find? How do you find sources that are relevant and credible? How do you select sources from among the often overwhelming number available on the internet? And perhaps most pressing of all, how do you find sources that you can fit together or synthesize as part of a common dialogue or debate?

Given how daunting such challenges can be, we have broken them down into the following issues, to be addressed one at a time.

DEVELOP A GOOD RESEARCH QUESTION

One big challenge of the research essay is navigating the sheer volume of sources that the internet makes available on almost any topic you want to write about. Students often come to our offices in a panic, having found many more sources than they can possibly read in a single semester. We reassure them, however, that they don't have to read everything that's been written on their topic, that they aren't expected to become experts on the subject (though nobody will complain if they do). Their goal instead should be to use a certain number of sources to develop some fundamental skills of intellectual inquiry, the central one of which, as we said before, is to enter a debate or conversation, terms that, as we suggest in our preface, are deeply related.

But still, students will ask, which sources do we focus on? How do we reduce a huge pile of sources to a manageable number? Our answer is pretty much the same one most writing instructors will give you: by coming up with a good research question. A good research question will help you cut through the clutter by identifying which sources are most important to you and how you'll approach them.

But what is a good research question?

In our view, you probably won't be surprised to hear, a good research question identifies a controversy, posing an issue that people can agree or disagree about. In other words, a good research question does more than identify a general topic, about which everything—and, hence, ultimately nothing—can be said. Instead, it focuses on a debate or conversation that both narrows down your sources and helps you integrate or synthesize those sources under a common umbrella issue. Consider these examples:

▸ Why did X happen? Was it, as _____ argues, because of _____ or, as _____ contends, because of _____?

▸ What should we do about X? Should we _____, as _____ urges, or _____, as _____ argues?

▸ Is X as harmful as _____ insists, or does it have benefits, as _____ claims?

▸ Is it true, as some assert, that _____?

▸ What is the relationship between _____ and _____? Is it X, as most assume, or could it be Y, as one source suggests?

In addition, good research questions often come by tapping into your own personal interests:

▸ Throughout the many years that I have taken an interest in _____, I, probably like most people, have assumed that _____. When I researched the topic for this essay, however, I was surprised to discover that _____.

▸ X argues _____. In my experience, however, _____.

Templates like these are tailor-made for sources, helping you put writers who may not even mention one another into a dialogue as part of a common conversation. But remember, a good research question is not something you can nail down once and for all at the start of your project. It is something you revise, refine, and in some cases radically alter as you work with your sources and better identify the unifying issue that you and they are concerned with.

To appreciate how important a research question is, consider how a hypothetical research paper that lacks one might open:

Robotics

Robotics is a very interesting topic in today's society. According to author X, human beings since time immemorial have been making tools to help them accomplish tasks, and in many respects artificial intelligence and robotics are no different. Authors Y and Z suggest that many companies are exploring robotics for ways it can help them make more money, and robots are a central concern in a lot of literature, film, and popular culture. The classic novel *Frankenstein* is basically about a robot. One study by author Z shows that young people take a special interest in robots, but many older people do, too.

Authors have touched on many different aspects of robotics. For example . . .

The problem with research papers like this is that they are untethered to any specific question or issue and therefore tend to lack direction, coming across as dumping grounds or grab bags of information without any unifying thread. As a result, such papers often take the form of a series of "and then" statements with references to sources sprinkled in—not unlike the "list summaries" we complained about in Chapter 2.

A controversial question or issue can remedy this type of unfocused writing. Compare, for example, the opening above with the opening to an essay reproduced in full at the end of this chapter by student writer Jason Smith:

> In recent years, many commentators have suggested that robots will take over most jobs in the next fifty years and leave the human workforce out in the cold. Experts even argue that this takeover is already happening. This paper challenges this alarmist way of thinking. The evidence, I argue, suggests that robots are not eliminating human jobs. In fact, they are creating new jobs.
>
> JASON SMITH, *Roe Butt, Cy Borg, Ann Droid:*
> *Hint, They're Not Taking Your Job*

Note here that Smith addresses the same topic—robots—as the hypothetical writer above, but he narrows it to the question of whether robots are likely to replace human workers. As a result, everything in this opening, as in the remainder of Smith's essay, is quietly devoted to this controversial question. Smith's title alone indicates that he is not going to just *talk about* robots but instead enter a conversation over whether or not robots should be feared.

You might also note here that Smith does not state his research question explicitly. But some exemplary writers do, as the environmental journalist Ben Alder illustrates when, in his very title, he asks, "Banning Plastic Bags Is Great for the World, Right? Not So Fast." In this way, Adler reaches out directly to his readers and draws them in, helping them invest in the conversation he's entering.

See pp. 320–26.

LET ONE GOOD SOURCE LEAD TO ANOTHER

Thus far we've suggested that a controversial question is central to academic research. But here you might wonder where a controversial question comes from. How do you find a question or issue that different people—you and your sources—disagree about? By looking in your sources themselves.

Sources frequently respond to other sources, either to confirm what those other sources are saying, contradict it, or some combination of both, as in:

▸ **X is far too pessimistic in her prediction that _____.**

▸ **Authors X and Y focus on the wrong issue. The issue is not _____ but _____.**

▸ **I agree with X in her critique of the view that _____, but _____.**

In such ways, sources are connected together in an intertextual network of conversation that the best researchers are always alert for. One major challenge of the research paper is to locate one of these conversations in your sources and then frame and enter that conversation.

This is no easy task. Nevertheless, you may be heartened to know that a single source alone can point you in the right direction. That is, just one effective source can provide you with a controversial issue or question that you can use in your own paper—as long as you appropriately credit the source, of course. If you're interested in writing about the environmental or green movement, for instance, you wouldn't have to go very far in Adler's article alone to find such a controversy, since Adler starts identifying positions he agrees and disagrees with as early as his third paragraph. You could also track down some of these sources—which online writing often makes easy when it provides clickable links—and read them next. You might also want to search to see if any of the sources Adler mentions extended the conversation by responding to Adler after his article was published, perhaps by using the Cited By function, which we discuss below (p. 213).

Using one source in this way to find other sources actually has a name. It's called "citation chaining" (or "reference mining") and involves following the trail of a conversation or debate from one source to another, in much the same way as you might follow a trail of bread crumbs. To start such a chain, you might ask questions like these: "In the material I have read, whom are the authors in dialogue with? Who are their 'they says'? What other sources are mentioned in this material that I might follow up on? Are there other texts these sources refer to that could be useful to me?"

BEWARE OF CONFIRMATION BIAS

Before you start searching for sources, though, it is important to understand what you're searching for—and *not* searching for. You're not just looking for sources that support your own viewpoint. Sure, you'll need some, or even many, sources that support your beliefs. But if you look only for the sources that you agree with, you will miss one of the central points of research—and of education itself—which is to get outside yourself and learn from different perspectives. Put another way, you could fall prey to so-called confirmation bias, the tendency to seek out and emphasize whatever confirms your preexisting beliefs and to ignore complicating and contradictory evidence.

Tips for Avoiding Confirmation Bias

- Try searching journal databases (like *JSTOR* for the humanities or *EBSCO* for the hard sciences) instead of relying solely on the internet search engine you usually use. This is an important step, because the most commonly used search engines prioritize results based on what they have learned about you from previous searches and are thus prone to reinforcing what you already believe. For this reason, when you do use your favorite search engine, try scrolling down in the list of entries that come up rather than relying solely on the first one or two that appear.

- Seek out sources with a variety of perspectives. Do all your sources agree or toe the same general line? Do they come from the same websites, journals, or group of authors?

- If you have trouble finding opposing points of view, try returning to the sources you agree with to see if they mention authors they differ from.

- Become your own naysayer. Ask yourself, "If I had to challenge or critique my own argument, what would I say? What is the strongest objection that could be made against my position?"

- But above all else, be sure to treat other perspectives with an open mind. Play the "believing game," as we discuss in Chapter 2, in which you try to understand what they are saying on their own terms before rushing to judgment.

APPRECIATE SCHOLARLY SOURCES

Some students might shy away from scholarly sources since they are usually a harder read than their nonscholarly counterparts. But such sources have many benefits, not least of which that they make chaining or tracking conversations relatively easy.

Unlike most popular and journalistic sources, academic sources provide all the citation information you need to track down any source or sources that have been referred to. That is, scholarly sources are scholarly precisely because they draw so heavily on other sources and include key elements like works-cited pages, references, or bibliographies that tell you exactly where those other sources can be found.

Our goal here, however, is not to cover all the ins-and-outs of scholarly documentation (MLA and APA style, endnotes, footnotes, parenthetical notes, works-cited lists, and so forth). Nor is our goal to explain how these distinctive documentation features of academic writing differ from one discipline to another. There are many excellent writer's handbooks and websites out there that provide this type of intricate instruction. And yet our discussion of research would be incomplete if it didn't underscore how helpful it is that scholarly writers tell you exactly which sources they are responding to in any particular passage and that they end their publications with all the documentation information you need to track these sources down.

In this way, scholarly, academic writers (like you!) are remarkably transparent, taking pains to identify their sources in ways that popular, journalistic, and literary writers do not. So, for instance, when Michelle Alexander, in the excerpt included in this book from *The New Jim Crow: Mass Incarceration in the Age of Colorblindness*, cites studies, she includes note numbers that direct readers to the precise studies she's referring to. One of her sentences on page 416, for instance, runs as follows:

Studies show that people of all colors *use and sell* drugs at remarkably similar rates.[9]

To locate these studies, all you need to do is flip to the end of Alexander's text and look for endnote 9, which cites several reports, such as the US Department of Health and Human Services and the National Household Survey on Drug Abuse. So, for example, if you were examining illegal drug use in your community compared to national averages, you could turn to the sources cited by Alexander for relevant data. Through devices like these, scholarly writers are remarkably transparent, inviting any reader to independently assess the conversation that they are engaged in.

But looking inside a scholarly source is not the only way to piece together or "chain" a debate or conversation. Because it is unlikely that any one scholarly source will be the last word in a published conversation, you might want to find out if any other sources have responded to your source, something you can do by using the handy Cited By or Cited Reference functions provided by *Google Scholar*, and journal repositories like *JSTOR* or *EBSCO*. For example, when we keyed in "Michelle Alexander, *The New Jim Crow*" into *Google Scholar*, here's what we got:

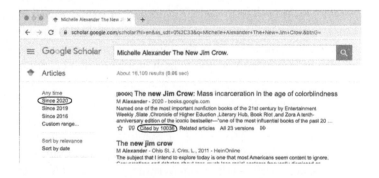

Librarians are usually more than happy to help you use this function. But the upshot is that, the number to the right of "Cited by" tells you that Alexander's book has inspired a tremendous amount of discussion, having been cited in no less than 10,036 other publications—far too many sources for you to possibly sort through. But no need to despair. By clicking on the "Cited by" link itself, you can do a more focused search by checking the box, "Search within citing articles," and then entering into the new search bar keywords tailored to your particular interests, as in: "presidential election, voter suppression, Black Lives Matter, Donald Trump." When we keyed in these more precise terms, we were able to reduce our list of 10,000+ publications to 1,480 results. And when we sorted by date, selecting, for example, only articles published "Since 2020," we further reduced that number to an even more manageable 86 that can be scanned for relevant titles.

EVALUATE YOUR SOURCES

Whether a source converges around a common question or issue is only one consideration when evaluating a source. Another factor is whether a source is reliable or not, which is often difficult to determine. Even as the internet greatly expands the amount of knowledge available to us, it is notoriously susceptible to misinformation and propaganda that look like objective fact. In their research article, "Lateral Reading: Reading Less and Learning More When Evaluating Digital Information," Sam Wineburg and Sarah McGrew of the Stanford History Education Group, found that even professional historians accustomed to online searches "often fell victim to easily manipulated features of websites such as official-looking logos and domain names."

So even as the internet has made academic research easier in many ways, it makes it hard to tell if what you are looking at is or isn't reliable. How are you to sort out one type of text from the other? How can you tell whether a source you're looking at has been discredited? One common answer is to restrict your searches to a type of scholarly writing we discussed earlier: the type that appears in academic journals and university presses that rely on the peer-review process of only publishing submissions that have been approved by other expert scholars.

Despite its merits, however, this approach excludes such indispensable venues as the *New York Times* and the *Wall Street Journal*, and general interest magazines like *Harper's* and the *Atlantic*, not to mention many popular books and most of what appears on the internet. Limiting yourself only to peer-reviewed sources is especially difficult when writing about current events and contemporary issues, which tend to be the purview of news periodicals.

For this reason, you might want to know about a second approach for determining whether a source is credible: the strategy that Wineburg and McGrew recommend of "reading laterally," which involves cross-checking all sources. Wineburg and McGrew suggest that in doing online research, we imitate professional fact-checkers, who tend to be more adept than even experienced academics at evaluating web sources. While most researchers, according to Wineburg and McGrew, "read vertically, staying within a website to evaluate its reliability," fact-checkers "read laterally," looking not just at what the source itself says but at what other sources say about it, too. In contrast to vertical readers, these savvy researchers are able to more accurately determine whether any group sponsors the website and who might have a financial stake in its claims.

Fact-checkers are also able to more accurately assess whether a website has a bias that needs to be taken into account and whether it promotes suspicious information.

Tips for Researching Like a Fact-Checker

- Open a browser tab and window and type in the website's name along with key terms like "funding," "credibility," and "bias." Hit Search and see what comes up.

- Go to the *Wikipedia* pages for the authors or website you're investigating, and consider following up on the links at the bottom of the page under "References," "Notes and References," and "Internal Links."

- Cross-check any claims presented by the source that strike you as improbable. In other words, when you come across claims that sound suspect, try investigating further to see if the claim is supported or refuted by other sources. That one source treats as factual what another source treats as questionable can, after all, be an excellent starting point for a paper.

- And again, if you're using a popular search engine, be sure not to rely exclusively on the first two or three results that come up but to scroll down to the lower items. Remember that the results given in nonscholarly search engines are based on your previous searches and are designed to get clicks.

If we could add anything to Wineburg's and McGrew's suggestions here, it would be to not underestimate how interesting in itself reading laterally like this can be. You may just find that investigating whether a given source is reliable is so fascinating that you just have to make it the central question that your research paper addresses, as in:

▸ While many observers seem to find website X trustworthy, others are suspicious of X because of _____ . I, however, am of two minds about this site and argue that we need to use this website with great caution.

▸ X challenges the reliability of Blog Y on the grounds that _____ _____ . My own view is _____ .

Templates like these can form the basis of a dynamite research paper. After all, throughout this chapter we have insisted that strong research writing requires a good controversial question, and it is hard to think of a controversial question that is better and more fundamental than whether the sources we rely on can be trusted.

DON'T LET ALL THOSE VOICES DERAIL YOU

Avoiding tangents is important in any piece of writing. As we explained in Chapter 8, regardless of the nature of the assignment, you need to stay focused throughout the entire length of your paper.

And yet, as we suggested at the start of this chapter, staying focused throughout a research paper can be especially challenging. This is not just because the research paper is relatively long but also because it requires you to synthesize a large number of sources that rarely come prepackaged in a ready-made conversation. In some cases, the sources you collect will not directly mention or address the others, and most will have an agenda that differs from your own. As a result, it can be difficult to reduce all your sources to a common conversation or issue and all too easy to let them throw you off track.

To see how one student manages to stay focused on his central research question over the full course of his research paper, let's return to the essay by student writer Jason Smith (pp. 222–31). As we noted earlier, Smith does an excellent job stating his central question—whether or not robots threaten to eliminate human jobs—at the start of his essay and even in his title. What we now want to note is that he does an equally good job staying focused on this issue while piloting through numerous sources.

On page 225, for instance, Smith opens one of his paragraphs with the following:

> A second alarming view of robots taking home the paycheck comes from . . . *McKinsey Quarterly.* . . .

This topic sentence, which introduces a new article, may look unremarkably simple. Nevertheless, this sentence does something that is actually quite difficult: it puts this new article in dialogue not only with the previous article that Smith had just addressed but also with the controversial question that Smith established in his opening paragraph a full three pages earlier. How can we tell that this sentence makes all these connections? In part because it relies on the same key terms, or their synonyms and antonyms, that Smith has already established in his preceding pages: terms like "robots," "alarmist," "fear," "taking over," "paycheck," "work," "employments," "workforce," and "jobs." Even the seemingly inconsequential word "second" makes connections, suggesting a parallel between this "second" article and the previous one that Smith addressed, suggesting that both adopt an "alarming view of robots taking home the paycheck." If you need help with such moves, you might want to do the exercises below, which are designed to help.

In this chapter, we've given you, we hope, some useful tips on how to write the college research essay. But as the chapter draws to a conclusion, we'd like to step back from this how-to discussion and say a word about what such research, as we see it, is essentially all about. For some students, the research essay may seem to be just one more pointless hoop that some authority is asking them to jump through. But for us, it's the highest expression of the conversational approach to writing that we discuss in this book, an opportunity to take off the training wheels and contribute to a conversation that instead of being preestablished by your instructor, you independently find and frame yourself. In this way, the academic research essay is far from merely academic in the negative sense. It is a chance to practice a set of skills that you can use the rest of your life: going out into the community, finding a space for yourself, and making a contribution of your own.

Exercises

1. Read Ayana Elizabeth Johnson's 2020 essay, "To Save the Climate, Look to the Oceans," on **theysayiblog.com** in light of the techniques addressed in this chapter. Working with a partner or a small group, answer the following questions:

   a. What do you take Johnson's central research question to be? What debate does that question frame or set up? Choose one of the templates from this chapter that corresponds with Johnson's question and then state that question using the template's language.

b. Look at the sources Johnson includes in her essay, which are hyperlinked, and analyze what Johnson does with each one. Does the source support or challenge her position? And how do you know? How does Johnson synthesize that source into her essay's central debate question?

c. Choose one of the sources Johnson includes and read it "laterally," as the term is used in this chapter, to evaluate its credibility. "Fact-check" the source to determine its commitments and biases. In the end, do you think the source is reliable? Why or why not?

d. Use *Google Scholar* to determine who has cited Johnson's essay and what conversations or debates her essay is part of. How might you enter this conversation in a research essay of your own?

2. Take a section of Johnson's essay and annotate it in the same ways that we annotated Jason Smith's essay (pp. 222–31). Identify as many "moves that matter" as you can, noting, for instance, how Johnson

- entertains counterarguments

- sets up a debate or conversation

- synthesizes sources to a common issue

- uses transition terms

- uses pointing words

- uses voice markers

- repeats herself with a difference

- includes metacommentary

- develops a constellation of key terms and phrases

- frames, or "sandwiches," quotations

3. To get going on a research essay, try the following steps:

Decide on a general topic for your essay, and then, working with a classmate, use the templates on page 206 to come up with at least two different research questions that address that topic. Analyze each question with your classmate, weighing its strengths and weaknesses until you decide which question you prefer.

Then, having decided on a question, continue working with your partner to develop a list of eight to ten key terms and phrases that you can use both in your paper itself and to search for sources on the internet.

After you've gathered your sources and written a draft of your paper, have a classmate read your draft to determine if it exhibits any of the confirmation bias discussed in this chapter. Do you use sources only to support your position, or do you bring in a variety of perspectives, including those of naysayers? Do other perspectives come to mind that could—or should— also be included in your text? Work together to either track down sources that represent any excluded perspectives or come up with language of your own to represent them, as in, "It is sometimes said that . . ."

Finally, have your partner evaluate how well you integrate or synthesize your sources. Are all your sources aligned with one another and with your essay's central debate question or issue? Can you come up with strategies to heighten the alignment and eliminate any misalignment?

Roe Butt, Cy Borg, Ann Droid: Hint, They're Not Taking Your Job

JASON SMITH

IN RECENT YEARS, many commentators have suggested that robots will take over most jobs in the next fifty years and leave the human workforce out in the cold. Experts even argue that this takeover is already happening. This paper challenges this alarmist way of thinking. The evidence, I argue, suggests that robots are not eliminating human jobs. In fact, they are creating new jobs. Throughout history, such innovative tools didn't end work but increased it.

JASON SMITH wrote this essay for his first-year writing course at Atlantic Cape Community College, where he is pursuing a general studies associate's degree in science. This essay was nominated for the Norton Writer's Prize and is documented in MLA style.

To be sure, in periods when innovations take hold, workers tend to fear their own dislocation. For example, as researcher James Lacey notes, during the industrialization of the French silk industry, "French weavers threw their wooden shoes (sabots) into textile machines to make them break down. (Thus the term sabotage.)." However, it is likely that those displaced workers found other jobs—as auto mechanics, gas station attendants, and car makers, for example—just as those who worked in carriage houses and were replaced by the automobile did. Changes happen in every industry over time: the airplane replaced the train, for example, and lightbulbs replaced the need for the candlemaker, but in every era, many displaced workers found new professions. A well-defined pattern is beginning to emerge here—all technological advances bring with them new opportunities.

> Makes a concession to the "they say" that actually bolsters his "I say."

Predictions about the downfall of the workforce due to technological innovation have been happening for nearly a century. Jeff Borland notes that "in the 1930s, John Maynard Keynes envisaged that innovations such as electricity would produce a world where people spent most of their time on leisure." Later, during the 1930s, as Richard Freeman notes, "US President Franklin D. Roosevelt blamed unemployment on his country's failure to employ the surplus labor created by the efficiency of its industrial processes." He also points out that

> Summarizes some "they say" sources from the past.

in the early 1960s, widespread fears that automation was eliminating thousands of jobs per week led the Kennedy and Johnson administrations to examine the link between productivity growth and employment.

Despite those worries and failed projections, studies done in the 1960s through the 1990s (a period that includes the advent of the modern computer) proclaimed the demise of work.

Two more recent studies demonstrate contemporary arguments for the impact robots will have on our future. *Race against the Machine*, a book by Erik Brynjolfsson and Andrew McAfee, focuses on the results of their study of the recovery from the Great Recession of 2008. In his TED talk based on the book, McAfee uses a chart that presents a dramatic correlation between productivity and the labor force and notes that his research with coauthor Brynjolfsson reveals that from 2008 through 2011, while the US working-age population increased, the actual number of available jobs declined, even though the economy was recovering during that time frame and productivity actually increased (00:0:51–1:56). Their inevitable conclusion, according to McAfee, is that robots are already replacing the human workforce.

However, the data gathered in *Race against the Machine* is shortsighted. Had the study continued only three more years, the authors would have seen the graph's job curve return to normal values. After any recession, the rebound

[margin note: Previews the first of two "they say" sources to be addressed.]

[margin note: Answers this first "they say," integrating sources.]

in employment has always taken longer than the rebound in the GDP, for several reasons. Manufacturers reduce their inventories, which makes it look like fewer people are producing more. In a recession, the remaining workers always find ways to pick up the slack left behind by laid-off workers, often through the use of overtime, which is cheaper in the short run than hiring new workers or rehiring those laid off. Once again, the greater productivity stems from existing workers, not automation. The most recent recession, moreover, produced some unusual employment data. Part-time workers are not counted as full-time employees, yet their work output is included in the overall productivity numbers.

A second alarming view of robots taking home the paycheck comes from Michael Chui and colleagues in a *McKinsey Quarterly* article titled "Where Machines Could Replace Humans—and Where They Can't." They write:

> Last year, we showed that currently demonstrated technologies could automate 45 percent of the activities people are paid to perform and that about 60 percent of all occupations could see 30 percent or more of their constituent activities automated, again with technologies available today.

The problem with this report is its use of probability for its logic: just because a thing *can* be done does not mean

> Summarizes and answers the second "they say," integrating yet more sources.

it *will* be done. As Gillian White points out in her reporting on a study by two economists, "The authors note that just because an industry can automate doesn't mean that it will." Costs in every case must be examined, as well as return on investment. Theoretical predictions only go so far; there is a real-world cost/benefit analysis that must be applied to each of these possible robot advancements. In addition, Chui and colleagues overlook arguments that it will require more humans to maintain and build robots than they replace (Metz).

In fact, convincing, well-researched papers that examine data over a much greater time span find there is no evidence of a robot takeover. These studies indicate that the opposite is true. For example, Jeff Borland and Michael Coelli, two Australian researchers, published an exhaustive study in 2017 that found that

> (i) the total amount of work available [in Australia] has not decreased following the introduction of computer-based technologies; and (ii) the pace of structural change and job turnover in the labor market has not accelerated with the increasing application of computer-based technologies. A review of recent studies that claim computer-based technologies may be about to cause widespread job destruction establishes several major flaws with these predictions. (377)

Continues to answer this second "they say," integrating even more sources.

Borland and Coelli found that fears about job losses have happened often throughout history: "Our suggested explanation for why techno-phobia has such a grip on popular imagination is a human bias to believe that 'we live in special times'" (377). In other words, we think that our particular era is unique—that now is truly the time that robots will take over our jobs—but such a scenario doesn't come to pass.

There are more practical reasons why robots will not replace humans in many fields, especially those areas of work that require direct interaction with humans. In his *Tech.Co* article "5 Reasons Why Robots Will Never Fully Replace Humans," Lanre Onibalusi notes that robots cannot "understand irrational thought," cannot "understand context," and "lack creative problem solving" abilities and that "people prefer to talk with a human." Additionally, as Ryan Nakashima reports, behind almost every form of robotization is an army of technocrats. This army of workers is considered the "dirty little secret" behind the artificially intelligent robot. Whether it be the hundreds of programmers or the vast numbers of call-center operators required to carry the load, robots require human helpers. It seems that robots simply cannot understand context, and enormous numbers of analysts are required to try to reteach an automated system every time it fails to understand a request

> Engages more sources in support of the "I say."

from a customer (Nakashima). In fact, according to a recent *New York Times* article, grocery retailers who have started using robots report that "the robots are good for their workers. They free up employees from mundane and sometimes injury-prone jobs like unloading delivery trucks to focus on more fulfilling tasks like helping customers" (Corkery). In this case, as in others, robots help increase productivity rather than replace humans.

Addresses a final naysayer.

Some of these alarmists argue that as robots become smarter, laws must be instituted to guard against a massive upheaval, or even elimination, of the human workforce. The problem with this preemptive approach is that no one can possibly imagine where or when those laws should exist or how to apply them. The normal course of events is to first have solid evidence that some event is "bad" and later proceed to legislate. For example, those who oppose self-driving cars, another kind of robot, call for governmental restrictions on them, but before such vehicles are on the road, there's no reason to fear them. In fact, they require human help. Many have heard of the self-driving truck that hauled two thousand cases of beer 120 miles in Colorado without a driver at the wheel (Isaac). What was not revealed was that there was a full police escort for the entire route and that the vehicle was incapable of negotiating the on- and off-ramps. I will admit that during the writing of this paper, a self-driving-car fatality did occur when an Arizona woman was struck and killed by a driverless vehicle owned by Uber. Uber immediately suspended all driverless test vehicles in the United States and Canada, and the following week Nvidia suspended all tests with the same product (Sage). Perhaps here is an example of a worthy event triggering the possibility of new laws, but an overall ban on automation itself in the workforce seems hasty.

As Jeff Borland has astutely observed, "The tale of new technologies causing the death of work is the prophecy that keeps on giving." It is sensational, alarmist, and grossly premature. I agree with those who believe society should not worry about robots taking away all the jobs. Most of the predictions for the future are countered by past facts. The reality is that all new technologies bring about new avenues of invention, experimentation, and work and that much of the new technology requires the intervention of humans. It is therefore unnecessary for governments to regulate robots to protect jobs.

> Succinctly recaps the essay's "I say" position.

WORKS CITED

Borland, Jeff. "Why We Are Still Convinced Robots Will Take Our Jobs despite the Evidence." *The Conversation*, 25 Nov. 2017, theconversation.com/why-we-are-still-convinced -robots-will-take-our-jobs-despite-the-evidence-87188.

Borland, Jeff, and Michael Coelli. "Are Robots Taking Our Jobs?" *The Australian Economic Review*, vol. 50, no. 4, 2017, pp. 377–97. *Wiley Online Library*, https://doi.org/10.1111/1467-8462.12245.

Brynjolfsson, Erik, and Andrew McAfee. *Race against the Machine*. Digital Frontier Press, 2011.

Chui, Michael, et al. "Where Machines Could Replace Humans—and Where They Can't (Yet)." *McKinsey Quarterly*, July 2016, www.mckinsey.com/business-functions/digital-mckinsey/our-insights/where-machines-could-replace-humans-and-where-they-cant-yet.

Corkery, Michael. "Should Robots Have a Face?" *The New York Times*, 26 Feb. 2020, www.nytimes.com/2020/02/26/business/robots-retail-jobs.html.

Freeman, Richard B. "Who Owns the Robots Rules the World." *IZA World of Labor*, May 2015, wol.iza.org/articles/who-owns-the-robots-rules-the-world/long.

Isaac, Mike. "Self-Driving Truck's First Mission: A 120-Mile Beer Run." *The New York Times*, 25 Oct. 2016, www.nytimes.com/2016/10/26/technology/self-driving-trucks-first-mission-a-beer-run.html.

Lacey, James. Comment on "Should Governments Limit Corporations' Abilities to Replace Human Workers with Technology?" *Quora*, 1 Jan. 2017, www.quora.com/Should-governments-limit-corporations-abilities-to-replace-human-workers-with-technology.

McAfee, Andrew. "Race against the Machine." *YouTube*, uploaded by TedxBoston, 17 July 2012, www.youtube.com/watch?v=QfMGyCk3XTw.

Metz, Cade. "Robots Will Steal Our Jobs, but They'll Give Us New Ones." *Wired*, 24 Aug. 2015, wired.com/2015/08/robots-will-steal-jobs-theyll-give-us-new-ones.

Nakashima, Ryan. "AI's Dirty Little Secret: It's Powered by People." *AP News*, 5 Mar. 2018, apnews.com/1f58465e55d643ea84e51713f35ad214.

Onibalusi, Lanre. "5 Reasons Why Robots Will Never Fully Replace Humans." *Tech.Co*, 2 Aug. 2017, tech.co/robots-replace-humans -work-2017-08.

Sage, Alexandria, and Sonam Rai. "Nvidia Halts Self-Driving Tests in Wake of Uber Accident." *Reuters*, 27 Mar. 2018, www.reuters.com/article/us-autos-selfdriving-nvidia /nvidia-halts-self-driving-tests-in-wake-of-uber-accident -idUSKBN1H32E0.

White, Gillian B. "How Many Robots Does It Take to Replace a Human Job?" *The Atlantic*, 30 Mar. 2017, www.theatlantic .com/business/archive/2017/03/work-automation/521364.

SIXTEEN

"ON CLOSER EXAMINATION"

Entering Conversations about Literature

———

IN CHINUA ACHEBE'S NOVEL *Things Fall Apart*, Okonkwo, the main character, is a tragic hero.

So what? Who cares?

Why does this typical way of opening an essay on a literary work leave readers wondering, "Why are you telling me this?" Because, in our view, such statements leave it unclear who would say otherwise. Would anyone deny that the main character of Achebe's novel is a tragic hero? Is there some other view of the subject that this writer is responding to? Since no such alternative interpretation is indicated, the reader thinks, "OK, Okonkwo is a tragic hero—as opposed to what?"

Now compare this opening with another possible one:

> Several members of our class have argued that Okonkwo, the main character of *Things Fall Apart*, is a hateful villain. My own view, however, is that, while it is true that Okonkwo commits villainous acts, he is ultimately a tragic hero—a flawed but ultimately sympathetic figure.

We hope you agree that the second version, which responds to what someone else says about Okonkwo, makes for more engaging writing than the first. Since the first version fails to present itself as a response to any alternative view of its subject, it comes at readers out of the blue, leaving them wondering why it needs to be said at all.

As we stress in this book, it is the views of others and our desire to respond to these views that gives our writing its underlying motivation and helps readers see why what we say matters, why others should care, and why we need to say it in the first place. In this chapter we suggest that this same principle applies to writing about literature. Literary critics, after all, don't make assertions about literary works out of the blue. Rather, they contribute to discussions and debates about the meaning and significance of literary works, some of which may continue for years and even centuries.

Indeed, this commitment to discussion animates most literature courses, in which students discuss and debate assigned works in class before writing papers about them. The premise is that engaging with classmates and teachers enables us to make discoveries about the work that we might not arrive at in simply reading the work alone.

We suggest that you think of writing about literature as a natural extension of such in-class discussions, listening carefully to others and using what they say to set up and motivate what you have to say.

START WITH WHAT OTHERS ARE SAYING

But in writing about literature, where do views to respond to— "they say"s—come from? Many sources. Published literary criticism is perhaps the most obvious:

▶ Critic X complains that author Y's story is compromised by his _____ perspective. While there's some truth to this critique, I argue that critic X overlooks _____.

▶ According to critic A, novel X suggests _____. I agree, but would add that _____.

But the view that you respond to in writing about literature can be far closer to home than published literary criticism. As our opening example illustrates, it can be something said about the literary work by a classmate or teacher:

▶ Several members of our class have suggested that the final message of play X is _____. I agree up to a point, but I still think that _____.

Another tactic is to start with something you yourself thought about the work that on second thought you now want to revise:

▶ On first reading play Z, I thought it was an uncritical celebration of _____. After rereading the play and discussing it in class, however, I see that it is more critical of _____ than I originally thought.

You can even respond to something that hasn't actually been said about the work but might hypothetically be said:

▶ It might be said that poem Y is chiefly about _____. But the problem with this reading, in my view, is _____.

▶ Though religious readers might be tempted to analyze poem X as a parable about _____, a closer examination suggests that the poem is in fact _____.

Sometimes the "they say" that you respond to in writing about a literary work can be found in the work itself, as distinct from what some critic or other reader has said *about* the work. Much great literary criticism responds directly to the literary work, summarizing some aspect of the work's form or content and then assessing it, in much the same way you can do in response to a persuasive essay:

▸ Ultimately, as I read it, *The Scarlet Letter* seems to say _____. I have trouble accepting this proposition, however, on the grounds that _____.

One of the more powerful ways of responding to a literary work is to address any contradictions or inconsistencies:

▸ At the beginning of the poem, we encounter the generalization, seemingly introducing the poem's message, that "_____." But this statement is then contradicted by the suggestion made later in the poem that "_____." This opens up a significant inconsistency in the text: is it suggesting _____ or, on the contrary, _____?

▸ At several places in novel X, author Y leads us to understand that the story's central point is that _____. Yet elsewhere the text suggests _____, indicating that Y may be ambivalent on this issue.

If you review the above templates, you'll notice that each does what a good discussion, lecture, or essay does: it makes an argument about some aspect of a work that can be interpreted in various ways. Instead of just making a claim about the work in isolation—character X is a tragic hero; sonnet Y is about the loss of a loved one—these templates put one claim as a response to another, making clear what motivated the argument to begin with. They thus act as conversation starters that can invite or even provoke other readers to respond with their own interpretations and judgments.

FIGURING OUT
WHAT A LITERARY WORK "MEANS"

In order to enter conversations and debates about literature, you need to meet the time-honored challenge of being able to read and make sense of literary works, understanding and analyzing what the text says. On the one hand, like the types of persuasive essays we focus on throughout this book, literary works make arguments their authors want to convey, things they are for and against, ideas they want to endorse or condemn. On the other hand, discovering "the argument" of a literary work—what it's "saying"—can be a special challenge because, unlike persuasive essays, literary works usually do not spell out their arguments explicitly. Though poets, novelists, and playwrights may have the same level of conviction as persuasive writers, rarely do they step out from behind the pages of their texts and say, "OK, folks, this is what it all means. What I'm trying to say in a nutshell is _____ ." That is, since literary texts do not include an explicit thesis statement identifying their main point, it's left up to us as readers to figure it out.

Because literary works tend to avoid such explicitness, their meanings often need to be teased out from the clues they provide: from the dialogue between characters, the plot, the imagery and symbolism, and the kind of language the author uses. In fact, it is this absence of overt argument that makes literature so endlessly debatable—and explains why scholars and critics argue so much about what literary works mean in ways similar to the classroom discussions that you have likely participated in as a student.

The Elusive Literary Author

Indeed, not even the use of the first person "I" in a literary work is an indication that you have located the author's own position or stance, as it usually is in an essay. When David Zinczenko, for example, in his essay "Don't Blame the Eater" (pp. 199–202) writes, "I tend to sympathize with these portly fast-food patrons" who file lawsuits against the fast-food industry, we can be confident that the "I" is Zinczenko himself and that the position he expresses is his own and informs everything else in his essay. But we cannot assume that the "I" who addresses us in a work of fiction or poetry is necessarily the author, for the person who "I" refers to is a fictional character—and one who may be unreliable and untrustworthy.

Take, for example, the first sentence of Edgar Allan Poe's short story "The Cask of Amontillado":

> The thousand injuries of Fortunato I had borne as I best could, but when he ventured upon insult I vowed revenge.

As soon becomes clear in the story, the "I" who speaks as the narrator here is not Poe himself but an insanely vengeful murderer whose words must be seen through to get at the point of Poe's story.

Instead of a readily identifiable position, literary works often present the perspectives of a number of different characters and leave it to readers to determine which if any speaks for the author. Thus when we encounter the seemingly eloquent lines in *Hamlet* "To thine own self be true, . . . / And canst thou not be false to any man," we can't assume, as we might if we encountered this statement in an essay, that it represents the author's own view. For these words are uttered by Polonius, a character whom Shakespeare presents as a tedious, cliché-spouting bore—not someone he leads us to trust. After all, part of Hamlet's problem is that it's not clear to him what being "true" to his own self would require him to do.

This elusive quality of literary texts helps explain why some of our students complain about the challenge of finding the "hidden meaning," as they sometimes call it, let alone summarizing that meaning in the way assignments often require. Sure, some students say, they enjoy reading literature for pleasure. But analyzing literature in school for its "meaning" or "symbolism"—that's another matter. Some even say that the requirement that they hunt for meanings and symbols robs literature of its fun.

In fact, as most students come to recognize, analyzing meanings, symbols, and other elements should enhance rather than stifle the pleasure we get from reading literature. But it can indeed be hard to figure out what literary works mean. How do we determine the point of stories or poems when the authors, unlike essayists like Zinczenko, do not tell us explicitly what they are trying to say? How do you go from a fictional event or poetic image (an insane man committing murder, two roads that diverge in the woods) or from a dialogue between fictional characters ("Frankly, my dear, I don't give a damn") to what these events, images, or lines of dialogue mean?

Look for Conflict *in* the Work

There is no simple recipe for figuring out what a literary work means, but one tactic that seems to help our own students is to look for the conflict or debate in the literary work itself and then ask what the text is leading us to think about that conflict. Asking these questions—what is the conflict in the work and which side, if any, should we favor?—will help you think about and formulate a position on what the work means. And since such claims are often ones that literary scholars argue about, thinking about the conflict *in* a literary work will often lead you to discussions and debates *about* the work that you can then respond to in your writing. Because literary authors don't tell us explicitly what the text means, it's always going to be *arguable*—and your task in writing about a literary work is to argue for what *you* think it means. Here are two templates to help get you started responding to other interpretations:

▸ **It might be argued that in the clash between characters X and Y in play Z, the author wants us to favor character Y, since she is presented as the play's heroine. I contend, however, that _____ .**

▸ **Several critics seem to assume that poem X endorses the values of discipline and rationality represented by the image of _____ over those of play and emotion represented by the image of _____ . I agree, but with the following caveat: that the poem ultimately sees both values as equally important and even suggests that ideally they should complement one another.**

This tactic of looking for the conflicts in literary works is part of a long tradition of critical thought that sees conflict as central to literature. In ancient Greece, Aristotle argued that conflict between characters or forces underlies the plots of tragic dramas such as *Oedipus*. Indeed, the ancient Greek word *agon*, which means antagonism, conflict, or debate, leaves its traces in the term "protagonist," the hero or leading character of a narrative work who comes into conflict with other characters or with the fates. And Plato noted the pervasiveness of conflict in literature when he banished poets from his ideal community on the grounds that their works depict endless conflict and division.

This emphasis on the centrality of conflict in literature has been echoed by modern theorists like the New Critics of the 1940s and '50s, who focused on such tensions and paradoxes as good and evil or innocence and experience—and more recently by poststructuralists and political theorists who see literature, like society, as saturated by such polarities as male/female, gay/straight, white/Black, and so on. Writers today continue to recognize conflict as the engine of good storytelling. As the Hollywood screenwriter Robert McKee puts it, "Nothing moves forward in a story except through conflict."

Building on this idea that conflict is central to literature, we suggest the following four questions to help you understand and formulate your own position on any literary work:

1. What is the central conflict?
2. Which side—if any—does the text seem to favor?
3. What's your evidence? How might others interpret the evidence differently?
4. What's your opinion of the text?

WHAT IS THE CENTRAL CONFLICT?

Conflicts tend to manifest themselves in different ways in different literary genres. In works that take a narrative or story form (novels, short stories, and plays), the central conflict will often be represented in an actual debate between characters. These debates between characters will often reflect larger questions and debates in the society or historical era in which they were written, over such issues as the responsibility of rulers, the consequences of capitalism and consumerism, or the struggle for gender equality. Sometimes these debates will be located within an individual character, appearing as a struggle in someone caught between conflicting or incompatible choices. Whatever form they may take, these debates can provide you with points of entry into the issues raised by the work, its historical context, and its author's vision of the world.

One narrative work that lends itself to such an approach is Flannery O'Connor's 1961 short story "Everything That Rises Must Converge." The story presents a running debate between a mother and her son, Julian, about the civil rights movement for racial equality that had erupted in the American South at the time the story was written, with Julian defending the outlook of this movement and his mother defending the South's traditional racial hierarchy. The story raises the debatable question of which character we should side with: Julian, his mother, both, or neither?

WHICH SIDE—IF ANY—DOES THE TEXT SEEM TO FAVOR?

When we teach this story, most of our students first assume the story sides with Julian's outlook, which to them as northern, urban college students in the twenty-first century seems the obviously enlightened position. Who, after all, could fail to see that the mother's views are backward and racist? As our class discussions unfold, however, most students come to reject this view as a misreading, one based more on their own views than on what's in the text. Sooner or later, someone points out that in several places Julian is presented in highly critical ways—and that his apparently progressive sympathy for racial integration rests on arid intellectual abstractions and a hypocritical lack of self-knowledge, in contrast with his mother's heartfelt loyalty to her roots. Eventually another possible interpretation surfaces, that both characters suffer from a common malady: that they're living in a mental bubble that keeps them from being able to see themselves as they really are.

The writing assignment we often give builds on this class discussion by offering students the following template for thinking about which character, if any, the text leads them to favor:

▶ **Some might argue that when it comes to the conflict between Julian and his mother over _____, our sympathies should lie with _____. My own view is that _____.**

WHAT'S YOUR EVIDENCE?

In entering the types of discussions and debates modeled by the above template, how do you determine where your "sympathies should lie"? More generally, how do you arrive at and justify an interpretation of what a literary text says?

The answer lies in the *evidence* provided by the work: its images, dialogue, plot, historical references, tone, stylistic details, and so forth.

It is important to remember, however, that evidence is not set in stone. Students sometimes assume that there exists some fixed code that unlocks the meaning of literary works, symbols, images, and other evidence. Characters die? This must mean that they are being condemned. A stairway appears? A symbol for upward mobility. A garden? Must be something sexual.

But evidence itself is open to interpretation and thus to debate. The mother's death in O'Connor's story, for instance, *could* be seen as evidence that we are supposed to disapprove of her as someone whose racial views are regressive and on the way out. On the other hand, her death may instead be evidence that she is to be seen as a heroic martyr too good for this cruel, harsh world. What a character's death means, then, depends on how that character is treated in the work, positively or negatively, which in turn may be subject to debate.

As we've repeatedly emphasized in this book, others will often disagree with you and may even use the same evidence you do to support interpretations that are contrary to your own. As with other objects of study, literary works are like the famous ambiguous drawing that can be seen as either a duck or a rabbit, depending how one views it.

Since the same piece of evidence in a literary work will often support differing, even opposing interpretations, you need to argue for what you think the evidence shows—and to acknowledge that others may read that evidence differently.

In writing about literature, then, you need to show that the evidence you are citing supports your interpretation and to anticipate other alternative ones:

▶ **Although some might read the metaphor of _____ in this poem as evidence that, for author X, modern technology undermines community traditions and values, I see it as _____.**

To present evidence in such a "they say / I say" way, you need to be alert for how others may read the work differently than you—and even use this very same evidence in support of an opposing interpretation:

▶ **Some might claim that evidence X suggests _____, but I argue that, on the contrary, it suggests _____.**

▶ **I agree with my classmate _____ that the image of _____ in novel Y is evidence of childhood innocence that has been lost. Unlike _____, however, I think this loss of innocence is to be read not as a tragic event but as a necessary, even helpful, stage in human development.**

Are Some Interpretations Simply Wrong?

No matter how flexible and open to debate evidence might be, not all interpretations we arrive at using that evidence are equally valid. And some interpretations are simply unsupported by that evidence. Let us illustrate.

As we noted earlier, some of our students first favored Julian over his mother. One student, let's call her Nancy, cited as evidence a passage early in the story in which Julian is compared to Saint Sebastian, a Christian martyr who is said to have exhibited exceptional faith under extreme suffering and persecution. As the mother stood preparing for Julian to take her to her weekly swimming class, Julian is described as standing "pinned to the door frame, waiting like Saint Sebastian for the arrows to begin piercing him."

Thinking this passage proves that Julian is the more sympathetic character, Nancy pointed to other evidence as well, including the following passage:

> [Julian] was free of prejudice and unafraid to face facts. Most miraculous of all, instead of being blinded by love for [his mother] as she was for him, he had cut himself emotionally free of her and could see her with complete objectivity. He was not dominated by his mother.

Citing passages like this in her essay, Nancy concluded: "Julian represents the future of society, a nonracist and an educated thinker."

After rereading the story, however, and hearing other students' views, Nancy came to realize that the passages she had cited—comparing Julian to a saint, suggesting that he is racially progressive, and that he is "free of" his mother and "objective" about her—were all intended ironically. Julian congratulates *himself* for being saint-like, free of prejudice, and objective, but the story ultimately implies that he deludes himself.

How did the supporters of the ironic reading convince Nancy to revise her initial reading—to see it as wrong, unsupported by the evidence? First, they pointed to the glaring discrepancy between the situations and kinds of suffering endured by Julian and Saint Sebastian. Could anyone be serious, they asked, in comparing something as mundane as being forced to wait a few minutes to go to the YMCA to a martyr dying for his faith? No, they answered, and the jarring incongruity of the events being compared, they argued, suggests that Julian, far from saint-like, is presented in this passage as an impatient, ungrateful, undutiful son. In addition, students pointed out that the gap between Julian's self-image as a progressive man of "complete objectivity" and "facts," "free of [his mother]," and the blubbering young man crying "Mama, Mama!" with "guilt and sorrow" at the end of the story suggests that Julian's righteous, high-minded image of himself is not to be taken at face value.

At this point you may be wondering, How can we say that some interpretations of literature must be ruled out as *wrong*? Isn't the great thing about interpreting literary works—in contrast to scientific texts—that there are no wrong answers? Are we saying that there is one "correct" way to read a literary work—the one way the work itself tells us we "should" read it?

No, we aren't saying that there is only one way to read a literary work. If we believed there were, we would not be offering a method of literary analysis based on multiple interpretations and debate. But yes, acknowledging that literary interpretations are open to debate is not to say that a work can mean anything we want it to mean, as if all interpretations are equally good. In our view, and that of most literature teachers, some interpretations are better than others—more persuasively reasoned and better grounded in the evidence of the text.

If we maintain that all interpretations are equally valid, we risk confusing the perspective of the work's author with our own, as did the students who confused their own views on the civil rights movement of the 1960s with Flannery O'Connor's. Such misreadings are reminiscent of what we call "the closest cliché syndrome," where what's summarized is not the view the author actually expresses but a familiar cliché—or, in O'Connor's case, a certain social belief—that the writer believes and mistakenly

assumes the author must too. The view that there are
no wrong answers in literary interpretation encourages
a kind of solipsism that erases the difference between
us and others and transforms everything we encounter
into a version of ourselves.

See p. 35 for more on the closest cliché syndrome.

As the literary theorist Robert Scholes puts it, reading, con-
ceived "as a submission to the intentions of another is the first
step" to understanding what a literary work is saying. For "if
we do not postulate the existence of [an author] behind the
verbal text," we will "simply project our own subjective modes
of thought and desire upon the text." In other words, unless we
do the best we can to get at what authors are saying, we will
never truly recognize their ideas except as some version of our
own. Scholes acknowledges that good reading often involves
going beyond the author's intention, pointing out contradictions and ideological blind spots, but he argues that we must
recognize the author's intention *before* we can try to see beyond
it in these ways.

WHAT'S YOUR OPINION OF THE TEXT?

In accord with the principle that we must try to understand the
text on its own terms before responding to it, we have thus far
in this chapter focused on how to understand and unpack what
literary texts say and do. Our approach to get at what they say
involves looking for the central conflict in the work and then
asking yourself how the author uses various types of evidence
(characters, dialogue, imagery, events, plot, etc.) to guide you
in thinking about that conflict. Ultimately, your job as a reader
of literature is to be open to a work as its author presents it, or

else your reading will fail to see what makes that work worth reading and thinking about.

But once you have reached a good understanding of the work, it is time to allow your own opinion to come into play. Offering your own interpretation of a work and opening that interpretation to response are crucial steps in any act of literary analysis, but they are not the end of the process. The final step involves offering your own insight into or critique of the work and its vision, assessing whether, as you see it, it is morally justified or questionable, unified or contradictory, historically regressive or progressive, and so forth. For example:

> Though she is one of the most respected Southern authors of the American literary canon, Flannery O'Connor continually denigrates the one character in her 1961 story who represents the civil rights movement and in so doing disparages progressive ideas that I believe deserve a far more sympathetic hearing.

Offering a critique, however, doesn't necessarily mean finding fault:

> Some criticize O'Connor's story by suggesting that it has a politically regressive agenda. But I see the story as a laudable critique of politics as such. In my view, O'Connor's story rightly criticizes the polarization of political conflicts—North vs. South, liberal vs. conservative, and the like—and suggests that they need to come together: to "converge," as O'Connor's title implies, through religious love, understanding, and forgiveness.

We realize that the prospect of critiquing a literary work can be daunting. Indeed, simply stating what you think an author is saying can be intimidating, since it means going out on a limb, asserting something about highly respected figures—works that are often complex, contradictory, and connected to larger historical movements. Nevertheless, if you can master these challenges, you may find that figuring out what a literary work is saying, offering an opinion about it, and entering into conversation and debate with others about such questions is what makes literature matter. And if you do it well, what *you* say will invite its own response: your "I say" will become someone else's "they say," and the conversation will go on and on.

SEVENTEEN

"THE DATA SUGGEST"

Writing in the Sciences

CHRISTOPHER GILLEN

CHARLES DARWIN DESCRIBED *On the Origin of Species* as "one long argument." In *Dialogue Concerning the Two Chief World Systems*, Galileo Galilei cast his argument for a sun-centered solar system as a series of conversations. As these historical examples show, scientific writing is fundamentally argumentative. Like all academic writers, scientists make and defend claims. They address disagreements and explore unanswered questions. They propose novel mechanisms and new theories. And they advance certain explanations and reject others. Though their vocabulary may be more technical and their emphasis more numerical, science writers use the same

---

CHRISTOPHER GILLEN is a professor of biology at Kenyon College and the faculty director of the Kenyon Institute in Biomedical and Scientific Writing. He teaches courses in animal physiology, biology of exercise, and introductory biology, all stressing the critical reading of primary research articles.

rhetorical moves as other academic writers. Consider the following example from a book about the laws of physics:

> The common refrain that is heard in elementary discussions of quantum mechanics is that a physical object is in some sense both a wave and a particle, with its wave nature apparent when you measure a wave property such as wavelength, and its particle nature apparent when you measure a particle property such as position. But this is, at best, misleading and, at worst, wrong.
>
> V. J. STENGER, *The Comprehensible Cosmos*

The "they say / I say" structure of this passage is unmistakable: they say that objects have properties of both waves and particles; I say they are wrong. This example is not a lonely argumentative passage cherry-picked from an otherwise nonargumentative text. Rather, Stenger's entire book makes the argument that is foreshadowed by its title, *The Comprehensible Cosmos*: that although some might see the universe as hopelessly complex, it is essentially understandable.

Here's another argumentative passage, this one from a research article about the role of lactic acid in muscle fatigue:

> In contrast to the often suggested role for acidosis as a cause of muscle fatigue, it is shown that in muscles where force was depressed by high $[K^+]_o$, acidification by lactic acid produced a pronounced recovery of force.
>
> O. B. NIELSEN, F. DE PAOLI, AND K. OVERGAARD,
> "Protective Effects of Lactic Acid on Force Production in
> Rat Skeletal Muscle," *Journal of Physiology*

In other words: many scientists think that lactic acid causes muscle fatigue, but our evidence shows that it actually promotes recovery. Notice that the authors frame their claim with a version of the "they say / I say" formula: "Although previous work suggests _____ , our data argue _____ ." This basic move and its many variations are widespread in scientific writing. The essential argumentative moves taught in this book transcend disciplines, and the sciences are no exception. The examples in this chapter were written by professional scientists, but they show moves that are appropriate in any writing that addresses scientific issues.

Despite the importance of argument in scientific writing, newcomers to the genre often see it solely as a means for communicating uncontroversial, objective facts. It's easy to see how this view arises. The objective tone of scientific writing can obscure its argumentative nature, and many textbooks reinforce a nonargumentative vision of science when they focus on accepted conclusions and ignore ongoing controversies. And because science writers base their arguments on empirical data, a good portion of many scientific texts *does* serve the purpose of delivering uncontested facts.

However, scientific writing often does more than just report facts. Data are crucial to scientific argumentation, but they are by no means the end of the story. Given important new data, scientists assess their quality, draw conclusions from them, and ponder their implications. They synthesize the new data with existing information, propose novel theories, and design the next experiments. In short, scientific progress depends on the insight and creativity that scientists bring to their data. The thrill of doing science, and writing about it, comes from the ongoing struggle to use data to better understand our world.

START WITH THE DATA

Data are the fundamental currency of scientific argument. Scientists develop hypotheses from existing data and then test those by comparing their predictions to new experimental data. Summarizing data is therefore a basic move in science writing. Because data can often be interpreted in different ways, describing the data opens the door to critical analysis, creating opportunities to critique previous interpretations and develop new ones.

Describing data requires more than simply reporting numbers and conclusions. Rather than jumping straight to the punch line—to what X concluded—it is important first to describe the hypotheses, methods, and results that led to the conclusion: "To test the hypothesis that _____, X measured _____ and found that _____. Therefore, X concluded _____." In the following sections, we explore the three key rhetorical moves for describing the data that underpin a scientific argument: presenting the prevailing theories, explaining methodologies, and summarizing findings.

Present the Prevailing Theories

Readers must understand the prevailing theories that a study responds to before they can fully appreciate the details. So before diving into specifics, place the work in context by describing the prevailing theories and hypotheses. In the following passage from a journal article about insect respiration, the authors discuss an explanation for discontinuous gas exchange (DGC), a phenomenon where insects periodically close valves on their breathing tubes:

> Lighton (1996, 1998; see also Lighton and Berrigan, 1995) noted the prevalence of DGC in fossorial insects, which inhabit microclimates where CO_2 levels may be relatively high. Consequently, Lighton proposed the chthonic hypothesis, which suggests that

DGC originated as a mechanism to improve gas exchange while at the same time minimizing respiratory water loss.

A. G. GIBBS AND R. A. JOHNSON, "The Role of Discontinuous Gas Exchange in Insects: The Chthonic Hypothesis Does Not Hold Water," *Journal of Experimental Biology*

Notice that Gibbs and Johnson not only describe Lighton's hypothesis but also recap the evidence that supports it. By presenting this evidence, Gibbs and Johnson set the stage for engaging with Lighton's ideas. For example, they might question the chthonic hypothesis by pointing out shortcomings of the data or flaws in its interpretation. Or they might suggest new approaches that could verify the hypothesis. The point is that by incorporating a discussion of experimental findings into their summary of Lighton's hypothesis, Gibbs and Johnson open the door to a conversation with Lighton.

Here are some templates for presenting the data that underpin prevailing explanations:

▶ **Experiments showing _____ and _____ have led scientists to propose _____.**

▶ **Although most scientists attribute _____ to _____, X's result _____ leads to the possibility that _____.**

Explain the Methods

Even as we've argued that scientific arguments hinge on data, it's important to note that the quality of data varies depending on how they were collected. Data obtained with sloppy techniques or poorly designed experiments could lead to faulty conclusions. Therefore, it's crucial to explain the methods used to collect data. In order for readers to evaluate a method, you'll need to indicate its purpose, as the following passage from a journal article about the evolution of bird digestive systems demonstrates:

> To test the hypothesis that flowerpiercers have converged with hummingbirds in digestive traits, we compared the activity of intestinal enzymes and the gut nominal area of cinnamon-bellied flowerpiercers (*Diglossa baritula*) with those of eleven hummingbird species.
>
> J. E. Schondube and C. Martinez del Rio,
> "Sugar and Protein Digestion in Flowerpiercers and
> Hummingbirds: A Comparative Test of Adaptive Convergence,"
> *Journal of Comparative Physiology*

You need to indicate purpose whether describing your own work or that of others. Here are a couple of templates for doing so:

▸ **Smith and colleagues evaluated _____ to determine whether _____.**

▸ **Because _____ does not account for _____, we instead used _____.**

Summarize the Findings

Scientific data often come in the form of numbers. Your task when presenting numerical data is to provide the context readers need to understand the numbers—by giving supporting information and making comparisons. In the following passage from a book about the interaction between organisms and their environments, Turner uses numerical data to support an argument about the role of the sun's energy on Earth:

> The potential rate of energy transfer from the Sun to Earth is prodigious—about 600 W m^{-2}, averaged throughout the year. Of this, only a relatively small fraction, on the order of 1–2 percent,

is captured by green plants. The rest, if it is not reflected back into space, is available to do other things. The excess can be considerable: although some natural surfaces reflect as much as 95% of the incoming solar beam, many natural surfaces reflect much less (Table 3.2), on average about 15–20 percent. The remaining absorbed energy is then capable of doing work, like heating up surfaces, moving water and air masses around to drive weather and climate, evaporating water, and so forth.

J. S. TURNER, The Extended Organism

Turner supports his point that a huge amount of the sun's energy is directly converted to work on Earth by quoting an actual value (600) with units of measurement (W m^{-2}, watts per square meter). Readers need the units to evaluate the value; 600 watts per square inch is very different from 600 W m^{-2}. Turner then makes comparisons using percent values, saying that only 1 to 2 percent of the total energy that reaches Earth is trapped by plants. Finally, Turner describes the data's variability by reporting comparisons as ranges—1 to 2 percent and 15 to 20 percent—rather than single values.

Supporting information—such as units of measurement, sample size (n), and amount of variability—helps readers assess the data. In general, the reliability of data improves as its sample size increases and its variability decreases. Supporting information can be concisely presented as:

▸ _____ ± _____ *(mean ± variability)* _____ *(units)*,
n = _____ *(sample size)*.

For example: before training, resting heart rate of the subjects was 56 ± 7 beats per minute, $n = 12$. Here's another way to give supporting information:

▸ We measured _____ (*sample size*) subjects, and the average response was _____ (*mean with units*) with a range of _____ (*lower value*) to _____ (*upper value*).

To help readers understand the data, make comparisons with values from the same study or from other similar work. Here are some templates for making comparisons:

▸ Before training, average running speed was _____ ± _____ kilometers per hour, _____ kilometers per hour slower than running speed after training.

▸ We found athletes' heart rates to be _____ ± _____ % lower than nonathletes'.

▸ The subjects in X's study completed the maze in _____ ± _____ seconds, _____ seconds slower than those in Y's study.

You will sometimes need to present qualitative data, such as that found in some images and photographs, which cannot be reduced to numbers. Qualitative data must be described precisely with words. In the passage below from a review article about connections between cellular protein localization and cell growth, the author describes the exact locations of three proteins, Scrib, Dlg, and Lgl:

> Epithelial cells accumulate different proteins on their apical (top) and basolateral (bottom) surfaces. . . . Scrib and Dlg are localized at the septate junctions along the lateral cell surface, whereas Lgl coats vesicles that are found both in the cytoplasm and "docked" at the lateral surface of the cell.

M. PEIFER, "Travel Bulletin—Traffic Jams Cause Tumors," *Science*

EXPLAIN WHAT THE DATA MEAN

Once you summarize experiments and results, you need to say what the data mean. Consider the following passage from a study in which scientists fertilized plots of tropical rainforest with nitrogen (N) and / or phosphorus (P):

> Although our data suggest that the mechanisms driving the observed respiratory responses to increased N and P may be different, the large CO_2 losses stimulated by N and P fertilization suggest that knowledge of such patterns and their effects on soil CO_2 efflux is critical for understanding the role of tropical forests in a rapidly changing global C [carbon] cycle.
>
> C. C. CLEVELAND AND A. R. TOWNSEND, "Nutrient Additions to a Tropical Rain Forest Drive Substantial Soil Carbon Dioxide Losses to the Atmosphere," *Proceedings of the National Academy of Sciences*

Notice that in discussing the implications of their data, Cleveland and Townsend use language—including the verbs "suggest" and "may be"—that denotes their level of confidence in what they say about the data.

Whether you are summarizing what others say about their data or offering your own interpretation, pay attention to the verbs that connect data to interpretations.

To signify a moderate level of confidence:

▸ The data *suggest / hint / imply* _____ .

To express a greater degree of certainty:

▸ Our results *show / demonstrate* _____ .

Almost never will you use the verb "prove" in reference to a single study, because even very powerful evidence generally falls short of proof unless other studies support the same conclusion.

Scientific consensus arises when multiple studies point toward the same conclusion; conversely, contradictions among studies often signal research questions that need further work. For these reasons, you may need to compare one study's findings to those of another study. Here, too, you'll need to choose your verbs carefully:

▸ Our data *support / confirm / verify* the work of X by showing that _____.

▸ By demonstrating _____, X's work *extends* the findings of Y.

▸ The results of X *contradict / refute* Y's conclusion that _____.

▸ X's findings *call into question* the widely accepted theory that _____.

▸ Our data *are consistent with* X's hypothesis that _____.

MAKE YOUR OWN ARGUMENTS

Now we turn toward the part of scientific writing where you express your own opinions. One challenge is that the statements of other scientists about their methods and results usually must be accepted. You probably can't argue, for example, that "X and Y claim to have studied six elephants, but I think they actually only studied four." However, it might be fair to say, "X and Y studied only six elephants, and this small sample size casts doubts on their conclusions." The second statement doesn't question what the scientists did or found but instead examines how the findings are interpreted.

When developing your own arguments—the "I say"—you will often start by assessing the interpretations of other scientists. Consider the following example from a review article about the beneficial acclimation hypothesis (BAH), the idea that organisms exposed to a particular environment become better suited to that environment than unexposed animals:

> To the surprise of most physiologists, all empirical examinations of the BAH have rejected its generality. However, we suggest that these examinations are neither direct nor complete tests of the functional benefit of acclimation.
>
> R. S. WILSON AND C. E. FRANKLIN, "Testing the Beneficial Acclimation Hypothesis," *Trends in Ecology & Evolution*

Wilson and Franklin use a version of the "twist it" move: they acknowledge the data collected by other physiologists but question how those data have been interpreted, creating an opportunity to offer their own interpretation.

For more on the "twist it" move, see p. 62.

You might ask whether we should question how other scientists interpret their own work. Having conducted a study, aren't they in the best position to evaluate it? Perhaps, but as the above example demonstrates, other scientists might see the work from a different perspective or through more objective eyes. And, in fact, the culture of science depends on vigorous debate in which scientists defend their own findings and challenge those of others—a give-and-take that helps improve science's reliability. So expressing a critical view about someone else's work is an integral part of the scientific process. Let's examine some of the basic moves for entering scientific conversations: agreeing, with a difference; disagreeing and explaining why; simultaneously agreeing and disagreeing; anticipating objections; and saying why it matters.

Agree, but with a Difference

Scientific research passes through several levels of critical analysis before being published. Scientists get feedback when they discuss work with colleagues, present findings at conferences, and receive reviews of their manuscripts. So the juiciest debates may have been resolved before publication, and you may find little to disagree with in the published literature of a research field. Yet even if you agree with what you've read, there are still ways to join the conversation—and reasons to do so.

One approach is to suggest that further work should be done:

▶ **Now that _____ has been established, scientists will likely turn their attention toward _____ .**

▶ **X's work leads to the question of _____ . Therefore, we investigated _____ .**

▶ **To see whether these findings apply to _____ , we propose to _____ .**

Another way to agree and at the same time jump into the conversation is to concur with a finding and then propose a mechanism that explains it. In the following sentence from a review article about dietary deficiencies, the author agrees with a previous finding and offers a probable explanation:

Inadequate dietary intakes of vitamins and minerals are widespread, most likely due to excessive consumption of energy-rich, micronutrient-poor, refined food.

B. AMES, "Low Micronutrient Intake
May Accelerate the Degenerative Diseases of Aging through
Allocation of Scarce Micronutrients by Triage,"
Proceedings of the National Academy of Sciences

Here are some templates for explaining an experimental result:

▸ **One explanation for X's finding of _____ is that _____ .
   An alternative explanation is _____ .**

▸ **The difference between _____ and _____ is probably
   due to _____ .**

Disagree—and Explain Why

Although scientific consensus is common, healthy disagreement is not unusual. While measurements conducted by different teams of scientists under the same conditions should produce the same result, scientists often disagree about which techniques are most appropriate, how well an experimental design tests a hypothesis, and how results should be interpreted. To illustrate such disagreement, let's return to the debate about whether or not lactic acid is beneficial during exercise. In the following passage, Lamb and Stephenson are responding to work by Kristensen and colleagues, which argues that lactic acid might be beneficial to resting muscle but not to active muscle:

The argument put forward by Kristensen and colleagues (12) . . . is not valid because it is based on observations made with isolated whole soleus muscles that were stimulated at such a high rate that >60% of the preparation would have rapidly become completely anoxic (4). . . . Furthermore, there is no reason to expect that adding more H+ to that already being generated by the muscle activity should in any way be advantageous. It is a bit like opening up the carburetor on a car to let in too much air or throwing gasoline over the engine and then concluding that air and gasoline are deleterious to engine performance.

G. D. Lamb and D. G. Stephenson,
"Point: Lactic Acid Accumulation Is an Advantage during
Muscle Activity," *Journal of Applied Physiology*

Lamb and Stephenson bring experimental detail to bear on their disagreement with Kristensen and colleagues. First, they criticize methodology, arguing that the high muscle stimulation rate used by Kristensen and colleagues created very low oxygen levels (anoxia). They also criticize the logic of the experimental design, arguing that adding more acid (H+) to a muscle that is already producing it isn't informative. It's also worth noting how they drive home their point, likening Kristensen and colleagues' methodology to flooding an engine with air or gasoline. Even in technical scientific writing, you don't need to set aside your own voice completely.

In considering the work of others, look for instances where the experimental design and methodology fail to adequately test a hypothesis:

▸ **The work of Y and Z appears to show that _____, but their experimental design does not control for _____ .**

Also, consider the possibility that results do not lead to the stated conclusions:

▸ **While X and Y claim that _____, their finding of _____ actually shows that _____ .**

OK, But . . .

Science tends to progress incrementally. New work may refine or extend previous work but doesn't often completely overturn it.

For this reason, science writers frequently agree up to a point and then express some disagreement. In the following example from a commentary about methods for assessing how proteins interact, the authors acknowledge the value of the two-hybrid studies, but they also point out their shortcomings:

> The two-hybrid studies that produced the protein interaction map for *D. melanogaster* (12) provide a valuable genome-wide view of protein interactions but have a number of shortcomings (13). Even if the protein-protein interactions were determined with high accuracy, the resulting network would still require careful interpretation to extract its underlying biological meaning. Specifically, the map is a representation of all possible interactions, but one would only expect some fraction to be operating at any given time.
>
> J. J. Rice, A. Kershenbaum, and G. Stolovitzky,
> "Lasting Impressions: Motifs in Protein-Protein Maps
> May Provide Footprints of Evolutionary Events,"
> *Proceedings of the National Academy of Sciences*

Delineating the boundaries or limitations of a study is a good way to agree up to a point. Here are templates for doing so:

▸ While X's work clearly demonstrates _____, _____ will be required before we can determine whether _____.

▸ Although Y and Z present firm evidence for _____, their data cannot be used to argue that _____.

▸ In summary, our studies show that _____, but the issue of _____ remains unresolved.

Anticipate Objections

Skepticism is a key ingredient in the scientific process. Before an explanation is accepted, scientists demand convincing evidence and assess whether alternative explanations have been thoroughly explored, so it's essential that scientists consider possible objections to their ideas before presenting them. In the following example from a book about the origin of the universe, Tyson and Goldsmith first admit that some might doubt the existence of the poorly understood "dark matter" that physicists have proposed, and then they go on to respond to the skeptics:

> Unrelenting skeptics might compare the dark matter of today with the hypothetical, now defunct "ether," proposed centuries ago as the weightless, transparent medium through which light moved. . . . But dark matter ignorance differs fundamentally from ether ignorance. While ether amounted to a placeholder for our incomplete understanding, the existence of dark matter derives not from mere presumption but from the observed effects of its gravity on visible matter.
>
> N. D. Tyson and D. Goldsmith,
Origins: Fourteen Billion Years of Cosmic Evolution

Anticipating objections in your own writing will help you clarify and address potential criticisms. Consider objections to your overall approach, as well as to specific aspects of your interpretations. Here are some templates for doing so:

▸ Scientists who take a _____ (*reductionist / integrative / biochemical / computational / statistical*) approach might view our results differently.

▶ This interpretation of the data might be criticized by X, who has argued that _____.

▶ Some may argue that this experimental design fails to account for _____.

Say Why It Matters

Though individual studies can be narrowly focused, science ultimately seeks to answer big questions and produce useful technologies. So it's essential when you enter a scientific conversation to say why the work—and your arguments about it—matter. The following passage from a commentary on a research article notes two implications of work that evaluated the shape of electron orbitals:

> The classic textbook shape of electron orbitals has now been directly observed. As well as confirming the established theory, this work may be a first step to understanding high-temperature superconductivity.
>
> C. J. HUMPHREYS, "Electrons Seen in Orbit," *Nature*

Humphreys argues that the study confirms an established theory and that it may lead to better understanding in another area. When thinking about the broad significance of a study, consider both the practical applications and the impact on future scientific work:

▶ These results open the door to studies that _____.

▶ The methodologies developed by X will be useful for _____.

▶ Our findings are the first step toward _____.

▸ **Further work in this area may lead to the development of**
_____ .

READING AS A WAY OF ENTERING
SCIENTIFIC CONVERSATIONS

In science, as in other disciplines, you'll often start with work done by others, and therefore you will need to critically evaluate their work. To that end, you'll need to probe how well their data support their interpretations. Doing so will lead you toward your own interpretations—your ticket into an ongoing scientific conversation. Here are some questions that will help you read and respond to scientific research:

How well do the methods test the hypothesis?

- Is the sample size adequate?
- Is the experimental design valid? Were the proper controls performed?
- What are the limitations of the methodology?
- Are other techniques available?

How fairly have the results been interpreted?

- How well do the results support the stated conclusion?
- Has the data's variability been adequately considered?
- Do other findings verify (or contradict) the conclusion?
- What other experiments could test the conclusion?

What are the broader implications of the work, and why does it matter?

- Can the results be generalized beyond the system that was studied?

- What are the work's practical implications?

- What questions arise from the work?

- Which experiments should be done next?

The examples in this chapter show that scientists do more than simply collect facts; they also interpret those facts and make arguments about their meaning. On the frontiers of science, where we are probing questions that are just beyond our capacity to answer, the data are inevitably incomplete and controversy is to be expected. Writing about science presents the opportunity to add your own arguments to the ongoing discussion.

EIGHTEEN

"ANALYZE THIS"

Writing in the Social Sciences

ERIN ACKERMAN

———————

SOCIAL SCIENCE is the study of people—how they behave and relate to one another, and the organizations and institutions that facilitate these interactions. People are complicated, so any study of human behavior is at best partial, taking into account some elements of what people do and why, but not always explaining those actions definitively. As a result, it is the subject of constant conversation and argument.

Consider some of the topics studied in the social sciences: minimum wage laws, immigration policy, health care, what causes aggressive behavior, employment discrimination. Got an opinion on any of these topics? You aren't alone. But in the writing you do as a student of the social sciences, you need to write about more

———————

ERIN ACKERMAN is the social sciences librarian at the College of New Jersey and formerly taught political science at John Jay College, City University of New York. Her research and teaching interests include American law and politics, women and law, and information literacy in the social sciences.

than just your opinions. Good writing in the social sciences, as in other academic disciplines, requires that you demonstrate that you have examined what you think and why. The best way to do that is to bring your views into conversation with those expressed by others and to test what you and others think against a review of evidence. In other words, you'll need to start with what others say and then present what you say as a response.

Consider the following example from an op-ed in the *New York Times* by two psychology professors:

> Is video game addiction a real thing?
>
> It's certainly common to hear parents complain that their children are "addicted" to video games. Some researchers even claim that these games are comparable to illegal drugs in terms of their influence on the brain—that they are "digital heroin" (the neuroscientist Peter C. Whybrow) or "digital pharmakeia" (the neuroscientist Andrew Doan). The American Psychiatric Association has identified internet gaming disorder as a possible psychiatric illness, and the World Health Organization has proposed including "gaming disorder" in its catalog of mental diseases, along with drug and alcohol addiction.
>
> This is all terribly misguided. Playing video games is not addictive in any meaningful sense. It is normal behavior that, while perhaps in many cases a waste of time, is not damaging or disruptive of lives in the way drug or alcohol use can be.
>
> Christopher J. Ferguson and Patrick Markey,
"Video Games Aren't Addictive"

In other words, "they" (parents, other researchers, health organizations) say that the video games are addictive, whereas Ferguson and Markey disagree. In the rest of the op-ed, they argue that video game critics have misinterpreted the evidence and are not being very precise with what counts as "addiction."

This chapter explores some of the basic moves social science writers make. Writing in the social sciences often takes the form of a research paper that generally includes several core components: a strong introduction and thesis, a literature review, and the writer's own analysis, including presentation of evidence/data and consideration of implications. The introduction sets out the thesis, or point, of the paper, briefly explaining the topic or question you are investigating and previewing what you will say in your paper and how it fits into the preexisting conversation. The literature review summarizes what has already been said on your topic. Your analysis allows you to present evidence (the information, or data, about human behavior that you are measuring or testing against what other people have said), to explain the conclusions you have drawn based on your investigation, and to discuss the implications of your research. Do you agree, disagree, or some combination of both with what has been said by others? What reasons can you give for why you feel that way? And so what? Who should be interested in what you have to say, and why?

You may get other types of writing assignments in the social sciences, such as preparing a policy memo, writing a legal brief, or designing a grant or research proposal. While there may be differences from the research papers in terms of the format and audience for these assignments, the purposes of sections of the research paper and the moves discussed here will help you with those assignments as well.

THE INTRODUCTION AND THESIS: "THIS PAPER CHALLENGES . . ."

Your introduction sets forth what you plan to say in your essay. You might evaluate the work of earlier scholars or certain widely held assumptions and find them incorrect when measured against new events or data. Alternatively, you might point out that an author's work is largely correct but that it could use some qualifications or be extended in some way. Or you might identify a gap in our knowledge—we know a great deal about topic X but almost nothing about some other closely related topic. In each of these instances, your introduction needs to cover both "they say" and "I say" perspectives. If you stop after the "they say," your readers won't know what you are bringing to the conversation. Similarly, if you were to jump right to the "I say" portion of your argument, readers might wonder why you need to say anything at all.

Sometimes you join the conversation at a point where the discussion seems settled. One or more views about a topic have become so widely accepted among a group of scholars or society at large that these views are essentially the conventional way of thinking about the topic. You may wish to offer new reasons to support this interpretation, or you may wish to call these standard views into question. To do so, you must first introduce and identify these widely held beliefs and then present your own view. In fact, much of the writing in the social sciences takes the form of calling into question that which we think we already know. Consider the following example from an article in the *Journal of Economic Perspectives*:

> Fifteen years ago, Milton Friedman's 1957 treatise A *Theory of the Consumption Function* seemed badly dated. Dynamic optimization theory had not been employed much in economics when Friedman wrote, and utility theory was still comparatively primitive, so his statement of the "permanent income hypothesis" never actually specified a formal mathematical model of behavior derived explicitly from utility maximization. . . . [W]hen other economists subsequently

found multiperiod maximizing models that could be solved explicitly, the implications of those models differed sharply from Friedman's intuitive description of his "model." Furthermore, empirical tests in the 1970s and 1980s often rejected these rigorous versions of the permanent income hypothesis in favor of an alternative hypothesis that many households simply spent all of their current income.

Today, with the benefit of a further round of mathematical (and computational) advances, Friedman's (1957) original analysis looks more prescient than primitive.

CHRISTOPHER D. CARROLL, "A Theory of Consumption Function, with and without Liquidity Constraints," *Journal of Economic Perspectives*

This introduction makes clear that Carroll will defend Milton Friedman against some major criticisms of his work. Carroll mentions what has been said about Friedman's work and then goes on to say that the critiques turn out to be wrong and to suggest that Friedman's work reemerges as persuasive. A template of Carroll's introduction might look something like this: "Economics research in the last fifteen years suggested Friedman's 1957 treatise was _____ because _____. In other words, they say that Friedman's work is not accurate because of _____, _____, and _____. Recent research convinces me, however, that Friedman's work makes sense."

In some cases, however, there may not be a strong consensus among experts on a topic. You might enter the ongoing debate by casting your vote with one side or another or by offering an alternative view. In the following example, Sheri Berman identifies two competing accounts of how to explain world events in the twentieth century and then puts forth a third view:

Conventional wisdom about twentieth-century ideologies rests on two simple narratives. One focuses on the struggle for dominance between democracy and its alternatives. . . . The other narrative focuses on the competition between free-market capitalism and its rivals. . . . Both of these narratives obviously contain some truth. . . . Yet both only tell part of the story, which is why their common conclusion—neoliberalism as the "end of History"—is unsatisfying and misleading.

What the two conventional narratives fail to mention is that a third struggle was also going on: between those ideologies that believed in the primacy of economics and those that believed in the primacy of politics.

SHERI BERMAN, "The Primacy of Economics versus the Primacy of Politics: Understanding the Ideological Dynamics of the Twentieth Century," *Perspectives on Politics*

After identifying the two competing narratives, Berman suggests a third view—and later goes on to argue that this third view explains current debates over globalization. A template for this type of introduction might look something like this: "In recent discussions of _____, a controversial aspect has been _____. On the one hand, some argue that _____. On the other hand, others argue that _____. Neither of these arguments, however, considers the alternative view that _____."

Given the complexity of many of the issues studied in the social sciences, however, you may sometimes agree *and* disagree with existing views—pointing out things that you believe are correct or have merit, while disagreeing with or refining other points. In the example below, anthropologist Sally Engle Merry agrees with another scholar about something that is a key trait of modern society but argues that this trait has a different origin than the other author identifies:

For more on different ways of responding, see Chapter 4.

Although I agree with Rose that an increasing emphasis on governing the soul is characteristic of modern society, I see the transformation not as evolutionary but as the product of social mobilization and political struggle.

> SALLY ENGLE MERRY, "Rights, Religion, and Community: Approaches to Violence against Women in the Context of Globalization," *Law and Society Review*

Here are some templates for agreeing and disagreeing:

- ▶ **Although I agree with X up to a point, I cannot accept his overall conclusion that _____ .**

- ▶ **Although I disagree with X on _____ and _____ , I agree with her conclusion that _____ .**

- ▶ **Political scientists studying _____ have argued that it is caused by _____ . While _____ contributes to the problem, _____ is also an important factor.**

- ▶ **While noting _____ , I contend _____ .**

In the process of examining people from different angles, social scientists sometimes identify gaps—areas that have not been explored in previous research.

In the following example, several sociologists identify such a gap:

Family scholars have long argued that the study of dating deserves more attention (Klemer, 1971), as dating is an important part of the life course at any age and often a precursor to marriage (Levesque & Caron, 2004). . . .

The central research questions we seek to answer with this study are whether and how the significance of particular dating rituals are patterned by gender and race simultaneously. We use a racially diverse data set of traditional-aged college students from a variety of college contexts. Understanding gender and racial differences in the assessment of dating rituals helps us explore the extent to which relationship activities are given similar importance across institutional and cultural lines. Most of the studies that inform our knowledge of dating and relationships are unable to draw conclusions regarding racial differences because the sample is Caucasian (e.g., Bogle, 2008), or primarily so (e.g., Manning & Smock, 2005). Race has been recently argued to be an often-overlooked variable in studies examining social psychological processes because of the prevalence of sample limitations as well as habitual oversight in the literature (Hunt, Jackson, Powell, & Steelman, 2000). Additionally, a failure to examine both gender and race prevents assessment of whether gendered beliefs are shared across groups. Gauging the extent of differences in beliefs among different population sub-groups is critical to advancing the study of relationship dynamics (see Weaver & Ganong, 2004).

PAMELA BRABOY JACKSON, SIBYL KLEINER, CLAUDIA GEIST, AND KARA CEBULKO, "Conventions of Courtship: Gender and Race Differences in the Significance of Dating Rituals," *Journal of Family Issues*

Jackson and her coauthors note that while other scholars have said that studying dating is important and have examined some aspects of dating, we have little information about whether attitudes about dating activities (such as sexual intimacy, gift exchange, and meeting the family) vary across groups by gender and race. Their study aims to fill this gap in our understanding of relationships.

Here are some templates for introducing gaps in the existing research:

- Studies of X have indicated _____. It is not clear, however, that this conclusion applies to _____.

- _____ often take for granted that _____. Few have investigated this assumption, however.

- X's work tells us a great deal about _____. Can this work be generalized to _____?

- Our understanding of _____ remains incomplete because previous work has not examined _____.

Again, a good introduction indicates what you have to say in the larger context of what others have said. Throughout the rest of your paper, you will move back and forth between the "they say" and the "I say," adding more details.

THE LITERATURE REVIEW: "PRIOR RESEARCH INDICATES . . ."

The point of a literature review is to establish the state of knowledge on your topic. Before you (and your reader) can properly consider an issue, you need to understand the conversation about your topic that has already taken place (and is likely still in progress). In the literature review, you explain what "they say" in more detail, summarizing, paraphrasing, or quoting the viewpoints to which you are responding. But you need to balance what they are saying with your own focus. You need to characterize someone else's work fairly and accurately

but set up the points you yourself want to make by selecting the details that are relevant to your own perspective and
observations.

It is common in the social sciences to summarize several
arguments in a single paragraph or even a single sentence,
grouping several sources together by their important ideas or
other attributes. The example below cites some key findings
and conclusions of psychological research that should be of
interest to motivated college students looking to improve their
academic performance:

> Some people may associate sacrificing hours of sleep with being
> studious, but the reality is that sleep deprivation can hurt your
> cognitive functioning without your being aware of it (e.g., becom-
> ing worse at paying attention and remembering things; Goel, Rao,
> Durmer, & Dinges, 2009; Pilcher & Walters, 1997).... Sleep affects
> learning and memory by organizing and consolidating memories
> from the day (Diekelmann & Born, 2010; Rasch & Born, 2013),
> which can lead to better problem-solving ability and creativity
> (Verleger, Rose, Wagner, Yordanova, & Kolev, 2013).
>
> ADAM L. PUTNAM, VICTOR W. SUNGKHASETTEE, AND
> HENRY L. ROEDIGER, III, "Optimizing Learning in College:
> Tips from Cognitive Psychology," *Perspectives on
> Psychological Science*

A template for this paragraph might look like this: "Students
believe _____, but researchers disagree because _____.
According to researchers, negative consequences of sleep deprivation include _____. The research shows that a positive
effect of sleep is _____, which improves _____."

Such summaries are brief, bringing together relevant
arguments by several scholars to provide an overview of

scholarly work on a particular topic. In writing such a summary, you need to ask yourself how the authors themselves might describe their positions and also consider what in their work is relevant for the point you wish to make. This kind of summary is especially appropriate when you have a large amount of research material on a topic and want to identify the major strands of a debate or to show how the work of one author builds on that of another. Here are some templates for overview summaries:

▸ In addressing the question of _____, researchers have considered several explanations for _____. X argues that _____. According to Y and Z, another plausible explanation is _____.

▸ What is the effect of _____ on _____? Previous work on _____ by X and by Y and Z supports _____.

▸ Scholars point to the role of _____ in _____.

▸ Existing research on _____ presents convincing evidence of _____.

Sometimes you may need to say more about the works you cite. On a midterm or final exam, for example, you may need to demonstrate that you have a deep familiarity with a particular work. And in some disciplines of the social sciences, longer, more detailed literature reviews are the standard. Your instructor and any assigned articles are your best guides for the length and level of detail of your literature review. Other times, the work of certain authors is especially important for your argument, and therefore you need to provide more details to explain what these authors have said. See how political scientists Hahrie Han and Lisa Argyle, in a report for the Ford Foundation, summarize an argument that is central to their investigation of improving democratic participation:

> [A]t the root of declining rates of participation is the sense that people do not feel like their participation matters. People do not feel like they have any real reason or opportunity to exercise voice in the political process. People's sense of agency is in decline, especially given negative or incomplete experiences of government in their lives.
>
> This lack of caring comes as no surprise when we examine research showing that most people have negative or, at best, incomplete experiences of the role of government in their lives. Suzanne Mettler, for instance, finds that many middle-class people who benefit from different government programs—ranging from education savings accounts to welfare to tax credits—believe that they "have not used a government social program." In addition, other scholars find a trend towards increasing privatization of public goods and political processes in the twenty-first century. As a result, government is what Mettler calls a "submerged state," since the role of government in people's lives is effectively submerged from view.
>
> HAHRIE HAN AND LISA ARGYLE, "A Program Review of the Promoting Electoral Reform and Democratic Participation (PERDP) Initiative of the Ford Foundation"

Note that Han and Argyle start by identifying the broad problem of lack of participation and then explain how Mettler's work describes how middle-class people may be unaware of the role of government in their lives, leading Mettler to argue for the idea of the "submerged state."

You may want to include direct quotations of what others have said, as Han and Argyle do. Using exact words helps you demonstrate that you are representing the author fairly. But you cannot simply insert a quotation; you need to explain to your readers what it means for your point. Consider the following example drawn from a political science book on the debate over tort reform:

> The essence of *agenda setting* was well enunciated by E. E. Schattschneider: "In politics as in everything else, it makes a great difference whose game we play" (1960, 47). In short, the ability to define or control the rules, terms, or perceived options in a contest over policy greatly affects the prospects for winning.
>
> WILLIAM HALTOM AND MICHAEL McCANN,
Distorting the Law: Politics, Media, and the Litigation Crisis

Notice how Haltom and McCann first quote Schattschneider and then explain in their own words how political agenda setting can be thought of as a game, with winners and losers.

Remember that whenever you summarize, quote, or paraphrase the work of others, credit must be given in the form of a citation to the original work. The words may be your own, but if the idea comes from someone else you must give credit to the original work. There are several formats for documenting sources. Consult your instructor for help choosing which citation style to use.

THE ANALYSIS

The literature review covers what others have said on your topic. The analysis allows you to present and support your own response. In the introduction you indicate whether you agree, disagree, or some combination of both with what others have said. You will want to expand on how you have formed your opinion and why others should care about your topic.

"The Data Indicate . . ."

The social sciences use evidence to develop and test explanations. This evidence is often referred to as data. Data can be quantitative or qualitative and can come from a number of sources. You might use statistics related to GDP growth, unemployment, voting rates, or demographics. You might report results from an experiment or simulation. Or you could use surveys, interviews, or other first-person accounts.

Regardless of the type of data used, it is important to do three things: define your data, indicate where you got the data, and then say what you have done with your data. For a chapter in their book assessing media coverage of female candidates, political scientists Danny Hayes and Jennifer Lawless explain how they assembled a data set:

> From the perspective of campaign professionals and voters, local newspaper coverage remains the most important news source during House campaigns....
>
> We began by selecting the appropriate newspaper for each House race in 2010 and 2014.... [W]e identified every news story during the thirty days leading up to the election that mentioned at least one of the two major-party candidates....
>
> Our data collection efforts produced 10,375 stories about 1,550 candidates who received at least some local news coverage in either the 2010 or 2014 midterms....
>
> Coders read the full text of each article and recorded several pieces of information. First, they tracked the number of times a candidate's sex or gender was mentioned.... Second, we recorded the number of explicit references to candidate traits, both positive and negative (e.g., "capable" and "ineffective")....
>
> Third, we tracked every time an issue was mentioned in connection with a candidate.... We then classified issues in two ways:

(1) We assigned each issue to one of the eight broad categories... and (2) we classified a subset of the topics as "women's" or "men's" issues.

> DANNY HAYES AND JENNIFER L. LAWLESS, *Women on the Run: Gender, Media, and Political Campaigns in a Polarized Era*

Hayes and Lawless explain how they collected their data—local newspaper coverage of congressional candidates—and explain how they coded and classified the coverage to allow them to perform statistical analysis of the news pieces. While you probably won't collect 10,000-plus news items for a class project, you could collect information (such as media coverage, interview responses, or legal briefs) and analyze and sort them to identify patterns such as repeated words and ideas.

If your data are quantitative, you also need to explain them. Sociologist Jonathan Horowitz's research concludes that job quality influences personal assessments of well-being by "improving social life, altering class identification, affecting physical health, and increasing amounts of leisure time." See how he introduces the data he analyzes:

> In this study, I use data from the General Social Survey (GSS) and structural equation modeling to test relationships between job quality and subjective well-being. The GSS is a nationally representative sample of adults in the United States that asks a large number of questions about experiences at work (Smith et al., 2010). In particular, the GSS introduced a new battery of questions titled "Quality of Working Life" in 2002 (and repeated in 2006 and 2010) which includes multiple questions about several job quality dimensions.
>
> JONATHAN HOROWITZ, "Dimensions of Job Quality, Mechanisms, and Subjective Well-Being in the United States," *Sociological Forum*

Here are some templates for discussing data:

▸ In order to test the hypothesis that _____, we assessed _____. Our calculations suggest _____.

▸ I used _____ to investigate _____. The results of this investigation indicate _____.

"But Others May Object . . ."

No matter how strongly your data support your argument, there are almost surely other perspectives (and thus other data) that you need to acknowledge. By considering possible objections to your argument and taking them seriously, you demonstrate that you've done your work and that you're aware of other perspectives—and most important, you present your own argument as part of an ongoing conversation.

See p. 408 for a selection from *The New Jim Crow.*   See how law professor Michelle Alexander acknowledges that there may be objections to her argument describing trends in mass incarceration as "the new Jim Crow."

> Some might argue that as disturbing as this system appears to be, there is nothing particularly new about mass incarceration; it is merely a continuation of past drug wars and biased law enforcement practices. Racial bias in our criminal justice system is simply an old problem that has gotten worse, and the social excommunication of "criminals" has a long history; it is not a recent invention. There is some merit to this argument.
>
> MICHELLE ALEXANDER, *The New Jim Crow: Mass Incarceration in the Age of Colorblindness*

Alexander imagines a conversation with people who might be skeptical about her argument, particularly her claim that this represents a "new" development. And she responds that they are correct, to a point. After acknowledging her agreement with the assessment of historical racial bias in the criminal justice system, she goes on in the rest of her chapter to explain that the expanded scope and consequences of contemporary mass incarceration have caused dramatic differences in society.

Someone may object because there are related phenomena that your analysis does not explain or because you do not have the right data to investigate a particular question. Or perhaps someone may object to assumptions underlying your argument or how you handled your data. Here are some templates for considering naysayers:

▸ _____ might object that _____.

▸ Is my claim realistic? I have argued _____, but readers may question _____.

▸ My explanation accounts for _____ but does not explain _____. This is because _____.

"Why Should We Care?"

Who should care about your research, and why? Since the social sciences attempt to explain human behavior, it is important to consider how your research affects the assumptions we make about human behavior. In addition, you might offer recommendations for how other social scientists might continue to explore an issue, or what actions policy makers should take.

In the following example, sociologist Devah Pager identifies the implications of her study of the way having a criminal record affects a person applying for jobs:

> [I]n terms of policy implications, this research has troubling conclusions. In our frenzy of locking people up, our "crime control"

policies may in fact exacerbate the very conditions that lead to crime in the first place. Research consistently shows that finding quality steady employment is one of the strongest predictors of desistance from crime (Shover 1996; Sampson and Laub 1993; Uggen 2000). The fact that a criminal record severely limits employment opportunities—particularly among blacks—suggests that these individuals are left with few viable alternatives.

> DEVAH PAGER, "The Mark of a Criminal Record,"
> *American Journal of Sociology*

Pager's conclusion that a criminal record negatively affects employment chances creates a vicious circle, she says: steady employment discourages recidivism, but a criminal record makes it harder to get a job.

In answering the "so what?" question, you need to explain why your readers should care. Although sometimes the implications of your work may be so broad that they would be of interest to almost anyone, it's never a bad idea to identify explicitly any groups of people who will find your work important.

Templates for establishing why your claims matter:

▸ **X is important because _____.**

▸ **Ultimately, what is at stake here is _____.**

▸ **The finding that _____ should be of interest to _____ because _____.**

As noted at the beginning of this chapter, the complexity of people allows us to look at their behavior from many different viewpoints. Much has been, and will be, said about how and why people do the things they do. As a result, we can look at writing in the social sciences as an ongoing conversation. When you join this conversation, the "they say / I say" framework will help you figure out what has already been said ("they say") and what you can add ("I say"). The components of social science writing presented in this chapter are tools to help you join that conversation.

READINGS

NINETEEN

WHY CARE ABOUT THE PLANET?

THESE DAYS, it's practically a cliché to care about the planet, like respecting one's parents or helping an old person cross the street. In fact, we hear so often about the precarious state of the planet that some of us may begin to tune out the messages as so much background noise. Just check out the news stories on almost any day: scientists raise the possibility of environmental disaster and predict a bleak future unless we reverse course immediately—if it isn't already too late. They remind us that the clean water and air on which we depend is threatened by industrial pollution and fracking. They point out that densely populated coastal areas could go underwater as sea levels rise due to rapidly melting polar ice caps. And they worry that we face the prospect of withered crops and water shortages as temperatures go up and rainfall declines. Activists urge us to do more, learn more, care more.

With all these potential catastrophes looming, could anyone seriously argue that we *shouldn't* care about the state of our planet? Well, not exactly. After all, the overwhelming majority of climate scientists analyze the data and show that the threat is urgent. But some critics of these projections suggest that concerns about the planet are exaggerated, that the situation isn't as dire as activists argue, that changes in temperature are a natural phenomenon not proven to be affected by human activity, or that policies meant to limit climate change could damage the economy and reduce our standard of living.

Where does all this discussion and debate leave us? Right now, we seem to be in a holding pattern, which many would surely describe more negatively as a state of paralysis, indecision, or denial. But understanding what's actually going on with the planet and what humans can do about it is a difficult undertaking indeed. For those of us who are nonscientists, we struggle to figure out the meaning of a mountain of complex technical data produced, analyzed, and explained to us by an array of experts representing different areas of expertise. We also struggle to decide—as people thinking about our future, as citizens desiring to take a constructive position, as residents of the planet whose fate is linked to our own—just what to think and what to do, given all the scientific studies and their political, economic, and policy implications.

The readings in this chapter offer a wealth of information and a variety of perspectives on environmental issues facing us today. Professor, author, and activist Naomi Klein provides evidence that climate change is already disrupting the planet in dangerous ways and is likely to get worse unless serious measures are taken; she praises youthful climate activists and supports the Green New Deal proposal. In contrast, Dan Crenshaw, a Republican congressman from Texas, while acknowledging the reality of climate change, critiques the large-scale changes proposed by progressives and offers a more measured, business-oriented set of proposals. Alice Chen and Vivek Murthy, distinguished physicians and leaders of major medical organizations, acknowledge the dangers of climate change but offer a more optimistic view of potential remedies, some of which are already under way.

Several readings examine ways in which poor people with little political clout suffer disproportionately from the impact of pollution and other environmental problems. Physician and researcher Mona Hanna-Attisha and her team of scientists analyze the disastrous effects of high levels of lead in drinking water of residents of Flint, Michigan, particularly on minority children in the city's poorest neighborhoods. Public health expert Michael R. Greenberg, in a response to Hanna-Attisha and colleagues, points out other areas of the United States that have recently experienced similar crises of lead poisoning from drinking water to make a larger point about the nation's crumbling infrastructure and the goal of environmental justice.

Other essays in this chapter deal with the effects of common consumer items on the environment. Marine life researcher and author Charles Moore discusses the dangers of plastic trash "choking the oceans," killing millions of sea creatures annually, and he argues that we must reduce the amount of plastic trash substantially or face long-term consequences to the health of the earth's waters. Reporter Ben Adler supports Moore's view of the dangers of plastic trash proliferation but goes on to argue that the solution of eliminating use of plastic grocery bags will have minimal if any effect on this crisis. Other, larger solutions are needed in his view. Finally, echoing calls from Indigenous peoples throughout the United States and around the world, Hawaiian college student Sandis Edward Waialae Wightman writes opposing construction of a large, extremely powerful telescope station atop the Mauna Kea, a dormant volcano long considered a sacred space by Hawaiians.

Reading the essays in this chapter and those in the accompanying *"They Say / I Blog"* will help you develop your own understanding of environmental issues now facing the planet. And you will have the opportunity to make your own contribution to this critically important discussion.

"We Are the Wildfire"
How to Fight the Climate Crisis

NAOMI KLEIN

—▭—

ON A FRIDAY IN MID-MARCH, they streamed out of schools in little rivulets, burbling with excitement and defiance at an act of truancy. The little streams emptied on to grand avenues and boulevards, where they combined with other flows of chanting children and teens. Soon the rivulets were rushing rivers: 100,000 bodies in Milan, 40,000 in Paris, 150,000 in Montreal. Cardboard signs bobbed above the surf of humanity: THERE IS NO PLANET B! DON'T BURN OUR FUTURE. THE HOUSE IS ON FIRE!

There was no student strike in Mozambique; on 15 March the whole country was bracing for the impact of Cyclone Idai,

---

NAOMI KLEIN, an award-winning journalist and author, is the inaugural Gloria Steinem Endowed Chair in Media, Culture, and Feminist Studies at Rutgers University. Cofounder of the climate justice organization The Leap, Klein is the author of several books, including *No Logo* (2000), *The Shock Doctrine* (2007), *This Changes Everything* (2014), and *No Is Not Enough* (2017). This selection, published in the *Guardian*, is excerpted from the introduction to her most recent book, *On Fire: The (Burning) Case for a Green New Deal* (2019).

one of the worst storms in Africa's history, which drove people to take refuge at the tops of trees as the waters rose and would eventually kill more than 1,000 people. And then, just six weeks later, while it was still clearing the rubble, Mozambique would be hit by Cyclone Kenneth, yet another record-breaking storm.

Wherever in the world they live, this generation has something in common: they are the first for whom climate disruption on a planetary scale is not a future threat, but a lived reality. Oceans are warming 40% faster than the United Nations predicted five years ago. And a sweeping study on the state of the Arctic, published in April 2019 in Environmental Research Letters and led by the renowned glaciologist Jason Box, found that ice in various forms is melting so rapidly that the "Arctic biophysical system is now clearly trending away from its 20th-century state and into an unprecedented state, with implications not only within but also beyond the Arctic." In May 2019, the United Nations' Intergovernmental Science-Policy Platform on Biodiversity and Ecosystem Services published a report about the startling loss of wildlife around the world, warning that a million species of animals and plants are at risk of extinction. "The health of ecosystems on which we and all other species depend is deteriorating more rapidly than ever," said the chair, Robert Watson. "We are eroding the very foundations of economies, livelihoods, food security, health and quality of life worldwide. We have lost time. We must act now."

It has been more than three decades since governments and scientists started officially meeting to discuss the need to lower greenhouse gas emissions to avoid the dangers of climate breakdown. In the intervening years, we have heard countless appeals for action that involve "the children," "the grandchildren," and "generations to come." Yet global CO_2 emissions have risen by more than 40%, and they continue to rise. The planet has warmed by about 1C since we began burning coal on an industrial scale and average temperatures are on track to rise by as much as four times that amount before the century is up; the last time there was this much CO_2 in the atmosphere, humans didn't exist.

As for those children and grandchildren and generations to come who were invoked so promiscuously? They are no longer mere rhetorical devices. They are now speaking (and screaming, and striking) for themselves. Unlike so many adults in positions of authority, they have not yet been trained to mask the unfathomable stakes of our moment in the language of bureaucracy and overcomplexity. They understand that they are fighting for the fundamental right to live full lives—lives in which they are not, as 13-year-old Alexandria Villaseñor puts it, "running from disasters."

On that day in March 2019, organizers estimate there were nearly 2,100 youth climate strikes in 125 countries, with 1.6 million young people participating. That's quite an achievement for a movement that began eight months earlier with a single teenager deciding to go on strike from school in Stockholm, Sweden: Greta Thunberg.

The wave of youth mobilization that burst on to the scene in March 2019 is not just the result of one girl and her unique way of seeing the world, extraordinary though she is. Thunberg is quick to note that she was inspired by another group of teenagers who rose up against a different kind of failure to protect their futures: the students in Parkland, Florida, who led a national wave of class walkouts demanding tough controls on gun ownership after 17 people were murdered at their school in February 2018.

Nor is Thunberg the first person with tremendous moral clarity to yell "Fire!" in the face of the climate crisis. Such voices have emerged multiple times over the past several decades; indeed, it is something of a ritual at the annual UN summits on climate change. But perhaps because these earlier voices belonged to people from the Philippines, the Marshall Islands, and South Sudan, those clarion calls were one-day stories, if that. Thunberg is also quick to point out that the climate strikes themselves were the work of thousands of diverse student leaders, their teachers, and supporting organizations, many of whom had been raising the climate alarm for years.

As a manifesto put out by British climate strikers put it: "Greta Thunberg may have been the spark, but we're the wildfire."

For a decade and a half, ever since reporting from New Orleans with water up to my waist after Hurricane Katrina, I have been trying to figure out what is interfering with humanity's basic survival instinct—why so many of us aren't acting as if our house is on fire when it so clearly is. I have written books, made films, delivered countless talks, and co-founded an organization (The Leap) devoted, in one way or another, to exploring this question and trying to help align our collective response to the scale of the climate crisis.

See Chapter 5 on effective ways to use "I."

It was clear to me from the start that the dominant theories about how we had landed on this knife edge were entirely insufficient. We were failing to act, it was said, because politicians were trapped in short-term electoral cycles, or because climate change seemed too far off, or because stopping it was too expensive, or because the clean technologies weren't there yet. There was some truth in all the explanations, but they were also becoming markedly less true over time. The crisis wasn't far off; it was banging down our doors. The price of solar panels has plummeted and now rivals that of fossil fuels. Clean tech and renewables create far more jobs than coal, oil, and gas. As for the supposedly prohibitive costs, trillions have been marshaled for endless wars, bank bailouts, and subsidies for fossil fuels, in the same years that coffers have been virtually empty for climate transition. There had to be more to it.

Which is why, over the years, I have set out to probe a different set of barriers—some economic, some ideological, but others related to the deep stories about the right of certain people to dominate land and the people living closest to it, stories that underpin contemporary western culture. And I have investigated the kinds of responses that might succeed in toppling those narratives, ideologies, and economic interests, responses that weave seemingly disparate crises (economic, social, ecological, and democratic) into a common story of civilizational transformation. Today, this sort of bold vision increasingly goes under the banner of a Green New Deal.

Because, as deep as our crisis runs, something equally deep is also shifting, and with a speed that startles me. Social movements rising up to declare, from below, a people's emergency. In addition to the wildfire of student strikes, we have seen the rise of Extinction Rebellion, which kicked off a wave of nonviolent direct action and civil disobedience, including a mass shutdown of large parts of central London. Within days of its most dramatic actions in April 2019, Wales and Scotland both declared a state of "climate emergency," and the British parliament, under pressure from opposition parties, quickly followed suit.

In the US, we have seen the meteoric rise of the Sunrise Movement, which burst on to the political stage when it occupied the office of Nancy Pelosi, the most powerful Democrat in Washington, DC, one week after her party had won back the House of Representatives in the 2018 midterm elections.

They called on Congress to immediately adopt a rapid decarbonization framework, one as ambitious in speed and scope as Franklin D Roosevelt's New Deal, the sweeping package of policies designed to battle the poverty of the Great Depression and the ecological collapse of the Dust Bowl.

The idea behind the Green New Deal is a simple one: in the process of transforming the infrastructure of our societies at the speed and scale that scientists have called for, humanity has a once-in-a-century chance to fix an economic model that is failing the majority of people on multiple fronts. Because the factors that are destroying our planet are also destroying people's lives in many other ways, from wage stagnation to gaping inequalities to crumbling services to surging white supremacy to the collapse of our information ecology. Challenging underlying forces is an opportunity to solve several interlocking crises at once.

In tackling the climate crisis, we can create hundreds of millions of good jobs around the world, invest in the most systematically excluded communities and nations, guarantee healthcare and childcare, and much more. The result of these transformations would be economies built both to protect and to regenerate the planet's life support systems and to respect and sustain the people who depend on them.

This vision is not new; its origins can be traced to social movements in ecologically ravaged parts of Ecuador and Nigeria, as well as to highly polluted communities of color in the United States. What is new is that there is now a bloc of politicians in the US, Europe, and elsewhere, some just a decade older than the young climate activists in the streets, ready to translate the urgency of the climate crisis into policy, and to connect the dots among the multiple crises of our times. Most prominent among this new political breed is Alexandria Ocasio-Cortez, who, at 29, became the youngest woman ever elected to the US Congress. Introducing a Green New Deal was part of the platform she ran on. Today, with the race to lead the Democratic party in full swing, a majority of leading presidential hopefuls claim to support it, including Bernie Sanders, Elizabeth Warren, Kamala Harris, and Cory Booker. It had been endorsed, meanwhile, by 105 members of the House and Senate.

The idea is spreading around the world, with the political coalition European Spring launching a green new deal for Europe in January 2019 and a broad green new deal coalition of organizations in Canada coming together (the leader of the New Democratic party has adopted the frame, if not its full ambition, as one of his policy planks). The same is true in the UK, where the Labour party is in the middle of negotiations over whether to adopt a green new deal-style platform.

Those of us who advocate for this kind of transformative platform are sometimes accused of using it to advance a socialist or anticapitalist agenda that predates our focus on the climate crisis. My response is a simple one. For my entire adult life, I have been involved in movements confronting the myriad ways that our current economic systems grind up people's lives and landscapes in the ruthless pursuit of profit. *No Logo*, published 20 years ago, documented the human and ecological costs of corporate globalization, from the sweatshops of Indonesia to the oil fields of the Niger Delta. I have seen teenage girls treated like machines to make our machines, and mountains and forests turned to trash heaps to get at the oil, coal, and metals beneath.

For more on answering objections, see Chapter 6.

The painful, even lethal, impacts of these practices were impossible to deny; it was simply argued that they were the necessary costs of a system that was creating so much wealth that the benefits would eventually trickle down to improve the lives of nearly everyone on the planet. What has happened instead is that the indifference to life that was expressed in the exploitation of individual workers on factory floors and in the decimation of individual mountains and rivers has instead trickled up to swallow our entire planet, turning fertile lands into salt flats, beautiful islands into rubble, and draining once vibrant reefs of their life and color.

I freely admit that I do not see the climate crisis as separable from the more localized market-generated crises that I have documented over the years; what is different is the scale and scope of the tragedy, with humanity's one and only home now hanging in the balance. I have always had a tremendous sense of urgency about the need to shift to a dramatically more humane economic model. But there is a different quality to that urgency now because it just so happens that we are all alive at the last possible moment when changing course can mean saving lives on a truly unimaginable scale.

Joining the Conversation

1. Naomi Klein is an author and activist who believes that countries throughout the world must work together to combat the climate change crisis. She begins her essay with examples of student protests, followed by descriptions of cyclones in Africa caused by climate change, before presenting her own arguments in subsequent paragraphs. How would you summarize her "they say" and "I say" arguments using the templates on page 42?

2. What evidence and arguments does Klein provide to support her position? Has she convinced you that we should take action against climate change? If so, how and where does she convince you?

3. In paragraph 3, the author quotes experts on climate change. Pick one of these quotes and provide a frame for it, as discussed in Chapter 3. The frame (or "quotation sandwich") should include one sentence describing who is speaking and why, the quote itself, and a follow-up statement explaining the meaning and significance of the quotation.

4. Near the end of the essay, in paragraph 19, the author inserts a naysayer: "Those of us who advocate for this kind of transformative platform are sometimes accused of using it to advance a socialist or anticapitalist agenda that predates our focus on the climate crisis." How effectively does she anticipate objections? How does Klein respond to this potential criticism from naysayers?

5. Write an essay responding to Klein with "they say" and "I say" statements, naysayers, and other argument strategies.

It's Time for Conservatives to Own the Climate-Change Issue

DAN CRENSHAW

THERE IS AN INTERESTING POLITICAL TACTIC often employed by the Left, and it follows a predictable pattern. First, identify a problem most of us can agree on. Second, elevate the problem to a crisis. Third, propose an extreme solution to said crisis that inevitably results in a massive transfer of power to government authorities. Fourth, watch as conservatives take the bait and vociferously reject the extreme solutions proposed. Fifth and finally, accuse those same conservatives of being too heartless or too stupid to solve the original problem on which we all thought we agreed.

DAN CRENSHAW is a member of the US House of Representatives. As a Navy SEAL, he achieved the rank of lieutenant commander and earned two Bronze Star Medals (one with valor), the Purple Heart, and the Navy Commendation Medal with valor. Wounded in Afghanistan, he lost his right eye and retired from the military in 2016. Crenshaw holds an MPA from Harvard University's Kennedy School of Government and is the author of *Fortitude: American Resilience in the Era of Outrage* (2020). This op-ed appeared in the *National Review* on March 3, 2020.

Dan Crenshaw.

This is the pattern we have seen play out with respect to climate change. With ever-more-extreme "solutions" such as the Green New Deal being proposed, conservatives have quickly taken the bait, falling into the tired political trap set by leftists. But I believe we no longer have to do this. We can fight back against the alarmism with tangible solutions based on reason, science, and the free market.

I recently joined House Republican leader Kevin McCarthy in unveiling a proposal that takes existing innovative technologies—ones that have proven to reduce emissions here in the United States—that the U.S. can then market and export to the world. After all, climate change is a *global* issue, and with global energy demand expected to increase by 25 percent over the next 20 years, there is a distinct need for the U.S. to export cleaner energy sources to the developing world, as well as to the biggest CO_2 emitters, such as China and India. Crushing our own economy, as the Green New Deal would have us do, will not stop worldwide growth in emissions or decrease worldwide energy demand.

My portion of the plan—called the New Energy Frontier—focuses specifically on carbon capture, a field in which there is already promising innovation. For instance, the company NET Power, located near my district in Houston, has developed a natural-gas electricity plant that has the capacity to power 5,000 homes, while capturing and recirculating CO_2 back through the plant via an innovative thermodynamic cycle. As a result, the system produces zero net emissions.

The New Energy Frontier devotes existing funds at the Department of Energy (DOE) to the research, development, and deployment of carbon-capture technology, so that these kinds of innovations may then be scaled up. I also propose creating a new "Carbon Utilization Energy Innovation Hub," which will exist within DOE for the sole purpose of exploring how we can make carbon dioxide useful. This hub relies on a bedrock environmental principle: recycling byproducts, in this case CO_2, into a useful commodity. Instead of presuming CO_2 is a waste product, we should think of it as a *commodity* and use the CO_2 that we are extracting from power plants for everything from enhanced oil recovery to cement production to plant growth.

Other parts of the GOP plan include simple improvements to the 45Q tax credit for carbon-capture projects. These would incentivize and reward those in the industry who choose to implement carbon-capture technology. Likewise, the "trillion trees" program assumes a simpler tack by directly encouraging the world to plant more trees, one of the best carbon-capture technologies in world history.

It is long past time for conservatives to point out the flawed reasoning of the radical environmentalists. Their dogmatic obsession with a wind-and-solar-only energy grid leads them to foolishly denounce other sources of carbon-free energy such as nuclear power. They call for a ban on fracking, thus ignoring the massive carbon-reducing effect of natural gas. They also ignore the simple fact that, right now, only fossil fuels can deliver the economic production the world relies upon. As Bill Gates astutely asks those who advocate fiercely for wind and solar, "What's your plan for steel?"

That is why conservatives must make the case for what has *actually worked*. Owing in part to the shale revolution and our emergence as a natural-gas superpower, the U.S. has reduced carbon emissions by around 15 percent since 2005. Contrast that success with countries such as Germany, which dove head-first into renewables with a $580 billion investment, but still saw an increase in per capita emissions. Why? After the self-imposed destruction of its own energy supply, Germany was forced to rely on Russian gas, which has a 40 percent higher carbon footprint than American natural gas. Good intentions and dogmatic obsessions with eliminating fossil fuels have utterly failed the environmental cause, yet activists continue to faithfully cling to them. The notion of "focusing on what works" has been lost in the conversation.

Calls for a carbon tax are similarly misguided. Even if we were to implement a carbon tax, such a policy might inadvertently *increase* emissions as our cleaner, better-regulated American oil-and-gas industry potentially cedes market share to less clean Russian and Saudi producers. At the risk of stating the obvious, the developing world won't stop demanding energy just because we decide to tax ourselves more.

See Chapter 10 for other templates that introduce meta-commentary.

Conservatives can either tackle the issue of carbon emissions 10 sensibly by proposing workable solutions, or run the risk of allowing the Democrats to do it for us—with policies that would offer marginal environmental benefits at a devastating cost to the economy.

See Chapter 1 for other ways to keep what "they say" in view.

As Representative Alexandria Ocasio-Cortez (D., N.Y.), my colleague, said of this dichotomy, "If you don't like the Green New Deal, then come up with your own ambitious, on-scale proposal to address the global climate crisis. Until then, we're in charge."

We don't want them in charge. It's time to start promoting conservative solutions. The New Energy Frontier is exactly that.

Joining the Conversation

1. Republican congressman Dan Crenshaw of Texas, unlike many in his party, accepts the reality of climate change and the need to address it. What are his "they say" and "I say" statements?

2. Look back at the preceding essay by Naomi Klein. In what ways, if any, does Klein employ the tactics that Crenshaw accuses the Left of using in political debates?

3. The author accuses liberals of "alarmism" in their calls to combat climate change. He says in paragraph 2 that conservatives can fight back with solutions "based on reason, science, and the free market." Read through the essay and consider how effectively he uses these three categories, particularly science, in proposing conservative solutions.

4. Can you find "so what?" or "who cares?" statements in the essay? If not, create one of each that meshes with Crenshaw's

argument, and state where in the text they should be located and why.

5. Consider the conflicting arguments offered by Naomi Klein and Dan Crenshaw. Then write a "they say / I say" essay offering your own views on the topic of climate change.

Should We Be More Optimistic about Fighting Climate Change?

ALICE CHEN AND VIVEK MURTHY

THERE ARE TWO STORIES ABOUT CLIMATE CHANGE. The first is the one you hear the most: that if we don't dramatically curb greenhouse gas emissions in the next decade, there will be dire consequences to our health and way of life. The second story is about optimism. It's about how innovations large and small are helping us to mitigate these dangers and transform our economy and our lives.

Both stories are true. But the second one is rarely told. It's also the reason why we believe that reining in climate change is possible. As doctors and entrepreneurs, we have witnessed the extraordinary capacity that people have to surmount challenges and maintain hope in the most difficult circumstances.

ALICE CHEN, an internal medicine physician, served as executive director and a founding board member of Doctors for America. She cowrote this essay, which appeared in *Harvard Business Review* on September 16, 2019, with her husband, VIVEK MURTHY, also a physician and the nineteenth surgeon general of the United States. He is the author of the book *Together: The Healing Power of Connection in a Sometimes Lonely World* (2020).

Alice is the former Executive Director of Doctors for America, and has practiced medicine in California and Washington, DC. Vivek, before serving as the 19th Surgeon General of the United States, co-founded a clinical trial optimization company and two organizations focused on improving health in India. From health care's frontlines we've witnessed the catastrophic costs of climate change, and have seen the public and private sectors—to varying degrees—respond. It is why we are both increasingly worried, and increasingly optimistic. And why we want you to be, too.

Diagnosis: Climate Change

When we think about the major health challenges facing the world, we tend to think about mental illness, violence, malnutrition, and chronic illnesses like heart and lung diseases. It surprises many to learn that climate change is the greatest public health challenge facing communities around the world. But where there is risk, there is also opportunity; Nielsen estimates that by 2021, one quarter of total store sales in the U.S. ($150 billion) will be sustainable products. What's more, those products are expected to outperform traditional products. We are heartened by this, but not altogether surprised. As physicians, we know that patients we have cared for throughout the years stand to be increasingly affected by climate change. We

See Chapter 7 for more on establishing why your claims matter.

also know that these people are not just our patients, but they are also your employees, colleagues, and customers, maybe even yourself and your family. The choices you make today—big ones about carbon neutrality and small ones like the kind of light bulb in your desk lamp—are going to influence their lives tomorrow.

The impact of climate change hits close to home for us. Our families still live in California and Miami where we each grew up—in neighborhoods at risk from increasing wildfires, drought, hurricanes, and sea level rise. Our young son and daughter are too young to understand, but they will live with the consequences of what we do today to protect their world. This became exceedingly evident to us in November 2018, when Northern California was bathed in a deep and noxious smoke.

Two hundred miles north of San Francisco the largest 5 wildfire in California's history—named the Camp Fire—was burning. In the Bay Area, home to over 7 million people, the smoke hovered overhead. Children couldn't go outside during recess, and many schools closed entirely. People wore masks whenever they stepped outside. Emergency rooms and doctors offices filled as people struggled to breathe. Many people with particularly sensitive family members—babies, the elderly, asthmatics, and others with chronic illnesses— temporarily fled from the area. By the time it was contained,

it had consumed more land than the city of Chicago and destroyed 500 businesses. In nearby Chico, 10% of their workforce lost their homes. Many were unable to find new housing they could afford, so they moved away, straining an already tight labor market.

A report by the global insurance group Munich RE found that the Camp Fire was the costliest natural disaster in the world in 2018 at $16.5 billion. PG&E, California's largest electric utility, cited wildfire liabilities of $30 billion from 2017 and 2018 fires when they filed for bankruptcy in early 2019. It was the sixth largest corporate bankruptcy filing ever. Their 16 million customers will see rate increases to pay for costly court-ordered wildfire prevention work, including clearing power lines from the branches of an estimated 120 million trees. Increasingly homes and businesses at the interface between city and natural spaces—some of the most sought after communities—are becoming uninsurable.

It's not just wildfires, and it's not just California. According to a survey released December 2018, nearly half of Americans (46%) said they have personally felt the effects of climate change. The number who actually have is almost certainly higher. Warmer oceans mean more frequent and severe hurricanes that are flooding cities, causing extended power outages, shuttering businesses including hospitals and clinics, and creating short- and long-term stress for all those in the potential path of the storm. When Florida residents went online to buy supplies ahead of Hurricane Irma, they found 2-day shipping that had extended to 13 days—after the storm would have passed. E-commerce increased to 14.3% of total retail sales in the U.S. in 2018, making extreme weather a threat to a growing segment of businesses and the economy.

Beyond the immediate economic impact, extreme weather increases the risks and costs of employees who work outdoors, in construction, delivering mail and packages, utility maintenance, farming, or policing, for example. These workers have the greatest exposure to not only catastrophic extremes, but also extended pollen seasons that are worsening people's allergies and asthma and, as the territories for tick- and mosquito-borne illnesses expand, are also increasingly at risk of getting sick from Lyme disease, dengue, and Zika.

A Dose of Optimism

It is easy to feel overwhelmed by the magnitude of the climate change crisis. But not only can this be dangerous, it ignores the progress we have made in the five decades since scientists first sounded the alarm on climate change. Now, for the first time, new renewable energy has become cheaper than existing coal in the U.S. Consumers are choosing

For more on how to disagree and explain why, see Chapter 4.

sustainable products at a higher rate each year. Even Royal Dutch Shell, the largest oil company in the world, is responding to shareholder pressure by looking to renewables and energy efficiency in transportation. Sweden is committed to eliminating fossil fuels from electricity generation by 2040 and is challenging every other country to race them to 100%. Germany's renewables have outstripped coal, and on one windy, sunny day this past Easter Monday, they generated 77% of the nation's electricity needs with renewables. This is climate change's second story. And it is one that should both give us hope and spur us to further action.

In 2017, Walmart launched Project Gigaton, an initiative to 10 reduce greenhouse gas emissions from the global value chain. More than 200 suppliers of products that are a part of our everyday lives have joined that effort, bringing sustainability—whether we know it or not—to our laundry piles, refrigerators, and showers. For example, because up to 90% of a washing machine's energy use goes toward heating water, Tide had reformulated their laundry detergent to clean well in cold water and launched a new campaign to challenge consumers to make the switch to cold. Similarly, Anheuser-Busch built a massive wind farm in Oklahoma that supplies enough electricity to cover all of the Budweiser beer brewed in the U.S. Kellogg has established a goal of training half a million U.S. farmers in techniques that lower greenhouse gas emissions, and Unilever has reached nearly 50% post-consumer recycled materials for plastic packaging.

For more evidence of progress, we look to Boston-based Indigo Ag and their Terraton Initiative, a private carbon market that will pay farmers to capture carbon in the soil by switching to regenerative farming practices—including no tilling, crop rotations, cover crops, and livestock grazing. Indigo Ag estimates that transitioning all of the world's agricultural lands to these more sustainable practices has the potential to take 1 terraton (1 trillion tons) of carbon dioxide out of the atmosphere, nearly as much as we have put into the atmosphere since the start of the Industrial Revolution.

Commitments in the private sector go hand in hand with what is happening in the public sector. In the U.S., more than 100 cities and 8 states plus the District of Columbia have committed to 100% renewable energy. China is outstripping the rest of the world in installation of solar power. Scotland harnessed so much wind energy in the first half of 2019 that it could power all Scottish homes twice for the year. Kenya gets half its power from geothermal sources, capturing heat coming from deep within the East African Rift. Morocco is building the world's largest concentrated solar plant.

In California, business and political leaders are not waiting for the wildfires and droughts of climate change to take apart the fifth largest economy in the world. In 2018, the state made a commitment to 100% zero-carbon energy sources by 2045. In that same year, the all-electric Tesla Model 3 became the top-selling passenger vehicle in the state. And this past July, four of the world's largest automakers—Ford, BMW, Honda, and Volkswagen—sided with California in a surprise deal to produce more fuel-efficient cars, rejecting Trump administration efforts to roll back Obama-era standards.

Each of these examples takes us one step closer to ensuring climate stability. Closer to managing the stress and destruction and loss that comes to increasingly frequent natural disasters. Closer to protecting ourselves and our most vulnerable—the elderly, children, and those with chronic disease like congestive heart failure—from increasingly common extreme heat.

Where We Need to Go Together

The Paris Agreement in 2015 has been adopted by every nation 15 on earth, even war-torn Syria, which was the last to join the global climate effort. And while the Trump administration has announced an intention to withdraw the United States from the Agreement, it cannot legally do so until November 2020. We should demand that governments play the bold leadership role that is needed in this moment. In the meantime, a groundswell of people in the private sector and state and local governments are rising to the challenge with the "We Are Still In" campaign. They recognize that every one of us must build on the successes to date and rapidly transform how we live and do business because the window of opportunity is small, and there is a job for all of us to do.

Consider how even changing a light bulb can make a difference. Thomas Edison changed the world when he invented the incandescent bulb in 1895 by dramatically expanding the hours during which it was possible to work, read, and socialize. But that the incandescent bulb has one major drawback: it only turns 10% of the energy it uses into light. The rest is lost as heat. Following the 1973 oil crisis, General Electric tried to popularize fluorescent lights, which were more energy efficient. But the blueish, flickering light felt jarring and most families opted to stick with Edison. Finally, in 2011, the first LED light bulbs to replace standard bulbs were introduced. They had the warmth and constant light of incandescents but used up to 90% less energy and lasted up to 25 times longer.

At first many of us were shocked that a light bulb could cost $50. But enough of us chose to try them—millions of us in fact—that the prices dropped rapidly. By 2017, the cost dropped to less than $2 per bulb, and for the first time, LED bulbs topped sales of household replacement light bulbs in the U.S. The U.S. Environmental Protection Agency now estimates that if every household in America switched to EnergyStar® LEDs in their top 5 most used light fixtures, we would save enough energy to light 33 million homes for a year, and save nearly $5 billion a year in energy costs, and prevent greenhouse gases equivalent to the emissions from nearly 6 million cars. This is a boon for businesses and cities, which are increasingly installing LEDs into offices, factories, street lights, and traffic lights. The wins here pile up; they are saving on the cost of energy, and also on productivity, as they spend less time switching out broken light bulbs and worn out fluorescent tubes.

This sounds like a good story on its own, but there's still another frontier when it comes to lighting. Solar powered LED lanterns are promising an even more dramatic reduction in traditional energy needs while expanding access to light for the more than 1 billion people who are not on the electricity grid. Here, again, we see the intersection of public health, climate change, and innovation. Before LEDs, kerosene lamps were a major contributor in many parts of the world to indoor air pollution that caused respiratory and eye problems, not to mention the risk of burns and fire. Solar powered LED lanterns—and other solar and local renewable energy sources—mean that people around the world can extend their lives by living in healthier conditions, but they are also a shining example of the possibilities ahead as we innovate and open new markets as solar panels, batteries, and LEDs converge.

Next week, the UN Climate Change Summit in New York is bringing together nations to share progress and commitments and to challenge one another to be bolder and faster in a global race to outpace climate change. One year ago, the UN Intergovernmental Panel on Climate Change released a special report that showed that we have to cut our carbon emissions in half in 11 years—by 2030—on our way to net zero emissions by 2050 and negative emissions after that in order to avoid the most catastrophic and irreparable changes. This is about the bottom line and productivity, yes. It is also about our health. None of us can wait for the biggest, most powerful players to take action.

Our research and experience tell us that now is the moment 20 to turn the tide. Ultimately, success in combating climate change will mean all of us working together with as much speed and thoughtfulness as we can. Each of us must find ways to have impact, whether that's launching bold initiatives to reduce carbon emissions in your company, connecting with your trade association to build strength in numbers, or even just changing the light bulb in your desk lamp. It is time to rapidly adopt solutions that are working and improve upon them. We do not have time to dwell too long on why we cannot win and must focus on why we can, and must, win.

Joining the Conversation

1. Alice Chen and Vivek Murthy use a classic "they say / I say" format in this article. Restate it in your own words, and summarize how the authors support their argument.
2. The authors are physicians and experienced leaders of major medical organizations. They published this article in the *Harvard Business Review*, a general management magazine read by managers in business, industry, government, and the nonprofit world. In what ways can you tell that the article is intended for an audience of executives as opposed to activists or general readers?

3. The article describes a number of climate-related disasters that would seem to offer strong reasons for pessimism. Why do you think the authors are so adamant about the importance of staying optimistic that the problems they discuss can be solved?

4. The authors bring in examples from their own and other people's experiences as well as statistical findings from research. What, in your view, is the power of this personal way of arguing? What, if any, are its limitations?

5. Write an essay responding to Chen and Murthy with your own view of optimism versus pessimism in fighting climate change. In developing your essay, feel free to draw on and enter into conversation with other readings from this chapter.

Banning Plastic Bags Is Great for the World, Right? Not So Fast

BEN ADLER

———

LIKE CIGARETTES, plastic bags have recently gone from a tolerated nuisance to a widely despised and discouraged vice.

Last month, the New York City Council passed a 5-cent-per-bag fee on single-use bags handed out by most retailers. Two weeks ago, the Massachusetts State Senate passed a measure that would ban plastic bags from being dispensed by many retail businesses and require a charge of 10 cents or more for a recycled paper or reusable bag. The Massachusetts proposal may not become law this year, but it's the latest sign that the plastic bag industry is losing this war. Already in Massachusetts, 32 towns and cities have passed bag bans or fees. So have at least 88 localities in California, including the cities of Los Angeles

———

BEN ADLER, a senior editor for *City & State New York*, writes widely about policy and the environment, including city planning, climate change, energy, and transportation. His writing has been published in *Politico*, the *Nation*, the *New York Times*, the *New Republic*, the *Atlantic*, and *Architectural Record*. He is originally from Brooklyn, NY, and is a graduate from Wesleyan University. This piece first appeared in *Wired* in 2016.

and San Francisco, plus cities and towns in more than a dozen other states and more than a dozen other countries.

The adverse impacts of plastic bags are undeniable: When they're not piling up in landfills, they're blocking storm drains, littering streets, getting stuck in trees, and contaminating oceans, where fish, seabirds, and other marine animals eat them or get tangled up in them. As longtime plastic bag adversary Ian Frazier recently reported in *The New Yorker*, "In 2014, plastic grocery bags were the seventh most common item collected during the Ocean Conservancy's International Coastal Cleanup, behind smaller debris such as cigarette butts, plastic straws, and bottle caps." The New York City Sanitation Department collects more than 1,700 tons of single-use carry-out bags every week, and has to spend $12.5 million a year to dispose of them.

Bag bans cut this litter off at the source: In San Jose, California, a plastic bag ban led to an 89 percent reduction in the number of plastic bags winding up in the city's storm drains. Fees have a smaller, but still significant, effect. Washington, DC's government estimates that its 5-cent bag tax has led to a 60 percent reduction in the number of these bags being used, although that figure is contested by other sources.

Is Plastic Really Worse Than Paper?

But advocates of these laws and journalists who cover the issue 5 often neglect to ask what will replace plastic bags and what the environmental impact of that replacement will be. People still need bags to bring home their groceries. And the most common substitute, paper bags, may be just as bad or worse, depending on the environmental problem you're most concerned about.

That's leading to a split in the anti-bag movement. Some bills, like in Massachusetts, try to reduce the use of paper bags as well as plastic, but still favor paper. Others, like in New York City, treat all single-use bags equally. Even then, the question remains as to whether single-use bags are necessarily always worse than reusable ones.

Studies of bags' environmental impacts over their life cycle have reached widely varying conclusions. Some are funded by plastic industry groups, like the ironically named American Progressive Bag Alliance. Even studies conducted with the purest of intentions depend on any number of assumptions. How many plastic bags are replaced by one cotton tote bag? If a plastic bag is reused in the home as the garbage bag in a bathroom waste bin, does that reduce its footprint by eliminating the need for another small plastic garbage bag?

If your chief concern is climate change, things get even muddier. One of the most comprehensive research papers on the environmental impact of bags, published in 2007 by an Australian state government agency, found that paper bags have a higher carbon footprint than plastic. That's primarily because more energy is required to produce and transport paper bags.

"People look at [paper] and say it's degradable, therefore it's much better for the environment, but it's not in terms of climate change impact," says David Tyler, a professor of chemistry at the University of Oregon who has examined the research on the environmental impact of bag use. The reasons for paper's higher carbon footprint are complex, but can mostly be understood as stemming from the fact that paper bags are much thicker than plastic bags. "Very broadly, carbon footprints are proportional to mass of an object," says Tyler. For example, because paper bags take up so much more space, more trucks are needed to ship paper bags to a store than to ship plastic bags.

Looking beyond Climate Change

Still, many environmentalists argue that plastic is worse than 10
paper. Climate change, they say, isn't the only form of environmental degradation to worry about. "Paper does have its own
environmental consequences in terms of how much energy it
takes to generate," acknowledges Emily Norton, director of the
Massachusetts Sierra Club. "The big difference is that paper
does biodegrade eventually. Plastic is a toxin that stays in the
environment, marine animals ingest it, and it enters their bodies and then ours."

Some social justice activists who work in low-income urban
neighborhoods or communities of color also argue that plastic
bags are a particular scourge. "A lot of the waste ends up in
our communities," says Elizabeth Yeampierre, execu- See Chapter 3
tive director of UPROSE, an environmental and social for more
on framing
justice-oriented community organization in Brooklyn. quotations.
"Plastic bags not only destroy the physical infrastructure," she
says, referring to the way they clog up storm drains and other
systems, "they contribute to emissions." And she points out that
marine plastic pollution is a threat to low-income people who
fish for their dinner: "So many frontline communities depend on
food coming from the ocean." That's why her group supported
New York City's bag fee even though it's more of a burden on
lower-income citizens. A single mom, or someone working two
jobs, is more likely to have to do her shopping in a rush on the
way home from work than to go out specifically with a tote bag
in hand. But for UPROSE, that concern is outweighed by the
negative impacts of plastic bags on disadvantaged communities.

Increasingly, environmentalists are pushing for laws that
include fees for all single-use bags, and that require paper bags to
be made with recycled content, which could lower their carbon

footprint. The measure now under consideration in Massachusetts, for example, would mandate that single-use paper bags contain at least 40 percent recycled fiber. That's the percentage the Massachusetts Sierra Club has advocated for at the state level and when lobbying for municipal bag rules.

It's Complicated

But what if reusable bags aren't good either? As the Australian study noted, a cotton bag has major environmental impacts of its own. Only 2.4 percent of the world's cropland is planted with cotton, yet it accounts for 24 percent of the global market for insecticides and 11 percent for pesticides, the World Wildlife Fund reports. A pound of cotton requires more than 5,000 gallons of water on average, a thirst far greater than that of any vegetable and even most meats. And cotton, unlike paper, is not currently recycled in most places.

The Australian study concluded that the best option appears to be a reusable bag, but one made from recycled plastic, not cotton. "A substantial shift to more durable bags would deliver environmental gains through reductions in greenhouse gases, energy and water use, resource depletion and litter," the study concluded. "The shift from one single-use bag to another single-use bag may improve one environmental outcome, but be offset by another environmental impact."

But studies conducted in Australia or Europe have limited 15 applicability in the US, particularly when you're considering climate impact, because every country has a different energy mix. In fact, every region of the US has a different energy mix.

"There's no easy answer," says Eric Goldstein, New York City environment director for the Natural Resources Defense

Council, which backed NYC's bag fee. "There are so very many variables. Here's just one tiny example: Does the paper for paper bags come from a recycled paper mill on Staten Island or a virgin forest in northern Canada? As far as I know, nobody has done the definitive analysis, which would necessarily need to have a large number of caveats and qualifications. Also, this question is something like asking, 'Would you prefer to get a parking ticket or a tax assessment?' It depends on the specifics, but it's better to avoid both wherever possible." Goldstein is confident that if people switch to reusable bags, even cotton ones, and use them consistently, that will ultimately be better for the environment.

The ideal city bag policy would probably involve charging for paper and plastic single-use bags, as New York City has decided to do, while giving out reusable recycled-plastic bags to those who need them, especially to low-income communities and seniors. (The crunchy rich should already have more than enough tote bags from PBS and Whole Foods.)

The larger takeaway is that no bag is free of environmental impact, whether that's contributing to climate change, ocean pollution, water scarcity, or pesticide use. The instinct to favor reusable bags springs from an understandable urge to reduce our chronic overconsumption, but the bags we use are not the big problem.

For more templates that guide your reader to your major point, see Chapter 10.

"Eat one less meat dish a week—that's what will have a real impact on the environment," says Tyler. "It's what we put in the bag at the grocery store that really matters."

Joining the Conversation

1. This essay is divided into four sections: a four-paragraph introduction, a section titled "Is Plastic Really Worse Than

Paper?," a section titled "Looking beyond Climate Change," and a conclusion titled "It's Complicated." Write down the primary point of each section. What does each contribute to the essay as a whole?

2. At the beginning of paragraph 3, Ben Adler states: "The adverse impacts of plastic bags are undeniable." He goes on to list some of the most serious impacts and in the following paragraph cites the apparent success of several cities' laws banning plastic bags. Why, then, in your view, does he later in the essay seem to question the value of such measures?

3. This essay makes extensive use of direct quotations from other authors, including writer Ian Frazier, chemistry professor David Tyler, environmentalist Emily Norton, community organizer Elizabeth Yeampierre, and activist Eric Goldstein. Analyze the way Ben Adler first introduces and then discusses a quotation from one of these authors, and explain why you think Adler included that particular quotation in his essay. In other words, what did the quotation and his discussion of it contribute to Adler's essay?

4. Read Charles J. Moore's essay, "Choking the Oceans with Plastic" (pp. 327–32). In it, he discusses the environmental dangers of the large amounts of plastic garbage polluting our oceans and other waterways, and he advocates taking serious measures to address this ongoing problem. Given what you have just read in Ben Adler's essay on the banning of plastic bags, how do you think Adler might respond to Moore? What in particular do you see in Adler's text that leads you to believe he would agree, disagree, or both agree and disagree with Moore's argument?

5. Write a response to both Moore and Adler in which you put forth your own arguments on the plastic bag issue while responding to their views.

Choking the Oceans with Plastic

CHARLES J. MOORE

———◻———

THE WORLD IS AWASH IN PLASTIC. It's in our cars and our carpets, we wrap it around the food we eat and virtually every other product we consume; it has become a key lubricant of globalization—but it's choking our future in ways that most of us are barely aware.

I have just returned with a team of scientists from six weeks at sea conducting research in the Great Pacific Garbage Patch— one of five major garbage patches drifting in the oceans north and south of the Equator at the latitude of our great terrestrial deserts. Although it was my 10th voyage to the area, I was utterly shocked to see the enormous increase in the quantity of plastic waste since my last trip in 2009. Plastics of every description, from toothbrushes to tires to unidentifiable fragments

———

CHARLES J. MOORE is an oceanographer and founder of the Algalita Marine Research and Education Institute in Long Beach, CA, an organization that works to educate about plastic pollution in the oceans and its connection to our increased reliance on and consumption of plastics. In 1997, while sailing across the Pacific Ocean, he and his crew discovered the Great Pacific Garbage Patch, a giant 670,000-square-mile expanse of plastic debris floating in the ocean. This op-ed was first published in 2014 in the *New York Times*.

too numerous to count floated past our marine research vessel *Alguita* for hundreds of miles without end. We even came upon a floating island bolstered by dozens of plastic buoys used in oyster aquaculture that had solid areas you could walk on.

Plastics are now one of the most common pollutants of ocean waters worldwide. Pushed by winds, tides and currents, plastic particles form with other debris into large swirling glutinous accumulation zones, known to oceanographers as gyres, which comprise as much as 40 percent of the planet's ocean surface—roughly 25 percent of the entire earth.

No scientist, environmentalist, entrepreneur, national or international government agency has yet been able to establish a comprehensive way of recycling the plastic trash that covers our land and inevitably blows and washes down to the sea. In a 2010 study of the Los Angeles and San Gabriel Rivers, my colleagues and I estimated that some 2.3 billion pieces of plastic—from polystyrene foam to tiny fragments and pellets—had flowed from Southern California's urban centers into its coastal waters in just three days of sampling.

The deleterious consequences of humanity's "plastic foot- 5 print" are many, some known and some yet to be discovered. We know that plastics biodegrade exceptionally slowly, breaking into tiny fragments in a centuries-long process. We know that plastic debris entangles and slowly kills millions of sea creatures; that hundreds of species mistake plastics for their natural food, ingesting toxicants that cause liver and stomach abnormalities in fish and birds, often choking them to death. We know that one of the main bait fish in the ocean, the lantern fish, eats copious quantities of plastic fragments, threatening their future as a nutritious food source to the tuna, salmon, and other pelagic fish we consume, adding to the increasing amount of synthetic chemicals unknown before 1950 that we now carry in our bodies.

We suspect that more animals are killed by vagrant plastic waste than by even climate change—a hypothesis that needs to be seriously tested. During our most recent voyage, we studied the effects of pollution, taking blood and liver samples from fish as we searched for invasive species and plastic-linked pollutants that cause protein and hormone abnormalities. While we hope our studies will yield important contributions to scientific knowledge, they address but a small part of a broader issue.

The reality is that only by preventing synthetic debris—most of which is disposable plastic—from getting into the ocean in the first place will a measurable reduction in the ocean's plastic load be accomplished. Clean-up schemes are legion, but have never been put into practice in the garbage patches.

The National Oceanic and Atmospheric Administration in the United States supports environmentalist groups that remove debris from beaches. But the sieve-like skimmers they use, no matter how technologically sophisticated, will never be able to clean up remote garbage gyres: There's too much turbulent ocean dispersing and mixing up the mess.

The problem is compounded by the aquaculture industry, which uses enormous amounts of plastic in its floats, nets, lines and tubes. The most common floats and tubes I've found in the deep ocean and on Hawaiian beaches come from huge sea-urchin and oyster farms like the one that created the oyster-buoy island we discovered. Those buoys were torn from their moorings by the tsunami that walloped Japan on March 11, 2011. But no regulatory remedies exist to deal with tons of plastic equipment lost accidentally and in storms. Government and industry organizations purporting to certify sustainably farmed seafood, despite their dozens of pages of standards, fail to mention gear that is lost and floats away. Governments, which are rightly concerned with depletion of marine food sources, should ensure that plastic from cages, buoys and other equipment used for aquaculture does not escape into the waters.

But, in the end, the real challenge is to combat an economic 10 model that thrives on wasteful products and packaging, and leaves the associated problem of clean-up costs. Changing the way we produce and consume plastics is a challenge greater than reining in our production of carbon dioxide.

See Chapter 8 for more on how to connect the parts of an essay.

Plastics are a nightmare to recycle. They are very hard to clean. They can melt at low temperatures, so impurities are not vaporized. It makes no difference whether a synthetic polymer like polyethylene is derived from petroleum or plants; it is still a persistent pollutant. Biodegradable plastics exist, but manufacturers are quick to point out that marine degradable does not mean "marine disposable."

Scientists in Britain and the Netherlands have proposed to cut plastic pollution by the institution of a "circular economy."

The basic concept is that products must be designed with end-of-life recovery in mind. They propose a precycling premium to provide incentives to eliminate the possibility that a product will become waste.

In the United States, especially in California, the focus has been on so-called structural controls, such as covering gutters and catch basins with screens. This has reduced the amount of debris flowing down rivers to the sea. Activists around the world are lobbying for bans on the most polluting plastics—the bottles, bags and containers that deliver food and drink. Many have been successful. In California, nearly 100 municipalities have passed ordinances banning throwaway plastic bags and the Senate is considering a statewide ban.

Until we shut off the flow of plastic to the sea, the newest global threat to our Anthropocene age will only get worse.

Joining the Conversation

1. According to Charles J. Moore, what dangers do plastic garbage in its many forms pose to the world? How widespread does his research reveal the problem of plastic garbage in the world's waterways to be?
2. Pick one sentence from the essay that you think best embodies its main argument and explain why you think so.
3. A key strategy in effective argumentative writing is for authors to raise possible objections to their own positions—what this book calls naysayers—and to respond to those views. In this short essay, Moore does not raise or respond to possible objections to his argument. Think of two or three possible naysayers, and respond to each of them from the author's perspective.

4. So what? Who cares? How does Moore make clear to readers why his topic matters? Or, if you don't think he does, how might he do so?
5. Do some research of your own on water pollution caused by plastic debris, and write an essay responding to Moore's argument. You may agree, disagree, or both agree and disagree with the author, but be sure to represent his views early in your text, both summarizing and quoting from his essay.

Mauna Kea: The Fight to Preserve Culture

SANDIS EDWARD WAIALAE WIGHTMAN

—▭—

UA MAU KE EA O KA 'AINA I KA PONO. This Hawaiian motto translates to "The life of the land is preserved in righteousness." Hawaiians have always felt the need to protect their land, but the threat they face today is the Thirty Meter Telescope, also known as the TMT, which is scheduled for construction atop Mauna Kea, a revered mountain on Hawaii's Big Island. Those building the telescope say that location is ideal and that the telescope will be an innovation in astronomical imagery. However, Mauna Kea, considered the birthplace of Hawaii, has maintained its cultural significance since King Kamehameha united the islands in 1810. The deep respect Hawaiians have

———

SANDIS EDWARD WAIALAE WIGHTMAN is a student at California State University, Dominguez Hills, where he is pursuing a double major in behavioral sciences and English. Born and raised on the US mainland, Wightman is Hawaiian and has danced hula for ten years. He wrote this essay for his first-year writing class and states that this piece allowed him to both reconnect with his culture and raise awareness about an important debate about culture and politics on the island of Hawaii. This essay was nominated for the Norton Writer's Prize. It is documented using MLA style.

for their land has resulted in a long-standing cultural practice of stewardship, especially of Mauna Kea. Construction of the TMT would restrict Hawaiians' access to Mauna Kea, leading to stewardship by outsiders, and it would separate Hawaiians from a significant source of their culture and a sacred space. While some might argue that those protesting the telescope are just resistant to science, the history of Hawaiian discoveries and their use of technology contradicts that, demonstrating that their resistance is not to science itself but to the takeover of an important part of their landscape.

Astronomers argue that mountaintops are desirable for telescope installation due to their remote locations and high vantage points; however, many mountains are also revered by Indigenous peoples. For example, Shannon Hall writes in *Scientific American* that the San Carlos Apache tribe battled astronomers over Mount Graham in Arizona during the 1980s. The mountain was a place of worship for the tribe, and astronomers wanted to build three telescopes on it. Eventually, all three telescopes were built (Hall).

Like the Apaches, Hawaiians are not strangers to having outsiders decide what gets done with their land. A history of the islands put together by the Hawaii Tourism Authority explains that in the 1700s, Captain Cook arrived and promptly attempted to rename Hawaii "the Sandwich Islands." Then, in the 1800s, Queen Liliuokalani was imprisoned in Iolani Palace during an American-led coup; this resulted in the annexation of the Kingdom of Hawaii, turning it into a US territory ("Brief History"). But even though Hawaii is no longer a sovereign nation, land disputes between Hawaiians and others continue to this day.

In fact, the dispute over Mauna Kea has been going on for decades: attempts to build on the mountain have been met with protests since the 1990s. As in Arizona, courts said that the construction should move forward, including the Supreme Court of Hawaii in 2018. However, protests continued after that decision. Since July 2019, a permanent camp of protesters has kept the construction from starting. In addition, according to an article from the American Association for the Advancement of Science, Hawaiian scientists recently asked that an important industry report "ensure that no federal money is used to build on state land without the consent of local Indigenous people" (Clery). Though the two sides declared a truce in late 2019—the protesters wouldn't block the roads, and construction wouldn't start on the telescope—the project remains delayed (Clery).

Protesters continue to fight because Mauna Kea, a dormant ⁵ volcano on Hawaii's Big Island, is considered a source of life and is revered by the Hawaiian people. Joseph Ciotti explains in *The Hawaiian Journal of History* that its name is Hawaiian for "White Mountain," referring to the snow that can often be found on the summit in the wintertime. When measured from its base at the ocean floor to its peak, it is the largest mountain on the planet. It is considered a source of life because the island of Hawaii was formed by the lava that erupted from Mauna Kea; the mountain birthed the island. Some parents even travel 750 feet below the summit to Lake Wai'au to offer the umbilical cord of their newborn children (Ciotti 148). Hawaiians respect Mauna Kea because just as it gave life to Hawaii, the people know that its eruptions can also destroy them. Mauna Kea didn't just create Hawaii; it provided for the Hawaiian people in other ways. Because Mauna Kea is the tallest point on the island, it was used as a lookout point to watch for invaders, and when the snow at the summit melted, it trickled down and watered the plant life and served as a water

For more on summarizing, see Chapter 2.

Mauna Kea volcano.

source for the people. Ancient Hawaiians, who were skilled astronomers, would even go to Mauna Kea to look at the stars and create maps, without the aid of telescopes.

The Hawaiian people's history with astronomy proves that the issue they have with the TMT does not stem from a lack of interest in astronomy or in scientific discovery. In fact, astronomy has been a part of Hawaiian culture for centuries. According to the University of Hawaii Institute for Astronomy, many stories told by ancient Hawaiians included the stars, and their navigators had a great appreciation for and understanding of the skies above them, as well as how wind, waves, cloud formations, birds, and fish could guide them. These travelers ventured on expeditions to places like Easter Island and New Zealand in their canoes. Captain Cook's arrival on Kauai in the late 1700s brought tools such as spyglasses, clocks, and charts. The Hawaiians easily adapted to this new technology, but the vast

Mauna Kea telescope.

and ancient knowledge of the sky was quickly forgotten, as was the lore ("Astronomy"). Historically, Hawaiians have been very innovative and welcoming of new technologies. The Hawaiian people have simply weighed the importance of the telescope against the importance of the birthplace of their homeland. To many Hawaiians, any benefits this telescope brings are not worth the effects it will have on their culture.

However, astronomers argue that the telescope is necessary for scientific innovation. According to the project's website, the TMT, or Thirty Meter Telescope, is currently being built by TMT International Observatory, a nonprofit organization established in May 2014. Members of this group include Caltech, the National Institutes of Natural Sciences of Japan, the Department of Science and Technology of India, and others ("Partners"). The website also explains that "the Thirty Meter Telescope is a new class of extremely

See Chapter 6 for tips on how to name your naysayers.

large telescopes that will allow us to see deeper into space and observe cosmic objects with unprecedented sensitivity" ("What Is TMT?"). The site claims that images from the TMT are more than twelve times sharper than images from the Hubble Space Telescope.

Scientists interested in seeing these images hope there can be compromise, and many Hawaiians agree. A 2015 article in *Nature* detailed the points of view of several people involved with the dispute, including Doug Simons, a thirty-year resident of Hawaii. "There is no way to make everybody happy on the mountain," he says. "Historically, these things have been worked through some sort of give-and-take process—I don't see why that can't happen here" (qtd. in Witze 28). The *Nature* article also profiles Alexis Acohido, part Native Hawaiian, who heard about the telescope construction during a summer astronomy internship: "'What they had planned sounded really awesome,' she says. 'I thought it would be cool to have for Hawaii'" (26).

But despite the willingness of some Hawaiians to compromise, others are worried about allowing outsiders to take control of the mountain. Respect for the *'aina*, or land, is a major part of Hawaiian culture. For centuries, Hawaiians have acted as stewards of the islands. They see it as their cultural responsibility, because of everything the land provides for them. This is especially true of Mauna Kea. Hawaiians often travel up the mountain to gather plants to use for medicine or to pick flowers for leis. When they do take from the mountain, they are sure not to damage the land or overharvest. Hawaiians have a familiarity with Mauna Kea and are able to observe any abnormalities that might require intervention. The TMT's construction will restrict the access Hawaiians have to the mountain, leaving outsiders who are not familiar with the landscape in charge of its well-being.

Hawaii's history with colonization is a long and tragic one. 10 From the Kingdom of Hawaii's annexation by the United States, to the current commercialization and gentrification of the islands, Hawaii has lost so much to outsiders who believe that the land is theirs to take, simply because they want it. The Hawaiians' fight to preserve their culture and their land has been going on for centuries. How much longer will it continue? In *Ka Wai Ola*, a free monthly newspaper, Sterling Wong quotes from a statement by the Office of Hawaiian Affairs, which argues that "OHA believes that the current proposed rules fall short of meaningfully ensuring the appropriate stewardship of Mauna Kea, including through the protections of Native Hawaiian traditional and customary rights" (7). They hope instead for more recommendations that "mitigate the impacts of public and commercial activities on Mauna Kea" (7). We can only hope that the historical trend of Indigenous people's losing access to their land stops here.

WORKS CITED

"Astronomy to the Early Hawaiians." *University of Hawaii Institute for Astronomy*, www.ifa.hawaii.edu/users/steiger/early_hawaiians.htm.

"A Brief History of the Hawaiian Islands." *The Hawaiian Islands*, 2020 Hawaiian Tourism Authority, 2020, www.gohawaii.com/hawaiian -culture/history.

Ciotti, Joseph E. "Historical Views on Mauna Kea: From the Vantage Points of Hawaiian Culture and Astronomical Research." *The Hawaiian Journal of History*, vol. 45, 2011, pp. 147–66. *eVols*, evols.library.manoa.hawaii.edu /bitstream/10524/33785/1/HJH45_147-166.pdf.

Clery, Daniel. "New Front Emerges in Battle to Build Giant Telescope in Hawaii." *American Association for the Advancement of Science*, 14 Jan. 2020, www.sciencemag.org/news/2020/01/new-front-emerges -battle-build-giant-telescope-hawaii.

Hall, Shannon. "Hawaii's Telescope Controversy Is the Latest in a Long History of Land-Ownership Battles." *Scientific American*, 11 Dec. 2015, www.scientificamerican.com/article/hawaii-s-telescope-controversy-is-the-latest-in-a-long-history-of-land-ownership-battles.

"Partners." *TMT International Observatory*, 2021, tmt.org/page/partners.

"What Is TMT?" *University of California Observatories*, 2021, www.ucobservatories.org/observatory/thirty-meter-telescope/.

Witze, Alexandra. "The Mountain-Top Battle over the Thirty Meter Telescope." *Nature*, vol. 526, no. 7571, 1 Oct. 2015, pp. 24–28. https://doi.org/10.1038/526024a.

Wong, Sterling. "UH's Proposed Rules Fall Short of Ensuring Appropriate Stewardship of Mauna Kea." *Ka Wai Ola*, 1 Nov. 2018, kawaiola.news/aina/uhs-proposed-rules-fall-short-of-ensuring-appropriate-stewardship-of-mauna-kea/.

Joining the Conversation

1. Coming from a composition class in which he learned to use "they say / I say" essay structure, student writer Sandis Edward Waialae Wightman employs the format in his essay. Paraphrase his "they say" and "I say" statements and the arguments he uses to support his views. Why, in his opinion, is this issue an important one?

2. In presenting his "they say," Wightman expresses the views of those in favor of building a huge telescope on top of a mountain that is special to the Hawaiian people for religious, cultural, and historical reasons. What words and phrases does he use to differentiate his own views from those with which he disagrees?

3. Find three examples in which Wightman anticipates naysayers and responds to possible objections to his argument. How effective is his strategy of including and discussing positions that would appear to work against his own views? What does the writer gain and/or lose through use of this strategy, and why?

4. So what? Who cares? Where does Wightman explain why his argument matters—and for whom?
5. Find out through news reports about a controversy over proposed construction on campus or in your local community. After reading about the various positions taken by supporters and opponents of the project, write an essay responding to those arguments and presenting your own position.

Elevated Blood Lead Levels in Children Associated with the Flint Drinking Water Crisis

MONA HANNA-ATTISHA, JENNY LACHANCE,
RICHARD CASEY SADLER, AND ALLISON
CHAMPNEY SCHNEPP

Objectives. *We analyzed differences in pediatric elevated blood lead level incidence before and after Flint, Michigan, introduced a more corrosive water source into an aging water system without adequate corrosion control.*

―――――

MONA HANNA-ATTISHA, JENNY LACHANCE, RICHARD CASEY SADLER, and ALLISON CHAMPNEY SCHNEPP published this article in February 2016 in the *American Journal of Public Health*. Together, they investigated blood lead levels in children under age five with samples taken by the Hurley Medical Center in Flint, MI, before and after the 2014 decision to change the city's water source. Hanna-Attisha is the C. S. Mott Endowed Professor of Public Health and an associate professor of pediatrics and human development at Michigan State University, where she also leads the Pediatric Public Health Initiative with Hurley Medical Center.

Methods. *We reviewed blood lead levels for children younger than 5 years before (2013) and after (2015) water source change in Greater Flint, Michigan. We assessed the percentage of elevated blood lead levels in both time periods, and identified geographical locations through spatial analysis.*

Results. *Incidence of elevated blood lead levels increased from 2.4% to 4.9% (P < .05) after water source change, and neighborhoods with the highest water lead levels experienced a 6.6% increase. No significant change was seen outside the city. Geospatial analysis identified disadvantaged neighborhoods as having the greatest elevated blood lead level increases and informed response prioritization during the now-declared public health emergency.*

Conclusions. *The percentage of children with elevated blood lead levels increased after water source change, particularly in socioeconomically disadvantaged neighborhoods. Water is a growing source of childhood lead exposure because of aging infrastructure. (Am J Public Health. 2016;106:283–290. doi:10.2105/AJPH.2015.303003)*

IN APRIL 2014, the postindustrial city of Flint, Michigan, under state-appointed emergency management, changed its water supply from Detroit-supplied Lake Huron water to the Flint River as a temporary measure, awaiting a new pipeline to Lake Huron in 2016. Intended to save money, the change in source water severed a half-century relationship with the Detroit Water and Sewage Department. Shortly after the switch to Flint River water, residents voiced concerns regarding water color, taste, and odor, and various health complaints including

Mona Hanna-Attisha.

skin rashes.[1] Bacteria, including *Escherichia coli*, were detected in the distribution system, resulting in Safe Drinking Water Act violations.[2] Additional disinfection to control bacteria spurred formation of disinfection byproducts including total trihalomethanes, resulting in Safe Drinking Water Act violations for trihalomethane levels.[2]

Water from the Detroit Water and Sewage Department had very low corrosivity for lead as indicated by low chloride, low chloride-to-sulfate mass ratio, and presence of an orthophosphate corrosion inhibitor.[3,4] By contrast, Flint River water had high chloride, high chloride-to-sulfate mass ratio, and no corrosion inhibitor.[5] Switching from Detroit's Lake Huron to Flint River water created a perfect storm for lead leaching into drinking water.[6] The aging Flint water distribution system contains a high percentage of lead pipes and lead plumbing, with estimates of lead service lines

See Chapter 14 for approaches to reading particularly challenging texts.

ranging from 10% to 80%.[7] Researchers from Virginia Tech University reported increases in water lead levels (WLLs),[5] but changes in blood lead levels (BLLs) were unknown.

Lead is a potent neurotoxin, and childhood lead poisoning has an impact on many developmental and biological processes, most notably intelligence, behavior, and overall life achievement.[8] With estimated societal costs in the billions,[9-11] lead poisoning has a disproportionate impact on low-income and minority children.[12] When one considers the irreversible, life-altering, costly, and disparate impact of lead exposure, primary prevention is necessary to eliminate exposure.[13]

Historically, the industrial revolution's introduction of lead into a host of products has contributed to a long-running and largely silent pediatric epidemic.[14] With lead now removed from gasoline and paint, the incidence of childhood lead poisoning has decreased.[15] However, lead contamination of drinking water may be increasing because of lead-containing water infrastructures, changes in water sources, and changes in water treatment including disinfectant.[16-18] A soluble metal, lead leaches into drinking water via lead-based plumbing or lead particles that detach from degrading plumbing components. ("Plumbing" is derived from the Latin word for lead, "plumbum.") Lead was restricted in plumbing material in 1986, but older homes and neighborhoods may still contain lead service lines, lead connections, lead solder, or other lead-based plumbing materials. Lead solubility and particulate release is highly variable and depends on many factors including water softness, temperature, and acidity.[19-21] The US Environmental Protection Agency (EPA) regulates lead in public water supplies under the Safe Drinking Water Act Lead and Copper Rule, which requires action when lead levels reach 15 parts per billion (ppb).

Lead in drinking water is different from lead from other [5] sources, as it disproportionately affects developmentally vulnerable children and pregnant mothers. Children can absorb 40% to 50% of an oral dose of water-soluble lead compared with 3% to 10% for adults.[22] In a dose–response relationship for children aged 1 to 5 years, for every 1-ppb increase in water lead, blood lead increases 35%.[23] The greatest risk of lead in water may be to infants on reconstituted formula. Among infants drinking formula made from tap water at 10 ppb, about 25% would experience a BLL above the Centers for Disease Control and Prevention (CDC) elevated blood lead level (EBLL) of 5 micrograms per deciliter (μg/dL).[24] Tap water may account for more than 85% of total lead exposure among infants consuming reconstituted formula.[25] A known abortifacient, lead has also been implicated in increased fetal deaths and reduced birth weights.[26]

As recommended by the CDC and supported by the American Academy of Pediatrics, blood lead screening is routine for high-risk populations and for children insured by Medicaid at age 1 and 2 years.[27] The CDC-recommended screening ages are based on child development (increased oral–motor behavior), which places a child most at risk for house-based lead exposure (e.g., peeling paint, soil, dust). State and national blood lead–screening programs, however, do not adequately capture the risk of lead in water because infants are at greatest risk.

Armed with reports of elevated WLLs and recognizing the lifelong consequences of lead exposure, our research team sought to analyze blood lead data before (pre) and after (post) the water source switch with a geographic information system (GIS) to determine lead exposure risk and prioritize responses.

This research has immediate public policy, public health, environmental, and socioeconomic implications.

This research includes Flint, Michigan, and surrounding municipalities in Genesee County (Greater Flint). Greater Flint is a postindustrial region of nearly 500 000 people struggling from years of disinvestment by the automobile industry and associated manufacturing activities: the region has lost 77% of its manufacturing employment and 41% of employment overall since 1980.[28] National and local data sources demonstrate dismal indicators for children, especially within Flint city limits.[29–32] Greater Flint ranks toward the bottom of the state in rates of childhood poverty (42% in Flint vs 16.2% in Michigan and 14.8% in the United States), unemployment, violent crime, illicit drug use, domestic violence, preterm births, infant mortality, and overall health outcomes (81st out of 82 Michigan counties).

Greater Flint's struggles have been amplified by a history of racial discrimination, whereby exclusionary housing practices were common.[33,34] Such attitudes toward integration later precipitated White flight and emboldened home-rule governance,[35,36] causing a massive decline in tax revenue for the city. The declining industrial and residential tax bases strained the city's ability to provide basic services and reversed the public health fortunes of the city and suburbs.[37] Severely reduced city population densities reduced water demand in the distribution system, exacerbating problems with lead corrosion.

Methods

This retrospective study includes all children younger than 5 years who had a BLL processed through the Hurley Medical Center's laboratory, which runs BLLs for most Genesee County children. The pre time period (before the water source change) was January 1, 2013, to September 15, 2013, and the post time period (after the water source change) was January 1, 2015, to September 15, 2015. The primary study group comprised children living within the city of Flint (n = 1473; pre = 736; post = 737) who received water from the city water system. Children living outside the city where the water source was unchanged served as a comparison group (n= 2202; pre = 1210; post = 992).

After institutional review board approval and Health Insurance Portability and Accountability Act waiver, we drew data from the Epic electronic medical record system including BLL, medical record number, date of birth, date of blood draw, full address, sex, and race. For each child, only the highest BLL was maintained in the data set. We coded timing (pre or post) of the BLL on the basis of the date of blood draw. We calculated age at time of blood draw.

We geocoded the data set with a dual-range address locator, and manually confirmed accuracy of geocoded addresses.

See Chapter 17 for more on explaining your methods in science writing.

We conducted a series of spatial joins to assign participant records to Greater Flint municipalities and Flint wards (including those with high WLL), enabling the calculation of the number and percentage of children with EBLLs in each geographic region for both time periods. The reference value for EBLL was 5 μg/dL or greater. We identified Flint wards with high WLLs with water lead sampling maps.[38] Wards 5, 6, and 7 had the highest WLLs; in each ward, more than 25% of samples had a WLL higher than 15 ppb. We theorized that children living in this combination of wards would have the highest incidence of EBLLs (referred to as "high WLL Flint"; the remainder of Flint was referred to as "lower WLL Flint").

We derived overall neighborhood-level socioeconomic disadvantage from census block group variables intended to measure material and social deprivation. We calculated these scores from an unweighted z score sum of rates of lone parenthood, poverty, low educational attainment, and unemployment (adapted from Pampalon et al.[39]; used previously in Flint by Sadler et al.[40]), and assigned these to each child on the basis of home address. Positive values denote higher disadvantage, and negative values denote lower disadvantage. Table 1 highlights the overall socioeconomic disadvantage score comparison by time period and area.

Table 1. Demographic Comparison of the Time Periods before (Pre) and after (Post) Water Source Change from Detroit-Supplied Lake Huron Water to the Flint River, by Area: Flint, MI, 2013 and 2015

	Outside Flint		All Flint		High WLL Flint		Lower WLL Flint	
Characteristic	Pre	Post	Pre	Post	Pre	Post	Pre	Post
Gender, %								
Male	51.6	49.5	48.6	52.9	47.6	54.4	49.1	52.3
Female	48.4	50.5	51.4	47.1	52.4	45.6	50.9	47.7
Race/ethnicity, %								
African American	24.3	24.5	69.4	70.6	74.9	78.8	67.0	66.9
Other categories	75.7	75.5	30.6	29.4	25.1	21.2	33.0	33.1
Age, y, mean	1.89	1.83	2.09	2.06	2.06	2.02	2.11	2.07
Overall socioeconomic disadvantage score	−0.83	−0.98	2.94	2.88	2.18	2.39	3.28	3.10

Note: WLL = water lead level. Nostatistically significant differences were found in any pre–post value within any of the 4 geographical areas.

We created spatial references for EBLL risk and a predictive surface for BLL by using GIS, providing the ability to see otherwise invisible spatial–temporal patterns in environmental exposure.[17] Because of the need to understand spatial variations and geographically target resources, we also ran ordinary Kriging with a spherical semivariogram model on the entire data set for Greater Flint, allowing interpolation of associated BLL risks with lead in water. Previous methods for evaluating spatial variation in lead levels have ranged from multivariable analyses at the individual level[41] to interpolation methods such as inverse distance weighting[42] and Kriging.[43] Given our assumption that lead risk is spatially correlated in Greater Flint because of the age and condition of pipes, interpolation methods are appropriate for building a preliminary risk surface. Both inverse distance weighting and Kriging derive such surfaces by calculating values at unmeasured locations based on weighting nearby measured values more strongly than distant values.[44] Whereas inverse distance weighting is a deterministic procedure and relies on predetermined mathematical formulae, Kriging has the added sophistication of using geostatistical models that consider spatial autocorrelation, thereby improving accuracy of prediction surfaces (ArcGIS Desktop version 10.3, Environmental Systems Research Institute, Redlands, CA). As well, Kriging can be run with relatively few input points: adequate ranges fall between 30 and 100 total points, although Kriging has been conducted with just 7.[44]

Our city of Flint sample included 736 children in the pre period and 737 children in the post period, which amounts to a density of approximately 22 points per square mile. Kriging has become an increasingly common method for measuring variations in soil lead, and is given more in-depth treatment elsewhere.[45] To examine change in proportion of children with

EBLL from the pre to post time periods, we used χ^2 analysis with continuity correction for each area (outside Flint, all Flint, high WLL Flint, and lower WLL Flint). In addition, we examined differences in overall socioeconomic disadvantage scores from the pre to post time periods by using the independent t test. Finally, we used both χ^2 analysis with continuity correction and 1-way ANOVA [analysis of variance] to assess demographic differences by area. We used post hoc least significant difference analysis following statistically significant 1-way ANOVAs.

Results

We uncovered a statistically significant increase in the proportion of Flint children with EBLL from the pre period to the proportion of Flint children in the post period. In the pre period, 2.4% of children in Flint had an EBLL; in the post period, 4.9% of children had an EBLL ($P < .05$). By comparison, outside of Flint water, the change in EBLL was not statistically significant (0.7% to 1.2%; $P > .05$). In high WLL Flint, EBLL increased from 4.0% to 10.6% ($P < .05$). Figure 1 shows the EBLL percentage change per area.

Results of the GIS analyses show significant clustering of EBLLs within the Flint city limits. According to ordinary Kriging, Figure 2 shows a predicted surface based on observations of actual child BLL geocoded to home address to visualize BLL variation over space (measured in μg/dL). The darkest shades of red represent the highest risk for EBLL based on existing observations. Outside Flint, the entire county falls entirely within the lowest half of the range (in shades of blue); the only locations where predicted BLL is greater than 1.75 μg/dL is within Flint city limits.

Figure 1. Comparison of Elevated Blood Lead Level Percentage, before (Pre) and after (Post) Water Source Change from Detroit-Supplied Lake Huron Water to the Flint River: Flint, MI, 2013 and 2015

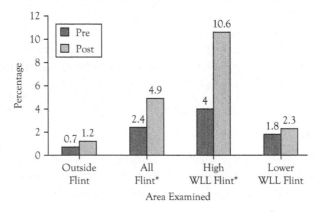

Note: WLL = water lead level.
*$p < .05$.

Within Figure 2, each ward is also labeled according to the percentage of water samples that exceeded 15 ppb. The areas with the highest WLLs strongly coincide with the areas with the highest predicted BLLs. In addition, the high percentage of EBLL in wards 5, 6, and 7 also correspond with the high WLLs in wards 5, 6, and 7 (the labels in Figure 2). Table 2 shows ward-specific WLLs, pre period and post period EBLL percentages, and predicted BLL and predicted change in BLL from Kriging.

Areas experiencing the highest predicted BLL in the post period (Figure 2) are generally also areas with greatest change in predicted BLL (measured in µg/dL) when compared with the pre period (Table 2; Figure A, available as a supplement to the online version of this article at http://www.ajph.org). Figure A quantifies this rate of change with a green to red scale: large increases are shown in increasingly darker shades of red, whereas large decreases are shown in increasingly darker shades of green. These once again match with city wards that experienced greater rates of EBLL percentage increase (Figure 1, Table 2). In wards 5 and 6 (which experienced a predicted 0.51 and 0.27 µg/dL increase, respectively), the EBLL percentage more than tripled. In ward 5, the EBLL percentage increased from 4.9% to 15.7% ($P < .05$). The area of intersection between wards 3, 4, and 5 (in the east side of the city) also appeared high in the Kriging analysis of Figure 2, and with a different unit of aggregation this neighborhood would also exhibit a significant increase in EBLL percentage. Ward 7 had high pre period and post period EBLL percentage levels above 5% (with a particularly high rate in the western portion of the ward). Citywide, 4 wards (1, 4, 7, and 9) experienced decreases in predicted BLL, 3 wards (2, 5, and 6) experienced large increases, and 2 wards (3 and 8) remained largely the same (Figure A).

Overall, statistically significant differences exist between the 20 areas examined (outside Flint, high WLL Flint, and lower WLL Flint) in all demographic characteristics except sex. The overall percentage of African American children is 24.4% outside Flint, compared with 76.8% in high WLL Flint and 67.0% in lower WLL Flint ($P < .001$). Children outside Flint were younger (mean = 1.86 years [SD = 1.10]) than high WLL Flint (mean = 2.04 years [SD = 1.02]) and lower WLL Flint (mean = 2.09 years [SD = 1.07]; $P < .001$). Differences in overall socioeconomic disadvantage scores are likewise significant ($P < .001$). Post hoc least significant difference analysis shows statistically significant differences for overall socioeconomic disadvantage between outside Flint and high WLL Flint ($P < .001$), between outside Flint and lower WLL Flint (P < .001), and between high WLL Flint and lower WLL Flint (P < .001).

Discussion

Our findings reveal a striking increase in the percentage of Flint children with EBLL when we considered identical seasons before and after the water source switch, with no statistically significant increase in EBLL outside Flint. The spatial and statistical analyses highlight the greatest EBLL increase within certain wards of Flint, which correspond to the areas of elevated WLLs.

A review of alternative sources of lead exposure reveals no other potential environmental confounders during the same time period. Demolition projects by the Genesee County Land Bank Authority (Heidi Phaneuf, written communication, October 29, 2015) showed no spatial relationship to the areas of increased EBLL rates. As well, no known new lead-producing factories nor changes in indoor lead remediation programs were implemented during the study period. Although Flint has a significant automobile history, the historical location of potentially lead-using manufacturing (e.g., battery plants, paint and pigment storage, production plants) do not align with current exposures.

Because there was no known alternative source for increased lead exposure during this time period, the geospatial WLL results, the innate corrosive properties of Flint River water, and, most importantly, the lack of corrosion control, our findings strongly implicate the water source change as the probable cause for the dramatic increase in EBLL percentage.

As in many urban areas with high levels of socioeconomic disadvantage and minority populations,[46] we found a preexisting disparity in lead poisoning. In our pre water source switch data, the EBLL percentage in Flint was 2.4% compared with 0.7% outside Flint. This disparity widened with a post water source switch Flint EBLL of 4.8%, with no change in socioeconomic or demographic variables (Table 1). Flint children already suffer from risk factors that innately increase their lead exposure: poor nutrition, concentrated poverty, and older housing stock. With limited protective measures, such as low rates of breast-feeding,[47,48] and scarce resources for water alternatives, lead in water further exacerbates preexisting risk factors. Increased lead-poisoning rates have profound implications for the life course potential of an entire cohort of Flint children already rattled with toxic stress contributors (e.g., poverty, violence, unemployment, food insecurity). This is particularly troublesome in light of recent findings of the epigenetic effects of lead exposure on one's grandchildren.[49]

For more on explaining why your argument matters, see Chapter 7.

The Kriging analysis showed the highest predicted BLLs within the city along a wide swath north and west of downtown. This area has seen significant demographic change, an increase in poverty, and an increase in vacant properties, especially over the past 25 years (Richard Sadler, written communication, October 5, 2015). Higher BLLs were also predicted northeast of downtown and in other older neighborhoods where poverty and vacancy rates have been high for many decades. Significantly, the biggest changes in predicted BLL since 2013 were also found in these impoverished neighborhoods; more stable neighborhoods in the far north and south of the city may have experienced improved predicted BLLs because of prevention efforts taken by the more-often middle-class residents in response to the water source change. Of considerable interest is that the areas shown as having the best public health indices by Board and Dunsmore in Figure 2

Figure 2. Predicted Surface of Child Blood Lead Level and Ward-Specific Elevated Water Lead Level after (Post) Water Source Change from Detroit-Supplied Lake Huron Water to the Flint River: Flint, MI, 2015

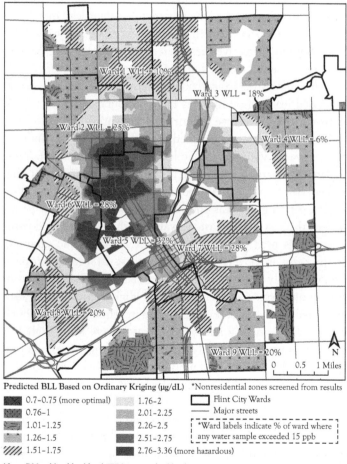

Note: BLL = blood lead level; WLL = water lead level.

of their 1948 article[37] are virtually identical to the areas with the worst lead levels today.

After our preliminary zip code–based findings (pre to post water source switch EBLL = 2.1% to 4.0%; $P < .05$) were shared at a press conference,[50] the City of Flint and the Genesee County Health Department released health advisories,[51] and the county health department subsequently declared a public health emergency.[52] Shortly after, the State of Michigan released an action plan with short- and long-term solutions focusing on additional sampling, filter distribution, and corrosion control.[53] One week later, Michigan's governor revealed WLLs in 3 schools to be in the toxic range with 1 school showing a water lead level of 101 ppb, almost 7 times the level that requires remediation.[54] A $12 million plan to reconnect to Detroit's water source was announced.[54]

We undertook our current spatial analytic approach to overcome limitations of zip code boundaries and to develop a more thorough understanding of specific areas in Flint where EBLL risk is more severe (post office addresses often do not align with municipal boundaries in Michigan, and one third of Flint mailing addresses are not in the city of Flint). This spatial analysis is valuable for understanding subneighborhood patterns in EBLL risk because aggregation by zip code or ward minimizes the richness of spatial variation and creates artificial barriers that may obscure hot spots (as in the confluence of wards 3, 4, and 5).

Such use of spatial analysis for estimating lead exposure risk has been used to target blood lead–screening programs. In our case, in addition to identifying areas of risk, spatial analysis helps guide municipal and nongovernmental relief efforts aimed at identifying vulnerable populations in specific neighborhoods for priority distribution of resources (e.g., bottled water, filters, premixed formula).

Limitations

Our research contains a few limitations. First, we may have underestimated water-based lead exposure. Our sample included all children younger than 5 years with blood lead screening, although the greatest risk from lead in water is in utero and during infancy when lead screening is not done. If lead screening were recommended at a younger age (e.g., 6 or 9 months) for children who live in homes with potential lead piping or lead service lines, more children with EBLL from water could be identified, although state and national

Table 2. Ward-Based Comparison of WLL Percentages, Pre- and Post-switch EBLL Percentages, and Predicted Post BLL and Change in Predicted BLL by Ordinary Kriging Geostatistical Analysis: Flint, MI, 2013 and 2015

Ward	WLL % > 15 ppb	Pre EBLL%	Post EBLL%	Predicted Post BLL[a]	Change in Predicted BLL from Pre to Post, µg/dL
1	10	0.0	2.8	1.4	−0.10
2	25	0.0	1.4	0.7	0.19
3	18	1.0	4.5	2.9	0.05
4	6	3.1	1.7	2.4	−0.15
5[b]	32	4.9	15.7	10.3	0.51
6[b]	28	2.2	9.3	5.5	0.27
7[b]	28	5.4	5.9	5.7	−0.26
8	20	2.7	1.4	2.0	0.01
9	20	3.4	1.6	2.5	−0.43

Note: BLL = blood lead level; EBLL = elevated blood lead level; WLL = water lead level.
[a]Ordinary Kriging geostatistical analysis.
[b]Indicates wards defined as high WLL risk in this study.

comparison rates would be lacking. Second, lead screening is not completed for all children. It is mandated by Medicaid and CDC-recommended for other high-risk groups; such data may be skewed toward higher-risk children and thus overestimate EBLL, especially in non–high-risk areas. Third, the underserved population of Flint has significant housing instability: lead levels may reflect previous environmental exposure, and exposure often cannot be adequately estimated on the basis of current residence alone.[55]

Fourth, although large, our sample does not reflect all lead [30] screening from Flint. We estimate that our data capture approximately 60% to 70% of the Michigan Childhood Lead Poisoning Prevention Program data for Flint. Annual data released from this program further support our findings, revealing an annual decrease in EBLL percentage from May to April 2010 to 2011 until the same period in 2013 to 2014 (4.1%, 3.3%, 2.7%, 2.2%, respectively[56]; Robert L. Scott, e-mail correspondence, September 25, 2015). Following the water switch in April 2014, the 4-year declining trend (as seen nationally) reversed with an annual EBLL of 3.0%.

We found consistent results (with control for age and methodology) when we analyzed Michigan Childhood Lead Poisoning Prevention Program data for both high WLL Flint (EBLL percentage increased: 6.6% to 9.6%) and outside Flint (EBLL percentage remained virtually unchanged: 2.2% to 2.3%). Our institution-processed laboratory blood lead tests, however, had an even greater proportion of children with EBLLs versus state data in the post period. This may reflect that the BLLs processed at Hurley Medical Center, the region's only safety-net public hospital, represent a patient population most at risk with limited resources to afford tap water alternatives.

Conclusions and Future Research

Future research directions include conducting more detailed geospatial analyses of lead service-line locations with locations of elevated BLLs and WLLs; repeating identical spatial and statistical analyses in the same time period in 2016 reflecting changes associated with the health advisory and return to Lake Huron source water; analyzing feeding type (breastfed or reconstituted formula) for children with EBLLs; analyzing cord blood lead of Flint newborns compared with non-Flint newborns; and conducting water lead testing from homes of children with EBLLs.

A once celebrated cost-cutting move for an economically distressed city, the water source change has now wrought untold economic, population health, and geopolitical burdens. With unchecked lead exposure for more than 18 months, it is fortunate that the duration was not longer (as was the case in Washington, DC's lead-in-water issue).[16] Even so, the Flint drinking water crisis is a dramatic failure of primary prevention. The legal safeguards and regulating bodies designed to protect vulnerable populations from preventable lead exposure failed.

The Lead and Copper Rule requires water utilities to notify the state of a water source or treatment change recognizing that such changes can unintentionally have an impact on the system's corrosion control.[57] Although a review is required before implementing changes, the scope of risk assessment is not specified and is subject to misinterpretation. In response to the Flint drinking water crisis, the EPA recently released a memo reiterating and clarifying the need for states to conduct corrosion control reviews before implementing changes.[58] This recommendation is especially relevant for communities with aging infrastructures, usurped city governance, and minimal water utility capacity; in such situations, there is an increased need for state and federal expertise and oversight to support decisions that protect population health.

Through vigilant public health efforts, lead exposure has [35] fallen dramatically over the past 30 years.[13] With the increasing recognition that no identifiable BLL is safe and without deleterious and irreversible health outcomes,[13] *Healthy People 2020* identified the elimination of EBLLs and underlying disparities in lead exposure as a goal.[59] Regrettably, our research reveals that the potentially increasing threat of lead in drinking water may dampen the significant strides in childhood lead-prevention efforts. As our aging water infrastructures continue to decay, and as communities across the nation struggle with finances and water supply sources, the situation in Flint, Michigan, may be a harbinger for future safe drinking-water challenges. Ironically, even when one is surrounded by the Great Lakes, safe drinking water is not a guarantee.

CONTRIBUTORS

M. Hanna-Attisha originated the study, developed methods, interpreted analysis, and contributed to the writing of the article. J. LaChance and R. Casey Sadler assisted with the development of the methods, analyzed results, interpreted the findings, and contributed to the writing of the article. A. Champney Schnepp assisted with the interpretation of the findings and contributed to the writing of the article.

REFERENCES

1. Associated Press. "I don't even let my dogs drink this water." *CBS News*. March 4, 2015. Available at: http://www.cbsnews.com/news/flint -michigan-break-away-detroit-water-riles-residents. Accessed October 3, 2015.

2. City of Flint 2014 Annual Water Quality Report. 2014. Available at: https://www.cityofflint.com/wp-content/ uploads/CCR-2014.pdf. Accessed September 30, 2015.

3. Edwards M, Triantafyllidou S. Chloride to sulfate mass ratio and lead leaching to water. *J Am Water Works Assoc.* 2007;99(7):96–109.

4. Edwards M, McNeill LS. Effect of phosphate inhibitors on lead release from pipes. *J Am Water Works Assoc.* 2007;94(1):79–90.

5. Edwards M, Falkinham J, Pruden A. Synergistic impacts of corrosive water and interrupted corrosion control on chemical/microbiological water quality: Flint, MI. National Science Foundation Grant abstract. Available at: http://www.nsf.gov/awardsearch/showAward? AWD_ID=1556258&Historical Awards=false. Accessed September 10, 2005.

6. Guyette C. Scary: leaded water and one Flint family's toxic nightmare. *Deadline Detroit.* July 9, 2015. Available at: http://www.deadlinedetroit.com /articles/12697/scary_leaded_water_and_one_flint_family_s_toxic_nightmare# .VfYm6eeZZJN. Accessed September 13, 2015.

7. Fonger R. Flint data on lead water lines stored on 45,000 index cards. *Mlive Media Group.* October 1, 2015. Available at: http://www.mlive.com /news/flint/index.ssf/2015/10/flint_official_says_data_on_lo.html. Accessed October 4, 2015.

8. Centers for Disease Control and Prevention. Preventing lead poisoning in young children. 2005. Available at: http://www.cdc.gov/nceh/lead /publications/PrevLeadPoisoning.pdf. Accessed September 30, 2015.

9. Gould E. Childhood lead poisoning: conservative estimates of the social and economic benefits of lead hazard control. *Environ Health Perspect.* 2009;117(7):1162–1167.

10. Landrigan PJ, Schechter CB, Lipton JM, Fahs MC, Schwartz J. Environmental pollutants and disease in American children: estimates of morbidity, mortality, and costs for lead poisoning, asthma, cancer, and developmental disabilities. *Environ Health Perspect.* 2002;110(7):721–728.

11. Schwartz J. Societal benefits of reducing lead exposure. *Environ Res.* 1994;66(1):105–124.

12. Pamuk E, Makuc D, Heck K, Reuben C, Lochner K. Socioeconomic status and health chartbook. Health, United States, 1998. Centers for Disease Control and Prevention. 1998. Available at: http://www.cdc.gov/nchs/data /hus/hus98cht.pdf. Accessed October 1, 2015.

13. Low level lead exposure harms children. A renewed call for primary prevention. Report of the Advisory Committee on Childhood Lead Poisoning Prevention. Centers for Disease Control and Prevention. 2012. Available at: http://www.cdc.gov/nceh/lead/acclpp/final_document_030712.pdf. Accessed September 2015.

14. Landrigan PJ, Graef JW. Pediatric lead poisoning in 1987: the silent epidemic continues. *Pediatrics.* 1987;79(4):582–583.

15. Shannon MW. Etiology of childhood lead poisoning. In: Pueschel SM, Linakis JG, Anderson AC, eds. *Lead Poisoning in Childhood.* Baltimore, MD: Paul H. Brookes Publishing Company; 1996:37–58.

16. Edwards M, Triantafyllidou S, Best D. Elevated blood lead in young children due to lead-contaminated drinking water: Washington, DC. *Environ Sci Technol.* 2009;43(5):1618–1623.

17. Miranda ML, Kim D, Hull AP, Paul CJ, Overstreet Galeano MA. Changes in blood lead levels associated with use of choramines in water treatment systems. *Environ Health Perspect*. 2007;111(2):221–225.

18. Edwards M. Designing sampling for targeting lead and copper: implications for exposure. Lecture presented to: the US Environmental Protection Agency National Drinking Water Advisory Group; September 18, 2014.

19. Davidson CI, Rabinowitz M. Lead in the environment: from sources to human receptors. In: Needleman HL, ed. *Human Lead Exposure*. Boca Raton, FL: CRC Press; 1991.

20. Gaines RH. The corrosion of lead. *J Ind Eng Chem*. 1913;5(9): 766–768.

21. Raab GM, Laxen DPH, Anderson N, Davis S, Heaps M, Fulton M. The influence of pH and household plumbing on water lead concentration. *Environ Geochem Health*. 1993;15(4):191–200.

22. Toxicological profile for lead. US Department of Health and Human Services, Public Health Service, Agency for Toxic Substances and Diseases Registry. 2007. Available at: http://www.atsdr.cdc.gov/toxprofiles/tp13.pdf. Accessed October 6, 2015.

23. Ngueta G, Belkacem A, Tarduf R, St-Laurent J, Levallois P. Use of a cumulative exposure index to estimate the impact of tap-water lead concentration on blood lead levels in 1- to 5-year-old children (Montreal, Canada). *Environ Health Perspect*. 2015; Epub ahead of print.

24. Triantafyllidou S, Gallagher D, Edwards M. Assessing risk with increasingly stringent public health goals: the case of water lead and blood lead in children. *J Water Health*. 2014;12(1):57–68.

25. US Environmental Protection Agency. Safe Drinking Water Act Lead and Copper Rule (LCR). *Fed Regist*. 1991;56:26460–26564.

26. Edwards M. Fetal death and reduced birth rates associated with exposure to lead-contaminated drinking water. *Environ Sci Technol*. 2014;48(1):739–746.

27. Advisory Committee on Childhood Lead Poisoning Prevention. Recommendations for blood lead screening of young children enrolled in Medicaid: targeting a group at high risk. *MMWR Recomm Rep*. 2000; 49 (RR-14):1–13.

28. Jacobs AJ. The impacts of variations in development context on employment growth: a comparison of central cities in Michigan and Ontario, 1980–2006. *Econ Dev Q*. 2009;23(4):351–371.

29. Kids Count Data Center. A project of the Annie E Casey Foundation. Available at: http://datacenter. kidscount.org/data#MI/3/0. Accessed September 26, 2015.

30. County health rankings and roadmaps: building a culture of health, county by county. Available at: http://www.countyhealthrankings.org/app /michigan/2015/overview. Accessed September 26, 2015.

31. Michigan MIECHV Needs Assessment FY2015. Available at: http://www.michigan.gov/documents/homevisiting/Updated_MHVI_Needs _Assessment_2014_All_counties_474015_7.pdf. Accessed October 5, 2015.

32. US Census Bureau. Quick Facts Beta. Available at: http://www.census .gov/quickfacts/table/PST045214/00, 2629000,26. Accessed September 2015.

33. Lewis PF. Impact of Negro migration on the electoral geography of Flint, Michigan, 1932–1962: a cartographic analysis. *Ann Assoc Am Geogr.* 1965;55(1):1–25.

34. Taeuber KE, Taeuber AF. *Negroes in Cities: Residential Segregation and Neighborhood Change.* Chicago, IL: Aldine Publishing Company; 1969.

35. Highsmith AR. Demolition means progress: urban renewal, local politics, and state-sanctioned ghetto formation in Flint, Michigan. *J Urban Hist.* 2009;35:348–368.

36. Zimmer BG, Hawley AH. Approaches to the solution of fringe problems: preferences of residents in the Flint metropolitan area. *Public Adm Rev.* 1956;16(4):258–268.

37. Board LM, Dunsmore HJ. Environmental health problems related to urban decentralization: as observed in a typical metropolitan community. *Am J Public Health Nations Health.* 1948;38(7):986–996.

38. Martin R, Tang M. Percent lead in water by Flint ward. Flint Water Study. 2015. Available at: http://i0.wp.com/flintwaterstudy.org/wp -content/uploads/2015/09/Flint-Ward-Map_252-989x1280-2.jpg. Accessed September 26, 2015.

39. Pampalon R, Hamel D, Gamache P, Raymond G. A deprivation index for health planning in Canada. *Chronic Dis Can.* 2009;29(4):178–191.

40. Sadler RC, Gilliland JA, Arku G. Community development and the influence of new food retail sources on the price and availability of nutritious food. *J Urban Aff.* 2013;35(4):471–491.

41. Hastings D, Miranda ML. Using GIS-based models to protect children from lead exposure in international series in operations research and management science. In: Johnson M, ed. *Community-Based Operations Research: Decision Modeling for Local Impact and Diverse Populations.* 1st ed. New York, NY: Springer-Verlag New York; 2012:173–187.

42. Schwarz K, Pickett STA, Lathrop RG, Weathers KC, Pouyat RV, Cadenasso ML. The effects of the urban built environment on the spatial distribution of lead in residential soils. *Environ Pollut.* 2012;163:32–39.

43. Griffith DA, Doyle PG, Wheeler DC, Johnson DL. A tale of two swaths: urban childhood blood-lead levels across Syracuse, New York. *Ann Assoc Am Geogr.* 1998;88(4):640–665.

44. Jernigan RW. *A Primer on Kriging.* Washington, DC: US Environmental Protection Agency; 1986.

45. Markus J, McBratney AB. A review of the contamination of soil with lead: II. Spatial distribution and risk assessment of soil lead. *Environ Int.* 2001;27(5):399–411.

46. Schulz A, Northridge ME. Social determinants of health: implications for environmental health promotion. *Health Educ Behav.* 2004;31(4):455–471.

47. Genesee County Health Department. Re: Breastfeeding initiation challenge. 2010. Available at: http://www.gchd.net/PressReleases /20100923bfeeding_challenge.asp. Accessed October 6, 2015.

48. Sherlock JC, Quinn MJ. Relationship between blood lead concentrations and dietary lead intake in infants: the Glasgow Duplicate Diet Study 1979–1980. *Food Addit Contam.* 1986;3(2):167–176.

49. Sen A, Heredia N, Senut M-C, et al. Multigenerational epigenetic inheritance in humans: DNA methylation changes associated with maternal exposure to lead can be transmitted to the grandchildren. *Sci Rep.* 2015;5:14466.

50. Fonger R. Elevated lead found in more Flint kids after water switch, study finds. *Mlive Media Group.* September 24, 2015. Available at: http://www.mlive.com/news/flint/index.ssf/2015/09/study_shows_twice_as _many_flin.html. Accessed November 8, 2015.

51. Fonger R. Flint makes lead advisory official, suggests water filters and flushing. *Mlive Media Group.* September 25, 2015. Available at: http://www .mlive.com/news/flint/index.ssf/2015/09/flint_makes_lead_advisory_offi.html. Accessed October 6, 2015.

52. Johnson J. Don't drink Flint's water, Genesee County leaders warn. *Mlive Media Group.* October 1, 2015. Available at: http://www.mlive.com /news/flint/index.ssf/2015/10/genesee_county_leaders_warn_do.html. Accessed October 6, 2015.

53. Erb R, Gray K. State to tackle unsafe water in Flint with tests, filters. *Detroit Free Press.* October 2, 2015. Available at: http://www.freep.com/story /news/local/michigan/2015/10/02/state-officials-outline-plan-flintwater/ 73200250. Accessed October 6, 2015.

54. Wisely, J. Snyder announces $12-million plan to fix Flint water. *Detroit Free Press.* October 8, 2015. Available at: http://www.freep.com/story/news /local/michigan/2015/10/08/snyder-flint-water-reconnect/73567778. Accessed October 8, 2015.

55. Kestens Y, Lebel A, Chaix B, et al. Association between activity space exposure to food establishments and individual risk of overweight. *PLoS One.* 2012;7(8):e41418.

56. Tanner K, Kaffer N. State data confirms higher blood-lead levels in Flint kids. *Detroit Free Press.* September 29, 2015. Available at: http://www .freep.com/story/opinion/columnists/nancy-kaffer/2015/09/26/state-data-flint -lead/72820798. Accessed October 7, 2015.

57. US Environmental Protection Agency, Office of Water. Lead and Copper Rule 2007 short-term regulatory revisions and clarifications state implementation guidance. June 2008. Available at: http://water.epa.gov /lawsregs/rulesregs/sdwa/lcr/upload/New-Lead-and-Copper-Rule-LCR-2007 -Short-Term-Regulatory-Revisions-and-Clarifications-State-Implementation -Guidance.pdf. Accessed October 25, 2015.

58. Grevatt PC. Lead and Copper Rule requirements for optimal corrosion control treatment for large drinking water systems. Memo to EPA Regional Water Division Directors, Regions I-X. November 3, 2015. Available at: http://flintwaterstudy.org/wp-content/uploads/2015/11/LCR-Requirements-for -OCCT-for-Large-DW-Systems-11-03-2015.pdf. Accessed December 8, 2015.

59. *Healthy People 2020*: topics and objectives index. Washington, DC: US Department of Health and Human Services; 2012. Available at: http://www .healthypeople.gov/2020/topicsobjectives2020. Accessed October 27, 2015.

Joining the Conversation

1. This article from a respected journal of public health discusses the causes and impact of excessive levels of lead on children in Flint, Michigan, a mainly low-income community near Detroit. As is common in scientific reports, after a short overall summary known as an abstract and a few opening paragraphs, the article includes the following sections: Methods, Results, and Discussion. Describe in your own words the purpose or function of each of these sections, including the opening text.

2. The Discussion section includes the article's main conclusions regarding the crisis in Flint. Write a paragraph summarizing the authors' conclusions. What specific evidence do they provide in the Results section to support those conclusions?

3. When originally published, the article featured a subtitle, "A Spatial Analysis of Risk and Public Health Response," describing the focus of the study. Where in the article is the meaning of the term "spatial" explained? In what sense is the research spatial, and what is so important about this aspect of the study in terms of its findings?

4. Examine Table 1 on page 349. What do the data that are displayed in this table tell us about the lead crisis in Flint?

Taken as a whole, what does the information included in this table contribute to the authors' argument? Why do you think they chose to present this information in a visual format?

5. We recommend that writers address "so what?" and "who cares?" questions when writing an essay. Read a *Wikipedia* entry about the effects of lead poisoning, focusing specifically on the section discussing its effects on children. Then consider the findings of the Flint study, and write the "so what?" and "who cares?" questions you'd include if you were writing an essay on the subject of lead in drinking water.

Delivering Fresh Water: Critical Infrastructure, Environmental Justice, and Flint, Michigan

MICHAEL R. GREENBERG

—▣—

THE ARTICLE BY HANNA-ATTISHA ET AL. about water-related lead poisoning in Flint, Michigan,[1] may be interpreted by some to mean that Flint was an aberration—a singular policy failure to both obtain and deliver a potable water supply. Flint may be among the worst water system contamination cases, but it is not the only one, as we are learning. Flint offers the chance to rethink what we mean by critical infrastructure and what environmental justice implies in regard to fresh water in the United States.

See Chapter 4 on agreeing, but with a difference.

MICHAEL R. GREENBERG is Distinguished Professor at the Edward J. Bloustein School of Planning and Public Policy at Rutgers University. He studies the political and economic relationships among public health and safety, environmental health, risk management, and urban planning. He has published more than thirty books and more than three hundred articles, and he has served on numerous boards and task forces, including the EPA Science Advisory Board and the National Research Council Committee. This article was published in *American Journal of Public Health* in August 2016.

Critical Infrastructure

Critical infrastructure is a term used to identify public and private assets that are required for society and the economy to function. The US Presidential Policy Directive 21 (PPD-21) defines 16 critical infrastructure sectors. Water and wastewater are one of the 16 and are assigned to the US Environmental Protection Agency (EPA). The national plan for water and wastewater, organized around risk assessment and management principles, is a good step forward.[2] But the national plan was formulated to address terrorism threats rather than to respond to a long-standing gradual deterioration of the guts of the critical fresh water systems. I am not criticizing the EPA; not to think of water as a target for terrorists would be inexcusable, and so the fact that some reservoirs now resemble fortresses with armed guards is unfortunate but necessary.

But how did we get so distracted by homeland security concerns that we forgot about public health principles regarding water sources and infrastructure? Flint is a painful reminder of the fact that we need to insist on assessment of the risks associated with changing a water source. Urban water systems were designed to deliver safe potable water. How ludicrous and sad it is that we have spent tens of billions of dollars to protect the public against terrorists and remove toxins from raw water before we push it through the system, only to find that the potable water is incompatible with the delivery system and is an equal or even worse threat than deliberate contamination and water pollution. Older cities such as Flint are undermined by badly deteriorated infrastructure. Unless a new project is built or a pipe bursts, there is a good chance that we will not know that the infrastructure is failing because it has gradually deteriorated, sometimes not able to deliver water for firefighting.

With more than 150 000 public water systems in the United States dispensing about 85% of the freshwater supply, rethinking what constitutes critical infrastructure requires a major intellectual recalibration and fiscal challenge.[2] Not only must the status of water sources be monitored but also the conveyance, treatment, storage, and other system elements that influence the quantity and quality of water. In very tight budget times, decisions need to be made about what to upgrade with the primary goal of protecting human health and safety, not other priorities related to water supply.

Environmental Justice and Potable Water

Flint's population is relatively poor, with a large proportion of 5 African Americans. Flint fits the pattern of poor living in many physically distressed neighborhoods. Such urban neighborhoods typically have relatively high burdens of environmental deterioration that includes water and other infrastructure systems, public problems such as crime and physical blight, poor public education systems, and a limited tax base. It is not surprising why water supply cases like Flint occur. Water supply problems are typically much less visible than many others.

Environmental justice issues with the water supply are not limited to our oldest, poorest, and resource-starved city neighborhoods. Balazs and Ray's outstanding paper[3] underscored these issues among the rural poor in California's San Joaquin Valley and provided provocative historical and social context for rural water environmental justice problems. Indeed, monitoring data comparing ground and surface water supplies collected as early as the 1970s document the reality that contaminated water is more likely in rural areas than in cities because pollutants in rural aquifers move slowly and take longer to dilute than the same contamination in a river or lake. I developed and implemented a risk communication protocol to explain to people who relied on their own wells that their potable water was contaminated and needed to be replaced. Many of them were angry, did not believe what we were telling them, and when they understood the data were afraid that they inevitably were going to contract cancer.

Outside the relatively water-secure parts of the United States, Europe and other fortunate locations around the world, potable water problems are often nearly intractable and often getting worse, especially in the already poor and underserved areas. For one third to one sixth of the world's population, primarily in Africa, the Middle East, and western Asia,[4,5] there may not be a good water source that can be reached, infrastructure to treat and deliver it, or enough water to meet rising demands. Many

Sign in Flint, Michigan.

No water sign in San Joaquin Valley, California.

of these places have already experienced serious droughts, rapid urbanization and industrialization, diversion and degradation of their local water supplies, and conflict over freshwater rights with their neighbors.[6]

The US Freshwater Challenge

I offer no simple solutions. We know that governments sell fresh water to their residential and commercial customers to create local jobs and raise revenue. But if they cannot afford to maintain their systems, they need to consider other options, such as mergers and selling their systems to private companies, to protect human health and safety. These companies, many large international water purveyors, can invest to maintain water systems. But they

For more on embedding references to others' arguments, see Chapter 5.

are profit-making organizations, and ultimately communities will pay for the upgrade. Local governments and states will need to decide whether they want to take this step to avoid potentially creating a self-inflicted human health wound on their communities.

The Flint case represents an opportunity to educate elected officials, their staff, and the public about what neglect of a critical infrastructure system delivering an irreplaceable resource must eventually bring. Once the Flint and related cases have died down, the political process will once again divert attention from dealing with the legacy of critical infrastructure deterioration.[7] The Safe Drinking Water Act was intended to protect drinking water quality, and has to some extent, but has not delivered what it could have with greater support.[8] It needs help from elected officials and public groups.

Public health practitioners need to press for and support assessment and management of local water quality and quantity problems before water ever reaches the tap. Their efforts may not be welcomed by elected officials and their administrative staff who will claim that public health is invading their turf. But public health practitioners can effectively insist that providing safe water distribution to homes, schools, and other consumer locations in all neighborhoods is essential and environmentally just. I do not view the US potable water supply problem as intractable, despite the legacy of neglect and ongoing unhelpful political decisions. The issue has been placed at or near the bottom of the "to do" and "to fund" piles on elected officials' desks. The Flint urban case and the San Joaquin, California, rural one tells us that freshwater is critical infrastructure that needs to be a much higher priority.

References

1. Hanna-Attisha M, LaChance J, Sadler RC, Schnepp AC. Elevated blood levels in children associated with the Flint drinking water crisis: a spatial analysis of risk and public health response. *Am J Public Health.* 2016;106(2):283–290.

2. US Environmental Protection Agency. *Water Sector-Specific Plan.* Washington, DC: US Department of Homeland Security; 2010.

3. Balazs CL, Ray I. The drinking water disparities framework: on the origins and persistence of inequities in exposure. *Am J Public Health.* 2014;104(4):603–611.

4. Greenberg M, Ferrer J. Global availability of water. In: Friis R, ed. *The Prager Handbook of Environmental Health. Vol. 3. Water, Air, & Sold Water.* Santa Barbara, CA; 2012:1–20.

5. Gleick P, ed. *The World's Water 2008-2009.* Washington, DC: Island Press; 2008.

6. Greenberg MR. Water, conflict, and hope. *Am J Public Health.* 2009;99(11):1928–1930.

7. Committee on Predicting Outcomes of Investments in Maintenance and Repair for Federal Facilities. *Predicting Outcomes of Investments in Maintenance and Repair of Federal Facilities.* Washington, DC: National Academy Press; 2012.

8. US Environmental Protection Agency. 25 years of the Safe Drinking Water Act. History and Trends. Available at: https://yosemite.epa.gov/water/owrccatalog.nsf/0/b126b7616c71450285256d83004fda48? OpenDocument. Accessed April 3, 2016.

Joining the Conversation

1. Michael R. Greenberg is responding in this essay to the research report by Dr. Mona Hanna-Attisha and her colleagues (see pp. 342–67) on the water-related lead poisoning crisis in Flint, Michigan. He begins his response by making a "they say / I say" distinction. Restate in your own words the "they say" and "I say" statements that he introduces. Judging from his "I say" statement, what view is the author advancing?

2. After reading through Greenberg's response as a whole, consider what the author is arguing in relation to the Hanna-Attisha et al. study. Cite three examples from his response to support your answer.

3. Find the official website of the government agency in charge of the water supply in your locality. What specifically does it say about the health and safety of your drinking water? How do you think Greenberg would evaluate this statement?

4. The author titles the final section of this short essay "The US Freshwater Challenge." He begins this section by stating, "I offer no simple solutions." Why not? What are the issues and challenges that make providing clean drinking water such a complex matter?

5. Write a "they say / I say" essay in which you analyze the argument made by Hanna-Attisha and colleagues and the response by Greenberg. Be sure to include your own views on the subject of clean drinking water and environmental justice.

TWENTY

HOW CAN WE BRIDGE THE DIFFERENCES THAT DIVIDE US?

A 2020 REPORT FROM THE NONPARTISAN Pew Research Center surveying more than 12,000 Americans across the political spectrum is titled "U.S. Media Polarization and the 2020 Election: A Nation Divided." The report, authored by researchers Mark Jurkowitz, Amy Mitchell, Elisa Shearer, and Mason Walker, found that "Republicans and Democrats place their trust in two nearly inverse news media environments." In other words, the sources that Democrats see as credible Republicans tend to view as untrustworthy, and vice versa. We have seen in the most recent presidential elections how such distrust on a nationwide scale can poison the country's political atmosphere.

Across these hardening divisions, many people are frustrated by the stress and dysfunction of living in such a polarized society, wishing to find at least some common ground on which we may work together as citizens of one nation. Many believe it's time to work in earnest at improving communication and understanding across communities, but where exactly to start? Possible steps involve venturing out of our comfort zones to listen and pay attention to viewpoints that might challenge our own, finding ways to respond thoughtfully, and attempting to establish at least some common ground. The readings in this chapter offer a much-needed effort to understand and move beyond those differences—most likely not to the point where we can all agree on the burning issues of the day but at least to where we can once again live, work, and progress together.

One set of readings in this chapter pinpoints existing divisions and offer possible means of bridging those divides. Sean Blanda, writer and technology entrepreneur, suggests that we show compassion and respect for "the Other Side," his term for how we label people who don't think exactly the way we do. And danah boyd, a scholar who examines the intersection of society and technology, illustrates how Americans have self-segregated in recent decades—online, in college, in the military, and in the workplace—arguing that "we must find a healthy way to diversify our social connections." Coryell examines the phrase "all lives matter" used in response to the Black Lives Matter movement. She concludes that, if Black Lives Matter and similar movements are ignored or silenced, the status quo of racial inequality will be perpetuated.

Another set of readings in this chapter explores the attitudes and backgrounds of groups that many see as having been left behind. Legal scholar Michelle Alexander takes us to prisons across America to describe the discrimination faced by incarcerated members of our society, who, she argues, are overwhelmingly African American. This prison system is at the core of what she calls "the new Jim Crow." Linguist John McWhorter, analyzing transcripts of actual court trials, shows another way in which courts often misrepresent African Americans. He demonstrates that court stenographers frequently misunderstand nonstandard dialects, such as Black English, in trial testimony and on wiretap recordings, and that such misunderstandings may at times affect the outcome of a trial. In telling his own story, author J. D. Vance writes about growing up poor and Appalachian in Ohio and Kentucky and making his way out of poverty to Yale University Law School and a career in investment banking. He finds that a sense of hopelessness and despair is undermining his community and prevents many from embracing available opportunities. Scholar Lisa Pruitt, from a background quite similar to Vance's, discusses the complicated role of race and attitudes toward it in the lives of working-class Appalachians.

A final set of readings in the chapter examines controversy over immigration to the United States. Journalist and professor Sudeku Mehta, whose family came to the United States from India when he was a child, cites evidence showing that immigration as a whole benefits the country economically as well as culturally. In contrast, writer and political consultant David Frum presents a less rosy view of immigration's impact on the nation.

As you read this chapter—and its companion website, *"They Say/I Blog"*—you will encounter a variety of perspectives, face the challenge to examine and perhaps reconsider your own views, and have the opportunity to contribute to this vital, ongoing conversation.

The "Other Side" Is Not Dumb

SEAN BLANDA

—▭—

THERE'S A FUN GAME I like to play in a group of trusted
friends called "Controversial Opinion." The rules are simple:
Don't talk about what was shared during Controversial Opinion
afterward and you aren't allowed to "argue"—only to ask questions about why that person feels that way. Opinions can range
from "I think James Bond movies are overrated" to "I think
Donald Trump would make an excellent president."

Usually, someone responds to an opinion with, "Oh my god!
I had no idea you were one of *those* people!" Which is really
another way of saying "I thought you were on my team!"

In psychology, the idea that everyone is like us is called the
"false-consensus bias." This bias often manifests itself when we
see TV ratings ("Who the hell are all these people that watch
NCIS?") or in politics ("Everyone I know is for stricter gun

SEAN BLANDA builds editorial products that serve a variety of communities. He is also the cofounder of Technical.ly, a startup based in
Philadelphia that "grows local technology communities by connecting organizations and people through news, events, and services."
This 2016 essay first appeared in *Medium*, a website for news and
commentary.

control! Who are these backwards rubes that disagree?!") or polls ("Who are these people voting for Ben Carson?").

Online it means we can be blindsided by the opinions of our friends or, more broadly, America. Over time, this morphs into a subconscious belief that we and our friends are the sane ones and that there's a crazy "Other Side" that must be laughed at—an Other Side that just doesn't "get it," and is clearly not as intelligent as "us." But this holier-than-thou social media behavior is counterproductive; it's self-aggrandizement at the cost of actual nuanced discourse, and if we want to consider online discourse productive, we need to move past this.

What is emerging is the worst kind of echo chamber, one ₅ where those inside are increasingly convinced that everyone shares their world view, that their ranks are growing when they aren't. It's like clockwork: an event happens and then your social media circle is shocked when a non–social media peer group public reacts to news in an unexpected way. They then mock the Other Side for being "out of touch" or "dumb."

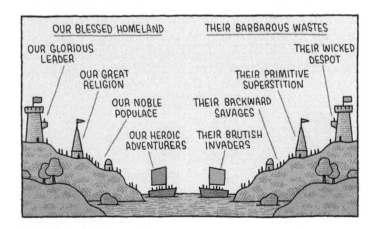

Fredrik deBoer, one of my favorite writers around, touched on this in his essay "Getting Past the Coalition of the Cool." He writes:

> [The Internet] encourages people to collapse any distinction between their work life, their social life, and their political life. "Hey, that person who tweets about the TV shows I like also dislikes injustice," which over time becomes "I can identify an ally by the TV shows they like." The fact that you can mine a Rihanna video for political content becomes, in that vague internety way, the sense that people who don't see political content in Rihanna's music aren't on your side.

When someone communicates that they are not "on our side" our first reaction is to run away or dismiss them as stupid. To be sure, there are hateful, racist people not worthy of the small amount of electricity it takes [for] just one of your synapses to fire. I'm instead referencing those who actually believe in an opposing viewpoint of a complicated issue, and do so for genuine, considered reasons. Or at least, for reasons just as good as yours.

This is not a "political correctness" issue. It's a fundamental rejection of the possibility to consider that the people who don't feel the same way you do might be right. It's a preference to see

About how often do you hear or read something in the news that makes you angry?

| 31% A few times a day | 37% Once a day | 20% Once a week | 5% Once a month | 6% Rarely |

the Other Side as a cardboard cutout, and not the complicated individual human beings that they actually are.

What happens instead of genuine intellectual curiosity is the sharing of *Slate* or *Daily Kos* or *Fox News* or *Red State* links. Sites that exist almost solely to produce content to be shared so friends can pat each other on the back and mock the Other Side. Look at the Other Side! So dumb and unable to see this the way I do!

Sharing links that mock a caricature of the Other Side isn't signaling that we're somehow more informed. It signals that we'd rather be smug assholes than consider alternative views. It signals that we'd much rather show our friends that we're like them than try to understand those who are not.

It's impossible to consider yourself a curious person and 10 participate in social media in this way. We cannot consider ourselves "empathetic" only to turn around and belittle those who don't agree with us.

On Twitter and Facebook this means we prioritize by sharing stuff that will garner approval of our peers over stuff that's actually, you know, true. We share stuff that ignores wider realities, selectively shares information, or is just an outright falsehood. The misinformation is so rampant that the *Washington Post* stopped publishing its Internet fact-checking column because people didn't seem to care if stuff was true.

> Where debunking an Internet fake once involved some research, it's now often as simple as clicking around for an "about" or "disclaimer" page. And where a willingness to believe hoaxes once seemed to come from a place of honest ignorance or misunderstanding, that's frequently no longer the case. Headlines like "Casey Anthony found dismembered in truck" go viral via old-fashioned schadenfreude—even hate.

...

Institutional distrust is so high right now, and cognitive bias so strong *always*, that the people who fall for hoax news stories are frequently only interested in consuming information that conforms with their views—even when it's demonstrably fake.

The solution, as deBoer says: "You have to be willing to sacrifice your carefully curated social performance and be willing to work with people who *are not like you*." In other words you have to recognize that the Other Side is made of actual people.

But I'd like to go a step further. We should all enter every issue with the very real possibility that *we might be wrong this time*.

Isn't it possible that you, reader of *Medium* and Twitter power user, like me, suffer from this from time to time? Isn't it possible that we're not right about everything? That those who live in places not where you live, watch shows that you don't watch, and read books that you don't read, have opinions and belief systems just as valid as yours? That maybe you don't see the entire picture?

Think political correctness has gotten out of control? Follow the many great social activists on Twitter. Think America's stance on guns is puzzling? Read the stories of the 31% of Americans that own a firearm. This is not to say the Other Side is "right" but that they likely have real reasons to feel that way. And only after understanding those reasons can a real discussion take place.

See pp. 140–41 for ways to clarify and elaborate on your point.

As any debate club veteran knows, if you can't make your opponent's point for them, you don't truly grasp the issue. We can bemoan political gridlock and a divisive media all we want. But we won't truly progress as individuals until we make an honest effort to understand those that are not like us. And you won't convince anyone to feel the way you do if you don't respect their position and opinions.

A dare for the next time you're in a discussion with someone you disagree with: Don't try to "win." Don't try to "convince" anyone of your viewpoint. Don't score points by mocking them to your peers. Instead try to "lose." Hear them out. Ask them to convince you and mean it. No one is going to tell your environmentalist friends that you merely asked follow-up questions after your brother made his pro-fracking case.

Or, the next time you feel compelled to share a link on social media about current events, ask yourself why you are doing it. Is it because that link brings to light information you hadn't considered? Or does it confirm your world view, reminding your circle of intellectual teammates that you're not on the Other Side?

I implore you to seek out your opposite. When you hear someone cite "facts" that don't support your viewpoint don't think "that can't be true!" Instead consider, "Hm, maybe that person is right? I should look into this." Because refusing to truly understand those who disagree with you is intellectual laziness and worse, is *usually* worse than what you're accusing the Other Side of doing.

Joining the Conversation

1. Sean Blanda begins his essay by defining "false-consensus bias." Explain what this concept is, and give an example from your own experience or observation that you think demonstrates this bias.

2. In paragraph 6, Blanda introduces a quotation by Fredrik deBoer, but he doesn't follow it with an explanation. How would you recommend that Blanda do so? (See pp. 51–52 for ways to create a "quotation sandwich.")

3. So what? Who cares? Where in this piece does Blanda explain why his argument matters? Has he persuaded you, and if not, why not?

4. In "Hillbilly Elegy," J. D. Vance (pp. 433–50) discusses why some Americans view liberals with disdain. What concrete suggestions do you think Blanda would make to encourage them to move beyond the stereotypes they might have of liberals?

5. Choose an issue of importance to you and write a tweet (280 characters or less) or a *Facebook* post that demonstrates respect for the "Other Side."

6. Go to **theysayiblog.com** and search for "(Alt) right and wrong" by Brendan Novak. How do Novak's views compare with Blanda's—how are they similar, and how are they different?

Why America Is Self-Segregating

DANAH BOYD

———————

THE UNITED STATES has always been a diverse but segregated country. This has shaped American politics profoundly. Yet, throughout history, Americans have had to grapple with divergent views and opinions, political ideologies, and experiences in order to function as a country. Many of the institutions that underpin American democracy force people in the United States to encounter difference. This does not inherently produce tolerance or result in healthy resolution. Hell, the history of the United States is fraught with countless examples of people enslaving and oppressing other people on the basis of difference. This isn't about our past; this is about our present. And today's battles over laws and culture are nothing new.

———————

DANAH BOYD is a researcher at Microsoft Research and an adjunct professor at New York University. She is the author of *It's Complicated: The Social Lives of Networked Teens* (2014) and the founder of Data & Society, a research institute "focused on the social and cultural issues arising from data-centric technological development." This essay first appeared in 2017 on *Points*, a blog of Data & Society.

Ironically, in a world in which we have countless tools to connect, we are also watching fragmentation, polarization, and de-diversification happen en masse. The American public is self-segregating, and this is tearing at the social fabric of the country.

Many in the tech world imagined that the Internet would connect people in unprecedented ways, allow for divisions to be bridged and wounds to heal. It was the kumbaya dream. Today, those same dreamers find it quite unsettling to watch as the tools that were designed to bring people together are used by people to magnify divisions and undermine social solidarity. These tools were built in a bubble, and that bubble has burst.

Nowhere is this more acute than with Facebook. Naive as hell, Mark Zuckerberg dreamed he could build the tools that would connect people at unprecedented scale, both domestically and internationally. I actually feel bad for him as he clings to that hope while facing increasing attacks from people around the world about the role that Facebook is playing in magnifying social divisions. Although critics love to paint him as only motivated by money, he genuinely wants to make the world a better place and sees Facebook as a tool to connect people, not empower them to self-segregate.

The problem is not simply the "filter bubble," Eli Pariser's 5 notion that personalization-driven algorithmic systems help silo people into segregated content streams. Facebook's claim that content personalization plays a small role in shaping what people see compared to their own choices is accurate. And they have every right to be annoyed. I couldn't imagine TimeWarner being blamed for who watches *Duck Dynasty* vs. *Modern Family*. And yet, what Facebook does do is mirror and magnify a trend that's been unfolding in the United States for the last twenty years, a trend of self-segregation that is enabled by technology in all sorts of complicated ways.

The United States can only function as a healthy democracy if we find a healthy way to diversify our social connections, if we find a way to weave together a strong social fabric that bridges ties across difference.

Yet, we are moving in the opposite direction with serious consequences. To understand this, let's talk about two contemporary trend lines and then think about the implications going forward.

See p. 144 for ways to provide a roadmap for your readers.

Privatizing the Military

The voluntary US military is, in many ways, a social engineering project. The public understands the military as a service organization, dedicated to protecting the country's interests. Yet, when recruits sign up, they are promised training and job opportunities. Individual motivations vary tremendously, but many are enticed by the opportunity to travel the world, participate in a cause with a purpose, and get the heck out of Dodge. Everyone expects basic training to be physically hard, but few recognize that some of the most grueling aspects of signing up have to do with the diversification project that is central to the formation of the American military.

When a soldier is in combat, she must trust her fellow soldiers with her life. And she must be willing to do what it takes to protect the rest of her unit. In order to make that possible, the military must wage war on prejudice. This is not an easy task. Plenty of generals fought hard to fight racial desegregation and to limit the role of women in combat. Yet, the US military was desegregated in 1948, six years before *Brown* v. *Board* forced desegregation of schools. And the Supreme Court ruled that LGB individuals could openly serve in the military before they could legally marry.

Morale is often raised as the main reason that soldiers should 10 not be forced to entrust their lives to people who are different than them. Yet, time and again, this justification collapses under broader interests to grow the military. As a result, commanders are forced to find ways to build up morale across difference, to actively and intentionally seek to break down barriers to teamwork, and to find a way to gel a group of people whose demographics, values, politics, and ideologies are as varied as the country's.

In the process, they build one of the most crucial social infrastructures of the country. They build the diverse social fabric that underpins democracy.

Tons of money was poured into defense after 9/11, but the number of people serving in the US military today is far lower than it was throughout the 1980s. Why? Starting in the 1990s and accelerating after 9/11, the US privatized huge chunks of the military. This means that private contractors and their employees play critical roles in everything from providing food services to equipment maintenance to military housing. The impact of this on the role of the military in society is significant. For example, this undermines recruits' ability to get training to develop critical skills that will be essential for them in civilian life. Instead, while serving on active duty, they spend a much higher amount of time on the front lines and in high-risk battle, increasing the likelihood that they will be physically or psychologically harmed. The impact on skills development and job opportunities is tremendous, but so is the impact on the diversification of the social fabric.

Private vendors are not engaged in the same social engineering project as the military and, as a result, tend to hire and fire people based on their ability to work effectively as a team. Like many companies, they have little incentive to invest in helping diverse teams learn to work together as effectively as possible. Building diverse teams—especially ones in which members depend on each other for their survival—is extremely hard, time-consuming, and emotionally exhausting. As a result, private companies focus on "culture fit," emphasize teams that get along, and look for people who already have the necessary skills, all of which helps reinforce existing segregation patterns.

The end result is that, in the last 20 years, we've watched one of our major structures for diversification collapse without anyone taking notice. And because of how it's happened, it's also connected to job opportunities and economic opportunity for many working- and middle-class individuals, seeding resentment and hatred.

A Self-Segregated College Life

If you ask a college admissions officer at an elite institution to describe how they build a class of incoming freshmen, you will quickly realize that the American college system is a diversification project. Unlike colleges in most parts of the world, the vast majority of freshmen at top tier universities in the United States live on campus with roommates who are assigned to them. Colleges approach housing assignments as an opportunity to pair diverse strangers with one another to build social ties. This makes sense given how many friendships emerge out of freshman dorms. By pairing middle class kids with students from wealthier families, elite institutions help diversify the elites of the future.

This diversification project produces a tremendous amount of conflict. Although plenty of people adore their college roommates and relish the opportunity to get to know people from different walks of life as part of their college experience, there is an amazing amount of angst about dorm assignments and the troubles that brew once folks try to live together in close quarters. At many universities, residential life is often in the business of student therapy as students complain about their roommates and dormmates. Yet, just like in the military, learning how to negotiate conflict and diversity in close quarters can be tremendously effective in sewing the social fabric.

In the spring of 2006, I was doing fieldwork with teenagers at a time when they had just received acceptances to college. I giggled at how many of them immediately wrote to the college in which they intended to enroll, begging for a campus email address so that they could join that school's Facebook (before Facebook was broadly available). In the previous year, I had watched the previous class look up roommate assignments on MySpace so I was prepared for the fact that they'd use Facebook to do the same. What I wasn't prepared for was how quickly they would all get on Facebook, map the incoming freshman class, and use this information to ask for a roommate switch. Before they even arrived on campus in August/September of 2006, they had self-segregated as much as possible.

A few years later, I watched another trend hit: cell phones. While these were touted as tools that allowed students to stay connected to parents (which prompted many faculty to complain about "helicopter parents" arriving on campus), they really ended up serving as a crutch to address homesickness, as incoming students focused on maintaining ties to high school friends rather than building new relationships.

Students go to elite universities to "get an education." Few realize that the true quality product that elite colleges in the US have historically offered is social network diversification. Even when it comes to job acquisition, sociologists have long known that diverse social networks ("weak ties") are what increase job prospects. By self-segregating on campus, students undermine their own potential while also helping fragment the diversity of the broader social fabric.

Diversity Is Hard

Diversity is often touted as highly desirable. Indeed, in profes- 20 sional contexts, we know that more diverse teams often outperform homogeneous teams. Diversity also increases cognitive development, both intellectually and socially. And yet, actually encountering and working through diverse viewpoints, experiences, and perspectives is hard work. It's uncomfortable. It's emotionally exhausting. It can be downright frustrating.

Thus, given the opportunity, people typically revert to situations where they can be in homogeneous environments. They look for "safe spaces" and "culture fit." And systems that are "personalized" are highly desirable. Most people aren't looking to self-segregate, but they do it anyway. And, increasingly, the technologies and tools around us allow us to self-segregate with ease. Is your uncle annoying you with his political rants? Mute him. Tired of getting ads for irrelevant products? Reveal your preferences. Want your search engine to remember the things that matter to you? Let it capture data. Want to watch a TV show that appeals to your senses? Here are some recommendations.

Any company whose business model is based on advertising revenue and attention is incentivized to engage you by giving you what you want. And what you want in theory is different than what you want in practice.

Consider, for example, what Netflix encountered when it started its streaming offer. Users didn't watch the movies that they had placed into their queue. Those movies were the movies they thought they wanted, movies that reflected their ideal self— *12 Years a Slave*, for example. What they watched when they could stream whatever they were in the mood for at that moment was the equivalent of junk food—reruns of *Friends*, for example. (This completely undid Netflix's recommendation infrastructure, which had been trained on people's idealistic self-images.)

The divisions are not just happening through commercialism though. School choice has led people to self-segregate from childhood on up. The structures of American work life mean that fewer people work alongside others from different socioeconomic backgrounds. Our contemporary culture of retail and service labor means that there's a huge cultural gap between workers and customers with little opportunity to truly get to know one another. Even many religious institutions are increasingly fragmented such that people have fewer interactions across diverse lines. (Just think about how there are now "family services" and "traditional services" which age-segregate.) In so many parts of public, civic, and professional life, we are self-segregating and the opportunities for doing so are increasing every day.

By and large, the American public wants to have strong 25 connections across divisions. They see the value politically and socially. But they're not going to work for it. And given the option, they're going to renew their license remotely, try to get out of jury duty, and use available data to seek out housing and schools that are filled with people like them. This is the conundrum we now face.

Many pundits remarked that, during the 2016 election season, very few Americans were regularly exposed to people whose political ideology conflicted with their own. This is true. But it cannot be fixed by Facebook or news media. Exposing people to content that challenges their perspective doesn't actually make them more empathetic to those values and perspectives. To the contrary, it polarizes them. What makes people willing to hear difference is knowing and trusting people whose worldview differs from their own. Exposure to content cannot make up for self-segregation.

If we want to develop a healthy democracy, we need a diverse and highly connected social fabric. This requires creating contexts in which the American public voluntarily struggles with the challenges of diversity to build bonds that will last a lifetime. We have been systematically undoing this, and the public has used new technological advances to make their lives easier by self-segregating. This has increased polarization, and we're going to pay a heavy price for this going forward. Rather than focusing on what media enterprises can and should do, we need to focus instead on building new infrastructures for connection where people have a purpose for coming together across divisions. We need that social infrastructure just as much as we need bridges and roads.

Joining the Conversation

1. Writer danah boyd argues that rather than becoming a more diverse nation, the United States is becoming a nation of self-contained identity groups. What evidence does she provide to support her argument? In what ways does your own experience support or challenge boyd's view?

2. In paragraph 4, boyd writes that Mark Zuckerberg is "naive as hell," using language that is informal, especially in contrast to her discussion of "fragmentation, polarization, and de-diversification," which are happening "en masse" (paragraph 2). How does this blend of styles affect your response to the essay?

3. According to boyd, we like the idea of diversity, but we're "not willing to work for it" (paragraph 25). How do you think Sean Blanda (pp. 380–86) might respond?

4. Write an essay responding to boyd, drawing on your own experiences in college, online, in the military, or with something else. Frame your argument as a response to boyd.

5. Self-segregation in college life is a topic on the minds of other writers, too. Go to **theysayiblog.com**, and search for Conor Friedersdorf. Read his essay on elitism in college dorms. What does he say about them?

All Words Matter: The Manipulation behind "All Lives Matter"

KELLY CORYELL

—◻—

I'VE NEVER UNDERSTOOD THE POPULAR SAYING "Sticks and stones may break my bones, but words will never hurt me." I grew up as a tomboy; I've had more than my fair share of scrapes, bruises, and stitches. But I've found that words inflict the most painful injuries. On sleepless nights when I toss and turn, I'm not replaying the time I broke my foot over and over in my head—I'm thinking about some embarrassing thing I said that still makes me physically cringe or a time someone said something hurtful to me. Broken bones heal—words stay with us.

This is because words have power. A skilled wordsmith can influence us by using evocative words that elicit an emotional response. The meanings of these "loaded" words aren't located in a dictionary. There is a context surrounding them that implies

———

KELLY CORYELL wrote this essay in her first-year writing course at Diablo Valley College in Pleasant Hill, CA. An English major, Coryell works as a tutor in the college's learning center and serves as a supplemental instruction leader for multilingual students. She plans to become an English professor. This essay, which is documented in MLA Style, was nominated for the Norton Writer's Prize.

a meaning beyond the basic information they convey. Loaded words and phrases appeal to our emotions, not our logic—they enter our hearts, not our minds. They can manipulate, so sometimes people use loaded language to distract us from a flawed argument.

Such is the case when people use the phrase "all lives matter" to oppose the phrase "Black lives matter." In 2012, neighborhood watch coordinator George Zimmerman shot and killed Trayvon Martin, an unarmed African American teenager returning home from a late-night snack run. In 2013, Zimmerman was acquitted of all charges. This sparked the birth of the Black Lives Matter (BLM) movement, when activists Alicia Garza, Opal Tometi, and Patrisse Cullors, frustrated with the systemic inequality and oppression exemplified by Zimmerman's trial, started using the hashtag #BlackLivesMatter on *Twitter*. As more and more Black people died during police confrontations or in police custody—Eric Garner, Michael Brown, Tamir Rice, Walter Scott, Freddie Gray—the movement, chanting the phrase "Black lives matter," gained momentum and media coverage, eventually becoming a major talking point in the 2016 presidential election. And in the spring of 2020, the deaths of Ahmaud Arbery, Breonna Taylor, George Floyd, Rayshard Brooks, Dominique "Rem'mie" Fells, and Riah Milton reignited the BLM movement, leading to an overdue reckoning with racism in this country.

As a direct response, Americans who either disagreed with the BLM movement as a whole or who supported the movement but were uncomfortable with its slogan, began to chant their own phrase: "all lives matter." It should be acknowledged that some of those who have used the phrase "all lives matter" did so naïvely aiming to unify people in a time of division, thinking of the words as a positive affirmation to which no one could object. However, saying

See Chapter 1 for templates that introduce an ongoing debate.

"all lives matter" as a response to "Black lives matter" is, in reality, sending a dangerous message: it steals attention from the systematic oppression of Black Americans and actively distorts the message behind the BLM movement, manipulating the American people into maintaining the oppressive status quo.

The phrase "all lives matter" belies the current racial inequal- 5 ity in America by implying that all lives are at equal risk. The racism and prejudice endured by African Americans didn't end when slavery was abolished in 1865, it didn't end when Congress passed the Civil Rights Act of 1964, and it didn't end when a Black man was elected president of the United States in 2008. Racial inequality in America persists to this day, ingrained and interwoven so deeply in American society that our prison systems and manufacturing industries depend on it. It's so expertly hidden under layers of celebrity gossip in our media and blatant and bold lies from our politicians, and so "normalized" in our culture, that many people may not even be aware of the plight of Black Americans.

But the statistics speak for themselves. According to the NAACP, African Americans are incarcerated at six times the rate of white Americans for drug crimes ("Criminal Justice"). The Center for American Progress reported that in 2016, the median wealth of Black families was *only 10 percent* of the median wealth of white families (Hanks et al.). Police shoot and kill Black Americans at *two and a half times* the rate of white Americans, according to a 2016 report (Lowery). All these statistics point to the fact that Black lives are valued less than white lives in America. The BLM movement aims to change this depressing reality by insisting that "Black lives matter."

For more on how to use reasons to disagree, see Chapter 4.

Responding to "Black lives matter" with "all lives matter" ignores the unique prejudices and discrimination Black people experience in America. Chimamanda Ngozi Adichie makes a parallel argument in her essay "I Decided to Call Myself a Happy Feminist." Adichie explains why she calls herself a feminist instead of a human-rights activist. She writes:

> Feminism is, of course, part of human rights in general—but to choose to use the vague expression *human rights* is to deny the specific and particular problem of gender. . . . For centuries, the world divided human beings into two groups and then proceeded to exclude and oppress one group. It is only fair that the solution to the problem should acknowledge that.

Adichie's point is that not every human being suffers the oppression that women suffer. Therefore, campaigning for all humans, while noble, is irrelevant. It would ignore the specific plights of women, as well as the historical fact that those behind the oppression of women were other human beings—men. In the same way, emphasizing *all* lives takes much-needed focus away from the oppression specifically felt only by Black Americans—which is a direct result of the centuries of oppression at the hands of white Americans.

Later in her essay, Adichie recalls a conversation she once had about gender:

> A man said to me, "Why does it have to be you as a woman? Why not you as a human being?" This type of question is a way of silencing a person's specific experiences. Of course I am a human being, but there are particular things that happen to me in the world because I am a woman.

Shifting attention away from the female gender to the entirety of humankind silences the hardships women face *simply because they are women.* Talking over them by questioning their commitment to the whole, and not allowing them to share their experiences, smothers their voices. The same is true when shifting focus from "Black lives" to "all lives." Saying "all lives matter" ignores the unique discrimination only Black Americans face, *simply because they are Black.* Dismissing the importance and relevance of their struggles because everyone has struggles misses the point entirely.

"All lives matter" implies that all lives endure an equal amount of hardship; therefore, the struggles of Black Americans deserve no more attention than the struggles of white Americans—which is demonstrably false statistically. Daniel Victor illustrates the harmful way the phrase "all lives matter" removes focus from the hardships of Black Americans in his article "Why 'All Lives Matter' Is Such a Perilous Phrase" for *The New York Times.* He writes:

> Those in the Black Lives Matter movement say black people are in immediate danger and need immediate attention. . . .
>
> Saying "All Lives Matter" in response would suggest to them that all people are in equal danger, invalidating the specific concerns of black people.
>
> "You're watering the house that's not burning, but you're choosing to leave the house that's burning unattended," said Allen Kwabena Frimpong, an organizer for the New York chapter of Black Lives Matter. "It's irresponsible."

To put it simply, focusing too much on the whole can divert much needed attention from crises affecting a specific group. As one *Twitter* user notes, "#AllLivesMatter is like I go to the Dr for a broken arm and he says 'All Bones Matter' ok but right now let's take care of this broken one" (SOAPbox). In this analogy, only one bone needs immediate attention—ignoring it because all bones are important to a person's health isn't an appropriate response to the situation. Nor would be putting the injured person in a full-body cast—though that would be treating every bone equally. "All lives matter" doesn't acknowledge that the lives of Black Americans are in greater danger due to the hundreds of years of systematic racism designed to devalue them. The point of saying "Black lives matter" is to bring attention to the fact that Black lives do not matter in our society. The BLM movement is not simply saying "Black people are shot and killed by the police," it's saying "Black people are shot and killed by the police *at two and a half times the rate of white people*." Replying with "all races are shot and killed by the police" can be an acceptable response to the first statement, *but not the second*. Yet that is exactly what saying "all lives matter" does—it ignores the second statement, ignores the voices of BLM activists.

Using "all lives matter" as a response to "Black lives matter" perpetuates the misconception that BLM activists do not believe both sentiments. The core of the BLM movement is the belief that *all* lives matter—*including* Black lives, which are treated differently than white lives, not just by law enforcement but America as a whole. As J. Clara Chan explains in her article "What Is 'All Lives Matter'? A Short Explainer":

> BLM supporters stress that the movement isn't about believing no other races matter. Instead, the movement seeks to highlight and change how racism disproportionately affects the black community, in terms of police brutality, job security, socioeconomic status, educational opportunities, and more.

The BLM movement's focus on particular inequities doesn't mean other races don't matter, but the phrase "all lives matter" is loaded language that implies they don't. Dave Bry explains this manipulation in his article titled "'All Lives Matter' Is and Always Was Racist—and This Weekend's Trump Rally Proved It" for the UK paper *The Guardian*. He writes:

> Often people who say "all lives matter" say it pointedly, correctively under the veneer of the idea that "all men are created equal." It is meant to refute the idea that "only" black lives matter.
>
> But understanding "black lives matter" to mean "only" black lives matter has been a misinterpretation from the beginning, one made in ignorance of the intent of the statement and the statistical facts that led to it.

That is to say, "all lives matter" misinterprets the point the BLM movement is making—that all lives do matter; therefore, Black lives need to matter as much as white lives in American society. It isn't "*only* Black lives matter"; it's "Black lives matter, *too*."

"All lives matter" manipulates people into believing those who say "Black lives matter" are against other lives. Jason Stanley explains the many ways language can be used as a tool for suppression in his *New York Times* opinion piece "The Ways of Silencing." Stanley writes, "Words are misappropriated and meanings twisted. I believe that these tactics . . . are, if you will, linguistic strategies for stealing the voices of others." In other words, a group can be silenced if the language vital to their ability to express themselves and their beliefs is co-opted by another group. Supporters of "all lives matter" co-opted the language of the BLM movement, forcing a separation between the two phrases. As a result, BLM activists cannot say "all lives matter" without sounding like they oppose the views of the BLM movement, since "all lives matter" is no longer just a phrase but a rebuttal—a counterargument.

Saying "all lives matter" is premature, since it presupposes that equality has already been achieved. If Black lives really did matter as much as white lives in American society, then saying so would be as uncontroversial as stating any other fact. In fact, America is not a postracial society: poverty, education, health, incarceration rates—all are unequal between different races in America. We must acknowledge this ugly truth if we are ever going to change it. "All lives matter" invokes a naïve reality in which all races are holding hands in a great big circle, singing "This Land Is Your Land" as the sun smiles down on the world. "All lives matter," like the statement "I don't see race, I just see people," may, at first, seem like a beautiful sentiment. Those who say such things may truly do so with the intent of creating a world where everyone is treated equally— regardless of race, gender, creed, orientation, and so on.

But upon close examination, these phrases—however well-meaning—are harmful because, aside from robbing people of their racial identities, they ignore race-based discrimination. How can one notice racism when one does not "see race"? How can one point out discrimination against African Americans if the only response one gets is "everyone matters"? If one insists that a goal has already been met when it hasn't, why would anyone put in more effort toward reaching that goal? This is why "all lives matter" is so manipulative and damaging. It's an attempt to convince us we don't have to keep reaching for equality and justice, even though every fact around us tells us this is far from the case. Only by consciously acknowledging racial inequality will we ever be able to put an end to it.

The root of "all lives matter" boils down to one thing: privi- 15 lege, and the reluctance to give it up in the name of equality. As Chris Boeskool puts it: "Equality can *feel* like oppression. But it's not. What you're feeling is just the discomfort of losing a little bit of your privilege." Evening the playing field can feel like a bad thing to the person benefiting from the imbalance. In the 1960s, a white bus rider may have felt oppressed when she started having to compete with Black bus riders for the front seat—she lost the privilege of getting a guaranteed front seat because of her race. In the 1970s, a man might have complained that he could no longer "compliment" his female coworkers without them accusing him of sexual harassment—he lost the privilege of being able to say offensive things because of his gender. If American society starts to accept that Black lives matter as much as white lives, white Americans will lose some of the privileges afforded to them as a result of the oppression of Black Americans. Therefore, people who either do not realize they have this privilege, or people who simply don't want to give it up, chant "all lives matter" in an effort to hold on to that privilege. If the BLM movement is silenced, the status quo of racial inequality will be maintained. The privileged must resist this unethical temptation and not mistake oppression as equality.

WORKS CITED

Adichie, Chimamanda Ngozi. "I Decided to Call Myself a Happy Feminist." *The Guardian*, 17 Oct. 2014, www.theguardian.com/books/2014/oct/17/chimamanda-ngozi-adichie-extract-we-should-all-be-feminists.

Boeskool, Chris. "When You're Accustomed to Privilege, Equality Feels Like Oppression." *HuffPost*, 14 Mar. 2016, www.huffpost.com/entry/when-youre-accustomed-to-privilege_b_9460662.

Bry, Dave. "'All Lives Matter' Is and Always Was Racist—and This Weekend's Trump Rally Proved It." *The Guardian*, 23 Nov. 2015, www.theguardian.com/commentisfree/2015/nov/23/all-lives-matter-racist-trump-weekend-campaign-rally-proved-it.

Chan, J. Clara. "What Is 'All Lives Matter'? A Short Explainer." *The Wrap*, 13 July 2016, www.thewrap.com/what-is-all-lives-matter-a-short-explainer.

"Criminal Justice Fact Sheet." *NAACP*, www.naacp.org/criminal-justice-fact-sheet. Accessed 12 Mar. 2019.

Hanks, Angela, et al. "Systematic Inequality: How America's Structural Racism Helped Create the Black–White Wealth Gap." *Center for American Progress*, 21 Feb. 2018, www.americanprogress.org/issues/race/reports/2018/02/21/447051/systematic-inequality.

Lowery, Wesley. "Aren't More White People Than Black People Killed by Police? Yes, but No." *The Washington Post*, 11 July 2016, www.washingtonpost.com/news/post-nation/wp/2016/07/11/arent-more-white-people-than-black-people-killed-by-police-yes-but-no.

SOAPbox [@djsoap92]. "#AllLivesMatter is like I go to the Dr for a broken arm and he says 'All Bones Matter' ok but right now let's take care of this broken one." *Twitter*, 5 July 2016, twitter.com/djsoap92/status/750563460921057280.

Stanley, Jason. "The Ways of Silencing." *The New York Times*, 25 June 2011, opinionater.blogsnytimes.com/2011/06/25/the-ways-of-silencing. Opinionator.

Victor, Daniel. "Why 'All Lives Matter' Is Such a Perilous Phrase." *The New York Times*, 15 July 2016, www.nytimes.com/2016/07/16/us/all-lives-matter-black-lives-matter.html.

Joining the Conversation

1. Paragraph 4 of this essay includes Kelly Coryell's "they say" and "I say" statements. Paraphrase these statements in your own words, and describe how the writer makes clear which statement is the "they say" and which the "I say."

2. What evidence and arguments does the author use in support of her position regarding the phrases "all lives matter" and "Black lives matter"?

3. The essay does not contain explicit responses to "so what?" and "who cares?" questions that explain why Coryell's arguments matter and for whom. See if you can construct these explanatory statements. Where in the essay would you insert them to best effect, and why?

4. The author quotes from a number of published works to develop her argument. Pick the quotation that you think offers the strongest support, and discuss how Coryell lays the groundwork for it beforehand and how she explains it afterward, a process described in Chapter 3 as the "quotation sandwich."

5. Write a response to this essay using at least one of each of the following "they say / I say" strategies: agree and disagree "I say" statement, "quotation sandwich," naysayer, and "so what?" and "who cares?" questions.

The New Jim Crow

MICHELLE ALEXANDER

—▢—

JARVIOUS COTTON CANNOT VOTE. Like his father, grandfather, great-grandfather, and great-great-grandfather, he has been denied the right to participate in our electoral democracy. Cotton's family tree tells the story of several generations of black men who were born in the United States but who were denied the most basic freedom that democracy promises—the freedom to vote for those who will make the rules and laws that govern one's life. Cotton's great-great-grandfather could not vote as a slave. His great-grandfather was beaten to death by the Ku Klux Klan for attempting to vote. His grandfather was prevented from voting by Klan intimidation. His father was barred from voting by poll taxes and literacy tests. Today, Jarvious Cotton

---

MICHELLE ALEXANDER is a lawyer and scholar known for her work to protect civil rights. She has taught at Stanford Law School and Ohio State University's law school, and she currently teaches at Union Theological Seminary in New York City. She is a contributing opinion writer for the *New York Times* and has written opinion pieces for the *Washington Post*, *Los Angeles Times*, *HuffPost*, and *Nation*, among other publications. She is the author of *The New Jim Crow: Mass Incarceration in the Age of Colorblindness* (2010); this selection is from the book's introduction and is documented using Chicago style.

cannot vote because he, like many black men in the United States, has been labeled a felon and is currently on parole.[1]

Cotton's story illustrates, in many respects, the old adage "The more things change, the more they remain the same." In each generation, new tactics have been used for achieving the same goals—goals shared by the Founding Fathers. Denying African Americans citizenship was deemed essential to the formation of the original union. Hundreds of years later, America is still not an egalitarian democracy. The arguments and rationalizations that have been trotted out in support of racial exclusion and discrimination in its various forms have changed and evolved, but the outcome has remained largely the same. An extraordinary percentage of black men in the United States are legally barred from voting today, just as they have been throughout most of American history. They are also subject to legalized discrimination in employment, housing, education, public benefits, and jury service, just as their parents, grandparents, and great-grandparents once were.

What has changed since the collapse of Jim Crow has less to do with the basic structure of our society than with the language we use to justify it. In the era of colorblindness, it is no longer socially permissible to use race, explicitly, as a justification for discrimination, exclusion, and social contempt. So we don't. Rather than rely on race, we use our criminal justice system to label people of color "criminals" and then engage in all the practices we supposedly left behind. Today it is perfectly legal to discriminate against criminals in nearly all the ways that it was once legal to discriminate against African Americans. Once you're labeled a felon, the old forms of discrimination— employment discrimination, housing discrimination, denial of the right to vote, denial of educational opportunity, denial of food stamps and other public benefits, and exclusion from jury service—are suddenly legal. As a criminal, you have scarcely more rights, and arguably less respect, than a black man living in Alabama at the height of Jim Crow. We have not ended racial caste in America; we have merely redesigned it.

I have reached [these conclusions] reluctantly. Ten years ago, I would have argued strenuously against the central claim made here—namely, that something akin to a racial caste system currently exists in the United States. Indeed, if Barack Obama had been elected president back then, I would have argued that his election marked the nation's triumph over racial caste—the final nail in the coffin of Jim Crow. My elation would have been tempered by the distance yet to be traveled to reach the promised land of racial justice in America, but my conviction that nothing remotely similar to Jim Crow exists in this country would have been steadfast.

Today my elation over Obama's election is tempered by a far more sobering awareness. As an African American woman, with three young children who will never know a world in which a black man could not be president of the United States, I was beyond thrilled on election night. Yet when I walked out of the election night party, full of hope and enthusiasm, I was immediately reminded of the harsh realities of the New Jim Crow. A black man was on his knees in the gutter, hands cuffed behind his back, as several police officers stood around him talking, joking, and ignoring his human existence. People poured out of the building; many stared for a moment at the black man cowering in the street, and then averted their gaze. What did the election of Barack Obama mean for him?

Like many civil rights lawyers, I was inspired to attend law school by the civil rights victories of the 1950s and 1960s. Even in the face of growing social and political opposition to remedial policies such as affirmative action, I clung to the notion that the evils of Jim Crow are behind us and that, while we have a long way to go to fulfill the dream of an egalitarian, multiracial democracy, we have made real progress and are now struggling to hold on to the gains of the past. I thought my job as a civil rights lawyer was to join with the allies of racial progress to resist attacks on affirmative action and to eliminate the vestiges of Jim Crow segregation, including our still separate and unequal system of education. I understood the problems plaguing poor communities of color, including problems associated with crime and rising incarceration rates, to be a function of poverty and lack of access to quality education—the continuing legacy of slavery and Jim Crow. Never did I seriously consider the possibility that a new racial caste system was operating in this country. The new system had been developed and implemented swiftly, and it was largely invisible, even to people, like me, who spent most of their waking hours fighting for justice.

I first encountered the idea of a new racial caste system more than a decade ago, when a bright orange poster caught my eye. I was rushing to catch the bus, and I noticed a sign stapled to a telephone pole that screamed in large bold print: THE DRUG WAR Is THE NEW JIM CROW. I paused for a moment and skimmed the text of the flyer. Some radical group was holding a community meeting about police brutality, the new three-strikes law in California, and the expansion of America's prison system. The meeting was being held at a small community church a few blocks away; it had seating capacity for no more than fifty people. I sighed, and muttered to myself something like, "Yeah, the criminal justice system is racist in many ways, but it really doesn't help to make such an absurd comparison. People will just think you're crazy." I then crossed the street and hopped on the bus. I was headed to my new job, director of the Racial Justice Project of the American Civil Liberties Union (ACLU) in Northern California.

Michelle Alexander speaks about her book, *The New Jim Crow.*

When I began my work at the ACLU, I assumed that the criminal justice system had problems of racial bias, much in the same way that all major institutions in our society are plagued with problems associated with conscious and unconscious bias. As a lawyer who had litigated numerous class-action employment-discrimination cases, I understood well the many ways in which racial stereotyping can permeate subjective decision-making processes at all levels of an organization, with devastating consequences. I was familiar with the challenges associated with reforming institutions in which racial stratification is thought to be normal—the natural consequence of differences in education, culture, motivation, and, some still believe, innate ability. While at the ACLU, I shifted my focus from employment discrimination to criminal justice reform and dedicated myself to the task of working with others to identify and eliminate racial bias whenever and wherever it reared its ugly head.

By the time I left the ACLU, I had come to suspect that I was wrong about the criminal justice system. It was not just another institution infected with racial bias but rather a different beast entirely. The activists who posted the sign on the telephone pole were not crazy; nor were the smattering of lawyers and advocates around the country who were beginning to connect the dots between our current system of mass incarceration and earlier forms of social control. Quite belatedly, I came to see that mass incarceration in the United States had, in fact, emerged as a stunningly comprehensive and well-disguised system of racialized social control that functions in a manner strikingly similar to Jim Crow.

In my experience, people who have been incarcerated rarely 10 have difficulty identifying the parallels between these systems of social control. Once they are released, they are often denied the right to vote, excluded from juries, and relegated to a racially segregated and subordinated existence. Through a web of laws, regulations, and informal rules, all of which are powerfully reinforced by social stigma, they are confined to the margins of mainstream society and denied access to the mainstream economy. They are legally denied the ability to obtain employment, housing, and public benefits—much as African Americans were once forced into a segregated, second-class citizenship in the Jim Crow era.

Those of us who have viewed that world from a comfortable distance—yet sympathize with the plight of the so-called underclass—tend to interpret the experience of those caught up in the criminal justice system primarily through the lens of popularized social science, attributing the staggering increase in incarceration rates in communities of color to the predictable, though unfortunate, consequences of poverty, racial segregation, unequal educational opportunities, and the presumed realities of the drug market, including the mistaken belief that most drug dealers are black or brown. Occasionally, in the course of my work, someone would make a remark suggesting that perhaps the War on Drugs is a racist conspiracy to put blacks back in their place. This type of remark was invariably accompanied by nervous laughter, intended to convey the impression that although the idea had crossed their minds, it was not an idea a reasonable person would take seriously.

Most people assume the War on Drugs was launched in response to the crisis caused by crack cocaine in inner-city neighborhoods. This view holds that the racial disparities in drug convictions and sentences, as well as the rapid explosion of the prison population, reflect nothing more than the government's zealous—but benign—efforts to address rampant drug crime in poor, minority neighborhoods. This view, while understandable, given the sensational media coverage of crack in the 1980s and 1990s, is simply wrong.

See p. 25 for more ways to introduce something implied or assumed.

While it is true that the publicity surrounding crack cocaine led to a dramatic increase in funding for the drug war (as well as to sentencing policies that greatly exacerbated racial disparities in incarceration rates), there is no truth to the notion that the War on Drugs was launched in response to crack cocaine. President Ronald Reagan officially announced the current drug war in 1982, before crack became an issue in the media or a crisis in poor black neighborhoods. A few years after the drug war was declared, crack began to spread rapidly in the poor black neighborhoods of Los Angeles and later emerged in cities across the country.[2] The Reagan administration hired staff to publicize the emergence of crack cocaine in 1985 as part of a strategic effort to build public and legislative support for the war. The media campaign was an extraordinary success. Almost overnight, the media was saturated with images of black "crack whores," "crack dealers," and "crack babies"—images that seemed to confirm the worst negative racial stereotypes about impoverished inner-city residents. The media bonanza surrounding the "new demon drug" helped to catapult the War on Drugs from an ambitious federal policy to an actual war.

The timing of the crack crisis helped to fuel conspiracy theories and general speculation in poor black communities that the War on Drugs was part of a genocidal plan by the government to destroy black people in the United States. From the outset, stories circulated on the street that crack and other drugs were being brought into black neighborhoods by the CIA. Eventually, even the Urban League came to take the claims of genocide seriously. In its 1990 report "The State of Black America," it stated: "There is at least one concept that must be recognized if one is to see the pervasive and insidious nature of the drug problem for the African American community. Though difficult to accept, that is the concept of genocide."[3] While the conspiracy theories were initially dismissed as far-fetched, if not downright loony, the word on the street turned out to be right, at least to a point. The CIA admitted in 1998 that guerrilla armies it actively supported in Nicaragua were smuggling illegal drugs into the United States— drugs that were making their way onto the streets of inner-city black neighborhoods in the form of crack cocaine. The CIA also admitted that, in the midst of the War on Drugs, it blocked law enforcement efforts to investigate illegal drug networks that were helping to fund its covert war in Nicaragua.[4]*

It bears emphasis that the CIA never admitted (nor has any evidence been revealed to support the claim) that it

---

*Covert war in Nicaragua In December 1981, the then president Ronald Reagan authorized the CIA to support the Contras, an opposition group that fought the Sandinistas, a revolutionary socialist group that the United States opposed in its fight against communism during the Cold War.

intentionally sought the destruction of the black community by allowing illegal drugs to be smuggled into the United States. Nonetheless, conspiracy theorists surely must be forgiven for their bold accusation of genocide, in light of the devastation wrought by crack cocaine and the drug war, and the odd coincidence that an illegal drug crisis suddenly appeared in the black community after—not before—a drug war had been declared. In fact, the War on Drugs began at a time when illegal drug use was on the decline.[5] During this same time period, however, a war was declared, causing arrests and convictions for drug offenses to skyrocket, especially among people of color.

The impact of the drug war has been astounding. In less than thirty years, the U.S penal population exploded from around 300,000 to more than 2 million, with drug convictions accounting for the majority of the increase.[6] The United States now has the highest rate of incarceration in the world, dwarfing the rates of nearly every developed country, even surpassing those in highly repressive regimes like Russia, China, and Iran. In Germany, 93 people are in prison for every 100,000 adults and children. In the United States, the rate is roughly eight times that, or 750 per 100,000.[7]

The racial dimension of mass incarceration is its most striking feature. No other country in the world imprisons so many of its racial or ethnic minorities. The United States imprisons a larger percentage of its black population than South Africa did at the height of apartheid. In Washington, D.C., our nation's capitol, it is estimated that three out of four young black men (and nearly all those in the poorest neighborhoods) can expect to serve time in prison.[8] Similar rates of incarceration can be found in black communities across America.

These stark racial disparities cannot be explained by rates of drug crime. Studies show that people of all colors *use and sell* illegal drugs at remarkably similar rates.[9] If there are significant differences in the surveys to be found, they frequently suggest that whites, particularly white youth, are more likely to engage in drug crime than people of color.[10] That is not what one would guess, however, when entering our nation's prisons and jails, which are overflowing with black and brown drug offenders. In some states, black men have been admitted to prison on drug charges at rates twenty to fifty times greater than those of white men.[11] And in major cities wracked by the drug war, as many as 80 percent of young African American men now have criminal records and are thus subject to legalized discrimination for the rest of their lives.[12] These young men are part of a growing undercaste, permanently locked up and locked out of mainstream society.

It may be surprising to some that drug crime was declining, not rising, when a drug war was declared. From a historical perspective, however, the lack of correlation between crime and punishment is nothing new. Sociologists have frequently observed that governments use punishment primarily as a tool of social control, and thus the extent or severity of punishment is often unrelated to actual crime patterns. Michael Tonry explains in *Thinking About Crime*: "Governments decide how much punishment they want, and these decisions are in no simple way related to crime rates."[13] This fact, he points out, can be seen most clearly by putting crime and punishment in comparative perspective. Although crime rates in the United States have not been markedly higher than those of other Western countries, the rate of incarceration has soared in the United States while it has remained stable or declined in other countries. Between 1960 and 1990, for example, official crime rates in Finland, Germany, and the United States were close to identical.

Yet the U.S. incarceration rate quadrupled, the Finnish rate fell by 60 percent, and the German rate was stable in that period.[14] Despite similar crime rates, each government chose to impose different levels of punishment.

Today, due to recent declines, U.S. crime rates have dipped 20 below the international norm. Nevertheless, the United States now boasts an incarceration rate that is six to ten times greater than that of other industrialized nations[15]—a development directly traceable to the drug war. The only country in the world that even comes close to the American rate of incarceration is Russia, and no other country in the world incarcerates such an astonishing percentage of its racial or ethnic minorities.

The stark and sobering reality is that, for reasons largely unrelated to actual crime trends, the American penal system has emerged as a system of social control unparalleled in world history. And while the size of the system alone might suggest that it would touch the lives of most Americans, the primary targets of its control can be defined largely by race. This is an astonishing development, especially given that as recently as the mid-1970s, the most well-respected criminologists were predicting that the prison system would soon fade away. Prison did not deter crime significantly, many experts concluded. Those who had meaningful economic and social opportunities were unlikely to commit crimes regardless of the penalty, while those who went to prison were far more likely to commit crimes again in the future. The growing consensus among experts was perhaps best reflected by the National Advisory Commission on Criminal Justice Standards and Goals, which issued a recommendation in 1973 that "no new institutions for adults should be built and existing institutions for juveniles should be closed."[16] This recommendation was based on their finding that "the prison, the reformatory and the jail have achieved only a shocking record of failure. There is overwhelming evidence that these institutions create crime rather than prevent it."[17]

These days, activists who advocate "a world without prisons" are often dismissed as quacks, but only a few decades ago, the notion that our society would be much better off without prisons—and that the end of prisons was more or less inevitable—not only dominated mainstream academic discourse in the field of criminology but also inspired a national campaign by reformers demanding a moratorium on prison construction. Marc Mauer, the executive director of the Sentencing Project, notes that what is most remarkable about the moratorium campaign in retrospect is the context of imprisonment at the time. In 1972, fewer than 350,000 people were being held in prisons and jails nationwide, compared with more than 2 million people today. The rate of incarceration in 1972 was at a level so low that it no longer seems in the realm of possibility, but for moratorium supporters, that magnitude of imprisonment was egregiously high. "Supporters of the moratorium effort can be forgiven for being so naïve," Mauer suggests, "since the prison expansion that was about to take place was unprecedented in human history."[18] No one imagined that the prison population would more than quintuple in their life-time. It seemed far more likely that prisons would fade away.

Far from fading away, it appears that prisons are here to stay. And despite the unprecedented levels of incarceration in the African American community, the civil rights community is oddly quiet. One in three young African American men will serve time in prison if current trends continue, and in some cities more than half of all young adult black men are currently under correctional control—in prison or jail, on probation or parole.[19] Yet mass incarceration tends to be categorized as a criminal justice issue as opposed to a racial justice or civil rights issue (or crisis).

The attention of civil rights advocates has been largely devoted to other issues, such as affirmative action. During the past twenty years, virtually every progressive, national civil rights organization in the country has mobilized and rallied in defense of affirmative action. The struggle to preserve affirmative action in higher education, and thus maintain diversity in the nation's most elite colleges and universities, has consumed much of the attention and resources of the civil rights community and dominated racial justice discourse in the mainstream media, leading the general public to believe that affirmative action is the main battlefront in U.S. race relations—even as our prisons fill with black and brown men. . . .

This is not to say that important criminal justice reform work 25 has not been done. Civil rights advocates have organized vigorous challenges to specific aspects of the new caste system. One notable example is the successful challenge led by the NAACP Legal Defense Fund to a racist drug sting operation in Tulia, Texas. The 1999 drug bust incarcerated almost 15 percent of the black population of the town, based on the uncorroborated false testimony of a single informant hired by the sheriff of Tulia. More recently, civil rights groups around the country have helped to launch legal attacks and vibrant grassroots campaigns against felon disenfranchisement laws and have strenuously opposed discriminatory crack sentencing laws and guidelines, as well as "zero tolerance" policies that effectively funnel youth of color from schools to jails. The national ACLU recently developed a racial justice program that includes criminal justice issues among its core priorities and has created a promising Drug Law Reform Project. And thanks to the aggressive advocacy of the ACLU, NAACP, and other civil rights organizations around the country, racial profiling is widely condemned, even by members of law enforcement who once openly embraced the practice.

Still, despite these significant developments, there seems to be a lack of appreciation for the enormity of the crisis at hand. There is no broad-based movement brewing to end mass incarceration and no advocacy effort that approaches in scale the fight to preserve affirmative action. There also remains a persistent tendency in the civil rights community to treat the criminal justice system as just another institution infected with lingering racial bias. The NAACP's Web site offers one example. As recently as May 2008, one could find a brief introduction to the organization's criminal justice work in the section entitled Legal Department. The introduction explained that "despite the civil rights victories of our past, racial prejudice still pervades the criminal justice system." Visitors to the Web site were urged to join the NAACP in order to "protect the hard-earned civil rights gains of the past three decades." No one visiting the Web site would learn that the mass incarceration of African Americans had already eviscerated many of the hard-earned gains it urged its members to protect.

Imagine if civil rights organizations and African American leaders in the 1940s had not placed Jim Crow segregation at the forefront of their racial justice agenda. It would have seemed absurd, given that racial segregation was the primary vehicle of racialized social control in the United States during that period. Mass incarceration is, metaphorically, the New Jim Crow and all those who care about social justice should fully commit themselves to dismantling this new racial caste system. Mass incarceration—not attacks on affirmative action or lax civil rights enforcement—is the most damaging manifestation of the backlash against the Civil Rights Movement. The popular narrative that emphasizes the death of slavery and Jim Crow and celebrates the nation's "triumph over race" with the election of Barack Obama, is dangerously misguided. The colorblind public consensus that prevails in America today—i.e., the widespread belief that race no longer matters—has blinded us to the realities of race in our society and facilitated the emergence of a new caste system.

. . .

The language of caste may well seem foreign or unfamiliar to some. Public discussions about racial caste in America are relatively rare. We avoid talking about caste in our society because we are ashamed of our racial history. We also avoid talking about race. We even avoid talking about class. Conversations about class are resisted in part because there is a tendency to imagine that one's class reflects upon one's character. What is key to America's understanding of class is the persistent belief—despite all evidence to the contrary—that anyone, with the proper discipline and drive, can move from a lower class to a higher class. We recognize that mobility may be difficult, but the key to our collective self-image is the assumption that mobility is always possible, so failure to move up reflects on one's character. By extension, the failure of a race or ethnic group to move up reflects very poorly on the group as a whole.

What is completely missed in the rare public debates today about the plight of African Americans is that a huge percentage of them are not free to move up at all. It is not just that they lack opportunity, attend poor schools, or are plagued by poverty. They are barred by law from doing so. And the major institutions with which they come into contact are designed to prevent their mobility. To put the matter starkly: The current system of control permanently locks a huge percentage of the African American community out of the mainstream society and economy. The system operates through our criminal justice institutions, but it functions more like a caste system than a system of crime control. Viewed from this perspective, the so-called underclass is better understood as an *undercaste*—a lower caste of individuals who are permanently barred by law and custom from mainstream society. Although this new system of racialized social control purports to be colorblind, it creates and maintains racial hierarchy much as earlier systems of control did. Like Jim Crow (and slavery), mass incarceration operates as a tightly networked system of laws, policies, customs, and institutions that operate collectively to ensure the subordinate status of a group defined largely by race. . . .

Skepticism about the claims made here is warranted. There 30 are important differences, to be sure, among mass incarceration, Jim Crow, and slavery—the three major racialized systems of control adopted in the United States to date. Failure to acknowledge the relevant differences, as well as their implications, would be a disservice to racial justice discourse. Many of the differences are not as dramatic as they initially appear, however; others serve to illustrate the ways in which systems of racialized social control have managed to morph, evolve, and adapt to changes in the political, social, and legal context over time. Ultimately, I believe that the similarities between these systems of control overwhelm the differences and that mass incarceration, like its predecessors, has been largely immunized from legal challenge. If this claim is substantially correct, the implications for racial justice advocacy are profound.

For more on ways to address a skeptical reader, see Chapter 6.

With the benefit of hindsight, surely we can see that piecemeal policy reform or litigation alone would have been a futile approach to dismantling Jim Crow segregation. While those strategies certainly had their place, the Civil Rights Act of 1964 and the concomitant cultural shift would never have occurred without the cultivation of a critical political consciousness in the African American community and the widespread, strategic activism that flowed from it. Likewise, the notion that the

New Jim Crow can ever be dismantled through traditional litigation and policy-reform strategies that are wholly disconnected from a major social movement seems fundamentally misguided.

Such a movement is impossible, though, if those most committed to abolishing racial hierarchy continue to talk and behave as if a state-sponsored racial caste system no longer exists. If we continue to tell ourselves the popular myths about racial progress or, worse yet, if we say to ourselves that the problem of mass incarceration is just too big, too daunting for us to do anything about and that we should instead direct our energies to battles that might be more easily won, history will judge us harshly. A human rights nightmare is occurring on our watch.

A new social consensus must be forged about race and the role of race in defining the basic structure of our society, if we hope ever to abolish the New Jim Crow. This new consensus must begin with dialogue, a conversation that fosters a critical consciousness, a key prerequisite to effective social action. My writing is an attempt to ensure that the conversation does not end with nervous laughter.

NOTES

1. Jarvious Cotton was a plaintiff in *Cotton v. Fordice*, 157 F.3d 388 (5th Cir. 1998), which held that Mississippi's felon disenfranchisement provision had lost its racially discriminatory taint. The information regarding Cotton's family tree was obtained by Emily Bolton on March 29, 1999, when she interviewed Cotton at Mississippi State Prison. Jarvious Cotton was released on parole in Mississippi, a state that denies voting rights to parolees.

2. The *New York Times* made the national media's first specific reference to crack in a story published in late 1985. Crack became known in a few impoverished neighborhoods in Los Angeles, New York, and Miami in early 1986. See Craig Reinarman and Harry Levine, "The Crack Attack: America's Latest Drug Scare, 1986–1992," in *Images of Issues: Typifying Contemporary Social Problems* (New York: Aldine De Gruyter, 1995), 152.

3. Clarence Page, "'The Plan': A Paranoid View of Black Problems," *Dover* (Delaware) *Herald*, Feb. 23, 1990. See also Manning Marable, *Race, Reform, and Rebellion: The Second Reconstruction in Black America, 1945–1990* (Jackson: University Press of Mississippi, 1991), 212–13.

4. See Alexander Cockburn and Jeffrey St. Clair, *Whiteout: The CIA, Drugs, and the Press* (New York: Verso, 1999). See also Nick Shou, "The Truth in 'Dark Alliance,'" *Los Angeles Times*, Aug. 18, 2006; Peter Kornbluh, "CIA's Challenge in South Central," *Los Angeles Times* (Washington edition), Nov. 15, 1996; and Alexander Cockburn, "Why They Hated Gary Webb," *The Nation*, Dec. 16, 2004.

5. Katherine Beckett and Theodore Sasson, *The Politics of Injustice: Crime and Punishment in America* (Thousand Oaks, CA: Sage Publications, 2004), 163.

6. Marc Mauer, *Race to Incarcerate*, rev. ed. (New York: The New Press, 2006), 33.

7. PEW Center on the States, *One in 100: Behind Bars in America 2008* (Washington, DC: PEW Charitable Trusts, 2008), 5.

8. Donald Braman, *Doing Time on the Outside: Incarceration and Family Life in Urban America* (Ann Arbor: University of Michigan Press, 2004), 3, citing D.C. Department of Corrections data for 2000.

9. See, e.g., U.S. Department of Health and Human Services, Substance Abuse and Mental Health Services Administration, *Summary of Findings from the 2000 National Household Survey on Drug Abuse*, NHSDA series H-13, DHHS pub. no. SMA 01-3549 (Rockville, MD: 2001), reporting that 6.4 percent of whites, 6.4 percent of blacks, and 5.3 percent of Hispanics were current users of illegal drugs in 2000; *Results from the 2002 National Survey on Drug Use and Health: National Findings*, NHSDA series H-22, DHHS pub. no. SMA 03-3836 (2003), revealing nearly identical rates of illegal drug use among whites and blacks, only a single percentage point between them; and *Results from the 2007 National Survey on Drug Use and Health: National Findings*, NSDUH series H-34, DHHS pub. no. SMA 08-4343 (2007), showing essentially the same finding. See also Marc Mauer and Ryan S. King, *A 25-Year Quagmire: The "War on Drugs" and Its Impact on American Society* (Washington, DC: Sentencing Project, 2007), 19, citing a study suggesting that African Americans have slightly higher rates of illegal drug use than whites.

10. See, e.g., Howard N. Snyder and Melissa Sickman, *Juvenile Offenders and Victims: 2006 National Report*, U.S. Department of Justice, Office of Justice Programs, Office of Juvenile Justice and Delinquency Prevention (Washington, DC: U.S. Department of Justice, 2006), reporting that white youth are more likely than black youth to engage in illegal drug sales. See also Lloyd D. Johnson, Patrick M. O'Malley, Jerald G. Bachman, and John E. Schulunberg, *Monitoring the Future, National Survey Results on Drug Use, 1975–2006*, vol. 1, *Secondary School Students*, U.S. Department of Health and Human Services, National Institute on Drug Abuse, NIH pub. no. 07-6205 (Bethesda, MD: 2007), 32, "African American 12th graders have

consistently shown lower usage rates than White 12th graders for most drugs, both licit and illicit"; and Lloyd D. Johnston, Patrick M. O'Malley, and Jerald G. Bachman, *Monitoring the Future: National Results on Adolescent Drug Use: Overview of Key Findings 2002*, U.S. Department of Health and Human Services, National Institute on Drug Abuse, NIH pub. no. 03-5374 (Bethesda, MD: 2003), presenting data showing that African American adolescents have slightly lower rates of illicit drug use than their white counterparts.

11. Human Rights Watch, *Punishment and Prejudice: Racial Disparities in the War on Drugs*, HRW Reports, vol. 12, no. 2 (New York, 2000).

12. See, e.g., Paul Street, *The Vicious Circle: Race, Prison, Jobs, and Community in Chicago, Illinois, and the Nation* (Chicago: Chicago Urban League, Department of Research and Planning, 2002).

13. Michael Tonry, *Thinking About Crime: Sense and Sensibility in American Penal Culture* (New York: Oxford University Press, 2004), 14.

14. Ibid.

15. Ibid., 20.

16. National Advisory Commission on Criminal Justice Standards and Goals, *Task Force Report on Corrections* (Washington, DC: Government Printing Office, 1973), 358.

17. Ibid., 597.

18. Mauer, *Race to Incarcerate*, 17–18.

19. The estimate that one in three black men will go to prison during their lifetime is drawn from Thomas P. Boncszar, "Prevalence of Imprisonment in the U.S. Population, 1974–2001," U.S. Department of Justice, Bureau of Justice Statistics, August 2003. In Baltimore, like many large urban areas, the majority of young African American men are currently under correctional supervision. See Eric Lotke and Jason Ziedenberg, "Tipping Point: Maryland's Overuse of Incarceration and the Impact on Community Safety," Justice Policy Institute, March 2005, 3.

Joining the Conversation

1. Michelle Alexander argues that in the United States mass incarceration is a "well-disguised system of racialized social control" (paragraph 9). Why, as she acknowledges in paragraph 4, did it take her so long to reach this conclusion?

2. Throughout the essay, Alexander presents and then responds to the views of others. Find two examples where Alexander introduces the views of others. In each case, how does she make clear to readers that the view in question is not hers?

3. The author states that "The racial dimension of mass incarceration is its most striking feature" (paragraph 17). What does she mean, and what evidence does she provide to support her claim?

4. According to Alexander, African Americans "are not free to move up at all" (paragraph 29), and "'the more things change, the more they remain the same'" (paragraph 2) What do you think John McWhorter (pp. 428–32) would say to that?

5. Write an essay responding to the reading in which you agree, disagree, or both with the author's argument that mass incarceration allows for continued discrimination against African Americans.

Could Black English Mean a Prison Sentence?

JOHN McWHORTER

—◻—

A BLACK MAN ON THE PHONE from a jail in San Francisco said, in 2015, "He come tell 'bout I'm gonna take the TV," which meant that this man was not going to do so. The transcriber listening in couldn't understand the first part, apparently, and recorded the whole statement as "I'm gonna take the TV."

It's impossible to know how often mistakes of this sort occur, but chances are they're common. An upcoming study in the linguistics journal *Language* found that 27 Philadelphia stenographers, presented with recordings of Black English grammatical patterns, made transcription errors on average in two out

———

JOHN McWHORTER is an associate professor of English and comparative literature at Columbia University. His research takes a comprehensive approach to American linguistic history: his numerous books and articles analyze the social, educational, and political dimensions of language in the United States, including studies on Black English and creole languages. This essay was published in the *Atlantic* in January 2019.

of every five sentences, and could accurately paraphrase only one in three sentences.

The Black English gap, as one might call it, matters: It can affect people's lives at crucial junctures. In 2007, a Sixth Circuit Court of Appeals dissent claimed that when a black woman said, in terror, "He finna shoot me," she may have been referring to something in the past, when in fact "finna" refers to the immediate future. "Why don't you just give me a lawyer, dog?" Warren Demesme asked the police when accused of sexual assault in 2017. The statements one makes to law enforcement after requesting a lawyer are inadmissible—but Demesme's rights were ignored because, it was argued, he'd requested a "lawyer dog," not an actual attorney.

For more examples of how to explain your argument's "so what?" factor, see Chapter 7.

Black people are overrepresented within the criminal-justice system, and race relations in America will never truly budge until "equality under the law" is more than a quaint phrase. But equality is, of course, impossible if the black people grappling with courts and imprisonment are routinely misunderstood.

Transcription mistakes can happen quite innocently. As far back as the 1930s, white men and women tasked with transcribing recordings of ex-slaves produced error-ridden manuscripts. One man was supposed to have said that after Emancipation Day, "the colored people sure went for!," which sounds odd grammatically and substantively; why wouldn't ex-slaves have been "for" their freedom? It turned out that the man was saying that ex-slaves "sure been poor," a straightforward statement.

I thought of this recently when I was staying at a hotel and asked a black woman working at the front desk where I could get a cup of coffee. When she pointed toward the restaurant, I said it was closed. Then she pointed more directly to a table with coffee urns *near* the restaurant—I was sleepy and hadn't seen it—and she said, with warm irony, "Dat table, dey close?" Her utterance could easily have thrown a foreigner, given that in Black English you can leave out the *are* of *Are they closed?* and the final *-d* of *closed*. Even some native English speakers may have misheard her without a certain amount of familiarity with the dialect.

When someone in a position of authority draws attention to the differences between standard and Black English, the response is often perplexity and derision. That was true in 2010 when the Drug Enforcement Administration put out a call for Black English translators so the agency could better understand conversations on wiretaps. Some in the media, poking fun at the whole project, suggested that Black English is simply a collection of slang words or even just a sloppy way of enunciating. The pervasive assumption was that black speech differs from mainstream speech only in some spicy lingo plus various instances of "broken" grammar.

See Chapter 6 for more on bringing in objections fairly.

In fact, Black English is not deficient but alternate. There is no scientific basis for judging Black English grammatical structures as faulty or unclear, and a Martian assigned to learn English who happened to land on the South Side of Chicago rather than in Scarsdale, New York, would have the same challenge in mastering the rules and nuances of the local speech. For example, the *come* in "He come tell 'bout I'm gonna take the TV" is used to convey indignation, and has inspired a linguistics article itself. Miss this and the man's whole meaning is lost—and to his possible detriment.

Even those who accept that Black English is more than slang may feel that a translation approach is unwarranted, condescending, or both. Sometimes it may be. In 1996, the Oakland, California, school district proposed to use Black English in the classroom as a sort of training wheel. The idea was that kids raised with Black English as a home language had trouble learning to read because standard English was so unfamiliar. But many (including me) thought that was a misdiagnosis: Black people, including kids, use Black English alongside standard English rather than exclusively.

The transcription issue is different. Most stenographers have not grown up with the bidialectal experience of poor black people and are thus encountering something genuinely unfamiliar, which they may not know how to get down on paper properly.

The solution here is not difficult. People who will spend their careers transcribing phrases such as "He come tell 'bout I'm gonna take the TV"—or even "Dat table, dey close?"—ought to learn the basics of how Black English works. They would need mastery of only about 25 grammatical traits, which are universal in Black English nationwide, despite local differences. For example, *be*, when used in a sentence such as *She be there on Sunday*, refers to something regular and habitual, as in "every Sunday," and is not simply a randomly unconjugated *be*. Another example: *We had went to the store then I got a text* conveys that the person was still in the store when the text came, not that it came after he left.

"Dat table, dey close?" is a passing anecdote, but "I'm gonna take the TV" could be the prelude to a man going to prison. A linguistically sophisticated America would understand that these speech patterns are not a pathology; they are the vessel of as much clarity and nuance as those of a privileged college kid. A sophisticated America would make sure those charged with distributing these words to the public sphere, or to a judge and jury, were aware of that fact.

Joining the Conversation

1. According to John McWhorter, how common are transcription mistakes by court stenographers in transcribing statements by speakers of Black English, and why do these mistakes matter?

2. Rather than employ a "they say / I say" format in this article, the author uses a problem/solution structure. He presents as a problem the frequent and sometimes consequential mistakes that court stenographers make when attempting to understand and transcribe statements made by Black English speakers; his solution is that court stenographers (and Americans more generally) should learn the basics of Black English. How might this piece be rewritten in an equally persuasive way using a "they say / I say" format? Sketch out how you would organize such a rewriting.

3. Relate the argument presented in this article to the discussion of "Black lives matter" in college student Kelly Coryell's essay (pp. 397–407). In what ways can each text be seen as supporting the argument of the other text?

4. Write an argument essay using "they say / I say" strategies about a time when your words and/or actions were misunderstood.

5. Read the essay "The Case for Black Optimism" by Coleman Hughes on **theysayiblog.com**. How do you think Hughes would respond to McWhorter?

Hillbilly Elegy

J. D. VANCE

I ARRIVED FOR ORIENTATION at Ohio State in early September 2007, and I couldn't have been more excited. I remember every little detail about that day: lunch at Chipotle, the first time Lindsay* had ever eaten there; the walk from the orientation building to the south campus house that would soon be my Columbus home; the beautiful weather. I met with a guidance counselor who talked me through my first college schedule, which put me in class only four days per week, never before nine thirty in the morning. After the Marine Corps and its five thirty A.M. wake-ups, I couldn't believe my good fortune.

Ohio State's main campus in Columbus is about a hundred miles away from Middletown, meaning it was close enough for weekend visits to my family. For the first time in a few years, I could drop

J. D. VANCE is cofounder and investor of the Ohio venture capital firm Narya and has written articles for the *National Review* and the *New York Times*. He is the author of *Hillbilly Elegy: A Memoir of a Family and Culture in Crisis* (2016), which describes his experiences growing up in Jackson, KY, and Middletown, OH. The selection reprinted here is a chapter from that book.

*Lindsay Vance's sister.

in on Middletown whenever I felt like it. And while Havelock (the North Carolina city closest to my Marine Corps base) was not too different from Middletown, Columbus felt like an urban paradise. It was (and remains) one of the fastest-growing cities in the country, powered in large part by the bustling university that was now my home. OSU grads were starting businesses, historic buildings were being converted into new restaurants and bars, and even the worst neighborhoods seemed to be undergoing significant revitalization. Not long after I moved to Columbus, one of my best friends began working as the promotions director for a local radio station, so I always knew what was happening around town and always had an in to the city's best events, from local festivals to VIP seating for the annual fireworks show.

In many ways, college was very familiar. I made a lot of new friends, but virtually all of them were from southwest Ohio. My six roommates included five graduates of Middletown High School and one graduate of Edgewood High School in nearby Trenton. They were a little younger (the Marine Corps had aged me past the age of the typical freshman), but I knew most of them from back home. My closest friends had already graduated or were about to, but many stayed in Columbus after graduation. Though I didn't know it, I was witnessing a phenomenon that social scientists call "brain drain"—people who are able to leave struggling cities often do, and when they find a new home with educational and work opportunities, they stay there. Years later, I looked at my wedding party of six groomsmen and realized that every single one of them had, like me, grown up in a small Ohio town before leaving for Ohio State. To a man, all of them had found careers outside of their hometowns, and none of them had any interest in ever going back.

By the time I started at Ohio State, the Marine Corps had instilled in me an incredible sense of invincibility. I'd go to classes, do my homework, study at the library, and make it home in time to drink well past midnight with my buddies, then wake up early to go running. My schedule was intense, but every-thing that had made me fear the independent college life when I was eighteen felt like a piece of cake now. I had puzzled through those financial aid forms with Mamaw* a few years earlier, argu-ing about whether to list her or Mom as my "parent/guardian." We had worried that unless I somehow obtained and submitted the financial information of Bob Hamel (my legal father), I'd be guilty of fraud. The whole experience had made both of us pain-fully aware of how unfamiliar we were with the outside world. I had nearly failed out of high school, earning Ds and Fs in English I. Now I paid my own bills and earned As in every class I took at my state's flagship university. I felt completely in control of my destiny in a way that I never had before.

I knew that Ohio State was put-up-or-shut-up time. I had left 5 the Marine Corps not just with a sense that I could do what I wanted but also with the capacity to plan. I wanted to go to law school, and I knew that to go to the best law school, I'd need good grades and to ace the infamous Law School Admissions Test, or LSAT. There was much I didn't know, of course. I couldn't really explain why I wanted to go to law school besides the fact that in Middletown the "rich kids" were born to either doctors or lawyers, and I didn't want to work with blood. I didn't know how much else was out there, but the little knowledge I had at least gave me direction, and that was all I needed.

I loathed debt and the sense of limitation it imposed. Though the GI Bill paid for a significant chunk of my education, and Ohio State charged relatively little to an in-state resident, I still needed to cover about twenty thousand dollars of expenses

*Mamaw   Vance's grandmother.

on my own. I took a job at the Ohio Statehouse, working for a remarkably kind senator from the Cincinnati area named Bob Schuler. He was a good man, and I liked his politics, so when constituents called and complained, I tried to explain his positions. I watched lobbyists come and go and overheard the senator and his staff debate whether a particular bill was good for his constituents, good for his state, or good for both. Observing the political process from the inside made me appreciate it in a way that watching cable news never had. Mamaw had thought all politicians were crooks, but I learned that, no matter their politics, that was largely untrue at the Ohio Statehouse.

After a few months at the Ohio Senate, as my bills piled up and I found fewer and fewer ways to make up the difference between my spending and my income (one can donate plasma only twice per week, I learned), I decided to get another job. One nonprofit advertised a part-time job that paid ten dollars an hour, but when I showed up for the interview in khakis, an ugly lime-green shirt, and Marine Corps combat boots (my only non-sneakers at the time) and saw the interviewer's reaction, I knew that I was out of luck. I barely noticed the rejection email a week later. A local nonprofit did work for abused and neglected children, and they also paid ten dollars an hour, so I went to Target, bought a nicer shirt and a pair of black shoes, and came away with a job offer to be a "consultant." I cared about their mission, and they were great people. I began work immediately.

With two jobs and a full-time class load, my schedule intensified, but I didn't mind. I didn't realize there was anything unusual about my commitments until a professor emailed me about meeting after class to discuss a writing assignment. When I sent him my schedule, he was aghast. He sternly told me that I should focus on my education and not let work distractions stand in my way. I smiled, shook his hand, and said thanks, but I did not heed his advice. I liked staying up late to work on assignments, waking up early after only three or four hours of sleep, and patting myself on the back for being able to do it. After so many years of fearing my own future, of worrying that I'd end up like many of my neighbors or family—addicted to drugs or alcohol, in prison, or with kids I couldn't or wouldn't take care of—I felt an incredible momentum. I knew the statistics. I had read the brochures in the social worker's office when I was a kid. I had recognized the look of pity from the hygienist at the low-income dental clinic. I wasn't supposed to make it, but I was doing just fine on my own.

Did I take it too far? Absolutely. I didn't sleep enough. I drank too much and ate Taco Bell at nearly every meal. A week into what I thought was just a really awful cold, a doctor told me that I had mono. I ignored him and kept on living as though NyQuil and DayQuil were magical elixirs. After a week of this, my urine turned a disgusting brown shade, and my temperature registered 103. I realized I might need to take care of myself, so I downed some Tylenol, drank a couple of beers, and went to sleep.

When Mom found out what was happening, she drove to Columbus and took me to the emergency room. She wasn't perfect, she wasn't even a practicing nurse, but she took it as a point of pride to supervise every interaction we had with the health care system. She asked the right questions, got annoyed with doctors when they didn't answer directly, and made sure I had what I needed. I spent two full days in the hospital as doctors emptied five bags of saline to rehydrate me and discovered that I had contracted a staph infection in addition to the mono, which explained why I grew so sick. The doctors released me to Mom, who wheeled me out of the hospital and took me home to recover.

My illness lasted another few weeks, which, happily, coincided with the break between Ohio State's spring and summer terms. When I was in Middletown, I split time between Aunt Wee's and Mom's; both of them cared for me and treated me like a son. It was my first real introduction to the competing emotional demands of Middletown in a post-Mamaw world: I didn't want to hurt Mom's feelings, but the past had created rifts that would likely never go away. I never confronted these demands head-on. I never explained to Mom that no matter how nice and caring she was at any given time—and while I had mono, she couldn't have been a better mother—I just felt uncomfortable around her. To sleep in her house meant talking to husband number five, a kind man but a stranger who would never be anything to me but the future ex–Mr. Mom. It meant looking at her furniture and remembering the time I hid behind it during one of her fights with Bob. It meant trying to understand how Mom could be such a contradiction—a woman who sat patiently with me at the hospital for days and an addict who would lie to her family to extract money from them a month later.

I knew that my increasingly close relationship with Aunt Wee hurt Mom's feelings. She talked about it all the time. "I'm your mother, not her," she'd repeat. To this day, I often wonder whether, if I'd had the courage as an adult that I'd had as a child, Mom might have gotten better. Addicts are at their weakest during emotionally trying times, and I knew that I had the power to save her from at least some bouts of sadness. But I couldn't do it any longer. I didn't know what had changed, but I wasn't that person anymore. Perhaps it was nothing more than self-preservation. Regardless, I couldn't pretend to feel at home with her.

After a few weeks of mono, I felt well enough to return to Columbus and my classes. I'd lost a lot of weight—twenty pounds over four weeks—but otherwise felt pretty good. With the hospital bills piling up, I got a third job (as an SAT tutor at the Princeton Review), which paid an incredible eighteen dollars an hour. Three jobs were too much, so I dropped the job I loved the most—my work at the Ohio Senate—because it paid the least. I needed money and the financial freedom it provided, not rewarding work. That, I told myself, would come later.

Shortly before I left, the Ohio Senate debated a measure that would significantly curb payday-lending practices. My senator opposed the bill (one of the few senators to do so), and though he never explained why, I liked to think that maybe he and I had something in common. The senators and policy staff debating the bill had little appreciation for the role of payday lenders in the shadow economy that people like me occupied. To them, payday lenders were predatory sharks, charging high interest rates on loans and exorbitant fees for cashed checks. The sooner they were snuffed out, the better.

To me, payday lenders could solve important financial prob- 15 lems. My credit was awful, thanks to a host of terrible financial decisions (some of which weren't my fault, many of which were), so credit cards weren't a possibility. If I wanted to take a girl out to dinner or needed a book for school and didn't have money in the bank, I didn't have many options. (I probably could have asked my aunt or uncle, but I desperately wanted to do things on my own.) One Friday morning I dropped off my rent check, knowing that if I waited another day, the fifty-dollar late fee would kick in. I didn't have enough money to cover the check, but I'd get paid that day and would be able to deposit the money after work. However, after a long day at the senate, I forgot to grab my paycheck before I left. By the time I realized the mistake, I was already home, and the Statehouse staff had left for the weekend. On that day, a three-day payday loan, with a few dollars of interest, enabled me to avoid a significant overdraft fee. The legislators debating the merits of payday lending didn't mention situations like that. The lesson? Powerful people sometimes do things to help people like me without really understanding people like me.

My second year of college started pretty much as my first year had, with a beautiful day and a lot of excitement. With a new job, I was a bit busier, but I didn't mind the work. What I did mind was the gnawing feeling that, at twenty-four, I was a little too old to be a second-year college student. But with four years in the Marine Corps behind me, more separated me from the other students than age. During an undergraduate seminar in foreign policy, I listened as a nineteen-year-old classmate with a hideous beard spouted off about the Iraq war. He explained that those fighting the war were typically less intelligent than those (like him) who immediately went to college. It showed, he argued, in the wanton way soldiers butchered and disrespected Iraqi civilians. It was an objectively terrible opinion—my friends from the Marine Corps spanned the political spectrum and held nearly every conceivable opinion about the war. Many of my Marine Corps friends were staunch liberals who had no love for our commander in chief—then George W. Bush—and felt that we had sacrificed too much for too little gain. But none of them had ever uttered such unreflective tripe.

As the student prattled on, I thought about the never-ending training on how to respect Iraqi culture—never show anyone the bottom of your foot, never address a woman in traditional Muslim garb without first speaking to a male relative. I thought about the security we provided for Iraqi poll workers, and how we studiously explained the importance of their mission without ever pushing our own political views on them. I thought about listening to a young Iraqi (who couldn't speak a

See pp. 116–18 for ways to repeat key terms and phrases.

word of English) flawlessly rap every single word of 50 Cent's "In Da Club" and laughing along with him and his friends. I thought about my friends who were covered in third-degree burns, "lucky" to have survived an IED attack in the Al-Qaim region of Iraq. And here was this dipshit in a spotty beard telling our class that we murdered people for sport.

I felt an immediate drive to finish college as quickly as possible. I met with a guidance counselor and plotted my exit—I'd need to take classes during the summer and more than double the full-time course load during some terms. It was, even by my heightened standards, an intense year. During a particularly terrible February, I sat down with my calendar and counted the number of days since I'd slept more than four hours in a day. The tally was thirty-nine. But I continued, and in August 2009, after one year and eleven months at Ohio State, I graduated with a double major, summa cum laude. I tried to skip my graduation ceremony, but my family wouldn't let me. So I sat in an uncomfortable chair for three hours before I walked across the podium and received my college diploma. When Gordon Gee, then president of the Ohio State University, paused for an unusually long photograph with the girl who stood in front of me in line, I extended my hand to his assistant, nonverbally asking for the diploma. She handed it to me, and I stepped behind Dr. Gee and down off the podium. I may have been the only graduating student that day to not shake his hand. *On to the next one,* I thought.

I knew I'd go to law school later the next year (my August graduation precluded a 2009 start to law school), so I moved home to save money. Aunt Wee had taken Mamaw's place as the family matriarch: She put out the fires, hosted family gatherings, and kept us all from breaking apart. She had always provided me with a home base after Mamaw's death, but ten months seemed like an imposition; I didn't like the idea of disrupting her family's routine. But she insisted, "J.D., this is your home now. It's the only place for you to stay."

Those last months living in Middletown were among the 20 happiest of my life. I was finally a college graduate, and I knew that I'd soon accomplish another dream—going to law school. I worked odd jobs to save money and grew closer to my aunt's two daughters. Every day I'd get home from work, dusty and sweaty from manual labor, and sit at the dinner table to hear my teenage cousins talk about their days at school and trials with friends. Sometimes I'd help with homework. On Fridays during Lent, I helped with the fish fries at the local Catholic church. That feeling I had in college—that I had survived decades of chaos and heartbreak and finally come out on the other side—deepened.

The incredible optimism I felt about my own life contrasted starkly with the pessimism of so many of my neighbors. Years of decline in the blue-collar economy manifested themselves in the material prospects of Middletown's residents. The Great Recession, and the not-great recovery that followed, had hastened Middletown's downward trajectory. But there was something almost spiritual about the cynicism of the community at large, something that went much deeper than a short-term recession.

As a culture, we had no heroes. Certainly not any politician— Barack Obama was then the most admired man in America (and likely still is), but even when the country was enraptured by his rise, most Middletonians viewed him suspiciously. George W. Bush had few fans in 2008. Many loved Bill Clinton, but many more saw him as the symbol of American moral decay, and Ronald Reagan was long dead. We loved the military but had no George S. Patton figure in the modern army. I doubt my neighbors could even name a high-ranking military officer. The space program, long a source of pride, had gone the way of the dodo, and with it the celebrity astronauts. Nothing united us with the core fabric of American society. We felt trapped in two seemingly unwinnable wars, in which a disproportionate share of the fighters came from our neighborhood, and in an economy that failed to deliver the most basic promise of the American Dream—a steady wage.

To understand the significance of this cultural detachment, you must appreciate that much of my family's, my neighborhood's, and my community's identity derives from our love of country. I couldn't tell you a single thing about Breathitt County's mayor, its health care services, or its famous residents. But I do know this: "Bloody Breathitt" allegedly earned its name because the county filled its World War I draft quota entirely with volunteers—the only county in the entire United States to do so. Nearly a century later, and that's the factoid about Breathitt that I remember best: It's the truth that everyone around me ensured I knew. I once interviewed Mamaw for a class project about World War II. After seventy years filled with marriage, children, grandchildren, death, poverty, and triumph, the thing about which Mamaw was unquestionably the proudest and most excited was that she and her family did their part during World War II. We spoke for minutes about everything else; we spoke for hours about war rations, Rosie the Riveter, her dad's wartime love letters to her mother from the Pacific, and the day "we dropped the bomb." Mamaw always had two gods: Jesus Christ and the United States of America. I was no different, and neither was anyone else I knew.

I'm the kind of patriot whom people on the Acela corridor laugh at. I choke up when I hear Lee Greenwood's cheesy anthem "Proud to Be an American." When I was sixteen, I vowed that every time I met a veteran, I would go out of my way

J. D. Vance.

to shake his or her hand, even if I had to awkwardly interject to do so. To this day, I refuse to watch *Saving Private Ryan* around anyone but my closest friends, because I can't stop from crying during the final scene.

Mamaw and Papaw taught me that we live in the best and greatest country on earth. This fact gave meaning to my childhood. Whenever times were tough—when I felt overwhelmed by the drama and the tumult of my youth—I knew that better days were ahead because I lived in a country that allowed me to make the good choices that others hadn't. When I think today about my life and how genuinely incredible it is—a gorgeous, kind, brilliant life partner; the financial security that I dreamed about as a child; great friends and exciting new experiences—I feel overwhelming appreciation for these United States. I know it's corny, but it's the way I feel.

If Mamaw's second God was the United States of America, then many people in my community were losing something akin to a religion. The tie that bound them to their neighbors, that inspired them in the way my patriotism had always inspired me, had seemingly vanished.

The symptoms are all around us. Significant percentages of white conservative voters—about one-third—believe that Barack Obama is a Muslim. In one poll, 32 percent of conservatives said that they believed Obama was foreign-born and another 19 percent said they were unsure—which means that a majority of white conservatives aren't certain that Obama is even an American. I regularly hear from acquaintances or distant family members that Obama has ties to Islamic extremists, or is a traitor, or was born in some far-flung corner of the world.

Many of my new friends blame racism for this perception of the president. But the president feels like an alien to many Middletonians for reasons that have nothing to do with skin color. Recall that not a single one of my high school classmates attended an Ivy League school. Barack Obama attended two of them and excelled at both. He is brilliant, wealthy, and speaks like a constitutional law professor—which, of course, he is. Nothing about him bears any resemblance to the people I admired growing up: His accent—clean, perfect, neutral—is foreign; his credentials are so impressive that they're frightening; he made his life in Chicago, a dense metropolis; and he conducts himself with a confidence that comes from knowing that the modern American meritocracy was built for him. Of course, Obama overcame adversity in his own right—adversity familiar to many of us—but that was long before any of us knew him.

President Obama came on the scene right as so many people in my community began to believe that the modern American meritocracy was not built for *them*. We know we're not doing well. We see it every day: in the obituaries for teenage kids that conspicuously omit the cause of death (reading between the lines: overdose), in the deadbeats we watch our daughters waste their time with. Barack Obama strikes at the heart of our deepest insecurities. He is a good father while many of us aren't. He wears suits to his job while we wear overalls, if we're lucky enough to have a job at all. His wife tells us that we shouldn't be feeding our children certain foods, and we hate her for it—not because we think she's wrong but because we know she's right.

Many try to blame the anger and cynicism of working-class whites on misinformation. Admittedly, there is an industry of conspiracy-mongers and fringe lunatics writing about all manner of idiocy, from Obama's alleged religious leanings to his ancestry. But every major news organization, even the oft-maligned Fox News, has always told the truth about Obama's citizenship status and religious views. The people I know are well aware of what the major news organizations have to say about the issue; they simply don't believe them. Only 6 percent of American voters believe that the media is "very trustworthy."[1] To many of us, the free press—that bulwark of American democracy—is simply full of shit.

With little trust in the press, there's no check on the Internet conspiracy theories that rule the digital world. Barack Obama is a foreign alien actively trying to destroy our country. Everything the media tells us is a lie. Many in the white working class believe the worst about their society. Here's a small sample of emails or messages I've seen from friends or family:

- From right-wing radio talker Alex Jones on the ten-year anniversary of 9/11, a documentary about the "unanswered question" of the terrorist attacks, suggesting that the U.S. government played a role in the massacre of its own people.

- From an email chain, a story that the Obamacare legislation requires microchip implantation in new health care patients. This story carries extra bite because of the religious implications: Many believe that the End Times "mark of the beast" foretold in biblical prophecy will be an electronic device. Multiple friends warned others about this threat via social media.

- From the popular website *WorldNetDaily*, an editorial suggesting that the Newtown gun massacre was engineered by the federal government to turn public opinion on gun control measures.

- From multiple Internet sources, suggestions that Obama will soon implement martial law in order to secure power for a third presidential term.

The list goes on. It's impossible to know how many people believe one or many of these stories. But if a third of our community questions the president's origin—despite all evidence to the contrary—it's a good bet that the other conspiracies have broader currency than we'd like. This isn't some libertarian mistrust of government policy, which is healthy in any democracy. This is deep skepticism of the very institutions of our society. And it's becoming more and more mainstream.

We can't trust the evening news. We can't trust our politicians. Our universities, the gateway to a better life, are rigged against us. We can't get jobs. You can't believe these things and participate meaningfully in society. Social psychologists have shown that group belief is a powerful motivator in performance. When groups perceive that it's in their interest to work hard and achieve things, members of that group outperform other similarly situated individuals. It's obvious why: If you believe that hard work pays off, then you work hard; if you think it's hard to get ahead even when you try, then why try at all?

Similarly, when people do fail, this mind-set allows them to look outward. I once ran into an old acquaintance at a Middletown bar who told me that he had recently quit his job because he was sick of waking up early. I later saw him complaining on Facebook about the "Obama economy" and how it had affected his life. I don't doubt that the Obama economy has affected many, but this man is assuredly not among them. His status in life is directly attributable to the choices he's made, and his life will improve only through better decisions. But for him to make better choices, he needs to live in an environment that forces him to ask tough questions about himself. There is a cultural movement in the white working class to blame problems on society or the government, and that movement gains adherents by the day.

Here is where the rhetoric of modern conservatives (and I say this as one of them) fails to meet the real challenges of their biggest constituents. Instead of encouraging engagement, conservatives increasingly foment the kind of detachment that has sapped the ambition of so many of my peers. I have watched some friends blossom into successful adults and others fall victim to the worst of Middletown's temptations—premature parenthood, drugs, incarceration. What separates the successful from the unsuccessful are the expectations that they had for their own lives. Yet the message of the right is increasingly: It's not your fault that you're a loser; it's the government's fault.

My dad, for example, has never disparaged hard work, but he mistrusts some of the most obvious paths to upward mobility. When he found out that I had decided to go to Yale Law, he asked whether, on my applications, I had "pretended to be black or liberal." This is how low the cultural expectations of working-class white Americans have fallen. We should hardly be surprised that as attitudes like this one spread, the number of people willing to work for a better life diminishes.

The Pew Economic Mobility Project studied how Americans evaluated their chances at economic betterment, and what they found was shocking. There is no group of Americans more pessimistic than working-class whites. Well over half of blacks, Latinos, and college-educated whites expect that their children will fare better economically than they have. Among working-class whites, only 44 percent share that expectation. Even more surprising, 42 percent of working-class whites—by far the highest number in the survey—report that their lives are less economically successful than those of their parents'.

In 2010, that just wasn't my mind-set. I was happy about where I was and overwhelmingly hopeful about the future. For the first time in my life, I felt like an outsider in Middletown. And what turned me into an alien was my optimism.

Note

1. "Only 6% Rate News Media as Very Trustworthy," *Rasmussen Report.* February 28, 2013, www.rasmussenreports.com/public_content/politics /general_politics/february_2013/only_6-rate_news_media_as_very_trustworthy.

Joining the Conversation

1. J. D. Vance tells his own story, in part, to illustrate how the optimism he felt about his future "contrasted starkly with the pessimism of so many of [his] neighbors" (paragraph 21). What other arguments does Vance make throughout his narrative? In addition to citing personal experience, what kinds of evidence does he offer to support his views?

2. Vance uses metacommentary to explain to readers how to interpret something he has just said. Find two examples in the reading where Vance uses this technique.

3. An elegy is a sad, mournful lament. Why do you think Vance called his book *Hillbilly Elegy*? How does his own story relate to the title?

4. College student Kelly Coryell (pp. 397–407) writes in support of the Black Lives Matter movement. She argues that those who criticize this movement and advocate the slogan "all lives matter" ignore the long history of discrimination against African Americans and inequalities, which continue to this day. How might Vance respond to Coryell's argument about the challenges facing African Americans?

5. Vance tells his own story and also makes observations about his greater community. Think of a challenge or experience you have had. Write an essay about what happened, making an argument about how your personal experience reflects a greater trend taking place in your community or hometown.

What Hillbilly Elegy *Reveals about Race in Twenty-First-Century America*

LISA R. PRUITT

—▢—

MY INITIAL RESPONSE to the publication of *Hillbilly Elegy* and the media hubbub that ensued was something akin to pride.[1] I was pleased that so many readers were engaged by a tale of my people, a community so alien to the milieu in which I now live and work. Like Vance, I'm from hillbilly stock, albeit the Ozarks rather than Appalachia. Reading the early chapters, I laughed out loud—and sometimes cried—at the antics of Vance's grandparents, not least because they reminded me of my childhood and extended, working-class family back in Arkansas. Vance's recollections elicited vivid and poignant memories for me, just as Joe Bageant's *Deer Hunting with Jesus: Dispatches from America's Class War* (2007) and Rick Bragg's *All Over but the Shoutin'* (1997) had in prior decades.

———

LISA PRUITT is the Martin Luther King Jr. Professor of Law at University of California–Davis. Her scholarship examines how the law impacts rural people and communities, whom she argues are underrepresented in legal studies. Her intersectional research, with its particular focus on women's rights and critical race theory, spans across social and economic issues. This selection first appeared in the 2019 collection *Appalachian Reckoning: A Region Responds to* Hillbilly Elegy.

I appreciated Vance's attention not only to place and culture, but to class and some of the cognitive and emotional complications of class migration. I'm a first-generation college graduate, too, and elite academic settings and posh law firms have taken some getting used to. Vance's journey to an intellectual understanding of his family instability and his experience grappling with the resulting demons were familiar territory for me. In short, I empathize with Vance on many fronts.

See Chapter 1 on how "they say" might be an idea you yourself once held.

Yet as I read deeper into *Hillbilly Elegy*, my early enthusiasm for it was seriously dampened by Vance's use of what was ostensibly a memoir to support ill-informed policy prescriptions. Once I got to the part where Vance harshly judges the food stamp recipients he observed while bagging groceries as a high school student, I was annoyed by his highly selective dalliances into the social sciences and public policy. A few more chapters in, Vance was advocating against the regulation of payday lenders, and I began to realize that *Hillbilly Elegy* was a net loss for my people.

Indeed, because so many readers have made Vance authoritative vis-à-vis the white working class, I have come to grips with the fact that *Hillbilly Elegy* represents a regression in our understanding of white socioeconomic disadvantage. And that's saying a lot given the decades—even centuries—of disdain for those often referred to as "white trash."[2] The attention that *Hillbilly Elegy* draws to low-income, low-education whites does not foster understanding or empathy for those Vance left behind; rather, it cultivates judgment.

Vance invites us not to see the white working class in their 5 full complexity but instead to cast all the blame on them for their often dire circumstances. Never mind neoliberal trade policies and the decimation of unions; never mind the rise of Walmart and contingent employment; never mind crummy public education and spatial inequalities with respect to a wide range of services and infrastructure. Never mind the demise of the safety net. According to Vance, "hillbillies" just need to pull themselves together, keep their families intact, go to church, work a little harder, and stop blaming the government for their woes.

In spite of this message—or perhaps because of it—*Hillbilly Elegy* has made J. D. Vance a very rich and famous man. Not only has the book spent dozens of weeks on the *New York Times* best-seller list, Vance has leveraged its commercial success into a gig as a CNN commentator. National media treat him like a celebrity, providing updates on his career and family.[3] The Brookings Institution even gave Vance a quasi-academic platform in late 2017, putting him into conversation with eminent Harvard sociologist William Julius Wilson to opine about "race, class, and culture."[4]

How is it that an unassuming and not especially artful memoir of white class migration—by definition anecdotal—has been elevated to the status of authoritative text? How has Vance parlayed three short decades of life into a small fortune and a career as America's "favorite white trash-splainer,"[5] "the voice of the Rust Belt,"[6] and "the Ta-Nehisi Coates, if you will, of White Lives Matter"?[7] How did Vance go from being just another "hillbilly" (albeit one with an Ivy League degree, two generations removed from the hills) to the man of the hour, his popularity compared to that of a boy band?[8] How did this contemporary Horatio Alger come to be fodder for a forthcoming Ron Howard film?

The sales figures for *Hillbilly Elegy* suggest a wide audience. That the book has been greeted with near universal acclaim in elite media outlets such as the *New York Times* and the *Washington Post* suggests that many highly educated folks are among its readers,[9] as does the fact that Bloomberg News and the *Economist* listed it as one of the most important books of the year.[10] One commentator called the book "all the rage in DC" in the run-up to the 2016 election,[11] and Frank Rich has referred to the book's "NPR-ish" readership,[12] implying that elected officials, policy makers, the professional class, and the professoriate dominate Vance's fawning audience. *Hillbilly Elegy* has become a must-read among those often referred to as the chattering classes, and many college campuses have been on Vance's speaking circuit. Tickets to hear him at my institution, UC Davis, ranged in price from twenty-five to fifty-five dollars. Not a bad day's work for a (former) hillbilly.

In this essay, I argue that elites and our nation more broadly have embraced *Hillbilly Elegy* and given Vance a national platform because, on some level, he confirms a story elites—and arguably Americans more broadly—tell ourselves, a story we want to believe is true. As Vance acknowledges, he is the American Dream personified. His tale—as he curates it—is one of industry and (apparent) meritocracy, a tale that affirms our nation's core values and aspirations.

For more on signaling who is saying what, see Chapter 5.

What Vance does not talk about is *his* privilege—male, whiteish,[13] . . . and urbanish—or at least not rural. He also does not talk about the role of the state as a positive force that facilitated his upward trajectory to the Ivy League and beyond. What also goes unacknowledged is that Vance is actually an outlier, the exception to the rule.[14] Upward mobility in the United States has been declining for decades, and indeed, many previously "working class" by some standard or definition (demarcations of socioeconomic class categories are notoriously squishy) are now facing downward mobility,[15] along with attendant despair.[16] Vance is a good role model for the average "hillbilly" child, yes, but the data trends suggest that only the very rare one will be able to achieve a fraction of what Vance has. Further, those children's outcomes will be shaped not only by the presence or absence of lay-about parents and/or inspiring teachers but also by the political economy of regions and of the nation, and by the opportunity structures engineered by government. . . .

Notes

Thanks to Ann M. Eisenberg, Christopher Chavis, Jasmine Harris, Emily Prifogle, and Amanda Kool for comments on earlier drafts and to Anujan Jeevaprakash for research assistance. Liliana Moore managed the manuscript capably, patiently, and with good cheer.

1. J. D. Vance, *Hillbilly Elegy: A Memoir of a Family and Culture in Crisis* (New York: HarperCollins, 2016).

2. Joe Bageant, *Deer Hunting with Jesus: Dispatches from America's Class War* (New York: Crown, 2007); John Hartigan, Jr., "Unpopular Culture: The Case of 'White Trash,'" *Cultural Studies* 11, no. 2 (May 1997): 316; Nancy Isenberg, *White Trash: The 400-Year Untold History of Class in America* (New York: Penguin, 2016); Matt Wray, *Not Quite White: White Trash and the Boundaries of Whiteness* (Durham, NC: Duke University Press, 2006).

3. Molly Ball, "*Hillbilly Elegy* Writer Won't Seek Office," *Atlantic*, September 14, 2017, https://www.theatlantic.com/politics/archive/2017/09/hillbilly-elegy-writer-wont-seek-office/539949/; James Hohmann, "The Daily 202: Why the Author of 'Hillbilly Elegy' Is Moving Home to Ohio," *Washington Post*, December 26, 2016, https://www.washingtonpost.com/news/powerpost/paloma/daily-202/2016/12/21/daily-202-why-the-author-of-hillbilly-elegy-is-moving-home-to-ohio/5859da6ee9b69b36fcfeaf48/?utm_term=.1ae48f2230a0.

4. Elanor Krause and Richard Reeves, "Rural Dreams: Upward Mobility in America's Countryside" (Brookings Institution, September 5, 2017), https://www.brookings.edu/research/rural-dreams-upward-mobility-in-americas-countryside/.

5. Sarah Jones, "J. D. Vance, the False Prophet of Blue America," *New Republic*, November 17, 2016, https://newrepublic.com/article/138717/jd-vance-false-prophet-blue-america.

6. Karen Heller, "'Hillbilly Elegy' Made J. D. Vance the Voice of the Rust Belt. But Does He Want That Job?," *Washington Post*, February 6, 2017, https://www.washingtonpost.com/lifestyle/style/hillbilly-elegy-made-jd

-vance-the-voice-of-the-rust-belt-but-does-he-want-that-job/2017/02/06
/fa6cd63c-e882-11e6-80c2-30e57e57e05d_story.html?utm_term=
.d848b73b94ab.

7. Frank Rich, "No Sympathy for the Hillbilly," *New York Magazine,*
March 19, 2017, http://nymag.com/daily/intelligencer/2017/03/frank-rich-no
-sympathy-for-the-hillbilly.html.

8. Mark Ferenchik, "J. D. Vance Draws Crowds, and Questions about
Political Future," *Columbus Dispatch,* July 31, 2017, http://www.dispatch.com
/news/20170731/jd-vance-draws-crowds-and-questions-about-political-future.

9. Amanda Erickson, "A Hillbilly's Plea to the White Working Class,"
Washington Post, August 4, 2016, https://www.washingtonpost.com/opinions
/a-hillbillys-plea-to-the-white-working-class/2016/08/04/5c1a7a56-51ca-11e6
-b7de-dfe509430c39_story.html?utm_term=.c60ef2dbf4d9; Jennifer Senior,
"Review: In 'Hillbilly Elegy,' a Tough Love Analysis of the Poor Who Back
Trump," *New York Times,* August 10, 2016, https://nyti.ms/2jAuPgc.

10. William R. Easterly, "Stereotypes Are Poisoning American Politics,"
Bloomberg News, December 16, 2016, https://www.bloomberg.com/view/articles
/2016-12-16/stereotypes-are-poisoning-american-politics; "Why Donald
Trump Speaks to So Many Americans," *Economist,* August 11, 2016,
http://www.economist.com/news/books-and-arts/21704774-why-donald-trump
-speaks-so-many-americans-promises-promises?fsrc=scn%2Ftw%2Fte%2Fpe%
2Fed%2Fpromisespromises.

11. James Hohmann, "The Daily 202: Want to Know Why Trump's
Winning Ohio? Drink a Beer with 'The Deplorables' in Boehner's Old
District," *Washington Post,* October 4, 2016, https://www.washingtonpost.com
/news/powerpost/paloma/daily-202/2016/10/04/daily-202-want-to-know-why
-trump-s-winning-ohio-drink-a-beer-with-the-deplorables-in-boehner-s-old
-district/57f288a6e9b69b0592430082/?postshare=1241475588947475&tid=ss_tw.

12. Rich, "No Sympathy for the Hillbilly."

13. Lisa R. Pruitt, "Acting White? Or Acting Affluent? A Book Review
of Carbado & Gulati's *Acting White? Rethinking Race in Post-racial America,"*
Journal of Gender, Race & Justice 18 (2015): 159; Jill Fraley, "Invisible
Histories & the Failure of the Protected Classes," *Harvard Journal on Racial
& Ethnic Justice* 29 (2013): 95.

14. J. D. Vance and William Julius Wilson, "Race, Class, and Culture:
A Conversation with William Julius Wilson and J. D. Vance," Interview by
Camille Busette (Brookings Institution, September 5, 2017). Wilson told
Vance that he was an outlier—that they were both outliers given where
they are now in relation to their childhood circumstances.

15. Jonathan Davis and Bhash Mazumder, "The Decline in
Intergenerational Mobility after 1980" (Federal Reserve Bank of
Chicago, 2017).

16. Anne Case and Angus Deaton, "Mortality and Morbidity in the
21st Century" (Brookings Papers on Economic Activity, 2017).

What Hillbilly Elegy *Reveals about Race*

Joining the Conversation

1. Lisa R. Pruitt emphasizes that she comes from a white, working-class background similar to that of J. D. Vance and at first felt sympathetic to Vance's portrait of his family and of his own struggles to achieve success, which mirror her own struggles. Given her initial sympathies, what does she find so objectionable about Vance's discussion? What specifically is it that she disagrees with? Also, why do you think Pruitt makes such a point of her own working-class upbringing?

2. Pruitt writes in paragraph 4, "The attention that *Hillbilly Elegy* draws to low-income, low-education whites does not foster understanding or empathy for those Vance left behind; rather, it cultivates judgment." What does Pruitt mean by this statement? How does she support it? What evidence and arguments does she provide?

3. The author does not insert a naysayer, or counterargument, to her own position regarding *Hillbilly Elegy*. Create such a naysayer, indicate where in Pruitt's text you would place it, and provide a response to the naysayer.

4. The author also does not state explicitly why her essay matters (so what?) or which audience she hopes to reach (who cares?). Construct responses to "so what?" and "who cares?" questions, and indicate where in the text you would place them.

5. Write your own "they say / I say" essay in response to the arguments presented by both Vance and Pruitt about the relationship among personal responsibility, social class, and the role of government in upward mobility.

Jobs, Crime, and Culture: The Threats That Aren't

SUKETU MEHTA

———

THE ARGUMENTS AGAINST IMMIGRATION are most often about jobs, crime, and culture: that immigrants take away native jobs; that they increase the crime rate; that they are an alien culture.

The first two arguments are demonstrably false.

When people first immigrate, they compete most not with the native-born, but with immigrants who've gotten off the boat just before them. But the previous year's immigrants don't mind, because many of the newcomers are related to them. And in any case, the difference it makes in their wages is minuscule.

In 2006, Mayor Bloomberg, then a Republican, testified in the Senate right after the mayor of Hazleton, Pennsylvania,

———

SUKETU MEHTA is an associate professor of journalism at New York University and an award-winning writer of fiction and nonfiction who has published in the New Yorker, Granta, and Harper's Magazine. His writing considers the politics of immigration and migration from both an academic and a personal lens. Mehta was raised in Mumbai, India, and immigrated to New York as a teenager. This essay is from his 2019 book, This Land Is Our Land.

who wanted landlords who rented to undocumented immigrants to be locked up.[1]

Bloomberg said there were half a million undocumented immigrants in New York City, "And let's be honest: they arrive for a good reason—they want a better life for themselves and their families, and our businesses need them and hire them! Although they broke the law by illegally crossing our borders or overstaying their visas, and our businesses broke the law by employing them, our City's economy would be a shell of itself had they not, and it would collapse if they were deported. The same holds true for the nation."

The self-made billionaire laid out the business case for immigration: many other countries are growing their economies faster than the United States is, reversing the century-long advantage America has enjoyed. Baby boomers are retiring, America's birthrate is slowing, and there aren't enough young workers to pay for the old folks' pensions. "The economics are very simple: We need more workers than we have."

He called for increasing immigration, because it's good for the economy, and for legalizing those who're already here. "There is only one practical solution, and it is a solution that respects the history of our nation: Offer those already here the opportunity to earn permanent status and keep their families together." It is a moral argument. "For decades, the Federal government has tacitly welcomed them into the workforce, collected their income and social security taxes, which about two-thirds of undocumented workers pay, and benefited immeasurably from their contributions to our country."

But just as there are climate change skeptics, there are immigration skeptics. There's a global consensus among 99 percent of legitimate economists that immigration is good for the economy. Then there's George Borjas, an economist at Harvard. He is among the very few to have presented any kind of serious evidence that it is not so. "Although immigration makes the aggregate economy larger, the actual net benefit accruing to natives is small, equal to an estimated two-tenths of 1 percent of GDP. There is little evidence indicating that immigration (legal and/or illegal) creates large net gains for native-born Americans."[2]

Borjas further argues that immigration has harmed those Americans who were already least able to withstand harm. He estimates that immigration has cut the wages of American high school dropouts by 3 to 5 percent, or an average of $1,800 a year. And, yes, for many, that $1,800 is a significant amount.

In 2015, Borjas published a study claiming that the arrival of the "Marielitos," the 125,000 prisoners that Castro emptied from his jails in 1980 and put on boats to Florida, made the wages of high school dropouts in the area plunge by 10 to 30 percent. This study was cited by none other than Trump's senior adviser Stephen Miller in support of his draconian restrictions on immigration.[3]

But later analysis showed that Borjas's study was, at the very least, deeply flawed—in part because it used sample sizes as small as seventeen to twenty-four people per year, and focused on the people who could confirm his hypothesis. Borjas eliminated Hispanic dropouts, women, and workers who're not between the ages of twenty-five and fifty-nine—who constitute a combined 91 percent of low-skilled workers in Miami—in his samples of people affected by the Marielitos. According to the U.C. Berkeley economists Giovanni Peri and Vasil Yasenov, the new immigrants may have actually had a positive effect on the local job market because they created a demand for services, from supermarkets to auto repair shops. In any case, the Marielitos are thriving, and the Florida job market quickly recovered from whatever short-term effects the influx might have had.[4]

Do immigrants steal jobs from the natives? Çağlar Özden, a lead economist for the World Bank's Development and Research Group, maintains that they don't. "In general Özden found that migrants often take jobs that locals don't want or can't fill . . . Özden also found that unskilled migrants tend either to have no impact on local wages and employment or to increase wages and employment," summarizes the analyst Ruchir Sharma, the chief global strategist at Morgan Stanley.[5] If you can have an immigrant nanny mind your children, you can go to work as a writer or a dentist and make more money than if you were home minding your children.

The economist Michael Clemens makes a similar point. As *The Atlantic* explains,

> he [Clemens] and his co-authors, through study of all the available economic literature, have found that decades of immigration of tens of millions of people to the United States has reduced real wages for the average American worker by fractions of a percent, if at all . . . Clemens's research also challenges the notion that immigrants take away jobs from Americans. In agriculture, for example, he has estimated that for every three seasonal workers who are brought in, one American job is created across all sectors. Directly, workers need managers, and more often than not those managers are Americans. Indirectly, workers buy things, which means more Americans are needed to sell and produce those things. And yet, Clemens told me, "when a bus of 60 Mexicans is coming up from the border, nobody looks at it and says 'Ah, there's 20 American jobs.'"[6]

Close to half of American farmworkers are here illegally.[7] Expelling them will not only decimate American agriculture;

it will make no difference to the wages of native farmworkers. When the Bracero "guest worker" program ended in 1964, and Mexican farmworkers, who had done backbreaking work in the fields to replace Americans shipped off to the battlefields of Europe, were asked to go back, they were not replaced by American workers. Their bosses simply shifted to less labor-intensive crops and introduced more machines in the fields.

Instead, the nation would be better served if the farmwork- 15 ers and most of the other undocumented who're already here, like the Dreamers, got amnesty. There's a precedent for this. In 1986, Ronald Reagan signed the Immigration Reform and Control Act, also known as the "Reagan amnesty," which gave green cards to 2.7 million undocumented people. After it passed, the wages of the legalized workers went up, tax revenues increased as they started filing tax returns, and the crime rate fell by 5 percent, as property crimes decreased because the undocumented could work legally.[8]

There will be winners from free trade and free movement of people—like technology corporations. And there will be losers, for a while—like the unskilled. But the winners could be made to give away a part of their winnings to the losers through taxes. One way to do this would be to make the earned income tax credit much more generous. This would help both immigrants and the high school dropouts whose prospects are most hurt by immigration. More federal funds should be made available for areas such as border towns that are struggling with the impact of rising migration, in the form of aid for schools and hospitals. These funds could also be raised through a fee that would be charged to companies for each skilled immigrant they sponsor.

Ultimately, whatever the merits of Borjas's argument, the solution isn't to keep low-skilled workers out, which would be catastrophic for entire sectors of the economy. (For example, four out of eight of Maryland's crab-picking businesses closed in 2018 because of the difficulty of finding seasonal migrant labor after Trump's restrictions.)[9] It's to get more students through high school. Then the migrants with lower skills can begin their climb on the ladder of economic opportunity working as apple pickers and nannies, while those born here can work as clerks and call-center workers. And both can dream of their children becoming doctors and presidents.

Migrant farm workers harvest strawberries in California.

If you want to make the economy grow, let in more immigrants—and legalize the ones already here.

Immigrants, particularly the undocumented, are presented by politicians and Fox anchors as a feral horde of drug dealers and rapists. How criminally inclined are immigrants, really?

Alex Nowrasteh of the Cato Institute analyzed crime statistics in Texas for 2016. Native-born Americans were convicted of crimes at a rate of 2,116 per 100,000 people. For legal immigrants, that number plunged to 292 per 100,000; for illegal immigrants, 879. "The native-born criminal conviction rate was thus 2.4 times as high as the criminal conviction rate for illegal immigrants in that year and 7.2 times as high as that of legal immigrants," writes Nowrasteh.[10]

A 2018 study in the journal *Criminology* studied the correla- 20 tion between levels of undocumented immigration in American states and the prevalence of crime, from 1990 to 2014. The conclusion was unambiguous: "Increases in the undocumented immigrant population within states are associated with significant decreases in the prevalence of violence," the study found. For every 1 percent increase in the undocumented population, there were 49 *fewer* violent crimes per 100,000 people. "Immigrants are driven by pursuit of education and economic opportunities for themselves and their families," said Michael Light, one of the study's coauthors. "Migration—especially undocumented migration—requires a lot of motivation and planning. Those are characters that aren't correlated with a high crime-prone disposition."[11]

According to a 2018 Yale survey, the number of undocumented immigrants in America now stands at 22.1 million— and could be as high as 29.5 million. This may mean that the undocumented commit crimes at half the rates originally attributed to them. "You have the same number of crimes but now spread over twice as many people as was believed before, which right away means that the crime rate among undocumented immigrants is essentially half whatever was previously believed," said Edward Kaplan, a coauthor of the study.[12]

If you want to make the country safer, let in more immigrants—legal or otherwise.

The third complaint, that immigrants bring in a culture different from an existing one, is the most valid. So, if you're living in a kind of Norman Rockwell America, you might not like a cantina to open up next door blaring salsa music. But your neighbor, bored out of his mind by the sterility of Norman Rockwell's America, might welcome it. You don't get to define what a national culture is. Americans don't; even Europeans don't, because go back a few decades and the definition of French, or British, or German culture—what religions and foods and ethnic origins constituted it—was radically different from what it is today.

For a discussion of effective transitions, see Chapter 8.

Might you consider that by our moving here we will make things better—not just economically but also culturally? That there is something worthwhile in the cultures we bring with us—all of us, not just the Asian model minorities—and some of it is something that you can learn from? It could be our work ethic, it could be our love of family, it could be our gorgeous dresses or soulful music, it could be our richly spiced cuisine or our complex myths. Our old gods will meet your newer gods and produce a hybrid better suited for worship by all.

The street food of Germany is doner kebab; of Great Britain, chicken tikka masala; of France, couscous. The most exciting music in Paris isn't Edith Piaf but the Afropop playing in dozens of clubs in and around the city.

We were also drawn here by your songs. My father moved himself, and his wife and three children, to America to expand his family diamond business. But there was a deeper, more long-standing attraction, which had begun in college in Calcutta, in the 1950s. It was when my father was first exposed to the great rock 'n' yell of Chuck Berry and Elvis—music that the Jesuit deans of St. Xavier's tried to ban because they couldn't stand to see their students gyrating their pelvises. My father had never heard such an awesome caterwaul before, and—along with America's decadent movies and books—it seeded the young man's desire to go live there someday.

And isn't that, after all, what makes America work: this messy mix, this barbaric yawp, this redneck rondeau, this rude commingling? Isn't this what permeates its films, movies, books; and isn't it the principal product it can still export? It is American culture's permissiveness, openness, and vigor that still attract the masses to the Golden Door, not its rigidity.

An argument that's been resurfacing is that this new crop of immigrants, unlike previous waves of migrants, doesn't assimilate. "The vast majority of past immigrants changed *their* values, not America's, when they came to this country. They came here to become American, not only in terms of language, citizenship, and national identity, but also in terms of values," wrote the radio host Dennis Prager in *National Review*. "But while some immigrants still do, the majority does not. They want to become American citizens in order to better their lives—a completely understandable motivation—not to embrace American values and identity. The majority of today's immigrants from Latin America, for example, wishes to become wealthier . . . Latin Americans."[13]

On this question, a lot of people on both sides throw around facts and figures out of their own hats. What was needed was an authoritative, thoroughly researched study conducted by a respected, impartial organization.

In 2015, the federal government—the U.S. Department of Citizenship and Immigration Services and the National Science Foundation—asked the National Academy of Sciences to undertake just such a study. It was, and remains, the definitive word on the subject. The 500-page report looked at 41 million immigrants and their 37 million children. It assembled research from 18 leading economists, demographers, and migration scholars—including immigration skeptics like George Borjas.[14]

English-language learning "is happening as rapidly or faster now than it did for earlier waves of mainly European immigrants in the 20th century," the report found. According to a 2013 Gallup poll, 95 percent of immigrants think learning English is essential or important. By the second generation, educational achievement catches up to the children of the native-born. By the third generation, most immigrant children speak only English.[15] Only 41 percent of third-generation Mexican American children, for example, speak exclusively Spanish at home.[16] The report also found that incarceration rates for immigrant men in the eighteen-to-thirty-nine age group are a quarter of those for native-born men. "Cities and neighborhoods with greater concentrations of immigrants have much lower rates of crime and violence."[17]

As for jobs, 86 percent of first-generation immigrant males participate in the labor force, which is a higher rate than the native-born. "Immigrant men with the lowest level of education are more likely to be employed than comparable native-born men, indicating that immigrants appear to be filling low-skilled jobs that native-born Americans are not available or willing to take."[18]

The study found that in almost all categories, immigrants do better than the native-born. "Foreign-born immigrants have better infant, child, and adult health outcomes than the U.S.-born population in general and better outcomes than U.S.-born members of their ethnic group. In comparison with native-born Americans, the foreign-born are less likely to die from cardiovascular disease and all cancers combined; they experience fewer chronic health conditions, lower infant mortality rates, lower rates of obesity, and fewer functional limitations. Immigrants also have a lower prevalence of depression and of alcohol abuse." They also get divorced less.

There were some caveats. The first to arrive need more government help than they contribute in taxes, such as public schooling for their children, as have newly arrived immigrants in the past. The total annual cost to all levels of government is $57 billion. But the children of these immigrants, by the second generation, contribute $30 billion in taxes; by the third generation, $223 billion.[19]

By the third generation, immigrants assimilate into 35 America—in all ways. Their crime, health, divorce, and education rates are the same as the native-born. They sit around on the couch and watch TV and grow obese; work or don't work; study or don't study; commit crimes; and dislike learning languages other than English at the same rates as the native-born. In other words, they've become fully American.

The report came down resolutely on one side of the debate:

Immigration is integral to the nation's economic growth. The inflow of labor supply has helped the United States avoid the problems facing other economies that have stagnated as a result of unfavorable demographics, particularly the effects of an aging work force and reduced consumption by older residents. In addition, the infusion of human capital by high-skilled immigrants has boosted the nation's capacity for innovation, entrepreneurship, and technological change.

Sometimes America isn't even aware of the talent coming to its shores, or the way somebody let in for one skill can later demonstrate another. A farmworker could become a political activist; an engineer could open a restaurant. And their children . . . do what children of immigrants have always done. Although a Mexican migrant may start out mowing lawns, his children quickly move up, according to the report:

See Chapter 3 for more on explaining quotations.

> Second generation children of immigrants from Mexico and Central America have made large leaps in occupational terms: 22 percent of second generation Mexican men and 31 percent of second generation men from Central America in 2003–2013 were in professional or managerial positions . . . The occupational leap for second generation women for this period was even greater, and the gap separating them from later generation women narrowed greatly.[20]

Immigrants also assimilate in other ways, less palatable to people like the Iowa representative Steve King, who famously declared, "We can't restore our civilization with somebody else's babies." The primal fear of nativists like King is *They're coming for our women!* Oh, yes, we are—and for your men, too. One out of every seven marriages in America is interracial or interethnic, twice the rate of the last generation. In 1970, only 1 percent of American babies were descended from parents of different races. By 2013, that number had risen tenfold. In the next four decades, the number of interracial births will go up by 174 percent.[21]

I've always found American definitions of "race" confusing. In India, I could understand categories of religion or caste. But what does it mean to be "black" or "white" in America? Is Obama half-white or half-black? The best answer to whites' fear of being overrun by 2044 may be this: by then, "race" might not matter anymore.

"More than 35 percent of Americans said that one of their 'close' kin is of a different race," says the National Academy of Sciences report. "Integration of immigrants and their descendants is a major contributor to this large degree of intermixing." In the future, the lines between what Americans today think of as separate ethnoracial groups may become much more blurred. Indeed, immigrants become Americans not just by integrating into our neighborhoods, schools, and workplaces, but also into our families. Very quickly, "they" become "us."

NOTES

1. Michael Bloomberg, "Mayor Bloomberg Testifies before the U.S. Senate Judiciary Committee Field Hearing on Federal Immigration Legislation." New York City, Office of the Mayor (July 5, 2006). https://wwwl.nyc.gov /office-of-the-mayor/news/230-06/mayor-bloomberg-testifies-before-u-s-senate -judiciary-committee-field-hearing-federal.

2. Jennifer Rubin, "What the Anti-Immigrant Movement Really Believes." *Washington Post* (May 9, 2013). https://www.washingtonpost.com /blogs/right-turn/wp/2013/05/09/what-the-anti-immigrant-movement-really -believes/.

3. George J. Borjas, "The Wage Impact of the Marielitos: A Reappraisal." *ILR Review* 7, no. 5 (September 2015). https://www.nber.org/papers/w21588.

4. Giovanni Peri and Vasil Yasenov, "The Labor Market Effects of a Refugee Wave: Applying the Synthetic Control Method to the Mariel Boatlift." National Bureau of Economic Research Working Paper no. 21801 (December 2015, revised June 2017). https://www.nber.org/papers/w21801.

5. Ruchir Sharma, *The Rise and Fall of Nations: Forces of Change in the Post-Crisis World* (New York: W. W. Norton, 2016), p. 51.

6. Shaun Raviv, "If People Could Immigrate Anywhere, Would Poverty Be Eliminated?" *Atlantic* (April 26, 2013). https://www.theatlantic.com

/international/archive/2013/04/if-people-could-immigrate-anywhere-would
-poverty-be-eliminated/275332/.

7. Tamar Haspel, "Illegal Immigrants Help Fuel U.S. Farms. Does
Affordable Produce Depend on Them?" *Washington Post* (March 17, 2017).
https://www.washingtonpost.com/lifestyle/food/in-an-immigration
-crackdown-who-will-pick-our-produce/2017/03/17/cc 1c6df4-0a5d-11e7-93dc
-00f9bdd74ed1_story.html.

8. Rachel Kleinfeld, "Wanna Cut Crime? Let in More Immigrants, Legal
and Illegal." *Newsweek* (September 7, 2017). https://www.newsweek.com
/wanna-cut-crime-let-more-immigrants-legal-and-illegal-661183.

9. Ryan Marshall, "Shortage of Blue Crab Pickers Forces Maryland
Seafood Shops to Shut Down." *Delmarva Now* (May 4, 2018).
https://www.delmarvanow.com/story/money/2018/05/04/shortage-maryland
-blue-crab-pickers-causes-seafood-shops-shutdown-h-2-b-visa-lottery
/577930002/.

10. Alex Nowrasteh, "Criminal Conviction Rates in Texas in 2016." Cato
Institute (April 23, 2018). https://www.cato.org/blog/criminal-conviction-rates
-texas-2016.

11. Christopher Ingraham, "Two Charts Demolish the Notion That
Immigrants Here Illegally Commit More Crime." *Washington Post* (June 19,
2018). https://www.washingtonpost.coin/news/wonk/wp/2018/06/19/two
-charts-demolish-the-notion-that-immigrants-here-illegally-commit-more
-crime/.

12. Mohammad M. Fazel-Zarandi, Jonathan S. Feinstein, and Edward
H. Kaplan, "The Number of Undocumented Immigrants in the United
States: Estimates Based on Demographic Modeling with Data from 1990 to
2016." *PLOS ONE* (September 21, 2018). https://journals.plos.org/plosone
/article?id=10.1371/journal.pone.0201193.

13. Dennis Prager, "Immigrants Change Cultures—Whether New
Yorkers in Florida or Latinos in America." *Townhall* (July 17, 2018).
https://townhall.com/columnists/dennisprager/2018/07/17/immigrants-change
-cultures--whether-new-yorkers-in-florida-or-latinos-in-america-n2500981.

14. National Academies of Sciences, Engineering, and Medicine. *The
Integration of Immigrants into American Society* (Washington, DC: National
Academies Press, 2015), p. 6. https://doi.org/10.17226/21746.

15. Jeffrey M. Jones, "Most in U.S. Say It's Essential That Immigrants
Learn English." Gallup (August 9, 2013). https://news.gallup.com/poll
/163895/say-essential-immigrants-learn-english.aspx.

16. Jens Manuel Krogstad and Ana Gonzalez-Barrera, "A Majority of
English-Speaking Hispanics in the U.S. Are Bilingual." Pew Research Center
(March 24, 2015). http://www.pewresearch.org/fact-tank/2015/03/24/a
-majority-of-english-speaking-hispanics-in-the-u-s-are-bilingual/.

17. Julia Preston, "Newest Immigrants Assimilating as Fast as Previous
Ones, Report Says." *New York Times* (September 21, 2015). https://www
.nytimes.com/2015/09/22/us/newest-immigrants-assimilating-as-well-as-past
-ones-report-says.html.

18. "Report Finds Immigrants Come to Resemble Native-Born Americans over Time, But Integration Not Always Linked to Greater Well-Being for Immigrants." National Academies of Sciences, Engineering, and Medicine (September 21, 2015). http://www8.nationalacademies.org/onpinews /newsitem.aspx?RecordID=21746.

19. Julia Preston, "Immigrants Aren't Taking Americans' Jobs, New Study Finds." *New York Times* (September 21, 2016). https://www.nytimes.com/2016 /09/22/us/immigrants-arent-taking-americans-jobs-new-study-finds.html.

20. National Academies of Sciences, Engineering, and Medicine, *The Integration of Immigrants into American Society* (Washington, DC: National Academies Press, 2015), p. 6. https://doi.org/10.17226/21746.

21. Kim Parker, Juliana Menasce Horowitz, Rich Morin, and Mark Hugo Lopez, "Multiracial in America: Proud, Diverse and Growing in Numbers." *Pew Research Center* (June 11, 2015). http://www.pewsocialtrends .org/2015/06/11/multiracial-in-america/.

Joining the Conversation

1. Suketu Mehta, writer and professor of journalism, immigrated to the United States from India with his family as a child. While beginning his essay by listing arguments against immigration ("they say"), he proceeds to argue for the benefits of immigration to the United States. Summarize his argument in two or three sentences.

2. Mehta employs quotations from several authors whose views differ from his own, such as economist George Borjas and politician Steve King. Find two examples where Mehta presents views that he opposes, and then show how he is able to clearly distinguish those views from his own.

3. The author responds to three different arguments against immigration: that immigrants take away native jobs, that they increase the crime rate, and that they are an alien culture. How does he use transitions and other connecting devices to link the various parts of his essay?

4. David Frum's "How Much Immigration Is Too Much? The Wrong Debate" (pp. 474–83), while acknowledging some

positive effects of immigration to the United States, takes a more critical view overall than does Mehta on immigration as it impacts Americans economically and culturally. Given Frum's specific concerns about immigration, how might he respond to Mehta's argument?

5. Ask some of your relatives about your own family's journey to the United States. If that is not possible, ask a friend or classmate. When and where did your family's arrival take place and where from, what did they do to make a living, and how is immigration now viewed by your family? Finally, how would your family's experience relate to the patterns described by Mehta?

How Much Immigration Is Too Much? The Wrong Debate

DAVID FRUM

—⌐◻⌐—

"WE WANTED WORKERS, but we got people instead." So quipped the Swiss writer Max Frisch about the guest workers who came to northern Europe seeking economic opportunity in the aftermath of World War II. Yet when immigration is the subject, policy makers tend to concede the microphone to the economists—precisely the profession that looks at people and sees workers instead.

From an economic point of view, immigration is good because it encourages specialization and thus efficiency. In a low-immigration world, an American accountant might have to pay $25 or $30 an hour for yard services by American-born landscapers. At that price, she might choose to do the yard work herself. If higher immigration lowers the price of landscaping work to

———

DAVID FRUM is a senior editor at the *Atlantic* and author of nine books. He writes on US domestic and foreign policy, and his essays and columns have been published in the *Wall Street Journal*, the *Weekly Standard*, *Time*, and *Foreign Affairs*. In 2001–2, Frum worked in the White House as a speechwriter for George W. Bush. This selection first appeared in the *Atlantic* in 2019.

$10 to $12 an hour, she may hire a landscaper and devote her newfound free time to extra accounting work. Instead of leaving the office at 5 p.m. to cook dinner for her family, she can stay until 6 o'clock and order from Postmates as she drives home. Or she can buy more services than she otherwise would. A lower bid from an immigrant-employing contractor might allow her to renovate her kitchen this year rather than postponing it to next year.

But all of this only happens because lower-earning immigrants displace the Americans who used to do the work at higher costs. You may ask, "So what happens to those displaced Americans?" The economist's answer is that, pressed by immigrant competition, displaced American workers are driven to "upskill." Perhaps a former landscaper learns some Spanish, and thus can act as the foreman of a crew of immigrants. Perhaps he shifts to sales or design work. Either way, the economic models say, everybody is better off.

You may further ask, "Does this really happen? Don't at least some displaced American workers end up unemployed or underemployed, unable to find work at anything close to their old wage level? Aren't both American-born men and American-born women of prime working age less likely to work today than in the 1990s?"

Yes, all of that is true. But when workers quit the work- 5 force, they disappear from the statistical samples on which the economic models are built. Labor-force statistics count only those in the labor force. If an American-born land-scaper successfully upskills to foreman, his higher pay is recorded and measured. If an American-born landscaper retires early on a disability benefit, his lower income is not recorded and not measured. From a labor economist's perspective, he has ceased to exist. Immigration's economic costs and benefits will be calculated without reference to him.

See Chapter 6 on answering objections.

The battles over the accuracy of the models of immigration's economic effects are as protracted and vicious as any in the social sciences. We can't settle them here, and don't need to. Instead, let's focus on what economists generally do agree on.

First, adding millions of additional immigrant workers every decade makes the American economy in the aggregate much bigger than it would otherwise be.

Second, immigration contributes very little to making native-born Americans richer than they would otherwise be. In 2007, in the course of arguing the economic case for more immigration, George W. Bush's White House tried to quantify the net economic benefits of immigration to native-born Americans. The advocates' own calculation yielded a figure of $37 billion a year. That's not nothing, but in the context of a then–$13 trillion economy, it's not much.

Third, the gains from immigration are divided very unequally. Immigrants reap most of them. Wealthy Americans claim much of the rest, in the form of the lower prices they pay for immigrant-produced services. Low-income Americans receive comparatively little benefit, and may well be made worse off, depending on who's counting and what method they use.

And finally, while the impact of immigration on what the typical American earns is quite small, its impact on government finances is big. Estimates from the National Academy of Sciences suggest that on average, each immigrant costs his or her state and local governments $1,600 more a year in expenditures than he or she contributes in revenues. In especially generous states, the cost is much higher still: $2,050 in California; $3,650 in Wisconsin; $5,100 in Minnesota.

Immigrants are expensive to taxpayers because the foreign-born population of the United States is more likely to be poor and stay poor. Even when immigrants themselves do not qualify for a government benefit—typically because they are in the country illegally—their low income ensures that their children do. About half of immigrant-headed households receive some form of social assistance in any given year.

Assertions that federal tax revenue from immigrants can stabilize the finances of programs such as Medicare and Social Security overlook the truth that immigrants will get old and sick—and that in most cases, the taxes they pay over their working life will not cover the costs of their eventual claims on these programs. No matter how many millions of immigrants we absorb, they can't help shore up these programs if they'll need more in benefits than they can ever possibly pay in taxes. If a goal of immigration policy is to strengthen Social Security and Medicare, it would be wise to accept fewer immigrants overall, but more high-earning ones, who will pay more in taxes over their working years than they will collect in benefits in retirement. Under the present policy favoring large numbers of low-wage earners, the United States is accumulating huge future social-insurance liabilities in exchange for relatively meager tax contributions now.

Yet the true bottom line is this: Neither the fiscal costs nor the economic benefits of immigration are large enough to force a decision one way or the other. Accept the most negative estimate of immigration's dollar costs, and the United States could still afford a lot of immigration. Believe the most positive reckoning of the dollar benefits that mass immigration provides, and they are not so large that the United States would be crazy to refuse them.

For good or ill, immigration's most important effects are social and cultural, not economic. What are these effects, then? Some are good, some are bad, and some depend on the eye of the beholder.

For more on agreeing and disagreeing simultaneously, see Chapter 4.

Immigrants Are Making America Safer

Generally, immigrants commit crimes at lower rates than native-born Americans do. And although the children of immigrants commit crimes at much higher rates than their parents do, some evidence suggests that cities with higher percentages of immigrants have experienced steeper reductions in crime. President Trump speaks often about the victims of crime committed by undocumented immigrants, but the years of high immigration since 1990 have seen the steepest declines in crime since modern recordkeeping began.

Immigrants Are Making America Less Self-Destructive

Asians, who comprise the nation's fastest-growing immigrant group, are half as likely to abuse drugs or alcohol as other population groups are. Only one-fifth of Hispanic households own a firearm, as opposed to one-half of white households.

The severest self-harm, suicide, is very much a problem of the native-born. Suicide rates have surged since 1999. But white people commit suicide at nearly three times the rate of ethnic minorities. The states with the highest percentages of immigrants have suffered least from the suicide surge; the states with the lowest percentages have suffered most.

Immigrants Are Lowering America's Average Skill Level

In 2007, ETS—the company that administers the SAT—warned of a gathering "perfect storm": "Over the next 25 years or so," it said, "as better-educated individuals leave the workforce they will be replaced by those who, on average, have lower levels of

education and skill." This warning shows every sign of being ful-
filled. About 10 percent of the students in U.S. public schools
are now non-native English speakers. Unsurprisingly, these
students score consistently lower on national assessment tests
than native speakers do. In 2017, nearly half of Hispanic fourth
graders had not achieved even partial mastery of grade-level
material. According to the Annie E. Casey Foundation, these
children are at significant risk of dropping out of high school.

But here's something more surprising: Evidence from North
Carolina suggests that even a fairly small increase in the non-
native-speaking presence in a classroom seriously depresses
learning outcomes for *all* students. The nation has under-
taken important educational reforms over the past generation.
In many ways, that commitment has yielded heartening results.
Yet since about 2007, progress has stalled, and in some cases
even reversed. Cuts to state budgets during the Great Recession
bear some of the responsibility. But so does immigration policy. *The Hechinger Report*, from Columbia University's Teachers College, observes that the 2017 National Assessment of
Educational Progress "was the first time that white students
dropped below 50 percent of fourth-grade test takers. Hispanics now account for 26 percent of the fourth-grade population,
up from 19 percent 10 years ago. Disproportionately poor, and
sometimes not speaking English at home, Hispanics tend to
score considerably lower than white students."

Immigrants Are Enabling Employers to Behave Badly

Most jobs are becoming impressively safer, year by year. You 20
may think of mining as a uniquely hazardous industry. Yet in
2006, after a tragic sequence of accidents, Congress enacted

the most sweeping mine-safety legislation in a generation. In the decade since, mining fatalities have declined by two-thirds.

Mining, however, is an industry dominated by native-born workers. Industries that rely on the foreign- born are improving much more slowly. Forestry, fishing, and farming are three of the most dangerous industries in the United States. They are 46 percent reliant on immigrant laborers, half of them undocumented. (Documented and undocumented immigrants together make up only 17 percent of the U.S. workforce as a whole.) Building and grounds maintenance is surprisingly dangerous work: 326 people died in 2017. Some 35 percent of grounds workers are immigrants. About 25 percent of construction workers are immigrants, but immigrants supply almost half the workers in the most dangerous areas, notably roofing and drywalling. When so many workers in a job category toil outside the law, the law won't offer much protection.

America was built on the revolutionary idea, never fully realized, that those who labor might also govern—that every worker should be a voter. The struggle toward this ideal has been slow, arduous, and sometimes violent. The immigration surge has had the effect of setting this ideal back. Half a century after the Voting Rights Act of 1965, the United States has again habituated itself to employing workers who cannot vote and therefore cannot protect their interests or even their lives.

Immigrants Are Altering the Relationship between Americans and Their Government, and Making the Country More Hierarchical

Visitors to the United States used to be startled by the casual egalitarianism of American manners. "Have you ever realized to yourself as a fact that the porter who carries your box has not made himself inferior to you by the very act of carrying that box?" Anthony Trollope asked readers back home in Victorian England. If not, brace yourself: "That is the very lesson which the man wishes to teach you."

That lesson may no longer be getting taught. In 1970, almost every U.S. resident was a U.S. citizen, enjoying all the political and civil rights of citizenship. Today, in immigration-dense states such as California, Texas, New Jersey, and New York, at least 10 percent of residents are not citizens. These people occupy a wide array of subordinated legal statuses. Some are legal permanent residents, lacking only the right to vote. Some are legal temporary residents, allowed to work but requiring permission to change employers. Some hold student visas, allowing them to study here but not to work. Some, such as the Dreamers, and persons displaced by natural disasters in the Caribbean or Central America, may have entered the country illegally but are authorized to remain and work under a temporary status that can continue for years or decades.

America is not yet Dubai or Qatar or ancient Athens, where citizenship is almost an aristocratic status rather than the shared birthright of all residents. But more and more of the people who live among Americans are not on equal legal footing with Americans. They cannot vote. They cannot qualify as jurors. If they commit a crime, they are subject not only to prison but to deportation. And because these noncitizens are keenly aware of those things, they adjust their behavior. They keep a low profile. They do not complain to the authorities if, say, their boss cheats them out of some of their pay, or if they've been attacked on the street, or if they are abused by a parent or partner at home.

Heavy immigration has enabled the powerful—and the policy makers who disproportionately heed the powerful—to pay less attention to the disarray in so many segments of the U.S. population. Because the country imports so many workers, employers do not miss the labor of the millions of men consigned to long-term incarceration. Without the immigrant workers less prone to abuse drugs than the native-born, American elites might have noticed the opioid epidemic before it killed more Americans than died in the Vietnam, Korean, and Iraq Wars and the 9/11 attacks combined. The demand for universal health coverage might gain political force if so many of the uninsured were not noncitizens and nonvoters. None of this is immigrants' fault, obviously. It is more true that America's tendency to plutocracy explains immigration policies than that immigration policies explain the tendency to plutocracy. Managing immigration better is only one element of restoring equity to American life. But it is an essential element, without which it is hard to imagine how any other element can be achieved.

Joining the Conversation

1. David Frum uses a "they say / I say" structure to frame his argument about the impact of immigration on the United States. Summarize his "they say" and corresponding "I say." How do these statements relate to the subtitle of his article, "The Wrong Debate"? In other words, what, in Frum's opinion, would be the right debate—that is, a more productive, relevant, insightful discussion on immigration?

2. The author states in paragraph 14 that "immigration's most important effects are social and cultural, not economic. . . . Some are good, some bad, and some depend on the eye of the beholder." Of the five social and cultural effects he

goes on to discuss, which do you think he would categorize as good, which as bad, and which as depending on the eye of the beholder? Provide evidence from the text to support your answer.

3. This article does not use metacommentary (as discussed in Chapter 10) to emphasize the significance of his argument. Write a sentence for him that includes metacommentary, beginning with the template "Essentially, I am arguing . . ." Where in the text would you place this statement, and why?

4. In "Jobs, Crime, and Culture: The Threats That Aren't" (pp. 458–73), Suketu Mehta offers a much more positive assessment of the effects of immigration on the US economy and culture. Take one or two of David Frum's arguments, such as his assertion that immigrants are lowering America's average skill level, and respond to it from Mehta's perspective, drawing on the evidence that Mehta provides in his article.

5. Do some research online about the package of bills known as "A Just Society" introduced by US representative Alexandria Ocasio-Cortez. What might Frum say in response to her proposed legislation, especially the Embrace Act?

TWENTY-ONE

WHAT'S COLLEGE FOR?

AS PEOPLE CONSIDER THE FUTURE in these uncertain times, the question "What's college for?" looms larger than ever. With a struggling economy, many people are thinking carefully about whether the costs of a college education, which can be considerable, justify the potential benefits or are even affordable at present. Ideally, college offers students a chance to gain foundational knowledge and skills guided by faculty in a supportive and stimulating environment, a time for personal and academic growth, a transitional step on the way to adulthood and independence. In promoting their strengths, colleges highlight such features as small classes, distinguished faculty, low teacher-student ratio, wide variety of majors, knowledgeable advising staff, quality internship and co-op opportunities, impressive job placement of alumni, and affordable tuition, in addition to a friendly atmosphere, attractive campus, successful sports programs, and an array of extracurricular activities. Small wonder, then, that a national study reported by the journal *Inside Higher Education* in 2019 found that over three-quarters of all high-school students planned to attend college, whether it be a community college, technical school, four-year institution, or university.

But we can also see another side to the college story: graduates unable to find good jobs or, in some cases, any job at all;

students with large amounts of college debt from loans that can take years, even decades, to pay off; stories of uncaring professors, huge classes, maze-like bureaucracies, distracted advisers; students who for a variety of reasons wake up one day to find themselves in academic trouble. As with all paths in life, it's possible to take a wrong turn in college. If students choose to attend, it's advisable for them to go in with their eyes open, with specific reasons for pursuing a so-called higher education, and with a plan for how best to succeed.

This chapter begins with Stephanie Owen and Isabel Sawhill's study showing that while college graduates on average make significantly more money over their lifetimes than high school graduates do, there is wide variation in the return on investment, based on such factors as college attended, major, whether or not the student graduates, and occupation. Political scientist Charles Murray advances the view that far too many American students currently go on to college but would be better off attending a vocational program or going right to work after high school.

Other authors in the chapter argue, in different ways, that faculty and institutions as a whole can support student success. Liz Addison, drawing on her own experiences, articulates the often underappreciated value of a community college education. Anna Clark similarly extols the advantages of community college while criticizing a recent national trend of many such institutions to drop the word "community" from their name due to its less-than-prestigious connotations. Clark argues that the community orientation of two-year institutions is one of their biggest strengths and selling points and should therefore be emphasized rather than obscured. Turning her attention away from the classroom experience, college student Gabriela Moro explores the role of minority student organizations at colleges.

She finds that while such groups offer a positive, supportive environment conducive to student success, such clubs should be supplemented with opportunities for students to meet and interact across groups. Alternatively, while not questioning the value of higher education, Gerald Graff argues that important learning can take place in settings other than college and about topics other than "academic" ones. He suggests that it matters less whether we read Macbeth or a Marvel comic book as long as we approach the subject with a critical eye and question it in analytic, intellectual ways.

Finally, two pieces raise awareness of potential problems that may be associated with the college experience. Sylvia Mathews Burwell writes of college students' increasing need for mental health services and offers suggestions for students, families, and institutions to address these concerns more effectively. Charles Fain Lehman concludes the chapter by highlighting the financial debt many students accrue in paying for college and the long-term difficulties many have in paying off their loans.

As a college student yourself, you'll find plenty to think about in this chapter—and on its companion blog, *"They Say / I Blog."*

Should Everyone Go to College?

STEPHANIE OWEN AND ISABEL SAWHILL

—▭—

Summary

For the past few decades, it has been widely argued that a college degree is a prerequisite to entering the middle class in the United States. Study after study reminds us that higher education is one of the best investments we can make, and President Obama has called it "an economic imperative." We all know that, on average, college graduates make significantly more money over their lifetimes than those with only a high school education. What gets less attention

See pp. 25–27 on introducing an ongoing debate.

STEPHANIE OWEN and ISABEL SAWHILL are the authors of *Should Everyone Go to College?*, a report published in 2013 by the Brookings Institution, a centrist think tank in Washington, DC. Owen was a senior research assistant at Brookings' Center on Children and Families at the time of the report's publication and is currently a PhD student in public policy and economics at the University of Michigan. Sawhill is a senior fellow in economic studies at Brookings and the author of *Generation Unbound: Drifting into Sex and Parenthood without Marriage* (2014).

is the fact that not all college degrees or college graduates are equal. There is enormous variation in the so-called return on education depending on factors such as institution attended, field of study, whether a student graduates, and post-graduation occupation. While the average return on obtaining a college degree is clearly positive, we emphasize that it is not universally so. For certain schools, majors, occupations, and individuals, college may not be a smart investment. By telling all young people that they should go to college no matter what, we are actually doing some of them a disservice.

The Rate of Return on Education

One way to estimate the value of education is to look at the increase in earnings associated with an additional year of schooling. However, correlation is not causation, and getting at the true causal effect of education on earnings is not so easy. The main problem is one of selection: if the smartest, most motivated people are both more likely to go to college and more likely to be financially successful, then the observed difference in earnings by years of education doesn't measure the true effect of college.

Researchers have attempted to get around this problem of causality by employing a number of clever techniques, including, for example, comparing identical twins with different levels of education. The best studies suggest that the return on an additional year of school is around 10 percent. If we apply this 10 percent rate to the median earnings of about $30,000 for a 25- to 34-year-old high school graduate working full time in 2010, this implies that a year of college increases earnings by $3,000, and four years increases them by $12,000. Notice that this amount is less than the raw differences in earnings between high school graduates and bachelor's degree holders of $15,000, but it is in the same ballpark. Similarly, the raw difference between high school graduates and associate's degree holders is about $7,000, but a return of 10 percent would predict the causal effect of those additional two years to be $6,000.

There are other factors to consider. The cost of college matters as well: the more someone has to pay to attend, the lower the net benefit of attending. Furthermore, we have to factor in the opportunity cost of college, measured as the foregone earnings a student gives up when he or she leaves or delays entering the workforce in order to attend school. Using average earnings for 18- and 19-year-olds and 20- and 21-year-olds with high school degrees (including those working part time or not at all), Michael Greenstone and Adam Looney of Brookings' Hamilton Project calculate an opportunity cost of $54,000 for a four-year degree. In this brief, we take a rather narrow view of the value of a college degree, focusing on the earnings premium. However, there are many non-monetary benefits of schooling which are harder to measure but no less important. Research suggests that additional education improves overall well-being by affecting things like job satisfaction, health, marriage, parenting, trust, and social interaction. Additionally, there are social benefits to education, such as reduced crime rates and higher political participation. We also do not want to dismiss personal preferences, and we acknowledge that many people derive value from their careers in ways that have nothing to do with money. While beyond the scope of this piece, we do want to point out that these noneconomic factors can change the cost-benefit calculus.

As noted above, the gap in annual earnings between young 5 high school graduates and bachelor's degree holders working full time is $15,000. What's more, the earnings premium associated with a college degree grows over a lifetime. Hamilton Project research shows that 23- to 25-year-olds with bachelor's degrees make $12,000 more than high school graduates but by age 50, the gap has grown to $46,500 (Figure 1). When we look at lifetime earnings—the sum of earnings over a career—the total premium is $570,000 for a bachelor's degree and $170,000 for an associate's degree. Compared to the average up-front cost of four years of college (tuition plus opportunity cost) of $102,000, the Hamilton Project is not alone in arguing that investing in college provides "a tremendous return."

It is always possible to quibble over specific calculations, but it is hard to deny that, on average, the benefits of a college degree far outweigh the costs. The key phrase here is "on average." The purpose of this brief is to highlight the reasons why,

Figure 1. Earning Trajectories by Educational Attainment

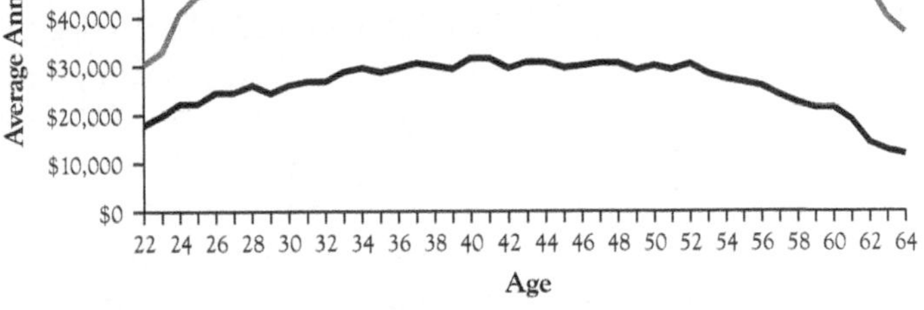

Source: Greenstone and Looney (2011).
Note: Sample includes all civilian U.S. citizens, excluding those in school. Annual earnings are averaged over the entire sample, including those without work. Source: March CPS 2007–2010.

for a given individual, the benefits may not outweigh the costs. We emphasize that a 17- or 18-year-old deciding whether and where to go to college should carefully consider his or her own likely path of education and career before committing a considerable amount of time and money to that degree. With tuitions rising faster than family incomes, the typical college student is now more dependent than in the past on loans, creating serious risks for the individual student and perhaps for the system as a whole, should widespread defaults occur in the future. Federal student loans now total close to $1 trillion, larger than credit card debt or auto loans and second only to mortgage debt on household balance sheets.

Variation in the Return on Education

It is easy to imagine hundreds of dimensions on which college degrees and their payoffs could differ. Ideally, we'd like to be able to look into a crystal ball and know which individual school will give the highest net benefit for a given student with her unique strengths, weaknesses, and interests. Of course, we are not able to do this. What we can do is lay out several key dimensions that seem to significantly affect the return on a college degree. These include school type, school selectivity level, school cost and financial aid, college major, later occupation, and perhaps most importantly, the probability of completing a degree.

Variation by School Selectivity

Mark Schneider of the American Enterprise Institute (AEI) and the American Institutes for Research (AIR) used longitudinal data from the Baccalaureate and Beyond survey to calculate lifetime earnings for bachelor's earners by type of institution attended, then compared them to the lifetime earnings of high school graduates. The difference (after accounting for tuition costs and discounting to a present value) is the value of a bachelor's degree. For every type of school (categorized by whether the school was a public institution or a nonprofit private institution and by its selectivity) this value is positive, but it varies widely. People who attended the most selective private schools have a lifetime earnings premium of over $620,000 (in 2012 dollars). For those who attended a minimally selective or open admission private school, the premium is only a third of that. Schneider performed a similar exercise with campus-level data on college graduates (compiled by the online salary information company PayScale), calculating the return on investment (ROI) of a bachelor's degree (Figure 2). These calculations suggest that public schools tend to have higher ROIs than private schools, and more selective schools offer higher returns than less selective ones. Even within a school type and selectivity category, the variation is striking. For example, the average ROI for a competitive public school in 2010 is 9 percent, but the highest rate within this category is 12 percent while the lowest is 6 percent.

Another important element in estimating the ROI on a college education is financial aid, which can change the expected return dramatically. For example, Vassar College is one of the most expensive schools on the 2012 list and has a relatively low annual ROI of 6 percent. But when you factor in its generous aid packages (nearly 60% of students receive aid, and the average amount is over $30,000), Vassar's annual ROI increases 50 percent, to a return of 9 percent (data available at http://www.payscale.com/college-education-value-2012).

Figure 2. Return on Investment of a Bachelor's Degree by Institution Type

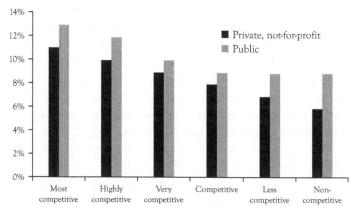

Source: Schneider (2010).
Note: Data uses PayScale return on investment data and Barron's index of school selectivity.

One of the most important takeaways from the PayScale 10 data is that not every bachelor's degree is a smart investment. After attempting to account for in-state vs. out-of-state tuition, financial aid, graduation rates, years taken to graduate, wage inflation, and selection, nearly two hundred schools on the 2012 list have negative ROIs. Students may want to think twice about attending the Savannah College of Art and Design in Georgia or Jackson State University in Mississippi. The problem is compounded if the students most likely to attend these less selective schools come from disadvantaged families.

Variation by Field of Study and Career

Even within a school, the choices a student makes about his or her field of study and later career can have a large impact on what he or she gets out of her degree. It is no coincidence that the three schools with the highest 30-year ROIs on the 2012 PayScale list—Harvey Mudd, Caltech, and MIT—specialize in the STEM fields: science, technology, engineering, and math. Recent analysis by the Census Bureau also shows that the lifetime earnings of workers with bachelor's degrees vary widely by college major and occupation. The highest paid major is engineering, followed by computers and math. The lowest paid major, with barely half the lifetime earnings of engineering majors, is education, followed by the arts and psychology (Figure 3). The highest-earning

Figure 3. Work-Life Earnings of Bachelor's Degree Holders by College Major

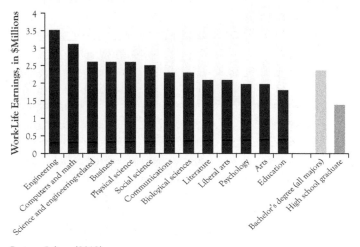

Source: Julian (2012).
Note: Synthetic work-life earnings estimates are calculated by finding median earnings for each 5-year age group between 25 and 64 (25–29, 30–34, etc.). Earnings for each group is multiplied by 5 to get total earnings for that period, then aggregated to get total lifetime earnings. This is done for high school graduates, bachelor's degree holders, and bachelor's degree holders by major.

occupation category is architecture and engineering, with computers, math, and management in second place. The lowest-earning occupation for college graduates is service (Figure 4). According to Census's calculations, the lifetime earnings of an education or arts major working in the service sector are actually lower than the average lifetime earnings of a high school graduate.

When we dig even deeper, we see that just as not all college degrees are equal, neither are all high school diplomas.

Figure 4. Work-Life Earnings of Bachelor's Degree Holders by Occupation

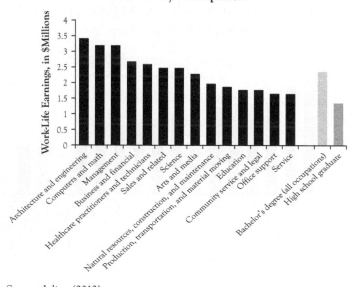

Source: Julian (2012).
Note: Synthetic work-life earnings estimates are calculated by finding median earnings for each 5-year age group between 25 and 64 (25–29, 30–34, etc.). Earnings for each group is multiplied by 5 to get total earnings for that period, then aggregated to get total lifetime earnings. This is done for high school graduates, bachelor's degree holders, and bachelor's degree holders by occupation.

Anthony Carnevale and his colleagues at the Georgetown Center on Education and the Workforce use similar methodology to the Census calculations but disaggregate even further, estimating median lifetime earnings for all education levels by occupation. They find that 14 percent of people with a high school diploma make at least as much as those with a bachelor's degree, and 17 percent of people with a bachelor's degree make more than those with a professional degree. The authors argue that much of this finding is explained by occupation. In every occupation category, more educated workers earn more.

But, for example, someone working in a STEM job with only a high school diploma can expect to make more over a lifetime than someone with a bachelor's degree working in education, community service and arts, sales and office work, health support, blue collar jobs, or personal services.

The numbers above are for full-time workers in a given field. In fact, choice of major can also affect whether a college graduate can find a job at all. Another recent report from the Georgetown Center on Education and the Workforce breaks down unemployment rates by major for both recent (age 22–26) and experienced (age 30–54) college graduates in 2009–2010. People who majored in education or health have very low unemployment—even though education is one of the lowest-paying majors. Architecture graduates have particularly high unemployment, which may simply reflect the decline of the construction industry during the Great Recession. Arts majors don't fare too well, either. The expected earnings (median full-time earnings times the probability of being employed) of a young college graduate with a theater degree are about $6,000 more than the expected earnings of a young high school graduate. For a young person with a mechanical engineering degree, the expected earnings of the college graduate is a staggering $35,000 more than that of a typical high school graduate.

Variation in Graduation Rates

Comparisons of the return on college by highest degree attained   15
include only people who actually complete college. Students
who fail to obtain a degree incur some or all of the costs of a
bachelor's degree without the ultimate payoff. This has major
implications for inequalities of income and wealth, as the students least likely to graduate—lower-income students—are also
the most likely to take on debt to finance their education.

Fewer than 60 percent of students who enter four-year
schools finish within six years, and for low-income students
it's even worse. Again, the variation in this measure is huge.
Just within Washington, D.C., for example, six-year graduation
rates range from a near-universal 93 percent at Georgetown
University to a dismal 19 percent at the University of D.C. Of
course, these are very different institutions, and we might expect
high-achieving students at an elite school like Georgetown to
have higher completion rates than at a less competitive school
like UDC. In fact, Frederick Hess and his colleagues at AEI
have documented that the relationship between selectivity and
completion is positive, echoing other work that suggests that
students are more likely to succeed in and graduate from college when they attend more selective schools (Figure 5). At the
most selective schools, 88 percent of students graduate within
six years; at non-competitive schools, only 35 percent do. Furthermore, the range of completion rates is negatively correlated
with school ranking, meaning the least selective schools have
the widest range. For example, one non-competitive school,
Arkansas Baptist College, graduates 100 percent of its students,
while only 8 percent of students at Southern University at
New Orleans finish. Not every student can get into Harvard,
where the likelihood of graduating is 97 percent, but students

Figure 5. Average Six-Year Graduation Rates by School Selectivity

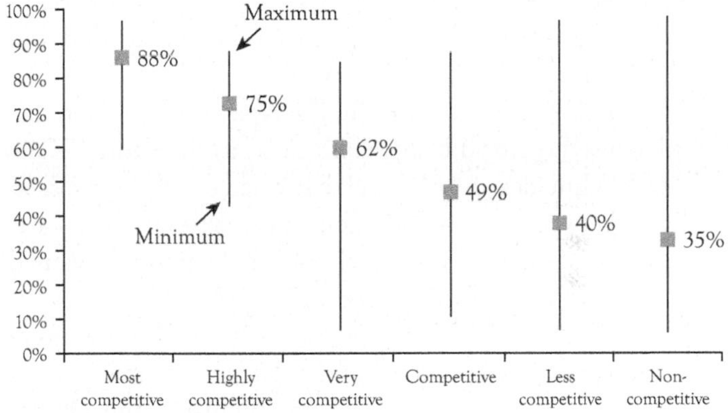

Source: Hess et al. (2009).

can choose to attend a school with a better track record within their ability level.

Unfortunately, recent evidence by Caroline Hoxby of Stanford and Christopher Avery of Harvard shows that most high-achieving low-income students never even apply to the selective schools that they are qualified to attend—and at which they would be eligible for generous financial aid. There is clearly room for policies that do a better job of matching students to schools.

Policy Implications

All of this suggests that it is a mistake to unilaterally tell young Americans that going to college—any college—is the best decision they can make. If they choose wisely and attend a school with generous financial aid and high expected earnings, and if they don't just enroll but graduate, they can greatly improve their lifetime prospects. The information needed to make a wise decision, however, can be difficult to find and hard to interpret.

One solution is simply to make the type of information discussed above more readily available. A study by Andrew Kelly and Mark Schneider of AEI found that when parents were asked to choose between two similar public universities in their state, giving them information on the schools' graduation rates caused them to prefer the higher-performing school.

The PayScale college rankings are a step in the right direction, giving potential students and their parents information with which to make better decisions. Similarly, the Obama Administration's new College Scorecard is being developed to increase transparency in the college application process. As it operates now, a prospective student can type in a college's name and learn its average net price, graduation rate, loan default rate, and median borrowed amount. The Department of Education is working to add information about the earnings of a given school's graduates. There is also a multi-dimensional search feature that allows users to find schools by location, size, and degrees and majors offered. The Student Right to Know Before You Go Act, sponsored by Senators Ron Wyden (D-OR) and Marco Rubio (R-FL), also aims to expand the data available on the costs and benefits of individual schools, as well as programs and majors within schools.

The College Scorecard is an admirable effort to help students and parents navigate the complicated process of choosing a college. However, it may not go far enough in improving transparency and helping students make the best possible decisions. A recent report by the Center for American Progress (CAP) showed a draft of the Scorecard to a focus group of college-bound high school students and found, among other things, that they are frequently confused about the term "net price" and give little weight to six-year graduation rates because they expect to graduate in four. It appears that the White House has responded to some of these critiques, for example showing median amount borrowed and default rates rather than the confusing "student loan repayment." Nevertheless, more information for students and their parents is needed.

There is also room for improvement in the financial aid system, which can seem overwhelmingly complex for families not familiar with the process. Studies have shown that students frequently underestimate how much aid they are eligible for, and don't claim the tax incentives that would save them money. Since 2009, the Administration has worked to simplify the FAFSA, the form that families must fill out to receive federal aid—but more could be done to guide low-income families through the process.

In the longer run, colleges need to do more to ensure that their students graduate, particularly the lower-income students who struggle most with persistence and completion. Research suggests that grants and loans increase enrollment but that aid must be tied to performance in order to affect persistence. Currently, we spend over $100 billion on Pell Grants and federal loans, despite a complete lack of evidence that this money leads to higher graduation rates. Good research on programs like Georgia's HOPE scholarships or West Virginia's PROMISE scholarships suggest that attaching strings to grant aid can improve college persistence and completion.

Finally, we want to emphasize that the personal characteristics and skills of each individual are equally important. It may be that for a student with poor grades who is on the fence about enrolling in a four-year program, the most bang for the buck will come from a vocationally oriented associate's degree or career-specific technical training. Indeed, there are many well-paid job openings going unfilled because employers can't find workers with the right skills— skills that young potential workers could learn from training programs, apprenticeships, a vocational certificate, or an associate's degree. Policymakers should encourage these alternatives at the high school as well as the postsecondary level, with a focus on high-demand occupations and high-growth sectors. There has long been resistance to vocational education in American high schools, for fear that "tracking" students reinforces socioeconomic (and racial) stratification and impedes mobility. But if the default for many lower-achieving students was a career-focused training path rather than a path that involves dropping out of traditional college, their job prospects would probably improve. For example, Career Academies are high schools organized around an occupational or industry focus, and have partnerships with local employers and colleges. They have been shown by gold standard research to increase men's wages, hours worked, and employment stability after high school, particularly for those at high risk of dropping out.

Conclusions

In this brief, we have corralled existing research to make the point that while on average the return on college is highly positive, there is a considerable spread in the value of going to college. A bachelor's degree is not a smart investment for every student in every circumstance. We have outlined three important steps policymakers can take to make sure every person does make a smart investment in their choice of postsecondary education. First, we must provide more information in a comprehensible manner. Second, the federal government should lead the way on performance-based scholarships to incentivize college attendance and persistence. Finally, there should be more good alternatives to a traditional academic path, including career and technical education and apprenticeships.

Additional Reading

Anthony P. Carnevale, Ban Cheah, and Jeff Strohl, "Hard Times: College Majors, Unemployment, and Earnings: Not All College Degrees Are Created Equal" (Washington, D.C.: The Georgetown University Center on Education and the Workforce, January 2012).

Anthony P. Carnevale, Stephen J. Rose, and Ban Cheah, "The College Payoff: Education, Occupations, Lifetime Earnings" (Washington, D.C.: The Georgetown University Center on Education and the Workforce, August 2011).

Michael Greenstone and Adam Looney, "Where Is the Best Place to Invest $102,000—In Stocks, Bonds, or a College Degree?" (Washington, D.C.: The Brookings Institution, June 2011).

Frederick M. Hess, Mark Schneider, Kevin Carey, and Andrew P. Kelly, "Diplomas and Dropouts: Which Colleges Actually Graduate Their Students (and Which Don't)" (Washington, D.C.: American Enterprise Institute for Public Policy Research, June 2009).

Harry J. Holzer and Robert I. Lerman, "The Future of Middle-Skill Jobs," (Washington, D.C.: The Brookings Institution, February 2009).

Caroline M. Hoxby and Christopher Avery, "The Missing 'One-Offs': The Hidden Supply of High-Achieving, Low Income Students" (Cambridge, MA, Working Paper, National Bureau of Economic Research, 2012).

Tiffany Julian, "Work-Life Earnings by Field of Degree and Occupation for People with a Bachelor's Degree: 2011" (Washington, D.C.: U.S. Census Bureau, October 2012).

Andrew P. Kelly and Mark Schneider, "Filling In the Blanks: How Information Can Affect Choice in Higher Education" (Washington, D.C.: American Enterprise Institute for Public Policy Research, January 2011).

Julie Margetta Morgan and Gadi Dechter, "Improving the College Scorecard: Using Student Feedback to Create an Effective Disclosure" (Washington, D.C.: Center for American Progress, November 2012).

Mark Schneider, "How Much Is That Bachelor's Degree Really Worth? The Million Dollar Misunderstanding" (Washington, D.C.: American Enterprise Institute for Public Policy Research, May 2009).

Mark Schneider, "Is College Worth the Investment?" (Washington, D.C.: American Enterprise Institute for Public Policy Research, October 2010).

Joining the Conversation

1. Stephanie Owen and Isabel Sawhill announce the "they say" in their second sentence—"Study after study reminds us that higher education is one of the best investments we can make"—and then proceed to report on how the return on that investment varies. What factors do they say make college a questionable investment?

2. This report draws on quite a bit of quantitative data on the economic effects of graduating from college. Look carefully at one of the graphs that Owen and Sawhill provide, and explain in your own words what the data say.

3. Owen and Sawhill's analysis seems to favor baccalaureate degree programs as conferring the greatest advantages on students. How might Liz Addison, whose essay appears on pages 527–30, respond to their argument?

4. In the essay's concluding paragraphs, the authors note information that students and parents should know before choosing a college. What information do they consider most important? What did you know and what did you not know

about colleges you were considering as you were deciding which school to attend? How might additional knowledge have helped you make a more informed choice?

5. According to Owen and Sawhill, "For certain schools, majors, occupations, and individuals, college may not be a smart investment" (paragraph 1). Taking this statement as a "they say," write a short essay responding with what you think. Discuss your own reasons for attending college, and refer to the authors' argument and data about the pros and cons of attending college.

Are Too Many People Going to College?

CHARLES MURRAY

—▢—

To ASK WHETHER too many people are going to college requires us to think about the importance and nature of a liberal education. "Universities are not intended to teach the knowledge required to fit men for some special mode of gaining their livelihood," John Stuart Mill told students at the University of St. Andrews in 1867. "Their object is not to make skillful lawyers, or physicians, or engineers, but capable and cultivated human beings." If this is true (and I agree that it is), why say that too many people are going to college? Surely a mass democracy should encourage as many people as possible to become "capable and cultivated human beings" in Mill's sense. We should not restrict the availability of a liberal education to a rarefied intellectual elite. More people should be going to college, not fewer.

———

CHARLES MURRAY is the W. H. Brady Scholar at the American Enterprise Institute, a "public policy think tank dedicated to defending human dignity, expanding human potential, and building a freer and safer world." He is the author, most recently, of *By the People: Rebuilding Liberty without Permission* (2015). This essay, adapted from his book *Real Education: Four Simple Truths for Bringing America's Schools Back to Reality* (2008) first appeared on September 8, 2008, in the *American*, the journal of the American Enterprise Institute.

Yes and no. More people should be getting the basics of a liberal education. But for most students, the places to provide those basics are elementary and middle school. E. D. Hirsch Jr. is the indispensable thinker on this topic, beginning with his 1987 book *Cultural Literacy: What Every American Needs to Know*. Part of his argument involves the importance of a body of core knowledge in fostering reading speed and comprehension. With regard to a liberal education, Hirsch makes three points that are germane here:

See Chapter 4 for ways to agree, but with a difference.

Full participation in any culture requires familiarity with a body of core knowledge. To live in the United States and not recognize Teddy Roosevelt, Prohibition, the Minutemen, Wall Street, smoke-filled rooms, or Gettysburg is like trying to read without knowing some of the ten thousand most commonly used words in the language. It signifies a degree of cultural illiteracy about America. But the core knowledge transcends one's own country. Not to recognize Falstaff, Apollo, the Sistine Chapel, the Inquisition, the twenty-third Psalm, or Mozart signifies cultural illiteracy about the West. Not to recognize the solar system, the Big Bang, natural selection, relativity, or the periodic table is to be scientifically illiterate. Not to recognize the Mediterranean, Vienna, the Yangtze River, Mount Everest, or Mecca is to be geographically illiterate.

This core knowledge is an important part of the glue that holds the culture together. All American children, of whatever ethnic heritage, and whether their families came here 300 years ago or three months ago, need to learn about the Pilgrims, Valley Forge, Duke Ellington, Apollo 11, Susan B. Anthony, George C. Marshall, and the Freedom Riders. All students need to learn the iconic stories. For a society of immigrants such as ours, the core knowledge is our shared identity that makes us Americans together rather than hyphenated Americans.

K–8 are the right years to teach the core knowledge, and the effort should get off to a running start in elementary school. Starting early is partly a matter of necessity: There's a lot to learn, and it takes time. But another reason is that small children enjoy learning myths and fables, showing off names and dates they have memorized, and hearing about great historical figures and exciting deeds. The educational establishment sees this kind of curriculum as one that forces children to memorize boring facts. That conventional wisdom is wrong on every count. The facts can be fascinating (if taught right); a lot more than memorization is entailed; yet memorizing things is an indispensable part of education, too; and memorizing is something that children do much, much better than adults. The core knowledge is suited to ways that young children naturally learn and enjoy learning. Not all children will be able to do the reading with the same level of comprehension, but the fact-based nature of the core knowledge actually works to the benefit of low-ability students—remembering facts is much easier than making inferences and deductions. The core knowledge curriculum lends itself to adaptation for students across a wide range of academic ability.

In the 20 years since *Cultural Literacy* was published, Hirsch and his colleagues have developed and refined his original formulation into an inventory of more than 6,000 items that approximate the core knowledge broadly shared by literate Americans. Hirsch's Core Knowledge Foundation has also developed a detailed, grade-by-grade curriculum for K–8, complete with lists of books and other teaching materials.

The Core Knowledge approach need not stop with eighth grade. High school is a good place for survey courses in the humanities, social sciences, and sciences taught at a level below the demands of a college course and accessible to most students in the upper two-thirds of the distribution of academic ability. Some students will not want to take these courses, and it can be counterproductive to require them to do so, but high school can put considerable flesh on the liberal education skeleton for students who are still interested.

Liberal Education in College

Saying "too many people are going to college" is not the same as saying that the average student does not need to know about history, science, and great works of art, music, and literature. They do need to know—and to know more than they are currently learning. So let's teach it to them, but let's not wait for college to do it.

Liberal education in college means taking on the tough stuff. A high-school graduate who has acquired Hirsch's core knowledge will know, for example, that John Stuart Mill was an important 19th-century English philosopher who was associated with something called Utilitarianism and wrote a famous book called *On Liberty*. But learning philosophy in college, which is an essential component of a liberal education, means that the student has to be able to read and understand the actual text of *On Liberty*. That brings us to the limits set by the nature of college-level material. Here is the first sentence of *On Liberty*: "The subject of this essay is not the so-called liberty of the will, so unfortunately opposed to the misnamed doctrine of philosophical necessity; but civil, or social liberty:

the nature and limits of the power which can be legitimately exercised by society over the individual." I will not burden you with *On Liberty*'s last sentence. It is 126 words long. And Mill is one of the more accessible philosophers, and *On Liberty* is one of Mill's more accessible works. It would be nice if everyone could acquire a fully formed liberal education, but they cannot.

Specifically: When College Board researchers defined "college readiness" as the SAT score that is associated with a 65 percent chance of getting at least a 2.7 grade point average in college during the freshman year, and then applied those criteria (hardly demanding in an era of soft courses and grade inflation) to the freshmen in a sample of 41 major colleges and universities, the threshold "college readiness" score was found to be 1180 on the combined SAT math and verbal tests. It is a score that only about 10 percent of American 18-year-olds would achieve if they all took the SAT, in an age when more than 30 percent of 18-year-olds go to college.

Should all of those who do have the academic ability to absorb a college-level liberal education get one? It depends. Suppose we have before us a young woman who is in the 98th percentile of academic ability and wants to become a lawyer and eventually run for political office. To me, it seems essential that she spend her undergraduate years getting a rigorous liberal education. Apart from a liberal education's value to her, the nation will benefit. Everything she does as an attorney or as an elected official should be informed by the kind of wisdom that a rigorous liberal education can encourage. It is appropriate to push her into that kind of undergraduate program.

But the only reason we can get away with pushing her is that the odds are high that she will enjoy it. The odds are high because she is good at this sort of thing—it's no problem for her to read *On Liberty* or *Paradise Lost*. It's no problem for her to come up with an interesting perspective on what she's read and weave it into a term paper. And because she's good at it, she is also likely to enjoy it. It is one of Aristotle's central themes in his discussion of human happiness, a theme that John Rawls later distilled into what he called the Aristotelian Principle: "Other things equal, human beings enjoy the exercise of the irrealized capacities (their innate or trained abilities), and this enjoyment increases the more the capacity is realized, or the greater its complexity." And so it comes to pass that those who take the hardest majors and who enroll in courses that look most like an old-fashioned liberal education are concentrated among the students in the top percentiles of academic ability. Getting a liberal education consists of dealing with complex intellectual material day after day, and dealing with complex intellectual material is what students in the top few percentiles are really good at, in the same way that other people are really good at cooking or making pottery. For these students, doing it well is fun.

Every percentile down the ability ladder—and this applies to all abilities, not just academic—the probability that a person will enjoy the hardest aspects of an activity goes down as well. Students at the 80th percentile of academic ability are still smart kids, but the odds that they will respond to a course that assigns Mill or Milton are considerably lower than the odds that a student in the top few percentiles will respond. Virtue has nothing to do with it. Maturity has nothing to do with it. Appreciation of the value of a liberal education has nothing to do with it. The probability that a student will enjoy *Paradise Lost* goes down as his linguistic ability goes down, but so does the probability that he works on double acrostic puzzles in his spare time or regularly plays online Scrabble, and for the identical reason. The lower down the linguistic ladder he is, the less fun such activities are.

And so we return to the question: Should all of those who have the academic ability to absorb a college-level liberal education get one? If our young woman is at the 80th percentile of linguistic ability, should she be pushed to do so? She has enough intellectual capacity, if she puts her mind to it and works exceptionally hard.

The answer is no. If she wants to, fine. But she probably 15 won't, and there's no way to force her. Try to force her (for example, by setting up a demanding core curriculum), and she will transfer to another school, because she is in college for vocational training. She wants to write computer code. Start a business. Get a job in television. She uses college to take vocational courses that pertain to her career interests. A large proportion of people who are theoretically able to absorb a liberal education have no interest in doing so.

And reasonably so. Seen dispassionately, getting a traditional liberal education over four years is an odd way to enjoy spending one's time. Not many people enjoy reading for hour after hour, day after day, no matter what the material may be. To enjoy reading *On Liberty* and its ilk—and if you're going to absorb such material, you must in some sense enjoy the process—is downright peculiar. To be willing to spend many more hours writing papers and answers to exam questions about that material approaches masochism.

We should look at the kind of work that goes into acquiring a liberal education at the college level in the same way that we look at the grueling apprenticeship that goes into becoming a master chef: something that understandably attracts only a few people. Most students at today's colleges choose not to take the courses that go into a liberal education because the capabilities they want to develop lie elsewhere. These students are not lazy, any more than students who don't want to spend hours learning how to chop carrots into a perfect eighth-inch dice are lazy. A liberal education just doesn't make sense for them.

For Learning How to Make a Living, the Four-Year Brick-and-Mortar Residential College Is Increasingly Obsolete

We now go from one extreme to the other, from the ideal of liberal education to the utilitarian process of acquiring the knowledge that most students go to college to acquire—practical and vocational. The question here is not whether the traditional four-year residential college is fun or valuable as a place to grow up, but when it makes sense as a place to learn how to make a living. The answer is: in a sensible world, hardly ever.

Start with the time it takes—four years. Assuming a semester system with four courses per semester, four years of class work means 32 semester-long courses. The occupations for which "knowing enough" requires 32 courses are exceedingly rare. For some professions—medicine and law are the obvious examples—a rationale for four years of course work can be concocted (combining pre-med and pre-law undergraduate courses with three years of medical school and law school), but for every other occupation, the body of knowledge taught in classrooms can be learned more quickly. Even Ph.D.s don't require four years of course work. The Ph.D. is supposed to signify expertise, but that expertise comes from burrowing deep in to a specialty, not from dozens of courses.

Those are the jobs with the most stringent academic require- 20 ments. For the student who wants to become a good hotel manager, software designer, accountant, hospital administrator, farmer, high-school teacher, social worker, journalist, optometrist, interior designer, or football coach, four years of class work is ridiculous. Actually becoming good in those occupations will take longer than four years, but most of the competence is acquired on the job. The two-year community college and online courses offer more flexible options for tailoring course work to the real needs of the job.

A brick-and-mortar campus is increasingly obsolete. The physical infrastructure of the college used to make sense for three reasons. First, a good library was essential to higher learning, and only a college faculty and student body provided the economies of scale that made good libraries affordable. Second, scholarship flourishes through colleagueships, and the college campus made it possible to put scholars in physical proximity to each other. Third, the best teaching requires interaction between teachers and students, and physical proximity was the only way to get it. All three rationales for the brick-and-mortar campus are fading fast.

The rationale for a physical library is within a few years of extinction. Even now, the Internet provides access, for a price, to all the world's significant technical journals. The books are about to follow. Google is scanning the entire text of every book in the libraries of Harvard, Princeton, Stanford, Oxford, the New York Public Library, the Bavarian State Library, Ghent University Library, Keio Library (Tokyo), the National Library of Catalonia, University of Lausanne, and an expanding list of others. Collectively, this project will encompass close to the sum total of human knowledge. It will be completely searchable. Everything out of copyright will be free. Everything still under copyright will be accessible for a fee. Libraries will still be a selling point for colleges, but as a place for students to study in pleasant surroundings—an amenity in the same way that an attractive student union is an amenity. Colleges and universities will not need to exist because they provide libraries.

The rationale for colleges based on colleagueships has eroded. Until a few decades ago, physical proximity was important because correspondence and phone calls just weren't as good. As email began to spread during the 1980s, physical proximity became less important. As the capacity of the Internet expanded in the 1990s, other mechanisms made those interactions richer. Now, regular emails from professional groups inform scholars of the latest publications in their field of interest. Specialized chat groups enable scholars to bounce new ideas off other people working on the same problems. Drafts are exchanged effortlessly and comments attached electronically. Whether physical proximity still has any advantages depends mostly on the personality of the scholar. Some people like being around other people during the workday and prefer face-to-face conversations to emails. For those who don't, the value of being on a college campus instead of on a mountaintop in Montana is nil. Their electronic access to other scholars is incomparably greater than any scholar enjoyed even within the world's premier universities before the advent of the Internet. Like the library, face-to-face colleagueships will be an amenity that colleges continue to provide. But colleges and universities will not need to exist because they provide a community of scholars.

The third rationale for the brick-and-mortar college is that it brings teachers together with students. Working against that rationale is the explosion in the breadth and realism of what is known as distance learning. The idea of distance learning is surprisingly old—Isaac Pitman was teaching his shorthand system to British students through the postal service in the 1840s, and the University of London began offering degrees for correspondence students in 1858—but the technology of distance learning changed little for the next century. The advent of inexpensive videocassettes in the 1980s opened up a way for students to hear and see lectures without being in the classroom. By the early 1990s, it was possible to buy college-level courses on audio or videotape, taught by first-rate teaching professors, on a wide range of topics, for a few hundred dollars. But without easy interaction between teacher and student, distance learning remained a poor second-best to a good college seminar.

Once again, the Internet is revolutionizing everything. As 25 personal computers acquired the processing power to show high-definition video and the storage capacity to handle big video files, the possibilities for distance learning expanded by orders of magnitude. We are now watching the early expression of those possibilities: podcasts and streaming videos in real time of professors' lectures, online discussions among students scattered around the country, online interaction between students and professors, online exams, and tutorials augmented by computer-aided instruction software.

Even today, the quality of student-teacher interactions in a virtual classroom competes with the interactions in a brick-and-mortar classroom. But the technology is still in its early stages of development and the rate of improvement is breathtaking. Compare video games such as Myst and SimCity in the 1990s to their descendants today; the Walkman you used in the 1990s to the iPod you use today; the cell phone you used in the 1990s to the BlackBerry or iPhone you use today. Whatever technical limitations might lead you to say, "Yes, but it's still not the same as being there in the classroom," are probably within a few years of being outdated.

College Isn't All It's Cracked Up to Be

College looms so large in the thinking of both parents and students because it is seen as the open sesame to a good job. Reaping the economic payoff for college that shows up in econometric analyses is a long shot for large numbers of young people.

When high-school graduates think that obtaining a B.A. will help them get a higher-paying job, they are only narrowly correct. Economists have established beyond doubt that people with B.A.s earn more on average than people without them. But why does the B.A. produce that result? For whom does the B.A. produce that result? For some jobs, the economic premium for a degree is produced by the actual education that has gone into getting the degree. Lawyers, physicians, and engineers can earn their high incomes only by deploying knowledge and skills that take years to acquire, and degrees in law, medicine, and engineering still signify competence in those knowledges and skills. But for many other jobs, the economic premium for the B.A. is created by a brutal fact of life about the American job market: Employers do not even interview applicants who do not hold a B.A. Even more brutal, the advantage conferred by the B.A. often has nothing to do with the content of the education. Employers do not value what the student learned, just that the student has a degree.

Employers value the B.A. because it is a no-cost (for them) screening device for academic ability and perseverance. The more people who go to college, the more sense it makes for employers to require a B.A. When only a small percentage of people got college degrees, employers who required a B.A. would have been shutting themselves off from access to most of the talent. With more than a third of 23-year-olds now getting a B.A., many employers can reasonably limit their hiring pool to college graduates because bright and ambitious high-school graduates who can go to college usually do go to college. An employer can believe that exceptions exist but rationally choose not to expend time and money to identify them. Knowing this, large numbers of students are in college to buy their admission ticket—the B.A.

But while it is true that the average person with a B.A. makes more than the average person without a B.A., getting a B.A. is still going to be the wrong economic decision for many high-school graduates. Wages within occupations form a distribution. Young people with okay-but-not-great academic ability who are thinking about whether to go after a B.A. need to consider the competition they will face after they graduate. Let me put these calculations in terms of a specific example, a young man who has just graduated from high school and is trying to decide whether to become an electrician or go to college and major in business, hoping to become a white-collar manager. He is at the 70th percentile in linguistic ability and logical mathematical ability—someone who shouldn't go to college by my standards, but who can, in today's world, easily find a college that will give him a degree. He is exactly average in interpersonal and intrapersonal ability. He is at the 95th percentile in the small-motor skills and spatial abilities that are helpful in being a good electrician.

He begins by looking up the average income of electricians and managers on the Bureau of Labor Statistics website, and finds that the mean annual income for electricians in 2005 was $45,630, only about half of the $88,450 mean for management occupations. It looks as if getting a B.A. will buy him a huge wage premium. Should he try to get the B.A. on economic grounds?

To make his decision correctly, our young man must start by throwing out the averages. He has the ability to become an excellent electrician and can reasonably expect to be near the top of the electricians' income distribution. He does not have it in him to be an excellent manager, because he is only average in interpersonal and intrapersonal ability and only modestly above average in academic ability, all of which are important for becoming a good manager, while his competitors for those slots will include many who are high in all of those abilities. Realistically, he should be looking at the incomes toward the bottom of the distribution of managers. With that in mind, he goes back to the Bureau of Labor Statistics website and discovers that an electrician at the 90th percentile of electricians' incomes made $70,480 in 2005, almost twice the income of a manager at the 10th percentile of managers' incomes ($37,800). Even if our young man successfully completes college and gets a B.A. (which is far from certain), he is likely to make less money than if he becomes an electrician.

Then there is job security to consider. A good way to make sure you always can find work is to be among the best at what you do. It also helps to have a job that does not require you to compete with people around the globe. When corporations downsize, they lay off mediocre managers before they lay off top electricians. When the economy gets soft, top electricians can find work when mediocre managers cannot. Low-level management jobs can often be outsourced to India, whereas electricians' jobs cannot.

What I have said of electricians is true throughout the American job market. The income for the top people in a wide variety of occupations that do not require a college degree is higher than the average income for many occupations that require a B.A. Furthermore, the range and number of such jobs are expanding rapidly. The need for assembly-line workers in factories (one of the most boring jobs ever invented) is falling, but the demand for skilled technicians of every kind—in healthcare, information technology, transportation networks, and every other industry that relies on high-tech equipment—is expanding. The service sector includes many low-skill, low-paying jobs, but it also includes growing numbers of specialized jobs that pay well (for example, in healthcare and the entertainment and leisure industries). Construction offers an array of high-paying jobs for people who are good at what they do. It's not just skilled labor in the standard construction trades that is in high demand. The increase in wealth in American society has increased the demand for all sorts of craftsmanship. Today's high-end homes and office buildings may entail the work of specialized skills in stonework, masonry, glazing, painting, cabinetmaking, machining, landscaping, and a dozen other crafts. The increase in wealth is also driving an increased demand for the custom-made and the exquisitely wrought, meaning demand for artisans in everything from pottery to jewelry to metalworking. There has never been a time in history when people with skills not taught in college have been in so much demand at such high pay as today, nor a time when the range of such jobs has been so wide. In today's America, finding a first-rate lawyer or physician is easy. Finding first-rate skilled labor is hard.

Intrinsic Rewards

The topic is no longer money but job satisfaction—intrinsic 35 rewards. We return to our high-school graduate trying to decide between going to college and becoming an electrician. He knows that he enjoys working with his hands and likes the idea of not being stuck in the same place all day, but he also likes the idea of being a manager sitting behind a desk in a big office, telling people what to do and getting the status that goes with it.

However, he should face facts that he is unlikely to know on his own, but that a guidance counselor could help him face. His chances of getting the big office and the status are slim. He is more likely to remain in a cubicle, under the thumb of the boss in the big office. He is unlikely to have a job in which he produces something tangible during the course of the day.

If he becomes a top electrician instead, he will have an expertise that he exercises at a high level. At the end of a workday, he will often be able to see that his work made a difference in the lives of people whose problems he has solved. He will not be confined to a cubicle and, after his apprenticeship, will be his own supervisor in the field. Top electricians often become independent contractors who have no boss at all.

The intrinsic rewards of being a top manager can be just as great as those of a top electrician (though I would not claim they are greater), but the intrinsic rewards of being a mediocre manager are not. Even as people in white-collar jobs lament the soullessness of their work, the intrinsic rewards of exercising technical skills remain undiminished.

Finally, there is an overarching consideration so important it is hard to express adequately: the satisfaction of being good at what one does for a living (and knowing it), compared to the melancholy of being mediocre at what one does for a living (and knowing it). This is another truth about living a human life that a 17-year-old might not yet understand on his own, but that a guidance counselor can bring to his attention. Guidance counselors and parents who automatically encourage young people to go to college straight out of high school regardless of their skills and interests are being thoughtless about the best interests of young people in their charge.

The Dark Side of the B.A. as Norm

It is possible to accept all that I have presented as fact and still 40 disagree with the proposition that too many people are going to college. The argument goes something like this:

The meaning of a college education has evolved since the 19th century. The traditional liberal education is still available for students who want it, but the curriculum is appropriately broader now, and includes many courses for vocational preparation that today's students want. Furthermore, intellectual requirements vary across majors. It may be true that few students can complete a major in economics or biology, but larger proportions can handle the easier majors. A narrow focus on curriculum also misses the important nonacademic functions of college. The lifestyle on today's campuses may leave something to be desired, but four years of college still give youngsters in late adolescence a chance to encounter different kinds of people, to discover new interests, and to decide what they want to make of their lives. And if it is true that some students spend too much of their college years partying, that was also true of many Oxford students in the 18th century. Lighten up.

If the only people we had to worry about were those who are on college campuses and doing reasonably well, this position would have something to be said for it. It does not address the issues of whether four years makes sense or whether a residential facility makes sense; nevertheless, college as it exists is not an intrinsically evil place for the students who are there and are coping academically. But there is the broader American society to worry about as well. However unintentionally, we have made something that is still inaccessible to a majority of the population—the B.A.—into a symbol of first-class citizenship. We have done so at the same time that other class divisions are becoming more powerful. Today's college system is implicated in the emergence of class-riven America.

The problem begins with the message sent to young people that they should aspire to college no matter what. Some politicians are among the most visible offenders, treating every failure to go to college as an injustice that can be remedied by increasing government help. American educational administrators reinforce the message by instructing guidance counselors to steer as many students as possible toward a college-prep track (more than 90 percent of high-school students report that their guidance counselors encouraged them to go to college). But politicians and educators are only following the lead of the larger culture. As long as it remains taboo to acknowledge that college is intellectually too demanding for most young people, we will continue to create crazily unrealistic expectations among the next generation. If "crazily unrealistic" sounds too strong, consider that more than 90 percent of high-school seniors expect to go to college, and more than 70 percent of them expect to work in professional jobs.

One aspect of this phenomenon has been labeled misaligned ambitions, meaning that adolescents have career ambitions that are inconsistent with their educational plans. Data from the Sloan Study of Youth and Social Development conducted during the 1990s indicate that misaligned ambitions characterized more than half of all adolescents. Almost always, the misalignment is in the optimistic direction, as adolescents aspire to be attorneys or physicians without understanding the educational hurdles they must surmount to achieve their goals. They end up at a four-year institution not because that is where they can take the courses they need to meet their career goals, but because college is the place where B.A.s are handed out, and everyone knows that these days you've got to have a B.A. Many of them drop out. Of those who entered a four-year college in 1995, only 58 percent had gotten their B.A. five academic years later. Another 14 percent were still enrolled. If we assume that half of that 14 percent eventually get their B.A.s, about a third of all those who entered college hoping for a B.A. leave without one.

If these numbers had been produced in a culture where the 45 B.A. was a nice thing to have but not a big deal, they could be interpreted as the result of young adults deciding that they didn't really want a B.A. after all. Instead, these numbers were produced by a system in which having a B.A. is a very big deal indeed, and that brings us to the increasingly worrisome role of the B.A. as a source of class division. The United States has always had symbols of class, and the college degree has always been one of them. But through the first half of the 20th century, there were all sorts of respectable reasons a person might not go to college—not enough money to pay for college; needing to work right out of high school to support a wife, parents, or younger siblings; or the commonly held belief that going straight to work was better preparation for a business career than going to college. As long as the percentage of college graduates remained small, it also remained true, and everybody knew it, that the majority of America's intellectually most able people did not have B.A.s.

Over the course of the 20th century, three trends gathered strength. The first was the increasing proportion of jobs screened for high academic ability due to the advanced level of education they require—engineers, physicians, attorneys, college teachers, scientists, and the like. The second was the increasing market value of those jobs. The third was the opening up of college to more of those who had the academic ability to go to college, partly because the increase in American wealth meant that more parents could afford college for their children, and partly because the proliferation of scholarships and loans made it possible for most students with enough academic ability to go.

The combined effect of these trends has been to overturn the state of affairs that prevailed through World War II. Now the great majority of America's intellectually most able people do have a B.A. Along with that transformation has come a downside that few anticipated. The acceptable excuses for not going to college have dried up. The more people who go to college, the more stigmatizing the failure to complete college becomes. Today, if you do not get a B.A., many people assume it is because you are too dumb or too lazy. And all this because of a degree that seldom has an interpretable substantive meaning.

Let's approach the situation from a different angle. Imagine that America had no system of postsecondary education and you were made a member of a task force assigned to create one from scratch. Ask yourself what you would think if one of your colleagues submitted this proposal:

First, we will set up a common goal for every young person that represents educational success. We will call it a B.A. We will then make it difficult or impossible for most people to achieve this goal. For those who can, achieving the goal will take four years no matter what is being taught. We will attach an economic reward for reaching the goal that often has little to do with the content of what has been learned. We will lure large numbers of people who do not possess adequate ability or motivation to try to achieve the goal and then fail. We will then stigmatize everyone who fails to achieve it.

What I have just described is the system that we have in 50 place. There must be a better way.

Joining the Conversation

1. The "I say" here is explicit: "too many people are going to college." We know what Charles Murray thinks. But why does he think this? In the rest of his essay, he tells us why. Summarize his argument, noting all the reasons and evidence he gives to support his claim.

2. Is Murray right—are too many people going to college? If you disagree, why? Whether or not you agree with him, do you find his argument persuasive?

3. In the middle of the essay is a lengthy narrative about someone who is trying to decide what to be when he grows up, an electrician or a manager. What does this narrative contribute to Murray's argument? Where would the argument be without the narrative?

4. Compare Murray's argument that college is a waste of time for many with Stephanie Owen and Isabel Sawhill's discussion of the value of college (pp. 488–505). What are the key differences between the two arguments, and which do you find more convincing?

5. In one or two paragraphs, reflect on why you chose your current school. Did you consider, first and foremost, how your college would help you "learn how to make a living," as Murray would recommend? Did you consider other potential benefits of your college education? If you could have a well-paying job without a college education, would you go to college anyway?

Two Years Are Better Than Four

LIZ ADDISON

—▢—

Oh, the hand wringing. "College as America used to understand it is coming to an end," bemoans Rick Perlstein and his beatnik friend of fallen face. Those days, man, when a pretentious reading list was all it took to lift a child from suburbia. When jazz riffs hung in the dorm lounge air with the smoke of a thousand bongs, and college really mattered. Really mattered?

Rick Perlstein thinks so. It mattered so much to him that he never got over his four years at the University of Privilege. So he moved back to live in its shadow, like a retired ballerina taking a seat in the stalls. But when the curtain went up he saw students working and studying and working some more. Adults

———

Liz Addison attended Piedmont Virginia Community College and Southern Maine Community College, where she graduated with a degree in biology in 2008. She received a graduate degree from the Royal Veterinary College in London in 2014 and now works as a veterinarian in Virginia. This essay, published in 2007, was a runner-up in a *New York Times Magazine* college essay contest. The essay responds to Rick Perlstein's opinion piece "What's the Matter with College?," in which he argues that universities no longer matter as much as they once did.

before their time. Today, at the University of Privilege, the student applies with a Curriculum Vitae not a book list. Shudder.

Thus, Mr. Perlstein concludes, the college experience—a rite of passage as it was meant it to be—must have come to an end. But he is wrong. For Mr. Perlstein, so rooted in his own nostalgia, is looking for himself—and he would never think to look for himself in the one place left where the college experience of self-discovery does still matter to those who get there. My guess, reading between the lines, is that Mr. Perlstein has never set foot in an American community college.

The philosophy of the community college, and I have been to two of them, is one that unconditionally allows its students to begin. Just begin. Implicit in this belief is the understanding that anything and everything is possible. Just follow any one of the 1,655 road signs, and pop your head inside—yes, they let anyone in—and there you will find discoveries of a first independent film, a first independent thought, a first independent study. This college experience remains as it should. This college brochure is not marketing for the parents—because the parents, nor grandparents, probably never went to college themselves.

Upon entry to my first community college I had but one 5 O'level to my name. These now disbanded qualifications once marked the transition from lower to upper high school in the Great British education system. It was customary for the average student to proceed forward with a clutch of O'levels, say eight or nine. On a score of one, I left school hurriedly at sixteen. Thomas Jefferson once wrote, "Everybody should have an education proportional to their life." In my case, my life became proportional to my education. But, in doing so, it had the good fortune to land me in an American community college and now, from that priceless springboard, I too seek admission to the University of Privilege. Enter on empty and leave with a head full of dreams? How can Mr. Perlstein say college does not matter anymore?

The community college system is America's hidden public service gem. If I were a candidate for office I would campaign from every campus. Not to score political points, but simply to make sure that anyone who is looking to go to college in this country knows where to find one. Just recently, I read an article in the *New York Times* describing a "college application essay" workshop for low-income students. I was strangely disturbed that those interviewed made no mention of community college. Mr. Perlstein might have been equally disturbed, for the thrust of the workshop was no different to that of an essay coach to the affluent. "Make Life Stories Shine," beams the headline. Or, in other words, prove yourself worldly, insightful, cultured, mature, before you get to college.

Yet, down at X.Y.C.C. it is still possible to enter the college experience as a rookie. That is the understanding—that you will grow up a little bit with your first English class, a bit more with your first psychology class, a whole lot more with your first biology, physics, chemistry. That you may shoot through the roof with calculus, philosophy, or genetics. "College is the key," a young African American student writes for the umpteenth torturous revision of his college essay, "as well as hope." Oh, I wanted desperately to say, please tell him about community college. Please tell him that hope can begin with just one placement test.

See Chapter 9 on mixing academic and colloquial styles.

When Mr. Perlstein and friends say college no longer holds importance, they mourn for both the individual and society. Yet, arguably, the community college experience is more critical to the nation than that of former beatnik types who, lest we forget, did not change the world. The community colleges of America cover this country college by college and community by community. They offer a network of affordable future, of accessible hope, and an option to dream. In the cold light of day, is it perhaps not more important to foster students with dreams rather than a building take-over?

I believe so. I believe the community college system to be one of America's uniquely great institutions. I believe it should be celebrated as such. "For those who find it necessary to go to a two-year college," begins one University of Privilege admissions paragraph. None too subtle in its implication, but very true. For some students, from many backgrounds, would never breathe the college experience if it were not for the community college. Yes, it is here that Mr. Perlstein will find his college years of self-discovery, and it is here he will find that college does still matter.

Joining the Conversation

1. What view is Liz Addison responding to? Write out a sentence or two summarizing the "they say."
2. Addison discusses her own educational experience as part of her argument. What role does this use of autobiographical narrative play in her argument?
3. How does Addison make it clear that her topic is important—and that it should matter to readers?
4. In closing, Addison writes of community colleges: "It is here that Mr. Perlstein will find his college years of self-discovery, and it is here he will find that college does still matter." Do you think college still matters? Write an essay responding to this point from your own perspective as a college student.

Why We Need to Keep the "Community" in Community Colleges

ANNA CLARK

—▫—

MY PARENTS TOOK TURNS going to college. While raising three kids, my father lost his left big toe in an accident at a tool-and-die shop and Mom babysat dozens of neighborhood rugrats. We didn't have enough. The kitchen cabinets were too bare. So, Dad signed up for classes at Lake Michigan College, the local two-year school formerly known as Benton Harbor Community College.

With his hands cupping his chin at a lamplit table, he softly read aloud from his textbooks; for years, his murmuring carried down the hallway to my bedroom, like a lullaby. When I was 11,

ANNA CLARK is a freelance journalist and author of *The Poisoned City*, an account of the water crisis in Flint, MI, which began in 2014. Her investigative reporting, published in *Politico*, the *New York Times*, and the *Washington Post*, focuses on the environment, education, politics, and her hometown, Detroit. She graduated from the University of Michigan and served as a Fulbright fellow in Nairobi, Kenya. This article appeared in *Next City* in 2015.

Bergen Community College commencement at MetLife Stadium in East Rutherford, NJ.

he earned his bachelor's degree through an extension program hosted by LMC and got a job at Whirlpool Corporation. Then it was Mom's turn. She did her homework alongside my siblings and I at the kitchen table. The same year I graduated high school, she earned her associate's degree, on her way to her own B.A. My mother and I posed in front of the fireplace, each in cap and gown, grinning for the camera, for each other, for wherever it was we were headed next.

It is not a coincidence that my parents are the only people I've witnessed who have worked their way out of poverty. With open admission and low-cost tuition, community colleges are the champions of people just like them: full-time workers and parents; older folks and younger ones; military veterans and people who speak English as a second language. That is, the true multiplicity of our communities.

But there is an escalating movement of community colleges dropping the word "community" from their names. The latest is Prince William Sound Community College in Valdez, Alaska, which announced this month that it will be known simply as Prince William Sound College. Henry Ford Community College outside Detroit has become Henry Ford College. Jackson Community College in Michigan is now Jackson College. Three Seattle community colleges began the fall semester with truncated names. Twenty-eight schools make up the Florida College System, which was known as the Florida Community College System until 2009; only three individual campuses still have "community" in their name. In all, more than 80 schools have cut "community" in the past 30 years, with at least 40 doing so in the last decade.

This is a bad move.   5

Administration officials insist that the name change does not signify a change in mission. Rather, they cite the broadening scope of their campuses. Many now offer bachelor's degrees in select fields, either through independent programs or in partnership with four-year schools. Twenty-five percent of community colleges offer on-campus housing. Not only do the schools want their name to broadcast the breadth of their offerings, but programming expansion also can coincide with shifts in accreditation or funding status.

See Chapter 1 for other examples of how to introduce what "they say."

You might even consider this part of their natural evolution. The first public two-year college was founded in 1901 in Illinois, Joliet Junior College. Shifting from an emphasis on liberal arts to Depression-era workforce training, these colleges were open to women at a time when few others were. Community colleges got their biggest boost in 1948, when the Truman Commission, combined with the GI Bill, catalyzed a national network of schools that were agile enough to meet local needs.

Today, there are around 1,100 community colleges in the U.S. In addition to offering credit courses and innovative training programs, these campuses are community nerve centers: They provide space for civic groups to meet, host blood drives and bring top-notch theater to small towns.

But the name change is also an attempt to heighten the prestige of community colleges. While nearly half of all undergraduates in the United States attend two-year schools, enrollment is unstable, riding the tides of economic trends. Better employment rates mean fewer students, which is why numbers have dropped for three consecutive years. Retention is a perpetual battle for open-access schools, and their reliance on underpaid adjunct faculty is troubling. Community colleges have a tremendous champion in the Obama Administration, with the President suggesting that they should be as "free and universal" as high school. But his "America's College Promise" initiative has struggled to get congressional support and funding. Some campuses are battling financial disorder, and dramatically hiking tuition. (Some states, however, are picking up the mantle themselves. This month, Oregon followed Tennessee in passing a law that offers free enrollment at community campuses.)

As well, the welcoming-to-all nature of these schools can be disparaged with unfortunate local nicknames—LMC, for example, is derided as "Last Minute College." The name change is supposed to inflate the appeal of these schools. But it is a decision that mistakes image for substance, an alarming precedent for an institution of higher learning. It has the reek of market research. When Jackson College announced its new name in 2013, officials boasted about how it will make them more marketable to international students. This is a surprising turn for a campus founded in 1928 to serve the people of rural mid-Michigan.

By assuming a name that has the ring of a traditional four- 10
year school, community colleges are playing into the stereotype
that they are less valuable than their counterparts. They give
credence to the second-class stigma. "I'm not sure at what point
'community college' was branded a dirty term," a columnist at
Lane Community College in Eugene, Oregon, wrote recently
in the school paper, "but I've found myself red in the face
when someone asked me where I go to school. In a room full
of university students."

Now, we are seeing that even top leaders of community colleges buy into this insecurity, to the point where they take the
drastic and expensive step of hiding behind a new name. They
would do better to save the money they're spending on changing logos, signage and stationery, and direct it toward telling
a more proud and truthful story about what these institutions
contribute to society.

Community colleges are a different animal than four-year
schools, after all. They deserve to be taken on their own terms.
Traditional education metrics, like the time it takes to graduate,
aren't neatly comparable. The Department of Education's measure of graduation rates is designed for students who enroll in
the fall as first-time degree-seeking undergraduates who attend
school full-time. None of that describes the majority of community college students. Most attend part-time, begin in "off"
semesters, transfer to other schools and, in many cases, they
are not seeking a degree or certificate when they sign
up for classes. All of this distorts the statistics on community colleges, confusing "graduation" as a synonym
for "educational completion."

For more on how reasons should support what you say, see Chapter 4.

Because they serve a different population—including working adults, like my parents—their singular value should be
recognized. And when it comes down to it, despite the snide

nicknames, people get this. A June Gallup poll revealed that Americans are about as likely to describe the education at a community college as "excellent" or "good" as they are to positively rate four-year schools. With the national student loan debt at a preposterous $1.2 trillion, that fact deserves a spotlight.

Community colleges are, at heart, a radical manifestation of the belief that access to education, knowledge and culture are a public good. By stripping the "community" from their names, these schools give up too much ground to those who believe otherwise.

Joining the Conversation

1. Why does Anna Clark believe that removing the term "community" from community colleges is such a bad idea? In her view, what role should community colleges play in their communities, and how does that role differ from that of other colleges and universities?

2. In paragraph 5, the author presents her "I say," which she goes on to explain for the remainder of the essay. What language strategy does she use to present her argument and to distinguish her view from those leading up to it? How effective is she in introducing her argument, and why?

3. Clark states in paragraph 10, "By assuming a name that has the ring of a traditional four-year school, community colleges are playing into the stereotype that they are less valuable than their counterparts. They give credence to the second-class stigma." How would you respond to this argument?

4. On what specific points do you think Clark would agree with Liz Addison's "Two Years Are Better Than Four" (pp. 527–30)? On what points might she be likely to disagree?

5. Go to **theysayiblog.com** and search for the commercial from San Joaquin Valley College in which a jug of laundry detergent tries to convey a serious message to a potential future student. How might author Anna Clark respond to this commercial?

6. Drawing on any of readings on **theysayiblog.com** or in this chapter, write an essay putting forth your own argument on the value of attending the community college.

Minority Student Clubs:
Segregation or Integration?

GABRIELA MORO

—▫—

MINORITY REPRESENTATION on US college campuses has increased significantly in recent years, and many schools have made it a priority to increase diversity on their campuses in order to prepare students for a culturally diverse US demo-cratic society (Hurtado and Ruiz 3–4). To complement this increase, many schools have implemented minority student clubs to provide safe and comfortable environments where minority students can thrive academically and socially with peers from similar backgrounds. However, do these minority groups amplify students' tendency to interact only with those who are similar to themselves? Put another way, do these groups inhibit students from engaging in diverse relationships?

Many view such programs to be positive and integral to minority students' college experience; some, however, feel that

———

GABRIELA MORO wrote this essay in her first-year composition class at the University of Notre Dame in South Bend, IN. It was published in the university's journal *Fresh Writing*, "an online archive of exemplary first-year writing projects." A neuroscience and behavior pre-health major, Moro is pursuing a career in medicine.

these clubs are not productive for promoting cross-cultural interaction. While minority clubs have proven to be beneficial to minority students in some cases, particularly on campuses that are not very diverse, my research suggests that colleges would enrich the educational experience for all students by introducing multicultural clubs as well.

To frame my discussion, I will use an article from *College Student Journal* that distinguishes between two types of students: one who believes minority clubs are essential for helping minority students stay connected with their cultures, and another who believes these clubs isolate minorities and work against diverse interaction among students. To pursue the question of whether or not such groups segregate minorities from the rest of the student body and even discourage cultural awareness, I will use perspectives from minority students to show that these programs are especially helpful for first-year students. I will also use other student testimonials to show that when taken too far, minority groups can lead to self-segregation and defy what most universities claim to be their diversity goals. Findings from research will contribute to a better understanding of the role minority clubs play on college campuses and offer a complete answer to my question about the importance of minority programs.

Before I go further, I would like to differentiate among three kinds of diversity that Patricia Gurin and colleagues identify in their article "Diversity and Higher Education: Theory and Impact on Educational Outcomes." The first type is *structural diversity*, "the numerical representation of diverse [racial and ethnic] groups." The existence of structural diversity alone does not assure that students will develop valuable intergroup relationships. *Classroom diversity*, the second type, involves gaining "content knowledge" or a better understanding about diverse peers and their backgrounds by doing so in the classroom. The third type of diversity, *informal interactional diversity*, refers to "both the frequency and the quality of intergroup interaction as keys to meaningful diversity experiences during college." Students often encounter this kind of diversity in social settings outside the classroom (Gurin et al. 332–33). Informal interactional diversity is the focus of my research, since it is the concept that leads colleges to establish social events and organizations that allow all students to experience and appreciate the variety of cultures present in a student body.

In a study published in *College Student Journal*, three admin- 5 istrators at Pennsylvania State University explore how biracial students interact with others on a college campus. The authors conclude that views of minority clubs and related programs, which the authors call race-oriented student services, tend to fall into two groups: "Although some argue that these race-oriented student services are divisive and damage white-minority relations, others support these services as providing a safe place and meeting the needs of minority students to develop a sense of racial pride, community and importance" (Ingram et al. 298). I will start by examining the point of view of those who associate minority clubs with positive outcomes.

A study by Samuel Museus in the *Journal of College Student Development* finds that minority student programs help students to stay connected with their culture in college and help ease first-year minority students' transition into the college environment. The study also shows that ethnic student organizations help students adjust and find their place at universities that have a predominantly white student body (584). Museus concludes that universities should stress the importance of racial and ethnic groups and develop more opportunities for minority students to make connections with them. This way, students can find support from their minority peers as they work together to face academic and social challenges. Museus's findings suggest that minority student groups are essential for allowing these students to preserve and foster connections to their own cultures.

In another study, Wendell Hall and colleagues evaluate how minority and non-minority students differ in their inclinations to take part in diversity activities and to communicate with racially and ethnically diverse peers at a predominantly white university. These scholars conclude that "engagement [with diverse peers] is learned" (434). Students who engaged with diverse students before going to college were more likely to interact with diverse peers by the end of their sophomore year. Minority students were more predisposed than their white peers to interact with diverse peers during their freshman year (435). These findings indicate that minority student clubs can be helpful for first-year minority students who have not previously engaged with other minority students, especially if the university has a predominantly white student body.

Professors and scholars are not the only ones who strongly support minority clubs. For example, three students at Harvard College—Andrea Delgado, Denzel (no last name given), and Kimi Fafowora—give their perspective on student life and multicultural identity on campus to incoming students via *YouTube* ("Student Voices"). The students explain how minority programs on campus have helped them adjust to a new college environment as first-year students. As Delgado puts it:

I thought [cultural clubs were] something I maybe didn't need, but come November, I missed speaking Spanish and I missed having tacos, and other things like that. That's the reason why I started attending meetings more regularly. Latinas Unidas has been a great intersection of my cultural background and my political views. (00:12:30–12:56)

The experiences these minority students shared support the scholarly evidence that minority clubs help incoming students transition into a new and often intimidating environment.

While the benefits of these clubs are quite evident, several problems can also arise from them. The most widely recognized is self-segregation. Self-segregating tendencies are not exclusive to minority students: college students in general tend to self-segregate as they enter an unfamiliar environment. As a study by Nathan Martin and colleagues finds, "Today, the student bodies of our leading colleges and universities are more diverse than ever. However, college students are increasingly self-segregating by race or ethnicity" (720). Several studies as well as interviews with students suggest that minority clubs exacerbate students' inclination to self-segregate. And as students become comfortable with their minority peers, they may no longer desire or feel the need to branch out of their comfort zone.

In another study, Julie Park, a professor at the University of 10 Maryland, examines the relationship between participation in college student organizations and the development of interracial friendships. Park suggests that "if students spend the majority of time in such groups [Greek, ethnic, and religious student organizations], participation may affect student involvement in the broader diversity of the institution" (642). In other words, if minority students form all of their social and academic ties within their minority group, the desired cultural exchange among the student body could suffer.

So what can be done? In the Penn State study mentioned earlier, in which data were collected by an online survey, participants were asked to respond to an open-ended question about what they think universities should do to create a more inviting environment for biracial students (Ingram et al. 303). On one hand, multiple students responded with opinions opposing the formation of both biracial and multiracial clubs: "I feel instead of having biracial and multiracial clubs the colleges should have diversity clubs and just allow everyone to get together. All these 'separate' categorizing of clubs, isn't that just separation of groups?" "Having a ton of clubs that are for specific races is counter-productive. It creates segregation and lack of communication across cultures" (304–05).

On the other hand, students offered suggestions for the formation of multicultural activities: "Encourage more racial integration to show students races aren't so different from each other and to lessen stereotypes" (305). "Hold cultural events that allow students of different races to express/share their heritage" (306). Patreese Ingram and colleagues conclude that while biracial and multiracial student organizations are helpful in establishing an inviting college environment for minority students,

> creating a truly inclusive environment...requires additional efforts: these include multicultural awareness training for faculty, staff, and students, and incorporation of multicultural issues into the curriculum. In addition to the creation of biracial/multiracial clubs and organization, the students in this study want to increase awareness of the mixed heritage population among others on college campuses. (308)

The two very different opinions reported in this study not only point to the challenges minority student programs can create but also suggest ways to resolve these challenges. Now that evidence from both research studies and student perspectives confirms that these clubs, while beneficial to minority students'

For tips on clarifying where you have been and where you are going, see p. 144.

experiences, can inhibit cultural immersion, I will continue with my original argument that the entire student body would benefit if campuses also implemented multicultural advocacy clubs, rather than just selective minority clubs. Gurin and colleagues, the researchers who identify the three types of diversity in higher education, contend that even with the presence of diverse racial and ethnic groups and regular communication among students formally and informally, a greater push from educators is needed:

> In order to foster citizenship for a diverse democracy, educators must intentionally structure opportunities for students to leave the comfort of their homogenous peer group and build relationships across racially/ethnically diverse student communities on campus. (363)

This suggestion implies that participation from students and faculty is needed to foster cultural immersion in higher education.

Another way to improve cross-cultural exchange is by developing a diverse curriculum. An article on multiculturalism in higher education by Alma Clayton-Pedersen and Caryn McTighe Musil in the *Encyclopedia of Education* review the ways in which universities have incorporated diversity studies into their core curriculum over the last several decades. The authors found that the numbers of courses that seek to prepare students for a democratic society rich in diversity have increased (1711, 1714). However, they recommend that institutions need to take a more holistic approach to their academic curricula in order to pursue higher education programs that prepare students to face "complex and demanding questions" and to "use their new knowledge and civic, intercultural capacities to address real-world problems" (1714). My research suggests that a more holistic approach to the importance of diversity studies in the college curriculum, as well as multicultural advocacy clubs, are necessary in order to prepare *all* students, not just minority students, for the diverse world and society ahead of them.

Thus, even though minority student clubs can lead to self-segregation among students and result in less cross-cultural interaction, their benefits to minority students suggest that a balance needs to be found between providing support for minorities and avoiding segregation of these groups from the rest of the student body. Besides sponsoring minority student programs, colleges and universities can implement multicultural events and activities for all students to participate in, especially during the freshman year. An initiative like this would enhance the diverse interactions that occur on campuses, promote cultural immersion, and garner support for minority student clubs.

Beyond the reach of this evaluation, further research should 15 be conducted, specifically on the types of cultural events that are most effective in promoting cultural awareness and meaningful diverse interactions among the student body. By examining different multicultural organizations from both public and private institutions, and comparing student experiences and participation in those programs, researchers can suggest an ideal multicultural program to provide an optimal student experience.

WORKS CITED

Clayton-Pedersen, Alma R., and Caryn McTighe Musil. "Multiculturalism in Higher Education." *Encyclopedia of Education*, edited by James W. Guthrie, 2nd ed., vol. 5, Macmillan, 2002, pp. 1709–16.

Gurin, Patricia, et al. "Diversity and Higher Education: Theory and Impact on Educational Outcomes." *Harvard Educational Review*, vol. 72, no. 3, 2002, pp. 330–37. *ResearchGate*, https://doi.org/10.17763/haer.72.3.01151786u134n051.

Hall, Wendell, et al. "A Tale of Two Groups: Differences between Minority Students and Non-Minority Students in Their Predispositions to and Engagement with Diverse Peers at a Predominantly White Institution." *Research in Higher Education*, vol. 52, no. 4, 2011, pp. 420–39. *Academic Search Premier*, https://doi.org/10.1007/s11162-010-9201-4.

Hurtado, Sylvia, and Adriana Ruiz. "The Climate for Underrepresented Groups and Diversity on Campus." *Higher Education Research Institute*, 2012, heri.ucla.edu/briefs/urmbrief.php.

Ingram, Patreese, et al. "How Do Biracial Students Interact with Others on the College Campus?" *College Student Journal*, vol. 48, no. 2, 2014, pp. 297–311.

Martin, Nathan D., et al. "Interracial Friendships across the College Years: Evidence from a Longitudinal Case Study." *Journal of College Student Development*, vol. 55, no. 7, 2014, pp. 720–25. *Academic Search Premier*, https://doi.org/10.1353/csd.2014.0075.

Museus, Samuel D. "The Role of Ethnic Student Organizations in Fostering African American and Asian American Students' Cultural Adjustment and Membership at Predominantly White Institutions." *Journal of College Student Development*, vol. 49, no. 6, 2008, pp. 568–86. *Project MUSE*, https://doi.org/10.1353/csd.0.0039.

Park, Julie J. "Clubs and the Campus Racial Climate: Student Organizations and Interracial Friendship in College." *Journal of College Student Development*, vol. 55, no. 7, 2014, pp. 641–60. *Academic Search Premier*, https://doi.org/10.1353/csd.2014.0076.

"Student Voices: Multicultural Perspectives." *YouTube*, uploaded by Harvard College Admissions and Financial Aid, 7 Aug. 2014, www.youtube.com/watch?v=djIWQgDx-Jc.

Joining the Conversation

1. What larger conversation is Gabriela Moro responding to in this essay?

2. What are some of the connecting words, phrases, and sentences Moro uses to transition from one paragraph to another? (See pp. 111–12 for a list of commonly used transitions.)

3. Notice how many direct quotations Moro includes. Why do you think she includes so many? What do the quotations contribute that a summary or paraphrase would not?

4. Writer danah boyd (pp. 387–96) criticizes the many ways in which Americans are now self-segregating. How might she respond to Moro's description of Notre Dame's campus and to Moro's proposal to support minority clubs *and* multiculturalism?

5. Develop an argument of your own that responds to Moro's proposal, agreeing, disagreeing, or both. However you choose to argue, be sure to consider other positions in addition to your own, including other authors in this chapter.

Hidden Intellectualism

GERALD GRAFF

———◻———

EVERYONE KNOWS SOME YOUNG PERSON who is impressively "street smart" but does poorly in school. What a waste, we think, that one who is so intelligent about so many things in life seems unable to apply that intelligence to academic work. What doesn't occur to us, though, is that schools and colleges might be at fault for missing the opportunity to tap into such street smarts and channel them into good academic work.

Nor do we consider one of the major reasons why schools and colleges overlook the intellectual potential of street smarts: the fact that we associate those street smarts with anti-intellectual concerns. We associate the educated life, the life of the mind, too narrowly and exclusively with subjects and texts that we consider inherently weighty and academic. We assume that it's possible to wax intellectual about Plato, Shakespeare,

———

GERALD GRAFF, a coauthor of this book, is a professor of English and education at the University of Illinois at Chicago. He is a past president of the Modern Language Association, the world's largest professional association of university scholars and teachers. This essay is adapted from his 2003 book, *Clueless in Academe: How Schooling Obscures the Life of the Mind.*

the French Revolution, and nuclear fission, but not about cars, dating, fashion, sports, TV, or video games.

The trouble with this assumption is that no necessary connection has ever been established between any text or subject and the educational depth and weight of the discussion it can generate. Real intellectuals turn any subject, however lightweight it may seem, into grist for their mill through the thoughtful questions they bring to it, whereas a dullard will find a way to drain the interest out of the richest subject. That's why a George Orwell writing on the cultural meanings of penny postcards is infinitely more substantial than the cogitations of many professors on Shakespeare or globalization (104–16). See pp. 62–63 for tips on disagreeing, with reasons.

Students do need to read models of intellectually challenging writing—and Orwell is a great one—if they are to become intellectuals themselves. But they would be more prone to take on intellectual identities if we encouraged them to do so at first on subjects that interest them rather than ones that interest us.

I offer my own adolescent experience as a case in point. Until I 5 entered college, I hated books and cared only for sports. The only reading I cared to do or could do was sports magazines, on which I became hooked, becoming a regular reader of *Sport* magazine in the late forties, *Sports Illustrated* when it began publishing in 1954, and the annual magazine guides to professional baseball, football, and basketball. I also loved the sports novels for boys of John R. Tunis and Clair Bee and autobiographies of sports stars like Joe DiMaggio's *Lucky to Be a Yankee* and Bob Feller's *Strikeout Story*. In short, I was your typical teenage anti-intellectual—or so I believed for a long time. I have recently come to think, however, that my preference for sports over schoolwork was not anti-intellectualism so much as intellectualism by other means.

In the Chicago neighborhood I grew up in, which had become a melting pot after World War II, our block was solidly middle class, but just a block away—doubtless concentrated there by the real estate companies—were African Americans, Native Americans, and "hillbilly" whites who had recently fled postwar joblessness in the South and Appalachia. Negotiating this class boundary was a tricky matter. On the one hand, it was necessary to maintain the boundary between "clean-cut" boys like me and working-class "hoods," as we called them, which meant that it was good to be openly smart in a bookish sort of way. On the other hand, I was desperate for the approval of the hoods, whom I encountered daily on the playing field and in the neighborhood, and for this purpose it was not at all good to be book-smart. The hoods would turn on you if they sensed you were putting on airs over them: "Who you lookin' at, smart ass?" as a leather-jacketed youth once said to me as he relieved me of my pocket change along with my self-respect.

I grew up torn, then, between the need to prove I was smart and the fear of a beating if I proved it too well; between the need not to jeopardize my respectable future and the need to impress the hoods. As I lived it, the conflict came down to a choice between being physically tough and being verbal. For a boy in my neighborhood and elementary school, only being "tough" earned you complete legitimacy. I still recall endless, complicated debates in this period with my closest pals over who was "the toughest guy in the school." If you were less than negligible as a fighter, as I was, you settled for the next best thing, which was to be inarticulate, carefully hiding telltale marks of literacy like correct grammar and pronunciation.

In one way, then, it would be hard to imagine an adolescence more thoroughly anti-intellectual than mine. Yet in retrospect, I see that it's more complicated, that I and the 1950s themselves were not simply hostile toward intellectualism, but divided and ambivalent. When Marilyn Monroe married the playwright Arthur Miller in 1956 after divorcing the retired baseball star

Joe DiMaggio, the symbolic triumph of geek over jock suggested the way the wind was blowing. Even Elvis, according to his biographer Peter Guralnick, turns out to have supported Adlai over Ike in the presidential election of 1956. "I don't dig the intellectual bit," he told reporters. "But I'm telling you, man, he knows the most" (327).

Though I too thought I did not "dig the intellectual bit," I see now that I was unwittingly in training for it. The germs had actually been planted in the seemingly philistine debates about which boys were the toughest. I see now that in the interminable analysis of sports teams, movies, and toughness that my friends and I engaged in—a type of analysis, needless to say, that the real toughs would never have stooped to—I was already betraying an allegiance to the egghead world. I was practicing being an intellectual before I knew that was what I wanted to be.

It was in these discussions with friends about toughness and sports, I think, and in my reading of sports books and magazines, that I began to learn the rudiments of the intellectual life: how to make an argument, weigh different kinds of evidence, move between particulars and generalizations, summarize the views of others, and enter a conversation about ideas. It was in reading and arguing about sports and toughness that I experienced what it felt like to propose a generalization, restate and respond to a counterargument, and perform other intellectualizing operations, including composing the kind of sentences I am writing now.

Only much later did it dawn on me that the sports world was more compelling than school because it was *more intellectual than school*, not less. Sports after all was full of challenging arguments, debates, problems for analysis, and intricate statistics that you could care about, as school conspicuously was not. I believe that street smarts beat out book smarts in our culture not because street smarts are nonintellectual, as we generally suppose, but because they satisfy an intellectual thirst more thoroughly than school culture, which seems pale and unreal.

They also satisfy the thirst for community. When you entered sports debates, you became part of a community that was not limited to your family and friends, but was national and public. Whereas schoolwork isolated you from others, the pennant race or Ted Williams's .400 batting average was something you could talk about with people you had never met. Sports introduced you not only to a culture steeped in argument, but to a public argument culture that transcended the personal. I can't blame my schools for failing to make intellectual culture resemble the Super Bowl, but I do fault them for failing to learn anything from the sports and entertainment worlds about how to organize and represent intellectual culture, how to exploit its gamelike element and turn it into arresting public spectacle that might have competed more successfully for my youthful attention.

For here is another thing that never dawned on me and is still kept hidden from students, with tragic results: that the real intellectual world, the one that existed in the big world beyond school, is organized very much like the world of team sports, with rival texts, rival interpretations and evaluations of texts, rival theories of why they should be read and taught, and elaborate team competitions in which "fans" of writers, intellectual systems, methodologies, and -isms contend against each other.

To be sure, school contained plenty of competition, which became more invidious as one moved up the ladder (and has become even more so today with the advent of high-stakes testing). In this competition, points were scored not by making arguments, but by a show of information or vast reading, by grade-grubbing, or other forms of one-upmanship. School competition, in short, reproduced the less attractive features of sports culture without those that create close bonds and community.

And in distancing themselves from anything as enjoyable 15 and absorbing as sports, my schools missed the opportunity to capitalize on an element of drama and conflict that the intellectual world shares with sports. Consequently, I failed to see the parallels between the sports and academic worlds that could have helped me cross more readily from one argument culture to the other.

Sports is only one of the domains whose potential for literacy training (and not only for males) is seriously underestimated by educators, who see sports as competing with academic development rather than a route to it. But if this argument suggests why it is a good idea to assign readings and topics that are close to students' existing interests, it also suggests the limits of this tactic. For students who get excited about the chance to write about their passion for cars will often write as poorly and unreflectively on that topic as on Shakespeare or Plato. Here is the flip side of what I pointed out before: that there's no necessary relation between the degree of interest a student shows in a text or subject and the quality of thought or expression such a student manifests in writing or talking about it. The challenge, as college professor Ned Laff has put it, "is not simply to exploit students' nonacademic interests, but to get them to see those interests through academic eyes."

To say that students need to see their interests "through academic eyes" is to say that street smarts are not enough. Making students' nonacademic interests an object of academic study is useful, then, for getting students' attention and overcoming their boredom and alienation, but this tactic won't in itself necessarily move them closer to an academically rigorous treatment of those interests. On the other hand, inviting students to write about cars, sports, or clothing fashions does not have to be a pedagogical cop-out as long as students are required to see these interests "through academic eyes," that is, to think and write about cars, sports, and fashions in a reflective, analytical way, one that sees them as microcosms of what is going on in the wider culture.

If I am right, then schools and colleges are missing an opportunity when they do not encourage students to take their nonacademic interests as objects of academic study. It is self-defeating to decline to introduce any text or subject that figures to engage students who will otherwise tune out academic work entirely. If a student cannot get interested in Mill's *On Liberty* but will read *Sports Illustrated* or *Vogue* or the hip-hop magazine *Source* with absorption, this is a strong argument for assigning the magazines over the classic. It's a good bet that if students get hooked on reading and writing by doing term papers on *Source*, they will eventually get to *On Liberty*. But even if they don't, the magazine reading will make them more literate and reflective than they would be otherwise. So it makes pedagogical sense to develop classroom units on sports, cars, fashions, rap music, and other such topics. Give me the student anytime who writes a sharply argued, sociologically acute analysis of an issue in *Source* over the student who writes a lifeless explication of *Hamlet* or Socrates' *Apology*.

Works Cited

DiMaggio, Joe. *Lucky to Be a Yankee*. Bantam, 1949.
Feller, Bob. *Strikeout Story*. Bantam, 1948.
Guralnick, Peter. *Last Train to Memphis: The Rise of Elvis Presley*. Little, Brown, 1994.
Orwell, George. *A Collection of Essays*. Harcourt, 1953.

Joining the Conversation

1. Gerald Graff begins his essay with the view that we generally associate "book smarts" with intellectualism and "street smarts" with anti-intellectualism. Graff then provides an extended example from his early life to counter this viewpoint. What do you think of his argument that boyhood conversations about sports provided a solid foundation for his later intellectual life? What support does he provide, and how persuasive is it?

2. Graff argues in paragraph 13 that the intellectual world is much like the world of team sports, with "rival texts . . . , rival theories . . . , and elaborate team competitions." Can you think of any examples from your own experience that support this assertion? In what ways do you think "the real intellectual world" is different from the world of team sports?

3. Imagine a conversation between Graff and Charles Murray (pp. 506–26) on the intellectual skills people can develop outside the realm of formal education and the benefits of those skills.

4. So what? Who cares? Graff does not answer these questions explicitly. Do it for him: write a brief paragraph saying why his argument matters, and for whom.

5. Graff argues that schools should encourage students to think critically, read, and write about areas of personal interest such as cars, fashion, or music—as long as they do so in an intellectually serious way. What do you think? Write an essay considering the educational merits of such a proposal, taking Graff's argument as a "they say."

Generation Stress: The Mental Health Crisis on Campus

SYLVIA MATHEWS BURWELL

—▣—

It is supposed to be the time of their life—the halcyon days of college, when young adults grow, acquire knowledge, and learn new skills. But according to the 2016–17 Healthy Minds Study, an annual survey of mental health on American college campuses, while 44 percent of students said that they were flourishing, 39 percent reported experiencing symptoms of depression or anxiety. The proportion of students experiencing suicidal ideation has grown from 6 percent in 2007 to 11 percent in 2017. The percentage of students receiving psychotherapy has jumped from 13 percent to 24 percent over the same period. Even though more students are getting help, only a

Sylvia Mathews Burwell is the president of American University. Previously, she served as the US secretary of health and human services under President Barack Obama from 2014 to 2017. She is a lifelong public servant, working in leadership positions in several federal government agencies and nonprofit organizations. A native of West Virginia, she is a graduate of Harvard University and University of Oxford, where she studied as a Rhodes Scholar. This essay was published in *Foreign Affairs* in 2018.

little more than half of those with symptoms of depression and anxiety had received treatment in the previous year.

The rise in mental health challenges is not limited to college students. One in every four adults in the United States will suffer from an anxiety disorder in the course of his or her lifetime, and suicide rates for men and women have risen since 2000. Whether these figures are a passing trend, the new normal, or a harbinger of greater challenges to come, one cannot fully know. But no matter what, universities need to deal with this uptick in psychological distress. No longer can they consider students' mental health to be outside their area of responsibility.

Nowadays, that responsibility has broadened to include increasing students' resiliency—that is, helping them not just avoid stress but also develop the tools to work through it. Resiliency is about decreasing students' sense of overwhelming stress while fostering their growing autonomy to tackle difficult life challenges. It's also about treating their very real depression and anxiety.

Taking responsibility for students' mental health needs is particularly complex at a time when universities are rightfully under pressure about cost and access. And it is all the more complex given that part of the core mission of higher education is to challenge students. To put it succinctly, college is supposed to be hard. How to balance the natural challenges and stress that university life presents while supporting students' mental health is an increasingly difficult tightrope to walk. Yet it needs to be walked, since students' mental health is a growing concern, and when that health is poor, it can inhibit the core mission of learning. To address the issue, universities must raise awareness of the problem through education inside and outside the academy; focus on prevention, detection, and treatment; and acknowledge the importance of community— all while recognizing that stress is a part of life.

Following World War II, the United States built a thriving 5 middle class and became the engine of the global economy thanks to the foundation of a thriving higher education system. Now, that same system must be a part of resolving today's mental health crisis, which presents a broad challenge to American competitiveness and productivity.

Stressed Out

In my first year as president of American University, I met with students from a variety of backgrounds and quickly learned that they have a great deal of insight into why they experience more stress and anxiety than previous generations. The answer boils down to three factors: safety, economics, and technology.

Students' concerns about safety stem from different sources. Most undergraduates have no memory of a world before 9/11. They have grown up with bag searches on subways, SWAT teams at stadiums, and body scanners at airports—constant visual reminders that the United States was attacked and could be again. Students of an older generation would note that those are no different from Cold War–era "duck and cover" drills. Yet today's students point out that Americans never experienced nuclear war, only the threat of it.

See Chapter 6 for more on answering objections fairly.

They have also grown up with increasingly deadly mass shootings. This fall, students arrived on campus with the 2018 attack at Marjory Stoneman Douglas High School, in Parkland, Florida, fresh in their minds, but they also remember the attacks in 2017 at a concert in Las Vegas, in 2016 at the Pulse nightclub in Orlando, in 2012 at Sandy Hook Elementary School, and in 2007 at Virginia Tech. For some students on campus, incidents that have involved racially motivated acts of violence—such as the events in Charlottesville, Virginia, in 2017—add to their fear, stress, and anxiety. Female students have additional cause for worry. While the increasing transparency about how often sexual assault occurs on campus has helped advance the conversation about the issue, it has also added to safety concerns.

Other fears are rooted in economics. A college education is essential to social mobility, but tuition at both public and private universities continues to rise. Many students, especially first-generation college students, come from families with already stretched budgets and little experience in the nuances of financing higher education, making the prospect of student debt particularly daunting.

Students also worry about the economy they are graduating 10 into—they are old enough to remember the Great Recession— and fear that they will end up jobless, unable to pay off their debt, and forced to live with their parents. Although unemployment is now low in the United States, wage growth has stayed relatively flat throughout the recovery, and early career salaries, in particular, dropped during the recession.

As a result, many students worry that they will do no better than their parents, and with good reason: in the United States, the likelihood that a child will earn more than his or her parents has dropped from 90 percent to 50 percent over the past half century. Students also see an economy that offers them not a single career choice but an ever-changing panoply of career steps. Such a path may be exciting, but it is nowhere as conducive to stable health insurance and a secure retirement as the one their parents and grandparents followed.

Then there is the anxiety that results from social media. Part of the stress has to do with the pressure on young people to constantly present a curated version of their lives on Instagram, Snapchat, and other platforms. The way I translate this concern to older generations is by asking, "What would it be like if you had to update your résumé every day?" The obvious answer: incredibly stressful. Another part of the stress comes from the observing side of social media. Because people tend to heavily curate what they present, it can sometimes seem as if everyone else has better internships, earns higher grades, and attends more exclusive parties.

Things Really Are Different

Some argue that all this is nothing new, that school has always been anxiety inducing. But regardless of whether today's students really do face a greater number of stressors than generations past, there is little doubt that the impact of those stressors is felt more than before. Today's young adults seem to arrive at college with less resiliency and a lower appetite for risk and failure.

In raising their children, parents have focused more on protecting them from stress and anxiety and less on teaching them how to cope. Today's incoming classes are of a generation that received athletic trophies merely for participating. Becoming so used to winning makes it all the harder to deal with losing. It makes it harder to learn resiliency. On top of this, parents have created a culture of risk aversion. Today's students were warned as children not to walk home alone, and they grew up playing on playgrounds designed to break their falls. In many ways, children have been taught both explicitly and implicitly to avoid risk, and for many of them, the resulting safety has made them less capable of coping with failure and disappointment.

When students have a panic attack because they received a B minus on a test, it becomes clear that parents have probably not done enough to prepare them for the fact that life involves both success and failure. Today, high school graduates arrive on

American University's campus with higher SAT scores, more Advanced Placement credits, and more International Baccalaureate degrees than ever before. They are book smart but perhaps less life ready. This problem can be seen not only in how they deal with bad news but also in what they know about basic life skills, from managing their finances to doing their laundry. There are exceptions, of course, but American University's faculty and staff are probably not unique in observing that students increasingly come to college with less mastery of such skills.

Another way that today's students differ from their predecessors is in their relationships with their parents and other adults in their lives. Gone are the days when a five-minute phone call every Sunday was the extent of communication with family. For many students, thanks in part to advances in technology, there is nearly constant communication with parents through texting and calls. In the interactions I see with faculty and staff on campus, students seem to seek more adult guidance and assistance with problem solving than previous generations did.

For more on how repeating key terms and phrases can help you connect the parts, see Chapter 8.

Stress can play out in different ways. One common type of student is the overachiever: a first-year student who was at the top of his class in high school and never needed to exert much effort to get there. In his first semester at college, he fails a couple of midterm exams and finds himself too embarrassed to lean on his support network from home. At night, when his friends have gone to bed, he heads to the library and immerses himself in his studies. Eventually, he's sleeping less than four hours a night. And only when he reaches a breaking point does he seek out counseling that can help him work through his own expectations and time management.

Another common type is the overcommitted student. She comes to college with a strong sense of what she wants to do afterward—say, work on a political campaign—and loads up on extracurricular activities in pursuit of that goal. In her first semester, she joins several political clubs, runs for student government, and takes on a part-time internship on Capitol Hill. She even adds an extra class to get ahead. Without this level of commitment, she fears, she won't be competitive for the best campaigns. The result is long days of meetings, work, and classes, along with late nights trying to catch up. Only after she breaks down emotionally does she confide in her dorm's resident assistant, who refers her to the counseling center.

Challenge and Response

According to a 2015 report from the Center for Collegiate Mental Health, the number of students visiting counseling centers increased by 30 percent between 2009 and 2015 (enrollment grew by only 6 percent). Across the country, colleges and universities are adding extra professional staff to help students, in part because the types of counseling needs have also expanded. Some students arrive with complex medication regimes, whereas others are part of the growing number of students experiencing thoughts of suicide, a trend that requires more emergency services, such as 24-hour rapid-response counseling. As student bodies become more diverse, schools need support staff who can reach across cultural divides. Adding all these resources is not easy, especially for schools in rural areas, where mental health providers are in short supply.

Universities are struggling to keep up with rising numbers 20 of students seeking support: according to the Association for University and College Counseling Center Directors, in 2016–17, 34 percent of college counseling centers had to put some students on a waitlist. And it's important to note that many students remain reluctant to talk to a professional: while stigma concerning mental health today is less than what it was in the past, it still impedes students from recognizing their challenges, seeking out help, and committing to treatment.

Universities are putting more effort into prevention. Harvard University has started the Success-Failure Project, a program that hosts discussions aimed at redefining success and dealing with rejection. Duke University offers a mindfulness program designed to help students manage stress. At American University, we introduced a mandatory, two-semester course aimed at helping students adjust to their first year in college. Of course, it's important to make sure such programs don't end up adding to the problem: when I asked students if stress-reduction seminars might be helpful, one responded, "Please don't add anything to my already packed schedule that will further stress me out!"

Campuses that focus on creating a sense of community and belonging find that students who have support networks to turn to are better able to work through their challenges and stress. This sense of belonging can act as a preventive tool, countering students' feelings of loneliness and depression and providing a way for them to alert others to the problems they are facing. Increasing a campus' sense of community can often mean running into long-standing questions—for instance, about the value of fraternities and sororities and about whether to increase student engagement by offering more activities and clubs. Universities must face these old questions in the new context of growing mental health issues.

Producing Happier Graduates

Universities are in the early stages of grappling with the increase in stress and anxiety. Although there is no agreed-on formula at this time, there are some approaches that show promise.

There is general agreement that the solution lies in more education about the issue, inside and outside the academy. Creating awareness of the problem and teaching faculty, staff, and students how to prevent, recognize, and respond to it can help. Just as many campuses have made progress on educating students about sexual assault, they can do the same when it comes to mental health.

Moreover, as odd as it may sound, universities should draw on 25 some of the lessons learned during the 2014 Ebola outbreak—a global health threat that emerged during my tenure as U.S. secretary of health and human services—and adopt a public health approach to the problem. With Ebola, the priorities were prevention, detection, and treatment. These core elements can also guide universities in framing their approach to mental health. Prevention can mean introducing courses that help students adjust to college life. Detection might mean developing ways to quickly notice when a student doesn't download an assignment or show up for classes.

As for treatment, universities need to secure adequate resources for counseling so that students seeking help receive timely and effective care. On many campuses, triage systems prioritize the most acute cases, determine which students can be treated in a limited number of sessions, and refer to other providers those who require long-term care. No university is capable of offering unlimited sessions and all kinds of care, so administrators need to determine which cases to refer and which to keep in house. They must also have the capacity to meet demand without long waitlists for treatment. To inform their investments, universities should use data about their campus' particular needs—especially at a time when the economics of higher education are under both scrutiny and pressure.

Universities also need to acknowledge the power of communities. Communities can not only act as a knowledge base and a source of referrals; at a more basic level, they can also stem the problem to begin with. Study after study has found that social connectedness is correlated with well-being and resiliency, so universities should strive to build inclusive communities. Encouraging in-person (not Instagram) connections can help. Administrators should make sure that students are aware of the clubs and groups on campus, offer a sense of belonging, and invest in first-year residence halls and other communities for living and learning. Faculty and staff should recognize the value of engaging with students.

Finally, students, parents, and universities should embrace the healthy idea that stress is a part of what makes college great. College students develop intellectually, socially, and morally through a combination of challenge and support. Their time on campus should be not so overwhelming that they retreat, yet not so comfortable that there is no incentive to grow. Thus, the college experience should teach students not to avoid challenges—life is full of them, after all—but how to handle the stress that results. Recognizing this is the first step to producing more resilient students, as well as happier, better-adjusted graduates.

Joining the Conversation

1. Sylvia Mathews Burwell is president of a major university in Washington, DC, and previously served as secretary of health and human services for the United States. What is the mental health crisis she is describing and what does she say needs to be done about it? How do her executive experience and background affect your response to her argument?

2. Burwell highlights student stress in three areas: "safety, economics, and technology" (paragraph 6). For the first two areas, she provides a naysayer, anticipating a possible objection that a critical reader might offer. Find each naysayer and examine how she responds to it. Specifically, how does she use her response to develop her own argument? For the third area, stress due to technology, come up with a naysayer and a potential response.

3. This article is divided into four sections. What is the specific focus of each, and what connecting language does Burwell provide to link one section to the next?

4. Investigate your college's approach to and resources supporting student mental health. How do your institution's offerings stack up against the author's recommendations? How, if at all, might they be improved?

5. Burwell concludes by asserting that "the college experience should teach students not to avoid challenges—life is full of them, after all—but how to handle the stress that results." Write a "they say / I say" essay responding to this conclusion and other relevant aspects of her argument.

The Student Loan Trap: When Debt Delays Life

CHARLES FAIN LEHMAN

—⌐回⌐—

RODNEY SPANGLER FIRST ENROLLED at the University of North Texas in 2001. There, he pursued a degree in what the school now calls "integrative studies," focusing on history, philosophy, and criminal justice. Rodney also worked full time, and so attended UNT on and off until 2007.

For every semester of classes, Spangler took out student loans. When he left—without a degree—he estimates that he had about $30,000 in outstanding student debt.

"At first I always intended to repay them, but the first time I took a semester off, I started getting due notices/bills for them," Spangler told *The American Conservative* by email. "[I s]tarted going back, but the ones that came due kept sending notices, like there was no 'pause' button."

———

CHARLES FAIN LEHMAN, a staff writer for the *Washington Free Beacon*, writes about immigration, social media, relationships, politics, and substance abuse. His articles have appeared in the *Wall Street Journal*, the *Weekly Standard*, and on the Institute for Family Studies' blog. He is a 2016 graduate of Yale University. This essay was published in the *American Conservative* in 2019.

Overwhelmed by bills, Spangler simply stopped paying. Today, thanks to interest and delinquency penalties, he estimates his outstanding debt is about $60,000—double what it was. "I just don't see how I can ever pay those off," Spangler wrote, "short of winning the lottery."

Of course, it's possible to go on living with a five-figure debt hanging over your head, but it imposes more than its fair share of limitations. When Spangler tried to get a job in law enforcement, he met all the requirements, but was denied because of his credit history.

"I had some of the highest placement scores they had seen," Spangler claims, "but my credit report had too many negative marks." With one or two exceptions, all of those marks were from student loans.

The weight of the debt has not only hindered Spangler's search for employment—it has also affected his family and romantic life. He has had to rely on his parents to cosign for loans. And, he says, he has been "a little reticent to pursue a serious relationship," thanks in part to fear of being judged for his debt.

Spangler is not alone: he's one of the 44 million Americans who holds student debt, 30 percent of the population who have attended college. Together, they owe about $1.5 trillion, a bigger burden than credit cards, auto loans, or any other non-mortgage debt.

That there is a student debt crisis is not news. Media sites report on it frequently; academics attend to it with increasing trepidation. But in focusing on the scale of the problem, we sometimes forget to think about how all that debt affects people's lives.

Specifically, the last 20 years of student debt accumulation— driven largely by federal policy—have radically shifted the life-courses of younger Americans, whether late Gen Xers like Spangler or Millennials. Millions of Americans now enter adulthood with a burden unfaced by their parents or grandparents, which in turn slows their family formation, alters labor market behavior, and represents a profound alteration to how they live out citizenship.

Americans, historically, had little schooling. In 1900, less than 10 percent went to or graduated from high school; by 1910, the median adult had completed only 8 years of schooling. Americans, since Tocqueville's time at least, have believed that education was the nursemaid of citizenship. But only recently has that come to mean more than primary schooling.

The modern, post-war economy, however, precipitated a radical change in America's educational composition. In 1962, just 19 percent had been to college; today, 61 percent have. The proportion actually graduating went from 9 to 35 percent in the same period. In short, over the past half century, higher education has gone from the exception to the norm.

Stretching back at least to the G.I. Bill, government has carried the lion's share for this transition. In 1965, the government began to offer its credibility as a guarantor of private student loans under the Federal Family Education Loan Program. In the early 1990s, the Department of Education started issuing student loans itself, under the Federal Direct Loan Program.

The amount of debt held by the DOE rose steadily through the 1990s and early 2000s, then exploded during the Great Recession. Preston Cooper, an education research analyst at the American Enterprise Institute, told [the *American Conservative*] that many Americans, forced out of the full-time workforce, opted to reskill—and took on lots of debt to do so. The feds funded that choice: as of 2015, 91 percent of all student loans were publicly held.

Publicly available data on federal student loans thus get us 15
most of the way to a picture of the student debtor population.
Those data show that as federal loans became readily available,
millions of Americans took them on.

Clearly, some older Americans—especially ages 35 to 49—
have debt, likely thanks to grad school and the Great Recession reskilling. But there is a pronounced disjuncture between
even that group and America's younger adults. Among those
who have attended (although not necessarily graduated from)
college, more than half are in debt.

We can look closer for an even starker picture. The mode
25- to 34-year-old debtor has between $20,000 and $40,000
of debt—the median annual salary for a recent college grad is
about $50,000. Americans currently in and fresh out of college
owe similarly high amounts.

Maybe student debt is not so bad. As David Leonhardt
argued in a recent *New York Times* op-ed, it is in large part
held by college-educated kids from the top income quartile,
who can expect a substantial wage premium. Student debtors
are likely to be well-off, and a college degree will make them
more so.

Two issues complicate this argument, however. The first
is what we might call the "Somes": those who, like Spangler,
have more than a high school degree but less than
a college degree, i.e. only "some" college experience.
Federal survey data show that "Somes" account for the
second-highest proportion of all adults and the highest
proportion of 25- to 34-year-olds.

For tips on
how to use
voice markers
to distinguish
who is saying
what, see
Chapter 5.

Whereas debt-holding college grads usually do well, Somes 20
don't. Essentially all of the college wage premium accrues upon
graduation, thanks to what economists call the "sheepskin
effect"—the earnings boost comes with the diploma.

Figure 7. Federal Student Debt Holders as a Percentage of College-Attended Population

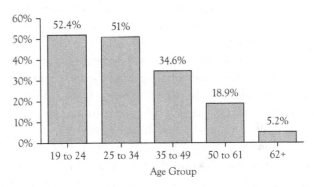

Source: U.S. Department of Ed.; Pop. figures from Current Population Survey ASEC/IPUMS.
Q1 2018, includes all with at least some college

The obverse of this is that Somes end up looking more like their peers with a high-school degree than a college one—except, that is, for a lot of student debt. As Leonhardt notes, 40 percent of Some borrowers defaulted on their loans, compared to just 8 percent who graduated. For a significant part of the student-loan-debtor population, then, there is no college-degree cushion.

There's a bigger problem: even among grads, student debt slows the set of life choices we commonly associate with adulthood. Even if most debtors eventually get their lives on track, debt has substantial effects on how long it takes them to do so.

Unsurprisingly, having debt shapes young Americans' job market decisions. Researchers at the University of California, Berkeley found that grads with debt pick higher salary jobs, often over "public-interest" positions. They also found that bearing debt may affect students' "academic decisions during college" in a way likely tied to their ultimate career trajectory. Young Americans may be more cautious about entering low-paying, high-social-significance roles—including politics, an area where older Americans are conspicuously over-represented.

Then there's homeownership. Americans in their 20s have always been unlikely to buy, but Millennials may be delaying well into their 30s. The couple profiled in a recent *Politico* article on Millennials' homebuying were 32 and 33, respectively; both cited their student debt as delaying their purchase. Analysis of British homeownership trends shows this is a common phenomenon, linking increased student debt levels to a "delay" in "first-time homeownership transition."

All of this contributes to late family formation. Fewer young 25 adults are married than ever and multiple analyses have found that student debt encourages cohabitation and reduces marriage among college-educated women (although, interestingly, not among men). That translates into less sex, and correspondingly fewer kids. A *New York Times*/Morning Consult poll found that 64 percent of young adults had fewer kids because of the cost of childcare (and, presumably, their ability to meet it); among those who claimed not to want kids, 13 percent explicitly cited their student debt as the reason.

All of this is fairly intuitive—if you have five figures of debt, paying it down will inevitably require trade-offs, which means delaying life. But it means that college debt directly slows young adults on the path their parents enjoyed—homes, marriage, children, etc.

See Chapter 7 for more about why it's important to say why your argument matters. That's the big problem. Even bracketing the Somes, spiraling student debt has had a lasting impact on how hard young Americans have to work just to make it to the same place as previous generations. The new normal of debt necessarily alters the shape of American life.

Figure 8. Federal Student Loan Distribution, by Debt Size and Age Group, 2018

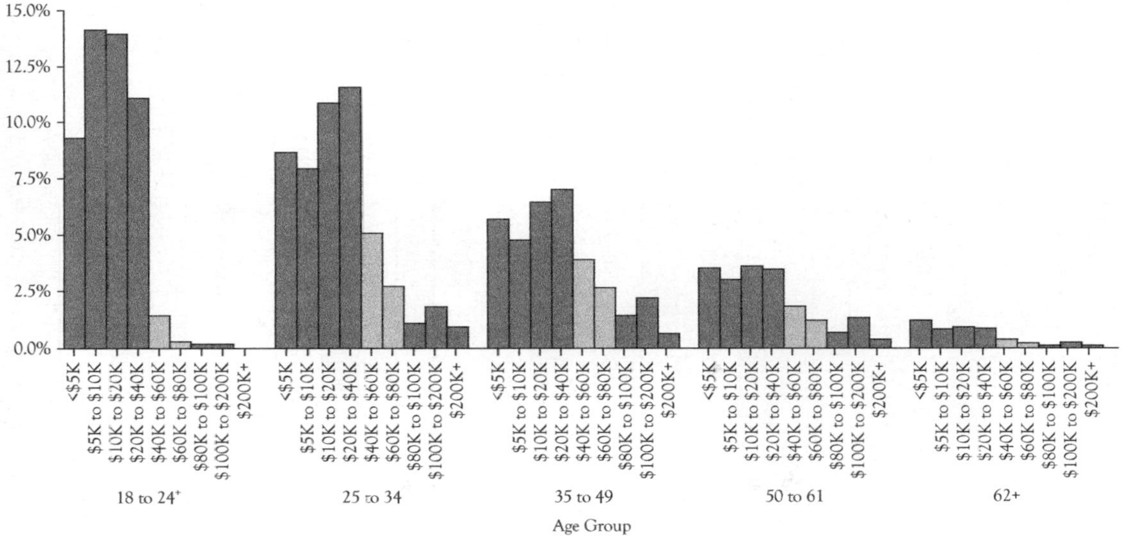

Source: U.S Department of Ed.; Pop. figures from Current Population Survey ASEC/IPUMS
(*18 to 24 group may include small number of borrowers below age 18).

Figure 9. Education Distribution, by Level and Age Group, Q1 2018

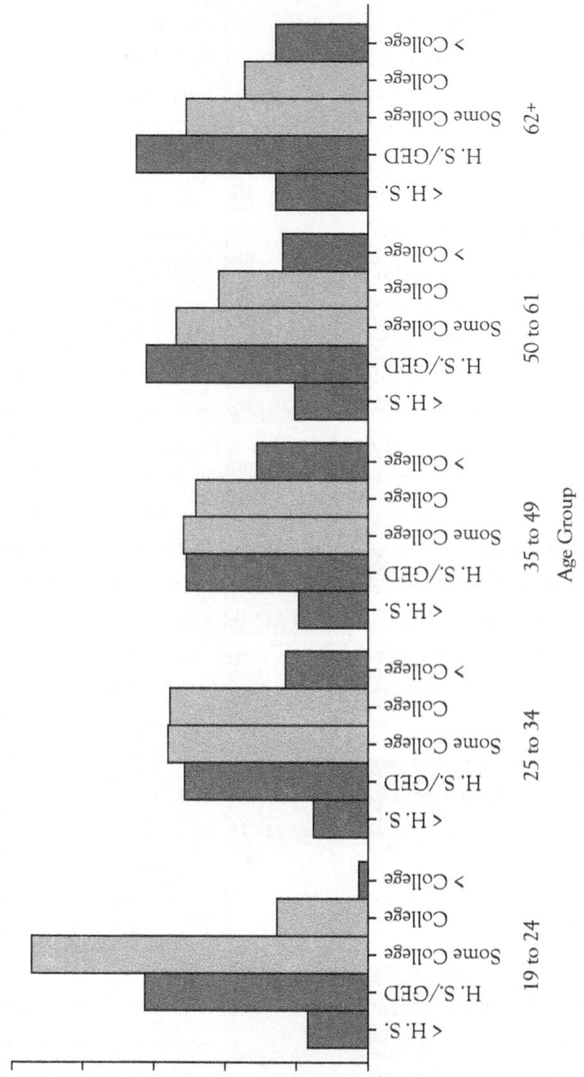

Source: Current Population Survey ASEC/IPUMS.

Crushing debt and delayed lives are of course unpleasant individual experiences, but there is a deeper problem of political equity. In America, there is a strong connection between education and the ideal of citizenship—a republic requires an educated populace. This connection implicates more than just reading and writing—Eleanor Roosevelt contended that every discipline, from Latin to mathematics, informs good citizenship.

In a society where education is a prerequisite for civic participation, raising the floor of expected educational attainment, we thought, would make better citizens. This was, for example, the instinct which induced President Barack Obama to call on "every American to commit to at least one year or more of higher education or career training. . . . every American will need to get more than a high school diploma."

But what is meant as inclusionary ends up exclusionary. The explosion of student debt, with its concurrent effects on debtors' lives, means that many who go to college struggle along on the path to full, independent American life. Deviations from life course constrain young Americans in their ability to give back to their communities, to raise families, to buy homes, to teach responsible membership in society—in short, to be a citizen. The debt-financed education revolution risks retarding precisely the democratic goal it was meant to serve.

When we spoke, Rodney Spangler was 39, almost 40. He intends to go back to school next fall. He will still be heavily in debt, although perhaps finally getting a degree will help. Even so, he'll have worked for decades for a position his parents could have reached with a high school education.

The proportion of the population that is college-exposed broke 50 percent in 2000 and has risen steadily since then. According to the Pew Research Center, the rising generation of "post-Millennials" are expected to be the most educated ever, with nearly 60 percent of those over 18 enrolled in college. If, as so many have argued, a new generation needs a renewed commitment to American citizenship, then they also need help surpassing the limitations stopping them from most fully living that commitment.

Joining the Conversation

1. Charles Fain Lehman begins this article with the story of one former college student whose life has been severely affected by college debt. How effective is this opening anecdote in drawing your attention and introducing his argument? How well does this student's plight reflect the overall problem of college debt that the author describes?

2. Paragraph 18 begins, "Maybe student debt is not so bad," then discusses and responds to a recent argument to that effect. Find where in this discussion the author addresses "so what?" and "who cares?" questions. What does he say, and what might you add to these statements?

3. In paragraph 28, Lehman states that former first lady Eleanor Roosevelt contended that "every discipline, from Latin to mathematics, informs good citizenship," and he goes on in paragraph 29 to say that "education is a prerequisite for civic participation." Do you agree with this view? According to Lehman, how does the student debt crisis relate to this argument? How would you respond to Lehman's argument?

4. Examine the bar graph on page 571 listing data on amount of student debt by age group. How do the data support Lehman's argument? Answer the same question with regard to the bar graph on page 574 showing average level of education by age group.

5. Read Charles Murray's essay (pp. 506–26), which argues that too many students in the United States choose to attend college in pursuit of bachelor's degrees, and relate what he says to what Lehman is arguing.

6. Research practical strategies for reducing college student debt, and write a "they say / I say" argument recommending what you see as the best strategies for an audience of prospective college applicants and their families.

TWENTY-TWO

HOW IS TECHNOLOGY
CHANGING US?

—◻—

How do our lives differ from the lives of Americans fifty years ago? Perhaps the major difference is our reliance today on digital technologies. According to a recent Pew Research poll, 90 percent of Americans use smartphones and other devices throughout the day for a constantly growing array of purposes: to communicate, conduct business, arrange transportation, gather information, take photos, make movies, watch shows, play games, find directions, exercise, listen to music, and much more. New applications are regularly emerging, and time spent on devices is increasing. That such digital activity enriches our lives has been particularly evident during the COVID-19 pandemic, with millions, unable to make personal contact, finding comfort in online communication—such as *Zoom* discussions with friends and loved ones.

But digital activity also serves as a source of anxiety and unease because it brings us continuous streams of news stories, social media posts, and text messages. Even more concerning, medical doctors, scientists, and educators worry that reliance on technology may negatively impact our brains and bodies. Concerns about the potential dangers of new technologies are nothing new; almost 2,400 years ago, in his dialogue now known as

The Phaedrus, Greek philosopher Plato expressed fears that use of the technology of writing would weaken people's capacity for in-depth learning and face-to-face communication. In 2015, Susan Greenfield, a neuroscientist, argued that as a result of technology use our "attention spans are shorter, personal communication skills are reduced and there's a marked reduction in the ability to think abstractly." Scientists used to believe that the human brain changed up through adolescence but was relatively stable before declining in old age. Now, however, there is strong evidence for what Greenfield calls "the malleability of the adult brain," with alterations in brain structure caused by the devices we have come to rely on—and even some indications that we are losing important mental skills.

But not everyone accepts these doomsday scenarios. Some experts argue that such alarmist views are seriously overstated. In their view, new technologies make us smarter, happier, and more productive. Kenneth Goldsmith writes that far from wasting time, much of what we do on the internet helps us develop new skills, learn about the world, and interact with others. Responding to fears that digital communication has led to a decline in personal connection and concern for our fellow humans in times of need, Jenna Wortham offers a more optimistic vision of connectivity, with evidence that people's most generous impulses are being tapped via the internet to help one another on an unprecedented scale. Similarly, Nicholas Brody argues that virtual communication has strengthened, not weakened, people's interconnections.

Still, many are concerned and think others should be, too. Nicholas Carr believes that extensive use of the internet is hurting our capacity for deep thinking and contemplation. Along similar lines, college student Justin Vinh argues that social media can cause feelings of envy, loneliness, depression, even addiction. Previously a strong proponent of digital technologies, Sherry Turkle now argues that they are leading to a decline in intimacy and a move away from self-reflection. Carole Cadwalladr shows how Google and Facebook use algorithms that make it easy to spread fake news and discriminatory speech, and Agustín Fuentes considers the prevalence of internet trolls spewing hateful comments and offers suggestions for increasing civility online. The readings in this chapter give us much to think about, raising a number of complex problems and providing no easy solutions. And while some commentators may paint an optimistic picture of technology and others a more pessimistic depiction, there's a little bit of optimism and pessimism in each reading, factors that make this conversation worth joining.

Go Ahead:
Waste Time on the Internet

KENNETH GOLDSMITH

———▢———

Is the Internet a waste of time? It's not so easy to say. When I click around news sites, am I wasting time because I should be working instead? What if I've spent hours working, and I need a break? Am I wasting time if I watch cat videos, but not if I read a magazine story about the Iran nuclear deal? Am I wasting time if I look up the latest presidential polling numbers, but not if I'm communicating with an old friend on Facebook?

The notion that the Internet is bad for you seems premised on the idea that the Internet is one thing—a monolith. In reality it's a befuddling mix of the stupid and the sublime, a shattered, contradictory, and fragmented medium. Internet

———

Kenneth Goldsmith is a poet and author of ten books, including *Seven American Deaths and Disasters* (2013) and *Uncreative Writing: Managing Language in the Digital Age* (2013). He is the founding editor of *UbuWeb*, an online archive, and senior editor of *PennSound*, a website for digital poetry recordings based at the University of Pennsylvania, where he teaches writing. This essay, first published on August 12, 2016, for the *Los Angeles Times*, is from his book *Wasting Time on the Internet* (2016).

detractors seem to miss this simple fact, which is why so many of their criticisms disintegrate under observation.

The way Internet pundits tell it, you'd think we stare for three hours at clickbait—those articles with hypersensational headlines—the way we once sat down and watched three hours of cartoons on Saturday morning TV. But most of us don't do any one thing on the Internet. Instead, we do many things, some of it frivolous, some of it heavy. Our time spent in front of the computer is a mixed time, a time that reflects our desires— as opposed to the time spent sitting in front of the television where we were fed shows we didn't necessarily enjoy. TV gave us few choices. Many of us truly did feel like we wasted our time—as our parents so often chided us—"rotting away" in front of the TV.

I keep reading—on screens—that in the age of screens we've lost our ability to concentrate, that we've become distracted. But when I look around me and see people riveted to their devices, I notice a great wealth of concentration, focus, and engagement.

And I keep reading—on the Internet—that the Internet 5 has made us antisocial, that we've lost the ability to have a conversation. But when I see people with their devices, what I see is people communicating with one another: texting, chatting, IM'ing. And I have to wonder, in what way is this not social? A conversation broken up into short bursts and quick emoticons is still a conversation. Watch someone's face while they're in the midst of a rapid-fire text message exchange: it's full of emotion—anticipation, laughter, affect.

The Internet has been accused of making us shallow. We're skimming, not reading. We lack the ability to engage deeply with a subject anymore. That's both true and not true: we skim and browse certain types of content, and read others carefully.

We're not all using our devices the same way. Looking over the shoulders of people absorbed in their devices on the subway, I see many people reading newspapers and books and many others playing Candy Crush. Sometimes someone will be glancing at a newspaper one moment and playing a game the next.

The other night, I walked into the living room and my wife was glued to her iPad, reading *Narrative of the Life of Frederick Douglass*. Hours later, when I headed to bed, she hadn't moved an inch, still transfixed by this 171-year-old narrative on her 21st-century device. When I said good night, she didn't even look up.

Internet critics tell us time and again that our brains are being rewired; I'm not so sure that's a bad thing. Every new media requires new ways of thinking. Wouldn't it be strange if in the midst of this digital revolution we were still expected to use our brains in the same way we read books or watched TV?

See pp. 25–27 for ways to introduce an ongoing debate.

The resistance to the Internet shouldn't surprise us: Cultural reactionaries defending the status quo have been around as long as media has. Marshall McLuhan tells us that television was written off by people invested in literature as merely "mass entertainment" just as the printed book was met with the same skepticism in the 16th century by scholastic philosophers. McLuhan says that "the vested interests of acquired knowledge and conventional wisdom have always been by-passed and engulfed by new media . . . The student of media soon comes to expect the new media of any period whatever to be classed as pseudo by those who have acquired the patterns of earlier media, whatever they may happen to be."

I'm told that our children are most at risk, that the excessive use of computers has led our kids to view the real world as fake. But I'm not so sure that even I can distinguish "real" from "fake." How is my life on Facebook any less "real" than what happens in my day-to-day life? In fact, much of what does happen in my day-to-day life comes through Facebook—work opportunities, invitations to dinner parties, and even the topics I discuss at those dinner parties.

After reading one of those hysterical "devices are ruining 10 your child" articles, my sister-in-law decided to take action. She imposed a system whereby, after dinner, the children were to "turn in" their devices—computers, smartphones, and tablets. They could "check them out" over the course of the evening, but only if they could prove they needed them for "educational purposes." Upon confiscating my nephew's cell phone one Friday night, she asked him on Saturday morning, "What plans do you have with your friends today?" "None," he responded. "You took away my phone."

On a vacation, after a full day of outdoor activities that included seeing the Grand Canyon and hiking, my friend and her family settled into the hotel for the evening. Her 12-year-old daughter is a fan of preteen goth girl crafting videos on YouTube, where she learns how to bedazzle black skull T-shirts and make perfectly ripped punk leggings. That evening, the girl selected some of her favorite videos to share with her mother. After agreeing to watch a few, her mother grew impatient. "This is nice, but I don't want to spend the whole night clicking around." The daughter responded indignantly that she wasn't just "clicking around." She was connecting with a community of girls her own age who shared similar interests.

Her mother was forced to reconsider her premise that her daughter was just wasting time on the Internet; instead, she was fully engaged, fostering an aesthetic, feeding her imagination, indulging in her creative proclivities, and hanging out with her friends, all from the comfort of a remote hotel room perched on the edge of the Grand Canyon.

Many Internet critics yearn for a return to solitude and introspection, quiet places far removed from the noises of our devices. But those places, away from the rabble, are starting to remind me of gated communities.

Joining the Conversation

1. Kenneth Goldsmith introduces a series of standard views followed by a series of "I say" statements. List each pair, noting the specific language the author uses in each instance.

2. So what? Who cares? Where does Goldsmith explain why his argument matters—and for whom?

3. In paragraph 8, Goldsmith quotes Marshall McLuhan, a scholar who wrote about the effects of technology on people. Why do you think Goldsmith is citing McLuhan here? How does the use of this quotation contribute to the author's argument?

4. Read Andreas Elpidorou's article "The Quiet Alarm" on **theysayiblog.com**. What do you think Goldsmith would say to Elpidorou's claim that the "next time boredom overcomes you . . . [i]t might be best not to cover it up with your smartphone"?

5. How do your friends, family, and/or coworkers spend time on the internet? How do they feel about it? Incorporating their views as evidence, write an essay responding to Goldsmith in which you agree, disagree, or both with his argument.

Has Coronavirus Made the Internet Better?

JENNA WORTHAM

—◻—

ON A RECENT SATURDAY NIGHT, Derrick Jones, a D.J. who performs under the name D-Nice, live-streamed himself working his turntables from his home in Los Angeles, where he was self-isolating. He started early in the afternoon and played deep into the night, pausing only to sip his drink, take the briefest of bathroom breaks and change into a new flamboyant hat. Despite all the chaos outside, here, online, was a safe harbor. The only thing contagious was the mood, which was jubilant. As names of friends—and increasingly, famous people—floated across his screen, he would grin and call out their names in greeting: Rihanna. Dwyane Wade. Michelle Obama. Janet Jackson. As the night stretched on, the party shifted into something more meaningful than a celebratory distraction. Time and space collapsed as tens of thousands of people experienced the

---

JENNA WORTHAM writes for the *New York Times*, where she also contributes to *Still Processing*, a podcast on culture. Her work has appeared in *Bust* magazine, *Jezebel*, the *Village Voice*, *Vogue*, and *Wired*. Her *Twitter* handle is @jennydeluxe. This essay first appeared in the *New York Times* on April 8, 2020.

same song, the same shared spirit, no matter who or where they were. Kind of like Covid-19 itself.

At one point, apparently inspired, Jones shouted out thanks to all the nurses, doctors and hospital workers. His eyes drifted to the number of people in the "room," surging toward 150,000, and paused, amazement shaping the contours of his eyes and mouth. "We should raise some money or something," he said.

What D-Nice seemed to realize in that moment was something many people have realized since Covid-19 gripped the country: Social media could be mobilized for something far greater than self-promotion. Artists have taken to YouTube or Instagram to provide some relief, to allow us to gather together and listen to an opera, or hear a standup set, or watch a poetry reading, all of us separate but still together. But more remarkable, it has become the medium by which people have organized to help others.

On Twitter, writers like Shea Serrano and Roxane Gay helped raise money for bills and groceries for those who are struggling. Programmers connected online to create a tool to schedule cooperative child care. Prison-reform organizations worked to bail out incarcerated people and send hand sanitizer to prisons and jails, where the virus is rampant. Google Docs files began circulating with information on food pantries and how to apply for unemployment. GoFundMes quickly popped up to distribute money to people hit hardest by the crisis, including sex workers, restaurant workers and underinsured artists. Healing practitioners made meditation sessions, yoga classes and other mental-health assistance available free online. Sewing patterns for masks and surgical caps were circulated online, and everyone from the rapper Future to the designer Collina Strada began efforts to produce them for front-line workers. Copper3D released its pending patent for 3-D printed masks, allowing anyone with a printer to churn them out and distribute them. In my own neighborhood, someone created a Slack channel where people shared strategies for deferring credit-card payments and rent and offered to run errands for families in need. Even the online performances, like D-Nice's dance party, felt as though they were really less about pure entertainment and more about serving a nation, a world even, that was suffering in isolation and fear.

For a time, futurists dreamed, optimistically, that cyberspace 5 might exist as a place where humankind could hit reset on society. The idea was that the arrival of networked computers would create an imaginary space where bodily markers of difference would be masked by a Utopian fog. In 1996, at the World Economic Forum in Davos, Switzerland, John Perry Barlow issued a manifesto titled "A Declaration of the Independence of Cyberspace," which stated, "We are creating a world that all may enter without privilege or prejudice accorded by race, economic power, military force or station of birth."

Barlow continued that the civilization he and others hoped to create would "be more humane and fair than the world your governments have made before."

By now we know that those dreams were a fantasy, informed by the same imperialistic and colonial urges that underpinned the creation of the internet itself. No dream internet Utopia ever emerged. Instead, societal woes have been compounded by the rise of technology. The internet has been oriented around an axis of maximizing profits, almost since its inception. In "The Know-It-Alls," the journalist (and my former colleague) Noam Cohen documents the emergence of Stanford University (nicknamed "Get Rich U.") as the birthplace of Silicon Valley, a place where a "hacker's arrogance and an entrepreneur's greed has turned a collective enterprise like the web into something proprietary, where our online profiles, our online relationships, our online posts and web pages and photographs are routinely exploited for business reasons." Today, it feels almost impossible to imagine another way of thinking about the internet.

See Chapter 5 for additional strategies on differentiating the writer's argument from the argument she is responding to.

And yet, in the aftermath of the arrival of the novel coronavirus, one has emerged that feels, at least for the moment, closer to John Perry Barlow's embarrassingly earnest speech. It's worth noting that he also said that cyberspace was an "act of nature, and it grows itself through our collective actions."

Historically speaking, new infrastructures tend to emerge as a response to disasters and the negligence of governments in their wake. In the 1970s, for example, an activist group called the Young Lords seized an X-ray truck that was administering tuberculosis tests in East Harlem, where the disease was prevalent, and extended the operating hours to make it more readily available to working residents. In the days since the crisis began, I've been turning to Adrienne Maree Brown's 2017 book, *Emergent Strategy*, which offers strategies for reimagining ways to organize powerful movements for social justice and mutual aid with a humanist, collective, anticapitalist framework. She describes the concept as "how we intentionally change in ways that grow our capacity to embody the just and liberated worlds we long for." Her book asks us not to resist change. That would be as futile as resisting the deeply embedded influence technology has on our lives. It's the same as resisting ourselves. But rather, it asks that we adapt, in real time, taking what we know and understand and applying it toward the future that we want. The internet will never exist without complications—already, many of the tools that are helping acclimate to this new cyberreality have been called out for surveillance—but perhaps people are learning how to work the tools to their advantage now.

For more on how to make concessions, see Chapter 6.

A few days after his marathon set, Jones talked to Oprah (over video) about his experience. "I've been in the music industry for over 30 years . . . but nothing felt like that, helping people." Shortly afterward, he announced that his next party would be a party with a cause: a voter-registration drive. In one night, he helped motivate 13,000 people to start registering.

Joining the Conversation

1. After reading this essay carefully, find the one sentence in it that you think best expresses its overall argument, and write a paragraph explaining why you chose that particular sentence.

2. Jenna Wortham begins her essay by relating how a well-known DJ livestreamed himself playing songs on his turntable from home, where he was self-quarantining during the coronavirus pandemic before a large virtual audience that included many famous people. Why is this an effective way

to begin the essay? What would be a more conventional "they say / I say" introduction?

3. The author ends paragraph 6 by writing "Today it feels almost impossible to imagine another way of thinking about the internet." How does she pivot at the beginning of the following paragraph to distinguish as clearly as possible between what she wants to say and what "they" say?

4. In "Are We Really as Awful as We Act Online?" (pp. 643–49), Agustín Fuentes examines the prevalence of hostile and hateful behavior on the internet. How might he respond to Wortham's discussion of more generous and positive online behavior during a world medical crisis?

5. In your own view, what are some ways that communicating to a large audience via the internet can result in positive outcomes? Write an essay developing your own argument about the potential of digital media to help people and support good causes, citing your own experiences and observations along with ideas from the readings in this chapter.

It Turns Out Our Tech Gadgets Aren't as Isolating as Experts Say

NICHOLAS BRODY

—▫—

WE ARE FACING a worldwide health crisis, and you can help. You don't need to enlist in the military or even sew homemade masks for healthcare workers (although the latter would certainly be appreciated).

No, you can help flatten the curve by doing one simple thing—staying home and texting your friends.

But isn't communicating via technology a poor substitute for "real" interaction? For over a decade journalists and scholars have lamented the detrimental effects of smartphones and social media on human relationships. Because of new forms of technology, we're supposedly lonelier than ever before, less connected, and battling a wider array of psychological maladies.

———

NICHOLAS BRODY is an associate professor of communication studies at the University of Puget Sound. His research focuses on technology and its social implications. He has published more than twenty journal articles and book chapters about cyberbullying and bystanders, technology use in relationships and breakups, and the cognitive similarities between social and physical pain. This article was originally published in the *News Tribune* on March 27, 2020.

But if new forms of technology are truly driving us apart, then why must governments issue legal edicts forcing people to stay at home and avoid socializing? In states such as New York and California, governors have issued shelter-in-place orders. Spain, Germany, and Italy are under lockdown.

See Chapter 6 on anticipating objections.

Here in Washington state, citizens took to (wait for it) social 5 media to demand shelter-in-place orders from Gov. Jay Inslee. He issued a stay-at-home order shortly thereafter.

The truth of the matter is that social media and smartphones never drove us away from one another. Rather, these tools highlighted the most fundamental need of all—to be connected.

Humans are driven by our need to communicate. We are social creatures, and we come to know ourselves and our world primarily through our interactions. Recent studies have shown that mobile phone use has about the same effect on mental health as eating potatoes.

As a professor and researcher of technology and communication, I teach a course on the social implications of technology. In one assignment I ask students to forego all communication technology use for a 24-hour period and document their experience.

Every semester I am struck by their observations. Students very rarely miss the technology itself. Rather, they miss each other. They use technology to connect with friends from afar and to coordinate in-person meetups.

As communication scholar Nancy Baym notes, we are not 10 addicted to our phones, we are addicted to each other.

Moreover, there are physiological benefits to being with one another. Expressing affection helps us better deal with stress. Extensive research has documented the health benefits of expressing our emotions to others.

All of which make the novel coronavirus especially frightening. The virus thrives by taking advantage of our basic need to be close to one another. Each carrier of the virus infects between 1 and 4 other individuals, primarily those with whom they live.

This virus is especially insidious because it presents us with a double bind. To survive, we must stay away from one another. To thrive, we need each other.

So what are we to do? We are incredibly lucky to live in a time of worldwide, instantaneous connection. Stay home. Stare at your screens. Send messages of hope and support to the people you are closest to.

And remember that your "addiction" isn't to your phone. It is to the humans on the other end of your texts. 15

Joining the Conversation

1. Why does communication professor Nicholas Brody believe that our increasing reliance on technology is a positive rather than a negative development in terms of human relations, particularly but not only during the COVID-19 pandemic? What evidence does he offer to support his argument?

2. At the beginning of paragraphs 3 and 4, Brody introduces naysayers, arguments against his own position, each starting with the word "But." Why do you think he argues against his own thesis here? How does he respond, and how do his responses strengthen his argument?

3. The author starts paragraph 6 by using metacommentary when he writes, "The truth of the matter is . . ." Look back at Chapter 10 on reasons and strategies for employing metacommentary, and explain how this essay benefits from its use here.

4. Relate Brody's view to Sherry Turkle's in "Stop Googling. Let's Talk." (pp. 614–23). How might Brody make use of the Turkle essay in constructing his own argument?

5. How do you, your friends, and family use technologies such as text messaging to communicate? How do they feel about these technologies, and why? Including their views as material for discussion, along with the arguments expressed in other readings in this chapter, write an essay responding to Brody in which you agree, disagree, or both with his argument.

How Smartphones Hijack Our Minds

NICHOLAS CARR

—▢—

So you bought that new iPhone. If you are like the typical owner, you'll be pulling your phone out and using it some 80 times a day, according to data Apple collects. That means you'll be consulting the glossy little rectangle nearly 30,000 times over the coming year. Your new phone, like your old one, will become your constant companion and trusty factotum—your teacher, secretary, confessor, guru. The two of you will be inseparable.

The smartphone is unique in the annals of personal technology. We keep the gadget within reach more or less around the clock, and we use it in countless ways, consulting its apps and checking its messages and heeding its alerts scores of times a day. The smartphone has become a repository of the self,

———

Nicholas Carr writes books and essays about technology and culture. His writing has appeared in the *Atlantic*, the *New York Times*, *Nature*, and *Wired*, and his essay "How Google Is Making Us Stupid" has been included in numerous anthologies. Carr's 2010 best-selling book, *The Shallows: What the Internet Is Doing to Our Brains*, has been translated into more than two dozen languages. This essay was published in the *Wall Street Journal* in 2017.

recording and dispensing the words, sounds and images that define what we think, what we experience and who we are. In a 2015 Gallup survey, more than half of iPhone owners said that they couldn't imagine life without the device.

We love our phones for good reasons. It's hard to imagine another product that has provided so many useful functions in such a handy form. But while our phones offer convenience and diversion, they also breed anxiety. Their extraordinary usefulness gives them an unprecedented hold on our attention and vast influence over our thinking and behavior. So what happens to our minds when we allow a single tool such dominion over our perception and cognition?

Scientists have begun exploring that question—and what they're discovering is both fascinating and troubling. Not only do our phones shape our thoughts in deep and complicated ways, but the effects persist even when we aren't using the devices. As the brain grows dependent on the technology, the research suggests, the intellect weakens.

Adrian Ward, a cognitive psychologist and marketing pro- 5 fessor at the University of Texas at Austin, has been studying the way smartphones and the internet affect our thoughts and judgments for a decade. In his own work, as well as that of others, he has seen mounting evidence that using a smartphone, or even hearing one ring or vibrate, produces a welter of distractions that makes it harder to concentrate on a difficult problem or job. The division of attention impedes reasoning and performance.

A 2015 *Journal of Experimental Psychology* study, involving 166 subjects, found that when people's phones beep or buzz while they're in the middle of a challenging task, their focus wavers, and their work gets sloppier—whether they check the phone or not. Another 2015 study, which involved 41 iPhone users and appeared in the *Journal of Computer-Mediated Communication*, showed that when people hear their phone ring but are unable to answer it, their blood pressure spikes, their pulse quickens, and their problem-solving skills decline.

The earlier research didn't explain whether and how smartphones differ from the many other sources of distraction that crowd our lives. Dr. Ward suspected that our attachment to our phones has grown so intense that their mere presence might diminish our intelligence. Two years ago, he and three colleagues—Kristen Duke and Ayelet Gneezy from the University of California, San Diego, and Disney Research behavioral scientist Maarten Bos—began an ingenious experiment to test his hunch.

The researchers recruited 520 undergraduate students at UCSD and gave them two standard tests of intellectual acuity. One test gauged "available cognitive capacity," a measure of how fully a person's mind can focus on a particular task. The second assessed "fluid intelligence," a person's ability to interpret and solve an unfamiliar problem. The only variable in the experiment was the location of the subjects' smartphones. Some of the students were asked to place their phones in front of them on their desks; others were told to stow their phones in their pockets or handbags; still others were required to leave their phones in a different room.

The results were striking. In both tests, the subjects whose phones were in view posted the worst scores, while those who left their phones in a different room did the best. The students who kept their phones in their pockets or bags came out in the middle. As the phone's proximity increased, brainpower decreased.

In subsequent interviews, nearly all the participants said 10 that their phones hadn't been a distraction—that they hadn't even thought about the devices during the experiment. They remained oblivious even as the phones disrupted their focus and thinking.

A second experiment conducted by the researchers produced similar results, while also revealing that the more heavily students relied on their phones in their everyday lives, the greater the cognitive penalty they suffered.

In an April article in the *Journal of the Association for Consumer Research*, Dr. Ward and his colleagues wrote that the "integration of smartphones into daily life" appears to cause a "brain drain" that can diminish such vital mental skills as "learning, logical reasoning, abstract thought, problem solving, and creativity." Smartphones have become so entangled with our existence that, even when we're not peering or pawing at them, they tug at our attention, diverting precious cognitive resources. Just suppressing the desire to check our phone, which we do routinely and subconsciously throughout the day, can debilitate our thinking. The fact that most of us now habitually keep our phones "nearby and in sight," the researchers noted, only magnifies the mental toll.

Dr. Ward's findings are consistent with other recently published research. In a similar but smaller 2014 study (involving 47 subjects) in the journal *Social Psychology*, psychologists at the University of Southern Maine found that people who had their phones in view, albeit turned off, during two demanding tests of attention and cognition made significantly more errors than did a control group whose phones remained out of sight. (The two groups performed about the same on a set of easier tests.)

See Chapter 8 on how to use transitions to connect the parts of your argument.

In another study, published in *Applied Cognitive Psychology* in April, researchers examined how smartphones affected learning in a lecture class with 160 students at the University of Arkansas at Monticello. They found that students who didn't bring their phones to the classroom scored a full letter-grade higher on a test of the material presented than those who brought their phones. It didn't matter whether the students who had their phones used them or not: All of them scored equally poorly. A study of 91 secondary schools in the U.K., published last year in the journal *Labour Economics*, found that when schools ban smartphones, students' examination scores go up substantially, with the weakest students benefiting the most.

It isn't just our reasoning that takes a hit when phones are 15 around. Social skills and relationships seem to suffer as well. Because smartphones serve as constant reminders of all the friends we could be chatting with electronically, they pull at our minds when we're talking with people in person, leaving our conversations shallower and less satisfying.

In a study conducted at the University of Essex in the U.K., 142 participants were divided into pairs and asked to converse in private for 10 minutes. Half talked with a phone in the room, while half had no phone present. The subjects were then given tests of affinity, trust and empathy. "The mere presence of mobile phones," the researchers reported in 2013 in the *Journal of Social and Personal Relationships*, "inhibited the development of interpersonal closeness and trust" and diminished "the extent to which individuals felt empathy and understanding from their partners." The down-sides were strongest when "a personally meaningful topic" was being discussed. The experiment's results were validated in a subsequent study by Virginia Tech researchers, published in 2016 in the journal *Environment and Behavior*.

The evidence that our phones can get inside our heads so forcefully is unsettling. It suggests that our thoughts and feelings, far from being sequestered in our skulls, can be skewed by external forces we're not even aware of.

Scientists have long known that the brain is a monitoring system as well as a thinking system. Its attention is drawn toward any object that is new, intriguing or otherwise striking—that has, in the psychological jargon, "salience." Media and communications devices, from telephones to TV sets, have always tapped into this instinct. Whether turned on or switched off, they promise an unending supply of information and experiences. By design, they grab and hold our attention in ways natural objects never could.

But even in the history of captivating media, the smartphone stands out. It is an attention magnet unlike any our minds have had to grapple with before. Because the phone is packed with so many forms of information and so many useful and entertaining functions, it acts as what Dr. Ward calls a "supernormal stimulus," one that can "hijack" attention whenever it is part of our surroundings—which it always is. Imagine combining a mailbox, a newspaper, a TV, a radio, a photo album, a public library and a boisterous party attended by everyone you know, and then compressing them all into a single, small, radiant object. That is what a smartphone represents to us. No wonder we can't take our minds off it.

The irony of the smartphone is that the qualities we find most appealing—its constant connection to the net, its multiplicity of apps, its responsiveness, its portability—are the very ones that give it such sway over our minds. Phone makers like Apple and Samsung and app writers like Facebook and Google design their products to consume as much of our attention as possible during every one of our waking hours, and we thank them by buying millions of the gadgets and downloading billions of the apps every year.

A quarter-century ago, when we first started going online, we took it on faith that the web would make us smarter: More information would breed sharper thinking. We now know it isn't that simple. The way a media device is designed and used exerts at least as much influence over our minds as does the information that the device unlocks.

For more on how to incorporate objections, see Chapter 6.

As strange as it might seem, people's knowledge and understanding may actually dwindle as gadgets grant them easier access to online data stores. In a seminal 2011 study published in *Science*, a team of researchers—led by the Columbia University psychologist Betsy Sparrow and including the late Harvard memory expert Daniel Wegner—had a group of volunteers read 40 brief, factual statements (such as "The space shuttle Columbia disintegrated during re-entry over Texas in Feb. 2003") and then type the statements into a computer. Half the people were told that the machine would save what they typed; half were told that the statements would be immediately erased.

Afterward, the researchers asked the subjects to write down as many of the statements as they could remember. Those who believed that the facts had been recorded in the computer demonstrated much weaker recall than those who assumed the facts wouldn't be stored. Anticipating that information would be readily available in digital form seemed to reduce the mental effort that people made to remember it. The researchers dubbed this phenomenon the "Google effect" and noted its broad implications: "Because search engines are continually available to us, we may often be in a state of not feeling we need to encode the information internally. When we need it, we will look it up."

Now that our phones have made it so easy to gather information online, our brains are likely offloading even more of the work of remembering to technology. If the only thing at stake were memories of trivial facts, that might not matter. But, as the pioneering psychologist and philosopher William James said in an 1892 lecture, "the art of remembering is the art of thinking." Only by encoding information in our biological memory can we weave the rich intellectual associations that form the essence of personal knowledge and give rise to critical and conceptual thinking. No matter how much information swirls around us, the less well-stocked our memory, the less we have to think with.

This story has a twist. It turns out that we aren't very good at distinguishing the knowledge we keep in our heads from the information we find on our phones or computers. As Dr. Wegner and Dr. Ward explained in a 2013 *Scientific American* article, when people call up information through their devices, they often end up suffering from delusions of intelligence. They feel as though "their *own* mental capacities" had generated the information, not their devices. "The advent of the 'information age' seems to have created a generation of people who feel they know more than ever before," the scholars concluded, even though "they may know ever less about the world around them."

That insight sheds light on our society's current gullibility crisis, in which people are all too quick to credit lies and half-truths spread through social media by Russian agents and other bad actors. If your phone has sapped your powers of discernment, you'll believe anything it tells you.

Data, the novelist and critic Cynthia Ozick once wrote, is "memory without history." Her observation points to the problem with allowing smartphones to commandeer our brains. When we constrict our capacity for reasoning and recall or transfer those skills to a gadget, we sacrifice our ability to turn information into knowledge. We get the data but lose the meaning. Upgrading our gadgets won't solve the problem. We need to give our minds more room to think. And that means putting some distance between ourselves and our phones.

Joining the Conversation

1. What is Nicholas Carr saying about the effects of smartphone use on the human mind? What evidence does he provide to support his view?

2. What possible objections to his own position does Carr introduce—and why do you think he does so? How effectively does he address these naysayers?

3. How does Carr use transition phrases and sentences to connect the parts of his text and to help readers follow his train of thought? (See Chapter 8 to help you think about how transitions help writers develop an argument and readers to process it.)

4. In "Go Ahead: Waste Time on the Internet" (pp. 582–86), Kenneth Goldsmith writes positively about internet activity: "When I look around me and see people riveted to their devices, I notice a great wealth of concentration, focus, and engagement." He adds, after observing his friend's twelve-year-old daughter's online behavior, that "she was fully engaged, fostering an aesthetic, feeding her imagination, indulging in her creative proclivities, and hanging out with her friends." Write a paragraph or two discussing how Carr might respond. What would he agree with, and what would he disagree with?

5. Keep track of your own smartphone activity for one day, noting the times and reasons for use. Then, keeping Nicholas Carr's argument in mind, write an essay on the benefits and dangers of smartphone use.

Social Media: The Screen, the Brain, and Human Nature

JUSTIN VINH

—◻—

As TECHNOLOGY ENABLES people to be increasingly connected, the following situation is a common morning routine: as dawn breaks, a teenager wakes up. But instead of jumping (or more likely rolling) out of bed, he pulls out his phone and opens the Facebook app. Twenty minutes of wasted time later, he closes the app and gets up. DING! He sees a notification of a new post on Twitter, goes back to bed, and checks out the notification. About an hour later, he *finally* gets out of bed and goes to make some coffee. Although this example may be slightly extreme, it is not a far cry from the actual routine of technology-reliant people. As more and more people become glued to their smartphone (and computer) screens, much of

---

JUSTIN VINH is an honors student at Northern Virginia Community College where he wrote this essay in his first-year writing class. He plans to pursue his bachelor's degree in biology or biomedical engineering and hopes to become a physician one day. Nominated for the Norton Writer's Prize, this essay is documented in APA style.

their time spent online will be dedicated to social media. These online hours beg the question: as social media becomes increasingly prevalent in modern society, how will it impact its users? Recent research indicates that despite social media's usefulness, its negative qualities—including how it contributes to depression and loneliness because of our tendencies toward comparisons to others and its addictive nature—outweigh any positive consequences.

A quick browse through any Facebook profile will show thousands of pictures of thrilling adventures, cute moments, happy mishaps, and perfectly framed photos. But no one really has such a perfect life. So why do most of the profiles on Facebook and other social platforms give the perception of a happy and adventurous life? The answer may lie in the core purpose of social media: sharing information about one's experiences and events with online friends. However, few people want to publish negative or dull experiences online, and teenagers in particular see social media as a way to gain popularity. Thus, in a world where their online status is often measured by their number of followers, teenagers who use social media feel like they should show only the bright and exciting moments of their lives. The result is that their followers will only ever see the sunny side of people's profiles and form the idea that they are without a care in the world.

This mentality might have negative mental consequences for users. As Copeland (2011) explored in a Slate article, to find out if this supposition is true, Alex Jordan, a psychology student studying for his PhD at Stanford, and other researchers conducted an experiment to try to gauge how participants judged their peers' emotions. The experiment revealed that the participants, all college students, consistently believed that their peers had more fun and fewer negative experiences than the peers actually did (Jordan et al., 2010, as cited in Copeland, 2011). In other words, the researchers' participants overestimated their peers' happiness. In another experiment, the researchers found that their participants were unhappier when they overestimated another person's happiness. Although a clear correlation exists between the two results, that fact does not necessarily mean the overestimation of happiness *causes* unhappiness.

Still, the relationship and possible causation makes sense: if happiness is a result of contentment, then comparisons, which sometimes end in dissatisfaction, would naturally lead to unhappiness. Social media welcomes its users to compare themselves to their peers, and it compels them to try to outdo their "opponents" to gain more followers and likes. This constant quest to create a better online image, along with the endless stream of photos and videos of people who seemingly have a better life, could lead to feelings of inferiority and worthlessness. Instead, everyone needs to be reminded occasionally that we all share troubles and difficulties (e.g., we all need to pay the bills).

Of course, another emotion may also lead to unhappiness: 5 loneliness. The need to spend so much time on social media must come from somewhere, and one activity that usually suffers from heightened screen time is face-to-face time with friends and family. Brown (2018) echoed these thoughts when describing the results of a recent study that was published in the *American Journal of Preventive Medicine*. The study, which involved young adults, found that that those who spent a great deal of time on social media reported being lonelier. The researchers said that social media users might feel like social outcasts because social media took over the time once spent interacting with people face-to-face (Primack et al., 2017, as cited in Brown, 2018). The results intuitively make sense. On social media, people cannot really interact because the forms of communication used are fairly shallow. Comments, short videos, and selfies—these are all abbreviated forms of communication that do not occur in real time. Also, one cannot usually see another person's face or emotions while conversing on social media. If people cannot engage in real interactions on social media, then they cannot form deep relationships there. Without really knowing who their "friends" are, many users may feel like they do not have any friends at all, and this feeling often leads to loneliness. To worsen the effects, the reduction in face-to-face interactions makes users feel even more lonely. They may be connected to thousands of people online yet feel like they are alone.

Others, especially those who enjoy social media, argue that using it in moderation surely would not cause a big impact. Some people do log on to platforms like Twitter and Snapchat only in moderation and display no signs of addiction. However, those rare users are massively outnumbered by those who do not. Teens, for example, are notorious for spending countless hours a day on their phones and, by extension, on social media; adults are not exempt from the allure of the social platforms either. Fuller (2017), who holds a medical degree, posited that two factors cause users to become addicted to social media: positive reinforcement and instant gratification. *Positive reinforcement* is the forming of a habit based on a reward, and it goes a long way toward making the use of social media habitual. One can always expect to see something new online when using social media. For example, a young teenager might fall into a habit of checking Facebook as soon as she comes home from school because she can expect to be entertained by her classmates' inevitable posts about their school day. According to Fuller (2017), "Positive reinforcement is difficult to resist and can lead people to become addicted to Facebook or other social media sites" (para. 5). *Instant gratification* also plays a role in

See Chapter 7 for more on how to address who cares about your argument.

making social media addictive. Everyone wants an instant reward, and social media provides it. If users do not like what they see on Facebook, they can instantly move on to something else. Social media provides users what they want when they want it, whether it be cat videos, pictures of exotic locales, or viral hits. In summary, instant entertainment can be a dangerous bait, luring many users toward the vice of addiction. As people use social media, they may become lonely or unhappy, but they will also find that despite those feelings, they keep coming back.

I acknowledge that there are some positive effects of social media. Obviously, the first benefit is the very reason why social media even exists: it helps connect friends and family who are separated by vast distances. However, a phone call, letter, or even an email could convey the same information while establishing a deeper relationship. Surely, if the goal of a relationship is to get to know each other and strengthen a bond, a two-sentence comment in text speak will not suffice. For most people, social media provides a way to be passively social. However, deep relationships can only be maintained by actively engaging in meaningful interactions. In addition to using social media to contact existing friends, many people, especially shy people, can also use social media to find new "friends" online. However, the anonymity that social media provides for its users allows them to curate their online personalities, thus tempting people to project distorted representations of themselves or even pose as different people. This same anonymity nearly guarantees that no one will ever truly know a user's true feelings, habits, or interests. Therefore, users may not know their "friends" as well as they think they do.

For more on making concessions, see Chapter 6.

In conclusion, based on recent research, social media may not be as good an idea as it first seems. Loneliness, unhappiness, stress, anxiety—these emotions are all very real, and they greatly affect people. Studies show that a strong relationship exists between these emotions and social media. The consequences that these social networks will bestow on society—whether good or bad—will come down to one choice: whether users can realize how much is too much. Social media promises the ability to connect with people, but instead it provides a disconnect from reality. In searching for happiness and fun, users find loneliness and sadness. In trying to make new friends, they lose their close friends. In seeking encouragement, they find stress and addiction instead. In this new age of social media, the social platforms' users are the only ones who stand to lose.

References

Brown, J. (2018, January 4). *Is social media bad for you? The evidence and the unknowns.* BBC Future. https://www.bbc.com/future/article/20180104-is-social-media-bad-for-you-the-evidence-and-the-unknowns

Copeland, L. (2011, January 11). *The anti-social network.* Slate. https://slate.com/human-interest/2011/01/is-facebook-making-us-sad-stanford-university-research-and-sherry-turkle-s-new-book-alone-together-suggest-that-social-networking-may-foster-loneliness.html

Fuller, K. (2017, December 7). Are we allowing social media to dictate our happiness? *Psychology Today.* https://www.psychologytoday.com/us/blog/happiness-is-state-mind/201712/are-we-allowing-social-media-dictate-our-happiness

Joining the Conversation

1. Justin Vinh makes an argument about the effects of social media on the human mind and emotions. What is his "they say" statement, and what is his "I say"? Does he agree, disagree, or both?

2. Make an outline listing the essay's thesis or overall argument, supporting points, and evidence provided.

3. List the naysayers Vinh inserts into the essay and how he responds to each of them in developing his argument. Are his responses persuasive—and if not, why not?

4. Vinh states that social media use can lead to, among other problems, loneliness. For example, in paragraph 5, he says that, when using social media, "people cannot really interact because the forms of communication used are fairly shallow." How might Sherry Turkle, author of "Stop Googling. Let's Talk." (pp. 614–23) respond to Vinh's comment?

5. Write a paragraph reflecting on the positive and negative aspects of social media use in your life. First, write it in the form of a text message you might send to a friend, and then revise it as more of a formal piece of academic writing. How do the two differ?

Stop Googling. Let's Talk.

SHERRY TURKLE

—◻—

COLLEGE STUDENTS TELL ME they know how to look someone in the eye and type on their phones at the same time, their split attention undetected. They say it's a skill they mastered in middle school when they wanted to text in class without getting caught. Now they use it when they want to be both with their friends and, as some put it, "elsewhere."

These days, we feel less of a need to hide the fact that we are dividing our attention. In a 2015 study by the Pew Research Center, 89 percent of cellphone owners said they had used their phones during the last social gathering they attended. But they weren't happy about it; 82 percent of adults felt that the way they used their phones in social settings hurt the conversation.

———

SHERRY TURKLE is the Abby Rockefeller Mauzé Professor of the Social Studies of Science and Technology at the Massachusetts Institute of Technology. Turkle's research examines how human relationships and communication are affected by digital technologies. She is the author of numerous studies and several books, including *Alone Together: Why We Expect More from Technology and Less from Each Other* (2017) and *Reclaiming Conversation: The Power of Talk in a Digital Age* (2015). This essay was published in the *New York Times* in 2015.

I've been studying the psychology of online connectivity for more than 30 years. For the past five, I've had a special focus: What has happened to face-to-face conversation in a world where so many people say they would rather text than talk? I've looked at families, friendships and romance. I've studied schools, universities and workplaces. When college students explain to me how dividing their attention plays out in the dining hall, some refer to a "rule of three." In a conversation among five or six people at dinner, you have to check that three people are paying attention—heads up—before you give yourself permission to look down at your phone. So conversation proceeds, but with different people having their heads up at different times. The effect is what you would expect: Conversation is kept relatively light, on topics where people feel they can drop in and out.

See Chapter 5 on why it can be helpful to use "I" in your writing.

Young people spoke to me enthusiastically about the good things that flow from a life lived by the rule of three, which you can follow not only during meals but all the time. First of all, there is the magic of the always available elsewhere. You can put your attention wherever you want it to be. You can always be heard. You never have to be bored. When you sense that a lull in the conversation is coming, you can shift your attention from the people in the room to the world you can find on your phone. But the students also described a sense of loss.

One 15-year-old I interviewed at a summer camp talked 5 about her reaction when she went out to dinner with her father and he took out his phone to add "facts" to their conversation. "Daddy," she said, "stop Googling. I want to talk to you." A 15-year-old boy told me that someday he wanted to raise a family, not the way his parents are raising him (with phones out during meals and in the park and during his school sports events) but the way his parents think they are raising him—

with no phones at meals and plentiful family conversation. One college junior tried to capture what is wrong about life in his generation. "Our texts are fine," he said. "It's what texting does to our conversations when we are together that's the problem."

It's a powerful insight. Studies of conversation both in the laboratory and in natural settings show that when two people are talking, the mere presence of a phone on a table between them or in the periphery of their vision changes both what they talk about and the degree of connection they feel. People keep the conversation on topics where they won't mind being interrupted. They don't feel as invested in each other. Even a silent phone disconnects us.

In 2010, a team at the University of Michigan led by the psychologist Sara Konrath put together the findings of 72 studies that were conducted over a 30-year period. They found a 40 percent decline in empathy among college students, with most of the decline taking place after 2000.

Across generations, technology is implicated in this assault on empathy. We've gotten used to being connected all the time, but we have found ways around conversation—at least from conversation that is open-ended and spontaneous, in which we play with ideas and allow ourselves to be fully present and vulnerable. But it is in this type of conversation—where we learn to make eye contact, to become aware of another person's posture and tone, to comfort one another and respectfully challenge one another—that empathy and intimacy flourish. In these conversations, we learn who we are.

Of course, we can find empathic conversations today, but the trend line is clear. It's not only that we turn away from talking face to face to chat online. It's that we don't allow these conversations to happen in the first place because we keep our phones in the landscape.

In our hearts, we know this, and now research is catching 10 up with our intuitions. We face a significant choice. It is not about giving up our phones but about using them with greater intention. Conversation is there for us to reclaim. For the failing connections of our digital world, it is the talking cure.

The trouble with talk begins young. A few years ago, a private middle school asked me to consult with its faculty: Students were not developing friendships the way they used to. At a retreat, the dean described how a seventh grader had tried to exclude a classmate from a school social event. It's an age-old problem, except that this time when the student was asked about her behavior, the dean reported that the girl didn't have much to say: "She was almost robotic in her response. She said, 'I don't have feelings about this.' She couldn't read the signals that the other student was hurt."

The dean went on: "Twelve-year-olds play on the playground like 8-year-olds. The way they exclude one another is the way 8-year-olds would play. They don't seem able to put themselves in the place of other children."

One teacher observed that the students "sit in the dining hall and look at their phones. When they share things together, what they are sharing is what is on their phones." Is this the new conversation? If so, it is not doing the work of the old conversation. The old conversation taught empathy. These students seem to understand each other less.

But we are resilient. The psychologist Yalda T. Uhls was the lead author on a 2014 study of children at a devicefree outdoor camp. After five days without phones or tablets, these campers were able to read facial emotions and correctly identify the emotions of actors in videotaped scenes significantly better than a control group. What fostered these new empathic responses? They talked to one another. In conversation, things go best if you pay close attention and learn how to put yourself in someone else's shoes. This is easier to do without your phone in hand. Conversation is the most human and humanizing thing that we do.

I have seen this resilience during my own research at a 15 device-free summer camp. At a nightly cabin chat, a group of 14-year-old boys spoke about a recent three-day wilderness hike. Not that many years ago, the most exciting aspect of that hike might have been the idea of roughing it or the beauty of unspoiled nature. These days, what made the biggest impression was being phoneless. One boy called it "time where you have nothing to do but think quietly and talk to your friends." The campers also spoke about their new taste for life away from the online feed. Their embrace of the virtue of disconnection suggests a crucial connection: The capacity for empathic conversation goes hand in hand with the capacity for solitude.

In solitude we find ourselves; we prepare ourselves to come to conversation with something to say that is authentic, ours.

If we can't gather ourselves, we can't recognize other people for who they are. If we are not content to be alone, we turn others into the people we need them to be. If we don't know how to be alone, we'll only know how to be lonely.

A virtuous circle links conversation to the capacity for self-reflection. When we are secure in ourselves, we are able to really hear what other people have to say. At the same time, conversation with other people, both in intimate settings and in larger social groups, leads us to become better at inner dialogue.

But we have put this virtuous circle in peril. We turn time alone into a problem that needs to be solved with technology. Timothy D. Wilson, a psychologist at the University of Virginia, led a team that explored our capacity for solitude. People were asked to sit in a chair and think, without a device or a book. They were told that they would have from six to 15 minutes alone and that the only rules were that they had to stay seated and not fall asleep. In one experiment, many student subjects opted to give themselves mild electric shocks rather than sit alone with their thoughts.

People sometimes say to me that they can see how one might be disturbed when people turn to their phones when they are together. But surely there is no harm when people turn to their phones when they are by themselves? If anything, it's our new form of being together.

But this way of dividing things up misses the essential con- 20 nection between solitude and conversation. In solitude we learn to concentrate and imagine, to listen to ourselves. We need these skills to be fully present in conversation.

For more on how to answer objections, see Chapter 6.

Every technology asks us to confront human values. This is a good thing, because it causes us to reaffirm what they are. If we are now ready to make face-to-face conversation a priority, it is easier to see what the next steps should be. We are not looking for simple solutions. We are looking for beginnings. Some of them may seem familiar by now, but they are no less challenging for that. Each addresses only a small piece of what silences us. Taken together, they can make a difference.

One start toward reclaiming conversation is to reclaim solitude. Some of the most crucial conversations you will ever have will be with yourself. Slow down sufficiently to make this possible. And make a practice of doing one thing at a time. Think of unitasking as the next big thing. In every domain of life, it will increase performance and decrease stress.

But doing one thing at a time is hard, because it means asserting ourselves over what technology makes easy and what feels productive in the short term. Multitasking comes with its own high, but when we chase after this feeling, we pursue an illusion. Conversation is a human way to practice unitasking.

Our phones are not accessories, but psychologically potent devices that change not just what we do but who we are. A second path toward conversation involves recognizing the degree to which we are vulnerable to all that connection offers. We have to commit ourselves to designing our products and our lives to take that vulnerability into account. We can choose not to carry our phones all the time. We can park our phones in a room and go to them every hour or two while we work on other things or talk to other people. We can carve out spaces at home or work that are device-free, sacred spaces for the paired virtues of conversation and solitude. Families can find these spaces in the day to day—no devices at dinner, in the kitchen and in the car. Introduce this idea to children when they are young so it doesn't spring up as punitive but as a baseline of family culture. In the workplace, too, the notion of sacred spaces makes sense: Conversation among employees increases productivity.

We can also redesign technology to leave more room for talking to each other. The "do not disturb" feature on the iPhone offers one model. You are not interrupted by vibrations, lights or rings, but you can set the phone to receive calls from designated people or to signal when someone calls you repeatedly. Engineers are ready with more ideas: What if our phones were not designed to keep us attached, but to do a task and then release us? What if the communications industry began to measure the success of devices not by how much time consumers spend on them but by whether it is time well spent?

It is always wise to approach our relationship with technology in the context that goes beyond it. We live, for example, in a political culture where conversations are blocked by our vulnerability to partisanship as well as by our new distractions. We thought that online posting would make us bolder than we are in person, but a 2014 Pew study demonstrated that people are less likely to post opinions on social media when they fear their followers will disagree with them. Designing for our vulnerabilities means finding ways to talk to people, online and off, whose opinions differ from our own.

Sometimes it simply means hearing people out. A college junior told me that she shied away from conversation because it demanded that one live by the rigors of what she calls the "seven minute rule." It takes at least seven minutes to see how a conversation is going to unfold. You can't go to your phone before those seven minutes are up. If the conversation goes quiet, you have to let it be. For conversation, like life, has silences—what some young people I interviewed called "the boring bits." It is often in the moments when we stumble, hesitate and fall silent that we most reveal ourselves to one another.

The young woman who is so clear about the seven minutes that it takes to see where a conversation is going admits that she often doesn't have the patience to wait for anything near that kind of time before going to her phone. In this she is characteristic of what the psychologists Howard Gardner and Katie Davis called the "app generation," which grew up with phones in hand and apps at the ready. It tends toward impatience, expecting the world to respond like an app, quickly and efficiently. The app way of thinking starts with the idea that actions in the world will work like algorithms: Certain actions will lead to predictable results.

This attitude can show up in friendship as a lack of empathy. Friendships become things to manage; you have a lot of them, and you come to them with tools. So here is a first step: To reclaim conversation for yourself, your friendships and society, push back against viewing the world as one giant app. It works the other way, too: Conversation is the antidote to the algorithmic way of looking at life because it teaches you about fluidity, contingency and personality.

This is our moment to acknowledge the unintended consequences of the technologies to which we are vulnerable, but also to respect the resilience that has always been ours. We have time to make corrections and remember who we are—creatures of history, of deep psychology, of complex relationships, of conversations, artless, risky and face to face. 30

Joining the Conversation

1. As a professor in the Science, Technology, and Society program at the Massachusetts Institute of Technology, Sherry Turkle used to be very hopeful about the power of technology to make our lives better, but she now has greater misgivings. What in your view does she mean by the title "Stop

Googling. Let's Talk."? What dangers does she observe in our reluctance to talk to one another?

2. In paragraphs 4 through 6, the author discusses young people's views of both the positive and negative aspects of our increasing tendency to focus on our phones. She quotes three young people in paragraph 5. How do their comments support Turkle's overall argument? Also, how does she lay the groundwork for these quotes in paragraph 4 and then explain their significance in paragraph 6?

3. Turkle inserts and responds to several naysayers in her essay. For example, in paragraph 19 she writes, "But surely there is no harm when people turn to their phones when they are by themselves." Explain how she responds to this naysayer and how her response fits her larger argument. Also, find and explain another example naysayer and response in her text.

4. Go to **theysayiblog.com** to find an interview with Sherry Turkle from 2015. Read the interview and come up with two or three questions of your own to ask Turkle about the possible effects of cell phone use.

5. Turkle argues that it is in face-to-face conversation "where we learn to make eye contact, to become aware of another person's posture and tone, to comfort one another and respectfully challenge one another—that empathy and intimacy flourish." She adds, "In these conversations, we learn who we are." Write an essay about your own views on communicating with social media, drawing on this and other readings in the chapter for ideas to consider, to question, and to support your view.

Google, Democracy, and the Truth about Internet Search

CAROLE CADWALLADR

—▫—

Tech-savvy right-wingers have been able to "game" the algorithms of internet giants and create a new reality where Hitler is a good guy, Jews are evil and . . . Donald Trump becomes president.

HERE'S WHAT YOU DON'T WANT TO DO late on a Sunday night. You do not want to type seven letters into Google. That's all I did. I typed: "a-r-e." And then "j-e-w-s." Since 2008, Google has attempted to predict what question you might be asking and offers you a choice. And this is what it did. It offered me a choice of potential questions it thought I might want to ask: "are jews a race?," "are jews white?," "are jews christians?," and finally, "are jews evil?"

———

CAROLE CADWALLADR is an award-winning journalist who writes features articles for the *Guardian* and the Observer, two British newspapers. She is well known for her investigative reporting that led to the downfall of Cambridge Analytica, the data analytics firm involved with Trump's 2016 campaign. She won the British Journalism Awards' Technology Journalism Award and the Orwell Prize for political journalism. She is also the author of the novel *The Family Tree* (2006).

Are Jews evil? It's not a question I've ever thought of asking. I hadn't gone looking for it. But there it was. I press enter. A page of results appears. This was Google's question. And this was Google's answer: Jews *are* evil. Because there, on my screen, was the proof: an entire page of results, nine out of 10 of which "confirm" this. The top result, from a site called Listovative, has the headline: "Top 10 Major Reasons Why People Hate Jews." I click on it: "Jews today have taken over marketing, militia, medicinal, technological, media, industrial, cinema challenges etc and continue to face the worlds [sic] envy through unexplained success stories given their inglorious past and vermin like repression all over Europe."

Google *is* search. It's the verb, to Google. It's what we all do, all the time, whenever we want to know anything. We Google it. The site handles at least 63,000 searches a second, 5.5 billion a day. Its mission as a company, the one-line overview that has informed the company since its foundation and is still the banner headline on its corporate website today, is to "organize the world's information and make it universally accessible and useful." It strives to give you the best, most relevant results. And in this instance the third-best, most relevant result to the search query "are Jews . . ." is a link to an article from stormfront.org, a neo-Nazi website. The fifth is a YouTube video: "Why the Jews are Evil. Why we are against them."

The sixth is from Yahoo Answers: "Why are Jews so evil?" The seventh result is: "Jews are demonic souls from a different world." And the 10th is from jesus-is-saviour.com: "Judaism is Satanic!"

There's one result in the 10 that offers a different point of view. 5 It's a link to a rather dense, scholarly book review from thetabletmag.com, a Jewish magazine, with the unfortunately misleading headline: "Why Literally Everybody In the World Hates Jews."

I feel like I've fallen down a wormhole, entered some parallel universe where black is white, and good is bad. Though later, I think that perhaps what I've actually done is scraped the topsoil off the surface of 2016 and found one of the underground springs that has been quietly nurturing it. It's been there all the time, of course. Just a few keystrokes away . . . on our laptops, our tablets, our phones. This isn't a secret Nazi cell lurking in the shadows. It's hiding in plain sight.

Stories about fake news on Facebook have dominated certain sections of the press for weeks following the American presidential election, but arguably this is even more powerful, more insidious. Frank Pasquale, professor of law at the University of

Maryland, and one of the leading academic figures calling for tech companies to be more open and transparent, calls the results "very profound, very troubling."

He came across a similar instance in 2006 when, "If you typed 'Jew' in Google, the first result was jewwatch.org. It was 'look out for these awful Jews who are ruining your life.' And the Anti-Defamation League went after them and so they put an asterisk next to it which said: 'These search results may be disturbing but this is an automated process.' But what you're showing—and I'm very glad you are documenting it and screen-shotting it—is that despite the fact they have vastly researched this problem, it has gotten vastly worse."

And ordering of search results does influence people, says Martin Moore, director of the Centre for the Study of Media, Communication and Power at King's College, London, who has written at length on the impact of the big tech companies on our civic and political spheres. "There's large-scale, statistically significant research into the impact of search results on political views. And the way in which you see the results and the types of results you see on the page necessarily has an impact on your perspective." Fake news, he says, has simply "revealed a much bigger problem. These companies are so powerful and so committed to disruption. They thought they were disrupting politics but in a positive way. They hadn't thought about the downsides. These tools offer remarkable empowerment, but there's a dark side to it. It enables people to do very cynical, damaging things."

Google is knowledge. It's where you go to find things out. 10 And evil Jews are just the start of it. There are also evil women. I didn't go looking for them either. This is what I type: "a-r-e w-o-m-e-n." And Google offers me just two choices, the first of which is: "Are women evil?" I press return. Yes, they are.

Every one of the 10 results "confirms" that they are, including the top one, from a site called sheddingoftheego.com, which is boxed out and highlighted: "Every woman has some degree of prostitute in her. Every woman has a little evil in her . . . Women don't love men, they love what they can do for them. It is within reason to say women feel attraction, but they cannot love men."

Next I type: "a-r-e m-u-s-l-i-m-s." And Google suggests I should ask: "Are Muslims bad?" And here's what I find out: yes, they are. That's what the top result says and six of the others. Without typing anything else, simply putting the cursor in the search box, Google offers me two new searches and I go for the first, "Islam is bad for society." In the next list of suggestions, I'm offered: "Islam must be destroyed."

Jews are evil. Muslims need to be eradicated. And Hitler? Do you want to know about Hitler? Let's Google it. "Was Hitler bad?" I type. And here's Google's top result: "10 Reasons Why Hitler Was One Of The Good Guys." I click on the link: "He never wanted to kill any Jews"; "he cared about conditions for Jews in the work camps"; "he implemented social and cultural reform." Eight out of the other 10 search results agree: Hitler really wasn't that bad.

A few days later, I talk to Danny Sullivan, the founding editor of SearchEngineLand.com. He's been recommended to me by several academics as one of the most knowledgeable experts on search. Am I just being naive, I ask him? Should I have known this was out there? "No, you're not being naive," he says. "This is awful. It's horrible. It's the equivalent of going into a library and asking a librarian about Judaism and being handed 10 books of hate. Google is doing a horrible, horrible job of delivering answers here. It can and should do better."

He's surprised too. "I thought they stopped offering autocomplete suggestions for religions in 2011." And then he types "are women" into his own computer. "Good lord! That answer at the top. It's a featured result. It's called a 'direct answer.' This is supposed to be indisputable. It's Google's highest endorsement." That every woman has some degree of prostitute in her? "Yes. This is Google's algorithm going terribly wrong."

I contacted Google about its seemingly malfunctioning auto- 15 complete suggestions and received the following response: "Our search results are a reflection of the content across the web. This means that sometimes unpleasant portrayals of sensitive subject matter online can affect what search results appear for a given query. These results don't reflect Google's own opinions or beliefs—as a company, we strongly value a diversity of perspectives, ideas and cultures."

Google isn't just a search engine, of course. Search was the foundation of the company but that was just the beginning. Alphabet, Google's parent company, now has the greatest concentration of artificial intelligence experts in the world. It is expanding into healthcare, transportation, To elaborate on a previous idea, see p. 144. energy. It's able to attract the world's top computer scientists, physicists and engineers. It's bought hundreds of start-ups, including Calico, whose stated mission is to "cure death" and DeepMind, which aims to "solve intelligence."

And 20 years ago it didn't even exist. When Tony Blair became prime minister, it wasn't possible to Google him: the search engine had yet to be invented. The company was only founded in 1998 and Facebook didn't appear until 2004. Google's founders Sergey Brin and Larry Page are still only 43. Mark Zuckerberg of Facebook is 32. Everything they've done, the world they've remade, has been done in the blink of an eye.

Google cofounders Larry Page and Sergey Brin.

But it seems the implications about the power and reach of these companies are only now seeping into the public consciousness. I ask Rebecca MacKinnon, director of the Ranking Digital Rights project at the New America Foundation, whether it was the recent furor over fake news that woke people up to the danger of ceding our rights as citizens to corporations. "It's kind of weird right now," she says, "because people are finally saying, 'Gee, Facebook and Google really have a lot of power' like it's this big revelation. And it's like, 'D'oh.'"

MacKinnon has a particular expertise in how authoritarian governments adapt to the internet and bend it to their purposes. "China and Russia are a cautionary tale for us. I think what happens is that it goes back and forth. So during the Arab spring, it seemed like the good guys were further ahead. And now it seems like the bad guys are. Pro-democracy activists are using the internet more than ever but at the same time, the adversary has gotten so much more skilled."

Last week Jonathan Albright, an assistant professor of com- 20 munications at Elon University in North Carolina, published the first detailed research on how right-wing websites had spread their message. "I took a list of these fake news sites that was circulating, I had an initial list of 306 of them and I used a tool—like the one Google uses—to scrape them for links and then I mapped them. So I looked at where the links went—into YouTube and Facebook, and between each other, millions of them . . . and I just couldn't believe what I was seeing.

"They have created a web that is bleeding through onto our web. This isn't a conspiracy. There isn't one person who's created this. It's a vast system of hundreds of different sites that are using all the same tricks that all websites use. They're sending out thousands of links to other sites and together this has created a vast satellite system of right-wing news and propaganda that has completely surrounded the mainstream media system."

He found 23,000 pages and 1.3 million hyperlinks. "And Facebook is just the amplification device. When you look at it in 3D, it actually looks like a virus. And Facebook was just one of the hosts for the virus that helps it spread faster. You can see the *New York Times* in there and the *Washington Post* and then you can see how there's a vast, vast network surrounding them. The best way of describing it is as an ecosystem. This really goes way beyond individual sites or individual stories. What this map shows is the distribution network and you can see that it's surrounding and actually choking the mainstream news ecosystem."

Like a cancer? "Like an organism that is growing and getting stronger all the time."

Charlie Beckett, a professor in the school of media and communications at [the London School of Economics], tells me: "We've been arguing for some time now that plurality of news media is good. Diversity is good. Critiquing the mainstream media is good. But now . . . it's gone wildly out of control. What Jonathan Albright's research has shown is that this isn't a byproduct of the internet. And it's not even being done for commercial reasons. It's motivated by ideology, by people who are quite deliberately trying to destabilize the internet."

Albright's map also provides a clue to understanding ²⁵ the Google search results I found. What these right-wing news sites have done, he explains, is what most commercial

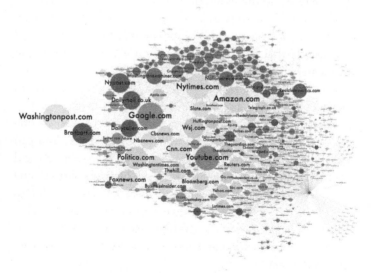

Jonathan Albright's map of the fake-news ecosystem.

websites try to do. They try to find the tricks that will move them up Google's PageRank system. They try and "game" the algorithm. And what his map shows is how well they're doing that.

That's what my searches are showing too. That the right has colonized the digital space around these subjects—Muslims, women, Jews, the Holocaust, black people—far more effectively than the liberal left.

"It's an information war," says Albright. "That's what I keep coming back to."

But it's where it goes from here that's truly frightening. I ask him how it can be stopped. "I don't know. I'm not sure it can be. It's a network. It's far more powerful than any one actor."

So, it's almost got a life of its own? "Yes, and it's learning. Every day, it's getting stronger."

The more people who search for information about Jews, 30 the more people will see links to hate sites, and the more they click on those links (very few people click on to the second page of results) the more traffic the sites will get, the more links they will accrue and the more authoritative they will appear. This is an entirely circular knowledge economy that has only one outcome: an amplification of the message. Jews are evil. Women are evil. Islam must be destroyed. Hitler was one of the good guys.

And the constellation of websites that Albright found—a sort of shadow internet—has another function. More than just spreading right-wing ideology, they are being used to track and monitor and influence anyone who comes across their content. "I scraped the trackers on these sites and I was absolutely dumbfounded. Every time someone likes one of these posts on Facebook or visits one of these websites, the scripts are then following you around the web. And this enables data-mining and influencing companies like Cambridge Analytica to precisely target individuals, to follow them around the web, and to send them highly personalized political messages. This is a propaganda machine. It's targeting people individually to recruit them to an idea. It's a level of social engineering that I've never seen before. They're capturing people and then keeping them on an emotional leash and never letting them go."

Cambridge Analytica, an American-owned company based in London, was employed by both the Vote Leave* campaign and the Trump campaign. Dominic Cummings, the campaign director of Vote Leave, has made few public announcements since the Brexit referendum but he did say this: "If you want to make big improvements in communication, my advice is—hire physicists."

Steve Bannon, founder of Breitbart News and the newly appointed chief strategist to Trump, is on Cambridge Analytica's board and it has emerged that the company is in talks to undertake political messaging work for the Trump administration. It claims to have built psychological profiles using 5,000 separate pieces of data on 220 million American voters. It knows their quirks and nuances and daily habits and can target them individually.

"They were using 40–50,000 different variants of ad every day that were continuously measuring responses and then adapting and evolving based on that response," says Martin Moore of Kings College. Because they have so much data on individuals and they use such phenomenally powerful distribution networks, they allow campaigns to bypass a lot of existing laws.

---

*Vote Leave An organization that campaigned for the United Kingdom to leave the European Union.

"It's all done completely opaquely and they can spend as 35 much money as they like on particular locations because you can focus on a five-mile radius or even a single demographic. Fake news is important but it's only one part of it. These companies have found a way of transgressing 150 years of legislation that we've developed to make elections fair and open."

Did such micro-targeted propaganda—currently legal—swing the Brexit vote? We have no way of knowing. Did the same methods used by Cambridge Analytica help Trump to victory? Again, we have no way of knowing. This is all happening in complete darkness. We have no way of knowing how our personal data is being mined and used to influence us. We don't realize that the Facebook page we are looking at, the Google page, the ads that we are seeing, the search results we are using, are all being personalized to us. We don't see it because we have nothing to compare it to. And it is not being monitored or recorded. It is not being regulated. We are inside a machine and we simply have no way of seeing the controls. Most of the time, we don't even realize that there are controls.

Rebecca MacKinnon says that most of us consider the internet to be like "the air that we breathe and the water that we drink." It surrounds us. We use it. And we don't question it. "But this is not a natural landscape. Programmers and executives and editors and designers, they make this landscape. They are human beings and they all make choices."

But we don't know what choices they are making. Neither Google or Facebook make their algorithms public. Why did my Google search return nine out of 10 search results that claim Jews are evil? We don't know and we have no way of knowing. Their systems are what Frank Pasquale describes as "black boxes." He calls Google and Facebook "a terrifying duopoly of power" and has been leading a growing movement of academics who are calling for "algorithmic accountability." "We need to have regular audits of these systems," he says. "We need people in these companies to be accountable. In the US, under the Digital Millennium Copyright Act, every company has to have a spokesman you can reach. And this is what needs to happen. They need to respond to complaints about hate speech, about bias."

Is bias built into the system? Does it affect the kind of results that I was seeing? "There's all sorts of bias about what counts as a legitimate source of information and how that's weighted. There's enormous commercial bias. And when you look at the personnel, they are young, white and perhaps Asian, but not black or Hispanic and they are overwhelmingly men. The world-view of young wealthy white men informs all these judgments."

Later, I speak to Robert Epstein, a research psychologist at the 40 American Institute for Behavioral Research and Technology, and the author of the study that Martin Moore told me about (and that Google has publicly criticized), showing how search-rank results affect voting patterns. On the other end of the phone, he repeats one of the searches I did. He types "do blacks . . ." into Google.

"Look at that. I haven't even hit a button and it's automatically populated the page with answers to the query: 'Do blacks commit more crimes?' And look, I could have been going to ask all sorts of questions. 'Do blacks excel at sports,' or anything. And it's only given me two choices and these aren't simply search-based or the most searched terms right now. Google used to use that but now they use an algorithm that looks at other things. Now, let me look at Bing and Yahoo. I'm on Yahoo and I have 10 suggestions, not one of which is 'Do black people commit more crime?'

"And people don't question this. Google isn't just offering a suggestion. This is a negative suggestion and we know that negative suggestions depending on lots of things can draw between five and 15 more clicks. And this is all programmed. And it could be programmed differently."

What Epstein's work has shown is that the contents of a page of search results can influence people's views and opinions. The type and order of search rankings was shown to influence voters in India in double-blind trials. There were similar results relating to the search suggestions you are offered.

"The general public are completely in the dark about very fundamental issues regarding online search and influence. We are talking about the most powerful mind-control machine ever invented in the history of the human race. And people don't even notice it."

Damien Tambini, an associate professor at the London School of Economics, who focuses on media regulation, says that we lack any sort of framework to deal with the potential impact of these companies on the democratic process. "We have structures that deal with powerful media corporations. We have competition laws. But these companies are not being held responsible. There are no powers to get Google or Facebook to disclose anything. There's an editorial function to Google and Facebook but it's being done by sophisticated algorithms. They say it's machines not editors. But that's simply a mechanized editorial function."

And the companies, says John Naughton, the *Observer* columnist and a senior research fellow at Cambridge University, are terrified of acquiring editorial responsibilities they don't want. "Though they can and regularly do tweak the results in all sorts of ways."

Certainly the results about Google on Google don't seem entirely neutral. Google "Is Google racist?" and the featured result—the Google answer boxed out at the top of the page—is quite clear: no. It is not.

But the enormity and complexity of having two global companies of a kind we have never seen before influencing so many areas of our lives is such, says Naughton, that "we don't even have the mental apparatus to even know what the problems are."

And this is especially true of the future. Google and Facebook are at the forefront of AI. They are going to own the future. And the rest of us can barely start to frame the sorts of questions we ought to be asking. "Politicians don't think long term. And corporations don't think long term because they're focused on the next quarterly results and that's what makes Google and Facebook interesting and different. They are absolutely thinking long term. They have the resources, the money, and the ambition to do whatever they want.

"They want to digitize every book in the world: they do it. They want to build a self-driving car: they do it. The fact that people are reading about these fake news stories and realizing that this could have an effect on politics and elections, it's like, 'Which planet have you been living on?' For Christ's sake, this is obvious."

"The internet is among the few things that humans have built that they don't understand." It is "the largest experiment involving anarchy in history. Hundreds of millions of people are, each minute, creating and consuming an untold amount of digital content in an online world that is not truly bound by terrestrial laws." The internet as a lawless anarchic state? A massive human experiment with no checks and balances and untold potential consequences? What kind of digital doommongerer would say such a thing? Step forward, Eric Schmidt— Google's chairman. They are the first lines of the book, *The New Digital Age*, that he wrote with Jared Cohen.*

---

*Jared Cohen Director of Jigsaw, formerly Google Ideas, a technology think tank.

We don't understand it. It is not bound by terrestrial laws. And it's in the hands of two massive, all-powerful corporations. It's their experiment, not ours. The technology that was supposed to set us free may well have helped Trump to power, or covertly helped swing votes for Brexit. It has created a vast network of propaganda that has encroached like a cancer across the entire internet. This is a technology that has enabled the likes of Cambridge Analytica to create political messages uniquely tailored to you. They understand your emotional responses and how to trigger them. They know your likes, dislikes, where you live, what you eat, what makes you laugh, what makes you cry.

And what next? Rebecca MacKinnon's research has shown how authoritarian regimes reshape the internet for their own purposes. Is that what's going to happen with Silicon Valley and Trump? As Martin Moore points out, the president-elect claimed that Apple chief executive Tim Cook called to congratulate him soon after his election victory. "And there will undoubtedly be pressure on them to collaborate," says Moore.

Journalism is failing in the face of such change and is only going to fail further. New platforms have put a bomb under the financial model—advertising—resources are shrinking, traffic is increasingly dependent on them, and publishers have no access, no insight at all, into what these platforms are doing in their headquarters, their labs. And now they are moving beyond the digital world into the physical. The next frontiers are healthcare, transportation, energy. And just as Google is a near-monopoly for search, its ambition to own and control the physical infrastructure of our lives is what's coming next. It already owns our data and with it our identity. What will it mean when it moves into all the other areas of our lives?

"At the moment, there's a distance when you Google 'Jews are' and get 'Jews are evil,'" says Julia Powles, a researcher at

Cambridge on technology and law. "But when you move into the physical realm, and these concepts become part of the tools being deployed when you navigate around your city or influence how people are employed, I think that has really pernicious consequences."

Powles is shortly to publish a paper looking at DeepMind's relationship with the NHS.* "A year ago, 2 million Londoners' NHS health records were handed over to DeepMind. And there was complete silence from politicians, from regulators, from anyone in a position of power. This is a company without any healthcare experience being given unprecedented access into the NHS and it took seven months to even know that they had the data. And that took investigative journalism to find it out."

The headline was that DeepMind was going to work with the NHS to develop an app that would provide early warning for sufferers of kidney disease. And it is, but DeepMind's ambitions—"to solve intelligence"—goes way beyond that. The entire history of 2 million NHS patients is, for artificial intelligence researchers, a treasure trove. And their entry into the NHS—providing useful services in exchange for our personal data—is another massive step in their power and influence in every part of our lives.

Because the stage beyond search is prediction. Google wants to know what you want before you know yourself. "That's the next stage," says Martin Moore. "We talk about the omniscience of these tech giants, but that omniscience takes a huge step forward again if they are able to predict. And that's where they want to go. To predict diseases in health. It's really, really problematic."

For the nearly 20 years that Google has been in existence, our view of the company has been inflected by the youth and liberal

---

***NHS** National Health Service, the name of the United Kingdom's public health care system.

outlook of its founders. Ditto Facebook, whose mission, Zuckerberg said, was not to be "a company. It was built to accomplish a social mission to make the world more open and connected."

It would be interesting to know how he thinks that's work- 60 ing out. Donald Trump is connecting through exactly the same technology.... And Facebook and Google are amplifying and spreading that message. And us too—the mainstream media. Our outrage is just another node on Jonathan Albright's data map.

"The more we argue with them, the more they know about us," he says. "It all feeds into a circular system. What we're seeing here is a new era of network propaganda."

We are all points on that map. And our complicity, our cre-dulity, being consumers not concerned citizens, is an essential part of that process. And what happens next is down to us. "I would say that everybody has been really naive and we need to reset ourselves to a much more cynical place and proceed on that basis," is Rebecca MacKinnon's advice. "There is no doubt that where we are now is a very bad place. But it's we as a society who have jointly created this problem. And if we want to get to a better place, when it comes to having an information ecosystem that serves human rights and democracy instead of destroying it, we have to share responsibility for that."

Are Jews evil? How do you want that question answered? This is our internet. Not Google's. Not Facebook's. Not right-wing propagandists.' And we're the only ones who can reclaim it.

Joining the Conversation

1. In what ways does Carole Cadwalladr believe that *Google* is jeopardizing democracy throughout the world? What sup-porting arguments and evidence does she provide?

2. Cadwalladr makes clear what her own views are, but she does not say much about other viewpoints. What objections could be raised to her argument, and where would you introduce them in her essay?

3. Cadwalladr frequently quotes others on the prominent representation of right-wing views in *Google* searches, but she doesn't always set up these quotations or follow them with explanations. Find two examples—in each case, how might she add a sentence or two to explain their meaning and significance? (See pp. 49–53 for ways to frame quotations.)

4. Compare the author's view of the internet with the view expressed by Jenna Wortham in "Has Coronavirus Made the Internet Better?" (pp. 587–92). How do their views differ? What do you think accounts for their differences?

5. Cadwalladr makes a number of debatable claims: "The right has colonized the digital space . . . far more effectively than the liberal left" (paragraph 26) and "Google and Facebook . . . are going to own the future" (paragraph 49). Write an essay responding to one of these claims or another claim that interests you, drawing on your own experiences to support your argument.

Are We Really as Awful as We Act Online?

AGUSTÍN FUENTES

—◻—

"YOU NEED TO HAVE your throat cut out and your decomposing, bug-infested body fed to wild pigs." An anonymous Facebook user wrote that—and more that's unprintable—to Kyle Edmund after the British pro tennis player lost in a 2017 tournament.

After University of Cambridge classics professor Mary Beard spoke about the history of male suppression of female voices, she received Twitter threats, including "I'm going to cut off your head and rape it."

On Martin Luther King Day this year, an anonymous Twitter user lionized the man who killed King some 50 years ago: "RIP James Earl Ray. A true fighter for the white race." The same month, U.S. President Donald Trump tweeted that his "Nuclear

———

AGUSTÍN FUENTES is the Rev. Edmund P. Joyce, C.S.C. Professor of Anthropology at the University of Notre Dame. His research investigates human behavior and human nature, from evolutionary studies of primates to explorations of how people interact with digital technologies. This selection appeared in *National Geographic* in 2018.

Button . . . is a much bigger & more powerful one" than Kim Jong Un's. This capped weeks of dueling statements in which Trump called the North Korean leader "Rocket Man" and "a madman" and Kim called Trump "a gangster" and a "mentally deranged U.S. dotard."

The internet is a particularly volatile place of late. Aggression on social media has reached such a pinnacle of acrimony that some U.S. House members proposed designating an annual "National Day of Civility." The proposal drew civil responses—but also tweets and posts of wrath, ridicule, and profanity.

Is this aggression on social media giving us a glimpse of 5 human nature, one in which we are, at our core, nasty, belligerent beasts?

No.

It's true that hate crimes are on the rise, political divisions are at record heights, and the level of vitriol in the public sphere, especially online, is substantial. But that's not because social media has unleashed a brutish human nature.

See Chapter 4 for more on how to agree and disagree simultaneously.

In my work as an evolutionary anthropologist, I've spent years researching and writing about how, over the past two million years, our lineage transformed from groups of ape-like beings armed with sticks and stones to the creators of cars, rockets, great artworks, nations, and global economic systems.

How did we do this? Our brains got bigger, and our capacities for cooperation exploded. We're wired to work together, to forge diverse social relationships, and to creatively problem-solve together. This is the inheritance that everyone in the 21st century carries.

I would argue that the increase in online aggression is due 10 to an explosive combination of this human evolutionary social skill set, the social media boom, and the specific political and economic context in which we find ourselves—a combination that's opened up a space for more and more people to fan the flames of aggression and insult online.

Let me explain. We've all heard the diet-conscious axiom "You are what you eat." But when it comes to our behavior, a more apt variation is "You are whom you meet." How we perceive, experience, and act in the world is intensely shaped by who and what surround us on a daily basis—our families, communities, institutions, beliefs, and role models.

See Chapter 9 on how to use colloquial expressions to make your argument.

These sources of influence find their way even into our neurobiology. Our brains and bodies constantly undergo subtle changes so that how we perceive the world plays off of, and maps to, the patterns of those people and places we see as most connected to us.

Lobbing Hostile Language Online

How—and why—are American adults abusing one another on the internet? In 2017 the Pew Research Center crunched the numbers. In a study of some 4,000 people, four out of 10 said they'd been subjected to harassing behavior. Politics was the issue most likely to trigger the harassment: About a third of those who'd been attacked—Democrats and Republicans equally—said it was due to their political beliefs. More than half those who'd been harassed said they didn't know the perpetrator's identity; nearly nine out of 10 said the anonymity online provides cover for vicious and harassing behavior. Among the adults polled, slightly less than a third said they responded or took some sort of action when witnessing someone being harassed online, and slightly more than a third said they made no response.

—Nina Strochlic

This process has deep evolutionary roots and gives humans what we call a shared reality. The connection between minds and experiences enables us to share space and work together effectively, more so than most other beings. It's in part how we've become such a successful species.

But the "who" that constitutes "whom we meet" in this system has been changing. Today the who can include more virtual, social media friends than physical ones; more information absorbed via Twitter, Facebook, and Instagram than in physical social experiences; and more pronouncements from ad-sponsored 24-hour news outlets than from conversations with other human beings.

We live in complicated societies structured around political and economic processes that generate massive inequality and disconnection between us. This division alone leads to a plethora of prejudices and blind spots that segregate people. The ways we socially interact, especially via social media, are multiplying exactly at a time when we are increasingly divided. What may be the consequences?

Historically, we have maintained harmony by displaying compassion and geniality, and by fostering connectedness when we get together. Anonymity and the lack of face-to-face interaction on social media platforms remove a crucial part of the equation of human sociality—and that opens the door to more frequent, and severe, displays of aggression. Being an antagonizer, especially to those you don't have to confront face-to-face, is easier now than it's ever been. If there are no repercussions for it, that encourages the growth of aggression, incivility, and just plain meanness on social media platforms.

Since we'll continue to be influenced by whom we meet virtually, the next question is: Whom do we *want* to meet? What kind of society do we want to shape and be shaped by?

That is, how do we modify the whom by which our brains and bodies are being molded—and thereby reduce the aggression?

Humans are evolutionarily successful because our big brains have allowed us to bond together and cooperate in more complex and diverse manners than any other animal. The capacity to observe how the world operates, to imagine how it might improve, and to turn that vision into reality (or at least make the attempt) is the hallmark of humanity.

And therein lies the solution to the problem. We are equipped with the skill set both to quell aggression and to encourage cohesion.

For countless millennia people have acted collectively to 20 punish and shame aggressive antisocial actions such as bullying or abuse. On social media, where the troll is remote and anonymous, even the best intentioned individual challenge may devolve into a shouting match. But confronting the bully with a group action—a reasoned, communal response rather than a knee-jerk, solo gesture—can be more effective at shutting down aggression.

Consider the impact of the #MeToo movement, the Time's Up movement, and the Black Lives Matter movement. Look at the public pressure brought to bear on media corporations to monitor "fake news" and hate speech.

These are excellent examples of how humans can leverage social media to nurture what's positive and sanction what's negative.

After the mass shooting at Marjory Stoneman Douglas High School in Parkland, Florida, activist students called out their Twitter trolls and shut them down. The neo-Nazi rallies have diminished, and some of the alt-right hate websites have been taken offline—all because thousands of people stood up to them and said, "No more."

Antisocial Media

When the Pew Research Center asked people how they handled their most recent exposure to online harassment, **61 percent** said they ignored it. The rest said they made some sort of response; within that group, the top six responses, ranked by popularity below, ranged from confronting the harasser online to deleting or changing the name on their own account online.

39% did not ignore online harassment. Here's what they did:

1. Confronted the person online
2. Unfriended/blocked the person
3. Reported the person responsible to website
4. Confronted the person face-to-face or via text/phone call
5. Discussed problem online
6. Changed username/deleted profile

Yes, it seems that the world is getting more aggressive, but that's not because we are aggressive at our core. It's because we haven't been stepping up, in unison, to do the difficult social work our contemporary world demands. That means standing up against bullying, abuse, and aggressive harassment, and fostering pro-social attitudes and actions. In person and on social media, we must do both.

Joining the Conversation

1. Agustín Fuentes does not provide an explicit "they say" statement in this essay but rather asks and answers the question

expressed in his title. What are his implicit "they say" and his explicit "I say" statements? How does he support his "I say" statement?

2. What makes Fuentes a credible source, one whose views on this topic the reader should seriously consider? That is, what expertise and experiences entitle him to speak as an expert? How and where in the article does he highlight his qualifications?

3. In Chapter 20, danah boyd also considers the powerful role of technology and social media in pushing the United States closer to an "us vs. them" nation of self-contained identity groups emphasizing differences rather than similarities. Compare the proposed solutions of both authors. Which seem to you more promising, and why? What other possible remedies can you think of?

4. At the beginning of his text, Fuentes includes quotations from social media posts expressing views quite different from his own. How does he clearly distinguish those views from his own position?

5. Write an argument using "they say / I say" strategies in which you agree, disagree, or both with Fuentes's discussion of online behavior and his ideas for reducing it.

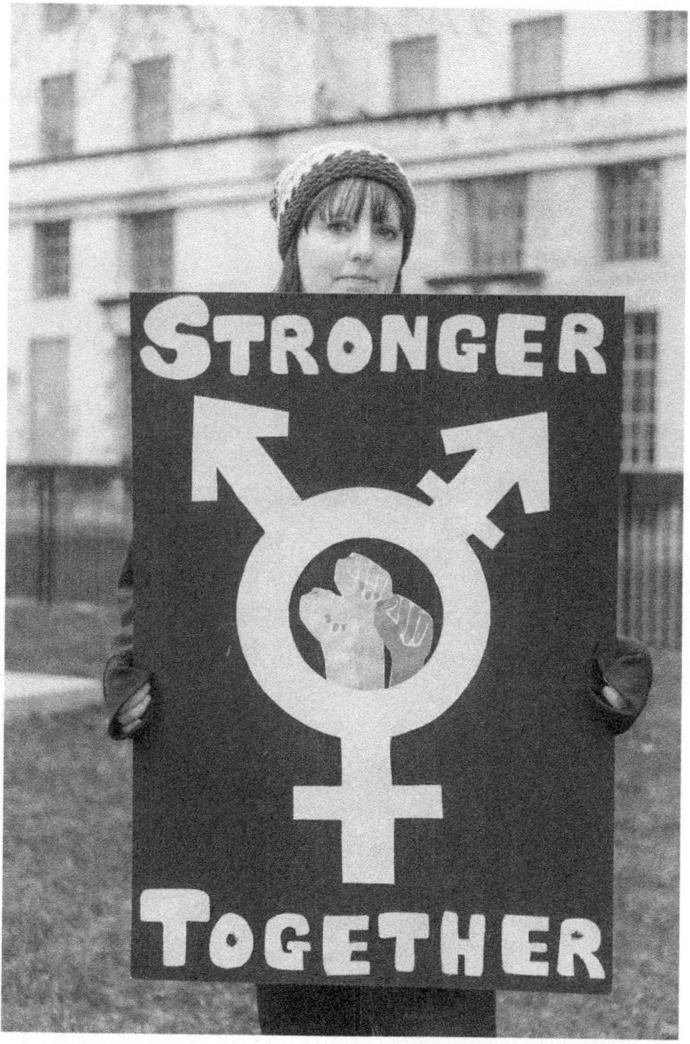
STRONGER
TOGETHER

TWENTY-THREE

WHAT'S GENDER GOT TO DO WITH IT?

—▣—

THE 1939 FILM CLASSIC *The Wizard of Oz* begins in sepia-toned black and white with scenes of rural Kansas, then shifts dramatically to Technicolor the moment a wide-eyed Dorothy and her little dog, Toto, enter the land of Oz. These days, where the concept of gender is concerned, our landscape seems to be shifting just as rapidly from drab black and white into living color.

Gender, as defined by the American Psychological Association, "refers to the attitudes, feelings, and behaviors that a given culture associates with a person's biological sex." Gender roles in our society have evolved considerably and are far less rigid than they were: more women are in the workforce, many doing jobs once held exclusively or primarily by men, and more men taking an active role in the raising of children, including a growing number of men who choose to stay at home with the children while their partner works outside the home. Moreover, while discrimination still exists, there is increasing acceptance of nonheterosexual relationships—most notably with same-sex marriage now legal in all of the United States—and, in the last few years, of people who choose to change their gender or sex.

No matter one's roles or beliefs, pressure still exists for people, particularly children, to maintain traditional gender roles—for males, playing sports, acting tough, and not showing emotion; for females, emphasizing physical appearance, attracting members of the opposite sex, and not acting "too intelligent." In this chapter, journalist Laurie Frankel writes about how her son went from "he to she in first grade," defying traditional gender expectations, and how the child experienced this transition at home and at school. Part of maintaining received gender roles has involved pronoun use, with men expected to use "he" and women "she," but many people are now challenging this linguistic and cultural constraint. Columnist Farhad Manjoo advocates the use of "they" as a singular pronoun that doesn't pigeonhole a person's identity, in order, as Manjoo puts it, to escape the "ubiquitous prison for the mind," while writer and editor Damon Linker rejects this argument on historical, philosophical, and linguistic grounds, championing the traditional gender-specific binary pronouns.

Other readings in the chapter focus on the unique expectations of women, arguing that while women have made substantial progress in the United States, serious obstacles remain. Anne-Marie Slaughter, a former government official and current CEO of the think tank New America, observes that women who want to advance in their careers find it difficult to also raise children—and that it's not possible to really "have it all." In response to this argument, journalist, husband, and father Richard Dorment asserts that the situation for men in contemporary American life is, in many ways, just as problematic as for women. He writes about the increasing difficulty men have in balancing work and home life. In a historical as well as contemporary analysis, journalist Helen Lewis focuses on the disproportionate suffering of women during pandemics, including the recent COVID-19 one. Looking most closely at women who are primary caregivers for young children and/or older adults while also holding paid employment, Lewis sees women's independence as "a silent victim of the pandemic." College student Sanjana Ramanathan highlights rampant sexism against women in online gaming communities and offers ways of fighting this hostile behavior. Finally, professional basketball player Monica Wright considers the greater support given to male athletes over their female counterparts in school-sponsored sports, as she argues for the strengthening of Title IX protections.

Gender is personal, part of one's own developing identity and web of relationships, but it is also political, related to questions of equity, fairness, and civil rights. In reading about some of the discussions taking place around gender, you will have the opportunity to learn more about this topic, formulate your views, and become part of this ongoing conversation.

From He to She in First Grade

LAURIE FRANKEL

—◻—

WHEN OUR SON TURNED 6, my husband and I bought him a puppet theater and a chest of dress-up clothes because he liked to put on plays. We filled the chest with 20 items from Goodwill, mostly grown-man attire: ties, button-down shirts, a gray pageboy cap and a suit vest.

But we didn't want his or his castmates' creative output to be curtailed by a lack of costume choices, so we also included high heels, a pink straw hat, a dazzling fairy skirt and a sparkly green halter dress.

He was thrilled with these presents. He put on the sparkly green dress right away. In a sense, he never really took it off.

For a while, he wore the dress only when we were at home, and only when we were alone. He would change back into

LAURIE FRANKEL is the author of three novels, *The Atlas of Love* (2010), *Goodbye for Now* (2012), and *This Is How It Always Is* (2017), which was inspired, in part, by the essay that appears here. Her writing has also appeared in publications such as the *Guardian*, *People*, and *Publishers Weekly*. Frankel is on the board of Seattle7Writers, a nonprofit organization that supports literacy and works to build relationships among writers, readers, librarians, and booksellers. This essay first appeared in the *New York Times* on September 16, 2016.

shorts and a T-shirt if we were running errands or had people coming over.

Then we would come home or our guests would leave, and he would change back to the sparkly green dress, asking me to tie the halter behind his neck and the sash around his waist.

Eventually he stopped changing out of it. He wore it to the grocery store and when he had friends over. He wore it to the park and the lake. He wore shorts for camp and trunks for swimming, but otherwise he was mostly in the dress.

My husband and I were never of the opinion that girls should not wear pants or climb trees or get dirty, or that boys should not have long hair or play with dolls or like pink, so the dress did not cause us undue alarm or worry. But school was about to start, and we found ourselves at a crossroads.

It seemed reasonable to say: "Wear whatever you're comfortable in to school. If that's what you want to wear, you don't have to keep changing in and out of it."

But it also seemed reasonable to say: "Dresses are for play at home only. The dress is fun, but you can't wear it to first grade."

The former had the advantage of being fair, what we believed, and what would make our child happiest. The latter had the advantage of being much less fraught.

So we asked him, "What do you think you'll do with your dress when school starts in a couple weeks?" We said: "You need new clothes for the new school year. What should we buy?"

For weeks, he wasn't sure.

And then, on the day before school started, he was.

I later learned that this is remarkably common, that children who make decisions like this often do so as push comes to shove. They achieve clarity when they are faced with two not-great options.

Our child could go to school dressed in shorts and a T-shirt 15 and feel wrong and awkward and not himself. Or he could wear what felt right and possibly face the wrath of his fellow elementary-school students.

When he woke up on that last day of summer vacation, the first thing he said was that he wanted to wear skirts and dresses to first grade.

"O.K.," I said, stalling for time, as my brain flooded with all the concerns I hadn't yet voiced. "What do you think other kids will say tomorrow if you wear a dress to school?"

For ways to let your naysayer speak informally, see pp. 88–90. "They'll say, 'Are you a boy or a girl?'" he replied. "They'll say: 'You can't wear that. Boys don't wear dresses.' They'll say, 'Ha, ha, ha, you're so stupid.'"

This seemed about right to me. "And how will that make you feel?" I asked.

He shrugged and said he didn't know. But he did know, with 20 certainty, what he wanted to wear to school the next day, even as he also seemed to know what that choice may cost him.

I hadn't met his new teacher yet, so I sent her a heads-up by email, explaining that this had been going on for some time; it wasn't just a whim. She emailed back right away, unfazed, and she promised to support our child "no matter what."

Then we went shopping. The fairy skirt and sparkly green dress were play clothes. He didn't have any skirts or dresses that were appropriate for school.

I didn't want to buy a whole new wardrobe when I didn't know if this was going to last. I envisioned a scenario in which he wore a skirt the first day, got made fun of, and never wore a skirt again. I envisioned another in which he got the skirt-wearing out of his system and happily donned pants every day thereafter. But mostly I was pretty sure the skirts were here to stay.

School started on a Wednesday, so we bought three outfits to get us through the week. Three school skirts. Three school tops. A pair of white sandals.

On the drive home, I asked, "What will you say back if kids 25 say the things you think they will?"

"I don't know," he admitted.

So we brainstormed. We role-played. We practiced saying, "If girls can wear pants or skirts, so can boys." We practiced saying: "You wear what you're comfortable wearing. This is what I'm comfortable wearing." We practiced polite ways of suggesting they mind their own business.

"Are you sure?" I asked him. I asked this while he was behind me in his car seat so he wouldn't see how scared I was. I asked casually while we ran errands so it wouldn't seem like a big deal.

"I'm sure," he said. He certainly sounded sure. That made one of us.

The question I couldn't stop asking myself was: Do we love 30 our children best by protecting them at all costs or by supporting them unconditionally? Does love mean saying, "Nothing, not even your happiness, is as important as your safety"? Or does love mean saying, "Be who you are, and I will love that person no matter what"?

I couldn't ask my child those questions. But the next morning I did ask one more time, "Are you sure?"

Which was ridiculous, given that he had gotten up before dawn to put on the new skirt and blouse and sandals and was grinning, glowing, with joy.

We put some barrettes in his very short hair and took the traditional first-day-of-school pictures. They're all a little blurry because he was too excited to stand still, but it doesn't matter because that joyful smile is all you see anyway.

My husband and I took deep breaths and walked him to school. For my son's part, he fairly floated, seemingly unconcerned. Having decided, he was sure.

The things I imagined happening fell into opposite catego- 35 ries, but both transpired. A lot of children didn't notice, didn't care or stared briefly before moving on. But there were a few who pestered him on the playground and in the hallways, who teased or pressed, who covered their mouths and laughed and pointed and would not be dissuaded by our carefully rehearsed answers.

That lasted longer than I had expected, but it was mostly over within the month.

At the end of that first week, when he was going to bed on Friday night, he was upset about something—weepy, cranky and irritable. He couldn't or wouldn't tell me what the problem was. His eyes were wet, his fists balled, his face stormy.

I tucked him in and kissed him good night. I asked, again, what the matter was. I asked, again, what I could do. I told him I couldn't help if he wouldn't talk to me. Finally I whispered, "You don't have to keep wearing skirts and dresses to school, you know. If kids are being mean, if it feels weird, you can absolutely go back to shorts and T-shirts."

He snapped out of it immediately, sitting up, his face clearing, his eyes drying and brightening. "No, Mama," he chided. I wish I could say that he did so sweetly, but his tone was more like, Don't be an idiot. "I already decided about that," he said. "I never think about that anymore."

It had been three days.   40

But it was also true. He had already decided. He didn't think about that anymore. And he—she—never looked back. She grew out her hair. She stopped telling people she was a boy in a skirt and started being a girl in a skirt instead.

And we, as a family, decided to be open and honest about it, too, celebrating her story instead of hiding it.

Two years later, our daughter still sometimes wears the green dress, for dress-up and to put on plays, as we imagined her doing in the first place. Now that she can be who she is on the inside and on the outside, on weekdays as well as on weekends, at home and everywhere else, the sparkly green dress has once again become just a costume.

Joining the Conversation

1. Laurie Frankel tells the story of her child's transition from "he to she" at home and at school. What's Frankel's point, and how does the story she tells support that point?

2. This essay appeared in the *New York Times*' "Modern Love" section, a "series of weekly reader-submitted essays that explore the joys and tribulations of love." These pieces are relatively short. If you were revising this one to be a longer essay, which strategies taught in this book could help?

3. So what? Frankel explains why gender identity is important to her child, herself, and her husband. Has she convinced you that you should care? If so, how? If not, how could she do better?

4. Write a one-page response to Frankel's essay in which you give your own reasons for supporting her argument, not supporting it, or both.

5. Go to **theysayiblog.com** and click on "What's Gender Got to Do with It?" Search for Frankel's essay and read the comments that readers have posted in response to her article. Consider how many posts incorporate personal stories, like Frankel does, as support.

It's Time for "They"

FARHAD MANJOO

—▢—

I AM YOUR STEREOTYPICAL, cisgender, middle-aged suburban dad. I dabble in woodworking, I take out the garbage, and I covet my neighbor's Porsche. Though I do think men should wear makeup (it looks nice!), my tepid masculinity apparently rings loudly enough online and in person that most people guess that I go by "he" and "him." And that's fine; I will not be offended if you refer to me by those traditional, uselessly gendered pronouns.

But "he" is not what you *should* call me. If we lived in a just, rational, inclusive universe—one in which we were not all so irredeemably obsessed by the particulars of the parts dangling between our fellow humans' legs, nor the ridiculous expectations signified by those parts about how we should act and speak and dress and feel—there would be no requirement for you to have to assume my gender just to refer to me in the common tongue.

There are, after all, few obvious linguistic advantages to the requirement. When I refer to myself, I don't have to

———

FARHAD MANJOO is an opinion columnist for the *New York Times* who writes about technology, the tech industry, and current politics. They have also worked as a writer for *Salon*, *Slate*, and the *Wall Street Journal*. This column was published in the *New York Times* in 2019.

announce my gender and all the baggage it carries. Instead I use the gender-nonspecific "I." Nor do I have to bother with gender when I'm speaking directly to someone or when I'm talking about a group of people. I just say "you" or "they."

So why does standard English impose a gender requirement on the third-person singular? And why do elite cultural institutions—universities, publishers and media outlets like *The Times*—still encourage all this gendering? To get to my particular beef: When I refer to an individual whose gender I don't know here in *The Times*, why do I usually have to choose either "he" or "she" or, in the clunkiest phrase ever cooked up by small-minded grammarians, "he or she"?

The truth is, I shouldn't have to. It's time for the singular 5 "they." Indeed, it's well past time—and I'd like to do my part in pushing "they" along.

Farhad Manjoo.

So: If you write about me, interview me, tweet about me, or if you are a Fox News producer working on a rant about my extreme politics, I would prefer if you left my gender out of it. Call me "they" or "them," as in: "Did you read Farhad's latest column—they've really gone off the deep end this time!" And—unless you feel strongly about your specific pronouns, which I respect—I would hope to call you "they" too, because the world will be slightly better off if we abandoned unnecessary gender signifiers as a matter of routine communication. Be a "him" or "her" or anything else in the sheets, but consider also being a "they" and "them" in the streets.

I suspect my call will be dismissed as useless virtue-signaling, but there are several clear advantages, both linguistic and cultural, to the singular "they." One of the main ones is that it's ubiquitous. According to linguists who study gender and pronouns, "they" and "them" are increasingly and widely seen as legitimate ways to refer to an individual, both generically and specifically, whether you know their gender or not—as I just did right in this sentence.

"In our latest study, 90 percent of the time when people refer to a hypothetical person, they use 'they,'" said Evan Bradley, who studies language and gender at Penn State.

But "they" is also used so commonly to refer to specific individuals that it doesn't trip people up. The same thing isn't true when you add a new, neutral pronoun to the language—something like "ze," which in Bradley's research was not recognized by many people, and when it was used, it was often taken to refer specifically to gender-nonconforming people.

By contrast, "they" is universal and purely neutral, Bradley 10 told me. When people encounter it, they infer nothing about gender. This makes singular "they" a perfect pronoun—it's flexible, inclusive, unobtrusive and obviates the risk of inadvertent misgendering. And in most circumstances, it creates perfectly coherent sentences that people don't have to strain to understand.

That's probably why the singular, gender-neutral "they" is common not just in transgender and nonbinary communities, for whom it is necessary, but also in mainstream usage, where it is rapidly becoming a standard way we refer to all people. If you watch closely, you'll see the usage in marketing copy, on social media, in app interfaces and just about everywhere else you look. For instance, when Uber or Lyft wants to tell you that your driver has arrived, they send you a notification that says something like: "Juan is almost here. Meet them outside."

Other than plainly intolerant people, there's only one group that harbors doubts about the singular "they": grammarians. If you're one of those people David Foster Wallace called a "snoot," Lyft's use of "them" to refer to one specific Juan rings grammatically icky to you. The singular, gender nonspecific "they" has been common in English as long as people have spoken English, but since the 18th century, grammar stylists have discouraged it on the grounds that "they" has to be plural. That's why institutions that cater to snoots generally discourage it. *The Times*, whose stylebook allows the singular "they" when the person being referred to prefers it, warns against its widespread usage: "Take particular care to avoid confusion if using they for an individual," the stylebook counsels.

See Chapter 7 for more on identifying groups that have a stake in the argument.

I think that's too cautious; we should use "they" more freely, because language should not default to the gender binary. One truth I've come to understand too late in life is how thoroughly and insidiously our lives are shaped by gender norms. These expectations are felt most acutely and tragically by those who don't conform to the standard gender binary—people who are transgender or nonbinary, most obviously.

But even for people who do mainly fit within the binary, the very idea that there is a binary is invisibly stifling. Every boy and girl feels this in small and large ways growing up; you unwittingly brush up against preferences that don't fit within your gender expectations, and then you must learn to fight those expectations or strain to live within them.

But it was only when I had a son and a daughter of my own 15 that I recognized how powerfully gendered constructs shape our development. From their very earliest days, my kids, fed by marketing and entertainment and (surely) their parents' modeling, seemed to hem themselves into silly gender norms. They gravitated to boy toys and girl toys, boy colors and girl colors, boy TV shows and girl TV shows. This was all so sad to me: I see them limiting their thoughts and their ambitions, their preferences and their identity, their very liberty, only to satisfy some collective abstraction. And there's little prospect for escape: Gender is a ubiquitous prison for the mind, reinforced everywhere, by everyone, and only rarely questioned.

We're a long way from eradicating these expectations in society. But we don't have to be wary about eradicating them in language.

"Part of introducing the concept of gender-neutral pronouns to people is to get them to ask, 'Why does this part of society need to be gendered in the first place?'" said Jay Wu, director of communications at the National Center for Transgender Equality. They continued: "Part of how we fix that is more and more people noticing that things are so gendered and being like, why does it have to be that way? What benefit does it bring us?"

None, I say, other than confusion, anxiety and grief. Call me "they," and I'll call you "them." I won't mind, and I hope you won't, either.

Joining the Conversation

1. Why does Farhad Manjoo believe in using "they" as a singular pronoun rather than the traditional male and female pronouns? What arguments do they provide to support their view?

2. Manjoo clearly believes that all English-language speakers and writers should make this recommended change in pronoun usage. However, Manjoo does single out a few groups, such as "elite cultural institutions" (paragraph 4), to criticize for continuing to "impose a gender requirement on the third-person singular." Write a response to a "who cares?" question, as discussed in Chapter 7, to convey the author's position on who should be concerned about this issue, and why.

3. The author begins by describing their own life as a "middle-aged suburban dad," and several other authors in this chapter also begin their argumentative essays by writing briefly about their own lives (for example, Anne-Marie Slaughter, "Why Women Still Can't Have It All," pp. 673–93, and Richard Dorment, "Why Men Still Can't Have It All," pp. 694–714). How does including personal details affect these authors' arguments? Do they strengthen them, weaken them, or both?

4. This short piece was written as a newspaper column. What strategies in this book could Manjoo use to revise their op-ed column as an academic essay? (See the advice in Chapter 11 for using the templates to revise.)

5. Consider your own use of personal pronouns where gender is concerned, and write an essay responding to the author in which you agree, disagree, or both with their argument.

Liberals' Astonishingly Radical Shift on Gender

DAMON LINKER

—▯—

SOMETIMES A PIECE of writing so perfectly distills a cultural moment and mood that it deserves to be given outsized attention. That's very much the case with Farhad Manjoo's op-ed column in Thursday's *New York Times*, ["It's Time For 'They.'"]

Little in the column is original to Manjoo. In 2019, one encounters similar arguments, assertions, and assumptions every day in published essays, on social media, in lavish advertising campaigns, and increasingly in the literature produced and enforced by corporate HR departments. Yet Manjoo's column is worth focusing on because it presents such a concise and cogent statement of the emerging elite-progressive consensus.

———

DAMON LINKER is a senior correspondent at *The Week*, where he writes about politics and religion. He was previously a senior editor at *Newsweek/the Daily Beast*, and his articles have been published in the *New York Times*, the *Washington Post*, and the *Wall Street Journal*. He is a lecturer in the Critical Writing Program at the University of Pennsylvania. This essay appeared in *The Week* in 2019.

What is this consensus? That "if we lived in a just, rational, inclusive universe . . . there would be no requirement for you to have to [assume] my gender just to refer to me in the common tongue." We would instead refer to Manjoo— along with everyone else in the world—by the gender-neutral pronoun "they." Not only would this help to avoid "the risk of inadvertent misgendering." It would also subvert the "very idea" of thinking about gender in binary terms.

See Chapter 2 for more on writing summaries.

In Manjoo's view, this idea—that the overwhelming majority of people are either men or women and so can be labeled either he or she, him or her, without causing offense or tyrannizing them—is "invisibly stifling" and "sad." Speaking of his own children, Manjoo laments how "silly gender norms" limit "their very liberty" with "little prospect for escape," relegating them to "a ubiquitous prison [for] the mind" that is "reinforced everywhere, by everyone." Hence the need to work toward "eradicating" these distinctions in language as a first step toward eradicating them "in society." As for the final element in the consensus, it holds that, other than "small-minded grammarians" (more on them below), the only people who would object to such a change in the use of "they" are those who are hopelessly "intolerant."

The first thing to be said about these convictions is that, apart from a miniscule number of transgender activists and postmodern theorists and scholars, no one would have affirmed any of them as recently as four years ago. There is almost no chance at all that the Farhad Manjoo of 2009 sat around pondering and lamenting the oppressiveness of his peers referring to "him" as "he." That's because (as far as I know) Manjoo is a man, with XY chromosomes, male reproductive organs, and typically male hormone levels, and a mere decade ago referring to such a person as "he" was considered to be merely descriptive of a rather mundane aspect of reality. His freedom was not infringed, or implicated, in any way by this convention. It wouldn't have occurred to him to think or feel otherwise. Freedom was something else and about other things.

The emergence and spread of the contrary idea—that "gender is a ubiquitous prison [for] the mind"—can be traced to a precise point in time: the six months following the Supreme Court's *Obergefell* decision, which declared same-sex marriage a constitutional right. Almost immediately after that decision was handed down, progressive activists took up the cause of championing transgender rights as the next front in the culture war—and here we are, just four short years later, born free but everywhere in chains.

How should we understand this astonishingly radical and rapid shift in self-understanding among highly educated progressive members of the upper-middle class? (In addition to calling himself a "cisgender, middle-aged suburban dad" at the opening of his column, Manjoo confesses that he "covet[s his] neighbor's Porsche," so it seems exactly right to describe him in this way.) I suspect Manjoo would say that his consciousness has been raised. Once he was blind, but now he sees. Once he slumbered, but now he's awake—or "woke."

Others have noted the religious connotations of the term. This has even been reflected in the prevalence of the formulation "Great Awakening" among sympathetic journalists seeking to explain the trend. It gets at something important. A kind of spiritual-moral madness periodically wells up and sweeps across vast swaths of the United States. In the 18th and 19th centuries, these Great Awakenings were decidedly "low church" affairs and invariably emerged from America's plethora of Protestant sects. Today, for perhaps the first time in American history, it is a nominally secular, progressive elite that finds itself swept up into a moral fervor and eager to overturn (linguistic and other) conventions in a surge of self-certainty and self-righteousness.

Yet the focus on religious antecedents can obscure as much as it clarifies about what's going on around us.

What is it, exactly, that Manjoo finds oppressive about the use of gendered pronouns? In addition to raising a fusty objection to the ungrammatical use of a gender-neutral plural pronoun to refer to single, gendered individuals, grammarians might also point out that English is far less gender-infused than many other languages. Latin, French, Spanish, Italian, German, and many other languages divide the world into masculine, feminine, and sometimes (but not always) neuter nouns. Masculine chairs, feminine houses, and so on, reflected in definite and indefinite articles and pronouns in every sentence ever read, written, spoken, or heard in languages across the world. Talk about a prison with little prospect for escape!

For more on how to disagree with reasons, see Chapter 4.

10

The comparatively slight fudging of the grammatical rules that Manjoo proposes for American English would be utterly impossible in these other languages, used by many hundreds of millions, without tearing them apart from top to bottom. Looks like Anglo-American culture stands at the forefront of human freedom after all.

But what is this freedom that Manjoo and so many others suddenly crave for themselves and their children? That's more than a little mysterious. Slaves everywhere presumably know that they are unfree, even if they accept the legitimacy of the system and the master that keeps them enslaved. But what is this bondage we couldn't even begin to perceive in 2009 that in under a decade has become a burden so onerous that it produces a demand for the overturning of well-settled rules and assumptions, some of which ("the gender binary") go all the way back to the earliest origins of human civilization?

The beginnings of an answer can be found in the writings of a number of thinkers who have analyzed, often critically but from a range of religious and political perspectives, the potential excesses of liberalism and democracy—and especially the antinomian logic of individualism. Alexis de Tocqueville, Robert Nisbet, Christopher Lasch, Walker Percy, Michel Houellebecq, and others have reflected deeply on what might be called the phenomenology of individualism—how a society devoted at the level of principle to the liberation of the individual from constraints can easily produce citizens who continually feel themselves to be newly enslaved and in need of ever new and more radical forms of liberation.

That's because all societies—as collectivities of individuals sharing a common culture as well as common laws, rules, and norms (including linguistic rules and norms)—invariably constrain individuals more than they would be if they lived in absolute isolation from others. Any one of those limits on the individual will can feel as if it's an intolerable constraint, and the principle of individual freedom can always be invoked in order to combat it.

This is how a progressive in 2014 can consider it an unac- 15 ceptable limitation on individual freedom for gay couples to be denied the right to marry—and base that argument on the claim that a gay man's love and natural desire for another man, like a lesbian's love and natural desire for another woman, is irreducible and ineradicable—and then insist just five years later that it is an unacceptable limitation on individual freedom for anyone to be presumed a man or a woman at all.

As Andrew Sullivan has powerfully argued, the two positions are fundamentally incompatible. The first, which morally justifies same-sex marriage, presumes that biological sex and binary gender differences are real, that they matter, and that they can't just be erased at will. The second, which Manjoo and many transgender activists embrace and espouse, presumes the opposite—that those differences can and should be immediately dissolved. To affirm the truth of both positions is to embrace incoherence.

But that assumes that we're treating them as arguments. If, instead, we view them as expressions of *what it can feel like* at two different moments in a society devoted to the principle of individualism, they can be brought into a kind of alignment. Each is simply an expression of rebellion against a different but equally intolerable constraint on the individual. All that's changed is the object of rebellion.

Will Manjoo's call for liberation from the tyranny of the gender binary catch on in the way that the push for same-sex marriage did before it? I have no idea. What I do know is that, whatever happens, it's likely to be followed by another undoubtedly very different crusade in the name of individual freedom, and then another, and another, as our society (and others like it) continues to work through the logic of its devotion to the principle of individualism.

The only thing that could halt the process is the rejection of that principle altogether.

Joining the Conversation

1. Damon Linker's essay is a direct response to Farhad Manjoo's argument in favor of gender-neutral pronoun usage in the previous reading. What exactly does Linker object to in Manjoo's essay? How does Linker use historical, philosophical, and grammatical arguments in opposing Manjoo's position?

2. In paragraph 16, Linker paraphrases journalist Andrew Sullivan's assertion that arguments in favor of gay marriage and against the idea that an individual should be presumed male or female "are fundamentally incompatible." What point exactly is Linker trying to make with this assertion, and how in particular does it relate to pronoun usage?

3. The author refers to the "Supreme Court's *Obergefell* decision, which declared same-sex marriage a constitutional right" in the United States in 2015. Research this court decision and its legal and cultural repercussions by finding three news articles about the decision. Select one to read in full, and draft a summary in response.

4. *Facebook*, *Instagram*, and other social media platforms have developed their own categories of gender and personal pronoun usage a person may choose for themselves when creating an account. Find the categories used by *Facebook* or another platform, examine how they explain the choices provided, and consider how their approach relates to the contrasting positions of Manjoo and Linker.

5. Write an essay discussing your own views on personal pronoun usage in which you consider the positions of both Manjoo and Linker. See if you can also bring in ideas from at least one other reading from this chapter in a way that enriches your own argument.

Why Women Still Can't Have It All

ANNE-MARIE SLAUGHTER

—▣—

Redefining the Arc of a Successful Career

Eighteen months into my job as the first woman director of policy planning at the State Department, a foreign-policy dream job that traces its origins back to George Kennan, I found myself in New York, at the United Nations' annual assemblage of every foreign minister and head of state in the world. On a Wednesday evening, President and Mrs. Obama hosted a glamorous reception at the American Museum of Natural History. I sipped champagne, greeted foreign dignitaries, and mingled. But I could not stop thinking about my 14-year-old son, who had started eighth grade three weeks earlier and was already resuming what had

ANNE-MARIE SLAUGHTER is the president and CEO of the New America Foundation, "a think tank and civic enterprise committed to renewing American politics, prosperity, and purpose in the digital age." She has taught at Princeton University and Harvard Law School and worked as director of policy planning for the US State Department. She is also the author and editor of several books, most recently *The Chessboard and the Web: Strategies of Connection in a Networked World* (2017). This reading is a selection from the essay that first appeared in the July/August 2012 issue of the *Atlantic*.

become his pattern of skipping homework, disrupting classes, failing math, and tuning out any adult who tried to reach him. Over the summer, we had barely spoken to each other—or, more accurately, he had barely spoken to me. And the previous spring I had received several urgent phone calls—invariably on the day of an important meeting—that required me to take the first train from Washington, D.C., where I worked, back to Princeton, New Jersey, where he lived. My husband, who has always done everything possible to support my career, took care of him and his 12-year-old brother during the week; outside of those midweek emergencies, I came home only on weekends.

As the evening wore on, I ran into a colleague who held a senior position in the White House. She has two sons exactly my sons' ages, but she had chosen to move them from California to D.C. when she got her job, which meant her husband commuted back to California regularly. I told her how difficult I was finding it to be away from my son when he clearly needed me. Then I said, "When this is over, I'm going to write an op-ed titled 'Women Can't Have It All.'"

She was horrified. "You *can't* write that," she said. "You, of all people." What she meant was that such a statement, coming from a high-profile career woman—a role model—would be a terrible signal to younger generations of women. By the end of the evening, she had talked me out of it, but for the remainder of my stint in Washington, I was increasingly aware that the feminist beliefs on which I had built my entire career were shifting under my feet. I had always assumed that if I could get a foreign-policy job in the State Department or the White House while my party was in power, I would stay the course as long as I had the opportunity to do work I loved. But in January 2011, when my two-year public-service leave from Princeton University was up, I hurried home as fast as I could.

A rude epiphany hit me soon after I got there. When people asked why I had left government, I explained that I'd come home not only because of Princeton's rules (after two years of leave, you lose your tenure), but also because of my desire to be with my family and my conclusion that juggling high-level government work with the needs of two teenage boys was not possible. I have not exactly left the ranks of full-time career women: I teach a full course load; write regular print and online columns on foreign policy; give 40 to 50 speeches a year; appear regularly on TV and radio; and am working on a new academic book. But I routinely got reactions from other women my age or older that ranged from disappointed ("It's such a pity that you had to leave Washington") to condescending ("I wouldn't generalize from your experience. *I've* never had to compromise, and my kids turned out great").

The first set of reactions, with the underlying assumption 5 that my choice was somehow sad or unfortunate, was irksome enough. But it was the second set of reactions—those implying that my parenting and/or my commitment to my profession were somehow substandard—that triggered a blind fury. Suddenly, finally, the penny dropped. All my life, I'd been on the other side of this exchange. I'd been the woman smiling the faintly superior smile while another woman told me she had decided to take some time out or pursue a less competitive career track so that she could spend more time with her family. I'd been the woman congratulating herself on her unswerving commitment to the feminist cause, chatting smugly with her dwindling number of college or law-school friends who had reached and maintained their place on the highest rungs of their profession. I'd been the one telling young women at my lectures that you *can* have it all and do it all, regardless of what field you are in. Which means I'd been part, albeit unwittingly, of making millions of women feel that *they* are to blame if they cannot manage to rise up the ladder as fast as men and also have a family and an active home life (and be thin and beautiful to boot).

Last spring, I flew to Oxford to give a public lecture. At the request of a young Rhodes Scholar I know, I'd agreed to talk to the Rhodes community about "work-family balance." I ended up speaking to a group of about 40 men and women in their mid-20s. What poured out of me was a set of very frank reflections on how unexpectedly hard it was to do the kind of job I wanted to do as a high government official and be the kind of parent I wanted to be, at a demanding time for my children (even though my husband, an academic, was willing to take on the lion's share of parenting for the two years I was in Washington). I concluded by saying that my time in office had convinced me that further government service would be very unlikely while my sons were still at home. The audience was rapt, and asked many thoughtful questions. One of the first was from a young woman who began by thanking me for "not giving just one more fatuous 'You can have it all' talk." Just about all of the women in that room planned to combine careers and family in some way. But almost all assumed and accepted that they would have to make compromises that the men in their lives were far less likely to have to make.

The striking gap between the responses I heard from those young women (and others like them) and the responses I heard from my peers and associates prompted me to write this article. See p. 145 for tips on indicating the importance of a claim. Women of my generation have clung to the feminist credo we were raised with, even as our ranks have been steadily thinned by unresolvable tensions between family and career, because we are determined not to drop the flag for the next generation. But when many members of the younger generation have stopped listening, on the grounds that glibly repeating "you can have it all" is simply airbrushing reality, it is time to talk.

I still strongly believe that women can "have it all" (and that men can too). I believe that we can "have it all at the same time." But not today, not with the way America's economy and society are currently structured. My experiences over the past three years have forced me to confront a number of uncomfortable facts that need to be widely acknowledged—and quickly changed.

Before my service in government, I'd spent my career in academia: as a law professor and then as the dean of Princeton's Woodrow Wilson School of Public and International Affairs.* Both were demanding jobs, but I had the ability to set my own schedule most of the time. I could be with my kids when I needed to be, and still get the work done. I had to travel frequently, but I found I could make up for that with an extended period at home or a family vacation.

I knew that I was lucky in my career choice, but I had no idea 10 how lucky until I spent two years in Washington within a rigid bureaucracy, even with bosses as understanding as Hillary Clinton and her chief of staff, Cheryl Mills. My workweek started at 4:20 on Monday morning, when I got up to get the 5:30 train from Trenton to Washington. It ended late on Friday, with the train home. In between, the days were crammed with meetings, and when the meetings stopped, the writing work began—a never-ending stream of memos, reports, and comments on other people's drafts. For two years, I never left the office early enough to go to any stores other than those open 24 hours, which meant that everything from dry cleaning to hair appointments to Christmas

*__Woodrow Wilson School__   Now called the Princeton School of Public and International Affairs.

shopping had to be done on weekends, amid children's sporting events, music lessons, family meals, and conference calls. I was entitled to four hours of vacation per pay period, which came to one day of vacation a month. And I had it better than many of my peers in D.C.; Secretary Clinton deliberately came in around 8 a.m. and left around 7 p.m., to allow her close staff to have morning and evening time with their families (although of course she worked earlier and later, from home).

In short, the minute I found myself in a job that is typical for the vast majority of working women (and men), working long hours on someone else's schedule, I could no longer be both the parent and the professional I wanted to be—at least not with a child experiencing a rocky adolescence. I realized what should have perhaps been obvious: having it all, at least for me, depended almost entirely on what type of job I had. The flip side is the harder truth: having it all was not possible in many types of jobs, including high government office—at least not for very long.

I am hardly alone in this realization. Michèle Flournoy stepped down after three years as undersecretary of defense for policy, the third-highest job in the department, to spend more time at home with her three children, two of whom are teenagers. Karen Hughes left her position as the counselor to President George W. Bush after a year and a half in Washington to go home to Texas for the sake of her family. Mary Matalin, who spent two years as an assistant to Bush and the counselor to Vice President Dick Cheney before stepping down to spend more time with her daughters, wrote: "Having control over your schedule is the only way that women who want to have a career and a family can make it work."

Yet the decision to step down from a position of power— to value family over professional advancement, even for a time—is directly at odds with the prevailing social pressures on career professionals in the United States. One phrase says it all about current attitudes toward work and family, particularly among elites. In Washington, "leaving to spend time with your family" is a euphemism for being fired. This understanding is so ingrained that when Flournoy announced her resignation last December, *The New York Times* covered her decision as follows:

> Ms. Flournoy's announcement surprised friends and a number of Pentagon officials, but all said they took her reason for resignation at face value and not as a standard Washington excuse for an official who has in reality been forced out. "I can absolutely and unequivocally state that her decision to step down has nothing to do with anything other than her commitment to her family," said Doug Wilson, a top Pentagon spokesman. "She has loved this job and people here love her."

Think about what this "standard Washington excuse" implies: it is so unthinkable that an official would *actually* step down to spend time with his or her family that this must be a cover for something else. How could anyone voluntarily leave the circles of power for the responsibilities of parenthood? Depending on one's vantage point, it is either ironic or maddening that this view abides in the nation's capital, despite the ritual commitments to "family values" that are part of every political campaign. Regardless, this sentiment makes true work-life balance exceptionally difficult. But it cannot change unless top women speak out.

Only recently have I begun to appreciate the extent to which many young professional women feel under assault by women my age and older. After I gave a recent speech in New York, several women in their late 60s or early 70s came up to tell me how glad and proud they were to see me speaking as a foreign-policy expert. A couple of them went on, however, to contrast my career with the path being traveled by "younger women today." One expressed dismay that many younger women "are just not willing to get out there and do it." Said another, unaware of the circumstances of my recent job change: "They think they have to choose between having a career and having a family."

A similar assumption underlies Facebook Chief Operating 15 Officer Sheryl Sandberg's widely publicized 2011 commencement speech at Barnard, and her earlier TED talk, in which she lamented the dismally small number of women at the top and advised young women not to "leave before you leave." When a woman starts thinking about having children, Sandberg said, "she doesn't raise her hand anymore . . . She starts leaning back [ellipsis in original]." Although couched in terms of encouragement, Sandberg's exhortation contains more than a note of reproach. We who have made it to the top, or are striving to get there, are essentially saying to the women in the generation behind us: "What's the matter with you?"

They have an answer that we don't want to hear. After the speech I gave in New York, I went to dinner with a group of 30-somethings. I sat across from two vibrant women, one of whom worked at the UN and the other at a big New York law firm. As nearly always happens in these situations, they soon began asking me about work-life balance. When I told them I was writing this article, the lawyer said, "I look for role models and can't find any." She said the women in her firm who had become partners and taken on management positions had made tremendous sacrifices, "many of which they don't even seem to realize . . . They take two years off when their kids are young but then work like crazy to get back on track professionally, which means that they see their kids when they are toddlers but not teenagers, or really barely at all [ellipsis in original]." Her friend nodded, mentioning the top professional women she knew, all of whom essentially relied on round-the-clock nannies. Both were very clear that they did not want that life, but could not figure out how to combine professional success and satisfaction with a real commitment to family.

I realize that I am blessed to have been born in the late 1950s instead of the early 1930s, as my mother was, or the beginning of the 20th century, as my grandmothers were. My mother built a successful and rewarding career as a professional artist largely in the years after my brothers and I left home—and after being told in her 20s that she could not go to medical school, as her father had done and her brother would go on to do, because, of course, she was going to get married. I owe my own freedoms and opportunities to the pioneering generation of women ahead of me—the women now in their 60s, 70s, and 80s who faced overt sexism of a kind I see only when watching *Mad Men*, and who knew that the only way to make it as a woman was to act exactly like a man. To admit to, much less act on, maternal longings would have been fatal to their careers.

But precisely thanks to their progress, a different kind of conversation is now possible. It is time for women in leadership positions to recognize that although we are still blazing trails and breaking ceilings, many of us are also reinforcing a falsehood: that "having it all" is, more than anything, a function of personal determination. As Kerry Rubin and Lia Macko, the authors of *Midlife Crisis at 30*, their cri de coeur for Gen-X and Gen-Y women, put it:

> What we discovered in our research is that while the empowerment part of the equation has been loudly celebrated, there has been very little honest discussion among women of our age about the real barriers and flaws that still exist in the system despite the opportunities we inherited.

I am well aware that the majority of American women face problems far greater than any discussed in this article. I am writing for my demographic—highly educated, well-off women who are privileged enough to have choices in the first place. We may not have choices about whether to do paid work, as dual incomes have become indispensable. But we have choices about the type and tempo of the work we do. We are the women who could be leading, and who should be equally represented in the leadership ranks.

Millions of other working women face much more difficult life 20 circumstances. Some are single mothers; many struggle to find any job; others support husbands who cannot find jobs. Many cope with a work life in which good day care is either unavailable or very expensive; school schedules do not match work schedules; and schools themselves are failing to educate their children. Many of these women are worrying not about having it all, but rather about holding on to what they do have. And although women as a group have made substantial gains in wages, educational attainment, and prestige over the past three decades, the economists Justin Wolfers and Betsey Stevenson have shown that women are less happy today than their predecessors were in 1972, both in absolute terms and relative to men.

The best hope for improving the lot of all women, and for closing what Wolfers and Stevenson call a "new gender gap"—measured by well-being rather than wages—is to close the leadership gap: to elect a woman president and 50 women senators; to ensure that women are equally represented in the ranks of corporate executives and judicial leaders. Only when women wield power in sufficient numbers will we create a society that genuinely works for all women. That will be a society that works for everyone.

. . .

Rediscovering the Pursuit of Happiness

One of the most complicated and surprising parts of my journey out of Washington was coming to grips with what I really wanted. I had opportunities to stay on, and I could have tried to work out an arrangement allowing me to spend more time at home. I might have been able to get my family to join me in Washington for a year; I might have been able to get classified technology installed at my house the way Jim Steinberg did; I might have been able to commute only four days a week instead of five. (While this last change would have still left me very little time at home, given the intensity of my job, it might have made the job doable for another year or two.) But I realized that I didn't just *need* to go home. Deep down, I *wanted* to go home. I wanted to be able to spend time with my children in the last few years that they are likely to live at home, crucial years for their development into responsible, productive, happy, and caring adults. But also irreplaceable years for me to enjoy the simple pleasures of parenting—baseball games, piano recitals, waffle breakfasts, family trips, and goofy rituals. My older son is doing very well these days, but even when he gives us a hard time, as all teenagers do, being home to shape his choices and help him make good decisions is deeply satisfying.

The flip side of my realization is captured in Rubin and Macko's ruminations on the importance of bringing the different parts of their lives together as 30-year-old women:

> If we didn't start to learn how to integrate our personal, social, and professional lives, we were about five years away from morphing into the angry woman on the other side of a mahogany desk who questions her staff's work ethic after standard 12-hour workdays, before heading home to eat moo shoo pork in her lonely apartment.

Women have contributed to the fetish of the one-dimensional life, albeit by necessity. The pioneer generation of feminists walled off their personal lives from their professional personas to ensure that they could never be discriminated against for a lack of commitment to their work. When I was a law student in the 1980s, many women who were then climbing the legal hierarchy in New York firms told me that they never admitted to taking time out for a child's doctor appointment or school performance, but instead invented a much more neutral excuse.

Today, however, women in power can and should change that environment, although change is not easy. When I became dean of the Woodrow Wilson School, in 2002, I decided that one of the advantages of being a woman in power was that I could help change the norms by deliberately talking about my children and my desire to have a balanced life. Thus, I would end faculty meetings at 6 p.m. by saying that I had to go home for dinner; I would also make clear to all student organizations that I would not come to dinner with them, because I needed to be home from six to eight, but that I would often be willing to come back after eight for a meeting. I also once told the Dean's Advisory Committee that the associate dean would chair the next session so I could go to a parent-teacher conference.

After a few months of this, several female assistant professors showed up in my office quite agitated. "You *have* to stop talking about your kids," one said. "You are not showing the gravitas that people expect from a dean, which is particularly damaging precisely because you are the first woman dean of the school." I told them that I was doing it deliberately and continued my practice, but it is interesting that gravitas and parenthood don't seem to go together.

Ten years later, whenever I am introduced at a lecture or other speaking engagement, I insist that the person introducing me mention that I have two sons. It seems odd to me to list degrees, awards, positions, and interests and *not* include the dimension of my life that is most important to me—and takes an enormous amount of my time. As Secretary Clinton once said in a television interview in Beijing when the interviewer asked her about Chelsea's upcoming wedding: "That's my real life." But I notice that my male introducers are typically uncomfortable when I make the request. They frequently say things like "And she particularly wanted me to mention that she has two sons"—thereby drawing attention to the unusual nature of my request, when my entire purpose is to make family references routine and normal in professional life.

This does not mean that you should insist that your colleagues spend time cooing over pictures of your baby or listening to the prodigious accomplishments of your kindergartner. It does mean that if you are late coming in one week, because it is your turn to drive the kids to school, that you be honest about what you are doing. Indeed, Sheryl Sandberg recently acknowledged not only that she leaves work at 5:30 to have dinner with her family, but also that for many years she did not dare make this admission, even though she would of course make up the work time later in the evening. Her willingness to speak out now is a strong step in the right direction.

Seeking out a more balanced life is not a women's issue; balance would be better for us all. Bronnie Ware, an Australian blogger who worked for years in palliative care and is the author of the 2011 book *The Top Five Regrets of the Dying*, writes that the regret she heard most often was "I wish I'd had the courage to live a life true to myself, not the life others expected of me." The second-most-common regret was "I wish I didn't work so hard." She writes: "This came from every male patient that I nursed. They missed their children's youth and their partner's companionship."

Juliette Kayyem, who several years ago left the Department 30 of Homeland Security soon after her husband, David Barron, left a high position in the Justice Department, says their joint decision to leave Washington and return to Boston sprang from their desire to work on the "happiness project," meaning quality time with their three children. (She borrowed the term from her friend Gretchen Rubin, who wrote a best-selling book and now runs a blog with that name.)

It's time to embrace a national happiness project. As a daughter of Charlottesville, Virginia, the home of Thomas Jefferson and the university he founded, I grew up with the Declaration of Independence in my blood. Last I checked, he did not declare American independence in the name of life, liberty, and professional success. Let us rediscover the pursuit of happiness, and let us start at home.

Innovation Nation

As I write this, I can hear the reaction of some readers to many of the proposals in this essay: It's all fine and well for a tenured professor to write about flexible working hours, investment intervals, and family-comes-first management. But what about the real world? Most American women cannot demand these things, particularly in a bad economy, and their employers have little incentive to grant them voluntarily. Indeed, the most frequent reaction I get in putting forth these ideas is that when the choice is whether to hire a man who will work whenever and wherever needed, or a woman who needs more flexibility, choosing the man will add more value to the company.

In fact, while many of these issues are hard to quantify and measure precisely, the statistics seem to tell a different story. A seminal study of 527 U.S. companies, published in the *Academy of Management Journal* in 2000, suggests that "organizations with more extensive work-family policies have higher perceived firm-level performance" among their industry peers. These findings accorded with a 2003 study conducted by Michelle Arthur at the University of New Mexico. Examining 130 announcements of family-friendly policies in *The Wall Street Journal*, Arthur found that the announcements alone significantly improved share prices. In 2011, a study on flexibility in the workplace by Ellen Galinsky, Kelly Sakai, and Tyler Wigton of the Families and Work Institute showed that increased flexibility correlates positively with job engagement, job satisfaction, employee retention, and employee health.

This is only a small sampling from a large and growing literature trying to pin down the relationship between family-friendly policies and economic performance. Other scholars have concluded that good family policies attract better talent, which in turn raises productivity, but that the policies themselves have no impact on productivity. Still others argue that results attributed to these policies are actually a function of good management overall. What is evident, however, is that many firms that recruit and train well-educated professional women are aware that when a woman leaves because of bad work-family balance, they are losing the money and time they invested in her.

Even the legal industry, built around the billable hour, is 35 taking notice. Deborah Epstein Henry, a former big-firm litigator, is now the president of Flex-Time Lawyers, a national consulting firm focused partly on strategies for the retention of female attorneys. In her book *Law and Reorder*, published by the

American Bar Association in 2010, she describes a legal profession "where the billable hour no longer works"; where attorneys, judges, recruiters, and academics all agree that this system of compensation has perverted the industry, leading to brutal work hours, massive inefficiency, and highly inflated costs. The answer—already being deployed in different corners of the industry—is a combination of alternative fee structures, virtual firms, women-owned firms, and the outsourcing of discrete legal jobs to other jurisdictions. Women, and Generation X and Y lawyers more generally, are pushing for these changes on the supply side; clients determined to reduce legal fees and increase flexible service are pulling on the demand side. Slowly, change is happening.

At the core of all this is self-interest. Losing smart and motivated women not only diminishes a company's talent pool; it also reduces the return on its investment in training and mentoring. In trying to address these issues, some firms are finding out that women's ways of working may just be better ways of working, for employees and clients alike.

Experts on creativity and innovation emphasize the value of encouraging nonlinear thinking and cultivating randomness by taking long walks or looking at your environment from unusual angles. In their new book, *A New Culture of Learning: Cultivating the Imagination for a World of Constant Change*, the innovation gurus John Seely Brown and Douglas Thomas write, "We believe that connecting play and imagination may be the single most important step in unleashing the new culture of learning."

Space for play and imagination is exactly what emerges when rigid work schedules and hierarchies loosen up. Skeptics should consider the "California effect." California is the cradle of American innovation—in technology, entertainment, sports, food, and lifestyles. It is also a place where people take leisure as seriously as they take work; where companies like Google deliberately encourage play, with Ping-Pong tables, light sabers, and policies that require employees to spend one day a week working on whatever they wish. Charles Baudelaire wrote: "Genius is nothing more nor less than childhood recovered at will." Google apparently has taken note.

No parent would mistake child care for childhood. Still, seeing the world anew through a child's eyes can be a powerful source of stimulation. When the Nobel laureate Thomas Schelling wrote *The Strategy of Conflict*, a classic text applying game theory to conflicts among nations, he frequently drew on child-rearing for examples of when deterrence might succeed or fail. "It may be easier to articulate the peculiar difficulty of constraining [a ruler] by the use of threats," he wrote, "when one is fresh from a vain attempt at using threats to keep a small child from hurting a dog or a small dog from hurting a child."

The books I've read with my children, the silly movies I've 40 watched, the games I've played, questions I've answered, and people I've met while parenting have broadened my world. Another axiom of the literature on innovation is that the more often people with different perspectives come together, the more likely creative ideas are to emerge. Giving workers the ability to integrate their non-work lives with their work— whether they spend that time mothering or marathoning—will open the door to a much wider range of influences and ideas.

Enlisting Men

Perhaps the most encouraging news of all for achieving the sorts of changes that I have proposed is that men are joining the cause. In commenting on a draft of this article, Martha Minow, the dean of the Harvard Law School, wrote me that one change she has observed during 30 years of teaching law at Harvard is that today many young men are asking questions about how they can manage a work-life balance. And more systematic research on Generation Y confirms that many more men than in the past are asking questions about how they are going to integrate active parenthood with their professional lives.

Abstract aspirations are easier than concrete trade-offs, of course. These young men have not yet faced the question of whether they are prepared to give up that more prestigious clerkship or fellowship, decline a promotion, or delay their professional goals to spend more time with their children and to support their partner's career.

Yet once work practices and work culture begin to evolve, those changes are likely to carry their own momentum. Kara Owen, a British foreign-service officer who worked a London job from Dublin, wrote me in an e-mail:

> I think the culture on flexible working started to change the minute the Board of Management (who were all men at the time) started to work flexibly—quite a few of them started working one day a week from home.

Men have, of course, become much more involved parents over the past couple of decades, and that, too, suggests broad support for big changes in the way we balance work and family. It is noteworthy that both James Steinberg, deputy secretary of state, and William Lynn, deputy secretary of defense, stepped down two years into the Obama administration so that they could spend more time with their children (for real).

Going forward, women would do well to frame work-family 45 balance in terms of the broader social and economic issues that affect both women and men. After all, we have a new generation of young men who have been raised by full-time working mothers. Let us presume, as I do with my sons, that they will understand "supporting their families" to mean more than earning money.

I have been blessed to work with and be mentored by some extraordinary women. Watching Hillary Clinton in action makes me incredibly proud—of her intelligence, expertise, professionalism, charisma, and command of any audience. I get a similar rush when I see a front-page picture of Christine Lagarde, the managing director of the International Monetary Fund, and Angela Merkel, the chancellor of Germany, deep in conversation about some of the most important issues on the world stage; or of Susan Rice, the U.S. ambassador to the United Nations, standing up forcefully for the Syrian people in the Security Council.

These women are extraordinary role models. If I had a daughter, I would encourage her to look to them, and I want a world in which they are extraordinary but not unusual. Yet I also want a world in which, in Lisa Jackson's* words, "to be a strong woman, you don't have to give up on the things that define you as a woman." That means respecting, enabling, and indeed celebrating the full range of women's choices. "Empowering yourself," Jackson said in a speech at Princeton, "doesn't have to mean rejecting motherhood, or eliminating the nurturing or feminine aspects of who you are."

I gave a speech at Vassar last November and arrived in time to wander the campus on a lovely fall afternoon. It is a place infused with a spirit of community and generosity, filled with

***Jackson** From 2009 until 2013, administrator of the United States Environmental Protection Agency.

benches, walkways, public art, and quiet places donated by alumnae seeking to encourage contemplation and connection. Turning the pages of the alumni magazine (Vassar is now coed), I was struck by the entries of older alumnae, who greeted their classmates with *Salve* (Latin for "hello") and wrote witty remembrances sprinkled with literary allusions. Theirs was a world in which women wore their learning lightly; their news is mostly of their children's accomplishments. Many of us look back on that earlier era as a time when it was fine to joke that women went to college to get an "M.R.S." And many women of my generation abandoned the Seven Sisters as soon as the formerly all-male Ivy League universities became coed. I would never return to the world of segregated sexes and rampant discrimination. But now is the time to revisit the assumption that women must rush to adapt to the "man's world" that our mothers and mentors warned us about.

I continually push the young women in my classes to speak more. They must gain the confidence to value their own insights and questions, and to present them readily. My husband agrees, but he actually tries to get the young men in his classes to act more like the women—to speak less and listen more. If women are ever to achieve real equality as leaders, then we have to stop accepting male behavior and male choices as the default and the ideal. We must insist on changing social policies and bending career tracks to accommodate *our* choices, too. We have the power to do it if we decide to, and we have many men standing beside us.

We'll create a better society in the process, for *all* women. We may need to put a woman in the White House before we are able to change the conditions of the women working at Walmart. But when we do, we will stop talking about whether women can have it all. We will properly focus on how we can help all Americans have healthy, happy, productive lives, valuing the people they love as much as the success they seek.

Joining the Conversation

1. According to Anne-Marie Slaughter, women can "'have it all.' . . . But not today, not with the way America's economy and society are currently structured" (paragraph 8). Summarize her "I say," noting the reasons and evidence she gives to support her claims.

2. In paragraph 19, Slaughter entertains a possible objection to her argument, saying that she is "well aware that the majority of American women face problems far greater than any discussed in this article." How does she answer this objection?

3. This essay consists of four sections: Redefining the Arc of a Successful Career, Rediscovering the Pursuit of Happiness, Innovation Nation, and Enlisting Men. Summarize each section in a sentence or two. Put yourself in Slaughter's shoes; your summary should be true to what she says. (See pp. 33–35 for guidance in writing this kind of summary.)

4. Slaughter claims that most young men today have not yet had to decide between accepting a promotion or other professional opportunity and delaying their own goals "to spend more time with their children and to support their partner's career" (paragraph 42). What would Richard Dorment (pp. 694–714) say to that?

5. Write a paragraph stating your own thoughts and perceptions on mixing family and career. Given Slaughter's arguments, how do you think she'd respond to what you say?

Why Men Still Can't Have It All

RICHARD DORMENT

—◻—

Lately, the raging debate about issues of "work-life balance" has focused on whether or not women can "have it all." Entirely lost in this debate is the growing strain of work-life balance on men, who today are feeling the competing demands of work and home as much or more than women. And the truth is as shocking as it is obvious: No one can have it all. Any questions?

THE BABY HAS A HEARTBEAT. The ultrasound shows ten fuzzy fingers and ten fuzzy toes and a tiny crescent-moon mouth that will soon let out the first of many wails. We have chosen not to find out the gender, and when the question comes, as it does every day, we say we have no preference. Ten fingers, ten toes. A wail in the delivery room would be nice. But in private, just us, we talk. About the pros and cons of boys versus girls, and about whether it would be better, more advantageous, to

---

RICHARD DORMENT is editor in chief for *Men's Health*. He was a senior editor for *Wired* and *Esquire* and has been a guest on television and radio programs including *Today, CNN Newsroom, Here and Now,* and *Upfront and Straightforward*. This essay first appeared in the June/July 2013 issue of *Esquire*.

be born a boy or a girl right now. It's a toss-up, or maybe just a draw—impossible to say that a boy *or* a girl born in America in 2013 has any conspicuous advantages because of his or her gender.

Consider the facts: Nearly 60 percent of the bachelor's degrees in this country today go to women. Same number for graduate degrees. There are about as many women in the workforce as men, and according to Hanna Rosin's 2012 book, *The End of Men*, of the fifteen professions projected to grow the fastest over the coming years, twelve are currently dominated by women. Per a 2010 study by James Chung of Reach Advisors, unmarried childless women under thirty and with full-time jobs earn 8 percent more than their male peers in 147 out of 150 of the largest U.S. cities. The accomplishments that underlie those numbers are real and world-historic, and through the grueling work of generations of women, men and women are as equal as they have ever been. Adding to that the greater male predisposition to ADHD, alcoholism, and drug abuse, women have nothing but momentum coming out of young adulthood—the big mo!—and then . . .

Well, what exactly? Why don't women hold more than 15 percent of *Fortune* 500 executive-officer positions in America? Why are they stalled below 20 percent of Congress? Why does the average woman earn only seventy-seven pennies for every dollar made by the average man? Childbirth plays a role, knocking ambitious women off their professional stride for months (if not years) at a time while their male peers go chug-chug-chugging along, but then why do some women still make it to the top while others fall by the wayside? Institutional sexism and pay discrimination are still ugly realities, but with the millions in annual penalties levied on offending businesses . . . they have become increasingly, and thankfully, uncommon.

College majors count (women still dominate education, men engineering), as do career choices, yet none of these on their own explains why the opportunity gap between the sexes has all but closed yet a stark achievement gap persists.

For a fuller explanation, the national conversation of late has settled on a single issue—work-life balance—with two voices in particular dominating: The first belongs to former State Department policy chief Anne-Marie Slaughter, whose essay "Why Women Still Can't Have It All" was the most widely read story ever on the *Atlantic*'s web site and landed her a book deal and spots on *Today* and *Colbert*. Slaughter's twelve-thousand-word story relies on personal anecdotes mixed with wonk talk: "I still strongly believe that women can 'have it all' (and that men can too). I believe that we can 'have it all at the same time.' But not today, not with the way America's economy and society are currently structured." The scarcity of

female leaders to effect public and corporate change on behalf of
women; the inflexibility of the traditional workday; the prevalence of what she calls "'time macho'—a relentless competition
to work harder, stay later, pull more all-nighters, travel around
the world and bill the extra hours that the international date
line affords you." All these factors conspire to deprive women
of "it all." (The "it" in question being like Potter Stewart's
definition of pornography: You know it when you have it.)

The second, and altogether more grown-up, voice belongs 5
to Facebook COO Sheryl Sandberg, whose "sort of feminist"
manifesto *Lean In* urges women to command a seat at any table
of their choosing. Like Slaughter, Sandberg references the usual
systemic challenges, but what it really boils down to, Sandberg
argues, is what Aretha Franklin and Annie Lennox prescribed
back in the eighties: Sisters Doin' It for Themselves. Sandberg
encourages women to negotiate harder, be more assertive, and
forget about being liked and concentrate instead on letting 'er rip.
She believes that women can, and should, determine the pace
and scope of their own careers, and for her audacity in assigning
some agency to the women of America, her critics (Slaughter
among them) say she blames women for their failure to rise far-
ther, faster, rather than the real culprits: society, corporations,
and men (which is to say: men, men, and men). Commenting
on the *Lean In* debate in a blog for *The New York Times,* Gail
Collins asked, "How do you give smart, accomplished, ambitious
women the same opportunities as men to reach their goals? What
about universal preschool and after-school programs? What
about changing the corporate mind-set about the time commitment it takes to move up the ladder? What about having more
husbands step up and take the major load?"

Her questions echo a 2010 *Newsweek* cover story, "Men's Lib,"
which ended with an upper: "If men embraced parental leave,

women would be spared the stigma of the 'mommy track'—and the professional penalties (like lower pay) that come along with it. If men were involved fathers, more kids might stay in school, steer clear of crime, and avoid poverty as adults. And if the country achieved gender parity in the workplace—an optimal balance of fully employed men and women—the gross domestic product would grow by as much as 9 percent. . . . Ultimately, [it] boils down to a simple principle: in a changing world, men should do whatever it takes to contribute their fair share at home and at work."

Two men wrote that, incidentally, which must make it true, and among those who traffic in gender studies, it is something of a truth universally acknowledged: Men are to blame for pretty much everything. And I freely admit, we do make for a compelling target. Men have oppressed their wives and sisters and daughters for pretty much all of recorded history, and now women are supposed to trust us to share everything 50-50?

Allow me to paint another picture. One in which women are asked to make the same personal sacrifices as men past and present—too much time away from home, too many weekends at the computer, too much inconvenient travel—but then claim some special privilege in their hardship. One in which universal pre-school and after-school programs would be a boon to all parents (and not, as Collins suggests, simply to women). In which men spend more time with their children, and are more involved with their home lives, than ever before. In which men work just as hard at their jobs, if not harder, than ever before. In which men now report higher rates of work-life stress than women do. In which men are tormented by the lyrics of "Cat's in the Cradle." In which men are being told, in newspapers and books, on web sites and TV shows, that they are the problem, that they need to help out, when, honestly folks, they're doing the best they can. In which men like me, and possibly you, open their eyes in the morning and want it all—*everything!*—only to close their eyes at night knowing that only a fool could ever expect such a thing.

My wife makes more money than I do. We majored in the same thing at the same college at the same time, and when I chose to go into journalism, she chose to go to law school. She works longer hours, shoulders weightier responsibilities, and faces greater (or at least more reliable) prospects for long-term success, all of which are direct results of choices that we made in our early twenties. She does more of the heavy lifting with our young son than I do, but I do as much as I can. (Someone else watches him while we are at work.) I do a lot of cooking and cleaning around our house. So does she. I don't keep score (and she says she doesn't), and it's hard to imagine how our life would work if we weren't both giving every day our all.

According to a study released in March by the Pew Research 10 Center, household setups like ours are increasingly the norm: 60 percent of two-parent homes with kids under the age of eighteen are made up of dual-earning couples (i.e., two working parents). On any given week in such a home, women put in more time than men doing housework (sixteen hours to nine) and more time with child care (twelve to seven). These statistics provoke outrage among the "fair share" crowd, and there is a sense, even among the most privileged women, that they are getting a raw deal. (In April, Michelle Obama referred to herself as a "single mother" before clarifying: "I shouldn't say single— as a busy mother, sometimes, you know, when you've got a husband who is president, it can feel a little single." Because really: The president should spend more time making sure the First Lady feels supported.)

But the complete picture reveals a more complex and equitable reality.

Men in dual-income couples work outside the home eleven more hours a week than their working wives or partners do (forty-two to thirty-one), and when you look at the total weekly workload, including paid work outside the home and unpaid work inside the home, men and women are putting in roughly the same number of hours: fifty-eight hours for men and fifty-nine for women.

How you view those numbers depends in large part on your definition of work, but it's not quite as easy as saying men aren't pulling their weight around the house. (Spending eleven fewer hours at home and with the kids doesn't mean working dads are freeloaders any more than spending eleven fewer hours at work makes working moms slackers.) These are practical accommodations that reflect real-time conditions on the ground, and rather than castigate men, one might consider whether those extra hours on the job provide the financial cover the family needs so that women can spend more time with the kids.

Also, according to women in the Pew study, it seems to be working out well. Working mothers in dual-earning couples are more likely to say they're very or pretty happy with life right now than their male partners are (93 percent to 87 percent); if anything, it's men who are twice as likely to say they're unhappy. (Pew supplied *Esquire* with data specific to dual-income couples that is not part of its published report. There is plenty of data relating to other household arrangements—working father and stay-at-home mom; working mother and stay-at-home dad; same-sex households—but since the focus of Slaughter, Sandberg, et al. is on the struggles of working mothers, and most working mothers are coupled with working fathers, the dual-income data set seems most relevant to examine here.)

Ellen Galinsky has been studying the American workplace 15
for more than thirty years. A married mother of two grown
kids with a background in child education and zero tolerance
for bullshit, she cofounded the Families and Work Institute
in part to chart how the influx of women in American offices
and factories would affect family dynamics. "In 1977," she says,
"there was a Department of Labor study that asked people, 'How
much interference do you feel between your work and your family life?' and men's work-family conflict was a lot lower than
women's." She saw the numbers begin to shift in the late 1990s,
and "by 2008, 60 percent of fathers in dual-earning couples
were experiencing some or a lot of conflict compared to about
47 percent of women. I would go into meetings with business
leaders and report the fact that men's work-family conflict was
higher than women's, and people in the room—who were so
used to being worried about women's advancement—couldn't
believe it."

What they couldn't believe was decades of conventional
wisdom—men secure and confident in the workplace, women
somewhat less so—crumbling away as more and more fathers
began to invest more of their time and energy into their home
lives. Though they still lag behind women in hours clocked at
the kitchen sink, men do more than twice as much cooking and
cleaning as they did fifty years ago, which probably comes as a
shock to older women who would famously come home from
work to a "second shift" of housework. In reporting her book,
Big Girls Don't Cry, a study of women's roles in the 2008 election, Rebecca Traister interviewed dozens of high-achieving
women who were in the thick of second-wave feminism and
encountered the generation gap for herself. "I remember one
day, right before Thanksgiving, a woman who had grown children said something like 'I would love to keep talking to you but

I have to start my two-day slog to Thanksgiving.' And I said very lightly, 'Oh, my husband does the cooking in our house.' This woman then got very serious, as if she had never heard of such a thing. For people [in their thirties], isn't it totally normal for guys to do a lot of cooking? In fact it's one of the things about today—dudes love food, right? But it was so foreign to her."

In speaking with a variety of men for this article, I found that most men say they share responsibilities as much as circumstances allow. One of the men who spoke with me, Dave from Atherton, California, runs a successful business, and both he and his wife (a fellow technology executive) say that they split their family duties 50-50. "We have a Google calendar that we share so that everyone is on the same page, and on the weekend, we plan out our week: who's doing what, who's driving the kids which day, what dinner looks like each night during the week."

Yet Dave still considers himself an anomaly. "There is still this expectation that women are going to do the majority of the housework, and deal with schools and stuff, while men can just make it home for dinner and show up at sporting events and be like, 'Wow, I'm being a great father.' It is a real issue, and it is something you really have to work at. You have to try and make sure that you're doing the other stuff around the house in a way that's fair and equal."

He makes a valid point, and in trying to figure out why men don't do more around the house, we could discuss any number of factors—men generally spend more time at work, out of the home, than women do, so they don't have as much time for chores; women are inherently more fastidious; men are lazy and/or have a higher threshold for living in filth—but the most compelling argument comes from writer Jessica Grose in *The New Republic*. "Women are more driven to keep a clean house because they know they—before their male partners—will be judged for having a dirty one." Rather than confront or ignore paternalistic expectations, some women seem willing to cede to them, and this whiff of put-upon-ness recalls something Slaughter acknowledged in an online chat with readers following her article's publication: "SO MUCH OF THIS IS ABOUT WHAT WE FEEL, or rather WHAT WE ARE MADE TO FEEL by the reactions of those around us." Between the all-caps (hers) and the sentiments expressed, this writing wouldn't be out of place on a teenage blog, and as anyone who's ever argued with a teenager knows, it's hard to reason with feelings.

However, I will try. The *validation of one's feelings* is the language of therapy, which is to say that it is how we all talk now. This is not to denigrate the language or the feelings; it is only to say that to use one's feelings as evidence of an injury is no way to advance a serious cause. And to imply that one has been *made* to feel any way at all— well, no grown man has ever won that argument before.

See p. 144 for ways to ward off potential misunderstandings.

A final point about housework: It is not always as simple as men volunteering to do what needs to be done. To give a small, vaguely pitiful example from my own life: We share laundry duty in my house, and yet whenever I'm through folding a pile of clothes, my wife will then refold everything, quietly and without comment. This used to annoy me—why do I even bother? or, conversely, Is this the Army?—but now it mostly amuses me. When I press her on it, she tells me that I'm doing it wrong, and this too used to annoy me, until I realized that it wasn't really about me. "If I've talked to one group of people about this, I've talked to hundreds," says Galinsky. "Women will say 'Support me more,' and men will say 'But you're telling me I'm doing it wrong.' I wouldn't say it's biological, because I'm not a biologist, but it feels biological to me in that it's very hard to let someone else do something different, because it might mean that the way you're doing it isn't right." When I asked Galinsky if this could explain why a wife would refold a pile of laundry that her husband had just done a perfectly good job folding, she laughed. "Exactly."

What you're about to read is a passage from "Why Women Still Can't Have It All," and though it's long and windy, I feel the need to quote from as much of it as possible. You will understand why:

> The proposition that women can have high-powered careers as long as their husbands or partners are willing to share the parenting load equally (or disproportionately) assumes that most women will *feel* as comfortable as men do about being away from their children, as long as their partner is home with them. . . . From years of conversations and observations . . . I've come to believe that men and women respond quite differently when problems at home force them to recognize that their absence is hurting a child, or at least that their presence would likely help. I do not believe fathers love their children any less than mothers do, but men do seem more likely to choose their job at a cost to their family, while women seem more likely to choose their family at a cost to their job.

(Dr. Slaughter, you had me at "I do not believe fathers love their children any less than mothers do. . . .")

Since Slaughter doesn't provide any evidence to support her claim, it's impossible to say whether the men she's referring to are the sole breadwinners in the family (meaning: the ones who feel the intense weight and pressure of being what one writer described as "one job away from poverty") or are in two-income households, or what, but it's worth keeping in mind that this comes from a person whose husband, by her own admission, sacrificed much in his own academic career to do the heavy lifting with their children, all so she could pursue her dream job and then complain about it, bitterly, in the pages of a national magazine.

The trouble with probing men's and women's emotional relationships with their children is that the subject is fraught with stereotypes and prone to specious generalities (see above), but here goes: In my own experience as both son and father, I've learned that one parent's relationship with a child (and vice versa) isn't inherently richer or deeper than the other parent's. It's just different, and with more and more fathers spending more and more time with their kids today—nearly three times as much as they did in 1965—that has become more true than ever. "There is a dramatic cultural shift among millennial and Gen X-ers in wanting to be involved fathers," says Galinsky. "And I don't just think it's just women who are telling men they need to share. Men want a different relationship with their children than men have had in the past. . . . They don't want to be stick figures in their children's lives. They don't want it on their tombstone how many hours they billed. That 'Cat's Cradle' song is very much alive and well in the male psyche."

"Men are being judged as fathers now in a way that I think 25 they never have been before," says Traister, and just as women are historically new to the workplace, men are new to the car-pool and negotiating these fresh expectations (their own and others') as they go along. Not only do working fathers from dual-income homes spend just as much time at work as their fathers and grandfathers did (all while putting in many, many more hours with kids and chores), they also spend more time at work than non-fathers. Seven hours more a week, according to Pew, a trend that Galinsky has noticed in her own research and that she attributes to the unshakable, if often illusory, sense of being the breadwinner. "There are these expectations, even among men whose wives bring in 45 percent of family income, that they were still responsible for the family."

There is the matter of guilt and whether women find it harder than men to be away from their children—which, if that's the case, would mean that women looking to advance in the work-place would have heavier emotional baggage than their male peers. Any husband who's watched his wife cry before taking a business trip (and wondering—silently, I hope—to himself, why?) will tell you that men and women have different ways of experiencing and expressing ambivalence, frustration, and, yes, guilt. "I have no idea if it's societal or genetic or whatever," says Dave, the California businessman, "but it's certainly real that I think my wife feels more guilty than I do when she's gone from the kids. There's no question." I can't claim to speak for Men Everywhere, but in the interviews I conducted for this article, nearly every subject admitted to missing his kids on late nights at the office or aching for home while on a business trip, yet they couch any guilt or regret in the context of sacrifice. Chalk this up to social conditioning (men are raised to be the providers, so it's easier for them to be absent) or genetic predisposition (men are not naturally nurturing) or emotional shallowness (men aren't as in touch with their feelings), but there is the sense, down to the man, that missing their kids is the price of doing business.

And so we all do the best we can. Dave and his wife make weekends sacrosanct and family dinners a priority. "My wife famously said she leaves her office at 5:30 so we can be home at 6:00 for dinner, and I do the same thing, though we're both back online doing work after the kids go to bed."

(Dave's last name, by the way, is Goldberg, and his wife is Sheryl Sandberg, and thanks to *Lean In*, she is famous. Goldberg is the CEO of a company named SurveyMonkey, which provides interactive survey tools for the masses, and he helped build it from a twelve-person operation to a staff of more than two hundred and a $1.35 billion valuation. All while splitting parenting responsibilities 50-50 with a really busy wife. They have the means, certainly, but more importantly, the will.)

Speaking of: In her commencement speech for Harvard Business School in 2012, Sandberg addressed an issue that comes up often—men need to do more to support women in the workplace. "It falls upon the men who are graduating today just as much or more than the women not just to talk about gender but to help these women succeed. When they hear a woman is really great at her job but not liked, take a deep breath and ask why. We need to start talking openly about the flexibility all of us need to have both a job and a life."

Among the various ways men can help women, paternity 30 leave is sometimes mentioned as a good place to start, the idea being that if more men took a few weeks off following the birth of a child, they would help remove the professional stigma surrounding maternity leave and level the playing field. Anyone who has watched any woman, much less one with a full-time job, endure third-term pregnancy, delivery, and the long, lonely nights of postpartum life would tell you how necessary a national paid maternity-leave policy is. Expectant and new mothers are put through the physical and emotional wringer, and they need that time to heal without worrying about losing their job or paying the bills. There are really no two ways about it.

Dads, however, are a different and more complicated story. In California, the first state to fund up to six weeks of paid leave for new moms and dads, only 29 percent of those who take it are men, and there have been numerous studies lately exploring why more men aren't taking greater advantage of the ability to stay home. The general consensus is reflected in a paper out of Rutgers University: "Women who ask for family leave are behaving in a more gender normative way, compared with men who request a family leave. . . . Because the concept of work-life balance is strongly gendered, men who request a family leave may also suffer a *femininity stigma*, whereby 'acting like a woman' deprives them of masculine agency (e.g., competence and assertiveness) and impugns them with negative feminine qualities (e.g., weakness and uncertainty)." This is some paleolithic thinking here, starting, for instance, with the idea that "acting like a woman" means anything at all, much less weakness and uncertainty.

I'm lucky enough to work for a company that provides paid paternity leave, but a few days after my son was born, I was back in the office. It's not because I was scared about appearing weak to my mostly male coworkers or employers, and it's not because I was any more wary of losing my job than usual. At work, I had a purpose—things needed to be done, people needed me to do them. At home, watching my wife feed and swaddle our son and then retreat to our bed to get some sleep of her own, I learned what many first-time fathers learn: assuming an absence of any health issues related to child or mother, the first six weeks of a child's life are fairly uneventful for men. A baby eats (with about 80 percent of women today choosing to breast-feed); he poops; he sleeps. There is potential for valuable bonding time, and a new mother could almost certainly use another pair of hands, but a man's presence is not strictly necessary. Baby book after baby book warns parents that new fathers typically feel "left out," and there's a reason for that: because they are typically left out. More and more companies offer paid and unpaid paternity leave, and a man should feel proud to exercise that option if that's what is best for him and his family. Maybe with the next baby I will. Maybe I won't. But when the doctor delivers a newborn to my exhausted, elated wife, I won't kid myself thinking that I, of all people, really deserve a little time off.

In her Harvard speech, Sandberg also evoked the specter of good old-fashioned sexism by claiming that ambitious, assertive women are generally less well liked than ambitious, assertive men. (In her book, she cites a now famous study conducted by a team of Columbia and NYU professors in which two groups were asked to assess two hard-charging executives, a man named Howard and a woman named Heidi, who were identical in every way except their names. Howard was considered the Man. Heidi, the Shrew.) It's a compelling and convincing study, and Sandberg is persuasive when she argues that too many women too often get an eye roll when they open their mouths. Two things I would hasten to add, though. One: Productivity, profitability, drive, and talent trump all. (I'm reminded of Tina Fey's defense of Hillary Clinton in 2008: "She is [a bitch]. So am I. . . . Bitches get stuff done.") Women might suspect that men don't like assertive, confrontational women, which is only half the truth, leading to my next point: that nobody wants to work with a nightmare of either gender. While the Howard-Heidi problem suggests that some men may get a longer leash than some women, the workplace is not every man's for the shitting all over.

"Advertising is a very small world and when you do something like malign the reputation of a girl from the steno pool on her first day, you make it even smaller. Keep it up, and even if you do get my job, you'll never run this place. You'll die in that corner office, a midlevel executive with a little bit of hair who women go home with out of pity. Want to know why? 'Cause no one will like you." Don Draper said that. Not me. And the wisdom he drops on Pete Campbell in the pilot of Mad Men shows that men can be just as vulnerable to office politics as women.

Finally, there is the issue of flex time, with some suggesting 35 that men should demand more options for when and where they can do their work so that women alone aren't penalized for requesting it. It has never been easier to work remotely for many professionals, yet many jobs—and in particular the top jobs, the leadership roles that history (men) has deprived women of in the past—don't have much give to them. Marissa Mayer at Yahoo was dragged into the flex-time debate when she decided that in order to save a struggling business with abysmal morale, she would do away with the company's generous work-from-home policy and require her employees to show up to an office. She was immediately painted as elitist and antiwoman, and it's easy to see why. Even though men and women are equally likely to telecommute, they typically don't place the same value on being able to do so. According to the Pew study, 70 percent of working mothers say a flexible schedule is extremely important to them, compared with just 48 percent of working fathers, and for many of those women (including my wife, who often works well past midnight at a crowded desk in our bedroom), the opportunity to do some work from home is the critical difference between a life that works and one that doesn't. That's what Mayer was messing with when she ordered all hands on deck, and it's what any employer faces when trying to balance family-friendly policies with the sometimes soul-destroying demands of a competitive marketplace.

When Barack Obama entered the White House, he talked about how he wanted his administration to be family-friendly, offering up Sasha and Malia's swing set to staffers so they could bring their own kids to work on the weekends. Rahm Emanuel famously assured him that it would be—"family-friendly to your family."

It was classic Obama—well-meaning, forward-thinking, mindful of the struggles of the common man—undermined by classic Emanuel, which is to say reality. The White House staff would be working at the highest levels of government, investing their love and labor into what can only be described as dream jobs at a time that can only be described as a national nightmare, and if that meant kids and partners had to take the backseat for a year or two, so be it. Man, woman, whoever: Get a shovel and start digging.

Slaughter, a tenured professor at Princeton, came on board as Hillary Clinton's head of policy planning at State, and in her *Atlantic* piece, she describes her grueling workweek in D.C., her weekend commute back to New Jersey, and her ultimate conclusion that "juggling high-level government work with the needs of two teenage boys was not possible." She talked about her struggles to a fellow wonk, Jolynn Shoemaker of Women in International Security, and Shoemaker offered her two cents on high-level foreign-policy positions: "Inflexible schedules, unrelenting travel, and constant pressure to be in the office are common features of these jobs." Slaughter acknowledges that it needn't be as difficult as all that: "Deputy Secretary of State James Steinberg, who shares the parenting of his two young daughters equally with his wife, made getting [secured access to confidential material] at home an immediate priority so that he could leave the office at a reasonable hour and participate in important meetings via videoconferencing if necessary. I wonder how many women in similar positions would be afraid to ask, lest they be seen as insufficiently committed to their jobs."

Slaughter makes an important point here, though probably not the one she intended to make. Steinberg did what he had to do to make a difficult situation work better for him; Slaughter's contention that a woman wouldn't feel as comfortable making the same request may or may not be true, but it doesn't matter. The option was apparently on the table. Fight for it, don't fight for it—it's entirely up to the individual. But don't complain that you never had a choice.

In the end, isn't this what feminism was supposed to be 40 about? Not equality for equality's sake—half of all homes run by men, half of all corporations run by women—but to give each of us, men and women, access to the same array of choices and then the ability to choose for ourselves? And who's to say, whether for reasons biological or sociological, men and women would even want that? When the Pew Research Center asked working mothers and fathers to picture their ideal working situation, 37 percent of women would opt for full time; 50 percent part time; and 11 percent wouldn't have a job at all. (Compare this with men's answers: 75 percent say full time, 15 percent say part time, and 10 percent wouldn't work at all.) Assuming that women had all the flexibility in the world, one of every two working mothers would choose to work part time. Perhaps with guaranteed paid maternity leave, universal daycare, and generous after-school programs, more women would be freed from the constraints of child care and would want to work full time. Or, possibly, they're just happy working part time, one foot in the workplace and one foot in the home. Hard to say.

"I can't stand the kind of paralysis that some people fall into because they're not happy with the choices they've made. You live in a time when there are endless choices. . . . Money certainly helps, and having that kind of financial privilege goes a long way, but you don't even have to have money for it. But you have to work on yourself. . . . Do something!"

Hillary Clinton said that. Not me. And while she wasn't referring to Slaughter in her interview with *Marie Claire*, she offers valuable advice to anyone who's looking to blame someone, or something, for the challenges they face in life. Getting ahead in the workplace is really hard. Getting to the top is really, really hard. And unless you are very fortunate indeed, there will always be somebody smarter, faster, tougher, and ready and willing to take a job if you're not up to the task. It's a grown-up truth, and it bites the big one, but for anyone to pretend otherwise ignores (or simply wishes away) what generations of working men learned the hard way while their wives did the backbreaking work of raising kids and keeping house. Hearing Gail Collins grumble about changing the corporate mind-set (as if competition weren't the soul of capitalism, and capitalism weren't the coin of the realm) or reading Slaughter complain that our society values hard work over family (as if a Puritan work ethic weren't in our national DNA) makes me feel like channeling Tom Hanks in *A League of Their Own*: There's no crying in baseball! If you don't want a high-pressure, high-power, high-paying job that forces you to make unacceptable sacrifices in the rest of your life, don't take the job. Or get another job that doesn't require those sacrifices. And if you can't get another job, take comfort knowing that the guy who sits across from you, the one with kids the same age as yours and a partner who's busting his or her ass to make it work, is probably in the very same boat. We are all equals here.

Then again, I would say that. I'm a man, with a working wife and a busy schedule and a little boy and another baby on the way, and I live with the choices that I've made. That is all I've ever asked for, and it is all I will ever need.

Joining the Conversation

1. Why, in Richard Dorment's view, can men still not "have it all"? What in particular does he mean by "it all," and what evidence does he provide to support his position?

2. In paragraph 33, the author paraphrases Sheryl Sandberg, Facebook's Chief Operating Officer and author of *Lean In: Women, Work, and the Will to Lead*, on the topic of sexism in the workplace. He then writes a response to Sandberg expressing both agreement and disagreement with her argument. What are the main points of Dorment's response? Taking Sandberg's perspective, write a brief counterresponse to Dorment's claims on this point.

3. Dorment published this article in *Esquire*, which calls itself "the magazine for men." How can you tell that he has written his article primarily for a male audience? How might he revise the article, keeping the same basic argument, to appeal to an audience of women?

4. Imagine you have a chance to speak with Dorment about this article. Write out what you'd say, remembering to frame your statement as a response to what he has said. (See Chapter 12 for advice on entering class discussions.)

5. Dorment's writing is quite informal—colorful and in places even irreverent. How does this informality suit his audience and purpose? How does it affect your response? Choose a paragraph in his article and dress it up, rewriting it in more formal, academic language. Which version do you find more appealing, and why?

The Coronavirus Is a Disaster
for Feminism

HELEN LEWIS

———□———

ENOUGH ALREADY. When people try to be cheerful about social distancing and working from home, noting that William Shakespeare and Isaac Newton did some of their best work while England was ravaged by the plague, there is an obvious response: *Neither of them had child-care responsibilities.*

Shakespeare spent most of his career in London, where the theaters were, while his family lived in Stratford-upon-Avon. During the plague of 1606, the playwright was lucky to be spared from the epidemic—his landlady died at the height of the outbreak—and his wife and two adult daughters stayed safely in the Warwickshire countryside. Newton, meanwhile, never married or had children. He saw out the Great Plague of 1665–6 on his family's estate in the east of England, and spent

———

HELEN LEWIS is a London-based journalist who has written for the *Guardian* and the *Sunday Times*. She is the former deputy editor of the *New Statesman* and she is now a staff writer at the *Atlantic*. Her first book, *Difficult Women: A History of Feminism in 11 Fights*, was published in 2020. This article was published in the *Atlantic* in March 2020.

most of his adult life as a fellow at Cambridge University, where his meals and housekeeping were provided by the college.

For those with caring responsibilities, an infectious-disease outbreak is unlikely to give them time to write *King Lear* or develop a theory of optics. A pandemic magnifies all existing inequalities (even as politicians insist this is not the time to talk about anything other than the immediate crisis). Working from home in a white-collar job is easier; employees with salaries and benefits will be better protected; self-isolation is less taxing in a spacious house than a cramped apartment. But one of the most striking effects of the coronavirus will be to send many couples back to the 1950s. Across the world, women's independence will be a silent victim of the pandemic.

Purely as a physical illness, the coronavirus appears to affect women less severely. But in the past few days, the conversation about the pandemic has broadened: We are not just living through a public-health crisis, but an economic one. As much of normal life is suspended for three months or more, job losses are inevitable. At the same time, school closures and household isolation are moving the work of caring for children from the paid economy—nurseries, schools, babysitters—to the unpaid one. The coronavirus smashes up the bargain that so many dual-earner couples have made in the developed world: *We can both work, because someone else is looking after our children.* Instead, couples will have to decide which one of them takes the hit.

Many stories of arrogance are related to this pandemic. Among 5 the most exasperating is the West's failure to learn from history: the Ebola crisis in three African countries in 2014; Zika in 2015–6; and recent outbreaks of SARS, swine flu, and bird flu. Academics who studied these episodes found that they had deep, long-lasting effects on gender equality. "Everybody's income was affected by the Ebola outbreak in West Africa," Julia Smith, a health-policy researcher at Simon Fraser University, told *The New York Times* this month, but "men's income returned to what they had made pre-outbreak faster than women's income." The distorting effects of an epidemic can last for years, Clare Wenham, an assistant professor of global-health policy at the London School of Economics, told me. "We also saw declining rates of childhood vaccination [during Ebola]." Later, when these children contracted preventable diseases, their mothers had to take time off work.

See Chapter 3 for more on how to create a quotation "sandwich."

At an individual level, the choices of many couples over the next few months will make perfect economic sense. What do pandemic patients need? Looking after. What do self-isolating older people need? Looking after. What do children kept home from school need? Looking after. All this looking after—this unpaid caring labor—will fall more heavily on women, because of the existing structure of the workforce. "It's not just about social norms of women performing care roles; it's also about practicalities," Wenham added. "Who is paid less? Who has the flexibility?"

According to the British government's figures, 40 percent of employed women work part-time, compared with only 13 percent of men. In heterosexual relationships, women are more likely to be the lower earners, meaning their jobs are considered a lower priority when disruptions come along. And this particular disruption could last months, rather than weeks. Some women's lifetime earnings will never recover. With the schools closed, many fathers will undoubtedly step up, but that won't be universal.

Despite the mass entry of women into the workforce during the 20th century, the phenomenon of the "second shift" still exists. Across the world, women—including those with jobs—do more housework and have less leisure time than their male partners. Even memes about panic-buying acknowledge that household tasks such as food shopping are primarily shouldered by women. "I'm not afraid of COVID-19 but what is scary, is the lack of common sense people have," reads one of the most popular tweets about the coronavirus crisis. "I'm scared for people who actually need to go to the store & feed their fams but Susan and Karen stocked up for 30 years." The joke only works because "Susan" and "Karen"—stand-in names for suburban moms—are understood to be responsible for household management, rather than, say, Mike and Steve.

Look around and you can see couples already making tough decisions on how to divide up this extra unpaid labor. When I called Wenham, she was self-isolating with two small children; she and her husband were alternating between two-hour shifts of child care and paid work. That is one solution; for others, the division will run along older lines. Dual-income couples might suddenly find themselves living like their grandparents, one homemaker and one breadwinner. "My spouse is a physician in the emergency dept, and is actively treating #coronavirus patients. We just made the difficult decision for him to isolate & move into our garage apartment for the foreseeable future as he continues to treat patients," wrote the Emory University epidemiologist Rachel Patzer, who has a three-week-old baby and two young children. "As I attempt to home school my kids (alone) with a new baby who screams if she isn't held, I am worried about the health of my spouse and my family."

Single parents face even harder decisions: While schools are closed, how do they juggle earning and caring? No one should be nostalgic for the "1950s ideal" of Dad returning to a freshly baked dinner and freshly washed children, when so many families were excluded from it, even then. And in Britain today, a quarter of families are headed by a single parent, more than 90 percent of whom are women. Closed schools make their life even harder.

The Coronavirus Is a Disaster for Feminism

Other lessons from the Ebola epidemic were just as stark—and similar, if perhaps smaller, effects will be seen during this crisis in the developed world. School closures affected girls' life chances, because many dropped out of education. (A rise in teenage-pregnancy rates exacerbated this trend.) Domestic and sexual violence rose. And more women died in childbirth because resources were diverted elsewhere. "There's a distortion of health systems, everything goes towards the outbreak," said Wenham, who traveled to west Africa as a researcher during the Ebola crisis. "Things that aren't priorities get canceled. That can have an effect on maternal mortality, or access to contraception." The United States already has appalling statistics in this area compared with other rich countries, and black women there are twice as likely to die in childbirth as white women.

For Wenham, the most striking statistic from Sierra Leone, one of the countries worst affected by Ebola, was that from 2013 to 2016, during the outbreak, more women died of obstetric complications than the infectious disease itself. But these deaths, like the unnoticed caring labor on which the modern economy runs, attract less attention than the immediate problems generated by an epidemic. These deaths are taken for granted. In her book *Invisible Women*, Caroline Criado Perez notes that 29 million papers were published in more than 15,000 peer-reviewed titles around the time of the Zika and Ebola epidemics, but less than 1 percent explored the gendered impact of the outbreaks. Wenham has found no gender analysis of the coronavirus outbreak so far; she and two co-authors have stepped into the gap to research the issue.

The evidence we do have from the Ebola and Zika outbreaks should inform the current response. In both rich and poor countries, campaigners expect domestic-violence

For more on writing transitions, see Chapter 8.

rates to rise during lockdown periods. Stress, alcohol consumption, and financial difficulties are all considered triggers for violence in the home, and the quarantine measures being imposed around the world will increase all three. The British charity Women's Aid said in a statement that it was "concerned that social distancing and self-isolation will be used as a tool of coercive and controlling behaviour by perpetrators, and will shut down routes to safety and support."

Researchers, including those I spoke with, are frustrated that findings like this have not made it through to policy makers, who still adopt a gender-neutral approach to pandemics. They also worry that opportunities to collect high-quality data which will be useful for the future are being missed. For example, we have little information on how viruses similar to the coronavirus affect pregnant women—hence the conflicting advice during the current crisis—or, according to Susannah Hares, a senior policy fellow at the Center for Global Development, sufficient data to build a model for when schools should reopen.

We shouldn't make that mistake again. Grim as it is to imag- 15 ine now, further epidemics are inevitable, and the temptation to argue that gender is a side issue, a distraction from the real crisis, must be resisted. What we do now will affect the lives of millions of women and girls in future outbreaks.

The coronavirus crisis will be global and long-lasting, economic as well as medical. However, it also offers an opportunity. This could be the first outbreak where gender and sex differences are recorded, and taken into account by researchers and policy makers. For too long, politicians have assumed that child care and elderly care can be "soaked up" by private citizens—mostly women—effectively providing a huge subsidy to the paid economy. This pandemic should remind us of the true scale of that distortion.

Wenham supports emergency child-care provision, economic security for small-business owners, and a financial stimulus paid directly to families. But she isn't hopeful, because her experience suggests that governments are too short-termist and reactive. "Everything that's happened has been predicted, right?" she told me. "As a collective academic group, we knew there would be an outbreak that came out of China, that shows you how globalization spreads disease, that's going to paralyze financial systems, and there was no pot of money ready to go, no governance plan . . . We knew all this, and they didn't listen. So why would they listen to something about women?"

Joining the Conversation

1. In what ways does Helen Lewis believe that women generally suffer more than men from the effects of a pandemic? What evidence does she cite?

2. Lewis does not incorporate or respond to positions other than her own, that is, naysayers (see Chapter 6). How might adding some naysayers strengthen her argument? List two or three objections she might have considered and how she could respond to them in ways that make her argument more powerful.

3. Supply one or two sentences of metacommentary, described in Chapter 10 as "a way of commenting on your claims and telling how—and how not—to think about them," and consider where the best place in the essay would be to insert it. See Chapter 10 for effective ways of expressing metacommentary.

4. Write an essay putting the Lewis reading in conversation with Anne-Marie Slaughter's argument (pp. 673–93) that women face an unfair share of responsibilities and obligations compared to men as well as Richard Dorment's argument (pp. 694–714) that men are similarly burdened. In particular, how might Lewis respond to Dorment?

5. Go to **theysayiblog.com** where this essay also appears and read the most recent remarks in the comment thread. Write a paragraph about your own experiences and observations of gender roles and responsibilities during the pandemic, in which you agree, disagree, or both with the author Helen Lewis's argument, and add it to the comment thread.

An End to Sexism in
Gaming Communities

SANJANA RAMANATHAN

—▣—

ON JUNE 18, 2016, sixteen-year-old Kim Se-Hyeon (competing under the gamer tag "Geguri") entered an amateur *Overwatch* esports tournament from her home in Seoul. Within twenty-four hours of her team's victory, rumors began circulating online that Geguri, who was the only female player in the tournament, had been cheating. Players "ELTA" and "Strobe" said her performance and mouse precision were too good and accused the teenager of using automated aim-assist software. Many people took the accusations seriously despite the lack of proof and began harassing Geguri, hurling gendered slurs and vulgar, often sexual insults. Strobe even resorted to death threats, saying "if there is a problem with our sponsors and

———

SANJANA RAMANATHAN wrote this paper in her first-year writing class at Drexel University in Philadelphia. Ramanathan is an English major with a concentration in writing, and she is on the staff of the *Triangle*, Drexel's independent student newspaper. This essay appeared in *The 33rd*, published by Drexel Publishing Group. It is documented in MLA Style.

such, I may visit Geguri's house with a knife in hand. I am not joking" (Kimes).

To any woman who plays video games, these remarks may seem uncomfortably familiar. Sexism appears at every level of the gaming community, from casual players to professionals. A female player who turns on her microphone to communicate with her male teammates may find herself instantly harassed because her voice gives away her gender. She may be accused of playing to attract men's attention. If she has skill, it is likely that she will be accused of cheating far more often than any male player. Reasonably, as two researchers from the academic journal *Feminism and Psychology* discovered, many women choose to use gender-neutral gamer tags and voice modifiers to hide that they are female (Easpaig and Humphrey).

Although blatant sexism has been present in gaming communities for decades, the most famous controversy occurred in 2014. "Gamergate" started with a harassment campaign targeting women in the gaming industry and feminist critics of video games. In an article in *The New Yorker*, Simon Parkin describes how these women were subjected to months of harassment, including death and rape threats. The campaign shed a light on the rampant and often violent sexism surrounding video games—in the industry, the communities of players, and the content of the games themselves. But even after the controversy died down, little change was made to solve the problem; two years later it made the media once again when sixteen-year-old Geguri was subjected to the same harassment.

As the online threats and abuse mounted, Geguri was invited by tournament casters to stage a demonstration proving her skill level. An *ESPN* article reports that when she arrived at the studio, caster Kim Young-Il noted that the high school girl "wasn't mentally ready" to face the public; she wore a white mask to hide her face and spoke very little during her introduction (Kimes). Geguri's demonstration proved once and for all that the accusations hurled at her were baseless. However, the scandal had shattered her self-confidence. "Because [my opponents] attacked me publicly, everyone in the community was attacking me, calling me a crazy bitch. I was scared," Geguri admitted in an interview with ESPN's Mina Kimes. For a year after clearing her name, Geguri disappeared almost entirely from esports.

For more on blending an author's words with your own, see Chapter 3.

Gender-based threats and stereotypes keep women from suc- 5 ceeding in professional esports, despite women accounting for 45 percent of today's gamers (Pugh 82). Although "female gamers don't have the same physical disadvantages against males as, say, female basketball players, very few have thrived on a professional level" due to harassment from male players and an unwillingness from professional teams to recruit them (Kimes). This toxic environment prevents women from succeeding in the game and engaging with other players.

The video game industry itself is where we must look to solve the problem. Despite more and more girls playing video games, there is a huge underrepresentation of women involved in making them. This "anomaly does not restrict itself to just one area of the industry, but affects the industry as a whole" (Pugh 82), causing casual gamers and esports to become affected as well. Because the industry is dominated by men, a majority of games are marketed to men and serve their perspective. Themes of misogyny and mistreated female characters are ever-present in today's video games, ones that are often picked off the shelf by teenage boys who pocket the harmful messages.

Involving more women in the gaming industry means creating a safe and fair environment for them to work. Two British researchers who studied the issue say that women are discouraged from even entering the "games industry because the nature of the industry is particularly restrictive to females," and those in the industry are restricted from higher-level jobs because it is assumed women will not be able work the long hours needed (Elliot and Prescott). In addition, Gamasutra's Game Developer Salary Survey revealed that on average, women who work in the field make 86 percent of what men make in the gaming industry (Graft). By eradicating this wage gap, game companies can create a more welcoming workplace for women interested in entering the field.

There are those who argue that the gaming industry is already seeing progress in its treatment of women. Joey Cisneros, in an op-ed for the University of Idaho's newspaper, points out that more games include female characters, including the best-selling *The Last of Us* series. "It would seem game studios and developers are now making diversity a priority," he says. Wong An Jie, a longtime gamer himself, also argues that "many critically acclaimed and best-selling video games feature female characters that are neither objectified nor sexualised while maintaining a healthy male fanbase; the Super Mario and Pokémon franchises are prominent examples." In his view, the existence of these two particular examples outweigh all of the others that feature oversexualized female images.

See Chapter 6 on adding a naysayer to your writing.

However, both of these arguments overlook the data: as Tom Faber points out in an opinion piece in the *Financial Times*, just 5 percent of the games at an influential 2019 expo "had female protagonists." In that piece, Faber does praise *The Last of Us* and other games that feature strong women, but he points out that the issue is about more than just characters:

Women are misrepresented in games because they are under-represented in the industry, with only 21 percent of game developers identifying as female in a 2017 survey. Women in the industry say they are put off by sexualisation of female characters, workplace harassment, gender pay gaps and a lack of interest in topics that matter to women.

In addition to those larger problems, just having women as characters might not be enough. Anita Sarkeesian and Carolyn Petit point out in *Wired* that there's "no guarantee whatsoever that those representations will be good ones. Games can and often do center women while also reinforcing harmful stereotypes or turning those women into sexual fantasies for the benefit of straight male players." If the industry wants to make advances, it needs to move beyond having a handful of games with female characters and include more women behind the scenes to avoid those sorts of portrayals.

By bringing more women into the industry, companies will 10 invite a new perspective of a game's script, character design, and marketing. The industry itself will benefit by having more diversity, as women will market to the untapped female player base. Gaming companies can encourage more women to enter the field by removing the deterrents. The 2014 Gamergate controversy revealed that the game industry was an unsafe place for women; it is up to companies to change their male-dominated workplaces and prove that change from the current mind-set is possible.

Already, the future is getting brighter for female players. As a 2018 *ESPN* article noted, Geguri decided to rejoin the esports scene and was recruited by the Shanghai Dragons, making her the first and only female player in the international Overwatch League. However, she is still one of the few women competing professionally in esports at an international level (Breslau). Big changes to end sexism in the industry itself may be enough to change the attitudes of the player base and the attitudes of professional teams. If game companies take steps to solve the problem of sexism within their own walls, other female players may be able to follow Geguri's success without the brutal struggle that came before.

WORKS CITED

Breslau, Rod. "Sources: Geguri Set to Join Shanghai Dragons, Become Overwatch League's First Female Player." *ESPN*, 14 Feb. 2018, www.espn.com/esports/story/_/id/22348024.

Cisneros, Joey. "Opinion: The Evolution of Women's Roles in Gaming." *The University of Idaho Argonaut*, 24 June 2020, www.uiargonaut .com/2020/06/24/opinion-the-evolution-of-womens-roles-in-gaming.

Easpaig, Bròna Nic Giolla, and Rhi Humphrey. "'Pitching a Virtual Woo': Analysing Discussion of Sexism in Online Gaming." *Feminism and Psychology*, vol. 27, no. 4, 2016, pp. 553–61. *Sage Journals*, https://doi .org/10.1177/0959353516667400.

Elliot, Lauren, and Julie Prescott. "The Only Girl in the Class! Female Students' Experiences of Gaming Courses and Views of the Industry." *Gender Considerations and Influence in the Digital Media and Gaming Industry*, edited by Julie Prescott and Julie Elizabeth McGurren, IGI Global, 2014, pp. 36–55. *IGI Global*, https://doi.org/10.4018/978 -1-4666-6142-4.

Faber, Tom. "Does Gaming Still Have a Woman Problem?" *Financial Times*, 23 July 2019, www.ft.com/content/8a7a4c1c-ac9b-11e9-b3e2 -4fdf846f48f5.

Graft, Kris. "Gender Wage Gap: How the Game Industry Compares to the U.S. Average." *Gamasutra*, 22 July 2014, www.gamasutra.com/view /news/221586/Gender_wage_gap_How_the_game_industry_compares _to_the_US_average.php.

Jie, Wong An. "Gen Y Speaks: Who Says Sexism Is Prevalent in Gaming?" *Today Online*, 25 Aug. 2019, www.todayonline.com/commentary /gen-y-speaks-who-says-sexism-prevalent-gaming.

Kimes, Mina. "Esports Is Dominated by Men. Can a 17-Year-Old Korean Girl Change That?" *ESPN*, 15 Sept. 2017, www.espn.com/espn/feature /story/_/id/20692051.

Parkin, Simon. "Gamergate: A Scandal Erupts in the Video-Game Community." *The New Yorker*, 17 Oct. 2014, www.newyorker.com/tech/annals-of -technology/gamergate-scandal-erupts-video-game-community.

Pugh, Vachon M. C. "A Look Inside the Current Climate of the Video Game Industry." *Gender Considerations and Influence in the Digital Media and Gaming Industry*, edited by Julie Prescott and Julie Elizabeth McGurren, IGI Global, 2014, pp. 82–91.

Sarkeesian, Anita, and Carolyn Petit. "Female Representation in Videogames Isn't Getting Any Better." *Wired*, 14 June 2019, www.wired.com/story /e3-2019-female-representation-videogames.

Joining the Conversation

1. What is the "toxic environment" in online gaming that college student Sanjana Ramanathan describes in paragraph 5 of her essay? How does it impact women gamers, and how does she think the problem can be solved?

2. The author does not include explicit "they say / I say" statements. Rather, she begins with a striking example of sexist behavior in paragraph 1 and then presents her argument in paragraph 2. Compose a "they say" statement to insert at the beginning of paragraph 2 and an "I say" statement that agrees, disagrees, or both.

3. Why is this issue important? Respond to this "so what?" question (see Chapter 7), addressing the reasons readers should be concerned about it. Where would be an appropriate place in the essay to include your response, and why?

4. Agustín Fuentes in "Are We Really as Awful as We Act Online?" (pp. 643–49) writes about the prevalence of trolling and other hostile online behavior. Given the specific advice he offers for reducing such behavior, how do you think he might respond to Ramanathan's essay?
5. Do some research on your own about sexism in the gaming world, and write a "they say / I say" essay responding to both Ramanathan and Fuentes.

Why We Need Title IX
Now More Than Ever

MONICA WRIGHT

—◻—

I'M GOING TO THROW a few names at you.

*Lauren Jackson. Tamika Catchings. Lisa Leslie. Maya Moore.
Tina Thompson. Sheryl Swoopes.* You've heard of these women.
Maybe you've watched them light it up in the WNBA or at
the Olympics. The point is, you know of them.

But you probably wouldn't, if not for a single sentence.

*"No person in the United States shall, on the basis of sex, be
excluded from participation in, be denied the benefits of, or be subjected to discrimination under any education program or activity
receiving Federal financial assistance."*

That's all Title IX, a federal civil rights law, is, give or take   5
some regulations. Without that sentence, the U.S. has eight

———

MONICA WRIGHT is an assistant coach for the University of Virginia
women's basketball team. She was the second pick in the 2010 WNBA
draft and won two WNBA championships. Wright played for the
University of Virginia Cavaliers from 2006–10 and holds the school's
all-time scoring record of 2,540 points. In her senior year, she was named
ACC Player of the Year and the WBCA National Defensive Player of
the Year. This essay was published in the *Players' Tribune* in 2017.

fewer gold medals. Without it, Dawn Staley and the University of South Carolina don't take the basketball world by storm. Without it, Lauren, Tamika, Lisa, Maya, Tina, Sheryl, Candace, Elena, and so, so many others, myself included, aren't where we are today.

I was your typical tomboy growing up. My older brother, Gerard, was a star in track and field, and I wanted to be just like him. I tried to follow him everywhere he went, play every sport he played. I started out running track, then took up soccer, then basketball at the age of nine. As it turned out, I was pretty darn good at basketball. I started playing on the AAU circuit, traveling all over the country and balling out everywhere I went. No one ever told me, "No, you can't play because you're a girl." Forty-five years ago, that wouldn't have been the case.

Title IX was passed in 1972. It's younger than my dad. He grew up in the Jim Crow South, before Title IX. When he was in high school in Texas, Tulane offered him a football scholarship. Even though Tulane had been integrated a few years before, my dad received a lot of death threats from white Tulane fans who didn't want to see him play there. He went to Lamar, in Beaumont, Texas, instead.

My dad liked to talk to me about those times as I was growing up and getting really serious about sports. He'd tell me how women could only play half-court basketball, and couldn't even continuously dribble until 1966. He wasn't trying to prove how much harder it was back then, he just wanted to make sure I appreciated the opportunities I had. And I did. I truly did. But I don't think I fully realized just how lucky I was until I met Debbie Ryan, my coach at the University of Virginia.

You have to understand, Coach Ryan is like royalty at UVA, and not just because she coached there for more than 30 years and won more than 700 games. Her legacy goes well beyond that.

"You guys are blessed," she used to tell us. "The fancy locker [10] room, the chartered planes . . . we didn't have that when I was playing. We used to share a locker room with the softball team. We used to have to ride a bus when the men's team would fly. We used to wash our own jerseys" . . .

Like my dad, she wasn't trying to shame us. She wanted us to know that we were playing for something bigger than ourselves. We're playing for those who came before us, who sacrificed so that we could play this game on equal footing. We're playing for those who will come after us, so they can enjoy the same, or maybe even better, opportunities than we currently have. I know that's why I bring it *every single game*. I know that's why Maya and Elena and Sue Bird and Nneka Ogwumike and every other WNBA player does, too.

I know there are those who think that Title IX isn't important. Or that it hasn't had that much of an impact. Well, for those people, here are a few numbers to consider. Since 1972, participation in women's sports in high schools has increased 900%. That's not a typo. Before Title IX, there were fewer than 30,000 NCAA female athletes. In 2012, that number was nearly 200,000. Just to top it off, in 2012, the United States sent more female than male athletes to the Olympics.

See Chapter 6 for more on answering objections.

And I would bet there are those who are saying that the time to talk about Title IX was last month. But is that really true?

We can and must celebrate the success gained by that simple sentence over the last 45 years. Not just on the anniversary of Title IX's passing, but every day. Because of that legislation, women have more access to opportunities in the classroom and in sports than ever before. Without Title IX, there probably wouldn't be enough basketball talent in our high schools, colleges or universities to fill the rosters in a professional women's league. And probably without the law, we probably would not be able to field a competitive Team USA to properly represent the country that gave us the opportunity in the first place!

But I also know we still have a long way to go until we have true equity between men and women. Some schools still fail to properly implement and enforce Title IX. But that's why we keep fighting and playing. Even if Title IX is one day completely enforced at every academic institution in the country, I still don't think our fight would be over. There's still the pros.

Have you ever wondered what sports would look like if Title IX or simple principles of fairness applied at the professional level?

I'm not necessarily arguing that leagues for women and men who play professional basketball or soccer or hockey or football should be precisely equal. Title IX, after all is built on principles of equity.

Monica Wright.

So, if those same principles applied to my league, for example, players in the WNBA would:

- Be given the same quality of equipment and supplies as their NBA counterparts

- Have similar locker rooms, practice gyms and competitive facilities

- Have access to the same medical, rehab and training services

- Enjoy the same travel arrangements, and per diems

Those are all Title IX considerations, which means that is what high school and college administrators are supposed to monitor for young athletes in their school programs. There is more to it, for sure. But this is a starting point for the larger conversation. Honestly, those kinds of improvements in travel, facilities, rehab services, etc., would be a significant step for professional athletes in my sport—a huge step for all those professional athletes who happen to be women. We would feel valued. And notice, I haven't even mentioned salaries—yet.

Just two years ago, the Women's Sports Foundation (WSF) reported that "college and professional sports continue to provide unequal funding for women." And the WSF went on to suggest that "paying men more for the same sport gives women in the sport less incentive to push themselves and discourages future female participants in the sport." Those are interesting findings. I understand the point the WSF is making; however, I am not sure that I fully agree.

For more on distinguishing what they say from what you say, see Chapter 5.

If you think any one of us has been less inclined to *bring it* 20 *every night*, well, I'll let you take that up with Tina or Britney or Alana or Skylar or Seimone or Sylvia or—anyone you dare to ask . . . ! But the overall point about the effects of inequities on long-term motivation is not lost on any of us.

In an ideal world there would be a Title IX for the pros. I get that because of market factors that's just not possible right now. But maybe through the lessons learned from Title IX and with the vision and passion of a generation who came of age under its provisions, we can change the culture. Think about the world that could create. One in which women are valued for their athletic pursuits, not compared to their male counterparts, and certainly not sexualized. One where the old stereotypes about female athletes don't exist, where there aren't any more barriers to access. Where the playing field is truly, completely, finally level.

I dropped a lot of names in this article. Those athletes deserve to be at the top of mind in your Title IX celebrations and discussions. Become a name dropper yourself. Attend a competition featuring athletes who happen to be women. There is at least one professional league playing this weekend.

Joining the Conversation

1. Monica Wright writes about her own basketball career and also paraphrases her father and quotes her college coach in arguing for the importance of Title IX. How do the examples she provides support her argument?

2. In paragraph 12, the author begins with a naysayer: "I know there are those who think Title IX isn't important. Or that it hasn't had much of an impact." What responses does she offer to these potential criticisms? What are two or three other arguments she could make in favor of Title IX? What evidence would she need to support these arguments?

3. Wright uses several connecting words to transition from one sentence to the next. Find some examples of these words and list them according to the categories laid out on pages 111–12. Then, using these same categories, come up with a connecting sentence to link two paragraphs in the essay to each other. Place this sentence at the beginning of the second paragraph.

4. The author mostly uses formal language in making her argument, but she occasionally uses a more personal voice, as discussed in Chapter 9. For example, in paragraph 6, while writing about her development as a young basketball player, she writes, "As it turned out, I was pretty darn good at basketball. I started playing on the AAU circuit, traveling all over the country, and balling out everywhere I went." How does the occasional use of informal language help Wright develop her argument? Find two other places where she might productively shift from formal to informal language, revise the sentences accordingly, and consider how the result affects her argument.

5. See what you can find out about the history of women's sports at your school, and interview a current or former (woman) scholarship athlete about her career and the influence of Title IX. Write a "they say / I say" research essay incorporating what you find and relating it to the Monica Wright essay and to "Coach Wears High Heels: Pau Gasol on Gender and the NBA" found on **theysayiblog.com**.

CREDITS

TEXT

Liz Addison: "Two Years Are Better Than Four." From *The New York Times*. © 2007 The New York Times Company. All rights reserved. Used under license.

Ben Adler: "Banning Plastic Bags Is Great for the World, Right? Not So Fast," Wired.com, June 10, 2016. Ben Adler, Wired © Condé Nast. Used with permission.

Michelle Alexander: Excerpt from *The New Jim Crow*–Copyright © 2010, 2012 by Michelle Alexander. Reprinted by permission of The New Press. www .thenewpress.com

Sean Blanda: "The 'Other Side' Is Not Dumb," from *Medium*, January 7, 2016. Reprinted by permission of the author.

danah boyd: "Why America Is Self-Segregating," by danah boyd. From Points, Data & Society, *Medium*, January 5, 2017. Reprinted by permission of the author.

Nicholas Brody: "It Turns Out Our Tech Gadgets Aren't as Isolating as Experts Say," *The News Tribune*, March 27, 2020. Reprinted by permission of the author.

Sylvia Matthews Burwell: Republished with permission of Council on Foreign Relations, from *Foreign Affairs*, Sylvia Matthews Burwell, Vol. 97, No. 6, 2018; permission conveyed through Copyright Clearance Center, Inc.

Carole Cadwalladr: "Google, Democracy and the Truth about Internet Search," *The Guardian*, December 4, 2016. Copyright Guardian News & Media Ltd 2020. www.theguardian.com. Used with permission.

Credits

Credits

PHOTOGRAPHS

ACKNOWLEDGMENTS

—🔲—

THIS BOOK WOULD NEVER HAVE seen print if it weren't for Marilyn Moller, our superb editor at Norton, and the extraordinary job she has done of inspiring, commenting on, rewriting (and then rewriting and rewriting again) our many drafts. Our friendship with Marilyn is one of the most cherished things to have developed from this project.

Our profound thanks go to Sarah Touborg for her excellent work in editing this new edition, her deft touch in helping to shape each readings chapter, and her calm expertise in keeping us on track and bringing the project to fruition; to Christine D'Antonio and Elizabeth Marotta for their superb work for managing the production and project editing; and to Joy Cranshaw and Katie Bolger for managing the digital resources that accompany the book. We appreciate Patricia Wong's excellent work as permissions editor and Ted Szczepanski's management of the photos for both versions of the book.

We thank John Darger, our Norton representative, who offered early encouragement to write this book, and to Debra Morton Hoyt and Mike Wood for their excellent work on the cover. Special thanks to Michele Dobbins, Elizabeth Pieslor, Kim Bowers, Emily Rowin, Lib Triplett and all the Norton travelers for the superb work they've done on behalf of our book.

We are deeply grateful to Laura Davies, Associate Professor of English and Director of Campus Writing Programs at SUNY Cortland, for her exceptional contributions in finding readings for this edition, writing the new exercises, revising the instructor's guide, and for her ongoing work on **theysayiblog.com**. We owe a special debt of gratitude to Erin Ackerman for her expert contributions to the new chapter on research, and for her chapter on writing in the social sciences. We also thank Chris Gillen for his chapter on writing in the sciences. We thank Lisa Ampleman for her terrific help editing and documenting the new student writing and for adding cross references throughout the readings.

A very special thanks goes to those who provided in-depth reviews of the new chapters on research and revising: Steven Bailey (Central Michigan University), Ana Cooke (Penn State University), Courtney Danforth (College of Southern Nevada), Africa Fine (Palm Beach State College), and Traci Klass (Palm Beach State College); and to those who provided detailed evaluations of the fourth edition: Joe Bizup (Boston University), Laura J. Panning Davies (SUNY Cortland), Karen Gocsik (University of California at San Diego), and Kelly Ritter (University of Illinois at Urbana–Champaign).

We are grateful to all of the instructors whose feedback was invaluable in shaping this fifth edition: Catherine Agar (Keuka College); Craig Albin (Missouri State University, West Plains Campus); Jason Barrett-Fox (Weber State); Jade Bittle (Rowan-Cabarrus Community College); Roberta Brown (Western New Mexico University); William Burgos (LIU Brooklyn); Jackson Connor (University of Rio Grande); Charles Cook (Red Creek High School/Finger Lakes Community College); Amanda Corcoran (American River College); Linda Cowling (North Central Missouri College); Ginny Crisco (California State University, Fresno); Tamera Davis, (Northern Oklahoma College, Stillwater); Matt Dube (William Woods University); Mei Mei Evans (Alaska Pacific University); Anna Eyre (Merrimack College); Audrey Fessler (Appalachian State

University); Jane Focht-Hansen (San Antonio College); Susan Gentry (Tunxis Community College); Sean Glassberg (Horry-Georgetown Technical College); Sarah Hallenbeck (University of North Carolina Wilmington); LewEllyn Hallett (University of Arkansas, Fayetteville); Natalie Hewitt (Hope International University); Lori Hughes (Lone Star College, Montgomery); Mark Hughes (Community College of Philadelphia); Elizabeth Inness-Brown (Saint Michael's College); Tim Jensen (Oregon State University); Alyssa Johnson (Horry-Georgetown Technical College); Gregory Johnson (Wake Technical Community College); Rhonda Jackson Joseph (Lone Star University Park); Alan Lindsay (New Hampshire Technical Institute); Jade Lynch-Greenberg (Purdue University Northwest); Gina MacKenzie (Holy Family University); Andrew Marvin (Three Rivers Community College); James Matthews (Fairmont State University); Gena McKinley (Rappahannock Community College, Warsaw Campus); Kelsey McNiff (Endicott College); Jeremy Meyer (Arizona State University, Tempe Campus); Jeannine Morgan (St. John's River State College); Janine Morris (Nova Southeastern University); Nichole Oechslin (Piedmont Valley Community College); Jessica Santini (Lake Region State College); Dagmar Scharold (University of Houston, Downtown); Greta Skogseth (Montcalm Community College); Joshua Smith (University of North Carolina at Chapel Hill); Christian Smith (Coastal Carolina University); Kristen Snoddy (Indiana University Kokomo); Nicholas Vick (Pitt Community College); Tobin von der Nuell (University of Colorado Boulder); Sarah White (Purdue University Northwest); Lacey Wootton (American University); and Ali Zimmerman Zuckerman (University of Minnesota).

We owe special thanks to our colleagues in the English department at the University of Illinois at Chicago: Mark

Canuel, our former department head, for supporting our earlier efforts overseeing the university's Writing in the Disciplines requirement; Walter Benn Michaels, our current department head; and Ann Feldman, former Director of University Writing Programs, for encouraging us to teach first-year composition courses at UIC in which we could try out ideas and drafts of our manuscript; Tom Moss, Diane Chin, Vainis Aleksa, and Matt Pavesich, who have also been very supportive of our efforts; and Matt Oakes, our former research assistant. We are also grateful to Ann, Diane, and Mark Bennett for bringing us into their graduate course on the teaching of writing, and to Lisa Freeman, John Huntington, Walter Benn Michaels, and Ralph Cintron, for inviting us to present our ideas in the keynote lecture at UIC's 2013 "Composition Matters" conference.

We are also especially grateful to Steve Benton and Nadya Pittendrigh, who taught a section of composition with us using an early draft of this book. Steve made many helpful suggestions, particularly regarding the exercises. We are grateful to Andy Young, a lecturer at UIC who has tested our book in his courses and who gave us extremely helpful feedback. And we thank Vershawn A. Young, whose work on code-meshing influenced our argument in Chapter 9, and Hillel Crandus, whose classroom handout inspired the chapter on "Entering Classroom Discussions."

We are grateful to the many colleagues and friends who've let us talk our ideas out with them and given extremely helpful responses. UIC's former dean, Stanley Fish, has been central in this respect, both in personal conversations and in his incisive articles calling for greater focus on form in the teaching of writing. Our conversations with Jane Tompkins have also been integral to this book, as was the composition course that Jane co-taught with Gerald entitled "Can We Talk?" Lenny Davis, too, offered both intellectual insight and emotional support, as did

ACKNOWLEDGMENTS

Heather Arnet, Jennifer Ashton, Janet Atwill, Kyra Auslander, Noel Barker, Jim Benton, Jack Brereton, Tim Cantrick, Marsha Cassidy, David Chinitz, Lisa Chinitz, Pat Chu, Duane Davis, Bridget O'Rourke Flisk, Steve Flisk, Judy Gardiner, Howard Gardner, Rich Gelb, Gwynne Gertz, Jeff Gore, Bill Haddad, Ben Hale, Scott Hammerl, Patricia Harkin, Andy Hoberek, John Huntington, Joe Janangelo, Paul Jay, David Jolliffe, Nancy Kohn, Don Lazere, Jo Liebermann, Steven Mailloux, Deirdre McCloskey, Maurice J. Meilleur, Alan Meyers, Greg Meyerson, Anna Minkov, Chris Newfield, Jim Phelan, Paul Psilos, Bruce Robbins, Charles Ross, Eileen Seifert, Evan Seymour, David Shumway, Herb Simons, Jim Sosnoski, David Steiner, Harold Veeser, Chuck Venegoni, Marla Weeg, Jerry Wexler, Joyce Wexler, Virginia Wexman, Jeffrey Williams, Lynn Woodbury, and the late Wayne Booth, whose friendship we dearly miss.

We are grateful for having had the opportunity to present our ideas to a number of schools: University of Arkansas at Little Rock, Augustana College, Brandeis University, Brigham Young University, Bryn Mawr College, Case Western University, Columbia University, Community College of Philadelphia, California State University at Bakersfield, California State University at Northridge, University of California at Riverside, University of Delaware, DePauw University, Drew University, Duke University, Duquesne University, Elmhurst College, Emory University, Fontbonne University, Furman University, Gettysburg College, Harper College, Harvard University, Haverford College, Hawaii Office of Secondary School Curriculum Instruction, Hunter College, University of Illinois College of Medicine, Illinois State University, John Carroll University, Kansas State University, Lawrence University, the Lawrenceville School, University of Louisiana at Lafayette, MacEwan University, University of Maryland at College Park, Massachusetts Institute of Technology,

University of Memphis, Miami University, University of Missouri at Columbia, New Trier High School, State University of New York at Geneseo, State University of New York at Stony Brook, North Carolina A&T University, University of North Florida, Northern Michigan University, Norwalk Community College, Northwestern University Division of Continuing Studies, University of Notre Dame, Ohio Wesleyan University, Oregon State University, University of Portland, University of Rochester, St. Ambrose University, St. Andrew's School, St. Charles High School, Seattle University, Southern Connecticut State University, South Elgin High School, University of South Florida, University of Southern Mississippi, Swarthmore College, Teachers College, University of Tennessee at Knoxville, University of Texas at Arlington, Tulane University, Union College, Ursinus College, Wabash College, Washington College, University of Washington, Western Michigan University, Westinghouse/Kenwood High Schools, University of West Virginia at Morgantown, Wheaton Warrenville English Chairs, and the University of Wisconsin at Whitewater.

We particularly thank those who helped arrange these visits and discussed writing issues with us: Jeff Abernathy, Herman Asarnow, John Austin, Greg Barnheisel, John Bean, Crystal Benedicks, Joe Bizup, Sheridan Blau, Dagne Bloland, Chris Breu, Mark Brouwer, Joan Johnson Bube, John Caldwell, Gregory Clark, Irene Clark, Dean Philip Cohen, Cathy D'Agostino, Tom Deans, Gaurav Desai, Lisa Dresdner, Kathleen Dudden-Rowlands, Lisa Ede, Alexia Ellett, Emory Elliott, Anthony Ellis, Kim Flachmann, Ronald Fortune, Rosanna Fukuda, George Haggerty, Donald Hall, Joe Harris, Gary Hatch, Elizabeth Hatmaker, Harry Hellenbrand, Nicole Henderson, Donna Heiland, Doug Hesse, Van Hillard, Andrew Hoberek, Michael Hustedde, Sara Jameson, T. R. Johnson, David Jones,

Ann Kaplan, Don Kartiganer, Linda Kinnahan, Dean Georg Kleine, Albert Labriola, Craig Lawrence, Lori Lopez, Tom Liam Lynch, Hiram Maxim, Michael Mays, Thomas McFadden, Sean Meehan, Connie Mick, Joseph Musser, Margaret Oakes, John O'Connor, Gary Olson, Tom Pace, Les Perelman, Emily Poe, Dominick Randolph, Clancy Ratliff, Monica Rico, Kelly Ritter, Jack Robinson, Warren Rosenberg, Laura Rosenthal, Dean Howard Ross, Deborah Rossen-Knill, Paul Schacht, Petra Schatz, Evan Seymour, Rose Shapiro, Mike Shea, Cecilia M. Shore, Erec Smith, Nancy Sommers, Stephen Spector, Timothy Spurgin, Ron Strickland, Trig Thoreson, Josh Toth, Judy Trost, Aiman Tulamait, Charles Tung, John Webster, Robert Weisbuch, Sandi Weisenberg, Karin Westman, Martha Woodmansee, and Lynn Worsham.

We also wish to extend particular thanks to two Chicago area educators who have worked closely with us: Les Lynn of the Chicago Debate League and Eileen Murphy of CERCA. Lastly, we wish to thank two high school teachers for their excellent and inventive adaptations of our work: Mark Gozonsky in his YouTube video clip, "Building Blocks," and Dave Stuart, Jr., in his blog, "Teaching the Core."

For inviting us to present our ideas at their conferences we are grateful to John Brereton and Richard Wendorf at the Boston Athenaeum; Wendy Katkin of the Reinvention Center of State University of New York at Stony Brook; Luchen Li of the Michigan English Association; Lisa Lee and Barbara Ransby of the Public Square in Chicago; Don Lazere of the University of Tennessee at Knoxville; Dennis Baron of the University of Illinois at Urbana–Champaign; Alfie Guy of Yale University; Irene Clark of the California State University at Northridge; George Crandell and Steve Hubbard, co-directors of the ACETA conference at Auburn University; Mary Beth

Acknowledgments

Rose of the Humanities Institute at the University of Illinois at Chicago; Diana Smith of St. Anne's Belfield School and the University of Virginia; Jim Maddox and Victor Luftig of the Bread Loaf School of English; Jan Fitzsimmons and Jerry Berberet of the Associated Colleges of Illinois; and Rosemary Feal, Executive Director of the Modern Language Association.

We are very grateful to those who reviewed the new readings for the fourth edition. Our thanks go to Steven K. Bailey (Central Michigan University); Edward Baldwin (College of Southern Nevada); Michal Brody (Sonoma State University); Courtney Danforth (College of Southern Nevada); Elias Dominguez-Barajas (University of Arkansas); Karen Gaffney (Raritan Valley Community College); Karen L. Henderson (Helena College University of Montana); Mark Hughes (Community College of Philadelphia); Lawrence J. Lehmann, Jr. (Camden County College); Kelly Ritter (University of Illinois Urbana–Champaign); Julia Ruengert (Pensacola State College); Sara Smith (Pensacola State College); and Debbie Williams (Abilene Christian University).

We also thank those who reviewed materials for the fourth edition: Teresa Alto (Itasca Community College); Darla Anderson (California State University, Northridge); Jan Andres (Riverside City College); Steven Bailey (Central Michigan University); Valerie Bell (Loras College); Tamara Benson (Kent State University); Jade Bittle (Rowan-Cabarrus Community College); Jill Bonds (University of Phoenix); William Cantrell (Johnson Central High School); David Chase (Raritan Valley Community College); Barbara Cook (Mount Aloysius College); Jonathan Cook (Durham Technical Community College); Lana Dalley (California State University, Fullerton); Carol Lynne D'Arcangelis (Memorial University of Newfoundland); Nicholas DeArmas (Seminole State College of Florida); Elias Dominguez-Barajas (University of Arkansas); Ember Dooling (St. Joseph High School); Andrew Dunphy (Massasoit Community College); Justin Eells (Minnesota State University, Mankato); Africa Fine (Palm Beach State College); Valerie Fong (Foothill College); Reese Fuller (Episcopal School of Acadiana); Karen Gaffney (Raritan Valley Community College); Jacquelyn Geiger (Bucks County Community College); Joshua Geist (College of the Sequoias); Ashley Gendek (Kentucky Wesleyan College); Sean George (Dixie State University); Karen Gocsik (University of California, San Diego); Sarah Gray (Middle Tennessee State University); George Grinnell (University of British Columbia Okanagan); Lindsay Haney (Bellevue College); Catherine Hayter (Saddleback College); Stephen V. Hoyt (Obridge Academy/St. Joseph's College); Timothy Jackson (Rosemont College); Julie Jung-Kim (Trinity International University); Hannah Keller (Campbell University); Michael Keller (South Dakota State University); Nina Kutty (DePaul University); Lisa Lipani (University of Georgia); Judi Mack (Joliet Junior College); Anna Maheshwari (Schoolcraft College); Sarah F. McGinley (Wright State University); James McGovern (Germanna Community College); Liz McLemore (Minneapolis Community and Technical College); Jason Melton (Sacramento State University); Michael Mendoza (Seminole State College of Florida); Carey Millsap-Spears (Moraine Valley Community College); Nicole Morris (Emory University); Shelley Palmer (Central Piedmont Community College); Jeff Pruchnic (Wayne State University); Tammy Ramsey (Bluegrass Community and Technical College); Cynthia Cox Richardson (Sinclair Community College); Rachel Rinehart (St. Edward's University); Kelly Ritter (University of Illinois at Urbana–Champaign); Deborah Rossen-Knill (University of Rochester); Laura Rossi-Le

(Endicott College); Julie Shattuck (Frederick Community College); Ellen Sorg (Owens Community College); Jennifer Stefaniak (Springfield Technical Community College); Heather Stringham (College of Southern Nevada); Stuart Swirsky (Seminole State College of Florida); Star Taylor (Riverside City College); Stephanie Tran (Foothill College); Alicia Trotman (Mercy College); Robert Williams (St. Edward's University); and Benjamin Woo (Carleton University).

We are very grateful to those who reviewed the new readings for the third edition. Our thanks go to Elias Dominguez Barajas (University of Arkansas), Christine Berni (Austin Community College), Wanda Fries (Somerset Community College), Leigh Hancock (Germanna Community College), Jennie Joiner (Keuka College), Elizabeth Kalbfleisch (Southern Connecticut State University), Jeanne McDonald (Waubonsee Community College), Roxanne Munch (Joliet Junior College), Michael O'Connor (Onondaga Community College), Kelly Ritter (University of Illinois, Urbana–Champaign), Gail Suberbielle (Baton Rouge Community College), Eleanor Welsh (Chesapeake College), and Debbie J. Williams (Abilene Christian University).

A very special thanks goes to those who reviewed materials for the third edition: Carrie Bailey (Clark College); Heather Barrett (Boston University); Amy Bennett-Zendzian (Boston University); Seth Blumenthal (Boston University); Ron Brooks (Oklahoma State University); Jonathan Cook (Durham Technical Community College); Tessa Croker (Boston University); Perry Cumbie (Durham Technical Community College); Robert Danberg (Binghamton University); Elias Dominguez Barajas (University of Arkansas); Nancy Enright (Seton Hall University); Jason Evans (Prairie State College); Ted Fitts (Boston University); Karen Gaffney (Raritan Valley Community College); Karen Gardiner (University of Alabama);

Stephen Hodin (Boston University); Michael Horwitz (University of Hartford); John Hyman (American University); Claire Kervin (Boston University); Melinda Kreth (Central Michigan University); Heather Marcovitch (Red Deer College); Christina Michaud (Boston University); Marisa Milanese (Boston University); Theresa Mooney (Austin Community College); Roxanne Munch (Joliet Junior College); Sarah Quirk (Waubonsee Community College); Lauri Ramey (California State University, Los Angeles); David Shawn (Boston University); Jennifer Sia (Boston University); Laura Sonderman (Marshall University); Katherine Stebbins McCaffrey (Boston University); K. Sullivan (Lane Community College); Anne-Marie Thomas (Austin Community College at Riverside); Eliot Treichel (Lane Community College); Rosanna Walker (Lane Community College); Mary Erica Zimmer (Boston University).

A very special thanks goes to those who reviewed materials for the second edition: Kathy Albertson (Georgia Southern University); Joseph Aldinger (State University of New York, Buffalo); Nicolette Amann (Humboldt State University); Sonja Andrus (Collin College); Gail Arnoff (John Carroll University); Lisa Siefker Bailey (Indiana University-Purdue University Indianapolis); John Berteaux (California State University, Monterey Bay); Sonya Blades (University of North Carolina, Greensboro); Elyse Blankley (California State University, Long Beach); Andrew Bodenrader (Manhattanville College); Rachel Bowman (University of North Carolina, Greensboro); Eric Branscomb (Salem State College); Harryette Brown (Eastfield College); Elena Brunn (Borough of Manhattan Community College/City University of New York); Rita Carey (Clark College); Julie Cassidy (Borough of Manhattan Community College); Catherine Chaterdon (The University of Arizona); Amy Lea Clemons (Francis Marion

Acknowledgments

University); Tracey Clough (University of Texas, Arlington); Julie Colish (University of Michigan, Flint); Matt Copeland (San Diego State University); Christopher Cowley (State University of New York, Buffalo); Angela Crow (Georgia Southern University); Susie Crowson (Del Mar College); Sean Curran (California State University, Northridge); Kate Dailey (Bowling Green State University, Firelands); Jill Darley-Vanis (Clark College); Virginia Davidson (Mount Saint Mary College); Page Delano (Borough of Manhattan Community College); Elisabeth Divis (University of Michigan); Will Dodson (University of North Carolina, Greensboro); Patricia Dowcett (Quinnipiac University); Laura Dubek (Middle Tennessee State University); William Duffy (University of North Carolina, Greensboro); Gary Eberle (Aquinas College); Alycia Ehlert (Darton College); Sarah Farrell (University of Texas, Arlington); Joseph Fasano (Manhattanville College); Benjamin Fischer (Northwest Nazarene University); Joan Forbes (Kean University); Courtney Fowler (California State University, Long Beach); Caimeen Garrett (American University); William Griswold (California State University, Long Beach); Deborah Greenhut (New Jersey City University); Charles Guy-McAlpin (University of North Carolina, Greensboro); Katalin Gyurian (Kean University); Jami Hemmenway (Eureka College); Jane Hikel (University of Hartford); Erin Houlihan (University of North Carolina, Greensboro); Erik Hudak (University of Texas, Arlington); Chris Hurst (State University of New York, Buffalo); Kristopher Jansma (Manhattanville College); Michael Jauchen (Colby-Sawyer College); Jeanine Jewell (Southeast Community College); Antonnet Johnson (University of Arizona); Donald Johnson (Santa Monica College); Lou Ann Karabel (Indiana University Northwest); Rod Kessler (Salem State College); Kristi Key (Newberry College); Kelly Kinney

ACKNOWLEDGMENTS

(Binghamton University); Francia Kissel (Indiana University-Purdue University Indianapolis); Geoff Klock, Debra S. Knutson (Shawnee State University); Morani Kornberg-Weiss (State University of New York, Buffalo); David LaPierre (Central Connecticut State University); Ann-Gee Lee (St. Cloud State University); Jerry Lee (University of Arizona); Jessica Lee (University of Arizona); Eric Leuschner (Fort Hays State University); Brian Lewis (Century College); Damon Kraft (Missouri Southern State University); Amy Losi (Hamburg Central School District); Aimee Lukas (Central Connecticut State University); Jaclyn Lutzke (Indiana University-Purdue University Indianapolis); John McBratney (John Carroll University); Heather McPherson (University of Minnesota); Cruz Medina (University of Arizona); Dawn Mendoza (Dean College); Rae Ann Meriwether (University of North Carolina, Greensboro); Catherine Merritt (University of Alabama); Gina Miller (Alaska Pacific University); Tomas Q. Morin (Texas State University); Jenny Mueller (McKendree University); Matt Mullins (University of North Carolina, Greensboro); Roxanne F. Munch (Joliet Junior College); Charles Nelson (Kean University); Pauline Newton (Southern Methodist University); Pat Norton (University of Alabama); Marsha Nourse (Dean College); Anne-Marie Obilade (Alcorn State University); Adair Olson (Black Hills State University); Nancy Pederson (University of Minnesota, Morris); Christine Pipitone-Herron (Raritan Valley Community College); D. Pothen (Multnomah University); Sarah A. Quirk (Waubonsee Community College); Clancy Ratliff (University of Louisiana, Lafayette); Kelly Ritter (University of North Carolina, Greensboro); Stephanie Roach (University of Michigan, Flint); Jeffrey Roessner (Mercyhurst College); Scott Rogers (Weber State University); Suzanne Ross (St. Cloud State University);

Keidrick Roy; Myra Salcedo (University of Texas, Arlington); Ronit Sarig (California State University, Northridge); Samantha Seamans (Central Connecticut State University); Rae Schipke (Central Connecticut State University); Michael Schoenfeldt (University of Michigan); Pat Sherbert (National Math and Science Initiative); Joyce Shrimplin (Miami University of Ohio); Leticia Slabaugh (Texas A&M, Galveston); Lars Soderlund (Purdue University); Summar Sparks (University of North Carolina, Greensboro); David Squires (State University of New York, Buffalo); Alice Stephens (Oldenburg Academy of the Immaculate Conception); Mary Stroud (The University of Arizona); Kimberly Sullivan (Clark College); Doug Swartz (Indiana University Northwest); William Tate (Covenant College); James Tolan (Borough of Manhattan Community College); Dawn Trettin-Moyer (University of Wisconsin–Oshkosh); Clementina Verge (Central Connecticut State University); Norma Vogel (Dean College); Nhu Vu (Seattle Central Community College); Christie Ward (Central Connecticut State University); Stephanie Wardrop (Western New England College); Rachael Wendler (University of Arizona); Cara Williams (University of North Carolina, Greensboro); Todd Williams (Kutztown University); Robert Wilson (Cedar Crest College); Courtney Wooten (University of North Carolina, Greensboro); Chuck Venegoni (John Hersey High School); William Younglove (California State University, Long Beach).

We also thank those who reviewed materials for the first edition: Marie Elizabeth Brockman (Central Michigan University); Ronald Clark Brooks (Oklahoma State University); Beth Buyserie (Washington State University); Michael Donnelly (University of Tampa); Karen Gardiner (University of Alabama); Greg Glau (Northern Arizona University); Anita

Helle (Oregon State University); Michael Hennessy (Texas State University); Asao Inoue (California State University at Fresno); Sara Jameson (Oregon State University); Joseph Jones (University of Memphis); Amy S. Lerman (Mesa Community College); Marc Lawrence MacDonald (Central Michigan University); Andrew Manno (Raritan Valley Community College); Sylvia Newman (Weber State University); Carole Clark Papper (Hofstra University); Eileen Seifert (DePaul University); Evan Seymour (Community College of Philadelphia); Renee Shea (Bowie State University); Marcy Taylor (Central Michigan University); Rita Treutel (University of Alabama at Birmingham); Margaret Weaver (Missouri State University); Leah Williams (University of New Hampshire); and Tina Žigon (State University of New York at Buffalo).

Finally, a special thank you to David Bartholomae for suggesting the phrase that became the subtitle of the book.

INDEX OF TEMPLATES

—▫—

LISTEN BEFORE YOU LEAP
(pp. 10–11)

▸ While I understand the impulse to _____, my own view
  is _____.

▸ While I agree with X that _____, I cannot accept her overall conclusion that _____.

▸ While X argues _____, and I argue _____, in a way
  we're both right.

THE TEMPLATE OF TEMPLATES
(p. 11)

▸ In recent discussions of _____, a controversial issue has
  been whether _____. On the one hand, some argue
  that _____. From this perspective, _____. On the other
  hand, however, others argue that _____. In the words of
  _____, one of this view's main proponents, "_____."
  According to this view, _____. In sum, then, the issue is
  whether _____ or _____.

My own view is that _____. Though I concede that _____, I still maintain that _____. For example, _____. Although some might object that _____, I would reply that _____. The issue is important because _____.

INTRODUCING WHAT "THEY SAY"
(p. 23)

▸ A number of _____ have recently suggested that _____.

▸ It has become common today to dismiss _____.

▸ In their recent work, Y and Z have offered harsh critiques of _____ for _____.

INTRODUCING "STANDARD VIEWS"
(pp. 23–24)

▸ Americans have always believed that _____.

▸ Conventional wisdom has it that _____.

▸ Common sense seems to dictate that _____.

▸ The standard way of thinking about topic X has it that _____.

▸ It is often said that _____.

▸ My whole life I have heard it said that _____.

▸ You would think that _____.

▸ Many people assume that _____.

hand, _____ contends _____. Others even maintain _____. My own view is _____.

▸ When it comes to the topic of _____, most of us will readily agree that _____. Where this agreement usually ends, however, is on the question of _____. Whereas some are convinced that _____, others maintain that _____.

▸ In conclusion, then, as I suggested earlier, defenders of _____ can't have it both ways. Their assertion that _____ is contradicted by their claim that _____.

CAPTURING AUTHORIAL ACTION
(pp. 41–44)

▸ X acknowledges that _____.

▸ X agrees that _____.

▸ X argues that _____.

▸ X believes that _____.

▸ X celebrates the fact that _____.

▸ X claims that _____.

▸ X complains that _____.

▸ X concedes that _____.

▸ X demonstrates that _____.

▸ X denies/does not deny that _____.

▸ X deplores the tendency to _____.

▸ X emphasizes that _____.

Index of Templates

- X insists that _____.

- X observes that _____.

- X questions whether _____.

- X refutes the claim that _____.

- X reminds us that _____.

- X reports that _____.

- X suggests that _____.

- X urges us to _____.

INTRODUCING QUOTATIONS
(p. 51)

- X states, "_____."

- As the prominent philosopher X puts it, "_____."

- According to X, "_____."

- X himself writes, "_____."

- In her book, _____, X maintains that "_____."

- Writing in the journal _____, X complains that "_____."

- In X's view, "_____."

- X agrees when she writes, "_____."

- X disagrees when he writes, "_____."

- X complicates matters further when he writes, "_____."

EXPLAINING QUOTATIONS
(p. 52)

▶ Basically, X is warning _____.

▶ In other words, X believes _____.

▶ In making this comment, X urges us to _____.

▶ X is corroborating the age-old adage that _____.

▶ X's point is that _____.

▶ The essence of X's argument is that _____.

DISAGREEING, WITH REASONS
(p. 62)

▶ I think X is mistaken because she overlooks _____.

▶ X's claim that _____ rests upon the questionable assumption that _____.

▶ I disagree with X's view that _____ because, as recent research has shown, _____.

▶ X contradicts herself / can't have it both ways. On the one hand, she argues _____. On the other hand, she also says _____.

▶ By focusing on _____, X overlooks the deeper problem of _____.

Index of Templates

AGREEING
(pp. 64–66)

- I agree that _____ because my experience _____ confirms it.

- X surely is right about _____ because, as she may not be aware, recent studies have shown that _____.

- X's theory of _____ is extremely useful because it sheds insight on the difficult problem of _____.

- Those unfamiliar with this school of thought may be interested to know that it basically boils down to _____.

- I agree that _____, a point that needs emphasizing since so many people believe _____.

- If group X is right that _____, as I think they are, then we need to reassess the popular assumption that _____.

AGREEING AND DISAGREEING SIMULTANEOUSLY
(pp. 68–69)

- Although I agree with X up to a point, I cannot accept his overall conclusion that _____.

- Although I disagree with much that X says, I fully endorse his final conclusion that _____.

- Though I concede that _____, I still insist that _____.

- X is right that _____, but she seems on more dubious ground when she claims that _____.

- While X is probably wrong when she claims that _____, she is right that _____.

- Whereas X provides ample evidence that _____, Y and Z's research on _____ and _____ convinces me that _____ instead.

- I'm of two minds about X's claim that _____. On the one hand, I agree that _____. On the other hand, I'm not sure if _____.

- My feelings on the issue are mixed. I do support X's position that _____, but I find Y's argument about _____ and Z's research on _____ to be equally persuasive.

SIGNALING WHO IS SAYING WHAT
(pp. 75–76)

- X argues _____.

- According to both X and Y, _____.

- Politicians, X argues, should _____.

- Most athletes will tell you that _____.

- My own view, however, is that _____.

- I agree, as X may not realize, that _____.

- But _____ are real and, arguably, the most significant factor in _____.

- But X is wrong that _____.

- However, it is simply not true that _____.

- Indeed, it is highly likely that _____.

- X's assertion that _____ does not fit the facts.

Index of Templates

▸ X is right that _____.

▸ X is wrong that _____.

▸ X is both right and wrong that _____.

▸ Yet a sober analysis of the matter reveals _____.

▸ Nevertheless, new research shows _____.

▸ Anyone familiar with _____ should agree that _____.

EMBEDDING VOICE MARKERS
(p. 79)

▸ X overlooks what I consider an important point about _____.

▸ My own view is that what X insists is a _____ is in fact a _____.

▸ I wholeheartedly endorse what X calls _____.

▸ These conclusions, which X discusses in _____, add weight to the argument that _____.

ENTERTAINING OBJECTIONS
(p. 86)

▸ At this point I would like to raise some objections that have been inspired by the skeptic in me. She feels that I have been ignoring _____.

▸ Yet some readers may challenge the view that _____.

▸ Of course, many will probably disagree with this assertion that _____.

NAMING YOUR NAYSAYERS
(pp. 87–88)

▸ Here many _____ would probably object that _____ .

▸ But _____ would certainly take issue with the argument that _____ .

▸ _____ , of course, may want to question whether _____ .

▸ Nevertheless, both followers and critics of _____ will probably argue that _____ .

▸ Although not all _____ think alike, some of them will probably dispute my claim that _____ .

▸ _____ are so diverse in their views that it's hard to generalize about them, but some are likely to object on the grounds that _____ .

INTRODUCING OBJECTIONS INFORMALLY
(pp. 88–89)

▸ But is my proposal realistic? What are the chances of its actually being adopted?

▸ Yet is it always true that _____ ? Is it always the case, as I have been suggesting, that _____ ?

▸ However, does the evidence I've cited prove conclusively that _____ ?

▸ "Impossible," some will say. "You must be reading the research selectively."

But a new body of research shows that fat cells are far more complex and that _____.

► If sports enthusiasts stopped to think about it, many of them might simply assume that the most successful athletes _____. However, new research shows _____.

► These findings challenge neoliberals' common assumptions that _____.

► At first glance, teenagers appear to _____. But on closer inspection _____.

ESTABLISHING WHY YOUR CLAIMS MATTER
(pp. 102–3)

► X matters / is important because _____.

► Although X may seem trivial, it is in fact crucial in terms of today's concern over _____.

► Ultimately, what is at stake here is _____.

► These findings have important consequences for the broader domain of _____.

► My discussion of X is in fact addressing the larger matter of _____.

► These conclusions / This discovery will have significant applications in _____ as well as in _____.

► Although X may seem of concern to only a small group of _____, it should in fact concern anyone who cares about _____.

COMMONLY USED TRANSITIONS
(pp. 111–12)

ADDITION

also	in fact
and	indeed
besides	moreover
furthermore	so too
in addition	

ELABORATION

actually	to put it another way
by extension	to put it bluntly
in other words	to put it succinctly
in short	ultimately
that is	

EXAMPLE

after all	for instance
as an illustration	specifically
consider	to take a case in point
for example	

CAUSE AND EFFECT

accordingly	so
as a result	then
consequently	therefore
hence	thus
since	

COMPARISON

along the same lines likewise
in the same way similarly

CONTRAST

although nevertheless
but nonetheless
by contrast on the contrary
conversely on the other hand
despite regardless
even though whereas
however while
in contrast yet

CONCESSION

admittedly of course
although it is true that naturally
granted to be sure

CONCLUSION

as a result in sum
consequently therefore
hence thus
in conclusion to sum up
in short to summarize

Index of Templates

TRANSLATION RECIPES
(pp. 126–27)

- Scholar X argues, "_____." In other words, _____.
- Essentially, X argues _____.
- X's point, succinctly put, is that _____.
- Plainly put, _____.

ADDING METACOMMENTARY
(pp. 140–46)

- In other words, _____.
- What _____ really means by this is _____.
- My point is not _____, but _____.
- Ultimately, my goal is to demonstrate that _____.
- To put it another way, _____.
- Chapter 2 explores _____, while Chapter 3 examines _____.
- Even more important, _____.
- Incidentally, _____.
- In sum, then, _____.
- My conclusion, then, is that, _____.
- In short, _____.
- Having just argued that _____, let us now turn our attention to _____.
- Although some readers may object that _____, I would answer that _____.

LINKING TO WHAT "THEY SAY"
(p. 182)

▸ As X mentions in <u>this article,</u> " _____."

▸ In making <u>this comment,</u> X warns that _____.

▸ Economists often assume _____; however, <u>new research</u> by X suggests _____.

DEVELOPING GOOD RESEARCH QUESTIONS
(pp. 205–8)

▸ Why did X happen? Was it, as _____ argues, because of _____ or, as _____ contends, because of _____?

▸ What should we do about X? Should we _____, as _____ urges, or _____, as _____ argues?

▸ Is X as harmful as _____ insists, or does it have benefits, as _____ claims?

▸ Is it true, as some assert, that _____?

▸ What is the relationship between _____ and _____? Is it X, as most assume, or could it be Y, as one source suggests?

▸ Throughout the many years that I have taken an interest in _____, I, probably like most people, have assumed that _____. When I researched the topic for this essay, however, I was surprised to discover that _____.

▸ X argues _____. In my experience, however, _____.

Index of Templates

LET ONE GOOD SOURCE LEAD TO ANOTHER
(p. 209)

▶ X is far too pessimistic in her prediction that _____.

▶ Authors X and Y focus on the wrong issue. The issue is not _____ but _____.

▶ I agree with X in her critique of the view that _____, but _____.

STARTING WITH WHAT OTHERS SAY
ABOUT A LITERARY WORK
(pp. 234–36)

▶ Critic X complains that author Y's story is compromised by his _____. While there's some truth to this critique, I argue that critic X overlooks _____.

▶ According to critic A, novel X suggests _____. I agree, but would add that _____.

▶ Several members of our class have suggested that the final message of play X is _____. I agree up to a point, but I still think that _____.

▶ On first reading play Z, I thought it was an uncritical celebration of _____. After rereading the play and discussing it in class, however, I see that it is more critical of _____ than I originally thought.

▶ It might be said that poem Y is chiefly about _____. But the problem with this reading, in my view, is _____.

▶ Though religious readers might be tempted to analyze poem X as a parable about _____, a closer examination suggests that the poem is in fact about _____.

RESPONDING TO OTHER INTERPRETATIONS OF A LITERARY WORK
(p. 239)

▶ It might be argued that in the clash between character X and Y in play Z, the author wants us to favor character Y, since she is presented as the play's heroine. I contend, however, that _____.

▶ Several critics seem to assume that poem X endorses the values of _____ represented by the image of _____ over those of _____ represented by the image of _____. I agree, but with the following caveat: _____.

SHOWING EVIDENCE WHEN WRITING ABOUT A LITERARY WORK
(p. 244)

▶ Although some might read the metaphor of _____ in this poem as evidence, that for author X, _____, I see it as _____.

▶ Some might claim that evidence X suggests _____, but I argue that, on the contrary, it suggests _____.

▶ I agree with my classmate _____ that the image of _____ in novel Y is evidence of _____. Unlike _____, however, I think _____.

Index of Templates

EXPLAIN WHAT THE DATA MEAN
(p. 258–59)

▸ Our data *support / confirm / verify* the work of X by showing that
_____.

▸ By demonstrating _____, X's work *extends* the findings
of Y.

▸ The results of X *contradict / refute* Y's conclusion that _____.

▸ X's findings *call into question* the widely accepted theory that
_____.

▸ Our data *are consistent with* X's hypothesis that _____.

EXPLAINING AN EXPERIMENTAL RESULT
(p. 262)

▸ One explanation for X's finding of _____ is that _____.
An alternative explanation is _____.

▸ The difference between _____ and _____ is probably due to _____.

INTRODUCING GAPS IN THE EXISTING RESEARCH
(p. 277)

▸ Studies of X have indicated _____. It is not clear, however,
that this conclusion applies to _____.

▸ _____ often take for granted that _____. Few have
investigated this assumption, however.

777

▸ X's work tells us a great deal about _____. Can this work be generalized to _____?

▸ Our understanding of _____ remains incomplete because previous work has not examined _____.

INDEX OF AUTHORS AND TITLES

Index of Authors and Titles

GERALD GRAFF, Emeritus Professor of English and education at the University of Illinois at Chicago and the 2008 president of the Modern Language Association of America, has had a major impact on teachers through such books as *Professing Literature: An Institutional History, Beyond the Culture Wars:*

How Teaching the Conflicts Can Revitalize American Education, and *Clueless in Academe: How Schooling Obscures the Life of the Mind.*

CATHY BIRKENSTEIN is a lecturer in English at the University of Illinois at Chicago. She has published essays on writing, most recently in *College English,* and, with Gerald Graff, in *The Chronicle of Higher Education, Academe,* and *College Composition and Communication.* She has also given talks and workshops with

Gerald at numerous colleges and is currently working on a study of common misunderstandings surrounding academic discourse.

RUSSEL DURST, who edited the readings in this book, is a professor of English at the University of Cincinnati, where he teaches courses in composition, writing pedagogy and research, English linguistics, and the Hebrew Bible as literature. A past president of the National Conference on Research in Language

and Literacy, he is the author of several books, including *Collision Course: Conflict, Negotiation, and Learning in College Composition.*